NIELS BOHR: REFLECTIONS ON SUBJECT AND OBJECT

The Theory of Interacting Systems | Volume 1

The Theory of Interacting Systems

Volume 1 | Niels Bohr: Reflections on Subject and Object

Volume 2 | Classical Theory

Volume 3 | Equilibrium Theory

Volume 4 | Quantum Theory

Volume 5 | Quantum Thermodynamics

Volume 6 | Relativity Theory

NIELS BOHR: REFLECTIONS ON SUBJECT AND OBJECT

The Theory of Interacting Systems | Volume 1 | Paul McEvoy

MICROANALYTIX
www.microanalytix.com   2001   San Francisco

This book is dedicated to my late teacher Norwood Russell Hanson.

This manuscript may not be published, copied, or distributed without the author's written permission.

Copyright ©, Paul McEvoy, 2001

ISBN 1-930832-00-1

First Edition, revision 1.3

Cover and title page designs and production by Julie R. Wheeler.

This book was typeset with $\mathcal{A}_{\mathcal{M}}\mathcal{S}$-TeX, the TeX macro system of the American Mathematical Society.

Illustrations were done with PiCTeX, the TeX macro package of Michael Wichura.

Typesetting, line illustrations, and production of this book were done by the author.

Translations are by the author, unless otherwise noted.

RSO Preface

This is the first volume of a six volume series on the relation of our macroscopic experience to the mechanics of the microscopic particle systems that give rise to it. The series begins with a study of the work of Niels Bohr on the conceptual issues underlying the relation of the microscopic and macroscopic worlds. It continues in the second volume with the development of a formalism for the general local thermodynamics in space and time of interacting macroscopic systems composed of microscopic particles that obey classical Hamiltonian mechanics. This leads in the third volume to a formalism for classical equilibrium thermodynamics that is consistent with the nonequilibrium formalism. The fourth volume presents a version of quantum mechanics that is closely based on Bohr's principles. This quantum formalism is extended into quantum thermodynamics in the fifth volume. The sixth volume, a work in progress, is devoted to the relativistic version of the theory.

Niels Bohr, the Danish physicist and philosopher, was one of the dominating intellects of the twentieth century. Bohr had come to understand, as quantum mechanics came into being and he faced the wave-particle duality, that a profound investigation was needed to determine what can be known and how and when we can know it. His analysis of the quantum representation of various experiments showed that the requirements for the consistent use of quantum concepts struck at the core of our shared notions of reality, being, knowledge, and intuition.

Within the physics community, there is general agreement that Bohr's work is significant, but little consensus on its importance to the working physicist. Part of the problem is understanding what Bohr meant. This is due to the fact that he expressed his ideas in a precise philosophical shorthand that is hard to interpret. Another difficulty stems from the fact that Bohr went farther than anyone else in embracing the wave-particle duality and rejecting materialist metaphysics.

Bohr's analysis showed maintaining the proper separation between the observing system and the observed system is required to make the interpretation of quantum experiments definite. He came to see this separation between measuring instrument and observed system as a physical parallel to the epistemological distinction between the knowing subject and the object of knowledge in philosophy. To justify the position he had reached, he devised an argument that draws on the requirements of language and communication to show what conditions the accounts of our experiments and their theoretical descriptions must meet if they are to yield objective knowledge of the world.

The challenge that Bohr offers those who would understand him is how to unpack his ideas in the contexts of both philosophy and physics while preserving the essence of his insights in both domains. Because he did not cite his sources or explain the meanings of the concepts he used, it is necessary to find the sources to uncover the meanings. To do justice to his work therefore requires a detailed knowledge of the development of these ideas in nineteenth century European thought and their roots in prior work.

Assessing the validity of Bohr's work is the second major challenge addressed in this book. This includes testing his ideas on complementarity using specific examples inside and outside physics. The most interesting of these tests is based on a suggestion he made in 1930 that we might find an example of complementarity in classical physics in the relation between thermodynamics and statistical mechanics. Pursuing this idea and its implications spawned a general inquiry that led me into a detailed investigation of the relation between thermodynamics and statistical mechanics.

My study of Bohr began in earnest in 1963 when professor Norwood Russell Hanson, a visiting German scholar Klaus Meyer-Abich, and I, spent the spring semester at Indiana University in a seminar discussing Bohr's work. After that semester, I moved on to further graduate work at M.I.T., Hanson moved to Yale, and Meyer-Abich returned to Germany to finish his dissertation. He published this work in 1965 under the title *Identität, Indivualität und Komplementarität*. It is an important piece of Bohr scholarship that has helped me to clarify a number of my own ideas.

I returned to Bohr in 1966 as the subject of my doctoral dissertation under Abner Shimony at the Massachusetts Institute of Technology. It was completed in 1971 under Robert Graves with the title "The Philosophy of Niels Bohr". This work was based in part on a careful textual analysis of what Bohr had written in chronological order over a 50-year period. The analysis of Bohr's work was supported by reference to a large literature on quantum mechanics and its interpretation that had grown up in the time since quantum mechanics had been introduced. While I felt that I had distilled the essence of what Bohr had said, I did not feel at that time that I understood its full meaning and deeper philosophical significance.

By 1974, I had become convinced that to understand Bohr it was necessary to examine the roots of his conceptions. This meant tracing the history of the important ideas he had used in his epistemological work. I then embarked on a study of the works of Harald Høffding, a professor of philosophy at the University of Copenhagen at the turn of the twentieth century who had been both a teacher and friend of Bohr's. This was followed by an examination of nineteenth century developments in philosophy, physics, biology, and language. To obtain a background on the key epistemological notions of subject, object, and reality, in the context of Bohr times, I went further and examined their philosophical roots in ancient eastern and western thought and traced their progression from there. In spite of Bohr's protestations to the contrary, these inquiries made it clear that many of the concepts he used in his epistemological work were inherited from previous philosophers. He combined them, however, in a way that was uniquely his own.

In 1975, I returned to direct work on Bohr with the goal of testing his ideas on complementarity outside of quantum physics. The most promising arena for that test was his suggestion of a possible example of complementarity in classical physics. It soon became clear that the tools available in standard equilibrium thermodynamics and statistical mechanics could not support the inquiry that was required. The direct work on Bohr was suspended and a fundamental investigation into these issues was initiated. Completing the portion of this investigation concerned with classical physics took more than twenty years and resulted in what are now Volume 2 on the theory of classical interacting systems and Volume 3 on the equilibrium version of the classical theory. The work on Bohr was taken up again in 1996, completed in 1997, and revised completely several times after that. The later volumes on quantum mechanics followed soon after. The general title of this series is the *Theory of Interacting Systems.*

In a nutshell, the Theory of Interacting Systems is a general nonequilibrium thermodynamics of interacting macroscopic systems that is consistent with the Hamiltonian statistical mechanics of the underlying microscopic particles. It turns out that the formalism of the macroscopic thermodynamics that emerged from these separate investigations using classical and quantum mechanics is relatively insensitive to the choice of the underlying particle mechanics. More important, I had come to realize that resolving the paradoxes of thermodynamics, which are rooted in the disjuncture between the irreversibility of thermodynamics and the reversibility of the underlying particle mechanics, requires an epistemological solution. I had also come to understand that the subject/object distinction, which Bohr had made a centerpiece of his epistemological theory, is not simply a philosophical distinction, but has direct implications for the mathematical representation in physics of macroscopic objects and their interactions.

The title of this volume, "Reflections on Subject and Object" (RSO), refers both to the fact that reflection is a necessary aspect of a knower and to the dichotomy of the knower and the known that played a central role in ancient Hindu, Buddhist, and Greek thought. Each component of this subject/object dichotomy reflects and is determined by the other. It is the job of a reflective subject, as the knower, to draw a boundary between him or herself and the object of study. The placement of this boundary depends on the knower, so it has aspects that are arbitrary and subjective. It was found that the need for this boundary, with its arbitrary and subjective elements, has consequences in both classical and quantum physics for the physical descriptions we give.

The overall goal of this book is to extract a usable epistemology from Bohr's work that can serve as a foundation for physics into the twenty-first century.

Table of Contents and Index.

The analytical Table of Contents presents the major headings within each chapter. This is the place to locate the treatments of various concepts important to the analysis of Bohr's work. The Index is a search tool that lists exhaustively the locations where various ideas are discussed or mentioned.

Bibliography.

Bibliographical references take the form Bohr [**1923a**]. The bibliography has more than 700 entries, so it has been broken into parts to make it more useful. These parts are listed by category in the Table of Contents, and include works by Bohr, works by Bohr and others, works on Bohr, works that are primarily philosophical in orientation, and works in physics, mathematics, language, biology, history, and others. To locate a reference requires locating the part of the bibliography to which it belongs, finding the author's name in alphabetical order within this part, and then finding the year in the left margin that corresponds to the date of the author's work that was cited.

Translation.

The English version of the quotation from Goethe's *Zur Farbenlehre* that appears at the beginning of Part III is taken from the translation titled *Theory of Colours,* Goethe [**1810**], listed in the Supplement section of the bibliography.

Acknowledgments.

I would like to thank all of those who have been supportive of my work over the years. Many have expressed enthusiasm and some have helped with bibliographical references during the more than 27 years required to complete the theory. A conservative estimate of the work time required to complete the first five volumes, beginning with the study of Bohr in 1963, is more than 40,000 hours.

I offer a very special thanks to the members of my family, Ruth Roberts, Heather Roberts McEvoy, and Kyle Roberts McEvoy, who have graciously borne the cost of many years of my hard labor. I would also like to thank Abner Shimony for conversations on a number of these topics many years ago. I express my appreciation to Clifford A. Truesdell IV, for suggesting the passage in Lewis Carroll's *Hunting of the Snark* and to Fred Glynn for supplying several translations of Lucretius' *De Rerum Natura* and helping with some aspects of the manuscript production. I thank Reza Jannatpour for references to scholarship on Omar Khayyám and to Maryam Saffari for discussions of the differences between the Farsi and English versions of his verse.

A number of others will be recognized in future volumes for their help on those volumes.

I reserve a final thanks for my late teacher Norwood Russell Hanson for his interest and support of my work on Bohr.

Paul McEvoy
MicroAnalytix, 2001

Table of Contents

RSO Preface	v
Table of Contents	xi
Part I: The Development of Bohr's Thought.	
Chapter 1. Reflections on Bohr	3
1.1 Prologue	4
1.2 The Theory of Interacting Systems	6
1.3 An Approach to Bohr	7
1.4 The Literature on Bohr	15
1.5 Bohr at Work	19
Chapter 2. The Development of Bohr's Thought: 1911–1925	24
2.1 The Crisis in Classical Theory	25
2.2 The Theory of the Hydrogen Atom	27
2.3 The Correspondence Principle	32
2.4 Reflection 1	36
2.5 The Bohr, Kramers, Slater Theory	36
2.6 Reflection 2	39
2.7 Precursors of Complementarity	40
2.8 Reflection 3	41
Chapter 3. The Quantum Formalism and Uncertainty Relations: 1925–1927	43
3.1 Development of the Quantum Formalism	44
3.2 The Quantum Formalism	46
3.3 Reflection 4	56
3.4 Discovery of the Uncertainty Relations	59
3.5 Reflection 5	64
3.6 The Uncertainty Relations and Thought Experiments	64
3.7 Reflection 6	67
3.8 Statistical Aspects of the Uncertainty Relations	68
3.9 Reflection 7	70

3.10 Bohr's 1927 Como Lecture ... 70

Chapter 4. Fields and Measurement: 1927–1934 ... 72
4.1 Further Developments in Quantum Theory ... 73
4.2 Interpreting the Uncertainty Relations ... 73
4.3 Reflection 8 ... 79
4.4 Uncertainty Relations in Field Measurements ... 80
4.5 The Bohr-Rosenfeld Thought Experiment ... 85
4.6 Von Neumann's Theory of Measurement ... 88
4.7 Reflection 9 ... 92
4.8 Exfoliation ... 93

Chapter 5. The Quantum State Description: 1935–1962 ... 97
5.1 Questions of Interpretation ... 98
5.2 The Einstein, Podolsky, Rosen Paradox ... 100
5.3 Einstein and Bohr on Reality ... 107
5.4 Reflection 10 ... 111
5.5 The Statistical Interpretation ... 112
5.6 Hidden Variable Theories ... 114
5.7 Bohr's Approach to the Quantum State ... 121
5.8 Reflection 11 ... 124
5.9 Bohr's Scientific Work after 1935 ... 125

Part II: The Synthesis of Bohr's Epistemology.

Chapter 6. Bohr's Philosophical Themes ... 129
6.1 The Search for Concepts ... 130
6.2 The Wave-Particle Duality ... 136
6.3 Reflection 12 ... 139
6.4 Bohr's View of Conceptual Frameworks ... 139
6.5 Reflection 13 ... 144
6.6 Observation ... 145
6.7 Reflection 14 ... 149
6.8 Description ... 150
6.9 Reflection 15 ... 154

Chapter 7. Bohr's Quantum Theory ... 156
7.1 Formulations of Complementarity ... 157
7.2 The Epistemological Significance of Complementarity ... 162
7.3 Bohr's Quantum Theory ... 166

Chapter 8. Bohr's Epistemological Theory ... 175
8.1 The Components of Bohr's Epistemology ... 176
8.2 Bohr's Main Argument ... 178
8.3 Bohr's Theory of Knowledge ... 181

8.4 Communication and the Subject/Object Distinction	186
8.5 Subjectivity and Objectivity	190
8.6 The Replacement of Concepts	192
8.7 Reflection 16	194

Part III: The Foundations of Bohr's Thought.

Chapter 9. The Natural History of Subject and Object	199
9.1 Bohr's Philosophical Themes	200
9.2 Wisdom of the East	201
9.3 Reflection 17	212
9.4 Wisdom of the West	213
9.5 Reflection 18	227
Chapter 10. Bohr and Kant	228
10.1 Kant's Theory of Knowledge	229
10.2 Bohr and Kant	238
10.3 Reflection 19	250
Chapter 11. Nineteenth Century Philosophy and Science	252
11.1 European Philosophy	253
11.2 Views of Language	257
11.3 The Study of Perception	263
11.4 The Foundations of Biology	265
11.5 Philosophical Aspects of Physics	271
11.6 Reflection 20	279
Chapter 12. Copenhagen: 1902–1935	281
12.1 Bohr and Høffding	282
12.2 Bohr on Language	289
12.3 Bohr and Wittgenstein	290
12.4 Fundamental Issues in Biology	296
12.5 The Maturation of Classical Physics	301
12.6 Reflection 21	303
Chapter 13. Complementarity, Observation, and Language	310
13.1 Quantum Theory and Views on Reality	311
13.2 Complementarity in Biology	315
13.3 Complementarity in the Social Sciences	322
13.4 An Assessment of Complementarity	327
13.5 Perception and Observation	329
13.6 Language and Epistemology	331
13.7 Reflection 22	338

Part IV: Reflections.

Chapter 14. Epistemological Issues in Classical Physics   341
14.1 Probability in Classical Physics   342
14.2 Thermodynamics in Bohr's Thought   347
14.3 The Relation of Thermodynamics to Statistical Mechanics   350
14.4 The Theory of Interacting Systems   352
14.5 Entropy   356
14.6 Attempts to Find Complementarity in Classical Physics   359
14.7 Subject and Object in Classical Physics   362
14.8 Microscopic and Macroscopic   364

Chapter 15. Bohr's Approach to Quantum Measurement   369
15.1 Measuring Instruments   370
15.2 Bohr and von Neumann   377
15.3 Reflection 23   390
15.4 Entropy and Observation   391
15.5 Bohr's Concept of Closure   394
15.6 Reflection 24   398

Chapter 16. Questions of Interpretation   400
16.1 Dynamical Theories of Wavefunction Reduction   401
16.2 Quantum Ergodic Theory and Decoherence Theory   402
16.3 Relative State Theories   409
16.4 The Transactional Interpretation   413
16.5 Quantum Entanglement   421
16.6 Reflection 25   423

Chapter 17. Epistemological Issues in Quantum Physics   425
17.1 Conceptual Issues in Electrodynamics   426
17.2 Locality and Superposition in Quantum Mechanics   430
17.3 Outstanding Issues in Quantum Physics   432

Chapter 18. What do Theories Tell Us?   442
18.1 Issues in the Theory of Knowledge   443
18.2 Components of the Conceptual Framework   445
18.3 What do Theories Tell Us?   451

Chapter 19. Subject and Object   462
19.1 Subject and Object in Theories of Knowledge   463
19.2 Remaining Questions   467
19.3 The Possibility and Limits of Knowledge   469
19.4 A Summing Up   473
19.5 Epilogue   478

RSO Bibliography	479
Bohr's Major Works	479
Bohr's Major Writings with Other Authors	481
The Bohr Archive	481
On Bohr	481
Philosophy	483
Physics	492
Mathematics	504
Language	504
Biology	505
History	506
Other	507
Supplement	507
Index	509

Part I

The Development of Bohr's Philosophical Thought

> Whose woods these are I think I know.
> ...
> He will not see me stopping here
> To watch his woods fill up with snow.
>
> Robert Frost, *"Stopping by the Woods on a Snowy Evening"*, 1923, *Complete Poems*

CHAPTER 1

Reflections on Bohr

1.1 Prologue

An inquiry into the theory of knowledge and the nature of reality is ultimately an exercise in poetry. It is a search for the ultimate grounding of what we can know about what may be and how we can know it. Basic to most of these attempts to understand the world has been the separation of the subject, as the knower, from the object that is known. Once this subject/object dualism has been introduced, the issue becomes explaining how these components interact to give rise to what we experience. While this division of reality into parts was fundamental to epistemological thought over several thousand years, the resulting dualism was itself one of the central philosophical problems. Ancient thinkers proposed ways of understanding this division and suggested how to take the measure of its parts. But reality does not come with signposts, so they differed on what is important and what they held to be true. Lao Tse, in the *Tao Te Ching,* verse 32, expressed the problem this way

Once the world is divided, the parts need names.
There are already enough names.
One must know when to stop.

The dualism between subject and object is mirrored in any division of the universe into objects for separate study. Another division that has also proved to be of epistemological significance is the division between the world of macroscopic experience and the microscopic world of particles and fields proposed to explain it. Drawing out the consequences of these divisions is the focus of this extended study titled the Theory of Interacting Systems. This book, the first in a series of volumes concerned with these matters, is devoted primarily to the philosophical issues underlying these divisions. Subsequent volumes explore the consequences for physics.

Thinking about epistemological issues becomes important in science when an existing theory cannot be extended and the theory replacing it cannot be fit within the current conceptual framework. By the early twentieth century, classical physics had been shown to be powerless for computing the emission curves of the full blackbody radiation spectrum as a function of temperature and had been replaced by Planck's theory. Classical theory had also not been successful in explaining the specific heats of substances and had been replaced by the theories of Albert Einstein and Peter Debye. Finally, classical theory was unable to account for atomic spectra, which still awaited a theoretical account. This was the situation in physics when the Danish physicist and philosopher Niels Bohr began his work.

Max Planck, at the turn of the century, was forced to introduce a nonclassical quantum of energy into his successful computation of blackbody radiation curves. Einstein subsequently introduced the concept of the photon as a heuristic device to explain the photoelectric effect and other phenomena concerning light and used it later in his explanation of specific heats. To reconcile the mismatch between the transformation properties of electrodynamics and mechanics, Einstein also introduced the special theory of relativity at the same time. Classical electrodynamics faced another challenge as experiments began to reveal the internal structure of the atom. The structure obtained in the investigations of the atom by Ernest Rutherford in the early twentieth century could not be accounted for by classical electrodynamics.

Shortly after he began work, Bohr developed his theory of the hydrogen atom. This was the beginning of a long career in which he played a central role in both physics and the development of a philosophical foundation for it. From the beginning, Bohr felt more deeply than his contemporaries did the need to understand the implications of the new theories based on quantum ideas. He experienced the failure of attempts to visualize the processes underlying these theories as a severe conceptual dislocation and came to realize that this situation required a philosophical analysis if we are to understand the proper scope and application of these theories.

Bohr's concern with putting the physics that he was helping to develop on a proper conceptual footing led him to an analysis of the role of theory and experiment in our scientific endeavors and to propose a theory of knowledge that supports their use. His goal was to find a consistent way to reconcile the apparently contradictory aspects of matter and electromagnetic radiation that the new observations seemed to imply and make the new theories predicting these observations intelligible. Out of this analysis, came a set of philosophical principles that he stated and reiterated over many years. Bohr's contributions, to both physics and epistemology, were central to the development and interpretation of quantum mechanics as it emerged.

Because Bohr was forced to clear a new path into these issues, he came to see more clearly than his colleagues did the inadequacy of the implicit philosophy underlying classical physics as most understood it. He also came to see the central importance to physics of the subject/object distinction in epistemology. Bohr felt his inquiry into epistemology had a much wider philosophical application than just the problems of quantum physics. In the form in which he presented it, however, Bohr's work is more of a prolegomena to an epistemology than a finished whole. He did, in fact, develop a general theory of knowledge based on this inquiry. But the full structure of his theory is implicit in his writings and needs to be pulled together and unpacked. The overall purpose of this volume is to extract that theory, explain it, test it, and extend it.

To understand what Bohr accomplished, I will need to take his theory apart, so to speak, and put the pieces on the shop floor so we can understand what they are and evaluate the validity of his conception of them. In the end, I will propose some modifications before putting the pieces back together. But I believe that the result preserves the spirit and intention of Bohr's work.

In this analysis of Bohr's epistemology we are opening a circle that connects intuition, knowledge, and perception. In rounding this circle, I will follow Bohr's philosophical inquiry into physics, philosophy, language, and biology, and explore the concepts of subject and object, reality, causality, perception, knowledge, and existence, as elements of the epistemology he developed.

1.2 The Theory of Interacting Systems

This is the first volume of a six volume series. The purpose of the series is to create a theory of the macroscopic world we occupy based on the physics of the microscopic world that underlies it. The formalism for a thermodynamics of local, time-dependent macroscopic physical quantities, which is based successively on the Hamiltonian statistical mechanics of classical, quantum, and relativistic particles, is developed in this series of volumes.

The epistemology presented by Bohr is an appropriate place to begin this work. Bohr was concerned with the relation between levels of experience and dug deeply into the issues that these connections raise. He was the first to recognize the importance of the subject/object distinction in physics and its formal expression in quantum mechanics. He also considered the issues involved when concepts based in ordinary experience are applied to microscopic settings. Bohr's perspective on the quantum state represented an important step away from the view of physical systems based on the conceptual framework of materialist metaphysics. All of these issues play an important role as aspects of physics in the work presented in this series.

The significance of thermodynamics to understanding issues connected with the relation of theories on different levels was hinted at by Bohr [**1930**], who was looking for aspects of classical theory in which complementarity might appear. He proposed at that time a possible complementarity between the 'spacetime coordination' and 'fixed temperature' descriptions of statistical mechanics and thermodynamics, respectively. An examination of the standard accounts of the relationship of thermodynamics to statistical mechanics showed that the equilibrium theories on which these accounts were based are not adequate to test Bohr's ideas. That realization led to the work in this series.

The examination of Bohr's ideas in connection with the relation of thermodynamics to statistical mechanics finally showed that Bohr's epistemological stance has a wider application than the atomic physics from which it emerged. Suitably extended, his epistemology provides a general approach to any pair of theories concerned with describing a system of particles on both macroscopic and microscopic levels.

The general title of this series is the Theory of Interacting Systems, which will be referred to as TIS. Although many of the topics and equations presented in TIS are based closely on work of particular authors, almost all analyses and equations will be expressed within a single TIS framework and notation that is common to all volumes. While this leads to the loss of some historical accuracy, the theoretical unification and the ability to compare work even between disparate theories within one notation far outweigh this disadvantage. An attempt will be made to notify the reader when, for example, a symbol or sign convention is used in a way that is different from that of the author under discussion.

This first volume will be referred to as RSO.[1] The succeeding volumes are primarily works of physics with a strong concern for the historical development of the concepts and their philosophical foundations. The second volume is titled *The Theory of Interacting Systems, Volume 2, Classical Theory*. This volume is referred to as CIS, which stands for the 'classical theory of interacting systems'. The fundamental principles of the Theory of Interacting Systems and the mathematical construction of a spacetime thermodynamics out of the classical Hamiltonian mechanics of systems of microscopic particles are presented in CIS. The third volume is *The Theory of Interacting Systems, Volume 3, Equilibrium Theory*, and is referred to as EIS. This volume specializes the spacetime theory of CIS to the equilibrium case. The equilibrium formalism, equations of state, thermodynamic coefficients, thermodynamic surfaces, phase transitions, asymptotic theory, and thermodynamic approximations are the main subjects of EIS. The fourth volume is called *The Theory of Interacting Systems, Volume 4, Quantum Theory*, or QIS. It contains a presentation of quantum mechanics that is based closely on Bohr's epistemology and his view of the quantum state. The resulting quantum mechanics differs significantly in its conceptual underpinnings from the versions presented by Schrödinger or von Neumann. The last completed volume, as of this date, is the fifth volume, *The Theory of Interacting Systems, Volume 5, Quantum Thermodynamics*, which is designated by QTS. QTS extends TIS thermodynamics to the quantum domain. The specialization of the theory to equilibrium quantum thermodynamics results in a different formalism than the one developed by von Neumann. The sixth volume on relativity theory is called *The Theory of Interacting Systems, Volume 6, Relativity Theory*, or RIS. It is in progress.

1.3 An Approach to Bohr

There has been a proliferation of books and articles on Bohr in recent years, each offering new insights and a new look at his ideas. Bohr has been viewed in this literature as a positivist, verificationist, idealist, realist, antirealist, instrumentalist, seer, obscurantist, transcendentalist, visionary, reactionary, a deep thinker, and a shallow thinker, among other things. Few other thinkers have been seen in so many widely diverse ways. This forest of

---

[1] This volume grew out of work that was first presented in 1971 in my doctoral thesis at MIT entitled "The Philosophy of Niels Bohr".

incompatible viewpoints is a testimony to the difficulty in coming to grasp with Bohr's work as well as to the unshakable feeling that there is something important to be found there. In spite of this plethora of books and articles, there are certain essential aspects of Bohr's work that have not been understood properly.

Bohr was driven to develop an epistemological response to the problems of quantum theory because he felt, more than any other physicist of the time, the discrepancy between the conceptual framework of classical physics and the requirements of some new conceptual framework that needed to replace it. Without significant formal philosophical training, Bohr nevertheless had a deep and strong philosophical intuition concerning fundamental physical matters that seemed to guide his thinking along a particular path over many years.

An adequate approach to Bohr must come to terms with his style of expressing himself and with certain core concepts that lie at the center of his thinking. Among these concepts are the subject/object distinction, observation, description, communication, and conceptual frameworks. Each of these concepts has a specific role in his epistemology. In addition, Bohr often used words important to philosophers, such as 'definition' and 'meaning', in the way physicists do and this seems to have caused some confusion in the philosophical literature. Finally, because he developed a novel argument in terms of the requirements of the subject/object distinction and communication to justify his new epistemological viewpoint, the careful analysis of the elements of this argument are central to understanding him.

The various discussions in the literature of the subject/object distinction are illustrative of the problems in understanding Bohr. Bohr expressed the requirement of maintaining a proper boundary between the subject and object as a requirement for the unambiguous definition, in communicable terms, of physical quantities in a measured system. Most authors present this point in the same way Bohr did and analyze it in terms of a philosophical theory of meaning and communication. In these terms, Bohr's argument seems to be an almost self-evident sequence of statements that objective scientific work must be communicable and that successful communication requires unambiguous concepts. This leaves these authors feeling a little uneasy because, as John Honner put it, there is so little to it. By contrast, I will show that the subject/object distinction, and the requirements Bohr imposed on experiments for establishing it, were introduced by Bohr for reasons of physics, not to meet the needs of communication or philosophy. In addition, his introduction of a philosophical argument concerning communication to support his epistemological ideas represents an after the fact justification for the epistemological requirements he had imposed. In a final step, I will argue that his justification in terms of language and communication is not supportable and must be replaced.

One of the recurring points that will be touched on concerning the analysis of Bohr's work and evaluating it is that he must be approached as a physicist and not as a philosopher. This is probably the greatest cause of misunderstanding Bohr and the source of a number of mistakes concerning his views. Another source of error is ignorance. My survey of the literature indicates that many, if not most, of the casual statements of Bohr's views made in passing in the physical and philosophical literatures are caricatures of his beliefs. The problem is pervasive in that statements in this literature of what is called the standard interpretation or the Copenhagen interpretation of quantum mechanics are often very far off the mark. Even those authors who do a better job characterizing standard views on the interpretation of quantum mechanics often attribute to Bohr conceptions that would more properly reflect those of Werner Heisenberg, Wolfgang Pauli, or John von Neumann.

The question of influences on Bohr, which by now has its own literature, will be discussed below. At this point, I will simply state that Bohr drew on nineteenth century conceptions for many of his philosophical ideas. Although Bohr did not make a systematic study of philosophy or other disciplines outside of physics, it is clear that he had absorbed a great deal from the milieu in which he worked and lived. A detailed historical and philosophical study of nineteenth and early twentieth century work in philosophy, physics, biology, language, and psychology, uncovered what I feel are the roots of many of the ideas that Bohr used.

For the most part, the focus in this book is on the parallel physical and philosophical issues underlying Bohr's work. I am less concerned with his scientific achievements or events in his life except as they illuminate his philosophy. A brief historical development of his ideas in the context of their times is used in Part I to show what problems Bohr and others faced in physics and the strategies they used to solve them. As part of this, just enough of the formalism of Bohr's theory of the hydrogen atom, quantum mechanics, the uncertainty relations, and von Neumann's theory of measurement, are introduced to provide a context for the points Bohr was making and the problems under discussion. A detailed examination of the foundations and mathematical representation of the quantum mechanics and quantum thermodynamics of macroscopic interacting systems is pursued in QIS and QTS.

A number of problems make the study and expression of Bohr's philosophy difficult and account for the divergent viewpoints in the literature. First, and foremost, is the well-known fact that Bohr himself never stated a full philosophical position on any of the topics that were central to him. Thus, in spite of having a general conception of the important features of an epistemology, Bohr never worked out the details necessary to fit these philosophical components into a sufficiently explicit epistemological system to support his ideas. In addition, although Bohr used a number of distinctly philosophical terms in his writing—such as individuality, irrationality, wholeness, and subject and object, among others—he did not attempt a deeper analysis from the philosophical perspective of the roles played by these ideas and how they are related to other similar inquiries that are part of the philosophical tradition. It is likely that he did not feel this was necessary, and, as will be discussed further below, he and others around him did not acknowledge any specific philosophical influences on his thought.

The second problem in the study of Bohr's work is that he tended to express his positions in terms of a small set of well turned phrases—almost aphorisms. He used these specific locutions repeatedly with a subtle shift in wording, meaning, and emphasis, as his views developed. In the end, his statements made at different times often have more of a family resemblance than equivalence. To discern the central core of meaning in these phases and statements requires a careful textual analysis and a timeline of the forms of speech he used in the context of his whole theory and the context of the physical problems he was considering over the fifty-year period of his work. Because of this, I have let Bohr and others speak for themselves as much as possible on issues where precision is paramount.

The third problem in Bohr's work is that he left some important things undone. The most significant of these is the incompleteness of his account of how we connect microscopic events, described in terms of probabilities by quantum mechanics, with the world of our macroscopic experience. He developed what I will present as an observation thesis and a description thesis to regulate how experiments should be represented theoretically and the observed results are to be interpreted. He used a communication thesis to place requirements on what an experiment must do to provide unambiguous results and what concepts can appear in statements of experimental results in a given experimental setting. I will also examine his mature concepts of a 'phenomenon', which refers to results obtained within a definite experimental context, and 'closure', which indicates that an experiment has been completed and its results recorded macroscopically. In his mature theory, he required that we refer only to closed phenomena when we are discussing the results of an experiment on the grounds that only closed phenomena are free of the quantum ambiguities associated with superpositions and nonlocalities. But he did not characterize these concepts further in his publications or indicate how they are to be reconciled with quantum mechanics itself.

In spite of these problems and slight shifts as Bohr's ideas developed, there is a consistency is his approach to understanding the issues and a depth of awareness of what is at stake that is not present in the thinking of his contemporaries on epistemological issues in physics. He maintained a close tie to the concrete and practical problems he was facing as a scientist, which has been widely recognized as one source of his strength. It is also the key to understanding him. He did not propound or indicate that he accepted a particular philosophical theory of meaning with regard to the description of physical systems, a particular theory of the truth of physical propositions, or anyone else's philosophical system. Each day he refocused on the physical problem at hand and brought to bear, often with the help of others, the concepts and insights he could for their solution. He approached the epistemological issues he faced in the same way and this close tie to concrete physical problems and examples continually guided him in this difficult terrain.

The evaluation of the validity of the elements Bohr used in the justification of his epistemological argument is of special interest. At the heart of Bohr's epistemology is a claim about the requirements on the communication of information obtained from experiments. This has been viewed variously as a simple statement of objective requirements on communication or as a part of a transcendental argument. Once again we see that there is not even general agreement on what Bohr was trying to do—quite apart from the question of whether he was successful or not. This thesis concerning communication is the linchpin of Bohr's work and I shall present a detailed case that Bohr's focus on the subject/object distinction and communication as the core justifications for his epistemology are translations into philosophical terms of points of physics.

Another issue by contrast, has received little attention recently from philosophers. This is the question of the significance of superposition in quantum mechanics. While this may be viewed as a technical aspect of the formalism, as the 'wave' part of the 'wave-particle duality', allowing superpositions of solutions is a radical innovation from the standpoint of the particle theories that were the precursors of quantum theory. Somehow, the 'both/and' relation of wave mechanics replaces the 'either/or' relation of particle mechanics. While this is often viewed by analogy with classical waves in terms of the interference between different microscopic entities, the situation is subtle and requires an understanding of what it implies in terms of the possibilities of observation in the context of a given experimental arrangement.

The subtitle of this book, *Reflections on Subject and Object*, refers to the central role of the subject/object distinction in Bohr's thought. Reflection is also one of the attributes of a knowing subject in almost any epistemological theory. In that spirit, this book will reflect on itself. In short sections entitled Reflections, set apart from the discussion of Bohr's work and its historical flow, I will consider what has been accomplished and what it means.

The book is organized into functional units. In Part I, the development of Bohr's philosophical thinking and work on quantum physics is examined in the context of the work of his contemporaries over his lifetime. The first concern in this historical context is how he fashioned out of the scientific issues he was facing his perspectives on theoretical description, observation, the place of complementarity, perception, language, and communication. As part of this discussion, I will examine briefly his attitude towards reality, causality, the uncertainty relations, the quantum formalism, measurement in quantum mechanics, and much more. A close analysis of his writings in chronological order, along with information on the work of his contemporaries and developments in physics, will be used to pursue the development in time and the proper characterization of these core concepts. Some of the issues, such as the philosophical classification of Bohr's views on reality, have recently acquired a large literature. Bohr's views on the issue of reality depend in part on his epistemological attitude toward quantum theory and experiment and will be taken up in stages throughout the book as the analysis progresses.

In Part II, the concern is with codifying the fundamental elements of Bohr's conceptual scheme. I will bring together his views on empirical observation and theoretical description and begin the process of organizing his philosophical position. This will show that there are a number of distinct philosophical commitments, which were designated above as *theses*, that are implicit in Bohr's work concerning the nature of observation, theoretical descriptions, perception, language, and communication. As part of this inquiry, these theses are stated in an explicit form that can then be evaluated in terms of their value in making sense of the scientific problems and their philosophical cogency. Bohr showed how these elements work together in what I will call his *main argument*. These theses and their links in the main argument are the primary focus of my exposition and subsequent assessment of Bohr's epistemology.

Reconstructing someone's thought in this way is always risky. However, without such a reconstruction, it is impossible to get at the deeper issues or even to see if Bohr's position is coherent in the larger sense. This detailed reconstruction of Bohr's philosophical views is one of the factors that set this work apart from most, but not all, other studies of Bohr. Opposition to an attempt to understand Bohr in this way was voiced by Leon Rosenfeld [1946], p. 9. He objected to an enterprise such as this on the grounds that it is a betrayal of the very spirit of Bohr's work, which he characterized as "pragmatic" and "supple". Rosenfeld was making an important point when he warned us that we may destroy Bohr's theory in our very attempt to pin it to the drawing board. Without a systematic approach and a clear idea of Bohr's commitments, however, we cannot really be sure of what he was saying or make a proper evaluation of it. What I will not do is assign Bohr to one or another philosophical position. Those who have categorized Bohr as, say, a positivist or attributed to him a philosophical theory of meaning, have projected a philosophical structure onto him that is unwarranted by his training and inclination. This approach also loses sight of the physical problems that Bohr was addressing with his terminology. Whenever this has been done in the literature on Bohr, it has obscured more than illuminated his views and led to serious errors in understanding him.[2]

Bohr justified his theory of knowledge by providing an account of the role of language, classical physics, and the subject/object distinction. In doing this, he used a vocabulary that is distinctly philosophical. In Part III, the possible sources of Bohr's philosophical ideas are examined. Because he did not make explicit reference to these sources, a circumstantial case must be constructed for the origin of his ideas.

For the sake of the larger perspective, Part III begins with a brief history of epistemological thinking that is focused on the subject and object distinction. Because Bohr was aware that elements of the issues of concern to him were present in what he referred to as "wisdom of the East", the examination of the roots Bohr's ideas begins with ancient Eastern thought concerning existence, causality, reality, and knowledge. This is followed by a discussion of parallel ideas in ancient Greek works. The subsequent expression of these ideas in Roman and Persian thought is touched on briefly followed by a discussion of the reemergence of these ideas in Western thought in the seventeenth and eighteenth centuries.

The influence of Kant on nineteenth century thought in philosophy and science was pervasive. This was still true in most of Europe, and at the University of Copenhagen in particular, at the beginning of the twentieth century. Bohr's thinking also shows some influences, however indirect, of Kant's ideas, so Kant's epistemology is presented in some detail. Both Kant and Bohr were engaged in creating epistemologies, so there is an opportunity to compare their approaches to a number of specific ideas with respect to these issues. The discussion of Kant also provides us with a valuable background for the examination of European thought during the nineteenth century.

The inquiry proceeds with a brief and focused historical account of the development of European thought in the areas of epistemology, biology, physics, and language during the nineteenth century.[3]

The objective is to assess just how much Bohr had absorbed from the scientists and philosophers that immediately preceded him in Europe. This account is used to show how ideas such as 'individuality', 'irrationality', and 'wholeness', among others, function in Bohr's thought and why he employed specific terms such as these in his work.

As we enter the twentieth century, and the beginning of Bohr's education at the University of Copenhagen, I will give a detailed account of the work

---

[2]More than one philosopher writing about Bohr has made this point. John Honner [**1987**] in particular has stressed it.

[3]Catherine Chevalley [**1994**], pp. 50–51, has emphasized the importance of both the history of science and the history of philosophy in developing an appreciation of the context in which the ideas of Bohr and other quantum physicists developed and bemoaned the fact that knowledge of this context is often missing in current writers. She observed that this fact has made Bohr's epistemological vocabulary unintelligible to many modern writers.

of the Danish philosopher Harald Høffding. Høffding's philosophical writings and the ideas of other philosophers discussed in Høffding's books are examined for ideas that Bohr drew on in the development of his philosophical thinking. This is not to say that Høffding himself is a direct influence on either Bohr's scientific thinking or his epistemology, but there is strong evidence I will present that the concepts Bohr chose for his epistemology exhibit the influence of transmitted ideas. Høffding is only one possible source among many that will be presented and that Bohr may have encountered during his education and reading, and in discussions with physicists, philosophers, and others.

The next step is an examination of Bohr's concern with the part that language plays in epistemology. I will collect the statements of his views on language and its role in knowledge and communication. A comparison between Bohr's ideas and those of Ludwig Wittgenstein shows some interesting parallels and differences.

The background provided by this specialized inquiry into the history of European philosophy, language, and science serves as the basis for a philosophical evaluation and critique of Bohr's work. At issue is the way Bohr tied these elements together in his *main argument*. Modern scientific research on language and concept acquisition will be used to evaluate some of Bohr's claims regarding the epistemological primacy of language. This will help in the examination of his perspectives on language and his statement of the need for classical physics and classical concepts to describe measuring instruments and experimental results. These inquiries will also help decide whether his claim that complementarity is a general aspect of epistemology and his applications of it outside of physics are plausible.

Part IV is devoted to reflecting on the epistemological theory that has emerged. As a test of Bohr's ideas, I follow a suggestion he made and look at epistemological issues in classical physics. I have outlined above his feeling that in the relation of classical thermodynamics to statistical mechanics a concept like that of complementarity is required to reconcile the proper application of the concepts of energy and temperature. Bohr's concern with the subject/object distinction also has a parallel in the relation of thermodynamics to statistical mechanics—but not in the form that he had expected it.

A detailed comparison of Bohr's approach to the theory of measurement in quantum mechanics with von Neumann's is the next concern. The notion of a measuring instrument is examined in term of the conditions a physical system must meet in order to qualify as a measuring instrument. The account of Bohr's approach to measurement comes out of the prior discussion of his understanding of the requirements on an observation. Because he allowed only a closed experiment to be subject to quantum analysis, there are significant differences in the ways that Bohr and von Neumann approached measurement in terms of both formalism and their views of the way a measurement works. This includes the reduction of the wavefunction by consciousness at the end of an experiment in von Neumann's approach versus the closure of the experiment in Bohr's approach.

Closure is a key concept in Bohr's theory because it represents the point at which quantum probabilities are converted into macroscopic observations. Because of the important role of the concept of closure, Bohr's speculations concerning how this might come about are examined. His hunch that closure might be explained in terms of an irreversible increase in entropy during an observation is shown not to be adequate. While Bohr would not have accepted an attempt to solve these problems within quantum dynamics, as many have tried with quantum ergodic theories and decoherence theories, I will use some other recent work to provide an epistemological solution to the problem of closure consistent with Bohr's perspective.

The interpretation of quantum mechanics is another area in which Bohr's viewpoint differs significantly from those of others. To contrast the way Bohr thought about these matters with some current approaches such as decoherence theory, some of the more recent work of other authors is reviewed briefly. Bohr's epistemological viewpoint is compared with the attempts of most of these authors to interpret the wavefunction realistically as a physical substance and to use quantum dynamics to provide a resolution of the problems.

A summary of significant epistemological and theoretical problems in quantum mechanics that are outstanding illustrates the conceptual problems that are still faced there. These involve specific issues such as the question of whether a photon interferes only with itself or with other photons. A number of other issues are connected with the relation of microscopic quantum theory to the macroscopic world we inhabit.

The work in this book is completed by returning to the question of the connection of subject and object. I bring together the study of the philosophical themes Bohr used in his work and the discussion of the physical implications of the subject/object distinction for an assessment. The final step is to review the threads in Bohr's work that have been separated during the course of this analysis. I tie them together and re-present Bohr's epistemological work in a form I feel preserves the harmony of his thought and meets the objections I have raised. An Epilogue closes the circle we have opened and echoes the poetry with which we began.

1.4 The Literature on Bohr

The articles written on Bohr and on his ideas in recent years are literally too numerous to mention. In addition, the response to the problem of interpreting quantum mechanics in the last 75 years has been a torrent of ideas, systems, and solutions. I have tried to do justice to as many of these sources as possible.

In terms of the general philosophical questions of concern to quantum mechanics, and the importance of the historical standpoint in both physics and philosophy to understanding it, the books by Max Jammer [1966], [1974], and earlier ones, stand out. Philosophical issues in Bohr's work were the main focus of book length treatments by Klaus M. Meyer-Abich [1965], Henry Folse [1985], David Murdoch [1985], John Honner [1987], Jan Faye [1991], David Favrholdt [1992], Sandro Petruccioli [1993]. There were also books by the physicists Wolfgang Pauli, Werner Heisenberg, Max Born, Leon Rosenfeld, and many others. Several scientific biographies of Bohr have been useful as well. There well over 600 other works that play an active role in this discussion of various aspects of Bohr's work.

While Bohr has fared relatively well in most of the full-length books in terms of careful treatments of his ideas and, recently, attention to their evolution over time, he has not done so well in the philosophical papers concerning his work. Many of the papers on Bohr by philosophers of physics, as opposed to historians of physics, place him in philosophical categories and then fault him for not representing these positions correctly or consistently. This approach fails to capture what Bohr was getting at and leads to a philosophical dead end. This unfortunate pattern seems to have infected papers on Einstein as well. Recently, however, a number of philosophers have begun to express doubts about this procedure and have tried to look more carefully at what Bohr said within his own framework as a physicist.

Quite a few papers were written in the 1960s and early 1970s concerning the philosophical aspects of Bohr's work and the interpretation of quantum mechanics. A second wave of interest in Bohr began in the mid 1980s and has lasted until the present. In the second wave, more historical materials have become readily available with the publications of the collected papers of both Bohr and Einstein and of collections of letters between Bohr and many other scientists.

The question of philosophical influences on Bohr has become a contentious issue and an ongoing controversy. Not too much was written about these issues until the 1950s and 1960s. Among the initial group of authors that considered influences of some kind are Carl-Friederich von Weizsäcker [1952], [1955], Rosenfeld [1963a], Åage Petersen [1963], the essays in Stefan Rozental [1964], Jammer [1966], and Gerald Holton [1970]. William James, Søren Kierkegaard, and Harald Høffding were the early favorites with some aspects of Immanuel Kant thrown in. In more recent books, some of the early favorites have lost favor and the roles of others enhanced. The study of this question has culminated in an ongoing controversy concerning influences on Bohr carried on primarily between the Danish philosophers David Favrholdt and Jan Faye.

David Favrholdt [1976] was an early dissenting voice concerning the influences on Bohr. He was concerned with refuting the "long-winded theories about the great inspiration" Bohr received from Danish philosophy. He justly criticized Jammer's account of Kierkegaard's influence on Bohr as insupportable either with regard to the means of transmission to Bohr or with respect to Bohr's ideas. He acknowledged that Bohr was acquainted with Poul Møller's book, *Adventures of a Danish Student*, from an early age, but questioned whether it had much influence on him. Favrholdt, p. 211, went on to mention the account in Høffding's *Memoirs* (*Eridringer*, 1928) of Høffding's friendship with Bohr's father, Christian Bohr, and his long acquaintance with Niels Bohr, but, referring to Niels, concluded that "there is no evidence whatsoever that he has been influenced philosophically by Høffding." He dismissed the discussions between Bohr and Høffding over the years as being of little philosophical significance except to Høffding in his later years. In this regard he mentioned that Høffding ended his last work with the statement: "A new step forward in the theory of knowledge will first be taken by a philosopher who in his younger days has acquainted himself with Einstein's and Niels Bohr's thoughts." He agreed with Rosenfeld that Bohr had probably not read James until about 1932. He also cited the letter by Rosenfeld to Holton [**1970**], p. 1059, in which Rosenfeld stated that Bohr had told him that he was "quite alone in working out these ideas, and had no help from anybody." Finally, Favrholdt discounted any influence on Bohr by philosophers at the University of Copenhagen after Høffding's death.

Faye is another Danish scholar who has studied Bohr extensively. Faye opposed Favrholdt's view in an article and proposed that not only was Høffding an influence on Bohr, but that Bohr had adopted specific elements of Høffding's philosophy for his work. Favrholdt replied to this in a second article and Faye [**1991**] then responded with a book length work in which he made a careful textual analysis of Bohr's work over time. He disagreed strongly with Favrholdt's dismissal of Høffding's philosophical influence on Bohr and presented evidence to establish the connection between Bohr and Høffding and its importance. Faye presented an overview of Høffding's philosophy and put forth a detailed argument concerning the scope and significance of the relationship between Bohr and Høffding. Faye expanded on his thesis that Bohr's philosophy is adapted directly from Høffding's philosophy.[4]

Faye examined some of the some major components of Høffding's philosophy that he claimed Bohr had accepted as his own. After stating that Bohr was very much influenced by Høffding's ideas when working on the interpretation of quantum mechanics in 1927, he, p. 127, argued that

"Over the preceding twenty years Bohr had identified himself so much with Høffding's approach to philosophical problems, his way of describing them and the solutions he put forward that this philosophy had become fundamental to Bohr's own philosophical outlook. We shall discover both Høffding's criterion of reality and his analysis of

---
[4]See also H. Kragh [**1992**].

the subject-object problem in Bohr's development of his conception of complementarity."

In this statement and many similar ones, Faye presented Høffding as not only a powerful influence on Bohr's philosophy, but essentially the only one. This is a persistent theme in Faye's approach to Bohr. In reference to Bohr's epistemological argument that classical concepts must be retained in the description of measuring instruments and the results of observation, Faye, p. 134, stated: "Thus, Bohr had learned from Høffding that the content of perception may not altogether comply with the forms of perception, which consist of the categories the mind applies to phenomena in order to make them intelligible. Bohr was well prepared for a situation where the classical framework might fail to apply to our experience of the physical world .... But, in spite of this fact, Bohr had also been taught that the forms of perception remain the only concepts we have with which we can apprehend that very same experience." As a final example, Faye, p. 225, spoke of what he called "Bohr's semantic theory". He characterized it in the statement "In general, Bohr holds that the objects of our perception, the phenomena, are not objective or well-defined in themselves; it is first when, and only when, they are grasped by virtue of their subsumption under the concept of continuity that the content of our experience can be said to be a concern with the real." These statements go far beyond what is warranted by Bohr's writings, his careful mode of expression, and the evidence given by others concerning what he intended. As rational reconstructions of Bohr's views, in other words, they seem wrong and Faye's attempts to reframe Bohr's thought as expressions of Høffding's philosophy feels very forced.

Favrholdt [1991] responded to Faye's earlier papers and then [1992] with a book length work, which was completed before Faye's 1991 book was published, in which he systematically debunked a sequence of what he called myths about influences on Bohr. Favrholdt examined the same sources that Faye did. These include records of meetings of the Danish scientific society of which Bohr was a member and at one time president, the published letters between Høffding and Bohr and between Høffding and the French philosopher Emile Meyerson, and records of friends and colleagues of Bohr, along with many others. He systematically discussed Bohr's family of origin, Høffding's *Filosofikum* course in the history of philosophy that Bohr attended, Bohr's relation to Høffding and his contact with him, the student group Ekliptika, Bohr's knowledge of philosophy, and the Kierkegaard, James, and Høffding myths as he called them. Favrholdt then went through a sequence of specific philosophical issues and inquired if Bohr acquired his views on them from Høffding. Favrholdt, pp. 119–122, concluded that if anyone was a significant philosophical influence on Bohr it was Bohr's fellow student, friend, and relative, Edgar Rubin. He, p. 122–126, also discounted possible influences by Mach and Kant that had been suggested by various authors.

Favrholdt, p. 32, mentioned that Bohr was interested in almost everything and was attentive at lectures at the Academy on many different topics when the lecturer was absorbed in the subject. He noted also that Bohr owned some books on philosophy, read a lot, read quickly, and would often pick a book at random to read before bed. Favrholdt, pp. 124–125, did acknowledge that "Bohr had to learn philosophy from somebody, but this does not imply that he was influenced by them." He went on to say that Bohr probably obtained his ideas from Anton Thomsen and Høffding and discussed them over the years with Rubin. He then quoted Honner's [**1987**] complaint that attempts to find influences on Bohr by various philosophers had been made many times "but the spoils have definitely been poor." Honner had also noted that attempts had been made to categorize Bohr as a pragmatist, idealist, positivist, etc., but felt that the risk of mistaken identification was high. Finally, Favrholdt quoted Honner's statement "In so far as one can describe Bohr as a philosopher, one must concede at the outset that his philosophy is *sui generis.*"

Favrholdt and Faye have both done a service in presenting many facts concerning Bohr's life and work in Copenhagen. Favrholdt's detailed analysis seems to be the best fit with the information available and with Honner's statement that Bohr's philosophy is *sui generis*. As a consequence, it seems clear that Bohr was not operating from a philosophical position that he inherited from someone else. This also means that Høffding, James, and Kant were not direct philosophical influences, although Bohr may have become acquainted with their ideas through Høffding, Thomsen, Rubin, his reading, and his many discussions with other physicists and philosophers.

In spite of the differences between the viewpoints expressed in the literature on Bohr, all have brought out new points of view and new materials that have contributed to understanding him. The books and articles mentioned above and in the Bibliography of this book offer in varying degrees a philosophical analysis and systematization of Bohr's work as he presented it. In almost all cases, this has meant accepting Bohr's *main argument* as the foundation of his epistemology and approaching it in essentially the same way he did. A different tack was taken in this book from the beginning because it was clear that to fully understand Bohr requires going beyond what he said and examining critically the justifications he gave for his epistemological positions. Accomplishing this task led me into distant waters for many years.

1.5 Bohr at Work

In spite of the fact that much of the information presented in this section has been reviewed in much more detail in the other books mentioned above, I will present briefly my independent investigation, done some time ago, of aspects of Bohr's working relations with others and his relations with Høffding in particular. For more details on Bohr's working relationships, see the books referred to.

Bohr's approach to the problems of early quantum theory was by way of conceptual analysis and a continual reexamination of the experiments and how to describe them. This offered a strong contrast to the more mathematical physicists who often surrounded him. It was both a source of strength for him and at times a weakness. He needed others to work as "sounding boards" for him as he worked out his ideas verbally. Those, such as Hendrik A. Kramers, could then render these ideas mathematically. Weizsäcker spoke of "Bohr's slaves" in this regard and felt that it inhibited some of them from being better physicists.[5]

With regard to the questions of philosophical influence, Bohr himself explicitly rejected the idea that there was much direct influence on his thought in the work of philosophers.[6] This view is also common among those who knew Bohr and worked with him.[7] Bohr also expressed skepticism concerning the work of professional philosophers.[8]

In spite of these views of Bohr and his coworkers, there is considerable evidence in Bohr's own words that he became familiar with the significant ideas of philosophy at an early age.[9] Harald Høffding, a philosopher at the University of Copenhagen for over 30 years, and Bohr's father, Christian Bohr, participated in the lively intellectual life of Copenhagen at end of the nineteenth century.[10] Many of those discussions were held in the Bohr household and the children were allowed to listen. These discussions continued until they were ended by Christian Bohr's death. Bohr recalled one discussion in which the physicist Christian Christiansen humorously chided Høffding about hidebound philosophers. He also spoke of the sweep of Høffding's work and of Høffding's full sympathy for the researcher in physics working at the far limit of scientific inquiry.

Leon Rosenfeld [**1946**] stated that Bohr's formal education in philosophy was limited to the lectures given by Høffding in his Filosofikum course on the history of philosophy and logic. This course was required of all entering students. In Høffding's Filosofikum lectures of 1903–1904, Bohr was certainly

---

[5] Wolfgang Pauli shared some of these feelings. The way Bohr worked was captured in detailed interviews with Heisenberg, Pauli, Victor F. Weisskopf, Weizsäcker, and others in the Bohr Archive.

[6] This is stated by Bohr [**Arch**], Interview, 11/17/62, in the last interview of Bohr before his death conducted by Thomas Kuhn, Åage Petersen and Erik Rüdinger.

[7] See, for example, Rosenfeld [**1946**], Oscar Klein [**1964**], p. 74, Rozental [**1964**], pp. 183–184, Abraham Pais [**1964**], p. 219, and Pais [**1991**], Chapter 19.

[8] See Pais [**1964**], p. 219. See also John Honner [**1987**], p. 72.

[9] In Part II of the "Oversigt over det Forhandlinger," for the period 1930–1933, of the Videnskabens Selskab (Scientific Association), Bohr discussed his encounters with Høffding.

[10] See also Bohr [**Arch**], 13:2, 1932, p. 1, where he mentioned that Høffding was an intimate friend of his father's in a manuscript titled "Høffding's views on Physics and Philosophy."

exposed to the ideas of Locke, Berkeley, Hume, Kant, and especially Høffding, among others. Bohr was actively interested in issues of epistemology at the University of Copenhagen and even thought then about writing a book on it. But, as mentioned before, Bohr did not acknowledge that these influences were very strong ones.[11]

On the other side, we do have some indirect evidence that Bohr was aware of some work done on mainstream issues in philosophy. For example, in 1924, Høffding spoke in a letter to Emile Meyerson of the contribution of "my friend Niels Bohr" in choosing a title for the Danish version of one of his essays.[12] Høffding also spoke in letters 4/23/26 and 12/30/26 of attending seminars that Bohr presented at the academy on his work. He was particularly proud of Bohr's statements concerning the importance of his work on the occasion of a volume published to commemorate his 85th birthday. He, p. 149, wrote of it to Meyerson in a letter on 3/30/28: "Among the eulogies which our press has published on the occasion of that day, an article by Mr. Niels Bohr in particular has been a source of great joy. Mr. Bohr declared that he has found in my books ideas which have aided thinkers in the understanding of their work and these have been a real help for them." In letters on 8/13/28, p. 156, 10/3/29, p. 169, and 10/21/29, p. 172, Høffding spoke of the warm friendship of Bohr, his interest in philosophy and literature and how important his visits had been when Høffding or his wife were ill. In a paper analyzing Kant's categories and his own, Høffding [**1930a**], p. 488, footnote, thanked Bohr for his help: "I allow myself here a personal note.— ... And now, as far as the meaning of the newest physics for philosophy is concerned, it has been of the greatest value to me that Professor Niels Bohr has helped me in his very instructive way during the study of his works."

Bohr was also engaged in the discussions of current ideas at the University of Copenhagen over many years. His son Hans Bohr [**1964**], pp. 331–332, wrote about his active interest in the intellectual life at the University of Copenhagen and his participation in it. He stated that Bohr was open to new ideas and went to the meetings of many societies with an open mind and listened with concentration. Faye and Favrholdt have mentioned a number of specific occasions on which Bohr participated in philosophical discussions of lectures at the scientific society.

One author that has been mentioned as a source of ideas for Bohr is William James. James [**1881**] wrote about the stream of consciousness and mentioned the word complementarity in relation to competing streams of thought. Most of the evidence, however, implies that Bohr did not read

---

[11]See Pais [**1991**], p. 423–424.
[12]See the letter dated 2/12/24 in Frithiof Brandt, Hans Høffding, and Jean Adigard Des Gautries, eds. [**1939**], p. 70. Harald Høffding subsequently spoke of "my friend Niels Bohr" in a discussion of participants in the Academy of Sciences in a letter to Meyerson dated 4/23/26, p. 123.

William James until 1932.[13] Høffding and James were friends and Høffding translated some of James' work into Danish. The thinking of James in relation to that of Høffding will be reviewed as part of the exploration of the ideas concerning consciousness, empiricism, and knowledge that were current in Copenhagen at the turn of the twentieth century and after.

The evidence is certainly clear that Bohr was not being disingenuous in his denial that there was a significant philosophical influence on him when he worked on the ideas of complementarity. There is no evidence that he studied philosophical writings outside of the classroom or searched these texts for answers to the problems he was facing.[14] It is also true that Bohr's discussions of Høffding's thought in relation to his own were in commemorative speeches and eulogies and not in an academic setting. However, as will be demonstrated in several places below, Bohr received a good deal of indirect and direct philosophical training in the Danish educational system. This was due to the nineteenth century European concern with the epistemological foundation of the sciences, the place of philosophy as part of a basic education, and the strong influence of Kant that was still felt at the beginning of the twentieth century. In addition, there is a good deal of evidence marshaled in the discussion of the sources of Bohr's ideas in Part III that leads to the conclusion that Bohr had absorbed many of his basic epistemological ideas from the philosophical environment in Europe at that time. While indirect, the weight of this evidence and the supporting textual data make a strong case. I conclude that, while Bohr did not study philosophy after his student days, these ideas were part of the atmosphere he grew up in, learned in, and lived in, so the ideas he used in his writings were almost certainly part of the furniture of the conceptual world he occupied.

Bohr felt troubled by his relationship to philosophers. In the last interview before his death, he [**Arch**], Interview 11/17/62, spoke of his concern for their lack of interest in the fundamental epistemological significance of complementarity. He asked the interviewers if any philosophers were working on his ideas or if they were being taught to schoolchildren. This self-portrait is consistent with the picture painted by Rozental [**1964**], pp. 183–184, of Bohr's concern with philosophy:

> "It was always a source of sorrow to Bohr that the professional philosophers, who after all should be the very people to apply more broadly the important viewpoints which had emerged during the development of atomic physics, did not seem sufficiently interested in

---

[13]See Holton [**1970**], pp. 1034–1035, and Favrholdt [**1992**].

[14]Most of the biographical information on Bohr contributed by his contemporaries supports this view. See, for example, Rosenfeld [**1946**], Ruth Moore [**1966**], and O. Klein [**1964**], p. 74. Weizsäcker [**Arch**], Interview 7/9/63, p. 23, felt that Bohr's general statements suffered from his lack of training in philosophy.

the problems. He made use of every opportunity to talk to philosophers both in Denmark and elsewhere, but most often without satisfactory result."[15]

Bohr reacted with humor when he suggested that "a specialist knows everything about nothing; a philosopher knows nothing about everything." But the disappointment was real.

The physicists and philosophers that have been influenced by Bohr since his early days are too numerous to mention here. I will discuss, however, in some detail the writings of Walter M. Elsasser, Max Delbrück, Gunter Stent, Viggo Brøndal, and Pascual Jordan because they did work outside physics that contributed ideas within the framework of Bohr's thinking.

---

[15] For more about Bohr's feelings about philosophers and his disappointment that some physicists—such as Planck and Einstein, as well as younger ones—still did not accept complementarity, see the last interview of Bohr in the Bohr Archive, Bohr [**Arch**], Interview, 11/17/62.

CHAPTER 2

The Development of Bohr's Thought: 1911–1925

Bohr's conceptual development in the context of the scientific issues he was involved in and struggling to understand is the central concern of Part I of this book. This brief history of Bohr's thought and work in physics between 1912 and 1962 is presented to show how the philosophical ideas that he ultimately settled on emerged out of the issues he was struggling with in physics.

2.1 The Crisis in Classical Theory

Problems in the use of classical theory for the explanation of observations began to develop in the late nineteenth century.[1] The approach to electrodynamics pioneered by Michael Faraday and completed by James Clerk Maxwell had just successfully widened the conceptual framework of physics beyond that of simple mechanics. Maxwell brought together a number of relations satisfied by electric and magnetic fields that had been obtained previously by C. A. Coulomb, André-Marie Ampére, and Faraday. He added to this collection the divergence free condition on the magnetic field and corrected Ampére's law by adding the displacement current. Maxwell's equations supported Faraday's concept of the electromagnetic field and predicted electromagnetic radiation, which was soon observed by Hertz.

The introduction of the field concept and the noncentral forces of electromagnetism were accompanied by some conceptual dislocation. For several years after the introduction of Maxwell's equations a number of workers, including Maxwell, tried to construct mechanical models based on central forces to explain the noncentral interactions of electrodynamics. These attempts failed. Nevertheless, electrodynamics was assimilated into physics without forcing at that time a serious revision of Newtonian mechanics.[2]

Classical mechanics and the theory of electrodynamics had been successfully applied to explaining an increasing number of observed phenomena during the last half of the nineteenth century. However, in the last quarter of the century, a number of observations had been made that could not be accounted for by these classical theories in any direct way. The specific heats of substances and the spectrum of blackbody radiation were the most important phenomena for which there were discrepancies between classical calculations and observations. An attempt had been made by Wilhelm Wien late in the nineteenth century to develop an equation describing the spectral distribution expected for blackbodies based on classical concepts. While this equation agreed with the experimental data in the high-energy region of the spectrum, it failed in the low frequency region. William Strutt, Lord Rayleigh, on the other hand, had worked out another radiation law (that was subsequently corrected by James Jeans) that was successful in the low frequency region, but failed in the high frequency region of the spectrum.

In 1900, Max Planck discovered a law, primarily by thermodynamic reasoning, for the spectrum of blackbody radiation that agreed with Rayleigh's formula in the low frequency region and with Wien's formula in the high frequency region—thereby successfully accounting for the whole spectrum.[3]

---

[1] For a contemporary account of the issues facing physicists in the late nineteenth century, see the work of Hendrik Antoon Lorentz [**1909**], Chapter II.

[2] See J. Turner [**1955**] on Maxwell's models and dynamical explanations.

[3] For a discussion of the development of Planck's work, see Kuhn [**1978**], Jammer [**1966**], and Martin J. Klein [**1963**]. A detailed critical review of Planck's use of Boltzmann's

Planck's formula implied, however, that electromagnetic radiation was not emitted continuously as classical theory would require, but is emitted in units, or 'quanta' as they soon came to be called, for which the energy is proportional to the frequency. This relation is expressed in the form $E = h\nu$, where E is the energy of the light quantum, ν is its frequency, and h is a constant called Planck's constant. By contrast, the energy of a radiation field in classical electrodynamics is proportional to the sum of the squares of the amplitudes of the fluctuating electric and magnetic field components but not to the frequency of the radiation.

In an important paper published in 1905, Einstein [**1905**] showed that both thermodynamic fluctuations and the photoelectric effect could be explained in terms of Planck's quanta.[4] In particular, the concept of a light quantum explained the experimental fact that photoelectrons are emitted immediately after a metallic surface is illuminated with low intensity light rather than after an interval during which a region of the metallic surface absorbs enough energy from a wave to expel an electron. Einstein [**1907**] continued his work on quanta of energy in his paper explaining the anomalous results for the specific heat of substances at low temperatures.

By the beginning of the twentieth century, the difference between the mechanical assumptions implicit in electrodynamics and those of Newtonian theory came to the fore in the work of H. A. Lorentz, Henri Poincaré, and Albert Einstein, and led to the development of the special theory of relativity. Einstein in particular understood in 1905 the need to reconcile the Galilean transformations appropriate to Newton's mechanical equations with the Lorentz transformation appropriate to electrodynamics. The changes in the perspective on coordinate transformations in Einstein's special theory of relativity included the elimination of Newton's absolute space and time. The subsequent development of the general theory of relativity eliminated inertial frames as privileged mechanical coordinate frames. What did not change significantly was the materialist metaphysics, which reflected Newton's assumptions concerning the matter described by his equations, that had come to be seen as the conceptual framework of classical physical theory.

1877 relation between entropy and probability in the derivation of his blackbody radiation formula is given in QTS, Part III.

[4]Einstein's [**1905**] statement of his conception of a light quantum is given on p. 368: "It seems to me that the observations associated with blackbody radiation, fluorescence, the production of cathode rays by ultraviolet light and other related phenomena connected with the emission or transformation of light are more readily understood if one assumes that the energy of the light is discontinuously distributed in space. In accord with the assumption to be considered here, the energy of a light ray spreading out from a point source is not continuously distributed over increasing space but consists of a finite number of energy quanta which are localized at points in space, which move without dividing and which can only be produced and absorbed in complete units."

2.2 The Theory of the Hydrogen Atom

Bohr's doctoral work at the University of Copenhagen was concerned with the properties of electrons in metals. He attempted to apply classical statistical mechanical ideas to this study. Direct attempts to do this failed, and in the introduction to his thesis, he indicated that the usual Hamiltonian mechanics does not apply to bound electrons in atoms. Soon after this work, Bohr left Denmark for England to do post-doctoral studies and, after visiting J. J. Thomson's laboratory, ended up working in Ernest Rutherford's laboratory. Rutherford had just completed scattering experiments that showed that the atom has a very small hard nucleus surrounded by a much larger volume of space, so Bohr naturally turned to the problem of the structure of the atom in the work he began in 1912.

By 1911, Rutherford had become convinced that atoms could not have the "plum pudding" configuration, with electrons embedded like raisins is a positively charged cloud, proposed for them by J. J. Thomson.[5] Rutherford's scattering experiments showed that the atom has a very small, positively charged, inner core, which contains almost all the mass of the atom, surrounded by negatively charged electrons at some distance from the core. It was known that classical electrodynamics could not account for an atom constructed of charged particles in a static configuration because, as was well-known by then, there is no solution of the laws of motion in classical electrodynamics that allows a collection of charged particles to remain in a static configuration. Nor could classical electrodynamics account for a stable atom constructed of moving charged particles because any localized system of charged particles will exert forces on each other and the particles will be accelerated. Classical theory requires that these particles radiate which means that the system will continuously radiate energy and decay after a finite lifetime—contrary to the stability observed for matter under ordinary conditions. Thomson's [**1913**] attempt to explain the structure of the atom using a combination of classical ideas with certain assumptions concerning the confinement of the internal distribution of charge in tubes inside the atom was not successful.

In 1913 Bohr proposed an answer to the problems of stability and structure of the atom by introducing the concept of a stationary state. He did assume that the atom is a classical dynamical system, but departed from classical theory by assuming that electrons do not radiate when the atom is in a stationary state. Bohr saw as his overriding task in this theory accounting for the stability of the atom from a theoretical perspective. He was also concerned in these papers with investigating the question of particle orbits and energy relationships within the atom. Since an excited atom will emit radiation, Bohr hoped to account for the energy emitted in terms of definite

---

[5]See Jammer [**1966**], Chapter 2, Section 2, for more on this.

energy changes within the atom. He was looking, moreover, for some mechanical changes or motions in the atom that would account for the frequency, intensity, and polarization of the spectral lines emitted by the atom.[6]

In applying this approach to the problem of explaining spectral lines, Bohr tried to relate the energy and form of the radiation to the motion of the electron within the atom as it makes a transition from one stationary state to another. He noted that under certain specific conditions the motion of the electrons in changing stationary states and emitting or absorbing radiation could be expected to be similar to that of classical electrons. He then maintained that calculations based on a new theory would be expected to agree with calculations of classical theory when these conditions are met.

As a consequence of his investigation, Bohr [1913] made several far-reaching hypotheses by means of which he was able—essentially by suspending classical electromagnetic theory in certain circumstances—to make headway on these problems. Bohr [1913], p. 19, summarized the problems connected with the nature and production of Röntegen rays, the problem of specific heats and the photoelectric effect, and then made the following working hypothesis:[7]

> "The result of the discussions of these questions seems to be a general acknowledgment of the inadequacy of the classical electro-dynamics in describing the behavior of systems of atomic size. Whatever the alteration in the laws of motion of the electron may be, it seems necessary to introduce in the laws in question a quantity foreign to classical electrodynamics, i.e., Planck's constant, or as it is often called, the elementary quantum of action. By the introduction of this quantity the question of the stable configuration of the electrons in the atoms is essentially changed, as this constant is of such dimensions and magnitude that it, together with the mass and charge of the particles, can determine a length of the order of magnitude required."

The only constant of length that can be constructed from h, m and e is proportional to $\lambda_C = \hbar^2/me^2$, where h is Planck's constant, $\hbar = h/2\pi$ and m and $-e$ are the mass and charge of the electron, respectively. The quantity λ_C is now called the Compton wavelength and is about 10^{-10} cm for an electron.

This work resulted in three papers published in 1913 on the structure of the hydrogen atom. Bohr discussed the implications of his work in an address to the Copenhagen Physical Society in 1913. He stated that he had given up the attempt to "explain" spectral laws, but wished "to indicate a way in which it appears possible to bring the spectral laws into close connection with other

---

[6]For a detailed study of the development of Bohr's theory of hydrogen atom, see John L. Heilbron and Thomas S. Kuhn [1969]. See also Sandro Petruccioli [1993].

[7]Bohr [1913], p. 2. See also Bohr's brief account of the origin of some of his ideas in 1912-1918 in Bohr [1961], pp. 36–40.

properties of the elements, which appear to be equally inexplicable on the basis of the present state of the science."[8] In addition to these problems concerning radiation, Bohr, p. 2, noted that phenomena involving collisions between two electrons, one of which is bound in an atom, might require different concepts as well.

Bohr's, p. 7, principal assumptions in setting up his theory were:

"(1) That the dynamical equilibrium of the systems in the ordinary stationary states can be discussed by help of the ordinary mechanics, while the passing of the systems between different stationary states cannot be treated on that basis. (2) That the latter process is followed by the emission of a *homogeneous* radiation, for which the relation between the frequency and the amount of energy emitted is the one given by Planck's theory."

Bohr then used these assumptions to compute the dimensions of the lowest stationary orbit an electron could have in an atom. He, p. 15, justified this calculation by an appeal to spectroscopic data.

Bohr expressed the radii of the allowed electron orbits, corresponding to the "stationary states", in terms of λ_C as (TIS notation) $(n^2 \lambda_C)/Z$, where n is the number of the orbit and Z is the number of positive charges in the nucleus. The formula he had obtained for the allowed radii took the form

$$(2.1) \qquad a_n = \frac{n^2 \hbar^2}{Z m e^2}.$$

From the relation $v = r\omega$ connecting the velocity of a particle in a circular orbit of radius r to the angular velocity ω in radians/sec, Bohr showed that the kinetic energy T of the electron in a stationary state is given by

$$(2.2) \qquad T = \tfrac{1}{2} m a_n^2 \omega^2.$$

He, p. 15, let U be the potential energy of the nucleus-electron system. This is the Coulomb potential at the radius a_n that is expressed as

$$(2.3) \qquad U = -\frac{Z e^2}{a_n}.$$

The virial theorem implies that $T = -\tfrac{1}{2} U$ for inverse square forces. It follows from this and the formula $E = T + U$ for the total energy E that

$$(2.4) \qquad E = -T = -\frac{Z^2 m e^4}{2 n^2 \hbar^2}.$$

Finally, Bohr used (2.2) with (2.4) to obtain the frequency of the electron in its orbit in terms of these quantities as

$$(2.5) \qquad \nu_n = \frac{\omega_n}{2\pi} = \frac{Z^2 m e^4}{2\pi n^3 \hbar^3}.$$

---

[8]This is quoted in Jammer [**1966**], p. 112.

Bohr, p. 15, then defined the "permanent" state of the system as the "one among the stationary states during the formation of which the greatest amount of energy is emitted." This is now called the ground state. From these calculations, Bohr, p. 15, concluded

> "According to the above considerations, we are led to assume that these configurations will correspond to states of the system in which there is no radiation of energy; states which consequently will be stationary as long as the system is not disturbed from the outside."

Since, by (2.5), the angular momentum of the electron in the atom is given by $p_\theta = mr^2\omega = ma_n^2\omega_n = n\hbar$, Bohr, pp. 22, 24–25, characterized these stationary states by the following condition on the angular momentum of an electron in the ground state ($n = 1$) of the atom

> "In any molecular system consisting of positive nuclei and electrons in which the nuclei are at rest relative to each other and the electrons move in circular orbits, the angular momentum of every electron around the center of its orbit will in the permanent state of the system be equal to $h/2\pi$ where h is Planck's constant."

This assumption was soon generalized by Sommerfeld and formed what came to be called the Bohr-Sommerfeld quantization condition:[9]

$$(2.6) \qquad \oint d\theta\, p_\theta = nh = J.$$

In the course of his discussion, Bohr [**1913**], pp. 15–16, moved from talking about orbits to talking about stationary states. His conception of a state, and a stationary state in particular, seems to be related to the concept of state as it was used in classical mechanics, statistical mechanics, and thermodynamics in some respects, but not in others.[10] However, Bohr's use of the term also differs sharply from the way it is used in other theories. Bohr used the discrete parameter n to characterize the state while for each of the other theories the state depends on parameters that can be varied continuously. Thus Bohr, in concert with Planck, has made a sharp break with the past.

Bohr [**1913**] also formulated the first version of what was to become his correspondence principle. He compared a bound electron to a free electron when both have the same energy. Since a free electron does not radiate, one could expect a correspondence between its motion and that of the bound electron as the radiation of the bound electron passing from one stationary state to another goes to zero. Using formula (2.4) for the energy levels of the

---

[9] See Jammer [**1966**], pp. 92–93. See also pp. 69–88 in Jammer for a further discussion of Bohr's early theory of the hydrogen atom.

[10] Compare Planck's use of the concept of state at about the same time, which has been discussed by Martin Klein [**1963**]. See also Meyer-Abich [**1965**], p. 56ff, for a discussion of some aspects of Bohr's use of "state".

atom, (2.5) for the frequency, and calculating the energy radiated in passing from one level to another, one can easily show that for large n we have

(2.7a) $$h\nu = \Delta T \approx 2T\frac{\Delta n}{n},$$

(2.7b) $$\Delta \nu_n \approx 3\nu_n \frac{\Delta n}{n}.$$

The radiation of the electron goes to zero as $\Delta n/n \to 0$. Bohr, pp. 16–17, concluded that we should therefore expect the two cases to coincide as n increases and $\Delta n/n$ becomes small. Using (2.7b), this can also be expressed as "the limit where the difference between the frequency of the rotation of the electron in successive states is very small compared with the absolute value of the frequency."[11] Bohr [1913], pp. 6–7, felt that this situation represents an 'analogy' between the motion of an electron in the atom and the motion of a free electron.

Another place that Bohr presented his ideas was to a meeting of the British Association for the Advancement of Science in 1913. James Jeans, in a review of the theory of blackbody radiation at that meeting, spoke approvingly of Bohr's theory. Lorentz also addressed the meeting concerning the transfer of energy between matter, resonators, and the ether. He pointed out that the transfer of a quantum of energy from a resonator to the ether was conceivable, but there is a problem understanding the transfer of dispersed energy from the ether to the resonator. Bohr emphasized the difficulty in distinguishing matter and resonators in Lorentz's scheme. Lorentz asked Bohr how he accounted mechanically for his atom and Bohr replied that his theory was not finished.[12]

Bohr's theory may be contrasted with that proposed simultaneously by Thomson [1913]. Thomson's theory included a specific structure for the atom, which does not radiate energy. He stated that it is not necessary to assume that electrostatic forces are the same in the atom as in electrodynamics because the laws of electrostatics represent large-scale averages. The only criterion he imposed on these forces is that the properties the atom possesses in virtue of them should correspond to the actual properties of the atom. There were two types of forces: an inverse cube radial force and an inverse square attractive force confined to a limited number of radial tubes. He was able to show that the emitted radiation in moving from one tube to another is $h\nu$.

In 1915, Bohr extended his 'analogy' concerning the motion of bound and free electrons and connected the mean of the frequency of the electron's orbital rotation in two stationary states with the frequency of the light emitted when

---

[11] Bohr [1915], p. 396. As van der Waerden [1967], pp. 6–7, has pointed out, however, this asymptotic behavior is not displayed by all quantum systems since it is does not hold for the harmonic oscillator.

[12] See the Inaugural Address by Oliver Lodge [1913], pp. 305–306, for these accounts.

the atom passes from one state to another.[13] Bohr also refined his angular momentum conditions in this paper so that it applied only to periodic orbits where, as he assumed before, ordinary mechanical laws apply. He [1915], p. 399, repeated that these laws are known to apply only to mean values of the variables characterizing the motion of the electrons.

2.3 The Correspondence Principle

Einstein [1916] introduced probabilities into atomic physics. He showed that the radiation field in equilibrium with atoms that absorb and emit radiation could be correctly described only by taking account of both the probability of a spontaneous emission or absorption of radiation by the atoms and the probability of an induced transition in the atoms due to the radiation field surrounding them. This was a sharp departure from the usual approach to accounting for these phenomena. The probabilities involved concerned events in individual atoms (assumed at that time to be determined at a deeper level) and could not be accounted for as averages over many atoms in the usual fashion of statistical mechanics.

When he used the concept of stimulated emission in the calculation of the energy of the radiation of a blackbody, Einstein obtained Planck's law.[14] Einstein felt that the necessity of introducing probabilistic laws into the physics of singular events at this juncture was due to our ignorance of the underlying structure that determined the phenomena we observe. As science advanced, one would thus expect that the probabilistic description would be replaced by one representing the causal structure underlying the emission and absorption process.[15] One of the important aspects of the introduction of probabilities into atomic theory at this time was that it provided a widening of the possible theoretical structures.

Bohr elaborated the analogy between classical systems and atomic systems further in his 1918 paper on the quantum theory of line spectra. Reexamining his previous assumptions, he [1918], p. 99, noted that it was obvious that ordinary mechanics does not apply, but

> "On the other hand, from the fact that it has been possible by means of ordinary mechanics and electro-dynamics to account for the phenomena of temperature radiation in the limiting region of slow vibrations, we may expect that any theory capable of describing this phenomenon in accordance with observations will form some sort of natural generalization of the ordinary theory of radiation."

---

[13] See Bohr [1915], p. 396. Meyer-Abich [1965], p. 53, noted that this reformulation of Bohr's ideas was stimulated by a criticism of J. W. Nicolson.

[14] See M. Jammer [1966], p. 112. See also my extended discussion of the work of Planck and Einstein on the theory of radiation in QTS, Part III.

[15] Einstein [1916]; see pp. 66, 76 in the translation in B. L. van der Waerden [1967]. See also Bohr [1918], pp. 130–131, and van der Waerden [1967], pp. 130–131. For other contemporary views, see N. R. Campbell [1920] and W. Campbell [1921], [1926].

Using Einstein's conception of the probability of a transition between two stationary states, he was able to pursue the connection between the classical theory of radiation and his theory of the atom:[16]

"In order to obtain the necessary relations to the ordinary theory of radiation in the limit of slow vibrations, we are therefore led directly to certain conclusions about the probability of transitions between two stationary states in this limit. This leads again to certain general considerations about the connection between the probability of a transition between any two stationary states and the motion of the system in these states, which will be shown to throw light on the question of the polarization and intensity of the different lines of the spectrum of a given system."

And,

"In order to obtain the necessary connection ... to the ordinary theory of radiation in the limit of slow vibrations, we must further claim that a relation as that just proved for the frequencies, will, in the limit of large n, hold also for the intensities of the different lines in the spectrum."

It was already clear to Bohr by this time that a fully mechanical solution to the problem of describing the internal structure of the atom was not to be expected due to the involvement of electrodynamics there. In reference to the effect of an external field on a stationary state of an atom, he [**1918**], p. 120, stated that "... we shall expect that, during the establishment of the field, *the system will in general adjust itself in some unmechanical way* ... ." In the absence of any other way to proceed, Bohr, pp. 98–99, noted that under the conditions in which electrostatic Coulomb forces would be predominant, we would expect a "... close approximation in the description of the motion of the stationary states ... we shall therefore ... for the present *calculate the motions of the particles in the stationary states as the motions of mass-points according to ordinary mechanics* including the modifications claimed by the theory of relativity ... ." Just before this, Bohr, pp. 95-96, had pointed out the validity of some aspects of classical (relativistic) particle mechanics in this domain: "Sommerfeld, by taking the small variation of the mass of the electron with its velocity into account, obtained an explanation of the fine-structure of the hydrogen atom which was found to be in brilliant conformity with measurements." At this point, Bohr felt that the difficulties in forming a coherent theory of the atom were due to the theory of radiation, and not with relativistic mass-point particle mechanics, and not with that part of electrodynamics dealing with the force exerted on charged particles by electrostatic fields.

---

[16]See the translation in van der Waerden [**1967**], pp. 101, 110.

By 1922, Bohr called this relation between classical theory and quantum theory a *correspondence principle*.[17] It was also in 1922 that Bohr pointed out the indispensability of classical concepts in dealing with quantum phenomena. But he felt that this is only necessary for the *present* standpoint of physics. He assumed that a future theory would dispense with classical concepts and introduce its own concepts,[18] and probably felt that quantum theory would follow the model of, say, the evolution of Maxwell's theory. In spite of the success of Einstein's application of statistical methods to radiation, Bohr was not then ready to accept the idea of a light quantum. He felt that although this "point of view" puts certain things "in a clear light," nevertheless it is "unreconcilable" with interference phenomena that are "our chief means of investigating the character of radiation."[19]

Bohr, pp. 157–158, continued his discussion of the light quantum hypothesis with the following passage that illustrates clearly how he approached the problem of analyzing the conceptual issues underlying quantum theory:

> "Certainly we can maintain that the picture which lies at the foundation of the light quantum hypothesis excludes in principle the possibility of a meaningful definition of the concept of the wave number ν, which even in this theory plays an important role. The light quantum hypothesis is therefore not suitable for giving a picture of the model in which the totality of the phenomena which come into question in the application of quantum theory can be arranged. The adequate ways in which this hypothesis renders certain aspects of the phenomena is, on the contrary, suited for the purpose of formulating the principles which lie at the base of the actual employment of quantum theory. This is in support of the point of view advocated on various sides that, in opposition to the description of natural phenomena in classical physics where it is always a question of the statistical results of a great number of individual processes, a complete space-time description of atomic processes cannot be carried out in a way free of contradiction with the help of concepts borrowed from classical electrodynamics, which up to now have been our only means."

Bohr later employed several of the ideas contained in this quotation in formulating complementarity. This is the first way in which he expressed himself

---

[17] Bohr [**1923a**]; see Sections 2, 3 and 4; pp. 142–153. For information on the various forms the correspondence principle has taken in the thought of Bohr and Heisenberg, see Patrick Heelan [**1965**], pp. 114–116. See also the philosophical analysis in Norman Russell Hanson [**1958b**], [**1959**]. For a general discussion of classical mechanics as a limiting form of quantum mechanics, see E. L. Hill [**1966**].

[18] Bohr [**1923a**], p. 117: "At the present standpoint of physics, each description must be grounded in an application of concepts that are introduced and defined in classical theory. The question arises as to the possibility of representing the principles of quantum theory in such a form that this application is free of contradiction."

[19] See Bohr [**1923a**], p. 157; [**1923b**], p. 32.

regarding the "picture which lies at the foundation of the light quantum hypothesis" and the exclusion in principle of "the possibility of a meaningful definition of the concept of the wave number ... ." The second is the concern with the prospect that it might be impossible to give a picture that will encompass the totality of phenomena of concern to quantum theory. The third is the idea that the significance of the light quantum hypothesis is not in giving such a picture, but rather as an aid to the formulation of principles underlying the *actual employment* of quantum theory. These ideas were precursors to the explicit concern on Bohr's part with the conditions under which a particular description may be employed without contradiction in quantum theory. The latter idea in turn was a precursor to, and formed a part of, Bohr's conception of complementarity.

Bohr [**1923a**], p. 142, felt that the probabilistic methods provided only a temporary solution because the duration of the transition process is not taken directly into account "the value of which, however, ... plays an important role in the description of the phenomena." This same argument was later used by Einstein against quantum theory. Bohr [**1923a**], p. 152, also spoke in this paper for the first time about the "definition" of the stationary state with respect to the description of the electron motion: "This deficiency in the sharpness of the description of the motion of electrons in atoms brings with it an unsharpness in the definition of stationary states, the consideration of which in certain cases receives an important meaning." In addition, he, p. 161, emphasized the formal nature of quantum theory.

As these quotations show, the theory of the atom and its interaction with radiation was, for Bohr in 1923, a web of theoretically unconnected heuristic hypotheses and principles.

In his Nobel Prize lecture, Bohr [**1923b**], pp. 38–39, sharpened his formulation of the correspondence principle:

"... the so-called *correspondence principle,* according to which the occurrence of transitions between the stationary states accompanied by the emission of radiation is traced back to the harmonic components, into which the motion of the atom may be resolved and which, according to the classical theory, determine the properties of the radiation to which the motion of the particles gives rise.

According to the correspondence principle, it is assumed that every transition between two stationary states can be correlated with a corresponding harmonic vibration component in such a way that the probability of the occurrence of the transition is dependent on the amplitude of the vibration."

Following the direction indicated in his 1918 paper, Bohr was able to relate the observed properties of radiation with the quantum processes. The amplitude of the classical vibration in a given direction was connected with the probability of the occurrence of a particular transition and was thus related to the intensity of that component in the radiation. From the relative intensities of the components of radiation polarized in different spatial directions, the total polarization can be derived.

2.4 Reflection 1

In the early period of Bohr's work, he came to grips with the physical problem of the stability of the atom and the related problem of explaining the spectra in terms of the structure of the atom and the motions of the electrons within it. It was clear that classical electrodynamics could not account for this structure in any reasonable or straightforward way, since it could offer no explanation for the stability of the atom. Later work demonstrated that the spectrum, although it could be connected to changes in the stationary state of an atom, could not be related in any simple way to the motions of the atomic electrons as would be required by classical theory. Because of the difficulties in applying classical ideas in the quantum domain, and in recognition of the growing difficulties with the requirement that a theory must provide a causal spacetime description of the phenomena, Bohr [**1925b**], pp. 34–35, 44–45, spoke of the impossibility of 'picturing' the events within the atom.[20] This viewpoint was associated with the "nonmechanical" adjustments in the system that Bohr had discussed in 1918.

Bohr consistently used the terms 'theoretical descriptions' or 'descriptions' in his discussions of the theoretical representation of atomic processes. I will discuss the origin of this terminology in Chapters 10 and 11. His choice of this terminology, and his consistent use of it over the lifetime of his work, indicates that he wished to remove any ontological implications from the theoretical terms in the developing quantum theory and remain neutral with respect to the ontological commitments of quantum theory. The perspective he maintained has implications for his views on what quantum theory can tell us about the nature of reality. His view of theories as descriptions, along with his views on reality in this domain, will be discussed in a later chapter.

Bohr's 1913 answer to problems in atomic theory was to propose a hypothesis that solved the stability problem by assumption. The problem concerning the spectrum was relegated in 1918 to the domain of probabilistic transitions, which Bohr felt at the time was a temporary step. These probabilities could be estimated using classical calculations and the correspondence principle.

2.5 The Bohr, Kramers, Slater Theory

While the concept of the photon fit well with Planck's theory that radiation is emitted only in quanta for which the energy is proportional to

---

[20]See also Meyer-Abich [**1965**], pp. 108–109, 110, 112, 127, 133.

the frequency of the light, Bohr had long resisted this concept because it could not be reconciled with the interference properties of electromagnetic waves clearly exhibited in simple experiments with light.[21] However, Louis de Broglie's postulation that matter has a wave aspect and the demonstration in 1924 of interference effects in the electron scattering experiments of C. J. Davisson and L. H. Germer showed that material particles also exhibit a "duality" similar to that of light. This paradoxical dualism occupied much of Bohr's subsequent thought.

Bohr carried this approach even further when he, with Kramers and Slater, developed in 1924 an idea of Slater's that virtual radiation fields determined the energy transitions in atoms associated with the emission of light. Bohr, Kramers and Slater, tried to encompass within one picture the continuous aspects of the wave nature of the propagation of radiation and the discontinuous aspects of the emission and absorption of radiation.[22] Using a conception introduced in Slater [**1924**], Bohr, Kramers and Slater [**1924**] (BKS) worked out a quantum theory of radiation.[23] They [**1924**], p. 785, began by pointing out the contradictory aspects of the attempts to give an "interpretation of the mechanism of interaction between radiation and matter." Interference effects that radiation exhibits under the proper circumstances shows its wave nature. On the other hand, individual events in the emission and absorption of light take place discontinuously, seemingly at an instant, and with a definite transfer of both momentum and energy. By means of the correspondence principle, BKS, pp. 785–786, hoped to connect the discontinuous aspects of the situation to the radiation field in a new way. Moreover, they, p. 788, referred to Einstein's work on the stimulated emission of photons from this perspective and pointed out: "At the present state of the science it seems necessary, as regards the occurrence of transition processes, to content ourselves with considerations of probability." These probabilities were given an operational meaning within the theory by employing the correspondence principle. This allowed them to estimate the transition probabilities using a classical calculation of the intensity of radiation to be expected. In this way, they, p. 789, attempted to obtain quantum electrodynamics as a "rational generalization" of classical electrodynamics.

To link the absorption and emission of radiation to an atom, the concept of a virtual oscillator within an atom was introduced along with its virtual radiation field. These elements were required to be virtual because of the failure to find any direct relation between the motions of the electrons making transitions within atoms and the radiation produced. Spontaneous transitions

---

[21] See also the discussion of Einstein's introduction of the photon concept in Arons and Peppard [**1965**].

[22] For details on the reception of the Bohr, Kramers and Slater paper by Einstein and others, see Martin Klein [**1970**].

[23] This paper was also an outgrowth of the ideas discussed in Bohr [**1923a**], pp. 158–161.

between stationary states within the atom were assumed to be probabilistically conditioned by the virtual oscillators and the virtual field within a single atom. Induced transitions between stationary states within the atom were assumed to be probabilistically conditioned by the virtual radiation in the space around the atom produced by the other atoms. There is no direct connection between the transitions in an atom and those in distant atoms because the virtual radiation field only determines the probability that such transitions will occur. This means that energy and momentum are conserved only in a statistical sense and not for each individual process. The relation between the actual radiation and the states of the atoms is maintained by means of the virtual field—but only on a statistical basis. If the relation were a causal one, then probabilistic concepts would have no place and the theory would be a version of the classical theory of the interaction of radiation and matter.

Anticipating the criticism they would receive, BKS, p. 799, emphasized that this picture constructed from the old quantum theory should not be rejected: "In view of the fundamental departures from the classical spacetime description, involved in the very idea of virtual oscillators, it seems at the present state of science hardly justifiable to reject a formal interpretation as that under consideration as inadequate."

BKS, p. 797, went on to warn the reader not to take the correspondence principle as a statement that classical theory and quantum theory have a conceptual union in some domain in the way that Newtonian theory and relativity theory do: "It must still be remembered that the analogy between the classical theory and the quantum theory as formulated through the correspondence principle is of an essentially formal character, which is especially illustrated by the fact that on the quantum theory the absorption and emission of radiation are coupled to different virtual oscillators." They, p. 795, also mentioned an "*a priori* limit to the accuracy with which the motion in these states can be described by means of classical electrodynamics ...". This limit is "... directly involved in the assumption that the virtual radiation field is not accompanied by a continuous change in the motion of an atom, but only acts by its induction of transitions involving finite changes of energy and momentum of the atom." Such limitations were a consequence of trying to meet the problems or paradoxes of quantum theory. Bohr, Kramers, and Slater continued that the difficulties concerning the time interval of the transition had " ... strengthened the doubt, expressed from various sides, whether the detailed interpretation of the interaction between matter and radiation can be given at all in terms of a causal description in space and time of the kind hitherto used for the interpretation of natural phenomena." [24]

The consequence of the Bohr, Kramers, Slater theory that momentum and energy are conserved only statistically and not in individual interactions

---

[24]The reference to previous doubts is to O. W. Richardson [**1916**], p. 507.

was soon disproved by the experiments of Compton and Simon [**1925**] and Bothe and Geiger [**1925**]. Compton and Simon showed that the angular predictions made by Compton in his theoretical discussion of the Compton effect, concerning the collision of a photon and an electron, were verified. Bothe and Geiger showed in an investigation of the Compton effect that the recoil electron and the scattered light are always observed simultaneously. Neither of these results would have been likely unless the conservation laws were valid in individual cases. This work showed that the conservation laws would have to be retained in any theory describing photon and electron interactions and, hence, in quantum theory.

2.6 Reflection 2

The possibility of the materiality of light had been addressed by Einstein [**1911**] in a discussion of the influence of gravitation on its propagation. By contrast, the BKS theory entertained the possibility that light does not have a material aspect. While this widened the possibilities for understanding light, the question of how a non-material entity could convey energy was left aside. The experiments of Compton and Simon and of Bothe and Geiger were reassuring in that the conservation laws for energy and momentum were not violated by light. This meant that, whatever light may be, its mechanics is connected with particle mechanics.

The conception in Bohr, Kramers and Slater of the formal interpretation of a theory was not defined precisely. They probably had in mind the use of the theory as an algorithm for predictions even though the theory violates certain principles thought to be required of every physical theory (e.g., causality or the conservation of energy). This opens the door to theories that are not "rigidly attached" to reality as currently conceived—an idea important to Bohr's later concept of complementarity.[25] It does emphasize the importance of the question of what grounds there are for rejecting a theory other than experimental inadequacy.

The use of the term 'rational generalization' in reference to the relation of one theory to another has been the source of some recent confusion in the philosophical community. Some have interpreted this to mean that individual concepts are generalized and that Bohr and others were seeking the limits to which concepts could be "stretched" to accommodate new experimental results. This misses the point that from a physical perspective only a theory as a whole is testable, so to call a concept in one theory a rational generalization of a concept in another depends on having both theories and showing the connection. This means that we can only see the "stretch" in a concept

---

[25]M. B. Hesse [**1953**], pp. 198–199, has spoken of the importance and use of mathematical formalisms, or models, such as mechanical models, when employed as hypotheses in the description of physical phenomena—without themselves having any mechanical or other physical interpretation.

from one theory to another after the fact and can certainly not view Bohr's problem to be that of stretching our concepts to fit quantum theory.

The general question of what elements can appear in our theories and what our theories tell us about reality has forced itself into the forefront here. The ontological issue of the virtual oscillators and virtual fields would have become important if the theory had been successful. Even so, the introduction of these elements at this time into physics, as part of the "conceptual broadening" that Bohr felt was needed, foreshadows the discussions of ontological issues and reality that were to be an aspect of quantum theory itself when it was developed soon after. These are among the most difficult conceptual issues that Bohr had to face in attempting to provide a philosophical grounding for physics.

2.7 Precursors of Complementarity

Bohr [**1925b**] moved even further in the direction of rejecting the possibility of a comprehensive spacetime description after the failure of the Bohr, Kramers, Slater theory. He restated [**1925b**], p. 29, the formal nature of the hypothesis of light quanta and spoke (pp. 34–36), of the failure of "an essential feature of the pictures in space and time on which the description of natural phenomena has hitherto been based. ... Nevertheless, the visualization of the stationary states by mechanical pictures has brought to light a far-reaching analogy between the quantum theory and the mechanical theory." This analogy is an expression of the correspondence principle, which, p. 37, " ... expresses the tendency to utilize in the systematic development of the quantum theory every feature of the classical theories in a rational transcription appropriate to the fundamental contrast between the postulates and classical theory." In reference to the classical Hamilton-Jacobi equations of motion as applied to the explanation of the Stark effect in hydrogen, Bohr [**1925b**], p. 39, stated that "Especially after the utilization of the correspondence principle ... can we say that in this effect every trait of Jacobi's solution can be recognized, although hidden by a quantum mask." But, p. 45, these " ... results do not allow of a unique association with mechanical pictures." The important point here is that every aspect of a mechanical picture appears in quantum theory; but these aspects cannot be uniquely associated within one picture.[26]

Bohr was struggling with the persistent presence of aspects of the mechanical description (or picture) of atomic phenomena coupled with the insufficiency of these pictures to give a full account of the situation. Bohr [**1925b**], p. 50, also observed that the conservation laws do not have their usual experimental or theoretical connection with mechanical concepts, but

---

[26]The use of the Hamilton-Jacobi equations of motion in quantum mechanics, and their employment in showing the correspondence between wave equations and particle equations in the limit of geometric optics, is discussed in QIS.

they still play an equally important role in accounting for the behavior of the atom. Bohr was at this time developing the particular locutions he used in his later works on these issues. He viewed experiments that provide information relevant to the kinematic particle picture as providing a 'spacetime coordination' and those that refer to the conservation laws as satisfying the 'claim of causality.' Thus, with regard to the stationary state of an atom, the dynamical laws apply to the calculation of the orbit as long as the atom is not under observation. When it is being observed closely enough to locate the electron within the atom, the stationary state is disrupted. This means that the validity of the classical laws cannot be either confirmed or denied with regard to the stationary state of an electron in an atom. The particle laws used to compute orbits cannot be dispensed with, however, because Sommerfeld's success in explaining the fine structure of the spectrum shows that the (relativistic) mechanical laws do apply within the atom.

In the 1923 proposal of de Broglie's [**1923**], [**1924**], [**1926**], that the wave and particle duality characteristic of light might also be true for material particles, he used the relation $E = h\nu$ for light to assign the photon a momentum according to the formula

$$(2.8) \qquad p = \frac{E}{c} = \frac{h\nu}{c} = \frac{h}{\lambda},$$

where (p, E) is the momentum-energy of the photon, c is the speed of light, ν is the frequency and λ is the wavelength.[27] De Broglie proposed that this relation between momentum and wavelength could be extended also to material particles:

$$(2.9) \qquad p = mv = \frac{h}{\lambda}; \qquad \lambda = \frac{h}{p}.$$

This conjecture was tested inadvertently by C. J. Davisson and L. H. Germer in 1925–26, when an accident changed the nickel powder in their experiment into nickel crystals, and they observed diffraction effects in the beam of scattered electrons that showed that the electrons had an effective wavelength that depended on the electron momentum.[28]

2.8 Reflection 3

It was clear in 1913 that a far-reaching revision in mechanics was necessary before the structure of the atom could be accounted for. Ten years later, Bohr [**1923b**], p. 32, still maintained his view that the interference effects of light are incompatible on logical grounds with Einstein's use of the photon or light quantum to explain of the photoelectric effect:

---

[27] For more details on de Broglie's theory, see Jammer [**1966**], Section 5.3.
[28] See Davisson and Germer [**1927**].

"In spite of its heuristic value, however, the hypothesis of light quanta, which is quite unreconcilable with so-called interference phenomena, is not able to throw light on the nature of radiation. I need only recall that these interference phenomena constitute our only means of investigating the properties of radiation and therefore of assigning any closer meaning to the frequency which in Einstein's theory fixes the magnitude of the light quantum."

On the other hand, arguments based on the behavior of Geiger counters and the photoelectric effect imply equally strongly that light is particulate in nature. Somewhat later, Bohr concluded from these and similar arguments that both the wave and particulate descriptions are "simple accounts of what is observed" in the appropriate situations and cannot be replaced or altered. For Bohr the experiments mentioned came to function as paradigms for the application of the terms wave or particle.[29] This means that attributing wave or particle properties to an entity in these experiments is not to be treated as a mere hypothesis.

Once the arguments are phrased in this form, the fundamental nature of the difficulty in quantum mechanics appears. An entity possessing wave properties must be extended in space in order that it may interfere with itself or other waves, while a particulate entity has all of its properties located in a small volume or at a point. These same conceptual difficulties hold for both material particles and light. Among the particulate properties we count mass, charge, spin, localized energy-momentum, etc., while a wave carries the properties of amplitude, wavelength, polarization, energy-momentum density, etc. Finally, particles attract or repel each other when they approach closely while waves that occupy the same spatial locations can be added or superimposed.

The necessity of using probabilistic concepts in the description of basic atomic processes meant that one could not give a causal account, in the usual (classical) sense, of the time development of the system. This difficulty is as important as the wave and particle duality recounted above. It was shown later that the two are very deeply related.

---

[29] See, for example, Bohr [**1930**], p. 4.

CHAPTER 3

The Quantum Formalism and the Uncertainty Relations: 1925–1927

The development of the new quantum theory in 1925 did not resolve the problem of the wave and particle duality of both light and matter as Bohr had hoped. Indeed, the discovery of the uncertainty relations by Heisenberg in 1927 gave what Bohr then called a quantitative measure of the incompatibility of the wave and particle concepts. Bohr discussed the severe epistemological problems raised by quantum theory in a lecture given to a meeting of physicists at Lake Como in Italy in 1927. The issues discussed in this lecture, and the answers he developed to address them, set him on a path he followed until the end of his life.

3.1 Development of the Quantum Formalism

Heisenberg made a definitive step in the creation of the formalism of quantum theory in 1925.[1] He restricted the concepts and representations that play a role in his formalism to those that are observable. He excluded electron paths, their orbits in atoms, and their periods of rotation, and limited himself to the arrays of observed transitions between electron states that resulted in the emission of radiation. He concerned himself in particular with the mathematical properties of these arrays and their multiplication rule, which represents a sequence of transitions. He was able to apply his formalism to the simple examples of the harmonic and anharmonic oscillators. His work was taken up immediately by Born and Jordan, who extended the formalism.[2] They then collaborated with Heisenberg in a paper called the "three man paper" that extended the applications of the formalism into new territory.

Heisenberg's theory soon came to be called "matrix mechanics" because of the representation of the probability of transitions within an atom as elements of a transition matrix. His work was based upon an attempt to "establish a basis for theoretical quantum mechanics founded exclusively upon relationships between quantities which are in principle observable."[3] He criticized the formal quantization rules of the previous quantum theory, which made use of the Bohr-Sommerfeld quantization condition, because they used concepts such as the position of the electron and its period of revolution to derive the observable energy levels of the atom. These quantities, he felt, were "apparently unobservable in principle." One could, of course, hope that these "hitherto unobservable quantities may later come within the realm of experimental determination." However, Heisenberg objected to this on the grounds that the rules used in the old quantum theory are not even internally consistent or applicable to a clearly defined range of quantum mechanical problems. This implied that the classical conceptions underlying them are not likely to find future application in a workable theory. The weight of the evidence that Heisenberg marshaled, especially Bohr's frequency condition for orbits and

---

[1] For a brief history of the developments at this time, see Born [**1964**] and the original references cited there. For more details on the history of this period, see Jammer [**1966**], [**1974**], Mehra and Rechenberg [**1987**], and many other sources. The three man paper referred to below is Born, Heisenberg and Jordan [**1925**].

[2] E. U. Condon [**1962**] has remarked on the frantic pace with which developments were occurring during this period. He recalled that when Born and Heisenberg had encountered the matrices, they went to the mathematician David Hilbert for help. He told them that he typically encountered matrices as by-products of the eigenvalues of a boundary-value calculation for a differential equation. He suggested that they look for a differential equation associated with the matrices. They thought this was a goofy idea and that Hilbert did not know what he was talking about. Hilbert had a good laugh after Schrödinger's work was published.

[3] Heisenberg [**1925**]. See p. 261 of the translation in van der Waerden [**1967**]. He [**1943**] returned to this point of view with the development of S-Matrix (Scattering Matrix) theory.

transitions, led him to the conclusion that "... even for the simplest quantum theoretical problems the validity of classical mechanics simply cannot be maintained. In this situation it seems sensible to discard all hope of observing hitherto unobservable quantities, such as the position and period of the electron, and to conclude that the partial agreement of the quantum rules with experience is more or less fortuitous."[4]

Through sponsorship by Einstein, de Broglie's hypothesis attracted the attention of many physicists soon after he proposed it. Schrödinger used it in 1925 in his work on the problem of the stationary states of an atom.[5] Proceeding from an analogy between wave optics and geometric optics, as expressed in the Hamilton-Jacobi equations, Schrödinger constructed a "wave mechanics" of a particle moving in a potential field. For an electron in an atom, he followed de Broglie [**1925**] and postulated that the only kinds of motions that would correspond to a stationary state are those for which the circumference of the orbit is an integral number of electron wavelengths. Since the momentum varies with the radius of the orbit, orbits can exist only for those momenta for which the corresponding wavelength and the circumference of the orbit are an integral multiple of each other. The discrete radii at which this relationship holds are the stationary states of the atom. From the wave point of view, those wavelengths that are an integral multiple of the circumference give rise to a standing wave through constructive interference, while those that are not integral multiples of the circumference will cancel themselves due to destructive interference.

Just before the publication of the three man paper, Dirac [**1925**] published his first paper on the quantum formalism. Shortly afterward, the validity of Heisenberg's matrix mechanics was confirmed by Pauli who applied it to the calculation of the stationary energy values in the hydrogen atom and found complete agreement with Bohr's formula. At about this time, Schrödinger [**1926a**] published his first paper using the wavefunction. Shortly after that, Schrödinger showed that the matrix mechanics formulation of Heisenberg and his wave mechanics were equivalent. Thus, by the end of 1926, the essential components of the quantum formalism were in place. Interpreting matrix elements or wavefunctions was no easy matter; intense debates, many of them taking place in Copenhagen, sprang up as to the meaning and interpretation of the various elements of the theory. The first important step was Schrödinger's [**1926b**] proof that wave mechanics and matrix mechanics are equivalent. But this did not slow the debate concerning the interpretation of the elements of the theory in terms of measurements, the wave-particle duality, and issues concerning a realistic interpretation of the

---
[4]Heisenberg [**1925**], p. 262. For further information on Heisenberg's theory, see Sinitiro Tomonaga [**1962**], Vol. I. While the position and the period of the electron have remained unobservable in quantum theory, the partial agreement of the old quantum rules with experience has been explained by subsequent work.

[5]See Schrödinger [**1925**], [**1926a**], [**1926b**].

theory. These problems were all intensified by Heisenberg's [**1927**] discovery of the uncertainty relations.

Neither the matrix elements of Heisenberg's quantum theory nor the waves of Schrödinger's theory were successfully interpreted in ways acceptable to classical intuition. Max Born [**1954**] recalled how the attempts by Schrödinger to interpret $e|\psi|^2$ as the density of electric charge had been rejected because ψ usually dissipates in time and, for $\mathcal{N}$ particles, it is defined in $3\mathcal{N}$-dimensional configuration space and not 3-dimensional coordinate space. He recalled the work of Einstein on photons in which Einstein, in an attempt to make his formulas intelligible, had interpreted the square of the optical amplitude as the probability of finding a photon. Using this as a basis, Born [**1926**], [**1927**], sought to interpret $|\psi(q,t)|^2$ as a probability density. To prove that this is appropriate, he finally hit on the idea of using scattering experiments.

While Born was able to provide a physical interpretation of the absolute square of the wavefunction as a probability density, and thereby solved the problem of using the theory, nevertheless, the question of the nature of the "waves" or "matrix elements" themselves had not been answered. The loss of the intuitive simplicity and visualizability of classical theory was deeply felt.

3.2 The Quantum Formalism

A brief exposition of the formalism of quantum theory will be useful for what follows. A number of issues, raised here and in later chapters, warrant a more detailed treatment to do them full justice. These issues are dealt with in much more detail in QIS and the focus here will remain on Bohr's epistemology.[6]

The *state* of a system is a theoretical entity that determines at a given time the subsequent dynamics of that system within some theory. In mechanics, whether classical or quantum, the change in the state with time is determined by the dynamical equations. The system state is therefore the time-dependent solution of these dynamical equations with appropriate initial and boundary conditions.

Let us begin with a brief discussion of the classical mechanics of a collection of $\mathcal{N}_k$ particles that is called the k system. The symbol k will also be used to represent the set of particles in the k system. These particles are indexed by a label that ranges from 1 to $\mathcal{N}_k$, and the notation $i \in k$ refers to particle i in system k. In classical Hamiltonian particle mechanics, the $\mathcal{N}_k$ particle system mechanical state of k can be represented as a point in

---

[6] For an exposition of the mature quantum formalism and its applications from a physical perspective, see the detailed work of Albert Messiah [**1961**]. There are also a number of treatises on the mathematical aspects of quantum theory, including the original ones by Dirac [**1930**] and von Neumann [**1932**]. Philosophical discussions are too numerous to mention.

the $6\mathcal{N}_k$-dimensional phase space of the system. The *phase space* of a system is defined as the direct product, also called the Cartesian product, of the 6-dimensional phase spaces for each of the particles. This space is the product space $\mathbf{R}^{6\mathcal{N}_k}$, where $\mathbf{R}$ is the set of real numbers. A point (Q_k, P_k) in phase space is given by the ordered sets $Q_k = (q_1, q_2, \ldots, q_{\mathcal{N}_k}) = \times_{i \in k} q_i$ and $P_k = \times_{i \in k} p_i$. The $3\mathcal{N}_k$-dimensional space in which Q_k is defined is called *configuration space*. The $3\mathcal{N}_k$-dimensional space in which P_k is defined is called *momentum phase space*. Because the coordinates and momenta of the particles are functions of time, the point representing system k at time t is written $(Q_k(t), P_k(t))$. This point traces a trajectory in phase space as the particle positions and momenta change in time. Each point (Q_k, P_k) in classical phase space represents a classical mechanical state of the k system and determines the results for each of the measurements that can be made on the system at a given time. Interactions between the particles are expressed in terms of the set $\{\phi_{ij}(q_i - q_j)\}$ of interparticle potential energies, defined for each pair of particles $i, j \in k$. For simplicity, these potentials are usually represented by instantaneous action at a distance potentials. Potentials due to particles outside system k are described by the external potential function $\Phi_{k,x}(Q_k, t)$.

The *kinetic energy, internal potential energy*, and *potential energy* of the k system are

(3.1a) $$\mathcal{K}_k(P_k) = \sum_{i \in k} \frac{p_i^2}{2m_i},$$

(3.1b) $$\Phi_{k,n}(Q_k) = \tfrac{1}{2} \sum_{i \in k} \sum_{j > i} \phi_{ij}(q_i - q_j),$$

(3.1c) $$\Phi_k(Q_k, t) = \Phi_{k,n}(Q_k) + \Phi_{k,x}(Q_k, t),$$

where $\sum_{i \in k}$ refers to the sum over the indices of the $\mathcal{N}_k$ particles in the k system from $i = 1$ to $i = \mathcal{N}_k$. In this case, $\mathcal{H}_k$ depends only on the set of particle momentum coordinates $\{p_i\}$, the set of masses $\{m_i\}$, the set of interparticle potential energy functions $\{\phi_{ij}(q_i - q_j)\}$, and the external potential $\Phi_{k,x}(Q_k, t)$. The k *Hamiltonian* energy is defined in terms of these quantities as a function of the coordinates and momenta of the particles by

(3.2) $$\mathcal{H}_k(Q_k, P_k) = \mathcal{K}_k(P_k) + \Phi_k(Q_k, t)$$

The classical time-independent equations of motion for this system are Hamilton's equations

(3.3) $$\frac{dq_i}{dt} = \frac{\partial \mathcal{H}_k}{\partial p_i}; \qquad \frac{dp_i}{dt} = -\frac{\partial \mathcal{H}_k}{\partial q_i}.$$

It is not hard to show that the classical conservation laws are valid for a distribution of one or more particles evolving in time in accord with Hamilton's equations.

In moving from the classical equations of motion to the quantum mechanical, let us begin with the classical Hamiltonian energy equation $\mathcal{E}_k = \mathcal{H}_k(Q_k, P_k)$ and make the following replacements:
1. replace the energy $\mathcal{E}_k$ with the operator $\mathbf{E}_k = i\hbar \partial/\partial t$;
2. replace the momentum p_i with the operator $\mathbf{p}_i = -i\hbar \partial/\partial q_i$;
3. replace the equation $\mathcal{E}_k = \mathcal{H}_k$ by the operator equation $\mathbf{E}_k \Psi = \mathcal{H}_k \Psi$ to obtain the non-relativistic *Schrödinger's equation*

$$(3.4) \qquad i\hbar \frac{\partial \Psi(Q_k, t)}{\partial t} = \mathcal{H}_k \left(Q_k, -i\hbar \frac{\partial}{\partial Q_k} \right) \Psi(Q_k, t),$$

where $\partial/\partial Q_k = (\partial/\partial q_1, \partial/\partial q_2, \ldots, \partial/\partial q_{\mathcal{N}_k}) = \times_{i \in k} \partial/\partial q_i$.

The solutions of Schrödinger's equation (3.4) preserve the conservation laws as do the solutions of Hamilton's equations for the classical case. In Hamiltonian mechanics, forces are expressed in terms of the potential by $F_k^\mu(Q_k, t) = -\nabla_k^\mu \Phi_k(Q_k, t)$ in both classical and quantum mechanics. There are some requirements that are usually imposed on solutions of Schrödinger's equation if they are to be states of a physical system. These requirements will be considered below.

To illustrate this formalism, let us consider a single neutral, spinless particle with mass m moving in a time-dependent external potential field $\Phi_{k,x}(q,t)$. The dynamical evolution of the quantum mechanical state $\psi(q,t)$ of the particle is determined by the non-time-dependent Schrödinger equation

$$(3.5) \qquad i\hbar \frac{\partial \psi(q,t)}{\partial t} = \mathcal{H}_k \psi(q,t),$$

where the quantum Hamiltonian, $\mathcal{H}_k$ is defined by

$$(3.6a) \qquad \mathcal{H}_k = -\frac{\hbar^2}{2m} \nabla^2 + \Phi_{k,x}(q,t),$$

with

$$(3.6b) \qquad \nabla^2 = \frac{\partial^2}{\partial q_x^2} + \frac{\partial^2}{\partial q_y^2} + \frac{\partial^2}{\partial q_z^2}.$$

The Hermitian conjugate function $\psi^\dagger(q,t)$ in this case is the complex conjugate of the state $\psi(q,t)$. If $\psi(q,t)$ is a vector or spinor function, the Hermitian conjugate $\psi^\dagger(q,t)$ is the complex conjugate transpose of $\psi(q,t)$.

The state function $\psi(q,t)$ is often called a wavefunction because of its resemblance to functions describing classical waves. Schrödinger's equation differs, however, from classical wave equations in that it is only of the first order in its time derivative, while classical wave equations in mechanics or electrodynamics are of the second order in their time derivatives. For this reason, the solutions of Schrödinger's equation differ significantly from the solutions of the classical wave equations and resemble the classical diffusion equation. The initial conditions also take a different form in quantum theory.[7]

Paul Ehrenfest [**1921**] addressed the relation between quantum mechanics and classical mechanics in a theorem.[8] In the theory of probability, the expected value or expectation function of a physical quantity expressed in terms of the microscopic particle variables is obtained by averaging the operator representing that quantity as a function of the particle variables over the particle variables weighted by the distribution of the particle variables. In quantum mechanics, the identification of the square of the wavefunction as a probability distribution and the interpretation of operators acting on the wavefunction as defining their values microscopically means that the expectation function of any operator **G** for a system in the state $\psi(q,t)$ takes the form

$$(3.7) \qquad G(t) = \langle \mathbf{G} \rangle = \int d^3q\, \psi^\dagger(q,t) \mathbf{G} \psi(q,t).$$

This definition can be used to compute the expected position $R^\mu(t) = \langle q^\mu \rangle$, the expected momentum $P^\mu(t) = \langle -i\hbar \nabla^\mu \rangle$, and the expected force $F^\mu(t) = -\langle \nabla^\mu \Phi(q,t) \rangle$. With these quantities, Ehrenfest's theorem[9]

$$(3.8) \qquad \frac{dR^\mu(t)}{dt} = \frac{1}{m} P^\mu(t), \qquad \frac{dP^\mu(t)}{dt} = F^\mu(t)$$

is obtained.

A particle with a precisely defined position at q_0 is represented by the *location measure* $\delta(q - q_0)$. Because this measure is not normalizable, it is not a quantum mechanical state. It is useful in asymptotic calculations and represents, as Bohr would put it, an *idealization of localizability* that we cannot attain with real particles. Similarly, a particle with a precisely defined momentum is represented by a plane wave $e^{ip \cdot q/\hbar}$. This function is also not normalizable, is not a quantum mechanical state, and represents the idealization of a precisely defined momentum state.

Consider next a moving particle localized within a volume. Under the proper circumstances, a wavefunction of limited spatial extent, called a wavepacket, can be used to represent the particle. A wavefunction with this description requires that many frequencies be superimposed in order that it will be nonzero only in a limited volume. The group velocity of the wavepacket

---

[7] The Hamilton-Jacobi formulation of classical mechanics is used to provide a classical approximation for quantum mechanics in Messiah [**1961**], Vol. I, pp. 222–228. See also his discussion, pp. 317–320, of the correspondence principle in the Heisenberg representation of Schrödinger's equation.

[8] See also the more recent work of N. Rosen [**1964a**], [**1964b**].

[9] For a more detailed treatment of Ehrenfest's theorem, issues connected with the Correspondence Principle, and the classical approximation of quantum mechanics, see QIS or Messiah [**1961**], Vol. I, Chapter VI.

as a whole is equal to the particle velocity. Because of the superposition of many frequencies, each representing a slightly different momentum for the particle (and therefore a different velocity), the wave will disperse in time. Wavepackets were often used by some authors such as von Neumann, but not by Bohr, as the quantum mechanical stand-ins for particles.

As an illustration of the behavior of a wavepacket, consider a particle moving along the x-axis. An initial wavepacket assigned to the particle at time $t = 0$ will disperse as time goes by. This dispersion can be illustrated, and the effects of the size of the wavepacket on it, can be computed by assuming at time $t = 0$ that the wavepacket has an extension along the x-axis of $b(0) = b > 0$ and has an expected momentum p. At time $t = 0$ this wavepacket is assumed to take the form $\psi(q,0) = [b^{\frac{1}{2}}\pi^{\frac{1}{4}}]^{-1} e^{-\frac{q^2}{2b^2}} e^{\frac{i}{\hbar}p \cdot q}$, which is used as an initial condition in Schrödinger's equation. At time $t > 0$ the probability density associated with this wavepacket is then given by

$$(3.9) \qquad |\psi(q,t)|^2 = \frac{1}{b(t)\pi^{\frac{1}{2}}} e^{-\frac{(q-vt)^2}{b^2(t)}},$$

where $b(t) = b[1 + (\hbar t)/(mb^2)]$. The maximum amplitude moves with a velocity $v = p/m$ and requires the time $T_d = 3^{\frac{1}{2}} mb^2/\hbar$ to double its width. For a 1 gram mass with $b = 0.1$ cm, the doubling time is 6×10^{17} years. For a mass 0.9×10^{-27} grams and $b = 10^{-8}$ cm, the doubling time is 2×10^{-16} seconds.

Consider next solutions of Schrödinger's equation with a time independent potential for which the particle has a definite energy E. The solution of Schrödinger's equation appropriate to this case can be written in the form $\psi(q,t) = \psi_E(q) e^{-iEt/\hbar}$. Substituting this function into the Schrödinger equation above yields

$$(3.10a) \qquad \left[\frac{\hbar^2}{2m}\nabla^2 + \Phi_{k,x}(q)\right]\psi_E(q) = E\psi_E(q)$$

or

$$(3.10b) \qquad \mathcal{H}_k \psi_E(q) = E\psi_E(q).$$

The effect of the Hamiltonian operator $\mathcal{H}_k$ on the state $\psi_E(q)$ of definite energy is to multiply the wavefunction by the Hamiltonian energy E. Mathematically, an equation of the form (3.10b) is called an eigenfunction equation for the Hamiltonian operator.

For an atom in a stationary state, the electrons are bound and their energies satisfy the condition $E < 0$. Schrödinger showed that equation (3.4) has solutions only for a discrete set of energies, $E_n < 0$, labeled by the integer n. It was easy to show that these states corresponded in the case of the hydrogen atom to Bohr's stationary states. The eigenvalues E_n are the same as those of Bohr's formula (1.4) and the radii of the orbits are given by

(1.1). These radii, as Bohr [**1915**], p. 399, pointed out, are only to be viewed as "mean values" and cannot be taken literally as the radii of orbits in the classical sense.[10]

The solution of the time-dependent Schrödinger equation requires the specification of initial conditions and boundary conditions. If, in addition, the wavefunction is to be physically meaningful, there are other conditions that it must also satisfy. Because $|\psi(q,t)|^2 = \psi^\dagger(q,t)\psi(q,t)$ is interpreted as a probability density function, it is required that the integral over the space accessible to the system must be 1.[11] The normalization condition means that the *norm* of ψ is 1:

$$(3.11) \qquad \|\psi\| = \sqrt{\int d^3q\, \psi^\dagger(q,t)\psi(q,t)} = 1.$$

Mathematically speaking, this condition is meaningful only if the wavefunction is square integrable. Moreover, for essentially physical reasons, it is usually required that $\psi(q,t)$ is single-valued and continuous.[12]

One property that equation (3.4) does share with other wave equations, as can be seen by immediate inspection, is that it is linear in ψ. This means that if ψ_1 and ψ_2 are both solutions of the equation, then their sum

$$(3.12) \qquad \phi = a_1\psi_1 + a_2\psi_2,$$

where a_1 and a_2 are complex numbers, is also a solution of the equation. In other words, the superposition of two solutions, to use terminology borrowed from wave theory, is also a solution. Physically, this means that the two "waves" do not modify each other, but their interference does modify where particles can be found. Thus, the superposition property has the observational consequence that a state that is a superposition of contributions from two coherent sources, as in Young's double slit experiment with light, can be zero at places for which it is not zero for either source alone. This is the basis for quantum mechanical interference phenomena that have no analogs in classical particle mechanics. Bohr [**1949**], p. 38, acknowledged the fundamental importance of superposition in quantum theory, as part of the wave aspect of the wave-particle duality, when he spoke of quantum theory as providing "... an essentially statistical description of atomic phenomena combining the features of individuality and the requirements of the superposition principle, equally characteristic of quantum theory."

---

[10]See Paul Ehrenfest [**1927**] for a further discussion of this.

[11]There are scattering experiments for which this condition is not met. These experiments use unnormalizable plane wavefunctions to approximate the initial state of a beam of particles that are all in a precise momentum state. Relative probabilities are used in scattering calculations.

[12]The requirement that ψ be single-valued is discussed in Section 4.7 and in more detail in QIS.

Requiring acceptable wavefunctions to be square-integrable means, as a consequence of the Cauchy inequality, that the integral of one acceptable wavefunction with the complex conjugate of another acceptable one yields a finite result.[13] Let us define an inner product of wavefunctions in terms of an integral over q by

$$(3.13) \qquad (\psi, \phi) = \int d^3q \, \psi^\dagger(q,t) \phi(q,t) \leq \|\psi\| \|\phi\|.$$

It follows that $(\psi, \phi) \leq \|\psi\| \|\phi\| < \infty$ when both ψ and ϕ are square integrable. It is easy to see from the definition (3.11) and the properties of the integral that the inner product for wavefunctions defined in this way obeys the following rules:

$$(3.14a) \qquad (\psi, a\phi) = a(\psi, \phi);$$
$$(3.14b) \qquad (\psi + \theta, \phi) = (\psi, \phi) + (\theta, \phi);$$
$$(3.14c) \qquad (\psi, \phi) = (\phi, \psi)^*;$$
$$(3.14d) \qquad (\psi, \psi) > 0 \quad \text{for } \psi \neq 0;$$
$$(3.14e) \qquad (\psi, \psi) = 0 \quad \text{for } \psi = 0.$$

The quantity a in (3.14a) is a complex scalar constant. These formulas can be used to show that the set of solutions of Schrödinger's equation form a *linear manifold* that is compatible with the inner product.[14]

Some additional mathematical formalism will be useful for the discussion of von Neumann's theory of measurement in relation to Bohr's approach. An abstract Hilbert space is defined as an infinite dimensional space that is a complete metric space with respect to the metric generated by the inner product. This metric may be defined by a function D, which, for any two elements of the space, gives the *distance* between them. The distance between the states ψ and ϕ is defined in terms of the norm by

$$(3.15) \qquad D(\psi, \phi) = \|\psi - \phi\| = (\psi - \phi, \psi - \phi)^{\frac{1}{2}}.$$

It can easily be shown that this definition satisfies the requirements of a distance function.[15]

---

[13] The following discussion is based on N. I. Akhiezer and I. M. Glazman [**1961**], Chapter 1. Consult this work for further details on the Cauchy inequality, linear manifolds, abstract Hilbert spaces, etc.

[14] The compatibility of the inner product and the linear structure is an important feature of current quantum mechanics. It would not hold in a non-linear version of the theory in which the addition of two wavefunctions could imply an interaction between them.

[15] A distance function is required to be a real, symmetric, positive definite function of two variables (points, functions, etc.) that is zero only when the norm of the difference between the two variables is zero. There are many different ways of defining the norm and each has its own distance function.

Let ψ_j be a wavefunction taken from a set of wavefunctions $\{\psi_i\}$ defined in a Hilbert space $\hat{H}$ and let r be a small positive real number. Consider the set of states ψ for which the following condition holds:

(3.16) $$D(\psi_j, \psi) < r.$$

The set of all states ψ that satisfy (3.16) is called a *ball* in $\hat{H}$ with center ψ_j and radius r. A sequence of elements, ψ_n, $n = 1, 2, \ldots$, is said to have a limit point ψ, written as

(3.17a) $$\lim_{n \to \infty} \psi_n = \psi,$$

if

(3.17b) $$\lim_{n \to \infty} D(\psi_n, \psi) = 0.$$

It need not be the case that such a ψ exists for every sequence of elements chosen from a given space. A space is said to be *complete* if every such sequence does converge to an element of the space.[16]

The *dimension* of a space is defined as the number of distinct elements in the set of elements of the space that can be chosen such that no member of the set can be expressed as a linear combination of other members of the set. For an infinite dimensional space, this set is arbitrarily large. The set of solutions of Schrödinger's equation for particular physical situations often forms an infinite dimensional manifold.

The wavefunction of a system refers to the description of the system of particles as a whole and cannot in general be decomposed into a product of wavefunctions representing the individual particles. The quantity $|\psi(q_1, q_2)|^2$, for example, which represents the probability that particle 1 will be at q_1 and particle 2 will be at q_2, cannot usually be represented as $\psi_1(q_1)\psi_2(q_2)$. If the particles are identical, there is an additional requirement, unique to quantum mechanics, that the wavefunction be either antisymmetric (for particles with half-integral spins called *fermions*) or symmetric (for particles with integral spins called *bosons*). The quantum symmetry requirements on the wavefunction in this case leads to some consequences, such as exchange forces, that are decidedly nonclassical.

A concrete realization of a Hilbert space, and the one we began with in connection with Schrödinger's equation, is the space L^2 of square integrable functions with the inner product structure introduced above. Following common usage, the elements of $\hat{H}$ are called either *vectors* or *wavefunctions*. An important feature of Hilbert space theory is the notion of a linear operator

---

[16]It is often possible to complete a space by adding to it all the elements defined by such sequences and showing that they satisfy the conditions defining the space. This cannot always be done. In particular, the Dirac delta measure can be obtained as the limit of a sequence of continuous, square-integrable functions but it is not an element in any Hilbert space.

acting on the vectors in the space. An operator maps a vector to a vector or a vector to a complex number, etc. The domain of an operator is the set of vectors on which it is defined. Its range is the set of quantities, such as vectors or complex numbers, that the vectors in the domain of the operator are mapped onto.

There is a complete mathematical analogy between the formulation of quantum mechanics in terms of differential equations and in terms of operator equations in Hilbert space. The Hilbert space formulation has the advantage of making the mathematical structure of the theory more transparent. However, other approaches can and have been used.[17]

An acceptable operator $\mathbf{T}$ maps a vector in the Hilbert space $\hat{H}$ to another vector in this Hilbert space: $\psi = \mathbf{T}\phi$. There is a special set of operators called *observables* that represent physical quantities in the quantum formalism. Because they represent physical quantities, observables must meet additional mathematical conditions that stem from this.

An operator $\mathbf{T}$ is *linear* if its domain is a linear manifold and if

$$(3.18) \qquad \mathbf{T}(a\psi + b\phi) = a\mathbf{T}\psi + b\mathbf{T}\phi$$

for any vectors ψ and ϕ in the domain of $\mathbf{T}$ and any complex numbers a and b. The range and domain of the operators used in quantum mechanics are important issues because an operator may map a vector not in its domain to a quantity that is not in $\hat{H}$. An example is the quantum momentum operator defined by

$$(3.19) \qquad \mathbf{p} = i\hbar \frac{\partial}{\partial q}.$$

This operator is not defined for some points q of some state vectors $\psi(q,t)$.

If $\mathbf{T}$ is a linear operator, its adjoint, $\mathbf{T}^\dagger$, if it exists, is defined by the relation

$$(3.20) \qquad (\mathbf{T}^\dagger \psi, \phi) = (\psi, \mathbf{T}\phi)$$

for arbitrary vectors ψ and ϕ. An operator is said to be *Hermitian* if $\mathbf{T}^\dagger = \mathbf{T}$. For some operators, $\mathbf{p}$ and $\mathbf{q}$, say, the product $\mathbf{pq}$ is defined as another operator by the sequence $\mathbf{p}\phi = \mathbf{p}(\mathbf{q}\psi) = \mathbf{pq}\psi$. In general the result of this operation is not the same as applying the operators in reverse order. If this is the case, the *commutator* of the operators is non-vanishing

$$(3.21) \qquad [\mathbf{p},\mathbf{q}]\psi = \mathbf{pq}\psi - \mathbf{qp}\psi \neq 0.$$

If $\mathbf{q}$ is the position operator and $\mathbf{p}$ is the momentum operator, then the commutator of these operators, introduced by Born and Jordan [**1925**], is (in

---

[17] See the references cited in Jammer [**1966**], pp. 376–377.

modern notation)

(3.22) $$[\mathbf{p}, \mathbf{q}] = i\hbar.$$

It is understood that commutators are valid only for vectors on both products are well defined.

Von Neumann [**1932**] investigated the foundations of quantum mechanics. He provided a standardized approach to analyzing quantum systems by combining some convenient mathematical tools with a requirement proposed by Bohr that a quantum system is in a determinate state with respect to some quantity only in an experimental arrangement designed to measure that quantity. Within a given experimental arrangement, von Neumann considered a complete set of commuting observables and the set of solutions of Schrödinger's equation that are simultaneous orthonormal eigenfunctions of all the operators in this set. He showed that a set of solutions of this form always exists. Every wavefunction that is a solution of Schrödinger's equation in this experiment can be represented as a series expansion in terms of this set of eigenfunctions.[18]

In von Neumann's theory, there is a one-to-one correspondence between the observable quantities of the theory and Hermitian operators that act on the wavefunctions. The expectation value of an observable operator is the quantity that is compared with experimental results. For an operator $\mathbf{R}$ and a system in the state described by the wavefunction ψ, the expectation value at time t will be expressed for later convenience in a bracket notation

(3.23) $$R(t) = (\psi, \mathbf{R}\psi) = \langle \mathbf{R} \rangle.$$

Let us define a *ray* in Hilbert space by $a\psi$, where ψ is a vector in Hilbert space and a is a complex number such that $|a|^2 = 1$. The form of the inner product (3.23) shows that all rays based on a given Hilbert vector have the same norm and expectation functions. Because only states with different expectation functions are physically distinct in a given experiment, it follows that only rays are physically distinct. The states represented by the ray $a\psi$ with different values of a are said to have different *phases*. Note that while states are represented by rays, (3.12) implies that only vectors may be added so that the relative phase of two superposed states ψ and ϕ is definite while the overall phase of their sum is undetermined. Next, because quantities that can be measured must be real, it is required that the operators representing them be Hermitian. This follows from the mathematical representation for the expected value for an observable $\mathbf{T}$ as the inner product $(\phi, \mathbf{T}\psi)$. By (3.14c), it follows that the Hermitian property expressed by (3.20) must be true for an observable.

---

[18] The requirement of a complete set of commuting observables in quantum electrodynamics has been discussed by F. J. Belinfante [**1962**].

A distinction was made in von Neumann's approach between what is called a pure state, which is represented by a vector ψ, and a mixture of states. A mixture is a collection of pure states used to represent a physical system in cases in which we know only the probabilities that the system is in one or another pure state. The pure states in a mixture are exclusive alternatives that may not be superimposed. Mixtures are used in quantum mechanics in the same way ensembles are used in classical statistical mechanics. To contrast a pure state with a mixture, let us first compute the expectation value of a pure state composed of a superposition of two states, $\psi = a\psi_1 + b\psi_2$, where a and b are complex numbers such that $|a|^2 + |b|^2 = 1$. The result is

(3.24)
$$\langle \psi^\dagger \mathbf{R} \psi \rangle = \langle (a\psi_1 + b\psi_2)^\dagger \mathbf{R}(a\psi_1 + b\psi_2) \rangle$$
$$= |a|^2 \langle \psi_1^\dagger \mathbf{R} \psi_1 \rangle + |b|^2 \langle \psi_2^\dagger \mathbf{R} \psi_2 \rangle$$
$$+ ab^* \int d^3q\, \psi_2^\dagger(q,t) \mathbf{R} \psi_1(q,t) + a^*b \int d^3q\, \psi_1^\dagger(q,t) \mathbf{R} \psi_2(q,t).$$

For a mixture M, on the other hand, in which the states ψ_1 and ψ_2 appear with probabilities w_1 and w_2, respectively, such that $w_1 + w_2 = 1$, the expectation value is computed by

(3.25) $\quad \mathcal{E}_M(\psi_1, \psi_2, \mathbf{R}) = w_1 \langle \psi_1^\dagger \mathbf{R} \psi_1 \rangle + w_2 \langle \psi_2^\dagger \mathbf{R} \psi_2 \rangle.$

These formulas show that in general a superposition, which corresponds to an "inclusive or" regarding alternatives, and a mixture, which represents an "exclusive or", are quite different. The terms called the "quantum interference terms" in (3.24) are missing in (3.25). The absence of quantum interference terms makes a mixture more like a set of classical alternatives.[19]

3.3 Reflection 4

The formalism of quantum mechanics represented a radical break with the formalism of classical mechanics. Deterministic calculations were replaced by probabilistic ones, the kinematic and dynamic visualizations of moving particles interacting with each other were replaced by abstract Hilbert space vectors changing in time. In addition, the existence of superpositions of states and von Neumann's view that an observable operator during a measurement projects the particle quantum state into one of its eigenstates (the projection postulate) cast doubt on the classical notion that particles are carriers of properties and independent of observation. It is no wonder that quantum theory has been hard to swallow and that many workers have searched for

---

[19]See the discussion of quantum mixtures in N. Rosen [**1965**]. See also the detailed discussion in QIS and the references cited there.

alternatives that would preserve our classical intuitions—even if the physical substrate in which these alternatives operated was hidden from us.

Bohr was not inclined to pursue abstract mathematical ideas and formalisms. For him the interpretation of the theory must be tied directly to the ways in which it encounters the world for us. For this reason he focused on real experiments or visualizable thought experiments and avoided abstract formal discussions of the theory of measurement. As we shall see in Chapter 15, this led him to an approach to measurement that is quite distinct from von Neumann's.

The most important aspect of the quantum state is that the predictions we can obtain from it are based on a measure of similarity between two states. If ψ_n is the eigenstate of the operator **T**, the quantity (ψ, ϕ_n) is the probability that the result n, corresponding to the eigenvalue t_n of **T**, will be obtained in a measurement. It represents, in a sense, a measure of how well the state ϕ_n matches the state ψ. According to von Neumann's *projection postulate*, measuring the observable **T** for a system described by the state ψ results in the operator **T** projecting ψ into one of the eigenvalues of **T**. After the measurement produces the result n, say, the state of the system is assumed in von Neumann's approach to be ϕ_n. It is also assumed that another measurement of the operator **T** will produce the same result as before. Underlying von Neumann's projection postulate is the assumption that the state is something possessed by the object under observation, that the operator changes this state during a measurement, and that the system possesses the new state after the measurement. This assumption, the projection postulate, and measurement issues will be examined below to see if they are compatible with Bohr's views.[20]

The proper employment of quantum mechanics requires following rules that are often counterintuitive. Moreover, the failure of the classical picture is profound enough that the accepted *façons de parler* in discussing the quantum state are often at odds with its proper employment in accord with the rules. These points illustrate the importance of Bohr's concern with establishing clearly what it is appropriate to say about a quantum system in a given circumstance.

As an example, let us look ahead and examine the work of James L. Park [**1991**] concerning the way occupation numbers for discrete energy distributions are referred to in heuristic discussions of the quantum representation of collections of particles. Park remarked that in many cases the way in which the states of these particles are discussed is not in accord with the lessons of the EPR paradox, concerning the relation of the correlated states of distant particles, and Bell's theorem, which is concerned with assessing the possibility that precisely defined hidden variables determine the quantum state. Park

---

[20]The projection postulate is not universally accepted. Criticisms of it will be discussed in QIS and QTS.

went on to show that the wrong results would be obtained if the heuristic statements were the actual basis for calculations.

To illustrate this point, Park computed the entropy for a given situation based first on a rigorous quantum treatment and then on a heuristic quantum treatment. He considered a pair of noninteracting fermions in the antisymmetric state

$$(3.26) \qquad \Psi_{\epsilon^a,\epsilon^b} = [\sqrt{2}]^{-1}[\phi_{\epsilon^a}(1) \otimes \phi_{\epsilon^b}(2) - \phi_{\epsilon^b}(1) \otimes \phi_{\epsilon^a}(2)],$$

which is represented in a basis of energy eigenfunctions composed of elements of the form $\phi_{\epsilon^a}(1)$ and $\phi_{\epsilon^b}(2)$, that refer to two particles, 1 and 2, each of which can be in one of a set of discrete energy states represented by the variables ϵ^a and ϵ^b. For two specific energy eigenvalues ϵ^1 and ϵ^2, the rigorous statistical matrix associated with the state $\Psi^A_{\epsilon^1,\epsilon^2}$ is expressed as a projection operator in the form

$$(3.27) \qquad \rho_r = \mathcal{P}_{\Psi_{\epsilon^1,\epsilon^2}} = \frac{\Psi_{\epsilon^1,\epsilon^2}}{\sum_{\epsilon^a,\epsilon^b} \|\Psi_{\epsilon^a,\epsilon^b}\|^2} \leq 1.$$

The sum is over all energy values that ϵ^a and ϵ^b can take on. According to the heuristic mode of discussion, one fermion has energy ϵ^1 and the other has energy ϵ^2. For the heuristic mode of discussion, Park showed that the statistical matrix takes the form

$$(3.28) \qquad \rho_h = \tfrac{1}{2}[\mathcal{P}_{\epsilon^1}(1) \otimes \mathcal{P}_{\epsilon^2}(2) + \mathcal{P}_{\epsilon^2}(1) \otimes \mathcal{P}_{\epsilon^1}(2)] \equiv \tfrac{1}{2}[\mathcal{P}_{\epsilon^1,\epsilon^2} + \mathcal{P}_{\epsilon^2,\epsilon^1}],$$

where $\mathcal{P}_{\epsilon^1}(1) = \mathcal{P}_{\phi_{\epsilon^1}(1)}$ is the projection operator, acting on particle 1, which is associated with the eigenstate $\phi_{\epsilon^1}(1)$ with eigenvalue ϵ^1, etc.

Park showed by an example that these two statistical matrices can give identical predictions for some calculations and not for others. He presented the rigorous and heuristic statistical matrices for the canonical ensemble representing this system at equilibrium in the form

$$(3.29a) \qquad \rho^A_r = [Z_A]^{-1} \sum_{\epsilon^a < \epsilon^b} e^{-\beta_k(\epsilon^a+\epsilon^b)} \mathcal{P}_{\Psi_{\epsilon^a,\epsilon^b}},$$

$$(3.29b) \qquad \rho^A_h = [Z_A]^{-1} \sum_{\epsilon^a < \epsilon^b} e^{-\beta_k(\epsilon^a+\epsilon^b)} \tfrac{1}{2}[\mathcal{P}_{\epsilon^a,\epsilon^b} + \mathcal{P}_{\epsilon^a,\epsilon^b}],$$

where the normalization is $Z_A = \sum_{\epsilon^a < \epsilon^b} e^{-\beta_k(\epsilon^a+\epsilon^b)}$. Park showed that the energy H^A computed from both of these statistical matrices is the same. However, when the entropy is computed for these normalized states, it is not hard to show (Park [**1991**], p. 90) that

$$(3.30a) \qquad S^A_r = -k_B \mathrm{Tr}\rho^A_r \ln \rho^A_r = k_B \beta_k H^A + k_B \ln Z_A,$$

$$(3.30b) \qquad S^A_h = -k_B \mathrm{Tr}\rho^A_h \ln \rho^A_h = k_B \beta_k H^A + k_B \ln[2Z_A],$$

where k_B is Boltzmann's constant. The result (3.30) implies

(3.31) $$S_h^A = S_r^A + \ln 2.$$

Park noted that there is a similar result for the boson case. In both cases, a higher value is attributed to the entropy in the heuristic case compared to the rigorous case.

It is easy to lose sight of these issues and to speak of elements as being definite when they are not. Bohr was aware of the problems involved in defining the quantum state of a system of particles and of the fact that it was an error to speak theoretically in ways that are incompatible with the information that can actually be provided by the experimental arrangement.

3.4 Discovery of the Uncertainty Relations

By 1925, Bohr had become convinced of the likelihood that a process in the atomic domain would not be visualizable in terms of spacetime pictures in the way they are in classical kinematics. In this context, Heisenberg set out in 1927 to clarify what visualizable or intuitive content there is in quantum mechanics. His intent was to come to an intuitive understanding of the kinematic and mechanical aspects of quantum mechanics by an exact analysis of how these concepts are actually used. He began [**1927**], p. 172, by stating what is meant by understanding a theory intuitively: "We believe that we understand a physical theory intuitively if we can think qualitatively of all the experimental consequences of this theory in simple cases and we know as well that the application of the theory never contains an internal contradiction." The employment of physical intuition has a long history and can often be successful when formal and mathematical approaches fail. In the nineteenth century, physical intuition became almost synonymous with a mechanical model.[21]

Heisenberg's next move was to develop the position he had adopted in his 1925 paper one step further. In his 1927 paper, he labeled statements employing quantities that could not be measured according to quantum theory as "having no sense." He [**1927**], p. 174, maintained that in order for the phrase "position of the electron" to have meaning, for example, it is necessary to state experiments by which the position could be measured. To this end, he introduced as an example of an experiment that could measure the position of the electron his famous γ-ray microscope. Although unrealizable in practice, there is no built-in or in principle limitation on measuring the position of an electron with an arbitrary degree of accuracy.

Heisenberg used this criterion as a way of distinguishing statements that can play a role in quantum physics from those that cannot. Heisenberg was

---

[21] For historical examples, see Alexandre Koyré [**1957**], Chapter VII, and Mary Hesse [**1953**]. See also the discussion in J. Hjort [**1920**], pp. 124–126, of Helmholtz's reaction to the model making of Kelvin and Maxwell.

therefore using the word 'meaning' in the way a physicist would and not philosophically. His statement meant that the "position of the electron" in quantum theory, by contrast to classical theory, can play a role in the theory only when it is possible to measure it. It is not a narrow operationalist position, which, roughly speaking, reduces the meaning of an observation to the actual measurements used to make it, because Heisenberg allowed idealized and thought experiments to serve as well as actual ones.[22] It is also not a statement about the meaning of individual terms in the statement. The word 'position' has a well-defined meaning in quantum mechanics just as in classical theory. His point was that the concept 'position' may not be applicable to the physical situation in a given experiment.

Heisenberg used the γ-ray microscope thought experiment to explain his reason for excluding a statement like "the 1S path of the electron in the hydrogen atom" from his theory. He observed that if we use light to measure the position of the electron, then the wavelength of light that must be used to establish the location precisely is of sufficient energy to remove the electron from the atom—making a second measurement of its position on a path impossible. On the other hand, p. 176, we do have the option of making a measurement of the position of the electron in many atoms so we are allowed to establish a probability function to describe where it is likely to be found. Moreover, he, p. 177 (see also p. 186), noted that we cannot make a determination at any one time of all the dynamical variables needed to define the classical state of the system.

Using the γ-ray microscope, Heisenberg made plausible the relation

$$(3.32) \qquad \Delta p \Delta q \approx h,$$

where Δp is the exactness with which the momentum p can be determined and Δq is the exactness with which the position q can be determined.[23] He, p. 175, felt that this relation is a "direct intuitive clarification of the relation $\mathbf{pq} - \mathbf{qp} = ih/2\pi$," where $\mathbf{q}$ is the quantum mechanical operator representing the position and $\mathbf{p}$ is the momentum operator. He noted that one can also obtain a similar relation from scattering experiments. Bohr [**1927**] pointed out, however, that Heisenberg's argument is not sufficient to establish (3.32) and corrected it. Bohr's argument will be discussed in Section 3.6.

Heisenberg, p. 179, extended this relation to the form $\Delta E \Delta t \approx h$. This represents the relation between the accuracy with which the energy of a system is determined and the time required to do so. He considered this relation a consequence of the commutation relation $\mathbf{Et} - \mathbf{tE} = ih/2\pi$. But this interpretation is controversial because there is no quantum mechanical

---

[22] See the discussion of meaning in Heisenberg [**1930**], p. 15.

[23] What I have called the "exactness" with which an operator representing a physical quantity can be measured is usually called the *dispersion*, in physics terminology, or the *variance*, in statistics terminology, of the operator.

operator corresponding to t. Pauli [**1933**], p. 140, objected to it on these grounds and maintained that the time t cannot be represented by an operator and that therefore the formal substitution of t into the operator relation $\mathbf{HF} - \mathbf{FH} = -i\hbar \mathbf{G}$ cannot be allowed.

Other authors subsequently created time operators by using combinations of operators such as $\mathbf{T} = m\mathbf{X}/\mathbf{P}_x$. L. Mandelstam and I. G. Tamm [**1945**], for example, defined the dispersion of a time-like quantity by $\Delta t = \Delta R/(\partial R/\partial t)$ and substituted this into the relation

$$(3.33) \qquad \Delta H \Delta R \geq \frac{\hbar}{2} \left| \frac{\partial R}{\partial t} \right|.$$

V. A. Fock and N. Krylov [**1947**] distinguished the Mandelstam-Tamm relation, derived from the Schrödinger equation, from what they called Bohr's relation for the uncertainty in the energy exchange during a measurement. The discussion was taken up again by Yakir Aharonov and David Bohm [**1961a**], [**1962**], [**1964**], Fock [**1962**], Chylinski [**1965**], E. P. Wigner [**1972**], and by others. Wigner [**1972**], p. 237, maintained that the time-energy relation applies only to the lifetime of a definite state of a system—such as when an atom is in an excited state, but there is no radiation present.[24]

Bohr's view [**1927**], pp. 60, 83, which will be discussed later in a more general context, is that $\Delta E \Delta t \geq \hbar$ represents a "general reciprocal relation ... between the maximum sharpness of definition of spacetime and energy-momentum vectors associated with individuals."[25] The quantity ΔE was later described by Bohr and Rosenfeld [**1933**], p. 29, as an uncertainty in energy transfer during a scattering experiment in which there is a latitude in the time Δt within which the scattering occurs. Bohr [**1949**], pp. 43–44, spoke also of a latitude ΔE in the energy ascribed to a particle and the interval Δt during which a shutter in an experiment was open.[26] If v is the velocity of the particle and ΔL is the length of the wave train associated with it as it passes through a shutter, then $\Delta t = \Delta L/v$.

The various attempts outlined above to provide an energy-time uncertainty relation in quantum mechanics were given a careful analysis by G. R. Allcock [**1969**], I. Allcock rejected the definition of a time operator as a ratio of two other operators that are averaged separately, as was done by Mandelstam and Tamm, on the grounds that calculating the expectation value of this operator requires two separate experiments and not a single measurement.[27]

---

[24]See Wigner [**1972**] for a discussion of this and references to other literature on the time-energy uncertainty relation.

[25]See also Pauli [**1933**], p. 146.

[26]This form for the energy uncertainty in certain types of experiments played a role in a number of papers in this period. It will appear again in the next chapter in the discussion of the work of Lev Landau and Rudolph Peierls.

[27]See also the discussion in B. Rankin [**1965**].

Von Neumann [**1932**] showed that the measurement of two operators in a single experiment requires that they are both functions of a third operator and that this third operator is the one measured. The proposal of Mandelstam and Tamm therefore does not represent the definition of a single operator representing a physical concept.

Allcock also elaborated on Pauli's [**1933**], p. 140, footnote 1, rejection of attempts to provide a Hermitian dynamic operator for the time. The candidate time operator $i\hbar\partial/\partial E$, for example, is not Hermitian when used with respect to the set of functions $\psi(E)$ usually used in quantum mechanics. No set of such functions, which is complete for $E > 0$, vanishing at $E = 0$, and closed under $\partial/\partial E$, as required by Hermiticity, exists.[28]

To justify his way of approaching quantum theory, Heisenberg, pp. 170–180, made an analogy with the theory of relativity: just as the definition of simultaneity depends on the existence of experiments to establish it, the definition and preparation of a state with simultaneous sharp values for dynamical variables requires the existence of an experimental arrangement that can do it. If there existed a signal that propagated infinitely fast, relativity theory would be impossible. Similarly, if there existed an experiment that permitted the sharp determination simultaneously of **p** and **q**, quantum mechanics would be impossible. But the relative inexactness in the simultaneous determination of these two variables (as expressed by the uncertainty relations) "allows therefore for the validity of the relations which find their pragmatic expression in the quantum mechanical commutation relations $\mathbf{pq} - \mathbf{qp} = ih/2\pi$."

Among the consequences of his investigation was Heisenberg's conclusion that we could never observe a conflict between the predictions of corpuscular theory and those of wave theory.[29] He considered in this regard the interference pattern of electrons reflected from a crystal or diffraction grating. If one attempts to trace accurately the electron paths between the grating and the screen, in order to observe the trajectory predicted by classical corpuscular theory, very precise observations of the electron position would be required. But this determination would add so much velocity (momentum) to the electron that its de Broglie wavelength would become extremely short and the electron would be scattered by the grating on an ordinary corpuscular trajectory. The interference pattern would therefore be destroyed by this procedure. Heisenberg, pp. 188–189, pointed out that this example shows that quantum theory does not differ from classical theory only in the microscopic domain,

---

[28] Several other candidate time operators share these difficulties. The work of Allcock will be mentioned again briefly in Chapter 15 in connection with his important challenge to the assumptions underlying von Neumann's theory of measurement in quantum mechanics. This challenge, along with a fuller discussion of Allcock's work on the time-energy uncertainty relation, including proposals that approximate energy eigenfunctions be used and a discussion of Pauli's proof, will be taken up in QIS.

[29] Bohr subsequently made this point often in his papers as well. See Bohr [**1935**], pp. 697–700, and [**1949**], pp. 43–47.

since the differences between the predictions of classical corpuscular theory and quantum theory are macroscopic in the case of interference phenomena.

Heisenberg, p. 180, also presented a version of the correspondence principle based on his approach:

"All concepts that in classical theory are used for the description of a mechanical system can also be defined exactly for atomic processes by analogy to the classical sources. The experiments that serve for such definitions have according to experience an inexactness in them if we require of them the simultaneous fixing of two canonically conjugate variables."

This is an interesting and significant variation on the formulations of the correspondence principle previously given by Bohr. Heisenberg was making the claim that all features of classical theory have a place and will find expression in quantum theory, which also echoes some statements by Bohr quoted earlier. Furthermore, these concepts can be "defined exactly" for atomic processes. The kind of definition that Heisenberg has in mind is the specification of an experimental procedure that would allow the precise measurement of a quantity. It should be kept in mind that, as above, this procedure may be a purely conceptual one.

Heisenberg concluded his paper with a discussion of the implications of his point of view for causality. He felt that the formulation of causality in physical theory is not a consequence of the theory but was a false pre-supposition of it. Nor should one "... be led to the opinion that an 'actual' world in which causal laws are valid is concealed behind the observed statistical world." In keeping with his overall point of view [**1927**], p. 197, such speculation seemed to him to be "unfruitful and meaningless." This viewpoint is an important consequence of the conceptual broadening that was part of the legacy of the Bohr, Kramers, Slater paper.

At the time of Heisenberg's work on the uncertainty relations, Bohr was developing the ideas that he put forth in his lecture at Como, Italy in September, 1927. As Heisenberg stated in a postscript to his paper, he had become acquainted with a draft of Bohr's paper and discussed it with Bohr. He [**1927**], pp. 197–198, acknowledged the influence of Bohr's ideas:

"After the completion of this work, new investigations by Bohr led to the point of view that a significant deepening and refinement of the analysis of quantum mechanical relations worked out in this paper can be made. In this connection, Bohr has informed me in a discussion of this work that I had overlooked several points. Above all, the uncertainty in the observations does not rest exclusively on the appearance of discontinuities, but depends directly on the demand that the different consequences be simultaneously valid that are expressed in the corpuscular theory on the one hand and the wave theory on the other."

These were the ideas that Bohr was shaping into his principle of complementarity.

3.5 Reflection 5

Bohr, along with Heisenberg, at this time located the origin and significance of the uncertainty relations in the disturbance of the system being measured by the measurement process. In the experiments they considered in their analysis of quantum measurement theory, they noted that there is always an unavoidable interference with the course of the phenomena by the measuring instrument. Not only is this interference unavoidable, but they also felt that it is uncontrollable and unpredictable as well.[30] This means that we cannot take account of a measurement or remove its effects through calculation or mechanical compensation as we can in classical theory. Bohr [**1927**], p. 53, who always looked for the most general viewpoint, pointed out that "... our usual description of physical phenomena is based entirely on the idea that the phenomena concerned may be observed without disturbing them appreciably." On a more general level, Bohr made it clear from the outset of his 1927 Como lecture that he was concerned with the possibilities for giving a description of physical phenomena and defining physical quantities in terms of this description. Thus, as indicated by Heisenberg in the above quotation, Bohr was already concerned with the consequences of the need for both wave and particle theories. This generality of approach is characteristic of Bohr's work and distinguishes him from all the other scientists working on quantum theory at that time.

3.6 The Uncertainty Relations and Thought Experiments

In Heisenberg's original analysis of the uncertainty relations, he looked upon the reciprocal location-momentum uncertainties that appeared when the γ-ray microscope is used to measure a sequence of particle positions as originating in the fact that the shorter wavelengths of light needed for a precise determination of the particle location resulted in a larger transfer of momentum to the particle. However, as Bohr soon pointed out, if it were possible to control the initial conditions of the experiment exactly, we could calculate the momentum transfer exactly and circumvent the uncertainty relations. Bohr [**1927**], pp. 62–64, showed that the relation of these uncertainties in the γ-ray microscope experiment was really due to the finite aperture of the microscope. As illustrated in Figure 3.1, a photon of definite momentum is scattered from an electron at some point A; if the photon is scattered within the cone of half-angle ϕ, it will be focused by the lens onto the photographic

---

[30] These are features of the 'disturbance theory of measurement' that will be discussed below. It is the basis for the representation of the energy uncertainty in certain experiments that were remarked on above. See also the contemporary discussion in G. N. Lewis and J. E. Mayer [**1929**].

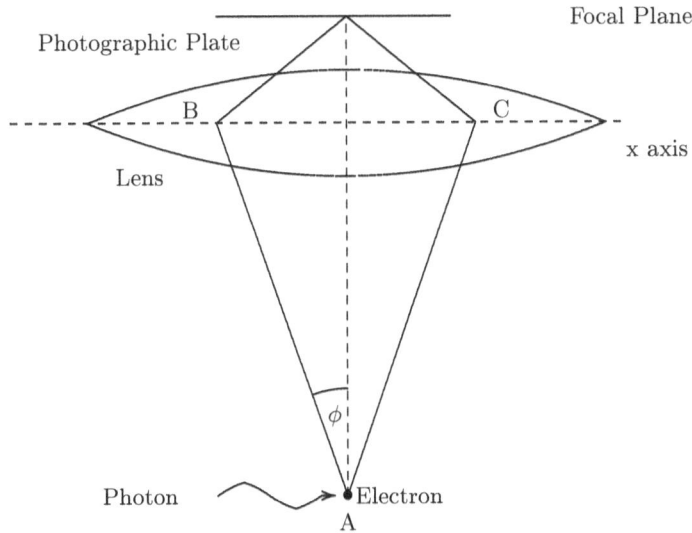

FIGURE 3.1. The γ-ray Microscope

plate. Since we cannot tell from which part of the cone the photon striking the plate has come, there is a resultant uncertainty in the momentum transferred to the electron from the photon.

The minimum distance between the points that can be separated by the lens (its resolving power) depends on the wavelength λ of the light and the angle 2ϕ of the lens aperture according to the following formula from optics:

$$\Delta x = \frac{\lambda}{2 \sin \phi}. \tag{3.34}$$

This can be called the uncertainty in the x measurement. The minimum uncertainty in the momentum transferred to the electron in the x direction by the photon, Δp_x, is the difference between the transfer if the photon passes through point B in the lens and the transfer if it passes through point C. The magnitude of the photon momentum is h/λ, so the uncertainty in the electron momentum in the x direction is

$$\Delta p_x = 2\frac{h}{\lambda} \sin \phi. \tag{3.35}$$

Combining these two relations gives

$$\Delta x \Delta p_x \approx h \tag{3.36}$$

as required.[31]

Modern derivations of the uncertainty relations make use of the commutation relations and the formalism of quantum mechanics as their basis. For any two operators that do not commute, **A** and **B**, say, such that

(3.37) $$[\mathbf{A}, \mathbf{B}] = i\hbar C,$$

where C is a constant, an uncertainty relation can be given. The *dispersions* of these operators for a system in state ψ are defined by the standard deviations

(3.38a) $$\Delta A_\psi = [(\psi, \mathbf{A}^2 \psi) - (\psi, \mathbf{A}\psi)^2]^{\frac{1}{2}},$$
(3.38b) $$\Delta B_\psi = [(\psi, \mathbf{B}^2 \psi) - (\psi, \mathbf{B}\psi)^2]^{\frac{1}{2}}.$$

It can then be shown that the product of the dispersions of these two operators for the state ψ is related to the commutator (3.6) by[32]

(3.39) $$\Delta A_\psi \Delta B_\psi \geq \tfrac{1}{2} \| [\mathbf{A}, \mathbf{B}] \psi \|.$$

If the state ψ is normalized, $\|\psi\| = 1$, we use the commutator (3.6) to obtain the uncertainty relations in the familiar form

(3.40) $$\Delta A \Delta B \geq \frac{\hbar C}{2}.$$

It should be noted that for some conjugate operators, the derivation mentioned above has to be modified.[33]

The uncertainty relations, as Heisenberg pointed out, do not set any lower limit to the exactness with which any given quantity in a system can be measured. In the language of states and operators, this means that the uncertainty relations do not set any lower limit to the dispersion of any given operator. We can construct states (at least mathematically) that are dispersion free for any operator. But the dispersion in the conjugate operator then increases without bound. The product of the uncertainties Δq and Δp of the operators **q** and **p** is a minimum for those states that have a Gaussian distribution in both the q and p spaces.[34]

---

[31]For another example of a calculation of this sort, see von Neumann [**1932**], pp. 241–242.

[32]See, for example, F. A. Kaempfer [**1965**], pp. 65–69.

[33]This is discussed in P. Carruthers and M. M. Nieto [**1968**]. Some errors in early work occurred because these limitations were not noticed.

[34]See R. Jackiw [**1968**].

3.7 Reflection 6

With regard to those thought experiments that claim to contradict the uncertainty relations, an examination indicates that it is usually the definitional criterion that they do not meet.[35] At some point in the experiment, information is assumed to be available that cannot be obtained from the experimental arrangement proposed. On the other hand, this objection has also been raised with respect to the use of thought experiments in support of quantum mechanics. One objection centers around the fact that no lens exists that could focus the γ rays of the wavelength needed to locate an electron within 10 Ångstroms inside the atom.[36] This objection concerns the acceptability of the idealization used in the experiment. While such an objection could be important to a future theory in which there might be an absolute lower limit on the definition of the position of the electron, say, it represents an unnecessary limitation from the standpoint of current theory.[37] From a philosophical point of view, the justification for completely excluding thought experiments would have to be made on rather extreme operationalist grounds—far beyond what most physicists, philosophers and quantum theorists in particular would be willing to accept. At any rate, this position would prove no threat to quantum theory since it has had to pass tests in the more restricted domain of actual experiments in tests of its validity.

By means of the γ-ray microscope, Heisenberg was trying to deal with the question of to what degree it makes sense to use the notions of position and momentum in conjunction with the quantum formalism. If he had discovered that the uncertainty relations could be circumvented, even if only in principle, this would imply that either the theory was not complete enough or that there were certain aspects of it that have not been understood properly and taken account of. These "hidden" aspects of physical objects, though not always directly observable with our instruments, could then be given meaning in Heisenberg's sense.

When the use of thought experiments in practice is examined, several features emerge. First, thought experiments can help in exploring the physical meaning and consequences of a theory. They can make clear the compatibility (or lack of it) of theoretical constructs with the kinds of (idealized) measurements envisioned by the theory. Einstein's elevator experiment was a demonstration that under certain circumstances the effects of the gravitational field cannot be distinguished from ordinary accelerated motion—giving support to his principle of equivalence. Second, thought experiments can be used to

---

[35] This is true of Karl Popper's [**1934**], pp. 243–246, thought experiment and the one proposed by Robison [**1969**]. See also J. Picht [**1965**].

[36] See E. Breitenberg [**1965**], pp. 357–358, footnote 9. See also Schrödinger's [**1934**], p. 519, warning against the indiscriminate use of thought experiments.

[37] This point was first made in connection with the γ-ray microscope by von Neumann [**1932**], p. 242, footnote 135.

compare the consequences of two theories. In this case, the procedure is to make a model of the situation and compare the consequences derived from the models to the facts. The defeat of Newton's corpuscular theory of light by Huyghens' wave theory rested on comparing the predictions of each theory concerning the reflection and refraction of light with the observations of these phenomena. Third, thought experiments can be used to indicate the nature of measurements allowed by a theory apart from any limitations outside the theory that prevent these measurements from being made. Heisenberg's γ-ray microscope is an illustration of what might be called a paradigmatic way of measuring the position of a particle. Any other accurate determination of the position of a particle should give results compatible with the results of this thought experiment. In this vein, Bohr [**1923b**], p. 32, considered the double slit interference experiment as paradigmatic for demonstrating wave properties.

Historically, as Kuhn [**1964**] has emphasized, thought experiments have played their most important roles in situations involving the analysis of natural phenomena according to competing theoretical structures. This was the case for Galileo's critique of Aristotle's conception of falling bodies and for Einstein's critique of simultaneity in classical mechanics. In situations such as these, the use of thought experiments to extract the physical meaning of a theory aids in the comparison of the applicability of concepts from the competing theories to physical situations. This inquiry does not establish that the concepts of the superseded theory are self-contradictory, but rather that associating them with aspects of the physical world requires the use of new conceptual structures.[38]

3.8 Statistical Aspects of the Uncertainty Relations

A clear and consistent interpretation of the uncertainty relations has not often been given by theorists discussing them. Quantities such as Δq and Δp have been variously called a "measure of the dispersion in physical variables", a "lower limit on the random fluctuation of physical variables", a "measure of the probable error in measuring physical variables", a "measure of the minimum disturbance of physical variables by measurement", and many others. Each version of the meaning of the uncertainty of the value of an operator for a given quantum state is related to a different perspective on the relation of this quantity to the data from measurements, to the underlying state, or to the measurement process. The differences in viewpoint are often based on ontological conceptions. On the one hand there is the statistical view in which the quantity $\Delta \mathcal{A}$ represents a feature of the data gathered from many measurements of $\mathcal{A}$ and is the standard deviation of the sample data. From this point of view, the reciprocal relation between Δq and Δp, say, is an additional factor of significance to quantum theory but not to the

---

[38] See Kuhn [**1964**], pp. 320, 322, 333–334.

interpretation of the quantities themselves. On the other hand, there is the physical approach that looks upon the quantities Δq and Δp as reflecting a physical or ontological property of the quantities themselves with respect to an atomic system. In one of the hidden variable theories, the uncertainties are attributed to "random fluctuations" of the values of the observables. In another hidden variable theory the uncertainties are attributed to the action of other variables that make the measured variable appear random. The Copenhagen Interpretation of quantum mechanics by contrast takes a middle stance on the ontological issue and the non-zero values of Δq and Δp are taken as a measure of the indefiniteness of the position and momentum of a system described by a quantum state.

The fact that the dispersion in $\mathcal{A}$ can be non-zero for measurements of $\mathcal{A}$ on systems in a single pure state—and not just for systems in a set of different states—indicates that caution must be used in interpreting these formulas in terms of standard statistics. In the classical case, a positive value for the dispersion of some observable is evidence that one is measuring that observable on an ensemble of systems in various states, since for each pure classical state, in either mechanics or statistical mechanics, the dispersion of an observable vanishes. The classical approach is in fact based on the assumption that the system may be characterized by a state with definite values for each of its variables and parameters. Every classical system can in principle be divided into components that are dispersion free for all its variables. In the quantum case, on the other hand, Heisenberg [**1930**] showed that the separation of systems into dispersion free classes cannot be done for even two quantum observables if the operators corresponding to these observables do not commute. Von Neumann [**1932**], Chapter IV, Sections 1 and 2, showed more generally that the existence of noncommuting operators in quantum theory implies that there are no dispersion free states for all the operators of quantum theory.[39]

There are other limitations on the employment of statistical functions in quantum mechanics. It is usually not possible to set up a joint probability distribution, which obeys the axioms of probability, for two noncommuting observables. Furthermore, attempts to define joint probability distributions for commuting observables do not seem to be well defined for certain states. The use of probability theory within quantum mechanics has been criticized, for example, by Patrick Suppes [**1963**], who also espoused a hidden variable approach to resolving the conceptual issues. The unambiguous application of probability theory to quantum mechanics has been discussed by V. S. Varadarajan [**1962**] and George W. Mackey [**1963**]. The reader is referred to these works for further details. I will return to the issue of probability in physics in Chapter 14.

---

[39]See also the discussion in J. Albertson [**1961**].

3.9 Reflection 7

As a terminological point, the uncertainty relations have been characterized variously as 'inexactness relations' (*Ungenauigheit*), 'unknowability relations' (*Unbekanntheit*), 'uncertainty relations' (*Unsicherheit*), and 'indeterminacy relations' (*Unbestimmtheit*). As mentioned above, Heisenberg initially used 'Ungenauigheit' to characterize the relations but later switched to 'Unbestimmtheit' and 'Unsicherheit'. Bohr [1927] used 'uncertainty', while Bohr and Rosenfeld [1933] used 'Unbestimmtheitsprinzip'. Pauli [1933], pp. 83, 86, 88, used the forms 'Unbestimmtheitsprinzip', 'Unsicherheitsrelation' and 'Unbekanntheit' in reference to the uncertainty relations. Pauli seems to have been the only one of the Copenhagen theorists to express the fact that these locutions do not all carry the same thrust. He made the point that "The distinction between (in principle) indeterminateness and unknowableness and the connection of both concepts is crucial for quantum mechanics." He [1933], pp. 88–89, illustrated this point by a brief discussion of the double-slit experiment.

The inconsistency regarding the choice of a term to characterize the uncertainty relations probably reflected a genuine ambivalence on the part of the quantum theorists as to whether the uncertainty relations describe a fact about the relation of the macroscopic world to the microscopic world or describe aspects of properties possessed by atomic entities. The answer to this question depends on the general answer given to the status of the quantum state description. I shall return to this issue several times below.

3.10 Bohr's 1927 Como Lecture

Immediately after Heisenberg's work on the uncertainty relations, Bohr presented his concept of complementarity at a conference at Lake Como in Italy. Most of the well-known physicists concerned with these matters at the time were present with the exception of Einstein. Bohr's lecture marked the first attempt to provide a genuine philosophical underpinning to the new advances in physics. The uncertainty relations had provided Bohr a concrete measure of the consequences of the wave-particle duality and thereby a physics-based justification for the ideas he was working on. Bohr had already embraced the wave-particle duality underlying quantum theory and he presented the concept of complementarity as the fundamental feature of a new conceptual framework broad enough to include it.

The lecture was published in Nature in 1928 in a revised form as Bohr [1927].[40] It sparked significant debate in the years that followed and solidified the boundaries between those who accepted Bohr's view of the consequences of quantum theory and those who were seeking a more "realistic" microscopic

---

[40] For comparisons between the 1927 form of the manuscript in the Bohr Archive and the slightly revised 1928 form published in Nature, see, for example, Faye [**1991**].

theory or a more realistic interpretation of quantum theory itself. At that time, and periodically afterward, Bohr was accused of being obscurantist and pessimistic by setting boundaries to where science could go. He responded that he was simply reflecting the way things were in a situation in which our previous intuitions, visualizations, and conceptions had failed.

In essence, Bohr stated that a principle of complementarity may be necessary in situations in which we must take account of the circumstances under which a measurement is made. For physical quantities that are not simultaneously compatible within a theory, the principle of complementarity states that it may be necessary to adopt one viewpoint or another when describing an experimental situation theoretically and that these viewpoints cannot be combined. Within each viewpoint, such as the wave or particle description of experimental results in quantum theory, the framework of theoretically associated concepts may be used consistently to represent experimental results and devise new experiments without further restriction.

The principle of complementarity is also connected with the possibilities of observation. It states that two complementary quantities cannot be measured within a single experimental arrangement. It this way, it preserves harmony between theory and experiment and assures us that our experiments will not contradict the theory and that the theory is compatible with the experiments. This means that competing and contradictory sets of complementary experimental results cannot be attributed simultaneously to a given system. It also means that members of a complementary pair of quantities cannot be assigned as properties to atomic entities.

The introduction of complementarity was accompanied by a discussion of what we need to take account of in describing an experiment theoretically and in stating the results of the experiments. Bohr initiated a set of themes in this lecture that he returned to over and over throughout his life. Because complementarity will be discussed in great detail in Part II, I will put off presenting more details until that time.

CHAPTER 4

Fields and Measurement: 1927–1934

After the rapid development of the new quantum mechanics between 1925 and 1927, quantum theory entered a time of testing and codification. Bohr was the primary defender of quantum mechanics and worked vigorously to answer the difficult challenges that emerged from these stringent tests of the consistency of quantum mechanics and its relation to experiment.

4.1 Further Developments in Quantum Theory

Between Bohr's Como lecture of 1927 and his work on the Einstein, Podolsky, Rosen paradox in 1935 a number of theoretical and experimental results became available. Von Neumann began in 1927 to codify the quantum formalism, the theory of measurement, and quantum thermodynamics. Dirac in 1927 paved the way into the quantization of the electromagnetic field. The relativistic Dirac equation for the electron and the Klein-Gordon equation were both introduced around this time. In the early 1930s the positron and the neutron were both discovered and the neutrino was postulated to account for energy discrepancies in weak decays. Work also began in earnest on quantum electrodynamics and quantum field theory. After the heady advances in quantum mechanics, it was felt that an adequate quantum field theory would soon follow. But that was not to happen.

This period was also a time of testing the basic conceptions of quantum mechanics. The uncertainty relations, for both particles and the electromagnetic field, were the subject of a number of analyses and subjected to stringent tests. Einstein and others presented serious challenges to non-relativistic quantum theory at the Solvay conferences held during this period. Landau and Peierls investigated relativistic quantum field theory and concluded that quantum mechanics may fail when applied to the electromagnetic field. Bohr reacted strongly to all of these suggestions of possible failures of quantum theory for he saw that a successful challenge to any component of quantum theory could be used as a successful assault on all of quantum theory. In response to the work of Landau and Peierls, Bohr and Rosenfeld investigated in 1933 the possibilities of measurement for the electromagnetic field.

One of the most important advances during this period was the development of a set of postulates to serve as the foundation of quantum mechanics and a theory of measurement based on these. This was completed by von Neumann and published in its definitive form in von Neumann [**1932**]. Von Neumann's work has served as the standard foundation for quantum mechanics since that time. Von Neumann's postulates and theory of measurement will be presented in this chapter, but critical analysis will be deferred until the differences between the views of Bohr and von Neumann are discussed in Chapter 15.[1]

4.2 Interpreting the Uncertainty Relations

Quantum theory was unpalatable for many people. The conflict between the implications of the uncertainty relations and the classical worldview stimulated a number of attempts to circumvent them. Einstein made such attempts at the 1927 and 1930 Solvay conferences. They cost Bohr, who also

---

[1] Von Neumann's postulates are not the only way a foundation can be provided for quantum mechanics. The construction of quantum mechanics using some alternative postulates proposed in the literature will be investigated in QIS and QTS.

attended, difficult times, but he was able to reply to them.[2] Max von Laue [**1932**], p. 916; [**1934**], p. 440, argued that it was premature to conclude that we would never overcome the uncertainty relations and expressed the hope that new discoveries might aid us.[3]

Several important questions came up when attempts were made to understand the uncertainty relations. One important issue was whether the uncertainty relations apply to a single system or only to an ensemble of systems all in the same state. Another was whether the relations implied (i) merely a limitation on the making of certain kinds of measurements simultaneously, (ii) a limitation in the possible knowledge obtainable about a system, or (iii) a limitation on the properties that can be ascribed to objects on the atomic level.[4]

Those who would maintain that the uncertainty relations apply only to an ensemble of systems view the quantum state itself is a statistical distribution that refers to an ensemble of systems. On this view, the quantum state is like a classical distribution function in many respects and represents the probability amplitude for the distribution of the values of variables that can be measured on the systems in the ensemble. In any given system, it is maintained that all variables have sharp values, and that the uncertainty relations refer to a limitation on measurement and not on possible knowledge about the system. Any well-defined measurement of a variable in quantum mechanics does in fact produce a value for the variable measured. The uncertainty, or spread, in the values of the variable in several measurements is interpreted as the spread in the values of the variable in the ensemble of systems over which it is measured. In the ensemble interpretation, the uncertainty relations have been called "statistical scatter relations".[5]

To examine these viewpoints, Heisenberg [**1930**], pp. 13–46, analyzed what he called "reconstructed" experiments from the Copenhagen point of

---

[2]This is discussed in Bohr [**1949**], pp. 41–47, 52–85.

[3]David Bohm [**1952a**], [**1952b**], later echoed Laue in hoping that the uncertainty relations might be found to be invalid outside of the domain in which they have presently been tested. This could happen, he felt, in the domain of high-energy reactions, small distances, or in the nucleus.

[4]A complete answer to these questions requires an analysis of the quantum state description and a decision as to the proper status to be accorded to it with respect to the objects it describes. This discussion will be deferred until Bohr's views of the quantum state have been presented.

[5]See Karl Popper [**1934**], Chapter IX. The uncertainty relations were called a "statistical dispersion principle" by L. E. Ballentine [**1970**], pp. 366–367 in a later version of these views. Ballentine characterized the latter in the following terms: " ... the uncertainty principle restricts the degree of statistical homogeneity which it is possible to achieve in an ensemble of similarly prepared states, and thus it limits the precision with which future predictions for any system may be made. But it does not impose any restriction on the accuracy to which an event can be reconstructed from the data of both state preparations and measurement in the time interval between these two operations."

4.2 INTERPRETING THE UNCERTAINTY RELATIONS

view.[6] He acknowledged that experiments could be performed that would yield information concerning a particle, for example, in which the products of the uncertainties involved violated the uncertainty relations. One may, for instance, measure the momentum of a beam of charged particles of known mass very accurately using a magnetic field. One may also observe very accurately the position at which a particle strikes a photographic plate. While the product of the uncertainties for the position and momentum of a particle moving through a magnetic field and striking a photographic plate is less than allowed by the uncertainty relations, Heisenberg claimed that this does not constitute a violation of quantum mechanics. His reason was that the position measurement made by having the electron strike the plate altered the precisely known momentum by an "unknown and indeterminable amount."[7] Heisenberg, p. 20, maintained further that this will occur in every such case:

"This may be expressed in concise and general terms by saying that every experiment destroys some of the knowledge of the system which was obtained by previous experiments. This formulation also makes it clear that the uncertainty relations do not refer to the past; if the velocity of the electron is at first known and the position then exactly measured, the position for times previous to the measurement may be calculated. For these past times $\Delta p \Delta q$ is smaller than the usual limiting value, but this knowledge of the past is of a purely speculative character since it can never (because of the unknown change in momentum caused by the position measurement) be used as an initial condition in any calculation of the future progress of the electron and thus cannot be subjected to experimental verification. It is a matter of personal belief whether such a calculation concerning the past history of the electrons can be ascribed any physical reality or not."

Heisenberg based his position on the disturbance theory of measurement: Every measurement of a quantity disturbs in an uncontrollable and unpredictable way the value of a quantity conjugate (in the quantum mechanical sense) to the one being measured.

Heisenberg's [1927], pp. 172, 186, statement of his relation as a "limit on the exactness" (*genauigheitsgrenzen*) with which two conjugate quantities may be measured, and Born's [1969], p. 26, reference in 1928 to the uncertainty relations as a "law of restricted measurability" reflect views stemming from the disturbance theory. The disturbance theory was based on an examination of various ways in which different quantities may be measured in atomic systems. In each case, the interaction of the measuring instrument could be shown to disturb the quantity being measured. The impossibility of circumventing the uncertainty relations by controlling the initial conditions

---

[6] Bohr [1938b], p. 23, has also discussed these experiments.
[7] Many examples of this approach are given in C. G. Darwin [1931a] and [1931b].

exactly is due to the universal validity of the uncertainty relations for all matter. The above discussion cannot therefore be used to establish the validity of the uncertainty relations for all matter, but it does suffice to show that the assumption of their universality does not lead to inconsistencies.[8]

Heisenberg did not limit his interpretation of the uncertainty relations to being merely a restriction on measurement. He [1930], p. 15, (see also [1952], p. 86), spoke of an indeterminateness in our knowledge:

> "The uncertainty principle refers to the degree of indeterminateness in the possible present knowledge of the simultaneous values of various quantities with which the quantum theory deals; it does not restrict, for example, the exactness of a position measurement alone or a velocity measurement alone."

This limitation on knowledge is not due merely to the impossibility of making the measurements needed to obtain it, but was based on a deeper conception of the epistemological status of quantum theory. This deeper conception, of course, was that arrived at by Bohr [1927] as part of the philosophical perspective he was developing toward quantum mechanics. In the investigation leading to the principle of complementarity, Bohr concentrated on the question of interpreting a measurement and what it means to say that we know something about an atomic system. Bohr developed his position in terms of the conditions that must be met in order that a measurement or a quantity is well defined in quantum mechanics. In this vein, he spoke of the uncertainty relations as "determining the highest possible accuracy in the definition of the energy and momentum of the individuals associated with the wave-field." With respect to the relation '$\Delta E \Delta t \approx \Delta x \Delta p_x \approx \Delta y \Delta p_y \approx \Delta z \Delta p_z$' designated by '(2)', Bohr went on to say[9]

> "The limitation in the classical concepts expressed through relation (2), is, besides closely connected with the limited validity of classical mechanics, which in the wave theory of matter corresponds to the geometric optics in which the propagation of waves is depicted through "rays". Only in this limit can energy and momentum be unambiguously defined on the basis of spacetime pictures. For a general definition of these concepts we are confined to the conservation laws, the rational formulation of which has been a fundamental problem for the symbolical methods to be mentioned below."

Although Bohr [1927], p. 73, spoke of a " ... maximum accuracy with which two canonically conjugate quantities can be observed," he made explicit his rejection of the interpretation of the uncertainty relations as being

---

[8]The disturbance theory will be discussed in more detail in the next chapter.

[9]Bohr [1927], pp. 59–60. See also [1929c], p. 18: "Obviously these facts not only set a limit to the extent of the information obtainable by measurements, but also set a limit to the *meaning* which we may attribute to such information." (Italics Bohr's.)

accurately characterized by the statement "the position and momentum of a particle cannot be simultaneously measured with accuracy":[10]

"On the contrary, the proper role of the indeterminacy relations consists in insuring quantitatively the logical compatibility of apparently contradictory laws which appear when we use two different experimental arrangements, of which only one permits an unambiguous use of the concept of position, while only the other permits the application of the concept of momentum defined as it is, solely by the law of conservation."

The uncertainty relations play an important role in Bohr's notion of complementarity by placing an explicit limit on the degree of mutual definition of conjugate concepts for atomic systems. This is turn places a limitation on the appropriateness of a description using such a concept for a particular atomic system under particular experimental conditions.

Heisenberg [**1930**], p. 20, adopted Bohr's view concerning the limits of applicability of certain descriptions and their attendant concepts, such as the particle description or the wave description, to atomic systems. He [**1930**], p. 15, termed "meaningless" any use of the words particle or velocity with an accuracy exceeding the uncertainty relations.[11] Pauli [**1936**], p. 740, spoke similarly of the position-momentum uncertainty relations: "This states that it is meaningless to coordinate *simultaneously* values of the position coordinate x of a material particle of light quantum and the component p_x of its momentum if the product of their exactness Δx and Δp_x is smaller than the order of the quantum of action h." He clarified his definition of meaning in [**1948**], p. 1110: "This definition of 'meaning' supposes a definition *a priori* of the quantum mechanical model, but it does not suppose an actual empirical verification." The use of the term 'meaning' in connection with statements concerning atomic systems is problematic. As the term meaning is being used by Heisenberg and Pauli, a concept is meaningful in application to a physical situation if it does not contradict theoretical restrictions on its application, such as the restriction imposed by the uncertainty relations. As mentioned before, this reference to meaning is clearly an elliptical one and it would be better to call a concept 'indefinite' or 'inappropriate' rather than 'meaningless' in a situation in which it cannot have a precise value. What is meant is that the simultaneous application of concepts is not physically meaningful when they are used outside the domain of their mutual validity.

---

[10]Bohr [**1937a**], pp. 292–293. See also Bohr [**1958b**], p. 5. The possibility for simultaneous measurements must, of course, be in accord with the uncertainty relations, but this fact does not determine the meaning of these relations. See E. Arthurs and J. L. Kelly [**1965**] and C. Y. She and H. Hefner [**1966**].

[11]See Josef M. Jauch [**1968**], Section 12.5, and George Mackey [**1968**], Section 3.2, for discussions of the definition of the velocity in quantum mechanics.

The interpretation of the uncertainties in physical variables representing actual physical properties of the atomic entities requires at least an implicit physical model of the entity to which these properties are attributed.[12] One such classical model of the uncertainty relations was proposed during this time by R. Fürth [**1933**]. His example, which was discussed by Bohm [**1957b**], p. 34, was based on Brownian motion. Let us consider one-dimensional motion only. Consider a particle of mass m suspended in a fluid. Suppose Δx is the distance moved by the particle in a short interval of duration Δt. The mean square of Δx turns out to be proportional to Δt. Using a as the constant of proportionality, it then follows

$$(4.1) \qquad \overline{(\Delta x)^2} = a\Delta t; \quad \text{or} \quad \delta x = \sqrt{\overline{(\Delta x)^2}} = a^{\frac{1}{2}}(\Delta t)^{\frac{1}{2}},$$

where δx is the root mean square of Δx. If the velocity is defined by $\bar{v} = \Delta x/\Delta t$, then $\bar{v}$ fluctuates at random, but its root mean square is

$$(4.2) \qquad \delta v = \sqrt{\frac{\overline{(\Delta x)^2}}{(\Delta t)^2}} = \frac{\delta x}{\delta t} = a^{\frac{1}{2}}(\Delta t)^{-\frac{1}{2}},$$

where $\delta t = \Delta t = \overline{\Delta t}$ was used. Using $p = mv$, so $\delta p = m\delta v = ma^{\frac{1}{2}}(\Delta t)^{-\frac{1}{2}}$, it follows that

$$(4.3) \qquad \delta x \delta p = ma.$$

Because ma is a constant independent of Δt, this relation is similar to the uncertainty relations.[13]

Later work along these lines refined some of these ideas. Bohm [**1957b**], [**1962a**], [**1962b**], for example, used this analysis as the basis for contending that quantum processes may be determined at a "subquantal" level and just appear to have a random element when observed on our level. This is analogous to the fact that the Brownian motion of a macroscopic particle is caused by deterministic interactions on the molecular level (classically speaking) but appears to be random when small macroscopic grains are observed under a microscope. This view claims that it is the crudeness of our measuring instruments prevents us from observing the interactions on the subquantal level and requires that the description of atomic systems be expressed in probabilistic terms.

---

[12] For example, to speak of the uncertainties in terms of random fluctuations as Bohm and Aharonov [**1957**], p. 1070, did, implies an essentially classical model with some additional mechanism causing the fluctuations.

[13] A similar classical model was proposed by Timothy Boyer [**1968**] in which he showed that a random classical electromagnetic field in conjunction with electrodynamics could reproduce Planck's [**1900**] predictions concerning blackbody radiation. This idea was similar to the concept of 'natural radiation' that Planck himself used in the late nineteenth century to calculate the entropy of the electromagnetic field.

Other models have been given by Louis de Broglie [**1953**], [**1957**], [**1960**], Bohm [**1952a**], [**1952b**], and others. In each of these models the essential problem is to show how the deterministic underlying structure can give rise to stochastic results compatible with quantum mechanics and the uncertainty relations in particular.

The very literal interpretation of the uncertainty relations in terms of a smearing of conjugate quantities has attracted few proponents. One reason is probably the difficulty in finding a testable model in which these features make sense. While an uncertainty in position might be visualized as a physical extension in space that may change in response to a change in the external conditions, it is more difficult to find a model of an object with an actual spread in the momenta.[14] In addition, the explanation of why two smeared conjugate observables are related in accord with the uncertainty relations encounters great difficulties. Furthermore, it is likely that such a model would also run into difficulties if it was applied to the explanation of most quantum mechanical experiments.

4.3 Reflection 8

The rapid application of quantum theory to the explanation of many physical phenomena and its experimental tests in the 1927–1934 period led to many innovations. These included Dirac's theory of the electron, the neutron, the positron, and the postulation of the neutrino to conserve energy in beta decay. Bohr was slow to accept these innovations, in both the quantum formalism and experimental observations. This was probably because he needed to understand how these new particles are related to concrete experimental arrangements that produce them—but he finally did accept them.[15]

Bohr and Einstein sparred on philosophical issues at the 1927 and 1930 Solvay conferences. Einstein was able to cut to the root issues in ways that forced Bohr to clarify his thinking. In each case, Bohr was able to answer the challenges posed by Einstein and make the answers part of his growing understanding of the philosophical issues that underlie an adequate interpretation of quantum theory.[16] I will return briefly to one of these debates below.

From the late twenties until the late thirties Bohr participated in many discussions concerning the interpretation of quantum theory in Copenhagen

---

[14]D. Bohm and L. de Broglie, in the references given above, have attempted such models with limited success.

[15]Bohr's reluctance to accept the new particles has been discussed by several interviewees and in a number of letters between Bohr and other physicists recorded in the Bohr Archive. In the case of the neutrino, it is said that it seemed as if he wanted the law of conservation of energy to fail.

[16]These discussions and thought experiments have been exhaustively reviewed at many times and in many places including Bohr [**1949**]. Consult these papers for details. For the purposes of the discussion here it is sufficient that Bohr was able to prevail, at least to his own satisfaction.

and elsewhere. These discussions included at various times Werner Heisenberg, Erwin Schrödinger, Wolfgang Pauli, Max Born, Pascual Jordan, V. A. Fock, George Gamow and many others. Out of these discussions came a rough consensus—accepted by a number of workers, but bitterly opposed by some—that was soon called the Copenhagen Interpretation of quantum mechanics. Of the group centered in Copenhagen, it was clearly Bohr who was most concerned with, and continued to struggle with, the philosophical issues underlying the interpretation of quantum mechanics. These issues occupied much of Bohr's work from 1927 until his death in 1962.

Bohr's initial problems vis á vis quantum mechanics were to understand the nature of measurement, interpret the uncertainty relations, show that the wave-particle duality does not lead to contradictions, and assess the role of the kinematic aspects (the spacetime picture) of a process versus its dynamical (conservation law) aspects. He saw the need to connect these new issues and principles of physics with an understanding of their philosophical implications. During this time, he introduced the notions of language, perception, communication, and the need to distinguish what he came to call the 'knowing subject' from the 'observed object', into his discussions of quantum physics and laid the foundations for his epistemology.

4.4 Uncertainty Relations in Field Measurements

Dirac extended quantum mechanics to the electromagnetic field in 1927 by finding a way to represent the quantities of classical electrodynamics in Hamiltonian form and then quantizing the commutation relations of the "location" and "momentum" analogs in the same way as for particles. Heisenberg [**1930**], p. 49, used Dirac's formalism to extend the uncertainty relations to the electromagnetic field. For the simultaneous measurement of the y component of the electric field vector and the z component of the magnetic field vector in a small cube of side δl, Heisenberg used the Lorentz force in the crossed electric and magnetic fields to obtain

$$(4.4) \qquad \Delta \mathfrak{E}_y \Delta \mathfrak{H}_z \geq \frac{hc}{(\delta l)^4},$$

with cyclic permutations of the directions x, y, and z. After Heisenberg's work, number of physicists took up the examination of how the quantized field strengths in Dirac's theory were to be measured and the status of the uncertainty relations with respect to these quantities. Heisenberg's result (4.4) was challenged by Jordan and Fock [**1930**] and Landau and Peierls [**1931**], and for a time it seemed that particle theory and field theory might be in conflict.[17] These investigations indicated that quantum mechanics might not be adequate to a proper characterization of the electromagnetic field or

---

[17]See Pauli [**1933**], p. 257.

generalizable to the relativistic domain. In addition, it soon became apparent that there are infinities associated with the total field energy computed using this quantum electromagnetic formalism.

Jordan and Fock [1930] obtained what they called "new uncertainty characteristics of the electromagnetic field." They used single electrons and protons as charged test bodies, Newton's second law in the form $e\Delta E_x = m\Delta a_x$, and then the position-momentum uncertainty relation for the test body to show that the uncertainty in the x component of the electric field strength is

(4.5) $$\Delta\mathfrak{E}_x = \frac{m}{e}\frac{\Delta v_x}{\delta t} \geq \frac{h}{e}\frac{1}{\Delta x \Delta t}.$$

They noted that this implies that we can only obtain a mean value of $\mathfrak{E}_x$ from our measurements and that this is associated with the space interval Δx and the time interval Δt. Next, using the curvature of the paths of charged particles in a magnetic field due to the Lorentz force law, they obtained for the magnetic field strength the result

(4.6) $$\Delta\mathfrak{H}_x \geq \frac{hc}{e}\frac{1}{\Delta y \Delta z}.$$

For an experiment in which both field quantities are measured simultaneously, they also obtained the result (4.4), in accord with Heisenberg [1930].

Shortly after his work on the electromagnetic field, Dirac developed a relativistic quantum theory of the electron.[18] In an analysis of its properties, he and others discovered that negative energy states were an integral part of the theory that could not be avoided because there was a finite probability that an electron would make the transition into one of these states under certain circumstances. Dirac's work and that of Felix Klein, W. Gordon, and E. Majorana, for integral spin particles, led to a flurry of activity in relativistic quantum particle theory. By analogy to the theory of the electromagnetic field, the particle wavefunction was soon quantized, given its own commutation relations, and renamed a quantum field function. This procedure was called "second quantization" at the time.

Landau and Peierls [1931] presented a strong critique of the quantum theory of the electromagnetic field and Dirac's relativistic wave mechanics. They stated that the purpose of their paper was to investigate whether the presuppositions for the applicability of wave mechanical methods are fulfilled. Their criticisms of the theory of the quantized electromagnetic field were based on questions of measurability of the fields, the associated uncertainty relations for the field strengths, and the infinite zero-point energy of the fields. For Dirac's relativistic theory of the electron, they mentioned the problems of the negative energy states and the infinite self-energy of the electron. The

---

[18] The formalism of Dirac's theory will be discussed briefly in QIS in the context of an investigation of the problem of localization in quantum mechanics.

quantum theory of measurement, in a form similar to that first presented by von Neumann in 1927 and subsequently in von Neumann [**1932**], was the basis for their critique. From this standpoint, Landau and Peierls [**1931**], p. 58, stated that if no measurement can determine the wavefunction then it can have no physical meaning. As a second criterion for the meaningfulness of a measurement, a repetition of the measurement is required to give with certainty the same result as the previous measurement. They maintained that neither of these assumptions is usually fulfilled in measurements in relativistic quantum mechanics because of limitation of the possible velocities of particles.

Landau and Peierls considered measuring the momentum of a particle, represented by a momentum-energy vector (P, E), by means of a collision with a plane mirror, which has a momentum-energy vector (p, ε). The conservation of momentum relation can be strictly employed in this case for the particle-mirror momenta (P, p) before the measurement and (P', p') after the measurement. On the other hand, the precision with which the interaction energy E_i between the particle with energy E and the mirror with energy ε can be fixed is limited to an uncertainty $\Delta E_i \sim h/\Delta t$ in E_i during the time Δt required to make the measurement.[19] In this analysis, the displacement Δx of the mirror during the interaction does not play a role. The equations satisfied by this collision are therefore

(4.7a) $$p + P - p' - P' = 0,$$

(4.7b) $$|\varepsilon + E - \varepsilon' - E'| \sim \frac{h}{\Delta t}.$$

Because the mirror is macroscopic, Landau and Peierls assumed its momentum and energy are known precisely both before, as (p, ε, p'), and after, as (ε'), the measurement. In the nonrelativistic case, it can be assumed also that $\Delta P = \Delta P'$ for the uncertainty in the particle momentum before and after the measurement. Using $\Delta E = v \Delta P$ and (4.7), this leads to

(4.8) $$(v - v') \Delta P > \frac{h}{\Delta t}.$$

This inequality, connected with the initial uncertainty of the particle momentum, is associated with the definite momentum change in the particle in this measurement, due to the interaction of the particle with the mirror as it is reflected. This inequality is separate from that associated with the uncertainty of the momentum itself, which is the concern of the uncertainty relations for a single particle.

---

[19]This assumption is a consequence of the disturbance theory of measurement, but has more general validity.

In relativity theory, $v < c$ and $|v - v'| < c$ for massive particles so the result

(4.9) $$\Delta P \Delta t > \frac{h}{c}$$

is obtained from (4.8). If the exact location q before the measurement is assumed given, then after the measurement the exactness is $\Delta q \sim c\Delta t$ because $v < c$. If it can be established that $\Delta P \Delta t < (h/c)$, it follows that $\Delta q \Delta P < h$ in contradiction to the uncertainty relations.

There is another source of uncertainty in this measurement due to radiation by the accelerated charged particle. The energy emission associated with this radiative damping is given by integrating Larmor's power formula over the time

(4.10) $$E^r = \frac{2e^2}{3c^3} \int dt \, \dot{v}^2.$$

This quantity is a minimum for uniform acceleration for which $\dot{v} = (v'-v)/\Delta t$. The radiated energy over the time Δt is therefore at least

(4.11) $$E^r \geq \frac{e^2}{c^3} \frac{(v'-v)^2}{\Delta t}.$$

This yields us a new uncertainty of the form

(4.12) $$(v' - v)\Delta P > \frac{e^2}{c^3} \frac{(v'-v)^2}{\Delta t}$$

that leads to

(4.13) $$\Delta P \Delta t > \frac{e^2}{c^3}(v' - v).$$

This additional uncertainty is not important for electrons because $e^2 < hc$ even when $v' - v \sim c$ so (4.13) is weaker than the uncertainty relation (4.9). It is important for larger bodies. Multiplying (4.13) by (4.8) to give a formula for $(\Delta P \Delta t)^2$, then yields

(4.14) $$\Delta P \Delta t > \frac{h}{c} \sqrt{\frac{e^2}{hc}}.$$

With respect to field measurements, Landau and Peierls, p. 62, observed that the simplest method is to observe the acceleration of a charged test body. For optimum results for an electric field measurement a body with a large mass and small velocity should be used to minimize the effects of the magnetic field. Assuming the momentum P of the test body is known before the measurement, its uncertainty after the measurement is related to the uncertainty $\Delta \mathfrak{E}$ in the electric field strength by

(4.15) $$e\Delta \mathfrak{E} \Delta t > \Delta P.$$

Using this with (4.14) yields the result

$$\Delta \mathfrak{E} > \frac{\sqrt{hc}}{(c\Delta t)^2}. \tag{4.16}$$

By means of similar methods, the uncertainty $\Delta \mathfrak{H}$ in the magnetic field strength, measured by the motion of a magnetized needle, is the same,

$$\Delta \mathfrak{H} > \frac{\sqrt{hc}}{(c\Delta t)^2}. \tag{4.17}$$

If we wish to measure the electric and magnetic field strengths simultaneously, then the magnetic field generated by the needle during its motion must be taken account of. The uncertainty of this magnetic field is on the order

$$\Delta \mathfrak{H} > \frac{e}{(\Delta l)^2} \frac{v'}{c}, \tag{4.18}$$

where Δl is the distance between the test body and the needle. If now (4.18) is multiplied by (4.15) and (4.9) is used, the result

$$\Delta \mathfrak{E}_x \Delta \mathfrak{H}_y > \frac{hc}{(c\Delta t)^2 (\Delta l)^2} \tag{4.19}$$

emerges. Using (4.17), (4.18), and (4.19), Landau and Peierls, p. 63, noted that for a long enough time interval, $\Delta t \to \infty$, the measurements of $\mathfrak{E}_x$ and $\mathfrak{H}_y$ can be made simultaneously and with arbitrary exactness. They concluded that static fields can be completely defined in the classical sense.

Extending their considerations to changing wave fields, which require different spacetime domains for the measurements, they concluded that (4.16) and (4.17) can be used simultaneously because the disturbances in the measurements of $\mathfrak{E}_x$ and $\mathfrak{H}_y$ occur in different spacetime domains. This implies that insofar as field strengths are definable, classical theory suffices. In the quantum domain, the field strengths are not measurable quantities because the atomicity of the charge and mass of the electron, for example, yields inequalities that far exceed (4.16) and (4.17).

After a further discussion of specific issues connected with measuring the location of light quanta and particles, Landau and Peierls investigated the mathematical difficulties of wave mechanics itself. They noted that the smallest wavepacket that can be constructed in Dirac's relativistic quantum theory of the electron using positive energy states alone has a dimension of h/mc. The collection of smaller wavepackets does not form a complete set of energy eigenfunctions and calculations with them imply that the electron has an average velocity that is nearly c. In addition, it is a consequence of quantum field theory that the zero-point energy of the vacuum is infinite. The results above and these considerations led Landau and Peierls to conclude that it is not surprising that there are infinities in the wave mechanics of relativistic systems because wave mechanics is not valid there. This is especially true for light, which they felt requires a relativistic treatment. They, pp. 68–69, drew from this investigation a pessimistic conclusion:

"In the correct relativistic quantum theory, which does not yet exist, there will be therefore no physical quantities and no measurements in the sense of wave mechanics. One can, however, bring the system into interaction with any sort of apparatus and ask what the apparatus does then. The theory will provide a probability for the result of this experiment. This cannot, however, be interpreted as a probability for a parameter of the system under investigation because one can in no way insure that the probability for a given result equals 1 and is zero for all others. Moreover, it is in principle not possible to make the time duration of such an experiment arbitrarily small."

The work of Landau and Peierls threatened the foundations of quantum mechanics and it stimulated a great deal of discussion. Pauli [1933], for example, discussed it in some detail. Rosenfeld [1961b], p. 125, observed that Bohr took the challenge of Landau and Peierls very seriously and worked on it for two years between 1931 and 1933. Bohr realized, as indicated above, that if the uncertainty relations are violated in this domain, then the electromagnetic field could be used to demonstrate violations elsewhere. In spite of the practical limitations on carrying out any of the experiments suggested by Landau and Peierls, Bohr could not let the challenge to the fundamental basis of quantum theory go unanswered. In this respect Bohr differed from many other physicists. His response to this challenge, for example, differed from Boltzmann's response to the challenge posed by Poincaré's recurrence theorem to his H theorem. Boltzmann dismissed this challenge because it would require longer than the age of the universe for the recurrence to happen, so he felt no need to be concerned with it. This was not an answer that Bohr could find acceptable.[20]

4.5 The Bohr-Rosenfeld Thought Experiment

Bohr, in collaboration with Rosenfeld, began in 1931 a thorough investigation of the compatibility of the electromagnetic field, as it is represented in quantum electrodynamics, with the uncertainty relations of quantum mechanics. Because this was an investigation into theoretical and experimental limits, similar to Carnot's investigation of the maximum possible efficiency of heat engines, they used a thought experiment for the purpose. They presented the results of this work in Bohr and Rosenfeld [1933] Later work from a field viewpoint was presented in Bohr and Rosenfeld [1950].[21]

---

[20] Boltzmann's work and Bohr's response are discussed further in Chapter 14.

[21] For a presentation of quantum electrodynamics in this era, see Josef Jauch and Fritz Rohrlich [1955].

At issue was whether quantum electromagnetic fields could be given meaning by the correspondence principle in the same way the correspondence principle gave meaning to the quantities in standard quantum mechanics. The critique of Landau and Peierls had indicated that they could not. However, on closer examination, Bohr and Rosenfeld felt that the problems of the relativistic electron and electromagnetic theory could be separated and that the formalism of electromagnetic theory could be treated in a way that is "independent of all considerations of the atomic structure of matter."

They began by noting that the only constants appearing in quantum electrodynamics are Planck's constant h and the speed of light c. Since these two constants are not sufficient to fix a magnitude of the dimensions of length, Bohr and Rosenfeld [**1933**], pp. 4, 36, maintained that they did not need to consider any limitations on their thought experiment due to questions of dimension or atomic structure. Next, they stated that measurements can be made only on finite volumes of space during finite time intervals. Finally, in reference to the charged bodies needed for field measurements, they [**1933**], p. 8, maintained that " ... their clear use as measuring instruments is limited precisely to those circumstances where we can handle the influence of the field on them and their action as field sources on the basis of classical electrodynamics." Because of these considerations, they explicitly allowed themselves the use of mechanical latches, massless flexible threads, and small weightless levers connecting charged bodies in their "thought apparatus". They, p. 36, made clear that the point of their discussion of field uncertainties by the use of this special apparatus was to show that "it is possible to strongly separate the limitations on the state of the test body connected with the atomic structure of matter and that based on the universal quantum of action and especially the limitation of the use of these bodies formulated in the uncertainty principle."

Bohr and Rosenfeld then described their apparatus and showed how various configurations of the levers, threads and latches could be used in principle to measure any of the field quantities sought. In the test body, they used charges that are much larger than the electron charge e and especially chosen extended and continuous charge distributions as well as continuous surface charge distributions. In order to quench unwanted radiation generated by the test body when the field accelerates it, the surface charge was arranged in layers of opposite charge moving in opposed directions. Removing this additional radiation is important because it would add to the field being measured and limit the accuracy of the measurement.

With this apparatus Bohr and Rosenfeld demonstrated that the field uncertainty relations arising from the quantum mechanical uncertainties in the position and momentum measurements on pieces of the apparatus are consistent with the theoretical predictions of the field uncertainties given by quantum electrodynamics. In this situation, when all limitations due to the atomic construction of matter can be avoided, they showed that the theoretical predictions of the mutual uncertainties of two conjugate field quantities given by quantum electrodynamics and the idealized possibilities for accurately measuring them are in accord.[22] In this way Bohr and Rosenfeld showed that the predictions of quantum electrodynamics are consistent with the possibilities of making any kind of field measurement.[23]

The argument that Bohr and Rosenfeld used in justifying their neglect of the atomic structure of their instruments in their considerations is reminiscent of that used by Bohr [**1913**] in discussing the radius of the electron orbit in his theory of the atom. The lack of an element in electrodynamics of the dimensions of length implies that fields do not have an intrinsic spatial structure the way an atom, for example, does. This means that the field strength at a given point does not depend on the simultaneous field strengths at other points. The field may therefore be treated as interacting locally with the apparatus; and correlations between distant parts of the apparatus (e.g., interference effects) represent correlations defining the nature of the field itself and not the result of some nonlocal interaction at each position in the field with the whole macroscopic apparatus.

There is, furthermore, no lower limit on the mass or size of the constituents of matter implied by electrodynamics. The laws of classical mechanics and quantum mechanics, which are made use of in interpreting the field strength measurements, do not contain any limitations as to a minimal possible mass or size either. If we then include in our range of possible measuring instruments those that contain idealizations as to mass or size, which are smaller, for example, than is actually possible with the particles we have to work with, we increase the range of possible tests of the theory without excluding any previous tests. The idealized equipment, therefore, does not violate the requirements of quantum electrodynamics or any limitations due to quantum mechanics and it provides a more severe test of quantum electrodynamics than would be provided by equipment in which the limitations due to the atomistic structure were observed.

The second claim of Bohr and Rosenfeld concerns the question of the need to use finite volumes of space and intervals of time for making measurements. They connected this claim to the question of the definition of the field itself. The field concept involves field strength and frequency as properties. In order to make sensible measurements of these properties, Bohr and Rosenfeld showed that a minimal volume and duration, which depend on the field strength and frequency, is required. This does not mean that

---

[22]Bohr [**1937a**], p. 294, recognized that the neglect of the atomic structure in reference to quantum theory would not be allowed by a more fundamental theory involving the " ... mutual interaction of the so-called constituents of matter but also the stability of their existence."

[23]The analysis of Bohr and Rosenfeld was reexamined in the light of the new methods of quantum field theory by E. Corinaldesi [**1953**] with similar results.

a point charge, such as an electron, cannot be used to provide some information, but rather that measurements using a distribution of charge over a volume during a finite time interval provide both a more stringent test of quantum electrodynamics and allow a sharper definition of the aspects of the field being studied.[24]

The third claim of Bohr and Rosenfeld, regarding the necessity of dealing classically with the fields generated by the motion of the charged bodies used in measuring the original field, is both the most important of their claims and the most difficult. It is woven into Bohr's general theory of quantum mechanics and will be taken up in Chapter 8 below.

The use of idealized equipment by Bohr and Rosenfeld meets Popper's [**1934**] criterion that idealizations must be concessions towards a more stringent test of the positions being examined. The second claim of Bohr and Rosenfeld is concerned with the need for a definition of the quantity being measured in terms of an appropriate experimental arrangement (even if idealized) to measure it. While this aspect of the inquiry is not too important in classical theory, where, for example, kinematic and dynamic variables may be dealt with independently, it is of crucial importance in quantum theory. A good portion of Bohr's approach to quantum theory involves showing that we must satisfy certain kinds of conditions in defining a physical quantity. For him, these conditions are implicitly involved in every statement of what we have observed. This means that the field cannot either be measured or made sense of outside the domain in which the conditions can be met for doing so. He went on to argue that it is not possible in quantum theory, as it often is in classical theory, to simply assume that the concepts of a field or of the position of a particle make sense when these cannot be part of the measurement being made or part of a consistent theoretical description of the system.

4.6 Von Neumann's Theory of Measurement

In classical theory the process of making an observation or measurement is assumed to offer no special difficulties. One can at least in principle arrange the situation so that the measurement process intrudes on the measured system to an arbitrarily small degree. When this is not possible for practical reasons, the perturbation of the measuring instrument may be calculated and compensated for. In quantum theory, on the other hand, it was clear, as emphasized by Bohr [**1927**] and others, that a detailed analysis of the measurement process was needed in order to establish that the quantum formalism can be applied meaningfully to the interpretation of experimental results.

---

[24]To require that field measurements must be made by electrons in very short time intervals was called an "idealization of limited application" by Bohr and Rosenfeld [**1933**], p. 5. An example of the calculation of field uncertainty relations and a field measurement experiment is given in Heisenberg [**1930**], Chapter III.

4.6 VON NEUMANN'S THEORY OF MEASUREMENT

A theory of measurement in quantum mechanics was introduced by John von Neumann in 1927 and extended in 1932. He contrasted the continuous development in time of a wavefunction in accord with Schrödinger's equation with the discontinuous change in the wavefunction accompanying a measurement. This latter change has been called the 'reduction of the wavefunction' and cannot be accounted for by Schrödinger's equation.

In von Neumann's measurement theory, there must be a separation between the quantum system being measured and the measuring instrument if Bohr's requirements on the subject/object distinction and his requirement of a classical description for the instrument, are to be maintained. Von Neumann showed that the choice of where the 'cut' is made between the measuring instrument, described classically, and the system being measured, described in quantum terms, is arbitrary. It is a further consequence of von Neumann's version of the theory of measurement that a measurement made at a time between the beginning and end of another measurements will cause an intermediate reduction of the wavefunction and will lead to different results than those predicted when there is no intermediate measurement. Attempts to explain or account for this difference using concepts of classical theory were not successful.[25]

One of the most important aspects of von Neumann's theory, and the most controversial, is the statement that the mechanism that causes the reduction of the wavefunction in an experiment is the intervention of the consciousness of the experimenter at the point he or she becomes aware of the result of the experiment.

Von Neumann [**1932**] pointed out that we do not directly observe the behavior of atomic entities, but rather make use of an apparatus suited for making the measurement. An interaction is set up between a system k and a measuring apparatus M for the purpose of relating the behavior of M, expressed in terms of a "pointer reading," with values of the quantity in k being measured. What has been called a pointer reading may actually be a speck on a photographic plate, a Geiger counter click, a spectral line, etc.

Given that we have an apparatus suitable for making a measurement of a given observable, the next step in the analysis is to show how the combined system $k + M$ may be described quantum mechanically. Using x to represent the variables of k and y to represent the variables of M, von Neumann represented the combined system $k + M$ before the interaction as

$$(4.20) \qquad \Psi_0(x, y) = \psi(x)\phi_0(y),$$

where $\phi_0(y)$ is the initial state of the apparatus and $\psi(x)$ is the state of the system being observed. Von Neumann's next important assumption was that the measurement of a given operator will give a definite result and the value of the variable represented by the operator will then be definite in the

---

[25]See A. Komar [**1962**] on the indeterminate character of this reduction.

system. This means that the quantum mechanical description appropriate to the system after the measurement will be an eigenstate of the variable being observed and its eigenvalue will be the result of the measurement. This assumption, usually called the *projection postulate,* led von Neumann to use a basis set $\{\psi_m(x)\}$ composed of wavefunctions that are eigenfunctions of the operator being measured to decompose the original system state as a weighted sum of these eigenfunctions:

(4.21a) $$\psi(x) = \sum_m a_m \psi_m(x),$$

where

(4.21b) $$\sum_m |a_m|^2 = 1.$$

For this to be meaningful for arbitrary states $\psi(x)$, the set of eigenfunctions must be a complete set that spans either the whole Hilbert space or an appropriate subspace to which the wavefunction $\psi(x)$ is confined. The initial state of the combined system is then expressed as

(4.22) $$\Psi_0(x,y) = \phi_0(y) \sum_m a_m \psi_m(x).$$

If the set $\{\psi_m(x)\}$ of eigenfunctions is not a complete set that spans $\hat{H}$, it is often possible to extend it into a complete set by adding wavefunctions to the set.

In this formalism, a good measurement for Von Neumann was one for which the state of the combined system after the interaction is

(4.23) $$\Psi_1(x,y) = \sum_m a_m \psi_m(x) \phi_m(y).$$

With (4.23), we have a correlation between the members of the set of possible states of the system, $\{\psi_n(x)\}$, and the set of states, $\{\phi_m(y)\}$, of the measuring instrument. Each state $\phi_m(y)$ corresponds to a distinct (macroscopic) pointer reading in von Neumann's terminology. The core of von Neumann's theory is the characterization of the effect of observing M on the state of the combined system. Von Neumann assumed that an experimenter, observing that the pointer reading corresponds to the state n of the measuring apparatus M, changes the state $\Psi_1(x,y)$ instantaneously and discontinuously into one definite product out of this superposition:

(4.24) $$\Psi_1 \to \Psi_2 = \psi_n(x) \phi_n(y).$$

The probability that this particular outcome will occur is $|a_n|^2$. Von Neumann called this a Type 1 discontinuous change in the wavefunction due to a measurement and distinguished it from a Type 2 change due to the normal evolution of the wavefunction in accord with Schrödinger's equation.

One important difference von Neumann pointed out between a Type 1 and a Type 2 change is that the Type 2 change in the state vector described by Schrödinger's equation is thermodynamically reversible, while the Type 1 change describing a measurement, expressed in (4.24), is not. Von Neumann's further conclusion, that irreversibility is an essential feature of any observation, was incorporated by Bohr into his later thought concerning the aspects of an observation.

Central to von Neumann's approach is the contention that at some stage the perception and consciousness of the observer must directly intervene. Based on his division of the world into "the observer" and the "observed system," he [**1932**], p. 420, concluded that at some point we must say: "and this is perceived by the observer." At this moment, the projection in (4.24) takes place.[26] One may in principle pursue the details of a particular measurement as far as desired. For example, one may simply observe the temperature registered by a mercury thermometer; or one may use statistical mechanics to calculate the relation between the temperature and the length of the mercury column, observe the length of the column, and conclude the temperature; or, proceeding further, one may relate the pattern of light going into the eye to the length of the mercury column and "observe" the image on the retina; and so on. But at some point this process must cease and what the observer directly perceives is stated.

Von Neumann went on to discuss the distinction, first made by Bohr [**1927**], between the subject and object of a measurement and the issue of where one places the "cut" between the object and the observer. He divided the world into three parts; part I is the system being observed, part II is the apparatus used to observe it and part III is the observer. He then posed the general question of the relation between a measurement viewed as an observation of system I by the system II + III and an observation of the system I + II by system III. The first problem to be dealt with is the question of the compatibility regarding predictions and mathematical structures defined in I and II separately with those defined in the product space I + II. Von Neumann [**1932**], Chapter VI, Section 2, and pp. 436–437 in particular, established that they are compatible; furthermore, he showed that the states of systems I and II are definite in the combined system if and only if the state in I + II can be written as a product of states in I and II: $\Psi(x,y) = \psi(x)\phi(y)$. A measurement must reduce the general state $\Psi(x,y)$ in I + II to a mixture of these products and then determine one particular product as its result in accord with equation (4.24).

Von Neumann then considered the possibility that the appearance of a mixture after a measurement might really be due to the unknown state of the measuring instrument before the measurement. That is, it was conjectured that the instrument itself is not in a pure state and that this mixture led to the

---

[26]See von Neumann [**1932**], Chapter VI, Section 1, pp. 417–421.

development of the final mixture. This means that the coefficients of the final mixture would depend only on the (unknown) coefficients of the mixture in II representing the state of the instrument. Von Neumann showed, however, that this cannot be the case because the coefficients of the resulting mixture in system I + II after the measurement depend on the initial state of system I.[27] He concluded from this that it is not the unknown state of the measuring instrument that is responsible for the noncausal behavior associated with measurement as symbolized by the arrow in (4.24).

After von Neumann's work, the theory of quantum measurement developed an extensive literature of its own. Because most of this work repeats previous positions and presents few new ideas, only the most significant and germane articles will be reviewed and referenced in the work below.[28]

4.7 Reflection 9

There is a difficulty in von Neumann's theory measurement concerning how we know a given piece of apparatus is suitable for making the measurement of a particular observable. Von Neumann, who felt that he was explicating Bohr's views in this matter and cited Bohr several times in this regard, simply assumed that the relationship is clear in the sense that observers will use a classical analysis to agree that a given piece of equipment is suitable for measuring a given observable. However, the steps (4.20) to (4.24) in von Neumann's theory were not congenial to Bohr's thinking. After the presentation of the 1935 thought experiment by Einstein, Podolsky, and Rosen (EPR), in which the possibility of changing the experimental arrangement or boundary conditions during the course of an experiment was envisioned, Bohr explicitly rejected this approach. This important point will come up again in the next chapter in the discussions of the EPR experiment and John S. Bell's analysis of von Neumann's theory.

Von Neumann's theory of measurement, accepted for the most part by those adopting some form of the Copenhagen Interpretation of quantum mechanics, had several features and implications that other theorists objected to strongly. The first is that the "consciousness" of the observer plays an important role in the measuring process. This was seen by some as the introduction of an element of subjectivity into physics and a violation of the requirement that physics and physical descriptions be independent of an particular observer. That is, if the observer plays an unavoidable role in quantum

---

[27]See von Neumann [**1932**], Section 3, pp. 437–439. Abner Shimony has stated (private communication) that this point was not established rigorously until the work of Wigner [**1963**], D'Espagnat [**1966**], and J. Earman and A. Shimony [**1968**].

[28]For typical mainstream analyses of the issues connected with quantum measurement at the time Bohr's work ended, see R. A. Mould [**1962**], J. M. Burgers [**1963**], and D. H. Holze and W. T. Scott [**1968**]. These articles are selected from a vast, and repetitive, literature on this topic that has appeared since 1926. Most are concerned with solving von Neumann's 'reduction of the wavepacket' problem.

theory as it is used, then the description of the world provided by quantum theory must be intertwined with mental processes of each observer and not independently valid. In its extreme form, this objection amounts to the claim that if observers are important in changing the states of physical objects, and in particular the states of macroscopic measuring instruments on which the observer has no significant perturbing physical influence, then quantum mechanics cannot provide a description of a real physical world independent of the existence of a particular observer.

Another objection was raised in a sharp form by Einstein, Podolsky, and Rosen [1935], who felt that quantum mechanics is not a complete description of "physical reality" in the sense that there are elements of the world that are not part of the quantum description. Still other objections centered on the possibility of finding another theory in which the controversial features of quantum theory (the uncertainty relations and the noncausal character of measurement, among other things) could be removed while the predictive success of quantum theory and its account of the discrete structure of atoms and radiation could be maintained.

Although von Neumann felt that his theory of measurement was in accord with Bohr's approach to quantum theory, his view of the role of the observer is not in agreement with the theory that Bohr developed. Whether or not Bohr explicitly rejected von Neumann's approach, he certainly would have disagreed with the emphasis placed by von Neumann on the movability of the 'cut' between the subject and the object of measurement, in which the apparatus is on one side and "direct perception" and consciousness is on the other. The differences between Bohr and von Neumann involve the nature of observation, the ascription of intrinsic properties to atomic entities, the characterization of measurement, and the role of the observer's consciousness in the description of experimental results. I will delve into these questions in Chapter 15 below.

4.8 Exfoliation

Bohr's ideas with regard to the epistemological aspects of quantum mechanics were very influential. Pauli [1933], p. 89, for example, made the statement that "By analogy to the term 'Relativity Theory' one can also call modern quantum theory 'Complementarity Theory'." He went on to say that "this complementarity has no analogy to classical gas theory even though both operate with statistical regularities." He also mentioned Bohr's [1930] Faraday lecture in which Bohr spoke of complementarity in a somewhat different sense as a complementarity between knowledge of the microscopic molecular motion on the one side and the macroscopic temperature of systems on the other.

The nonintuitive character of the predictions made by quantum mechanics motivated researchers to explore the formalism and test it. The uncertainty relations, superpositions of states, and the wave-particle duality, were the subject of study after study and debate. In every case where a definitive test could be devised, quantum mechanics was supported. The conceptual structure of quantum mechanics also survived the quantization of electrodynamics and the inclusion of relativistic concepts when it was extended into quantum electrodynamics and field theory.

While Bohr was interested in the conceptual issues and experimental results of quantum mechanics, he did not participate much in the exploration of its mathematical details. He was interested in situations in which the interplay between the formalism, physical intuition, and experiment could help us understand the new conceptual issues we are facing.

The central importance of the wave-particle duality, along with the uncertainty relations and the superposition of quantum states, made it important to Bohr's thinking to be able to show that any experiment in which the wave description is appropriate is unsuitable for showing particle properties and vice versa. Bohr generalized this into a central theme that connected the impossibility of violating quantum mechanics to the impossibility of constructing an explicit real or thought experiment to do so. This close connection between quantum theory, which Bohr characterized as representing the 'possibilities of description', and possible experiments to test it, which Bohr referred to as the 'possibilities of observation', caused Bohr to respond vigorously when presented with the claim that some experiment, whether a thought experiment or a real one, could exhibit both the wave and particle aspects of matter simultaneously. Bohr's method of answering these challenges was to demonstrate that the information required for the contradiction of quantum mechanical predictions could not be obtained experimentally. He showed, for example, that suspending the double slit apparatus on a spring, so that the slit through which the particle passed could be determined (by the transfer of momentum from the particle to the slit system), leads to an indeterminacy in the slit position that is just sufficient to wipe out the wave interference effects. Since that time, many others have, as a matter of course, used similar arguments to show that their experimental arrangements cannot be used to violate the uncertainty relations.[29]

Those practicing quantum mechanics also imposed a number of requirements on the quantum state. These requirements began to be investigated in the late 1920s and afterward. Among these requirements are mathematical conditions that an acceptable state must meet, such as being single-valued and in some cases either symmetric or antisymmetric under exchange of identical particles. Other requirements will be considered below.

---

[29]W. H. Furry and A. S. Ramsey [**1960**], for example, demonstrate this for the experiment they proposed in order to measure the Aharonov-Bohm effect. See also the discussion in R. Serber and C. N. Townes [**1960**] on the experimental aspects of complementarity. A general analysis of the interaction of a microsystem with a measuring instrument was presented by D. I. Blokhintsev [**1968**].

4.8 EXFOLIATION

As an illustration of the physical and philosophical issues involved, let us review briefly the discussion of whether the quantum wavefunction should be single valued. In his doctoral thesis, De Broglie presented a wave equation representing the force-free motion of matter. He added as a subsidiary condition that the function ψ representing the waves be single-valued. Schrödinger extended de Broglie's work to include forces in the wave equation and applied it successfully, along with de Broglie's single-valuedness condition, to the structure of the hydrogen atom.[30] The requirement of singlevaluedness was studied in detail by Pauli [**1933**] and revisited by him in [**1939**]. The issue was revived again in the 1960s in relation to the discussions of the Aharonov-Bohm effect.[31] D. Pandres [**1962**] took up the issue from a general perspective. He examined the mathematical behavior of products used in quantum mechanical expectation calculations that take the form $\Psi^\dagger \mathbf{G} \Psi$, where $\mathbf{G}$ is a Hermitian operator, at the boundary of the space accessible to the wavefunctions. He claimed, using a suitable choice of boundary surfaces and operators, that well-defined calculations require that (1) the wavefunctions must vanish outside a region accessible to particles, (2) the phase and amplitude of the wavefunctions must be continuous across any boundary between regions of space, and (3) the wavefunctions cannot possess a singularity as strong as r^{-1} and must vanish for large r faster than r^{-1}. Finally, he used this same method to show that the wavefunction must also be single valued.

The point concerning single-valuedness was opposed by Martin Kretzschmar [**1965a**], [**1965b**], [**1965c**], who argued that the requirement that the quantum wavefunction be single-valued is a *conventional* requirement made for mathematical or computational convenience and is not required by the formalism or needed for its interpretation. He concluded that it is the representation of the operators being measured that determines whether the wavefunction needs to be single-valued or not.[32]

Another issue that was discussed at some length was the relation between force and potential in quantum mechanics. In 1959, Yakir Aharonov and David Bohm showed that, if we require that interactions between particles and fields be local, the electromagnetic potential has a physical significance even in regions of space that are free of fields and forces. This was an unexpected result—given the standard classical view that only the forces have physical reality and that potentials are just convenient fictions that are used to simplify calculations. Because this result was counterintuitive, a number of papers appeared in rapid succession discussing different aspects of the issues raised by Aharonov and Bohm and agreeing or disagreeing with their conclusions. The Aharonov-Bohm effect was also confirmed experimentally in a number of

---

[30]These developments were discussed by Max Born [**1954**] in his Nobel prize lecture.
[31]See Pandres [**1962**] and the references cited there. See also E. Merzbacher [**1962**] and F. Lenz [**1962**].
[32]This issue will be pursued in much more detail in QIS.

papers. The reason that this paper stimulated discussions of whether single-valuedness should be required of wavefunctions is because the Aharonov-Bohm effect applies to experiments containing multiply connected regions.

Within eleven years after their first paper, the Aharonov-Bohm effect had become part of the accepted furniture of quantum mechanics and was no longer surprising. At this point, Herman Erlichson [**1970**] wondered why there had been any fuss because the calculation of the Aharonov-Bohm effect is a simple consequence of a proper application of the quantum mechanical formalism. He then wrote to Bohm and stated "As for myself, I cannot see why the Aharonov-Bohm effect is any more mysterious than other quantum effects, such as the double-slit diffraction, for example." He then asked Bohm in essence what was special about the Aharonov-Bohm effect. Bohm replied that it is a contribution to clarifying the *informal* language that physicists use when they are talking about particles, forces and local interactions as opposed to the formal calculations with the formalism itself.[33]

In point of fact, there is much more to the Aharonov-Bohm effect than Erlichson realized that more recent papers dealing with forces and gauge fields have recognized. In addition, Bohm's point concerning the informal language of physicists is also much more important than is often realized. At several places I have discussed persistent misunderstandings concerning the proper use or interpretation of the quantum formalism due to these often-unconscious habits of thought.

Bohr emphasized the importance of using an appropriate (quantum mechanical) description in a given context; but he also emphasized the importance of physical intuition in understanding and solving physical problems. In many cases, this informal language has been more important than the formal one in making progress in understanding new phenomena. Discussions of the uncertainty relations, for example, helped to wean people from the compelling classical pictures with they viewed the world. Moreover, Born [**1969**], p. 144, has also pointed out that without our classical intuition concerning how to devise experiments we would be paralyzed in our efforts.[34]

The important issues that have been raised concerning acceptable wavefunctions, the role of potentials and forces, the Aharonov-Bohm effect, and issues of locality will be discussed further in Chapter 17 below and in much more detail in QIS.

---

[33] See the conclusions of the review in Erlichson [**1970**], pp. 169–171. Excerpts from Erlichson's letter to Bohm and Bohm's reply are in the Appendix to this paper.

[34] As one example of the importance physicists attach to physical intuition, consider the statement of David L. Goodstein [**1975**], p. 316: "The fact is that if one inquires closely enough, even our elegant and eminently successful theories of solids have their quantitative shortcomings. Their success lies in that we believe that we have a firm grasp of the basic principles of the problem. It is that kind of grasp that we lack in the liquid problem. All the formalism we have gone through is no substitute for the intuition we need." Dirac [**1963**] has emphasized the importance of "beauty" as well.

CHAPTER 5

The Quantum State Description: 1935–1962

One implicit consequence of the uncertainty relations and the interference aspects of quantum particle theory was the failure of the materialist conceptual framework. This prospect brought a strong reaction from many physicists and philosophers. Some spoke in apocalyptic terms of the end of physics if the conception of complementarity introduced by Bohr is accepted. For these authors, it was imperative to find an alternative theory or an alternative interpretation that preserved the predictions of quantum theory but did not have the philosophically objectionable features of what came to be called the Copenhagen Interpretation.

5.1 Questions of Interpretation

After his work with Rosenfeld on the measurability of electromagnetic fields in quantum theory, Bohr continued to extend and refine his conception of complementarity. Bohr also made significant conceptual contributions to nuclear physics during the 1930s. In the late 1930s Bohr was also concerned with consolidating his philosophical position and published several papers and lectures that were devoted to this. These philosophical concerns occupied much of his published work until his death in 1962. The detailed exposition and discussion of his philosophical ideas will be deferred to Part II.

Soon after quantum mechanics was introduced, attempts were made to interpret it in ways that preserved more of the classical conceptual framework than Bohr had allowed. One natural attempt was based on the view that the square of the quantum state $|\Psi(Q_k, t)|^2$ is a probability distribution over an ensemble of systems in each of which the particle variables all have precisely defined values as they do for a classical ensemble. In this view, the quantum state does not apply to individual systems. Another natural approach assumed that the behavior of the particles is determined by precisely defined variables but that these are "hidden" from us and we have access in experiments only to variables that give rise to the quantum effects we measure. These two approaches are called the *statistical ensemble theory* and the *hidden variables theory*. Because these interpretations were mentioned by Bohr and stimulated von Neumann, later followed by others, to reply to them mathematically, they will be discussed in this chapter.[1] Two recent theories, decoherence theory and the transactional interpretation of quantum mechanics, appeared after Bohr's death, and will be discussed in Chapter 16.

The objections to quantum mechanics that led to these reinterpretations took several basic forms. One set of objections was concerned with the loss of the comfortable materialist ontology associated with Newtonian physics and their proponents looked for ways to recover what aspects of materialist ontology that one could from quantum theory. Another set of objections was concerned with issues of objectivity and subjectivity in quantum mechanics. These objections were critical of von Neumann's inclusion of the observer in physics. Yet another set of objections was concerned with questions of the locality of quantum interactions and the separability of distant systems.

Bohr rarely, if ever, spoke in terms of interpreting the wavefunction. For him, the unit of interpretation came to be a whole experiment, performed with

---

[1] Other major ontologically based interpretations of quantum mechanics are the macroscopic state theory, quantum ergodic theory, and the 'many worlds theory', which is also called the 'relative state theory'. The others, which make physical or philosophical assumptions that are less plausible than those of quantum mechanics, are outside the scope of this discussion. For a further discussion of these theories, see Shimony [**1963**] and D'Espagnat [**1965**]. See also articles advocating particular theories by Josef Jauch [**1964**], Jauch, E. P. Wigner and A. Yanase [**1967**], A. Loinger [**1968**], Rosenfeld [**1968**], B. DeWitt [**1968**], L. N. Cooper and D. van Vechten [**1969**], and many, many others.

definite initial and boundary conditions, and completed with the macroscopic registration of the observed results. His discussed his ideas in the context of concrete examples that were often based on the double slit experiment or on simple scattering experiments. Almost everyone else focused on the wavefunction itself and described particles in terms of moving wavepackets. The purpose of this inquiry is to understand why Bohr did not find these other approaches satisfying and developed an epistemology of his own that went in many ways much further outside the confines of classical physics.

The Disturbance Theory of Measurement.
Bohr initially attempted to understand the quantum mode of description in terms of the disturbance theory of measurement.[2] Heisenberg and von Neumann [**1932**], along with many others, also subscribed to the disturbance theory of measurement at that time. According to the disturbance theory of measurement, the unavoidable and unpredictable interference of measuring instruments with the course of phenomena is responsible for the mutual uncertainties in conjugate variables and for the indefiniteness of possible descriptions of a system. These disturbances are unavoidable and unpredictable because any attempt to fix closely the variables in the instrument determining the interaction will require yet another instrument to determine them and so on to an infinite regress. At each stage the uncertainty of the values of these variables will thwart our efforts to compute the disturbance of the original measurement.

The attractiveness of the disturbance theory lies in the fact that the uncertainty relations do not have to be accorded any unusual ontological import. Quantum theory provides, on this view, the most complete description that can be given of atomic phenomena in the face of the unavoidable disturbance in any information gathering measurement. The disturbance theory by itself, however, leaves open the question of whether a more complete description of physical objects could be given, at least in principle, than that provided by quantum theory. Many of the early objections to quantum theory were in fact made on the grounds that quantum theory did not provide the most complete description possible. The most severe challenge of the quantum state description on these grounds, and the one with undeniably the greatest impact, was the "paradox" proposed by Einstein, Podolsky and Rosen (EPR) in 1935.

Einstein, Tolman and Podolsky [**1931**] had considered the possibility of knowledge of the past and future in quantum mechanics. The subtler

---

[2]This conclusion is an inductive one based on an examination of the way Bohr expressed himself in Bohr [**1927**], [**1930**] and with regard to the subject/object interaction. Bohr did not directly commit himself to the disturbance theory in his early writings. And while Bohr after 1935 does not contradict what he said before 1935, he did not reject it explicitly until 1935 and after. Meyer-Abich [**1965**], pp. 146–147, and C. A. Hooker [**1972**], pp. 110–111, 120–121, have reached the opposite conclusion.

issues of locality and separability were raised in the work of EPR. Locality, which refers to whether interactions are required to be spatially localized or not, and separability, which refers to whether widely separated systems are independent or not, were destined to play a central role in future discussions of quantum mechanics from then on. These issues soon became more important than the issue of completeness.

5.2 The Einstein, Podolsky, Rosen Paradox

A significant event that did have an effect on Bohr's conceptions was the assault on quantum theory in the form of a paper introducing the Einstein, Podolsky, Rosen paradox. This paper focused his attention on problems with the disturbance theory of measurement and on certain implicit assumptions about the independence of distant systems.

Einstein, Podolsky and Rosen [**1935**] began their famous critique of quantum theory by distinguishing "the objective reality, which is independent of any theory" and "the physical concepts with which the theory operates." [3] By objective reality is meant that there is a world external to the observer comprised of objects that have intrinsic properties whether they are observed or not. The concepts of a theory are to be judged satisfactory only if the theory is correct and the description given by the theory is complete. The correctness of the theory is to be judged by comparing the agreement of the conclusions from the theory with experimental results. As for the judgment of the completeness of a theory, EPR [**1935**], p. 777, stated a necessary condition: *"every element of the physical reality must have a counterpart in the physical theory."* As a sufficient condition for an element of physical reality, they [**1935**], p. 777, proposed:

> "If, without in any way disturbing a system, we can predict with certainty (i.e., with probability equal to unity) the value of a physical quantity, then there exists an element of physical reality corresponding to this physical quantity."

EPR went on to point out that for an observable, **A**, and for the particular state function ψ that is an eigenfunction of that operator (so that $\mathbf{A}\psi = a\psi$), the physical quantity **A** has with certainty the value a for a system in that state. This means, according to the above criterion, that an element of physical reality corresponds to that physical quantity. The plane wave state $\psi = e^{\frac{i}{\hbar}p \cdot x}$ is an eigenstate of the operator $\mathbf{p} = -i\hbar\partial/\partial x$; and EPR [**1935**], p. 778, maintained that quantum mechanics implies (by their criterion) that the momentum of the particle described by this state is real while the position of the particle is not. Two quantities are related in this way with respect

---

[3]For details on the historical context of the work of Einstein, Podolsky, and Rosen, see Jammer [**1985**]. On the issue of physical reality, see also H. Margenau [**1950**] and [**1963**] and Born [**1953a**], [**1953b**], [**1953c**].

to their mutual reality, EPR noted, when the operators corresponding to the physical quantities do not commute. They, p. 778, concluded:

> "From this it follows that either (1) *the quantum mechanical description of reality given by the wavefunction is not complete or (2) when the operators corresponding to two physical quantities do not commute the two physical quantities cannot have simultaneous reality.* For if both of them had simultaneous reality—and thus definite values—these values would enter into the complete description according to the condition of completeness."

Since the measurement of a noncommuting observable can change the wavefunction, the values for noncommuting physical observables cannot be measured sequentially without altering the state. Thus the statements of quantum mechanics seem to be in accord with what can be measured without altering the wavefunction. But EPR demonstrated that the assumption that the wavefunction is a complete description of the physical reality of the system in combination with their criterion of physical reality leads to a contradiction.

In order to make their case, EPR considered two systems, I and II, each in known states that are permitted to interact during a given time interval. Let us call x_1 and x_2 the spatial coordinates of the systems I and II, respectively. During the interaction process, certain physical quantities in the two system become correlated. Let us designate the wavefunction of the combined system by $\Psi(x_1, x_2)$ at some particular time after the two systems have separated and there is no longer a physical interaction between them. Consider now the measurement in system I of some particular Hermitian operator **A** that has discrete eigenvalues. Von Neumann's projection postulate states that the system will be projected into one of the eigenfunctions of **A**. Similarly, the discrete Hermitian operator **B** can be measured in system I, where **B** does not commute with **A**, leaving the system in an eigenstate of **B**. The combined wavefunction $\Psi(x_1, x_2)$ can be expanded in terms of the system I eigenfunctions $u_i(x_1)$ of **A** or $v_i(x_1)$ of **B**:

$$(5.1) \quad \Psi(x_1, x_2) = \sum_{i=1}^{\infty} \psi_i(x_2) u_i(x_1)$$

$$= \sum_{i=1}^{\infty} \phi_i(x_2) v_i(x_1).$$

The functions $\psi_i(x_2)$ and $\phi_i(x_2)$ are, for the moment, considered to be the coefficients of the functions $u_i(x_1)$ and $v_i(x_1)$ in these expansions. If **A** is measured with the result a_k, the first sum is reduced to $\psi_k(x_2) u_k(x_1)$. Measuring **B** with result b_r would reduce the second sum to $\phi_r(x_2) v_r(x_1)$. From this EPR concluded:

> "We see therefore that, as a consequence of two different measurements performed on the first system, the second system may be left

in states with two different wavefunctions. On the other hand, since at the time of measurement the two systems no longer interact, no real change can take place in the second system as a consequence of anything that may be done to the first system. This is, of course, merely a statement of what is meant by the absence of an interaction between the two systems. Thus, *it is possible to assign two different wavefunctions* (in our example ψ_k and ϕ_r) *to the same reality* (the second system after interaction with the first)."

Suppose the distance between particles 1 and 2 is x_0 at time t. The wavefunction for the state of the combined system of two particles in the example given by EPR is

$$(5.2) \qquad \Psi(x_1, x_2) = \int_{-\infty}^{\infty} d^3p \, e^{\frac{i}{\hbar} p \cdot (x_1 - x_2 + x_0)}.$$

Rewriting this in terms of the momentum eigenfunctions of the first system, i.e.,

$$(5.3) \qquad u_p(x_1) = e^{\frac{i}{\hbar} p \cdot x_1}$$

gives

$$(5.4a) \qquad \Psi(x_1, x_2) = \int_{-\infty}^{\infty} d^3p \, \psi_p(x_2) u_p(x_1),$$

where

$$(5.4b) \qquad \psi_p(x_2) = e^{-\frac{i}{\hbar} p \cdot (x_2 - x_0)}.$$

On the other hand, writing the state of the combined system in terms of the position of the first particle, i.e.,

$$(5.5) \qquad v_x(x_1) = \delta(x_1 - x)$$

gives

$$(5.6a) \qquad \Psi(x_1, x_2) = \int_{-\infty}^{\infty} d^3x \, \phi_x(x_2) v_x(x_1).$$

where

$$(5.6b) \qquad \phi_x(x_2) = \int_{-\infty}^{\infty} d^3p \, e^{\frac{i}{\hbar} p \cdot (x - x_2 + x_0)} = (2\pi\hbar)^3 \delta(x - x_2 + x_0).$$

The function ψ_p is an eigenfunction of the operator **p** and ϕ_x is an eigenfunction of the operator **q**. By making a momentum measurement on the first system, the momentum of the second system can be predicted with certainty due to the correlation between the two systems expressed in the combined wavefunction. Similarly, if a position measurement is made on the first system, the position of the second system can be predicted with certainty. in accord with their criterion of reality, EPR [**1935**], p. 779, concluded that the quantity **p** is an element of reality in the first case and the quantity **q** is an element of reality in the second case. In addition, the two wavefunctions $\psi_k(x_2)$ and $\phi_r(x_2)$ both refer to the second system.

This situation leads then to the conclusion sought by EPR. Assuming that the wavefunction is a complete description of physical reality leads to the conclusion that two physical quantities with noncommuting operators can have simultaneous reality. The negation of alternative (1) above leads to the negation of alternative (2). This, combined with the original alternative possibilities, implies, p. 780, logically that alternative (1) is correct: the quantum mechanical description of reality given by the wavefunction is not complete.

EPR anticipated the criticism that their criterion of physical reality might be too broad. In defense against this criticism, they stated:

"Indeed, one would not arrive at our conclusion if one insisted that two or more physical quantities can be regarded as simultaneous elements of reality only when they can be simultaneously measured or predicted. On this point of view, since either one or the other, but not both simultaneously, of the quantities **p** and **q** depend upon the process of measurement carried out on the first system, which does not disturb the second system in any way. No reasonable definition of reality could be expected to permit this."

Bohr [**1935**] replied swiftly. He began by pointing out that quantum theory is adequate to handle the example proposed by EPR. He, pp. 696–697, proceeded by stating that "The contradiction in fact discloses only an essential inadequacy of the customary viewpoint of natural philosophy for a rational account of physical phenomena of the type with which we are concerned in quantum mechanics." He, p. 697, went on to state his reasons:

"Indeed, the finite interaction between the object and measured agencies conditioned by the very existence of the quantum of action entails—because of the impossibility of controlling the reaction of the object on the measuring instruments if these are to serve their purpose—the necessity of a final renunciation of the classical ideal of causality and a radical revision of our attitude towards the problems of physical reality."

To make his case, Bohr analyzed the possibility of measuring both the momentum and position of a particle passing through a slit. Assuming that the momentum of the particle is known before it passes through the slit, it will not be completely known after passing through the slit due to the possibility of an exchange of momentum between the particle and the slit. This is reflected in the diffraction of the wavefunction of the particle by the slit. Assume next that behind the first slit is a double slit system and behind that a photographic plate. Electrons will pass through the first slit and some of them will pass through one of the two slits behind the first. Those passing through one of the double slits will then strike the photographic plate.

The first slit acts as a rough position measurement for the electrons in the beam. The narrower the slit, the greater the diffraction of the wave associated with each electron and the more momentum will be transferred between the electron and the slit system and its supports. If we could ascertain the momentum of the electrons precisely, we could predict their paths after the first slit and discover for each electron which slit of the double slit system it will pass through. In the case in which the slits and screen are rigidly attached to a support, there is no way of measuring the amount of momentum absorbed by the system and its supports. On the other hand, Bohr showed that we can mount the first slit on a spring system so that we can monitor by its deflection the amount of momentum transferred to it by each electron passing through. However, allowing the slit to move in this fashion means that the measurement of the position will be less precise. By considering the effects of this broadening on the system, one can see that the interference pattern, which depends on waves emanating from a fixed position over a period of time, will be wiped out. Thus we have the choice, Bohr, p. 693, pointed out, of fixing accurately the space and time relations using a fixed slit system or an accurate control of the momentum at each stage of the experiment using a movable slit system. But we cannot do both at once.

Bohr's, p. 699, purpose in presenting these considerations was to emphasize that his choice of elements in the analysis was not an arbitrary one but was concerned with a

" ... rational discrimination between essentially different experimental arrangements and procedures which are suited either for an unambiguous use of the idea of space location, or for a legitimate application of the conservation theorem of momentum. Any remaining appearance of arbitrariness concerns merely our freedom of handling the measuring instruments, characteristic of the very idea of experiment."

This choice of experimental procedures is forced on us because of the impossibility of finding a way of measuring both spatial location and momentum accurately together. Furthermore, Bohr, p. 698, maintained

"The impossibility of a closer analysis of the reactions between the particle and the measuring instrument is indeed no peculiarity of the experimental procedure described, but is rather an essential property of an arrangement suited to the study of the phenomena of the type concerned, where we have to do with a feature of *individuality* completely foreign to classical physics."

The notion of individuality, as Bohr expressed it in the above quotation, does not follow from his inability to find a suitable experimental arrangement for making the simultaneous measurements, but rather expresses, as we shall see, one of the consequences of Bohr's concept of complementarity as applied in this situation.

Bohr used his example to expose what he called an essential ambiguity in the EPR criterion of physical reality when it is applied to the actual problems of atomic physics. He located the ambiguity in the meaning of the expression "without in any way disturbing the system." There is no question of a mechanical disturbance of one system due to measurement made on the other system, but[4]

" ... there is essentially the question of *an influence on the very conditions which define the possible types of predictions regarding the future behavior of the system.* Since these conditions constitute an inherent element of the description of any phenomenon to which the term "physical reality" may be attached, we see that the argumentation of the mentioned authors does not justify their conclusion that quantum-mechanical description is essentially incomplete."

I shall return to this important point below.

In his discussion of the work of EPR, Furry [**1936b**] considered the possibility that during the initial interaction systems I and II each made a transition into a definite but unknown state. The later results of the measurements would then be determined by these states.[5] Furry showed that this assumption is equivalent quantum mechanically to having made an intermediate, but unrecorded, measurement. Thus, if one takes an expansion of the combined wavefunctions into eigenfunctions of a particular operator (as in (5.1)) and assumes that the system had made a transition into one of these products of eigenfunctions of that operator, then a contradiction with quantum mechanics can be demonstrated. The EPR conclusion is thereby avoided, but at the cost of changing quantum dynamics. This intermediate step, which in the double slit experiment would convert the superposition of the waves emanating from each slit into a mixture of states each representing the probability that the electrons pass through a particular slit, would manifest itself in the absence of interference effects that would be expected of the superposition but not of the mixture. Furry then went on to show that if the above assumption were true, the uncertainty relations could be violated—at least in a thought experiment.

Bohm and Aharonov [**1957**], [**1960**], reviewed the status of the EPR discussion with respect to experiments. They indicated that the assumption examined by Furry to the effect that definite transitions occurred during interactions would imply quantities made definite by this transition, such as angular momentum for example, would be conserved only statistically and not in individual cases. Another possibility, not then adequately examined by experiment, is that the correlation of quantum mechanics breaks down when the subsystems are far enough apart. A third possibility is that there is a hidden instantaneous interaction between the distant systems that maintains

---
[4]Bohr [**1935**], p. 700. See also Bohr [**1949**], p. 60.
[5]See also the discussion in Hooker [**1972**], Section 7.

the correlations between them when different kinds of measurements are made on them.

The experiment discussed by Bohm and Aharonov is the measurement of the polarization of radiation produced in the annihilation of electron-positron pairs. According to the theory, polarization states of photons are similar to spin states of particles in their mathematical properties and behavior under observation. In the simplest electron-positron annihilation, two photons are emitted in opposite directions with equal and opposite momenta. If the direction of propagation for the photons is in the plus and minus z directions, the plane of polarization of these photons may be measured along any axis perpendicular to z for either photon. Annihilation photons always exhibit orthogonal linear polarizations on observation; there is a correlation between the measurements made along any chosen x axis for one photon and the corresponding y axis for the other photon. Since any (x, y) axes may be used, there is a correlation between observations on a measurable and indefinite property of distant photons as required for an EPR experiment.

The actual experiment Bohm and Aharonov discussed is that performed by C. S. Wu and I. Shaknov [1950]. (For reasons of experimental feasibility, it was a little more complicated than the one described above.) Bohm and Aharonov compared the results that would have been expected on the basis of quantum mechanics to the results expected on the basis of several other hypotheses (including ones considered by Furry) concerning particular transitions by photons into polarization states after the photon wavepackets no longer overlap. Their conclusion was that "... this experiment is explained adequately by the current quantum theory which implies distant correlations, of the type leading to the paradox of EPR, but not by any reasonable hypotheses implying a breakdown of the quantum theory that could avoid the paradox of EPR."[6] The other possibility, raised but not considered by Bohm and Aharonov, was that these results could be determined by hidden dynamical variables that maintain the correlations by instantaneous interactions over macroscopic distances. Hidden variables will be discussed below in connection with Bell's theorem and modern experiments of the EPR type in Chapter 15.

Einstein was not convinced by the reasoning in Bohr's [1935] reply to the EPR paradox and in Bohr's other writings. He repeated on many other occasions his contention that quantum mechanics, while successful in dealing with experimental data, must be incomplete.[7] Schrödinger [1954] contended that quantum mechanics is incomplete since it does not include any prescription for the construction of macroscopic observables, such as the Euler angles of a rigid body or the angle between two crystal faces. He [1958] also argued that quantum mechanics includes features that do not have physical reality.

---

[6]Bohm and Aharonov [1957], p. 1075. The criticism of these conclusions by A. Peres and P. Singer [1960] is correctly rebutted in the reply by Bohm and Aharonov [1960].

[7]See Einstein [1936], [1949] and R. S. Shankland [1963].

The "reduction of the wavepacket" does not occur at the same time for all observers and hence is not "shared by everybody." Since this is a hallmark of physical reality for him, he concluded that quantum mechanics, with the Copenhagen Interpretation, contains elements that have no physical reality and is therefore not a complete or satisfactory theory.

Later scholarship has indicated that Einstein at the time of the EPR paper may have been more concerned with issues of the locality of quantum interactions and the separability of the quantum wavefunction for two distant components of the physical system than he was with the completeness issue.[8] It is usually assumed in quantum mechanics that interactions are local. It is also usually assumed that distant systems can be treated as independent and studied separately. If the distant systems are independent, then the joint wavefunction $\Psi(q_1, q_2)$ can be written as the product $\phi_1(q_1)\phi_2(q_2)$. The EPR experiment showed clearly that both of these assumptions cannot be true at the same time in quantum theory. The usual conclusion is that the EPR experiment showed that distant systems cannot be represented by separable states if they have interacted in the past. This connection was dubbed "entanglement" of the states by Schrödinger [**1935a**].

Both locality and separability were important to Bell's reexamination of von Neumann's work demonstrating the impossibility of hidden variable theories if quantum mechanics is valid. In addition, the notion of entanglement introduced by Schrödinger has become a mainstay of modern analyses of quantum states and their properties. All three of these concepts will be revisited below.

5.3 Einstein and Bohr on Reality

The issue of reality in quantum mechanics and in Bohr's work in particular has been discussed for many years. Recently there has been a surge of concern and it seems as if this is the major topic of interest to those in the philosophical community writing about Bohr and Einstein.[9] The discussion in this section will be limited to the work of Bohr and Einstein, the view of reality they were discussing, and the arguments each side presented. A general discussion of the relation of theories to what we can say is real and the question what kind of philosophical viewpoint towards reality might be compatible with his epistemology will be taken up in Chapter 18.

Einstein was the most articulate of those presenting an alternative to the, mostly implicit, view of reality inherent in Bohr's perspective. Changes in

---

[8]See the paper Einstein [**1936**] and its analysis in Arthur Fine [**1986**].

[9]The analysis of the concept of reality from a philosophical perspective has been pursued in recent years by Michael Dummett, Richard Boyd, Hilary Putnam, Bas van Frassen, and others. The concept of reality in Bohr's work has been pursued in many books and papers. See, for example, the articles and their references in Faye and Folse [**1994**] and in the book length discussions of Bohr's work mentioned in Chapter 1.

the ways physicists approach the notion of reality were discussed by Einstein and L. Infeld [**1938**]:

> "The reality created by modern physics is, indeed, far removed from the reality of the early days. But the aim of physical theory still remains the same. With the help of physical theories we try to find our way through the maze of observed facts, to order and understand the world of our sense impressions. We want the observed facts to follow logically from our concept of reality. Without the belief that it is possible to grasp the reality with our theoretical constructions, without the belief in the inner harmony of our world, there could be no science. This belief is and always will remain the fundamental motive for all scientific creation." [10]

Einstein and Infeld were clearly arguing here that our conception of reality is primary and that the physical theories we fashion must follow from this. While they acknowledged that this conception can change and has changed, they did not specify how or why it has changed. They did state that the belief that we can "grasp the reality with our theoretical constructions" is essential for science. Given Einstein's other statements of his conception of reality, this must interpreted to mean that we grasp reality through our theoretical conceptions but these theoretical conceptions must also conform to certain metaphysical requirements.

Einstein and Infeld went on to state that our concepts are related to the objects of this reality in a one-to-one fashion, as a mail box number is to a mailbox, and not distilled from it, as soup is made out of beef. They maintained that science is not just a catalog of unrelated facts or a collection of laws. It is a freely invented creation of the human mind that provides us with a picture of reality. Physical theories try to connect this picture with sense impressions. The only justification for these mental structures that Einstein allowed is the validity of that link.[11] EPR further elaborated the connection between our concepts and reality by stating that without a physical interaction between two objects, which we may assume means a force acting between them, one can have no effect on the other.

In his "Reply to Criticisms," Einstein [**1949**], p. 667, further maintained that quantum theory does not satisfy "the programmatic aim of all physics: the complete description of any (individual) real situation (as it supposedly exists irrespective of any act of observation or substantiation.)." Because quantum mechanics cannot describe the decay time of a single radioactive atom, he maintained further that quantum mechanics is not complete.[12] In his discussion of the nature of reality, Einstein, pp. 673–674, elaborated on his earlier ideas. He stated that the distinction between sense-impressions

---

[10] Einstein and Infeld [**1938**], pp. 312–313.
[11] Einstein and Infeld [**1938**], p. 310.
[12] Einstein [**1936**], p. 374, [**1949**], p. 668.

and ideas cannot be conceptually defined, but is required to avoid solipsism. Sense-impressions themselves are conditioned by an objective and a subjective factor. The objective factor he meant is the "totality of such concepts and conceptual relations as are thought of as independent of experience, viz., of perceptions." Einstein considered this to be a form of Kantianism in which the categories are not fixed and determined by the understanding, but are free conventions chosen for their efficacy in allowing us to grasp experience intellectually and thereby to have "knowledge of the real".

The sufficient condition for a physical quantity to be an element of reality, according to EPR, is that the value of this physical quantity *can* be predicted with certainty without disturbing the system. They then noted that *if* it is required for the reality of two quantities that one be able to *simultaneously* measure or predict them, then their conclusion concerning the incompleteness of quantum theory would not follow because the position and momentum of a particle cannot be measured simultaneously with complete accuracy. And in their thought experiment, only the value of the operator **p** or the operator **q**, but not both, may be predicted for the second system based on measurements made on the first. EPR therefore did not make an actual measurement a criterion of reality because, for the two distant systems they were considering, the reality of the momentum would depend on whether a position or a momentum measurement was made on the first system. Since the measurements on the first system will have no physical effect on the second system, EPR concluded that no reasonable definition of reality could permit the reality of elements in the second system to depend in this way on the first system.

This conception of objective reality is independent of any theory, per se. It has been characterized as a "God's eye" view of the world and corresponds philosophically to metaphysical realism. The view of reality Einstein presented does depend on the totality of concepts and conceptual relations that are independent of perceptions and is his version of what Bohr would call a conceptual framework. In this terminology, Einstein's view is that it is the job of theories to connect the picture of the world provided by our conceptual framework to sense impressions. The picture is that of a universe out there, independent of us, with events transpiring over eons on a giant stage on which each of us plays a very small part for a very short time. We construct this picture by choosing elements and principles (Categories) based on their efficacy in helping us "grasp experience intellectually." The scientific concepts that play a role in this picture are in a one-to-one relation with objects in this reality. Our theories, in spite of being "free creations", must still conform to this underlying picture of reality. The deeper issues of what it means to grasp experience intellectually or how something from which the observed facts must follow logically can itself change was not addressed.

Bohr's reply began with the statement that the customary viewpoint of natural philosophy is essentially inadequate for a rational account of physical phenomena of the type with which we are concerned in quantum mechanics. Bohr [1935], p. 697, claimed that the source of the difficulty in the EPR view of reality is a failure to take proper account of the subject/object interaction that requires a "... final renunciation of the classical ideal of causality and a radical revision of our attitude towards the problems of physical reality." Bohr's purpose was to construct an adequate philosophical position within which quantum theory could be considered a complete and adequate theory. For Bohr, a "reasonable definition of reality" could include the element of nonlocality that was rejected by EPR. He [1935], p. 700, emphasized this by his concern with the conditions involving the *whole* experimental arrangement since this alone can define the possible types of predictions we can make regarding the future behavior of the system.

As an example, recall that Bohr recounted one of Einstein's philosophical reservations towards quantum theory along with his reply:

"On his side, Einstein mockingly asked us whether we could really believe that the providential authorities took recourse to dice-playing (*"... ob der liebe Gott würfelt"*), to which I replied by pointing at the great caution, already called for by ancient thinkers, in ascribing attributes to Providence in everyday language. I remember also how at the peak of the discussion Ehrenfest, in his affectionate manner of teasing his friends, jokingly hinted at the apparent similarity between Einstein's attitude and that of the opponents of relativity theory."

The argument between Bohr and Einstein was thus carried out on grounds virtually independent of the experimental success of quantum theory itself. The use of the phrase "... whether we could really believe ..." shows that the difference between them was with regard to the possible ways in which the world could be intelligibly represented.

One of the reasons that Einstein was not able to accept quantum theory and a conceptual framework associated with it is very likely the result of his previous analysis of the concepts underlying classical theory in connection with relativity theory. In this analysis, the concepts of locality and causality, along with that of the continuous field, played a crucial role. He may have felt that the foundations of relativity theory required them. Indeed, he spent the last part of his life working on a unified field theory that would unite electrodynamics, relativistic mechanics and the theory of gravitation with field ideas as the basis. To give up causality or locality for quantum ideas would have undermined the very presuppositions on which this work was based.[13] Since these ideas guided Einstein's thinking throughout his life, it is likely that he was impelled to see quantum theory as a statistical theory and retain the view of reality that underlies his work in relativity theory.

---

[13] This point has been emphasized by Hooker [1972], p. 152, and others.

The thinking behind the examples he chose as problems for quantum theory reflect this view of reality.

Bohr [1935], p. 696, went on to make his approach to the question of reality clear in his reply to Einstein, Podolsky and Rosen: "The extent to which an unambiguous meaning can be attributed to such an expression as "physical reality" cannot of course be deduced from *a priori* philosophical concepts, but ... must be founded on a direct appeal to experiments and measurements."[14] By this Bohr meant that we cannot simply adopt a philosophical position on the nature of physical reality and require that all physical theories conform to this standard. He was also referring, as part of his answer to EPR, to those aspects of his theory that he felt were necessary conditions for the unambiguous statement of the results of experiments and their interpretation in terms of theoretical descriptions. In this regard he [1929c], p. 12, had stated much earlier that "... the concept of the stationary states may indeed be said to possess, within its field of application, just as much, or, if one prefers, just as little "reality" as the elementary particles themselves." While in his earlier essays, Bohr [1929b], pp. 103, 104, [1930], p. 349, made clear that he felt that atoms themselves are real, the quotations given above [1954], p. 79, [1929c], p. 12, raise legitimate doubts as to what Bohr's later view were concerning the reality of atomic objects. It is clear that he preferred to avoid the question and focus on the epistemological aspects of his theory.

5.4 Reflection 10

Although Bohr did not acknowledge it, the EPR paper seems to have had a very important impact on his thinking. The importance of the EPR paradox lies in its clear demonstration that the notion of the quantum state and its relation to measurement are not determined simply by direct physical interaction in quantum theory. The EPR example pointed out that there are experiments in which there is no physical interaction between a particle and a macroscopic apparatus, say, but the experiments nevertheless do provide some information concerning the particle and thereby cause a change in the system state.[15] These considerations were fatal to the disturbance theory of measurement. Thus Bohr, while retaining phrases such as "interaction with the measuring instrument" in some of his later writings,[16] did not always mean them as physical interactions in the literal classical sense.[17]

---

[14]See also Bohr [1949], pp. 40–41.
[15]These were called "negative measurements" by M. Renninger [1960] and Rosenfeld [1968] pointed out that they are a variant of the EPR experiment. See also Hans Reichenbach [1944], p. 41, footnote 2.
[16]See Bohr [1949], p. 39, for example.
[17]Bohr [1938b], p. 24, [1948], p. 15, [1949], pp. 63–64, [1954], p. 73, [1958b], p. 5. See also Fock [1957], p. 646.

Another factor that played an important role in Bohr's thinking from 1935 on is the significance of the "whole experimental arrangement" in the assessment of the proper description of quantum systems. Thus, the truth of the statement by EPR that "no real change can take place in the second system as a consequence of anything that may be done to the first system" because that is "what is meant by an absence of an interaction between the two systems" is denied by Bohr. His reason is that we are dealing with a whole that cannot be subdivided in a given experiment and the two particles are not correctly described by separate states. The lack of a physical interaction between the two particles in quantum mechanics is not sufficient by itself to declare them independent, or 'separable' in the currently fashionable terminology, and represent them as a product of one-particle states.

The nonlocal consequences of this idea introduced a further separation from the conceptions underlying the classical state for which it is assumed that we can characterize a system by its properties that are independent of the context in which the system finds itself. The break with classical epistemology begun in Bohr [**1927**] was completed in Bohr [**1935**] when Bohr at least implicitly acknowledged these nonlocal aspects of quantum theory.[18]

Bohr [**Arch**], 16:2, 10/17/41, succinctly summarized the meaning of the elements employed in his theory in an unpublished sequence of notes: "Classical concepts mean elements of description defined in ordinary language. Use of language is never well defined since the immediate application of any word is complementary to an attempt to its definition. By ordinary language we mean such use of words where a sharp separation between subject and object can be maintained. This last point must not be confounded with the whole relativity of any description (the subjectivity of essential qualities)." These were the elements he later fashioned into what I will call his *main argument*, which provides the foundation and justification of his epistemology.

Bohr and Einstein have staked out distinct views of what reality is and our relation to it. This includes their conceptions of the role of theories, what a theory must do, and the form of the conceptual framework that theories belong to. These are all important themes to which I shall return in Part IV.

5.5 The Statistical Interpretation

Standard quantum mechanics was criticized by H. Freistadt [**1957**] and Bohm [**1957a**] because it does not allow a conceptual model of the kind comprehensible to them (like that of classical theory, say). In a similar vein, D'Espagnat [**1965**] reviewed the interpretations of quantum mechanics and concluded that "no realistic interpretation of quantum mechanics exists." Similar realizations, in a less sophisticated form, came out of the analysis of quantum mechanics from its beginning. One attractive possibility, which

---

[18] Faye [**1991**], pp. 168–169, also saw this change in Bohr's thought and has emphasized its importance.

would cause the least disruption in our usual worldview, was the possibility of interpreting quantum mechanics as a purely statistical theory. According to this interpretation, which was referred to as the 'statistical interpretation' above, the absolute square of the wavefunction represents a probability distribution in the sense of statistical mechanics. This point of view attracted many distinguished proponents: A. E. Ruark [**1928**], Slater [**1929**], J. H. van Vleck [**1929**], Schrödinger [**1935a**], Einstein [**1936**], p. 374, E. C. Kemble [**1929**], [**1935**], [**1937**], J. B. Hartle [**1968**], A. Landé [**1960**], pp. 89–90, and many others. If a statistical interpretation were successful, we would not need complementary descriptions of individual systems and we could retain a more or less classical description of the atomic realm.[19]

Extended arguments to the effect that quantum theory must be considered a statistical theory that cannot properly be applied to individual systems were made by J. L. Park [**1968**] and L. E. Ballentine [**1970**]. Park placed as a requirement for the attribution of a state to an individual system that this attribution can be done uniquely and that the state determines completely the behavior of the components of the system. In other words, Park required that the state of a system have all the properties of a classical state. The discussion of the EPR experiment above showed that at times distinct subsystems of the total system cannot be said to be in definite states. In addition, quantum mechanics does not provide a description of a system that is deterministic with regard to the state variables in the way classical theory does. Park [**1968**], p. 226, concluded from this that it is wrong to apply the quantum state description to a single quantum system and that quantum systems should be regarded as never being in any state.[20]

Ballentine [**1970**], p. 360, presented the central claims of the two points of view as follows:

1. A pure state (and hence also a mixture) provides a description of certain statistical properties of an ensemble of similarly prepared systems, but need not provide a complete description of an individual system;
2. A pure state provides a complete and exhaustive description of an individual system (e.g., an electron).

Ballentine [**1970**], p. 361, chose the first alternative and concluded:

"We see that a quantum *state* is a mathematical representation of the result of a certain state preparation procedure. Physical systems which have been subjected to the same state preparations will be similar in some of their properties, but not in all of them. ... Indeed, the physical interpretation of the uncertainty principle ... is that no state preparation procedure is possible which would yield

---

[19] For a recent version of the statistical interpretation under the name "ensemble interpretation", see D. Home and M. A. B. Whitaker [**1992**].

[20] Elsasser [**1969**] also supported this view.

an ensemble of systems identical in all their observable properties. Thus is it most natural to assert that a quantum state represents an ensemble of similarly prepared systems, but does not provide a complete description of an individual system."

Ballentine attributed the apparent indeterminateness of quantum variables to a limitation on the possibility of preparing an ensemble of systems in a certain way. There are several possible explanations why this might be the case. The first possibility is that the indeterministic results of quantum theory might be due to the measuring instrument being in an unknown mixture of states. This possibility was discussed previously, and rejected. The second possibility is that the act of making a measurement on the system disturbs it uncontrollably and unpredictably and this disturbance is the source of indeterminism. But this possibility was contradicted by the results of the EPR thought experiment. It followed from experiments of this type that a disturbance theory cannot account for the lack of determinism in quantum phenomena. The question of why a system or set of systems cannot be prepared or measured in such a way as to contradict quantum mechanics still requires explanation.

The crux of the matter is whether there exists or *can* exist a full successful hidden variable theory that will provide a more complete description than quantum mechanics. This point, while often glossed over by those advocating the statistical interpretation, is the important one. As long as quantum theory retains its experimental validity, experiments involving superpositions and sequences of measurements with intermediate superpositions make the attribution of intrinsic classical properties to individual particles difficult to explain. It is up to those advocating the statistical interpretation to show why the concepts used in the description of atomic systems have only a statistical significance; and they must also show that the embedding of quantum mechanics in a more detailed hidden variable theory is mathematically possible.[21] In the absence of some account of why we cannot make measurements on individual systems and select a group of these for which the product of the dispersions of conjugate variables is less than expressed in the uncertainty relations, the statistical interpretations will share the difficulties of the disturbance theory of measurement. The claim, in other words, that a more complete description of atomic systems may be given than allowed by quantum theory must be made good if the statistical position is to have a chance of success.

5.6 Hidden Variable Theories

The question of hidden variables, or of a causal world underlying the observable world, was also considered very soon after the discovery of quantum

---

[21] See Jeffrey Bub [**1968**] for a review discussion of this in relation to Bohr's views.

mechanics itself.[22] As pointed out in Chapter 2, Heisenberg [**1927**] rejected (for essentially operationalistic reasons) the possibility of such an underlying world in his discussion of the uncertainty relations. In Bohr's [**1927**] discussion of the conflicting requirements of observation, which requires an interaction with the system under observation, and of causality, which requires isolation of the system, he implicitly rejected hidden variable possibilities. The discussion was formalized by von Neumann [**1932**]. Von Neumann, pp. 209-210, 313-328, interpreted the "hidden parameters" or "hidden coordinates" as coordinates that could be supplied in addition to the quantum state description in much the same way that individual particle coordinates can be supplied in the form of a distribution function of particle variables in statistical mechanics to supplement the macroscopic description provided by thermodynamics. The quantum state on this interpretation would represent an average over the hidden variables just as a thermodynamic quantity represents an average of a particle analog quantity over a distribution that is a function of particle variables in classical statistical mechanics.

Hidden variable theories have been developed from a variety of models in which particular features were adopted as primary. Schrödinger initially tried to interpret the wavefunction, and then its absolute square after Born's work, in "tangibly real" terms as "fluctuations in the electric space density."[23] He was nevertheless aware that the wavefunction is in general a function in configuration space, not in real space. He revived these ideas in the early 1950s.[24] Others, notably Renninger [**1953**], Landé [**1955**], [**1960**], [**1965**], [**1966**], [**1969**], and W. Yourgrau [**1964**], have maintained that only particles are physically real and that the wavefunctions merely represent the probabilities for the particles to behave in certain ways. Bohm [**1952a**], p. 170, [**1957a**], pp. 111-113, on the other hand, attributed reality to the "ψ field" also. De Broglie [**1926**], [**1927**] assumed in his pilot wave theory that both the particle and wave are real and that the wave guides the particle. In his more ambitious Theory of the Double Solution, de Broglie [**1953**], [**1957**], [**1960**] and [**1969**] interpreted the "particle" as a singularity in a real wave field. The singularity is presumed to be due to a non-linear interaction of the wave with itself; the motion of the singularity is determined by the rest of the wave that surrounds it.

I shall not discuss the particular features of these theories here except to note that each of them has encountered serious difficulties in its physical interpretation. More sophisticated theories, such as the one proposed by Bohm and Bub [**1966**], [**1968**], do not have the same difficulties as the previous theories; but they do have others. Discussions of particular theories and further

---

[22] According to von Neumann [**1932**], p. 209, the question of whether or not an explanation of quantum mechanics by means of hidden parameters is possible " ... is a much discussed question."

[23] See Schrödinger [**1928b**], pp. 120-121, 126.

[24] See Schrödinger [**1950**] and the paper by Schrödinger in A. George [**1953**].

references to them may be found in Freistadt [**1957**], S. Körner [**1957**], Bell [**1964**], Bohm and Bub [**1966**], [**1968**], B. Misra [**1967**], J. M. Jauch and C. Piron [**1963**], [**1968**], S. P. Gudder [**1968**], [**1970**], and Wigner [**1970**].

In his proof that hidden variable theories contradict quantum mechanics, Von Neumann [**1932**], pp. 305–325, employed the following quantum mechanical axioms:
  (i) If an observable is represented by **R**, then a function f of that observable is represented by $f(\mathbf{R})$;
  (ii) the sum of several observables represented by **R**, **S**, ... is represented by the operator $\mathbf{R} + \mathbf{S} + \ldots$;
  (iii) the correspondence between Hermitian operators and observables is one to one;
  (iv) if the observable **R** is non-negative, then its expectation value is non-negative, i.e., $\mathcal{E}_\mathbf{R} \geq 0$;
  (v) for arbitrary observables **R**, **S**, ..., and arbitrary real numbers $a, b, \ldots$, the relation
$$\mathcal{E}_{a\mathbf{R}+b\mathbf{S}+\ldots} = a\mathcal{E}_\mathbf{R} + b\mathcal{E}_\mathbf{S} + \ldots$$
holds for all possible states for which the averages may be calculated.

The incompatibility between the claims of von Neumann and those of the hidden variable theorists that came afterward prompted a reexamination of these axioms and their use in von Neumann's proof. Even some of those who support the standard interpretation of quantum mechanics have criticized axioms (ii), (iii) and (v). It was not spelled out, for instance, in the original formulations of quantum theory how operators such as **pq** or **p** + **q** are to be understood and dealt with either theoretically or experimentally. This problem, which will appear below in another context, is especially important if the operators do not commute. In other words, there are no clear general rules of correspondence in von Neumann's quantum theory connecting the theoretical entities and the experimental arrangements used to measure them.

Since von Neumann's purpose was to establish whether or not hidden variables could be used to supplement the information provided by the quantum state function, he limited his discussion to those variants of quantum theory that satisfy these axioms.[25] Von Neumann did not require that the expectation values, calculated by averaging over the hidden states, be calculated by (3.23). The axioms do express on the other hand the Hilbert space formulation of the theory, an implicit algebra of operators and a one to one connection between (hypermaximal) Hermitian operators and observables. Von Neumann's purpose was to show that *any* expectation function meeting these axioms would exclude hidden variables.

Von Neumann reduced the question of hidden variables to that of whether the existence of a supplemented state, which is dispersion free for all operators of the theory, is compatible with that part of quantum theory he retained

---

[25]This point was emphasized by J. Albertson [**1961**], p. 484.

for his investigation.[26] Von Neumann observed that a system may not necessarily be in some pure state, which is the eigenstate of some operator, at a given time. We may therefore need to represent it as being in a mixture of pure states in which each pure state appears with a certain probability. Von Neumann represented a mixture by the Hermitian operator **U** and called it the density matrix for the system. However, because **U** determines the statistical properties of a system rather than the density of its states, it is called the *statistical matrix* in TIS. Von Neumann [**1932**], pp. 313–316, then obtained for the general expression of the expectation value of an operator **R** the following result:

$$(5.7) \qquad \mathcal{E}_{\mathbf{R}}(\mathbf{U}) = \text{Tr}(\mathbf{UR}) = \sum_i (\phi_i, \mathbf{UR}\phi_i),$$

where the set $\{\phi_i\}$ is an orthogonal set of state vectors that span the Hilbert space and Tr represents the *trace operator*. The mixture **U** is independent of **R** but depends on the set of states on which $\mathcal{E}_{\mathbf{R}}$ is calculated. Von Neumann [**1932**], pp. 317–324, examined the implications of Axiom (iv) for **U** and concluded that **U** is a non-negative definite operator, i.e., that $(f, \mathbf{U}f) \geq 0$ for an arbitrary vector f. Von Neumann then showed that the assumption that dispersion free ensembles exist implied certain properties for the statistical matrix **U** that contradicted its definition.

As S. Kochen and E. P. Specker [**1967**] have shown, von Neumann's results follow from less restrictive axioms using a theorem by Andrew Gleason.[27] Gleason [**1957**] proved that all measures on closed subspaces of a separable Hilbert space of dimension greater than two can be represented in the form

$$(5.8) \qquad \mathcal{E}_A = Tr(\mathbf{UP}_A),$$

where A is a closed subspace, $\mathbf{P}_A$ is the projection operator for this subspace, and **U** is an operator that satisfies the same conditions as von Neumann's statistical matrix operator. This means that for separable Hilbert spaces of dimension greater than two and for Hermitian operators, the representation given by von Neumann is completely general. Von Neumann's axioms concerning non-negativity and additivity of expectations, Axioms (iv) and (v), are then unnecessary since they follow from Gleason's representation.[28] The implication of this result is that no hidden variable theory can be formulated in Hilbert space of dimension greater than 2 where the complete set of Hermitian operators are the observables. For dimension 2, hidden variable theories have been constructed by Bell [**1966**], p. 448, and by Kochen and Specker [**1967**], pp. 75–81.

---

[26]The proof has been improved and put in a particularly clear form by Kochen and Specker [**1967**], pp. 81–82.
[27]See also Bell [**1966**].
[28]See also Jauch [**1968**], p. 132.

Bell [**1966**] made an incisive critique of these proofs of the impossibility of hidden variables. He objected to von Neumann's proof on the grounds that von Neumann's assumption (v) concerning the expectation values of sums of observables is unnecessarily restrictive if applied to hypothetical dispersion free states. Von Neumann's essential assumption (combining most of the above axioms) was restated by Bell as: *"Any real linear combination of any two Hermitian operators represents an observable, and the same linear combination of expectation values is the expectation value of the combination."* Bell [**1966**], p. 449, summarized his objection to von Neumann's assumptions very succinctly:[29]

"A measurement of a sum of noncommuting observables cannot be made by combining trivially the results of separate observations on the two terms—it requires quite a distinct experiment. For example, the measurement of σ_x for a magnetic particle might be made with a suitably oriented Stern-Gerlach magnet. The measurement of σ_y would require a different orientation, and of $(\sigma_x + \sigma_y)$ a third and different orientation. But this explanation of the non-additivity of allowed values also establishes the nontriviality of the additivity of expectation values. The latter is a quite peculiar property of quantum mechanical states, not to be expected *a priori*. There is no reason to demand it initially of the hypothetical dispersion free states, whose function it is to reproduce the *measurable* peculiarities of quantum mechanics when averaged over."

Bell [**1966**] discussed hidden variable theories using a formalism expressed in terms of a logic of propositions and showed that dispersion free states can be ruled out. Bell also discussed the results of Gleason and showed directly that if the dimensionality of the Hilbert space is greater than two, the additivity requirement for the expectation values of commuting operators (a weaker requirement than von Neumann's) cannot be met by dispersion free states. For a state to be dispersion free, the expectation value of an operator, and in particular a projection operator, must be unique for that state. This means that a projection operator always has either the expectation value 0 or 1 on the state. Bell made the assumptions: (i) if the expectation value of projections into a subspace orthogonal to the first is 0, and (ii) if the expectation value of the projections into two subspaces is 0 for a given state then the expectation

---

[29]These criticisms were anticipated by von Neumann [**1927**], p. 248. He considered the problem of measuring two quantum mechanical quantities **A** and **B** simultaneously. He observed that to measure them simultaneously requires two experiments, one measuring **A** and one measuring **B**, that do not disturb each other. If these two experiments are combined into one experiment, then a third quantity **C** and two functions f_1 and f_2 such that $\mathcal{E}(\mathbf{A}) = f_1(\mathcal{E}(\mathbf{C}))$ and $\mathcal{E}(\mathbf{B}) = f_2(\mathcal{E}(\mathbf{C}))$ must be found and the quantity **C** measured. Von Neumann observed that this step makes the concept of "degree of freedom" foreign to quantum mechanics because **A**, **B**, and **C** each have 1 degree of freedom, but **C** actually represents both **A** and **B**.

5.6 HIDDEN VARIABLE THEORIES

value of the projection into a subspace specified by any linear combination of vectors from the original subspaces is also 0.[30] These assumptions are slight reformulations of the ones discussed above. Bell showed in essence that these assumptions implied the continuity of the expectation value over the projection operators on neighboring subspaces.[31] From this it follows that a vector spanning a one-dimensional subspace and having an expectation value of 1 cannot have a direction that is arbitrarily close (as measured by the angle between them) to that of another vector spanning a subspace for which the expectation value is 0. Thus the expectation value for a given projection operator is a continuous function of the angle between the two vectors; a jump between 0 and 1 in the expectation value on arbitrarily close dispersion free states cannot occur. This result essentially reproduces that obtained by von Neumann [**1932**] and Bell [**1966**] without the objectionable assumption (iv).

Bell [**1966**], p. 451, added to his previous criticism of the axiom concerning the additivity of expectation values the statement that the problem arises here with the tacit assumption that the measurement of an observable must yield the same value independently of what other measurements may be made simultaneously. One may measure a projection operator on a subspace and on one or two other subspaces orthogonal to it. But it is possible that the second and third subspaces are not orthogonal to each other. The dual measurements on subspaces 1 and 2 and on subspaces 1 and 3 require different experimental arrangements and Bell pointed out that we have no *a priori* reason for believing that the expectation value of a projection operator on the first subspace must be the same in these two different situations.

The importance of this point, as stated by Bell [**1966**], p. 451, is that it allows the reasonable possibility that the result of an observation may depend not only on the state of the system, including the hidden variables, but also on the complete description of the apparatus used to make measurements on the system. Bell [**1966**], p. 447, cited Bohr's emphasis on the "... impossibility of a sharp separation between the behavior of atomic objects and the interaction with the measuring instrument which serve to define the conditions under which the phenomena appear," as a justification for allowing the possibility that a description of the whole experimental apparatus might be important in determining the result of an observation. This opens the door to what Shimony has called "contextualistic hidden variable theories," in which the

---

[30] These assumptions, as Abner Shimony has pointed out to me (private communication), are a consequence of imposing a probability measure on each Boolean sublattice of the lattice of propositions.

[31] The definition of neighboring vectors is given in terms of the Hilbert space metric. One can use, for example, the distance function $D(\phi, \psi)$ defined in (3.14).

result of an observation is determined by the hidden variables and by the other measurements that are being made simultaneously on an atomic system.[32]

Bell [1966], p. 452, turned to the question of what other acceptable and experimentally meaningful condition could be imposed on the hidden states. He suggested 'locality' as one possibility. Bell had pursued the consequences of assuming locality in reference to contextual hidden variable theories in Bell [1964]. In this paper, Bell discussed a form of the EPR experiment, involving the spins of two particles, that was originally proposed by Bohm [1951]. He assumed that the results of measuring the spin can be only +1 and −1 (these are normalized), and the hidden variables determining the results of the experiment act only locally, i.e., the result of measuring the spin on one system does not depend on the orientation of the apparatus used to measure the spin of the second particle. This assumption is now called *local realism*. Bell then proved that the expectation values for measurements made on these two particles cannot reproduce those of quantum mechanics to an arbitrary degree of accuracy.

Clauser, Horne, Shimony, and Holt [1969] generalized Bell's work and proposed a photon correlation experiment similar to that of Wu and Shaknov [1950]. In the Clauser, Horne, Shimony, and Holt experiment, distant polarizations of paired visible photons emitted by a cascade decay of excited Calcium atoms are measured in order to compare the predictions of quantum mechanics with a family of local hidden variable theories. More recent experiments use beam splitters to create correlated photons. Actual experiments of these types have been performed in which the correlations of two and three photons are examined. In the two photon case, the assumption of local realism violated the statistical predictions of quantum mechanics, and in the three photon case, this assumption violated individual predictions of quantum mechanics. In each case, quantum mechanical predictions were confirmed at the expense of local realism.[33] It should be noted that some hidden variable theories, e.g., Bohm [1952a], [1952b], are not tested in this experiment because they are not local.[34]

One of the main forces behind the search for a hidden variable theory is the desire to find a theory that is experimentally adequate but which does not have the philosophical and conceptual difficulties of quantum mechanics. The Clauser, Horne, Shimony and Holt experiment and those like it are important because one of the features to be desired of a hidden variable theory is locality. If, in a hidden variable theory, measurements made at one point are influenced

---

[32]For further information on various versions of Bell's theorem, generalizations of it by several authors, and experimental tests of it, see the review article by Clauser and Shimony [1978].

[33]See the experiments discussed in F. Salleri [1988], Chapter 7. For the three photon experiments and extensive references to recent work, see Jian-Wei Pan, Dik Bouwmeester, Matthew Daniell, Harald Weinfurter and Anton Zeilinger [2000].

[34]The "quantum potential" in Bohm's theory is not a local function.

by distant instruments, e.g., if the result obtained in a measurement of a particle's spin with one Stern-Gerlach magnet depends on the orientation of another distant Stern-Gerlach magnet to be used to measure the spin of another particle, then no improvement over quantum mechanics has been achieved. It was in fact this nonseparable aspect of quantum theory that made it possible to give more than one description of a physical system and led Einstein, Podolsky and Rosen to propose their paradox.

5.7 Bohr's Approach to the Quantum State

Bohr was very careful in his characterization of the quantum state. He introduced the notion of the 'state' of an atom, referring to the whole atom, in his 1913 paper. But he did not attribute this state to the electron in the atom in the usual classical dynamical sense. By the time of his 1927 Como lecture, Bohr had rejected the possibility of picturing the behavior of objects on the atomic scale because of the evidence he had marshaled for "... an essential failure of the pictures in space and time on which the description of natural phenomena has hitherto been based."[35] In this lecture, his only reference to the quantum mechanical state of a system is enclosed in quotation marks. He also at one point enclosed the term wavefunction in quotation marks.

Bohr's approach to the problem of understanding and using quantum mechanics was to choose particular experiments and show how a proper description could be given of them that would satisfy the requirements of quantum mechanics. This was also the way, as indicated above, he approached the analysis of the uncertainty relations. In these discussions the state could be used to make predictions that could be compared to experiments. In conjunction with the uncertainty relations, the state can be used to show the limits of applicability of certain classical concepts to the physical situation at hand. When dealing with incompatible operators, the statistical calculations using the probability distribution density description provided by quantum state are of fundamental importance (Bohr [**1927**], p. 72). Bohr [**1927**], p. 53, called these statistical aspects of the quantum state a consequence of the *quantum postulate* "... which attributes to any atomic process an essential discontinuity, or rather individuality, completely foreign to classical theories and symbolized by Planck's quantum of action." And [**1929b**], p. 113:[36]

> "Indeed, the inevitability of using, for atomic phenomena, a mode of description which is fundamentally statistical arises from a closer investigation of the information which we are able to obtain by direct measurement of these phenomena and of the meaning which we may ascribe in this connection to the application of the fundamental physical concepts."

---

[35]Bohr [**1927**], p. 72. See also Bohr [**1938b**], pp. 21–22, 23.
[36]See also Bohr [**1927**], p. 79.

Bohr [**1938b**], p. 13, also stated that statistical considerations are the only means we have of sufficiently generalizing physical descriptions to encompass the quantum phenomena.

Bohr paid attention to the implications of his approach to the analysis of quantum phenomena. In his examination of the proper application of the concepts of 'stationary state' and 'free particles' he concluded that there were domains for the proper application of both concepts to atomic systems and that one should not distinguish one as more fundamental than the other. In fact,[37]

" ... it might be said that the concepts of stationary states and individual transition processes within their proper field of application possess just as much or as little "reality" as the very idea of individual particles."

This point of view emphasizes how strongly Bohr felt that the wave and particle aspects of quantum theory are both on an equal footing. It represented quite a departure from a more traditional one embodied in von Neumann's approach to measurement in which the particle is treated as the fundamental entity and the state is attributed to it.

Bohr [**1927**], p. 75, went further: "In fact, wave mechanics, just as matrix theory, on this view represents a symbolic transcription of the problems of motion in classical mechanics and only to be interpreted by an explicit use of the quantum postulate." Bohr emphasized the purely symbolic character of the calculations of wave mechanics in several places in his 1927 lecture. In later essays, Bohr repeated his view that the quantum formalism is a "purely symbolic scheme."[38] Even more emphatically, Bohr [**1961**], p. 60, stated "Strictly speaking, the mathematical formalism of quantum mechanics and electrodynamics merely offers rules of calculation for the deduction of expectations about observations obtained under well-defined experimental conditions specified by classical physical concepts."

The concept of the quantum state, as it appears in most presentations of the quantum formalism and discussions of the theory of measurement, was foreign to Bohr's way of thinking. He did not enter into discussions of the quantum state in the way Schrödinger [**1935a**], p. 812, did when he proposed his famous 'cat paradox'. Schrödinger considered a situation in which a cat is placed in a box that is sealed to observation from the outside. There is a mechanism in the box that can kill the cat. This mechanism is controlled by some quantum phenomenon, such as radioactive decay or a photon passing through a half silvered mirror, that has a 50% chance of occurring during a specified period of time. The paradox lies in Schrödinger's claim that, according to von Neumann's theory of measurement, the wavefunction for the cat is a superposition of "alive" and "dead" states until we open the box to observe

---

[37] Bohr [**1927**], p. 87.
[38] Bohr [**1949**], p. 40, [**1958b**], p. 5.

it. The general issue is whether quantum mechanics applies to macroscopic systems, and, if so, whether there are superpositions of macroscopic states. If we do assume that quantum mechanics applies to macroscopic collections of matter, the question, as Leggett [1985], p. 47, has put it, is not how we get a particular result, but how it is possible to get a result at all. Thus, if we do assume that quantum mechanics applies to macroscopic collections of matter, the question is what result would we obtain.[39] In Chapter 15, it is established that the approaches of von Neumann and Bohr to the quantum state and measurement differ in their approach to this question.

Bohr [1929c], p. 17, also rejected explicitly, for example, the use of terms like "probability amplitude" in reference to the state. He did make clear, in opposition to the statistical interpretation of quantum mechanics, his view that the state concept applies to individual systems.[40] In his reply to EPR, Bohr [1935] maintained that quantum mechanics provided as complete a description of physical systems as possible in the light of the failure of classical theory. He thus rejected the possibility of a hidden variable explanation of quantum phenomena that he had already implicitly rejected when he spoke of the breakdown of visualization in reference to atomic phenomena and of limitations on the possibility of giving a causal description of these phenomena. He [1938b], p. 16, also accepted " ... the elegant axiomatic exposition of von Neumann, which in particular makes it evident that the fundamental superposition principle of quantum mechanics logically excludes the possibility of avoiding the non-causal features of the formalism by any conceivable introduction of additional variables." In other words [1937a], p. 294:

"The repeatedly expressed hopes of avoiding the essentially statistical character of quantum mechanical description by the assumption of some causal mechanism underlying the atomic phenomena and hitherto inaccessible to observation would indeed seem to be as vain as any project of doing justice to the increased profundity of the picture of the world achieved by the general theory of relativity by means of the ordinary conceptions of absolute space and time."

And [1961], p. 52:

"A crucial point, irrevocably excluding the possibility of reverting to a causal pictorial description, was the recognition that the scope of unambiguous application of the general conservation laws of momentum and energy is inherently limited by the circumstances that any experimental arrangement, allowing the location of objects in space

---

[39]For a discussion of this issue from an earlier perspective, see G. Ludwig [1961].

[40]Bohr always discussed individual systems in discussing the interpretation and application of quantum mechanics. This point of view was implicit in his reply to EPR. See also Bohr [1929b], pp. 103, 107.

and time, implies a transfer, uncontrollable in principle, of momentum and energy to the fixed scales and regulated clocks indispensable for the definition of the reference frame."

This last point, an echo of the disturbance theory of measurement, was another way of expressing the fact that every observation requires the specification of an experimental arrangement that serves as a "reference frame" for its interpretation. In addition, for an experiment that involves localizing a quantum system, there must be a physical interaction that connects the system to this reference frame. The analysis of Bohr's justification for claiming that the loss of a causal pictorial description is irrevocable will occupy much of what follows.

In his reply to EPR, Bohr [1935] emphasized that the very definition of the state of a system depends on the whole experimental arrangement in which it is observed. This is a nonlocal conception since a change in one part of the total apparatus can affect instantly the description of portions of the physical system at a quite distant place. The description (wavefunction) of the whole system changes when a measurement is made on part of it and this in turn may change the probabilities that will be computed for events in other parts of the system no matter how distant they are from the part measured. This idea of the state being defined as a relation between an atomic system and the experimental apparatus rather than being a property of the atomic system was called by Feyerabend [1968] a "relational" view of the quantum state.[41] From Bohr's point of view, the change in the wavefunction when part of a system is measured would be better characterized by saying that the original wavefunction has become invalid and a new wavefunction must be used to represent the whole system for rest of the experiment.

5.8 Reflection 11

The quantum state of a system, in Bohr's mature view of it, requires the specification of the experimental arrangement before it can be defined. The experimental arrangement, in turn, establishes the initial and boundary conditions for the system. With these in place, an appropriate and definite quantum state may be used to describe the system.

A comparison of Bohr's requirement that the experimental arrangement be specified before a definite state can be attributed to a system with the mathematical requirements for obtaining a definite solution to Schrödinger's equation indicates that Bohr's view of the circumstances needed for the attribution of a quantum state to a system is virtually a restatement of the mathematical requirements for a solution to exist. The quantum state can then be equated with the solution of Schrödinger's equation for the system with the given initial and boundary conditions.

---

[41] Bohr's conception of the state in these terms is discussed further in historical context by Jammer [1974], pp. 197–211.

This view of the state accommodates experiments that exhibit distant correlations, such as the one proposed by EPR, as well as so-called "delayed choice" experiments, in which there are changes in the boundary conditions during the experiment as the experimenter makes choices of what to measure. The state is computed in these cases just as it is for any differential equation with time varying or abruptly changing boundary conditions.

The advantage of Bohr's standpoint is that it carries little of the metaphysical baggage left over from mechanism. The implication of this perspective is that the state cannot be attributed to an entity in any way divorced from the experimental context. It is therefore not an intrinsic aspect or property of the quantum system itself, but reflects what a macroscopic knowing subject can say about that microscopic system in the given experimental context. Furthermore, it recognizes that apart from these conditions, there is no definite solution to Schrödinger's equation and no definite state can be attributed to a system.

5.9 Bohr's Scientific Work after 1935

Bohr's main contributions to physics in the 1930s were in the domain of nuclear theory. In the early 1930s he speculated on several possible ways to explain the anomalous energy spectrum in β decay. Most of his speculations on this issue appear in his correspondence with other scientists and with Pauli in particular. He held onto the idea of the nonconservation of energy as long as he could and it seemed to others that he hoped that energy is not conserved.[42]

Bohr presented the 'compound nucleus model' in a lecture to the Copenhagen Scientific Society (Bohr [**1936a**]). In a brief historical discussion, David Kaiser [**1994**] has pointed out that this qualitative conceptual model of nuclear reactions was very influential and led to a sequence of papers by others in which the consequences of this description of nuclear interactions were calculated. He noted that J. M. Blatt and V. Weisskopf [**1952**], Chapter VIII, had stated that Bohr's 1936 address to the Copenhagen Academy had a profound effect on the study of nuclear physics.

Kaiser, pp. 259–262, discussed both what Bohr had done and its impact. In his compound nucleus model, Bohr had replaced the nuclear reaction

(5.9) $$A + B \to D + E$$

with the two step sequence

(5.10) $$A + B \to C \to D + E.$$

---

[42]The history of this particular era in Bohr's work, and the impact on him of the discovery of the neutron and the speculation about the neutrino, has been discussed by Joan Bromberg [**1971**]. The idea the energy is only conserved statistically was revived by Schrödinger [**1958**].

This was called 'scattering through the resonance C' in the 1950s. Bohr conceptualized the intermediate state C as having "remarkable stability" and made as his basic assumption that the final interaction that takes C to $D+E$ is independent of the interaction that took $A+B$ to C. This postulate of independence was soon used to compute the total cross section of the reaction (5.10) in the form $\sigma_{\text{tot}} \propto \Gamma_{AB}\Gamma_{DE}$, where Γ_{AB} is proportional to the probability of the reaction $A+B \to C$ and Γ_{DE} is proportional to the probability of the reaction $C \to D+E$.

Bohr, as quoted by Kaiser, p. 261, spoke of the "essential feature" of nuclear reactions as a "free competition" between possible processes from the semi-stable intermediate state to the final state. Each reaction that is not forbidden is part of this free competition and each has a specific probability that it will occur. Kaiser illustrated Bohr's ideas with the scattering of an electron and a positron to produce a negative and a positive tau meson with a neutral Z^0 particle as the intermediate state. He showed that the total cross section was a product of the cross sections for the $e^- + e^+ \to Z^0$ and the $Z^0 \to \tau^- + \tau^+$ states. The result is a Breit-Wigner formula that is proportional to the product of Γ_{ee} and $\Gamma_{\tau\tau}$. It takes the form

$$(5.11) \qquad \sigma(e^-e^+ \to \tau^-\tau^+) = \frac{C\Gamma_{ee}\Gamma_{\tau\tau}}{(s^2 - M_Z^2)^2 + M_Z^2\Gamma^2}.$$

The Mandelstam variable s is the square of the energy in the center of mass frame and M_Z is the mass of the Z^0 particle. The Γ in the denominator is the "width of the Z^0 resonance" that represents the sum of the Γs for all Z^0 decay channels.

Kaiser, p. 262, observed that Bohr's three principles, (1) independence of initial and final states, (2) free competition of all possible decay reactions, and (3) the width of the decay channel of the intermediate state is the sum of the probabilities of all possible decays, all play a role, albeit in a modified form, in modern particle physics.

Bohr also contributed to the liquid-drop model of the nucleus that was important in understanding nuclear fission. There are notes of his work in the Bohr archive and in his collected papers Bohr [**1986**]. This work led to the paper N. Bohr and John A. Wheeler [**1939**]. It was used in the study of nuclear fission during World War II. After the war, Bohr played a relatively minor role in CERN and other installations for pursuing particle physics.

The later work of Bohr in physics is tangential to the epistemological concerns of this book, so these aspects of Bohr's work will not be pursued further. Consult Kaiser [**1994**] and the references cited there for more details on this aspect of Bohr's work.

Part II

The Synthesis of Bohr's Epistemology

Yet, how difficult it is to avoid substituting the sign for the thing; how difficult to keep the essential quality still living before us, and not to kill it with the word.

Johann Wolfgang Goethe, *Farbenlehre*, 1810

CHAPTER 6

Bohr's Philosophical Themes

The focus in Part II is on the philosophical issues Bohr raised and showing how they fit together. The goal is to systematize the theory of knowledge that is implicit in his writings. Up to now, I have let Bohr speak for himself as much as possible. The next step is to select and then employ consistently one mode of expression for each of the ideas that Bohr may have expressed in a variety of ways in a variety of settings. This will allow us to get at the core of meaning behind Bohr's locutions and pin down what his epistemological commitments really were. I will hold back my criticisms of Bohr's positions until they have been given a full exposition, systematized, and provided with a philosophical context.

6.1 The Search for Concepts

The consistency of Bohr's work, in his many discussions of the elements of his theory and even in his very choice of locutions, indicates that he was operating from a comprehensive epistemological viewpoint. Many of his papers on physics and almost all of his essays were directed to expressing his ideas, albeit tersely and somewhat obscurely, on the epistemological questions central to quantum mechanics and their justification.

In spite of working from a vantage point that guided him in philosophical matters, Bohr did not operate from a worked-out philosophical position. He must be viewed not as a philosopher who spoke physics, but a physicist who spoke philosophy. This means that his philosophy must always be understood in terms of, and grounded in, his physics. As noted above, Bohr, along with Heisenberg, Pauli, von Neumann, and many others, for example, characterized of certain statements in quantum mechanics as "meaningless". Philosophers who see this as a reflection of a philosophical position about meaning miss this important point and miss the chance to understand what these physicists really meant.

In the course of his work, Bohr tried out several different words and modes of expression for some of his key ideas before either abandoning the idea or settling on a locution that he felt would best express his point of view. One example of this evolution was his use of the word 'choice' in reference to atomic transitions. Bohr [**1927**], p. 69, mentioned choice first in his 1927 lecture concerning the behavior of atoms. In his 1928 survey of his 1927 lecture, he [**1929c**], p. 13, said: "... the description of the state of a single atom contains absolutely no element of referring to the occurrence of transition processes, so that in this case we can scarcely avoid speaking of a choice on the part of the atom."[1] However, in the same essay [**1929c**], pp. 19–20, Bohr qualified his use of such a term: "... properly speaking, such a phrase requires the idea of an external chooser, the existence of which, however, is denied already by the use of the word nature." Soon afterward, in the typescript of the notes for his Bristol lecture of 1931, Bohr [**Arch**], 12:5, p. 13, put a question mark in the margin of the manuscript at the point where he mentioned the need to use statistical methods and "speak of nature making a choice between possibilities."[2] In 1938, Bohr [**1938b**], p. 13, used

---

[1] See also Bohr [**1927**], p. 60, [**1929c**], p. 4.

[2] Other physicists spoke similarly, but clearly with a rhetorical meaning. For example, to highlight a problem for Bohr's theory of the atom, Rutherford had asked the question "How does an electron decide what frequency it is going to vibrate at when it passes from one stationary state to another?" Rutherford saw this as a grave difficulty in Bohr's theory of the atom. See Bohr [**1961**], p. 41. See also Meyerson [**1930**], p. 316, for a discussion of Poincaré's views on least action principles in terms of choice and Høffding [**1925**] for a discussion of Meyerson's epistemology. As Mehra [**1972**], p. 44, pointed out, Dirac used the phrase 'choice of Nature' concerning the outcome of an experiment at the 1930 Solvay conference, but Heisenberg preferred the term 'observation' instead.

'choice' again without qualification in reference to atomic transitions. By 1949, however, he had become critical of this terminology from the point of view of his overall philosophical position. He [**1949**], pp. 50–51, referred to Einstein's example of the photon and the half-silvered mirror as an illustration of the difficulty one gets into when trying to give a pictorial representation of the behavior of a photon—a situation in which one would be tempted to use the term 'choice' in describing its behavior. He [**1949**], p. 51, then reconsidered the whole issue:

> "The question was whether, as to the occurrence of individual effects, we should adopt the terminology proposed by Dirac, that we were concerned with a choice on the part of "nature", or, as suggested by Heisenberg, we should say that we have to do with a choice on the part of the "observer" constructing the measuring instruments and reading their recording. Any such terminology would, however, appear dubious since, on the one hand, it is hardly reasonable to endow nature with volition in the ordinary sense, while, on the other hand, it is certainly not possible for the observer to influence the events may appear under the conditions he has arranged. To my mind, there is no other alternative than to admit that, in this field of experience, we are dealing with individual phenomena and that our possibilities of handling the measuring instruments allow us only to make a choice between the different complementary types of phenomena we want to study."

He had already experimented with the idea that 'measurements may create phenomena' in Bohr and Rosenfeld [**1933**], p. 48: "Already in the case of a position or momentum measurement of the electron of a hydrogen atom in a given stationary state, one can maintain with certain correctness, that the results of the measurement are created by the measurement itself." He later rejected statements like this because, [**1949**], p. 64, this phrase is being "... used in a way hardly compatible with common language and practical definition." We see in both of these examples how much Bohr was aware that a deep philosophical inquiry is required in order to avoid apparent paradoxes in quantum theory.

In terms of conventional philosophical categories, Bohr was clearly instrumentalistic, as opposed to realistic, in statements of his approach to quantum theory. Beginning in 1927, he [**1927**], pp. 76–77, 90, spoke of the "symbolical method" of Schrödinger. Bohr [**1929c**], p. 18, subsequently developed this into a full-fledged instrumentalism: "We meet here in a new light the old truth that in our description of nature the purpose is not the disclose the real essence of the phenomena but only to track down, so far as it is possible, relations between the manifold aspects of our experience."[3] Bohr also called

---

[3] The philosophical history of this idea is pursued in Part III.

the quantum formalism a "purely symbolic scheme" on several occasions.[4] Thirty-four years after the first statement, he [**1961**], p. 60, wrote: "Strictly speaking, the mathematical formalism of quantum mechanics and electrodynamics merely offers rules of calculation for the deduction of expectations about observations obtained under well defined experimental conditions specified by classical physical concepts." Bohr's reluctance to attribute properties to atomic objects was complete. This is, moreover, a required feature of his viewpoint since he put the particle and the wave descriptions on an equal footing with respect to their "reality". Meyer-Abich [**1965**], p. 102, has called this approach to quantum theory and the individuality of atomic systems a concern not with objects in themselves but with "objects as the subjects of physics". I will sort out the meaning of these ideas below.

In his attempt to show that Bohr's philosophy was adopted from the philosophy of Høffding, Faye [**1991**], p. 165, stated that "the concept of continuity was as essential to Bohr's theory of knowledge as it was to Høffding's in virtue of its being for both a precondition for the acquisition of objective empirical knowledge." He, pp. 77–78, based this on his analysis of that aspect of Høffding's philosophy that he quoted from Høffding's [**1882b**] discussion of Kant. There Høffding stated that the law of continuity is valid for all phenomena because it formulates the general conditions under which we can have real experience. Because Høffding subscribed to this position, and Faye viewed Bohr's epistemology as derived from Høffding's, Faye argued that continuity plays an important role in Bohr's philosophy. However, even though Bohr occasionally used the term continuity, primarily in reference to mental phenomena, and sometimes spoke of avoiding "breaks in the causal chain", the concept of continuity plays no real role in his epistemology or its justification.

One of the most important tools that Bohr used in his analysis of quantum issues is thought experiments. As Kuhn [**1962**], p. 88, pointed out, it is no accident that quantum mechanics and relativity theory were both preceded and accompanied by philosophical analyses of the foundations of Newtonian theory. Kuhn also pointed out that thought experiments played an important role, in their critical function, in exposing the old framework to new information with a clarity unattainable in the laboratory. Kuhn concluded from his investigation that the point of the thought experiment analysis is not, as is sometimes believed, to make clear the untenability of the old theory, but rather to pave the way for the introduction of a new conceptual framework. The purpose of the analysis of the pertinent ideas related to the old conceptual framework is to prevent the new ideas from being rejected out of hand simply because they do not follow the form implicitly required by the old conceptual framework. Einstein's discussion of the concept of simultaneity made clear that the notion of universal simultaneity is not, nor could it be,

---

[4]Bohr [**1938b**], pp. 16, 25–26; [**1949**], p. 40; [**1958b**], p. 5.

supported by experiments. This, by itself, did not make the old conception wrong or inapplicable. The change from the old to the new was due in part to Einstein's analysis, and in part to two necessary factors: the experimental success of electrodynamics and the fact that the Lorentzian transformation laws for electrodynamic quantities under a change in coordinate frame are incompatible with the Galilean transformation laws of Newtonian mechanics. Because charged matter and electromagnetic fields interact, it is necessary that they share a similar relation to the reference frames. To make these theories consistent, Einstein showed that a change in the transformation laws of mechanics was required.

Similar factors were at work in Bohr's reply to Einstein, Podolsky and Rosen. In this reply, Bohr was arguing against the rejection of his views for traditional reasons in the same way that Bohr, Kramers and Slater had argued against the rejection of their formal quantum theory.

One of Bohr's ways of thinking in reference to conceptual change is embodied in the idea he [**1949**], p. 66, expressed that there are two kinds of truth:

"To the one kind belong statements so simple and clear that the opposite assertion obviously could not be defended. The other kind, the so-called "deep truths," are statements in which the opposite also contains deep truth. Now the developments in a new field will usually pass through stages in which chaos is gradually replaced by order; but it is not least in the intermediate stage where deep truth prevails that the work is really exciting and inspires the imagination to search for a firmer hold. ... we are nearing the goal where logical order to a large extent allows us to avoid deep truths .... "

Wittgenstein presented an idea with some similarity to Bohr's in his concept of a "depth grammar".[5] The idea of deep truths is also reminiscent of Kierkegaard's qualitative dialectic, in which the opposed components of reality cannot be embraced in a higher unity.[6]

In reference to philosophical inquiry itself, Bohr [**1937a**], pp. 289–290, spoke of

"... how often the development of physics has taught us that a consistent application of even the most elementary concepts indispensable for the description of our daily experience, is based on assumptions initially unnoticed, the explicit consideration of which is, however, essential if we wish to obtain a classification of more extended domains of experience as clear and as free from arbitrariness as possible. I also need hardly emphasize how much this development has contributed to the general philosophical clarification of the presuppositions underlying human knowledge."[7]

---

[5]See Wittgenstein [**1953**], pp. 47, 63, and Dirac [**1963**].
[6]See Høffding [**1882b**], v. 2, pp. 286–287.

In spite of his connection to Høffding and his recognition that philosophical ideas are important in resolving some of the conceptual problems surrounding quantum mechanics, Bohr had serious reservations about the usefulness of philosophical analysis. In unpublished notes on the unity of science, he expressed admiration for the work that the schools of sophistic, empirical, and realistic philosophy have contributed to the general background for the discussion of the issues of existence. However he felt that this work is not directly connected with his task. He viewed phrases such as 'external world' or 'consciousness of others' as being as elementary as the words "be," "will," and "know." He referred to the practical use of language in our daily life and stated that we cannot exclude these words from our vocabulary and must view them in the sense of practical communication with the meanings that are directly accessible to everyone.[8]

In his references to the "purely symbolic scheme" of quantum mechanics, and on several other occasions, Bohr indicated his view that the attribution of properties to objects, a mainstay of classical theory and the materialism that preceded it, can no longer be carried out without contradiction. In reference to the interpretation of the uncertainty relations, he declared that they should not be interpreted as a limitation on measurement, since this would imply that, in the accurate measurement of one quantity, there is still another quantity that is not being measured that could be taken account of in some future theory. He [**1937a**], p. 293, went on to say that "On the contrary, the proper role of the indeterminacy relations consists in assuring quantitatively the logical compatibility of apparently contradictory laws . . . ." And, "From the above considerations it should be made clear that the whole situation in atomic physics deprives of all meaning such inherent attributes as the idealizations of classical physics would ascribe to an object."

Inquiries into the nature of ontological questions, such as those of Rudolph Carnap [**1950**], [**1963**], Willard van Ormond Quine [**1953**], [**1960**], W. P. Alston [**1958**], and Alonzo Church [**1958**], fare no better with regard to the problems posed by complementarity. The approach to ontological questions recommended by Carnap requires adopting a linguistic framework and then dealing with questions of reality and existence within this framework.[9] Carnap did not discuss the question of what one should do when faced with an situation in which a linguistic framework seems to be adequate in terms of the properties it "contains" and the descriptions that can be formulated

---

[7] See also Bohr [**1954**], pp. 68–69, 78–79.

[8] Bohr [**Arch**], 21:1, 3/29/54, pp. 1–2.

[9] Carnap's concern with a special linguistic framework was not new. Gottfried Wilhelm von Leibniz considered a philosophical language for the discussion and resolution of philosophical problems and John Stuart Mill [**1846**], pp. 400–401 analyzed principles for a philosophical language. A number of other thinkers have also discussed a philosophical language that would be free of the ambiguities and associations of natural language. See the discussion of philosophical aspects of language in Chapter 11.

within it, but we are also forced to try to attribute incompatible properties to the objects involved. We cannot overcome this problem by a mere extension of our linguistic framework any more than the introduction of a new term for atomic sized entities will solve the conceptual problems surrounding them.

For Quine ontological commitments are determined by a theory and those elements in it that play the role of bound variables. However, Quine is also faced with the problem of incompatible proposition systems that have different bound variables, but are concerned with the same physical system.[10]

Bohr was clear that adopting an artificial language or linguistic framework is not a solution to the problems of quantum theory. He emphasized the fact that our shared language is uniquely adapted to describing our experience. Bohr also felt that theories are part of a conceptual framework and do not exist in isolation. So it is not simply the language we choose or the bound variables in our theories that tell us what is real. We must recognize that issues of reality involve the interplay between a theory and the conceptual framework in which it is embedded.

Petersen [**1963**], p. 12, has quoted a somewhat cryptic statement by Bohr with a bearing on Bohr's global view concerning ontological questions:

"There is no quantum world. This is only an abstract physical description. It is wrong to think that the task of physics is to find out how nature is. Physics concerns what we can say about nature."

There are two possible interpretations of this statement. The first, and most plausible interpretation, is that Bohr is not making a physical distinction between the microscopic and the macroscopic worlds. This statement is consistent with Bohr's discussion of measuring instruments as composed of atoms. The other interpretation is that Bohr is operating from a position that is realistic with respect to the macroscopic world and phenomenalistic with respect to the microscopic world. This view of Bohr's work has been adopted by a number of authors.[11] But, as indicated above, this latter view does not reflect Bohr's own view of what he was doing.

---

[10] The theorem of W. Craig [**1953**], [**1956**] is merciless in this regard. It refers to the replacement of theoretical terms, like the term 'electron', with a recursively generated infinite conjunction of statements containing only those terms designated as observational. If the terms 'wave' and 'particle' are both observational then their simultaneous unconditioned appearance in the replacement will lead to contradictions. To place conditions on them would trivialize Quine's thesis. See also the discussion in H. Putnam [**1965**].

[11] See Adolph Grünbaum [**1957**], pp. 717–718, Mario Bunge [**1955**], p. 6, Paul Feyerabend [**1958a**], p. 82, and Anthony J. Leggett [**1998**]. See also Roger Penrose [**1989**], p. 226, who interpreted Bohr as stating that there is *no* objective picture of the world and that "Nothing is actually 'out there,' at the quantum level." Penrose felt that this position is too defeatist and adopted the view that "attributes *objective physical reality* to the quantum description: the *quantum state.*" This view, as it is worked out in Penrose's subsequent discussion, involves particles that can appear in two places at once and throwing away physical reality (reduction of the wavepacket) after a measurement—all this without other physical consequences. Aside from the fact Penrose has misstated Bohr's views, his

6.2 The Wave-Particle Duality

The wave-particle duality is an aspect of all matter and radiation. Bohr came to see it as a touchstone for the ideas he was developing vis á vis the relation of theoretical descriptions to experimental observations. The importance of the concepts of wave and particle is that certain experiments are considered almost paradigmatic of wave and particle behavior. For this reason, resolving contradictions in the employment of these concepts and using them consistently in the quantum mechanical setting have paramount importance.

The wave properties of light were well known in classical physics. Numerous experiments, such as the measurement of the angle of refraction of light in changing media, interference effects, and diffraction effects were expressions of these properties. The interference patterns observed in Young's double slit experiment constituted a decisive demonstration that light is a wave phenomenon. This evidence was so compelling that the wave theory of Huyghens won out over the particulate theory of Newton. During the nineteenth century, Maxwell presented his equations relating electric fields, magnetic fields and charges. Maxwell showed that these equations imply a wave equation for the propagation of an electromagnetic field in the form of free radiation. This electromagnetic field was successfully associated with light. So, by the end of the nineteenth century, the wave theory of light was firmly established.

There were some problems with this theory, however. A wave requires a medium in which to propagate since it is simply a 'vibration' in this medium. The name 'ether' was given to this medium and its properties were calculated by analogy to the theory of elasticity. As a consequence of the high frequency of light, the values obtained for the tension in the ether and its energy were very high. While these values were felt to be unobservable, other effects were considered observable. According to various hypotheses concerning the relative motion of the ether and the earth, certain effects due to such motion should have been within range of observability. But the experiments of Michelson and Moreley in 1884, which were designed to measure this motion, and attempts to measure the aberration of starlight due to this motion, failed to detect these effects.

The introduction of the photon threatened to shift the balance from wave back to particle. While some embraced the photon fairly soon and adopted the view that light is particulate, Bohr was not able to accept the idea until 1925. Even after accepting the particulate description of light, Bohr [**1934**], p. 4, emphasized that "These interference patterns offer so thorough a test of the wave picture of light propagation that this picture cannot be considered as a hypothesis in the usual sense of this word, but may rather be regarded as the

---

viewpoint, as presented, is much less plausible than Bohr's approach. I will take up the associated philosophical issues again in Part IV.

adequate account of the phenomena observed."[12] This way of understanding the experimental results in both kinds of cases ultimately forced him to accept the wave-particle duality as fundamental and he concluded: "From these results, it seems to follow that, in the general problem of quantum theory, one is faced not with a modification of the mechanical and electrodynamical theories describable in terms of the usual physical concepts, but with an essential failure of the pictures in space and time on which the description of natural phenomena has hitherto been based."[13]

Having accepted the duality and pointed out a consequence, Bohr turned to the question of how one could make sense of a situation in which our customary spacetime pictures are no longer usable—a question first discussed by Bohr in Bohr, Kramers and Slater [**1924**], p. 799. Bohr looked to the interpretation of the experiments themselves, and possible alternative interpretations, as a guide to understanding the difficulties presented by the wave-particle duality. He [**1927**], p. 54, noted that

"Just as in the case of light, we have consequently in the question of the nature of matter, so far as we adhere to classical concepts, to face an inevitable dilemma which has to be regarded as the very expression of experimental evidence."

The difficulty lies in the direct connection between interference effects and the conception of light as a wave phenomenon, as well as the direct connection between the photoelectric effect and the conception of light as a particulate phenomenon:

"The situation which we meet here is characterized by the fact that we are apparently forced to choose between two mutually contradictory conceptions of the propagation of light: one, the idea of light waves, the other the corpuscular view of the theory of light quanta, each conception expressing fundamental aspects of our experience."[14]

Because of the paradigmatic nature of the experiments defining both the wave and particle properties of light and matter, new concepts cannot help us evade these consequences. Theoretical ideas are not lacking; the problem lies in the duality of our experience of nature. Bohr turned to an analysis of how we experience the world to help understand this situation. The result of this analysis was presented for the first time in his 1927 Como lecture.

At the beginning of the Como lecture, Bohr stated (p. 51): "... our interpretation of the experimental material rests essentially upon classical concepts." With this as a starting point, he emphasized later both the need for the "concept of the free particles" in interpreting solutions of the Schrödinger equation (p. 79) and the "necessity of the wave concept" (p. 66), where these

---
[12]See also Bohr [**1949**], p. 34.
[13]Bohr [**1925b**], pp. 34–35. See also Bohr [**1927**], p. 55, and [**1930**], p. 376.
[14]Bohr [**1929b**], p. 107.

are understood to have their ordinary classical meanings. This conception of the necessity of classical concepts for the interpretation of nature was one of the key epistemological insights on which Bohr constructed his interpretation of physics. He later extended these ideas into an interpretation of experience in general.

Bohr [**1930**], p. 370, warned on several occasions that the concepts of wave and particle in application to atomic phenomena must not be misinterpreted as a "complete analogy with ordinary wave propagation in material media." Indeed,

> "Just as in the case of radiation of quanta, often termed "photons", we have here to do with symbols helpful in the formulation of the probability laws governing the occurrence of elementary processes which cannot be further analyzed in terms of classical physical ideas. In this sense, phrases such as the "corpuscular nature of light" or "the wave nature of electrons" are ambiguous, since such concepts as corpuscle and wave are only well defined within the scope of classical physics, where, of course, light and electrons are electromagnetic waves and material corpuscles respectively."

Bohr [**1938b**], p. 23, went further and stated that wave and particle quantum phenomena, though useful for the purposes of illustration, were "only limiting cases of special simplicity." Bohr was not thinking of "real particles" or "real waves" but rather of appropriate descriptions of phenomena.[15]

Bohr [**1927**], p. 53, located the "essence" of quantum theory, in regard to its not having a full interpretation in classical terms, in what he called the "... quantum postulate, which attributes to any atomic process an essential discontinuity, or rather individuality, completely foreign to the classical theory and symbolized by Planck's quantum of action." Bohr [**1929b**], p. 108, initially characterized this postulate concerning the individuality of atomic phenomena by saying that "every change of state of an atom should be regarded as an individual process incapable of a more detailed description, by which the atom goes over from one so-called stationary state to another."[16] From a more general position, Bohr [**1935**], p. 699, [**1937b**], p. 16, discussed individuality in terms of an "impossibility" of giving a full account of the "course" of a particle experiment, say, due to the uncontrollable and unpredictable interaction between the particle and the instruments of observation. In his later work, Bohr [**1961**], p. 60, used the term "wholeness" and refined it into what we may call its final form:

---

[15] Problems connected with the use of analogies in quantum theory has been discussed by Bungé [**1968**].

[16] Bohr [**1927**], pp. 54, 75, 91, [**1929c**], pp. 7, 19, felt that the quantum postulate had an element of "irrationality" in it. By irrationality, he [**1929c**], p. 19, meant essentially the idea of "not comprehensible within the framework of the 'customary forms of perception' or concepts." See Meyer-Abich [**1965**], pp. 103–104, 128–133, 141–144. I will discuss the philosophical roots of the concepts of individuality and irrationality in Part III.

"The element of wholeness, symbolized by the quantum of action and completely foreign to classical physical principles has, however, the consequences that in the study of quantum processes any experimental inquiry implies an interaction between the atomic object and the measuring tools which, although essential for the characterization of phenomena, evades a separate account if the experiment is to serve its purpose of yielding unambiguous answers to questions."

The relation between the terms introduced here and Bohr's theory will be made clear in a discussion of these separate elements below.

6.3 Reflection 12

As shown in the last chapter, Bohr's discussion of the application of wave concepts to atomic systems contrasts greatly with those who have discussed things like the wavefunction in terms of 'probability amplitudes' or 'probability waves.' He accepted Born's probability interpretation of the wavefunction, but used it only in the special circumstance of a completed experiment. He did not, for example, describe particles by "wavepackets" and discuss how to interpret in particle terms what the wavepacket does at the surface of a diffraction grating or in a double slit interference experiment. He accorded equal "reality" to both the wave and the particle aspects of matter and radiation. This is why he did not interpret the wavefunction as being the wave itself, and subordinate the particle aspect, or interpret it as simply describing our knowledge of the particle behavior, and subordinate the wave aspect. The contrast between Bohr and most of the other thinkers in this regard is due to his concern for, and constant references to, conditions under which concepts are properly applied to atomic systems. He was not willing to accept the modes of speech used by most physicists in discussing the interpretation of the wavefunction. And many of the difficulties that I have examined in previous discussions of the interpretation of the uncertainty relations and the quantum state description, do not appear in Bohr's approach.

6.4 Bohr's View of Conceptual Frameworks

It is time to begin the process now of extracting what I will call Bohr's 'epistemological theory' out of his writings. This requires extracting a stable core of meaning from his statements that expresses the epistemology he was suggesting. The results of this inquiry will be tested in Chapter 14 by applying his epistemological theory to an area of classical physics that he felt showed the need for a wider conceptual framework. This will be followed in Chapter 16 by an examination of his approach vis á vis current thinking in quantum mechanics. While the epistemological theory that emerges from this process will be referred to as "Bohr's theory", I emphasize that Bohr never consolidated his work in this way himself and might not have agreed with the result.

In the initial consideration of his theory, a particular set of phrases or terms will be selected from those that he used. This set is limited to just those elements that are distinct and necessary for Bohr's theory. For example, Bohr does not distinguish between 'observation' and 'measurement' so they will not be distinguished in this analysis. The word 'observation' will be used in this case to represent the concept involved.

In Bohr's 1927 analysis of the concept of observation, he stated that it contained an element of "arbitrariness" in that we have a choice of which objects are to be included in the systems to be observed and those that are used in the observing. Part of what he meant by this is that we can choose where to place the 'boundary' between a system under observation, the system observing it, and the rest of the world.[17] The choice of where to put the boundaries and what to put on each side is determined by what you want to measure. This choice is important, for example, when we are attempting to establish the conservation of energy and momentum in a process because the choice of this boundary and observation or control of what crosses through it can have practical significance. For Bohr, this choice of boundaries and boundary conditions has an epistemological significance as well. It determines some aspects of the experimental arrangement.

For clarity, let us consider the elements of a generic experiment. The system under observation will be labeled by k, the measuring instrument by M, the knowing subject by S and the environment of the experiment, which is the rest of the universe, by E. In the division of the universe into the systems $k + M + S + E$, a boundary b_i may be placed at any + sign, where the label i refers to the system to the left of the + sign. Thus, the boundary b_k appears in the sequence as $k\ b_k\ M + S + E$. This is interpreted as the combined system $M + S + E$ observing system k. The choice of what to include in each of these systems determines where to put the boundary. This boundary determines what is in the system k and what is associated with the measuring instrument used to observe it.

Consider first the boundary b_k and the question of where one might meaningfully draw a line between what is considered to be the system under observation, the system k, and the instrument used to observe it, M.[18] In the case of a star and a telescope, there is not much question of what an appropriate choice would be. But in the case of measuring the temperature of a cup of water with an ordinary glass thermometer, the question of what is to be part of the system and what is not assumes more importance since the thermometer itself can exchange a significant amount of heat with the system and give a reading for the system that does not represent its temperature before the measurement. In this case, of course, we have the option of recording the

---

[17] As discussed above, von Neumann [**1932**] was the first to make these concerns with boundaries explicit in the formalism.

[18] This discussion is taken from von Neumann [**1932**].

temperature of the thermometer before the measurement and measuring or computing its heat capacity at that temperature and calculating the average heat exchanged with the measured system. This information can then be used to correct the temperature reading. Adding or subtracting the same amount of heat to or from the system can also compensate for the heat exchanged with the thermometer so that the net heat change in the system is zero. Even if a single correction does not suffice, there is still the option of making more corrections—using the same or a different method. In principle, at least, this can always be done in a converging series of corrections. In quantum theory, however, this option is not open even in principle.

There is yet a second sense, not concerned with boundaries separating what is to be included in each system, in which an observation is arbitrary. This is the arbitrariness in our choice of what aspect to observe in a given atomic system. While this arbitrariness is trivial in a classical system because the elements that can be observed in a system are usually independent of our choice of how to measure them, it assumes a special importance in atomic physics where this is not the case. Part of what we observe in the atomic domain, Bohr emphasized, is inextricably tied up with our choice of how to observe it. Bohr located this arbitrariness in our freedom to choose an "experimental arrangement" and what to include in it. He felt that the statement and description of this choice has to form part of our account of what we observed. Thus, with reference to the measuring system M above, there are further choices about how to use the instruments to make various different measurements.

The practical consequence of the boundary between measured system and measuring instrument for Bohr is that classical concepts must be used to describe the components included on the measuring instrument side of the boundary. In this way, the boundary helps to determine the kinds of experiments that can be done on the system. Bohr went on to assert that the choice of boundary has the equally importance consequence that it also determines the theoretical description that is appropriate for the system in this setting as well.

Implicit in this discussion of boundaries and choices of measuring instruments is the idea that the mathematical representation of the experimental situation, and therefore the possible wavefunction solutions of the Schrödinger equation and the predictions that can be made, depend on these choices. Bohr made use of this point, although not in a completely explicit form, in his solution for the problem posed by the EPR paradox. He subsequently expanded on this idea in his concept of a closed phenomenon as the proper way to interpret quantum theory and experiment.

In examining further the concept of observation Bohr [**1927**], p. 54, stated at one point that "Ultimately, every observation can, of course, be reduced to our sense perceptions." But he followed this immediately with the claim that the interpretation and expression of observations must always make use of theoretical concepts. Proceeding with his argument, he maintained that the point at which the "concept of observation", involving the quantum postulate, is introduced is a matter of convenience depending on where we have chosen to draw the line between the observing system and the observed system. The juxtaposition of these ideas shows that Bohr did not intend to be positivistic in his "reduction to sense perceptions" but just the opposite. He wished to emphasize that any observation involves theoretical notions when we state what we have observed. These, often implicit, theoretical ideas are noticed when we are required to justify that the experiment performed is adequate for measuring the quantity under investigation.

In reference to observation, Bohr often used terms like 'perception' and locutions such as 'forms of perception': "... any new experience makes it appearance within the frame of our customary points of view and forms of perception."[19] Or Bohr [1929c], p. 5, "... we are concerned with the recognition of physical laws which lie outside the domain of ordinary experience and which present difficulties to our accustomed forms of perception." Bohr [1929c], p. 5, gave a clue to his meaning for these phrases by his characterization of the role they play: "We learn that these forms of perception are *idealizations,* the suitability of which for reducing our sense impressions to order depends upon the practically infinite velocity of light and upon the smallness of the quantum of action." Bohr was thus really referring to classical descriptions of phenomena by his 'forms of perception'; but he was also emphasizing an element of indispensability concerning the need for these descriptions—very much in a Kantian sense. I shall for the time being replace this terminology with 'classical description', which better expresses what Bohr was trying to get at in relation to the functioning of his theory.

This terminological reduction is justified by comparing the way in which Bohr uses these various terms in his writing. Compare, for example, "... causality may be considered as a mode of perception by which we reduce our sense impressions to order" (Bohr [1929b], pp. 116–117), with "the causal mode of description" (Bohr [1929b], pp. 1, 5) or with "causal spacetime pictures" (Bohr [1927], pp. 55, 67). Favrholdt [1992], pp. 34–35, maintained that Bohr was using the word 'Anschauungsformen', or the Danish 'anskuelsesform', in an ordinary language sense when he characterized causality as a 'form of perception' and not as a philosophical term. He felt that Bohr was trying to express himself clearly, and was not speaking from a philosophical perspective, with the terminology he chose.

Moving to a still more general viewpoint, Bohr claimed that more than just the introduction of theoretical notions is involved in the interpretation of observations. What is needed in addition is what he called a "conceptual

---

[19]Bohr [1929c], p. 1. See also Bohr [1927], p. 91, [1929a], p. 93, and [1929c], pp. 18, 22.

6.4 BOHR'S VIEW OF CONCEPTUAL FRAMEWORKS

framework" or a "frame of reference" in which these theoretical notions play a part. A conceptual framework may be useful at a given time, but
"The main point to realize is that all knowledge presents itself within a conceptual framework adapted to account for previous experience and that any such frame may prove too narrow to comprehend new experience."[20]

Inquiry in many fields of knowledge has "... time and again proved the necessity of abandoning or remolding points of view which, because of their fruitfulness and apparently unrestricted applicability, were regarded as indispensable for rational explanation." He [**1954**], p. 68, continued:
"In fact, the widening of the conceptual framework not only has served to restore order within the respective branches of knowledge, suggesting the possibility of an ever more embracing objective description."

As we shall see, Bohr felt that the insights developed in physics concerning the possibility of encompassing experience that does not fit within old explanatory frameworks have application in many other fields of inquiry.

Bohr [**1954**], p. 68, characterized his idea of a conceptual framework as follows:
"When speaking of a conceptual framework, we refer to the unambiguous logical representations of relations between experiences. ... A special role is played by mathematics which has contributed so decisively to the development of logical thinking, and by which its well-defined abstractions offers invaluable help in expressing harmonious relationships."

What Bohr meant by this statement is that we express our experience by the use of a particular set of concepts some of which are related to each other by explicit or implicit definitions. It is a feature of the conceptual framework of classical physics that a wave, for example, exhibit undulation, distant phase correlations, amplitude, and the like. A wave can also be defined in terms of other concepts such as spatial displacements in time and frequency or in a theory by its laws of propagation and interaction. Quantum theory retains most, but not all, of the basic aspects of the concepts 'particle', 'wave', 'field', 'location', 'momentum', etc., that are present in the usual classical conceptual framework, while rejecting higher level aspects such as classical laws of propagation or classical modes of interaction.

Bohr did not explicitly make a clear distinction between a conceptual framework and a fundamental theory that is expressed within it. But this distinction is implicit in his discussion of the broadening of the conceptual framework (not just a change in theory) necessary for quantum mechanics; he was referring in this discussion to the need to dispense with spacetime pictures

---

[20]Bohr [**1954**], p. 67. See also Bohr [**1949**], p. 65.

and determinism, and the need for the adoption of a less mechanistic view of causality. It is also important to Bohr's theory that a conceptual framework is not replaced, but is widened to encompass new theories required by new experience. Bohr argued on many occasions that the concepts suited for the characterization of experience in our ordinary conceptual framework must be retained if we are to formulate a comprehensible theory. In sum, the classical conceptual framework embodies the metaphysics of classical theory; and this metaphysics is too narrow for quantum theory.[21]

6.5 Reflection 13

In addition to 'conceptual framework', Bohr used 'conceptual pictures' and 'frames of reference', but I shall only use 'conceptual framework' here as most representative of what Bohr was getting at.[22]

In his 1927 lecture, Bohr took note of and discussed the significance of the 'unvisualizability' or 'unpicturizability' of quantum mechanics.[23] By this he meant that we could not visualize the quantum processes according to our usual images based on classical physics, e.g., a particle as a point moving through space on a well-defined and continuous path. In this connection, Bohr used the terms 'spacetime pictures',[24] 'spacetime descriptions',[25] 'visualizable conceptions'[26] and 'wave pictures.'[27] All of these locutions refer to the same basic idea, namely, a description of some phenomenon in familiar terms that is visualizable in the sense of being analogous to a wave or particle process occurring in our ordinary frame of reference. In keeping with my attempt to reduce the terminology to a set of terms representing necessary and distinct ideas in Bohr's theory, the term 'description' will be used for all of them. Thus 'wave pictures' in Bohr's writing will be called 'wave descriptions' in this distillation of his ideas.

Questions concerning the possibilities for giving a coherent, consistent description of atomic objects occupied much of Bohr's thinking. A description for Bohr is a set of statements or formulas related to each other within a conceptual framework that can be applied to the interpretation of data. Because a wave description of an entity involves the concepts of extension, wavelength, amplitude, and phase as identifiable aspects of that entity, to say that a wave description can be properly applied to something means that this thing can be made to exhibit interference or diffraction patterns and will show phase correlations over an extended area. A particle description, on the

---

[21] The discussion of conceptual frameworks will be resumed in Chapter 18.
[22] For these locutions, see Bohr [**1929b**], pp. 112–113, [**1930**], p. 7, [**1937a**], p. 291, and [**1949**], pp. 34, 41.
[23] Bohr [**1925b**], pp. 34–35, 39, [**1927**], pp. 60, 77, 79, 90, [**1929b**], pp. 102, 107, 114.
[24] Bohr [**1927**], pp. 60, 77.
[25] Bohr [**1927**], p. 77.
[26] Bohr [**1929b**], p. 114.
[27] Bohr [**1930**], p. 4, [**1948**], pp. 10–11, [**1949**], p. 34, [**1955**], p. 90.

other hand, involves the used of the ideas of localizability, path, mass, charge, etc.

This approach to the foundations of Bohr's thinking differs significantly from that of Faye [1991]. He, p. 136, for example, characterized Bohr's views in a systematic manner as including the following aspects: "Explicitly or implicitly he rejected an *ontological* defense of the external world, a correspondence theory of truth, a picture theory of knowledge, strong objectivism, and a sharp distinction between subject and object. Instead he adhered to an *epistemological* defense of the external world, a coherence theory of truth, a non-picturing theory of knowledge, weak objectivism, and to there being a blurred distinction between subject and object." From my point of view, Bohr exhibited no systematic general philosophy of this sort. He did not try to "defend" the external world in the ways philosophers sometimes feel is needed; he spoke of 'ordinary truth' and 'deep truth' but not of 'coherent truth', 'correspondence truth', or other philosophical aspects of truth; he talked of the failures in our attempts to visualize atomic processes without rejecting the aspects of knowledge we gain from pictures and analogies that work, and his philosophical view of the subject/object distinction was based on the needs of his physics. Faye, p. 139, later stated that Bohr did require a sharp subject/object distinction for the measuring instrument and the object measured "in spite of their causal inseparability" and he, p. 173, also acknowledged that "Bohr never spoke about truth." Bohr's epistemological requirement of a sharply separated subject and object makes it hard to understand what Faye, p. 138, intended by his previous statement that Bohr meant in reference to observation that the "breakdown of the forms of perception in quantum mechanics, ..., is a special case of the general epistemic situation in that the distinction between subject and object becomes blurred." This raises the question of what other cases there are of this "general epistemic situation" and how we know when we are in it.

6.6 Observation

Bohr usually discussed concrete experiments when expressing his views. By this method, he drew a close relationship between his conception of what he called the 'possibilities of observation' and the 'possibilities of description' (or, sometimes, the 'possibilities of definition'). By the 'possibilities of observation', Bohr was referring to the kinds of observations that could be made on a particular system in a given experimental setting. This makes explicit the standard procedure for establishing that the observation of a quantity is possible by specifying an experiment arrangement and then showing by a theoretical analysis that it can make the measurement required. However, Bohr was emphasizing that this standard procedure has a special meaning when quantum theory is being used in that the choice of an experimental arrangement to measure one quantity may exclude the possibility of measuring some other quantity.

Using this method of analysis, Bohr [1927], p. 81, [1949], first discussed the possibilities for violating the uncertainty relations in certain thought experiments. While, in parallel with von Neumann, Bohr had spoken of an 'initial description' in the account of an experiment, he later dropped it as a separate component and concentrated on the "whole experimental arrangement". From this perspective, the initial conditions reflect our antecedent knowledge of how the system is set up and initialized and this information becomes part of the (possibly changing) boundary conditions in effect during the course of the experiment. As an example, Bohr discussed observation and description with regard to the stationary state of an atom. When dealing with a stationary state, he maintained that we must face a complete renunciation of a time description. In terms of the possibilities of observation, on the other hand, we must keep in mind the nature of the tools with which we can probe the atom:

> "In fact, all our knowledge concerning the internal properties of atoms is derived from experiments on their radiation or collision reactions, such that the interpretation of experimental facts ultimately depends on the abstractions of radiation in free space, and free material particles. Hence, our whole spacetime view of physical phenomena, as well as our definition of energy and momentum, depends ultimately on these abstractions. In judging the application of these auxiliary ideas, we should only demand inner consistency in which connection special regard has to be paid to the possibilities of observation and definition."[28]

Once a suitable experimental arrangement has been chosen, the possibilities of definition for a particular observable refer to the sharpness of the value for that observable in the state attributed to the system.

The possibilities of observation refer to the kinds of experiments that can be used to establish the value of a quantity in a given state. In reference to the stationary state of an electron in an atom, the position of the electron in its orbit as a function of time is completely undetermined. Any attempt to establish the electron position at a given time will require radiation of such short wavelength (high energy) or the use of a suitable particle with high enough momentum that the electron will be moved into a new orbit or completely removed from the atom. In order not to fall into error in this situation, we must pay attention to what is expressed concerning these quantities within the state description in question. From this point of view, the question of

---

[28] Bohr [1955], p. 77. These "abstractions" of free radiation and free particles play an important role in quantum field theory. See the paper on asymptotic quantum field theory by H. Lehman, K. Symanzik and W. Zimmerman [1955].

what position an electron occupies in its orbit at a given time when the atom is in a stationary state cannot even be answered in principle since it cannot be obtained from the quantum description (the wavefunction) of the stationary state. It is therefore not a question of a limitation in measurability, since the measurement of the position of the electron would give some value, but a question of whether this measurement provides us any missing information concerning the electron in the stationary state. As pointed out before, the answer to this question is that making a measurement of the electron position does not provide us with information significant for the determination of the stationary state of the atom or tell us anything further that could be incorporated into the description of the electron in the atom.

Bohr [**1927**], p. 68, stated in his analysis of the concept of observation that there is a "... distinction between the object and agency of measurement, inherent in our very idea of observation." Bohr often characterized this in terms of an interaction between the subject and object of measurement. It is impossible to avoid this "interaction", because some interaction between the object and agency of measurement is necessary in order to make a measurement.[29] But, as Bohr acknowledged in 1935 and thereafter, this interaction need not be a direct physical one. His other statements concerning the impossibility of making a sharp distinction between the subject and object of measurement, and avoiding the term 'interaction', are less subject to misunderstandings on this count. Bohr [**1927**], p. 54, also phrased the problem in terms of the impossibility of ascribing an independent reality to the phenomena and the agencies of observation.

The requirement of a sharp separation between the subject and the object of a measurement in quantum theory has, for Bohr's theory, the consequence that in some way a distinction must be made between them if observations are to be interpreted:

"... the observation problem of quantum physics in no way differs from the classical physical approach. The essentially new feature in the analysis of quantum phenomena is, however, the introduction of a *fundamental distinction between the measuring apparatus and the objects under investigation*. This is a direct consequence of the necessity of accounting for functions of the measuring instruments in purely classical terms, excluding in principle any regard to the quantum of action."[30]

Bohr looked upon making the subject and object distinct as a necessary condition for the interpretation of observation. In Part IV, it is shown that the requirement that the measuring instruments be classically described in fact makes the separation of subject and object.

---

[29]Bohr [**1929a**], p. 43, [**1929b**], p. 114, [**1929c**], pp. 4–5, 11–12, [**1937a**], p. 290, [**1938a**], p. 26, [**1938b**], p. 19, [**1949**], pp. 39–40, 50, 52, [**1962a**], p. 78.
[30]Bohr [**1958b**], pp. 3–4.

Bohr first made an explicit statement of the close relationship between a description and an experimental arrangement in [**1929c**], p. 17: "... the use made of the symbolic expedients will in each individual case depend upon the particular circumstances pertaining to the experimental arrangement ... ." He [**1930**], p. 5, then interpreted his earlier formulation of complementarity (in terms of mutually exclusive descriptions) as referring to mutually exclusive experimental arrangements:

> "Indeed, the spatial continuity of our picture of light propagation and the atomicity of light effects are complementary aspects in the sense that they account for equally important features of the light phenomena which can never be brought into direct contradiction with one another, since their closer analysis in mechanical terms demands mutually exclusive experimental arrangements."

This reference to the experimental arrangement in the description and definition of quantum phenomena became in 1935 and afterwards a requirement for the complete description of the object. Bohr even spoke occasionally (e.g., [**1938b**], p. 25), of individual atomic processes being determined by an interaction between the objects under investigation and the instruments. But he did not go too far in this direction and later warned against misinterpreting phrases such as these.[31] At any rate, the required reference to an experimental arrangement for the description of an observation became one of the foundations of Bohr's theory.[32] The implication of this requirement (Bohr [**1938b**], p. 26) is that "... no results of an experiment concerning a phenomenon which, in principle, lies outside the range of classical physics can be interpreted as giving information about independent properties of objects ...."

In 1938, Bohr [**1938b**], p. 24, introduced the term 'phenomenon' as a technical term that he proposed to mean 'observations made within a definite experimental context.' By 1949, Bohr [**1949**], p. 64, extended this idea to include the macroscopic registration of the results of the experiment. In later essays, he called this latter notion 'closure' and maintained that "the quantum mechanical formalism permits well-defined applications referring only to such closed phenomena."[33] In a closed experiment (Bohr [**1949**], pp. 51, 64), all observations are expressed by "... unambiguous statements referring, for instance, to the registration of the point at which an electron arrives at a photographic plate." This statement was later extended (Bohr [**1954**], p. 73) to "... every atomic phenomenon is closed in the sense that its observation

---

[31] Meyer-Abich [**1965**], pp. 108–109, has emphasized the point that Bohr did not make an operationalist reduction or "definition" of a physical concept in terms of a measuring procedure.

[32] Bohr [**1937a**], p. 291, [**1938a**], p. 26, [**1938b**], pp. 30, [**1949**], p. 50, [**1956**], p. 87.

[33] Bohr [**1954**], p. 73, [**1955**], p. 90. See also Petersen [**1968**] and Rosenfeld [**1967**], p. 124.

is based on registrations obtained by means of suitable amplification devices with irreversible functioning such as, for example, permanent marks on a photographic plate, caused by the penetration of electrons into the emulsion." Bohr [1961], pp. 60–61, [1962b], p. 92, turned his position into an emphasis on the "fundamentally irreversible character of the concept of observation itself." The introduction of the notion of the closure of a phenomenon, with its attendant irreversibility, as an element of observation was the culmination of Bohr's inquiry into the nature of observation and its role in quantum theory begun in 1927. The requirement of an irreversible registration of results moved his theory one step further from the traditional interpretation of physical theories.

6.7 Reflection 14

The progression in Bohr's concept of an observation can be seen as an attempt to ground observation, and the knowledge it produces, solidly in the macroscopic world of experimental arrangements and photographic plates, the behavior of which is presumed to be 'unambiguous'. Out of Bohr's original consideration of the possibilities of observation in relation to the possibilities of description there came first in 1929 a mention of the connection of particular descriptions and certain experimental arrangements. The direct connection between theoretical expressions and particular experimental arrangements, established by an analysis of the possibilities of observation, was made in 1932 when Bohr spoke of mutually exclusive experimental arrangements in reference to measuring complementary quantities. The need for mutually exclusive experimental arrangements for the measurement of variables in complementary descriptions meant that these variables were not accessible to observation simultaneously. This step maintained the accord between the possibilities of observation and the possibilities of description since, according to the uncertainty relations, only one of the two conjugate variables from complementary pictures can be made precise by observation at any one time.

After the EPR paper, Bohr moved to the position that the interpretation of an observation on an atomic system, that is, the attribution of the proper description to the system, requires reference to and specification of the *whole* experimental arrangement. This was an important step in Bohr's thinking because it made the proper description of an atomic system depend on global macroscopic factors rather than just local aspects of parts of the system. His expression of his conception of the subject/object distinction was modified so as to be clearly consistent with this position.

By 1938, Bohr moved to the idea that in order to be definite in reference to an observation, and to avoid the problems associated with superpositions of final states of the 'system plus apparatus' in von Neumann's theory, it is necessary that the experiment be completed and the results registered on a photographic plate or otherwise. By moving to completed observations with irreversible registration of the results of the experiment, and claiming that quantum theory dealt *only* with these 'phenomena', Bohr was able to achieve a completely definite situation without any remaining ambiguity as to the proper description. The quantum description of the system at the end of the experiment before an observation is registered can be employed as a predictive device, while the attribution of the final quantum state description to the observed system becomes an after-the-fact business that depends on which result actually occurred. This final quantum state is useful for future predictions. The price that Bohr had to pay for this definiteness regarding the final outcome was the impossibility of using the quantum state description as a property of the system in the same way classical state descriptions are often used.[34] Thus, the quantum state description was reduced, in Bohr's view, to a "purely symbolic" calculating device for establishing the probabilities of certain final results.

The concept of a closed phenomenon in Bohr's approach to quantum measurement contrasts sharply with the employment of consciousness in von Neumann's account. They are both attempts to give an account of the juncture between the quantum description of the dynamics of microscopic particles and the familiar macroscopic description of the world of our ordinary experience. As such, they represent pivotal points for both theories. A detailed analysis of the differences between Bohr and von Neumann's approach to measurement in quantum mechanics is given in Chapter 15.

6.8 Description

Two kinds of theoretical description occupied much of Bohr's thinking. The first is the spacetime description, or 'picture', of the kinematic motions of particles in the usual sense of classical physics. The second is the causal description in which the momentum and energy of a particle have a definite value over a period of time and for which the conservation laws apply. The spacetime description of the motion of a particle was called by Bohr [**1927**], pp. 54–55, "the idealization of observation" probably on the grounds that working towards increasing accuracy in measurements usually involves fixing more closely the exact spacetime history of a physical system. The causal description was called the 'idealization of definition' on the grounds that when a system is undisturbed by observation or other external interaction, the energy and momentum attributed to the particles in that state can be well-defined—as is the case for a stationary state. These ideas, and others that Bohr associated with them, form the nucleus of what will be introduced later as Bohr's Observation Thesis and Bohr's Description Thesis.

---

[34]I will argue in Chapter 14 that the equilibrium state is often treated this way in thermodynamics and statistical mechanics.

6.8 DESCRIPTION   151

Bohr used the terms 'definition', 'well-defined', 'ambiguous' and 'unambiguous' frequently. He employed the term 'definition', in particular, in several different senses. He [**1927**], pp. 59–60, used the term in one sense in speaking of the uncertainty relations as "... determining the highest possible accuracy in the definition of the energy and momentum of the individuals associated with the wave-field." This 'limitation in definition' is a consequence of the need to use in the wave description a superposition of waves with different frequencies in order to have a limited wave-field (or wave packet) for the description of a particle. But [**1927**], p. 59, this superposition is "... necessarily accompanied by a lack of sharpness in the definition of the corresponding energy and momentum ...." The sense of the term 'definition' that Bohr is using here is that of being well-defined within a description: variables playing a role in the description are well-defined or have a sharp definition if they can have a definite, unique value within that description.

The energy and momentum are well defined for Bohr in a plane wave description, while the position is well defined in a delta measure description. Although they are not states, these descriptions are often used to approximate incoming or outgoing states in an interaction when such an idealization does not do too much violence to the predictions of the evolution of the system in time. A true stationary state is also one for which the energy and momentum are well defined, but the particles involved are not interacting with a changing external environment. This state is of course unobservable. Variables that are not well defined or, equivalently, are not unambiguous are called 'ambiguous' by Bohr.[35]

Bohr also used the term 'definition' to mean 'expressing one concept in terms of others.' This can be done unambiguously (in his sense of the term) only if the concept and the ones defining it can be simultaneously definite within the theory. As an example, Bohr [**1927**], pp. 66, considered the concept of velocity and concluded that the velocity cannot be given in the usual way in terms of two position measurements: "Indeed, the position of an individual at two given moments can be measured with any desired degree of accuracy: but if, from such measurements, we would calculate the velocity of the individual in the ordinary way, it must be clearly realized that we are dealing with an abstraction, from which no unambiguous information concerning the previous or future behavior of the individual can be obtained." Thus the concept of velocity may not be defined with its usual predictive significance in terms of the measured distance divided by the time in the quantum context. It can at best be a concept derived from that of the momentum.

In a third sense of the term 'definition', Bohr [**1923a**], p. 152, [**1927**], p. 54, spoke of the conditions for the 'unambiguous definition of the state of

---

[35]See Bohr [**1949**], p. 40, where he says "... an essential element of ambiguity is involved in ascribing conventional physical attributes to atomic objects ...." See also Bohr [**1936a**], p. 26.

the system.' In this vein he [**1927**], p. 80, remarked that "the conception of a stationary state involves, strictly speaking, the exclusion of all interactions with individuals not belonging to the system." The sense of the term 'definition' being used by Bohr here is that of meeting the conditions required for the application of a particular concept or description. Bohr made this more explicit in subsequent essays, e.g. [**1938b**], p. 24, in discussing experimental conditions: "These conditions, which include the account of the properties and manipulation of all measuring instruments essentially concerned, constitute in fact the only basis for the definition of the concepts by which the phenomena are described." In his reply to Einstein, Podolsky and Rosen, Bohr [**1935**], p. 700, spoke of the experimental arrangement as constituting a part of *"the very conditions which define the possible types of predictions regarding the future behavior of the system."* While this perspective is a natural outgrowth of the considerations that Bohr had used in dealing with the conditions under which certain variables could be defined, e.g., conditions required for a well-defined stationary state in an atom, nevertheless, the *essential* involvement of the macroscopic world in the definition of the states or the variables of atomic physics was an even more radical break with traditional physics.

Bohr's emphasis on the proper choice of the description of quantum phenomena and on meeting the conditions required for the definition of states or variables as a means of avoiding paradoxes in quantum theory shows its value especially in cases in which there are no classical analogs. The tunneling of electrons through potential barriers, i.e., through regions from which they would be classically excluded, involves the localization of the electron first within the potential barrier and later outside it. During this process, we are not allowed, for example, to attribute to the electron any sort of definite energy.[36] This restriction holds true as well for the attribution of properties to entities involved in other 'virtual processes'.

There is a close relation between measurement and two of the senses of definition that Bohr used. In the first place, Bohr [**1938b**], p. 20, stated that a measurement involves the fixing of the external conditions that 'define' the initial state of the system and the possible predictions regarding it: "The essential lesson of the analysis of measurement in quantum theory is thus the emphasis on the necessity of taking the whole experimental arrangement into consideration, in complete conformity with the fact that all unambiguous interpretation of the quantum mechanical formalism involves the fixation of the external conditions, defining the initial state of the atomic system concerned and the character of possible predictions as regards subsequent observable properties of that system." In the second place, a measurement can change

---

[36]Bohr's early concern with the problem of attributing independent properties to atomic objects is in [**1929b**], p. 112. See also Bohr [**1938b**], p. 26, [**1949**], p. 58. Bohr also discussed tunneling in connection with the disintegration of nuclei in the 1929b reference.

the description of an atomic system and thus serve to make a variable well defined (or less well-defined). In other words, we can measure the variable or some variable it depends on and use this information as the basis for a new description of the atomic system.

One possible misconception of Bohr's use of 'definition' in reference to the experimental arrangement (that "serves to define the conditions under which phenomena appear") is that Bohr was being operationalistic and that the apparatus itself defines the classical concepts in application to the atomic system.[37] But this is not an accurate statement of either Bohr's views or those of Heisenberg [**1927**]. Bohr did not reduce the definition of concepts to particular experiments or even to an equivalence class of experiments. Rather, as we shall see, he established that a particular experimental arrangement is suitable for measuring a certain variable by analyzing it classically and then concluding that it was suitable for this purpose.[38]

As pointed out in the first chapter, Bohr in 1922 viewed the need to use classical concepts as a feature of physics that would be superseded later. And in Bohr [**1925b**], p. 48, he noted that Heisenberg's quantum theory avoids the use of spacetime description of the motion of the particles and thereby avoids the difficulties of the mechanical picture. The implication is that new concepts might come out of this. But by 1927, Bohr [**1927**], p. 53, maintained that the interpretation of experimental material rests *essentially* upon classical concepts. He [**1929a**], pp. 24–25, further amplified this view: "It lies in the nature of physical observation, nevertheless, that all experience must ultimately be expressed in terms of classical concepts, neglecting the quantum of action." And [**1929c**], p. 16, it is the application of classical concepts that "... makes possible the connection between the quantum symbolism and the content of experience."

In Bohr's theory it is classical concepts that provide meaning for the physical concepts of quantum theory:

"Indeed, the inevitability of using, for atomic systems a mode of description which is fundamentally statistical arises from a closer investigation of the information which we are able to obtain by direct measurement of these phenomena and of the meaning which we may ascribe, in this connection, to the application of the fundamental physical concepts. ... we must bear in mind that the meaning of these concepts is wholly tied up with the customary ideas ... "[39]

---

[37] Rosenfeld [**1955**], p. 79, [**1965**], p. 243, seems to hold this point of view. See also the discussion in Howard [**1994**].

[38] See Meyer-Abich [**1965**], p. 166, for a brief discussion of these points.

[39] Bohr [**1929b**], pp. 113–144. Redlich [**1962**], [**1968**] has maintained for similar reasons that the basic concepts in all science must be expressed in ordinary language.

Bohr [**1937a**], p. 251, went further and claimed that classical concepts would always be necessary for the interpretation of quantum theory and its successors:

> "No more is it likely that the fundamental concepts of the classical theories will ever become superfluous for the description of physical experience. The recognition of the indivisibility of the quantum of action, and the determination of its magnitude, not only depend on an analysis of measurements based on classical concepts, but it continues to be the application of these concepts alone which makes it possible to relate the symbolism of the quantum theory to the data of experience. At the same time, however, we must bear in mind that the possibility of an *unambiguous* use of these fundamental concepts solely depends upon the self-consistency of the classical theories from which they are derived and that, therefore, the limits imposed upon the application of these concepts are naturally determined by the extent to which we may, in our account of the phenomena, disregard the element that is foreign to classical theories and symbolized by the quantum of action."[40]

Bohr [**1929c**], p. 16, further emphasized the importance of classical concepts in another way: "... only with the help of classical ideas is it possible to ascribe an unambiguous meaning to the results of observation."

6.9 Reflection 15

A possible objection to Bohr's contention concerning the role and necessity of classical concepts is that we are trying to explain newly discovered features of matter and radiation using old classical concepts. On this view, the conceptual problem comes, so to speak, out of our attempt to force new conceptual wine into old conceptual bottles. Eddington, for example, proposed the term "wavicle" for entities that could function as both particles and as waves, but is not reducible to either, while Bungé [**1967a**], pp. 235, 246, proposed the term "quanton" for such an entity. One can, of course, give a name to an entity that sometimes exhibits wave properties and sometimes particle properties. But such a procedure does not by itself provide a solution to the problems involved in the wave-particle duality. The real question is how one can understand an entity that interacts with a whole diffraction grating in experiments in which wave effects are being observed, but whenever it is absorbed by a photographic plate or scintillation counter it always behaves as if it is located at a point. Giving an entity that behaves in this way a name, calling it a new concept, and pointing to the wavefunction as its description, does not solve the problem.

---

[40]See also Bohr [**1938a**], p. 26, [**1938b**], pp. 20, 22, [**1949**], p. 50, [**1956**], p. 87, for some examples among many.

The retention of classical descriptions and concepts is one of the most important features of Bohr's theory. At the expense of the bifurcation of the interpretation of the theory for epistemological reasons between the macroscopic level and the microscopic level, Bohr has gained important benefits. First, he has available to him descriptions that do not have the ambiguity (to use his terminology) associated with quantum descriptions. He does not have to worry about problems of interpretation concerning superpositions of wavefunctions associated with measuring instruments or problems connected with two separate observers 'reducing the wavefunction' at different times. Second, Bohr has available to him as a matter of principle all those descriptions of macroscopic instruments provided by classical theory that, according to his position, are fully adequate when the instruments are suited for use in making observations. This means that he has built a completeness into his theory in that, from his point of view, every conceivable experimental arrangement of macroscopic instruments can be adequately described by classical theory.[41]

---

[41]See Bohr [**1949**], p. 57, [**1957a**], p. 99.

CHAPTER 7

Bohr's Quantum Theory

Bohr's approach to quantum mechanics differed from that of his contemporaries and later textbook writers. While many of these paid lip service to his work, and subscribed to what they called the Copenhagen Interpretation, it seems that few of them really understood how profoundly Bohr's views differed from those considered to be standard in quantum mechanics. When Bohr embraced the wave-particle duality in the mid 1920s, he did not look back. He took on the task of providing an epistemology with this duality as a central feature and rejected those interpretations, some of which were offered under the umbrella of the Copenhagen Interpretation, that favored particles or waves at the expense of the other.

7.1 Formulations of Complementarity

Bohr considered complementarity to be the central feature of his work. It was presented for the first time in Bohr's 1927 Como lecture and he expanded upon it during the rest of his life.[1] He [**1929c**], p. 19, recalled that he had used the term 'reciprocity' instead of 'complementarity' in [**1929a**], p. 95, but rejected it because it was already used in physics with a different meaning.[2] Bohr viewed the concept of complementarity as having general significance in epistemology and proposed that it can contribute to the solution of problems in widely different disciplines. He used slightly different locutions in characterizing complementarity in his earlier work as compared to his later work. As indicated in the previous chapter, there was a subtle development in Bohr's conception of observation and description over the years. This development was accompanied by changes in the formulation of complementarity, which do not, however, represent a substantial change in the idea itself.[3]

Bohr's views on complementarity grew out of the difficulties he faced trying to reconcile the problems inherent in the wave-particle duality. He repeatedly compared the wave picture of the propagation of light or material particles to the localization of their energy (and mass and charge for material particles) when they are observed. He used the double slit experiment, particles striking a photographic plate, and the stationary state of an electron in an atom as touchstones for his ideas. He always avoided discussions based on the mathematical formalism typified, for example, by von Neumann's discussion of the measurement problem. In this way, he tried to keep his ideas as closely connected as possible with actual experiments and their results.

Bohr [**1927**], p. 54, began his Como lecture by pointing out that the "quantum postulate" attributes to any quantum transition a wholeness not further analyzable in spacetime, and this "implies that any observation of atomic phenomena will involve an interaction with the agency of observation not to be neglected." Bohr [**1927**], pp. 54–55, used the reciprocal relationship between the 'spacetime coordination' (successive position measurements) and the 'claim of causality' (validity of classical dynamical and conservation laws) in reference to the stationary state of an atom to introduce complementarity: "The very nature of quantum theory thus forces us to regard the spacetime coordination and the claim of causality, the union of which characterizes the

---

[1] See Meyer-Abich [**1965**] and Jammer [**1966**], [**1974**], for information on the historical and philosophical background of Bohr's development of the idea of complementarity.

[2] In a letter, Bohr [**Arch**], BSC 20, Bohr to Heisenberg, 5/20/30, Bohr told Heisenberg that he was staggering between the terms reciprocity and complementarity to express his ideas and asks Heisenberg what he thinks.

[3] General discussions of complementarity have been given by Weizsäcker [**1952**], Rosenfeld [**1961b**], [**1967**], Petersen [**1963**], and Meyer-Abich [**1965**]. Specific logical analyses have been given by H. Bedau and P. Oppenheim [**1961**] and Elsasser [**1969**]. Some criticisms are contained in Feyerabend [**1958a**], [**1962**], [**1964**], and in Popper [**1934**], [**1967**]. More recent discussions are contained in the books on Bohr referred to in Chapter 1.

classical theories, as complementary but exclusive features of the description . . . ."

In discussing complementarity, Bohr spoke in this same essay of "the complementary nature of descriptions,"[4] "complementary possibilities of description,"[5] "complementary pictures,"[6] and "complementary formulations of a problem."[7] The first of these two locutions played a role in his later work while the last two did not reappear. Bohr used both 'description' and 'picture', throughout most of his writings.[8] In keeping with my identification of 'description' and 'picture' in Bohr's work, I shall combine the first two formulations and say that at this point Bohr was concerned with 'complementary descriptions'.

In his reply to Einstein, Podolsky and Rosen, Bohr [**1935**], pp. 699, 700, used the phrases 'complementary classical concepts' and 'complementary physical quantities', but he did not use these forms in his writings again; and I shall argue below that these forms do not fit his general conception of complementarity. He briefly used a form like "incompatible information or experience obtained in mutually exclusive experimental arrangements" in 1937 and 1938.[9] In 1938, just after introducing the technical term 'phenomenon', Bohr [**1938b**], pp. 24–25, characterized complementarity as follows: ". . . phenomena defined by different concepts, corresponding to mutually exclusive experimental arrangements, can unambiguously be regarded as complementary aspects of the whole obtainable evidence concerning the objects under investigation." Bohr used 'complementary phenomena' and similar forms on several later occasions.[10]

A general statement concerning complementarity was given in a work on human cultures and philosophy by Bohr [**1938a**], p. 26:

"Information regarding the behavior of an atomic object obtained under definite experimental conditions may, however, according to a terminology often used in atomic physics, be adequately characterized as *complementary* to any information about the same object obtained by some other experimental arrangement excluding the fulfillment of the first condition. Although such kinds of information cannot be combined into a single picture by means of ordinary concepts, they represent indeed equally essential aspects of any knowledge of the object in question which can be obtained in this domain."

---

[4]Bohr [**1927**], pp. 57, 59, 63, 68, 73, 78.
[5]Bohr [**1927**], p. 78.
[6]Bohr [**1927**], pp. 56, 84.
[7]Bohr [**1927**], p. 75.
[8]*complementary descriptions:* Bohr [**1929a**], p. 96, [**1930**], p. 377, [**1930**], p. 10, [**1935**], p. 700, [**1948**], pp. 11, 16, [**1949**], p. 55, [**1961**], p. 61; *complementary pictures:* Bohr [**1930**], p. 350, [**1937a**], p. 294, [**1938a**], p. 26, [**1938b**], p. 18, [**1949**], p. 39.
[9]Bohr [**1937a**], p. 291, [**1938a**], p. 26.
[10]Bohr [**1948**], pp. 11, 15, [**1949**], pp. 40, 41, [**1955**], p. 90, [**1957a**], p. 99.

By 1955, he [**1955**], p. 90, shortened this to: "However great the contrasts exhibited by atomic phenomena under different experimental conditions, such phenomena must be termed complementary in the sense that each is well defined and that together they exhaust all definable knowledge about the objects concerned." There is a definite progression in the formulation of complementarity from the initial 'spacetime coordination versus the claim of causality' in 1927, to the need for 'mutually exclusive experimental arrangements' to 'complementary phenomena.' This progression was attached to the progression in Bohr's concept of observation, and was impelled by his idea that observational knowledge by definition must be unambiguous.

The movement in Bohr's formulation of complementarity from 'spacetime descriptions versus claim of causality' to 'mutually exclusive experimental arrangements' came because he was trying to ground his position as much as possible on a direct analysis of the possibilities of observation. If the accurate measurement of complementary quantities really does require mutually exclusive experimental arrangements, then Bohr has established the strong connection he was seeking. To establish the connection between complementary descriptions and mutually exclusive experimental arrangements without being circular, however, is not at all easy as we shall see below. Bohr's next step from 'mutually exclusive experimental arrangements' to 'complementary phenomena' was a consequence of the progression already noted with respect to the discussion of quantum observations and descriptions in terms of quantum phenomena.

This statement of the final point of Bohr's views is not universally recognized, but Bohr confirmed it himself. Meyer-Abich [**1965**], pp. 155–157 discussed a letter sent by Bohr to von Weizsäcker objecting to von Weizsäcker's interpretation of Bohr's position on complementarity. Bohr stated in this letter that in the meaning he used for the word, "... complementarity can only be between phenomena." Meyer-Abich examined this position and concluded that complementarity between "phenomenons" is compatible with the development of Bohr's thinking.[11] On the other hand, Bohr's claim that in 1927 he had intended complementarity only between phenomena is not historically accurate since, as Meyer-Abich has pointed out, 'spacetime description' and 'claim of causality' are not phenomena. This conception of complementary phenomena also reflects Bohr's contention, expressed on several occasions, that the experimental arrangement participates in the appearance of the phenomenon itself.

Weizsäcker [**1955**], in a discussion of the philosophical aspects of complementarity, had distinguished two forms that he called *parallel* and *circular* complementarity, respectively. He, p. 521, expressed this idea in terms of

---

[11] Meyer-Abich preferred the term phenomenons to phenomena as the plural for Bohr's concept to distinguish it from the standard use of this term. Because Bohr uses the form 'phenomena' as the plural for his concept, I will not adopt Meyer-Abich's usage.

'complementary concepts' and said that such concepts are in a parallel relation if they are in the same conceptual structure (picture) and are in a circular relationship if they are in different conceptual structures. Weizsäcker discussed Pauli's [1933] example, using position and momentum as two complementary classical concepts operating in the same picture (the particle picture), as an example of parallel complementarity. Another example he gave is the use of 'position' and 'wave number' that he felt were complementary aspects of the wave picture. He stated that 'position' does not seem the same in both cases since these are different pictures. The complementarity of 'particle' and 'wave', on the other hand, he [1955], pp. 522–523, considered as an example of circular complementarity. In his analysis of Bohr's complementarity between 'spacetime coordination' and 'claim of causality', Weizsäcker [1955], pp. 525, 527, concluded that this is "... exactly the complementarity between describing nature by classical concepts and by the ψ function."[12] This example, and the complementarity between what he called 'particle-place' and 'de Broglie wave-momentum', are examples of circular complementarity in Weizsäcker's view.

Bohr did not accept Weizsäcker's analysis of his views because for him it was essential that the incompatibility between complementary phenomena be reflected in an incompatibility of the experiments associated with them so contradictory results could never be exhibited simultaneously in one experiment. Two concepts themselves could never be in direct conflict as such because a concept never functions alone in Bohr's theory.

In an observation designed to fix the value of a variable representing a concept, an *appropriate* experimental arrangement is required. The judgment that an experimental arrangement is appropriate already involves other aspects of the situation in a necessary way. For example, to show that the γ-ray microscope is a valid way of measuring the position of a particle, from Bohr's point of view, requires showing that the apparatus is classically suited to this task. Initially no quantum limitations are assumed in the classical calculation demonstrating that the instrument can serve the proposed purpose. It is then shown that the accuracy attributed to the instrument in the measurement is compatible with any quantum limitations there are on using it in this way and that no other classical limitations on it are being violated.[13] The judgment of whether two concepts are incompatible in application really requires reference to the descriptions in which they play a role and reference to the experimental arrangements deemed suitable to measure them. To speak of complementarity between conjugate concepts, even though Bohr [1935] once

---

[12]Heisenberg [1955], p. 27, also made a similar statement about the same time. Murdoch [1985], p. 67, and Faye [1991], pp. 144–145, have also made a similar distinction between "wave-particle complementarity" and "kinematic-dynamic" complementarity.

[13]An example of a calculation of this type for the γ-ray microscope appears in G. R. Allcock [1969], III, pp. 314–316.

did so, is then elliptical at best and does not constitute an adequate account of the situation as regards Bohr's later views.

Weizsäcker's analysis in terms of a classical description versus a quantum mechanical one and his characterization of Bohr's position in terms of circular complementarity, i.e., concepts from two conceptual structures, is also not a correct analysis of Bohr.[14] In cases of complementarity, the incompatibility is demonstrated within the classical conceptual framework by associating the observations, obtained under mutually exclusive experimental arrangements, with incompatible classical descriptions. On the other hand, there should never be any conflict as to when the quantum description is appropriate. Except when instruments are being used for the purpose of making measurements, the quantum description is always appropriate. Bohr made this point often.[15] At times, however, when the quantum effects are negligible compared to the values of the variables of the system, that is, the macroscopic case in general, the classical description may be used.[16] Thus Weizsäcker's approach does not at all reflect Bohr's view of complementarity or capture its meaning. There is still a sense, however, in which an analysis similar to Weizsäcker's may be useful. This is with respect to quantities without a classical analog, like electron spin, that have components that do not commute. I shall return to this in the next section.

In analyzing a situation with respect to the possibility that it might exhibit complementarity, care must be exercised that complementarity not be confused with what Grünbaum [**1957**] has called 'operational incompatibility'. Operational incompatibility with respect to two physical concepts refers to the unavailability of a single experimental arrangement for the measurement of the two quantities. As Grünbaum has pointed out, operational incompatibility is not sufficient for theoretical incompatibility of the sort required by complementarity. It would therefore be a mistake to claim that incompatibilities in the 'possibilities of observation' for two variables imply or determine incompatibilities in the 'possibilities of description' using them. As an example consider measuring the positions and momenta of all the particles in a gram of a gas under standard conditions. Although this measurement cannot possibly be made, there is no theoretical limitation in classical physics on doing so. There is always the possibility that another method of measurement may provide us with the information. This means that technical

---

[14] Abner Shimony has pointed out (private communication) that many textbooks, e.g., Bohm [**1951**], have given accounts of Bohr's view of complementarity similar to Weizsäcker's.

[15] See Bohr [**1930**], pp. 9–10, [**1949**], p. 57, [**1961**], p. 39.

[16] This is not always the case. Fritz London [**1938**] discussed correlations over macroscopic distances for fluids near absolute zero. Such effects, as well as many other "macroscopic correlation effects," have been observed. See Shimony [**1963**], p. 764, and W. F. Vinen [**1968**]. There is a more recent discussions in Leggett [**1985**], [**1998**] and Shimony's [**1998**] comments on Leggett's work.

and physical limitations on measuring two quantities in the same system are necessary but not sufficient grounds for calling two theoretical descriptions complementary.

In summary, two quantum descriptions of an entity are *complementary* if[17]

(i) they meet the requirements of a description for Bohr;
(ii) the concepts being measured have classical counterparts;
(iii) they are both associated with possible observations that meet the requirements of an observation for Bohr; and
(iv) the classical observation statements associated with the quantum descriptions by the classically described experimental arrangements are incompatible.

The incompatibility of the classical descriptions referred to in (iv) is that of attributing to an entity contradictory classical properties (e.g., extension over a macroscopic volume versus localization in a microscopic volume).

One attempt to generalize complementarity within quantum mechanics was given by Elsasser.[18] Elsasser [**1937**], p. 989, spoke of a complementarity between the complexity of a system, as measured by its degrees of freedom, and the possibility of preparing it (to use a modern terminology) in a pure quantum mechanical state.[19] This alleged complementarity is like that mentioned above. It is a case of operational incompatibility rather than a genuine case of complementarity. In examining the possibilities of observation, there is no *in principle* or theoretical reason from Bohr's point of view why a complex system cannot be viewed as in a pure state if so desired. Similarly, the possibilities for description imply no such limitation either. I conclude that this suggestion cannot be accepted.

7.2 The Epistemological Significance of Complementarity

Not every element that plays a role in classical mechanics can be defined directly in quantum mechanics. The velocity, for example, can only be defined indirectly in terms of its relation to the momentum operator. Bohr [**1927**], pp. 65–66, was aware of this and considered it a consequence of the general distinction between the kinematic and the dynamic variables used to describe the system. Bohr focused on the tension between the sharpness with which the 4-dimensional kinematic spacetime position vector associated

---

[17] Bedau and Oppenheim [**1961**] have given a similar statement.

[18] See Elsasser [**1937**], [**1968**], [**1969**]. See also an interesting formulation of Edwin T. Jaynes [**1957b**], p. 176.

[19] Bohr [**Arch**], Set I, 5/10/60, disagreed with Elsasser's view. Bohr stated that it is just the "inexhaustible complexity" of organisms that leads to complementarity. The question of what it means to prepare a system in a particular kind of state assumes that the state is a property of the system and is foreign to Bohr's thinking. The question of whether the distinction between pure states and mixtures makes sense will be discussed in QIS.

with an atomic individual can be defined and the sharpness with which the dynamic momentum-energy vector can be simultaneously defined in quantum mechanics. This tension is expressed [**1927**], pp. 60–61, in the uncertainty relations as a reciprocal limitation on "... the maximum sharpness of definition of the space-time and energy-momentum vectors associated with individuals." Furthermore, " ... the general character of this relation makes it possible to a certain extent to reconcile the conservation laws with the spacetime coordination of observations, the idea of a coincidence of well-defined events in a spacetime point being replaced by that of unsharply defined individuals within finite spacetime regions."

The kinematic variables refer to fixing the system in some frame of reference external to the system. It is this information that allows us to locate the system and follow its motion. The dynamical variables, on the other hand, refer to the conserved quantities carried by the atomic entity and are responsible in a causal sense for its future motion. The symmetry in the characterizations of the kinematic and dynamic variables and the reciprocal limitation on how closely they can be mutually defined were a recurring theme in Bohr's thinking in the form of the 'spacetime description' versus the 'claim of causality'.

Bohr [**1927**], p. 68, located the origin of complementarity in the implications of the quantum postulate (individuality, wholeness) and on the need for a sharp distinction between the object and agency of measurement. The concept of complementarity emerged initially from a consideration of wave and particle descriptions in reference to the "conditions of observation" in the quantum domain.[20] Bohr [**1938b**], p. 27, [**1949**], p. 41, later characterized complementarity as a rational or consistent generalization of the ideal of causality, i.e., of the ideal of a complete causal spacetime description. These different aspects were finally synthesized [**1955**], p. 91, to "... the notion of complementarity points to the logical conditions for description and comprehension of experience in atomic physics."

Beginning in 1927, Bohr looked at the problem of observation in quantum mechanics as being analogous to that in special relativity. He repeated often that one must pay attention to the situation in which observations are made, just as in using relativity theory one must relate observations made to some particular frame of reference. He went on to argue that just as the paradoxes of relativity theory are avoided by reference to the framework within which observations are made, so too in quantum theory the experimental arrangement serves to define the "reference frame" within which observations are made and interpreted. Moreover, Bohr went on, the need in relativity theory to limit the application of some of our concepts in physical situations is paralleled in quantum theory. Finally, I might add, just as relativity has brought the classically unrelated concepts of space and time into an intimate

---

[20]Bohr [**1954**], p. 73, [**1956**], p. 87, [**1958b**], p. 4.

relationship, quantum theory has brought spacetime and momentum-energy also into a non-classical reciprocal relationship.

Bohr viewed the change from classical theory to relativity theory and to quantum theory as examples of rational generalizations of classical theory. Bohr obviously had correspondence arguments in mind when he spoke in this way. As Bohr [1929c], p. 6, observed, and Hooker [1972], p. 147, has emphasized, in each case the departure from classical physics was marked by the pervasive appearance of a small constant of nature $(1/c, h)$ assumed not to play a role in the basic classical laws. Bohr's real emphasis in his reference to relativity theory was on the relativization of the "position of the observer" in these two theories. In relativity the limitation on universal simultaneity was accompanied by the fact that events with a space-like separation could have their time order reversed by a coordinate transformation. Similarly, complementarity places a limit, needed to avoid errors, on combining concepts in quantum mechanics.

Bohr felt that the notion of complementarity could contribute significantly in helping solve fundamental conceptual problems in many different disciplines.[21] The usefulness of the concept of complementarity both to physics and to other disciplines lies in [1957], p. 1, "... the opportunities which time and again it has offered for examination and refinement of our conceptual tools." And [1954], pp. 78–79, "In return for the renunciation of accustomed demands on explanation, it offers a logical means of comprehending wider fields of experience, necessitating proper attention to the placing of the object-subject separation."

Because he characterized complementarity in terms of a renunciation of accustomed demands on explanation and as a statement of the impossibility of encompassing the descriptions associated with every possible observation that can be made on atomic systems within one descriptive framework, Bohr has been accused by some critics of antiscientific dogmatism.[22] But Bohr was careful to point out that there is no renunciation involved as far as the analysis of the situation is concerned: "The notion of complementarity does not imply any renunciation of detailed analysis limiting the scope of inquiry, but simply stresses the character of objective description, independent of subjective judgment, in any field of experience where unambiguous communication essentially involves regard to the circumstances in which evidence is obtained."[23] Furthermore, complementarity places no restrictions on our ability to arrange our experimental apparatus as we like. It is the limitation

---

[21] See Holton [1970], pp. 1046–1055, for additional evidence of Bohr's view that complementarity would be found to be a feature of descriptions in all fields of human inquiry.

[22] See, for example, Popper [1934], p. 454, Feyerabend [1961], Bungé [1967a], p. 235, [1956], p. 142. Meyer-Abich [1965], pp. 177–178, defended Bohr against these charges. See also Hooker [1972], p. 127, and Rosenfeld [1963b].

[23] Bohr [1961], p. 60. See also Bohr [1937b], p. 19, [1956], p. 87.

7.2 THE EPISTEMOLOGICAL SIGNIFICANCE OF COMPLEMENTARITY

on our ability to measure exactly certain quantities simultaneously that constitutes the limitation embodied in complementarity: "Far from restricting our efforts to put questions to nature in the form of experiments, the notion of *complementarity* simply characterizes the answers we can receive by such inquiry, whenever the interaction between the measuring instruments and objects forms an integral part of the phenomena."[24]

Bohr's concern with the nature of physical explanation recurred several times in connection with his views on complementarity. He spoke [1930], p. 7, of a "revision in the foundation of mechanics, ... , extending to the very idea of physical explanation ...." On another occasion, Bohr [1949], p. 39, spoke of the phenomena as "transcending the scope of classical physical explanation." In connection with the wave-particle duality and the conceptual problems associated with that, Bohr [1955], p. 90, made his position clearer: "Here, of course, we seek a physical explanation in the customary sense, but all we can demand in a new field of experience is the removal of any apparent contradiction." Not all physicists shared Bohr's views on the expendability of traditional notions of explanation nor did they agree with Bohr on the need to dispense with them so thoroughly in quantum mechanics.[25]

For Bohr, the indispensability of classical concepts was also indirectly related to complementarity. In this view, classical concepts form a "given" in the epistemological situation that cannot be further analyzed because we need to use them, and, according to Bohr, the use of these concepts and the analysis of them are complementary:

"We here come upon an fundamental feature in the general problem of knowledge, and we must realize that, by the very nature of the matter, we shall always have last recourse to a word picture in which the words themselves are not further analyzed ... we must, indeed, remember that the nature of our consciousness brings about a complementary relationship, in all domains of knowledge, between the analysis of a concept and its immediate application."[26]

The 'use' versus the 'analysis' of concepts mentioned in the quotation is an interesting epistemological claim that will be pursued below.

Some workers in quantum mechanics proposed that the mathematical concepts of quantum mechanics (e.g., the wavefunction) and a new form of logic, the so-called "quantum logic", might provide the new concepts that, if properly understood, would solve the physical and philosophical problems

---

[24]Bohr [1958b], p. 4.
[25]R. A. Millikan [1935], p. 266, seems representative of many "pragmatic" physicists in his statement: "Just why light quanta, passing through holes or slits, or lenses or gratings or any kind distribute themselves so as to produce in all cases precisely the patterns computed by the classical wave theory seems to transcend at present *physical* explanation." Hooker [1970] expressed similar views. See also Einstein [1949] and Schrödinger [1952].
[26]Bohr [1929c], p. 20. This position is reminiscent of Wittgenstein [1922], pp. 15, 30, 37, 45.

of quantum mechanics.[27] But Bohr felt that new concepts of the kind useful in the solution of problems of quantum mechanics could not come from mathematics (or anywhere else) because mathematics and logic are "... not a special branch of knowledge based on the accumulation of experience, but rather ... a refinement of general language, supplementing it with appropriate tools to represent relations for which ordinary verbal expression is imprecise or too cumbersome."[28] For this reason, and others given in the preceding chapter regarding a "third concept", Bohr [1948], p. 16, [1960a], p. 3, rejected the introduction of three-valued logics recommended by Reichenbach [1944], p. 145ff, and Weizsäcker [1955], p. 102.

7.3 Bohr's Quantum Theory

I will now assemble the elements of Bohr's quantum theory. This involves consideration of how the conditions on description and observation are to be met as well as a statement of the role of complementarity in application. The goal is to introduce these concepts in the way Bohr did and to discuss them in the context of the dialogue between those who developed the ideas at the time. In Part IV, more detailed comparisons will be made between the views of von Neumann and Bohr.

The scientific problem that complementarity posed for Bohr was how to characterize a quantum state and how to interpret an observation so that we are not faced with contradictions or inconsistencies. Bohr looked at how an experiment actually functions and examined the role of the quantum state as the theoretical description of the system in that context to find the answer. As mentioned in Section 5.8, to make a solution of Schrödinger's equation definite, the proper initial and boundary conditions must be supplied. These are not part of the quantum system but are part of the experimental arrangement. His answer to the problem of making a quantum state definite in an experiment was to make the classical description of the experimental arrangement an integral part of the quantum description. By this deceptively simple solution, unanticipated in classical physics, he was then able to show in each case that the contradictory aspects of complementary quantities could never be simultaneously exhibited because they required different experimental arrangements.

A measurement is usually made by setting up an instrument to provide a particular potential field or specific barriers that serve to sort out various possible system states. The Stern-Gerlach experiment, with its inhomogeneous magnetic field, is an example of the use of special potentials. The macroscopic boundary conditions provided by the slits and screens makes

---

[27]Issues connected with quantum logic were introduced by Birkhoff and von Neumann [1936].

[28]Bohr [1960a], p. 9. See also Bohr [1961], p. 60.

the double-slit experiment determinate. In considering wave-particle complementarity, Bohr showed that adding detectors to the double slit experiment, so that the slit a photon or particle has passed through can be determined, changes the experimental arrangement in such a way that it is no longer suitable for exhibiting interference effects. This demonstrates the tight linkage between the experimental arrangement, the quantum state, and the interpretation of observations to which Bohr was referring.

Although a description is not restricted for Bohr in the same way that an observation is, there must be some way to connect descriptions to experiments and observations. Bohr looked to the role of descriptive elements in classical theory to provide a guide to the relationships between concepts, their use in theoretical descriptions, and their association with experiments. This means that those concepts of quantum theory without classical analogs present a special difficulty for Bohr's theory and occupy a special place in it. Bohr and those who worked with him were aware of the special theoretical status of these concepts in Bohr's theory. This led to a many discussions of the concept of electron spin that, in spite of its name, has no classical analog.

Quantum Concepts without Classical Analogs: Spin.

The question of how to understand and deal theoretically with quantum concepts that do not have a classical analog arose in the late 1920s. The concept of electron spin had emerged out of an analysis of the Zeeman effect in the spectra of atoms. The orbital angular momentum of the electrons is an integral multiple of $\hbar$ and would lead to a spectral multiplet with an odd number of members in atoms with an odd number of electrons. However, it was observed that the multiplets of these atoms had an even number of members. This implies that the total angular momentum j of the atom, which gives rise to a multiplet with $2j + 1$ members, is half-integral. This half-integral component of the angular momentum of the atom contributed by each electron was given the name electron spin by Uhlenbeck and Goudsmidt in 1925. The name was based on an analogy between the magnetic moment of the electron, which couples to the magnetic field in the Zeeman effect experiment to split the multiplet, and the generation of a magnetic field by a circulating charge.

The spin of a point entity cannot have a classical interpretation. As the radius of the spinning entity is reduced to zero, the spin itself will either vanish or at some point the velocity of a point on the surface of the entity will exceed the speed of light. Neither of these alternatives is suitable for attempting to interpret the spin of an electron even if the radius of the electron is greater than zero (assuming some sense can be made out of this statement in reference to an electron). Bohr [**1929c**], p. 13, stated his position explicitly: "The fact that experiments, which so far have been explained by ascribing a magnetic moment to electrons, have been given a natural interpretation by Dirac's theory ..., is, indeed, equivalent to saying that it is not possible to detect the magnetic moment of the electron by experiments based upon a direct observation of its motion."[29] The question of the possibility of the direct observation of the magnetic moment of the electron is thus a direct test of one aspect of Bohr's views.

Pauli [1932] showed quantitatively at the 1930 Solvay congress that the magnetic moment of the free electron could not be measured by (a) arresting an oriented electron by a field, (b) using a Stern-Gerlach experiment with free electrons, (c) compensating the Lorentz force on the magnetic moment by an electric field, or (d) measuring directly the magnetic field produced by the electron.[30]

In his 1933 *Handbüch* article, Pauli [1933], pp. 236–240, demonstrated that the nonrelativistic wave mechanics of particles with spin, which includes the Thomas precession, is a first approximation of the Dirac equation. This gave support to what Pauli, p. 242, called a thesis of Bohr's: "The spin moment of the electron can never be separated uniquely from the path moment in experiments in which the classical concept of the particle path is applicable." The separation into diverging paths of a collection of moving charged particles with spin in an inhomogeneous magnetic field is due to the coupling of the spin with the gradient of the magnetic field. The impossibility of observing the electron spin using this method is a consequence of the uncertainty relations for the particle locations and momenta when one attempts to define their paths in quantum mechanics with sufficient precision to observe this effect. Pauli [1933], p. 242, also referred to his work as a "confirmation of the Bohr thesis" with respect to the measurability of the electron in " ... *those experiments to which the classical concept of the particle path is applicable."*

In later essays, Bohr warned against being fooled by the term "intrinsic spin" in reference to an electron. He emphasized that measurements involving the "spin" are not concerned with direct measurements of classically defined action or angular momentum. On the contrary, these results " ... are logically interpretable only by consistent use of the mathematical formalism of quantum theory."[31] Pauli's results indicated that Bohr's approach to the question of the interpretation of quantum theory has a deep consistency.[32]

---

[29] See also Bohr [1930], pp. 368–369.

[30] See also Nevill Francis Mott [1929] and Charles Galton Darwin [1931a]. Calculations supporting Bohr's argument are given in Mott and Harrie F. W. Massey [1965], pp. 214–219. R. Schiller [1967], p. 154, objected to the Bohr-Pauli results but did not provide a mathematical or other analysis to prove his point. For a straightforward discussion of Pauli's 1930 Solvay conference calculation of the unmeasurability of the magnetic moment (and therefore spin) of a free electron, see Hendrik B. G. Casimir [1985], pp. 14–16.

[31] Bohr [1961], p. 61. See also Bohr [1962b], p. 94.

[32] Pauli [1933], pp. 188–189, has given a bibliography of papers on spin and Pauli's 1925 exclusion principle. This includes the work of Dirac and Heisenberg in 1926 on the quantum mechanics of identical particles. It also includes the work of Bose in 1924 and Einstein in 1924 and 1925 on the statistics of particles with symmetric states and Fermi and then Dirac in 1926 on the statistics of particles with antisymmetric states. Wigner

The spin of an atomic particle does not appear in either the particle or the wave picture. (Pauli's initial characterization of what came to be called spin as a "non-classical two valuedness" is helpful in avoiding errors in this regard.) The same holds true for other concepts that have found application to atomic particles such as isospin, strangeness, parity, etc. Spin is measured only indirectly as in a Stern-Gerlach experiment. There is no classical conceptual model analogous to the γ-ray microscope or the interference experiments to guide us. The nonclassical aspect of the result observed in the Stern-Gerlach experiment is that two distinct two beams always emerge, which represent oppositely oriented spins, and not the classical single beam result expected for spins with random orientations.

The component of the spin to be measured is determined by the orientation of the pole pieces in the Stern-Gerlach magnet. Since only one orientation is possible at a time, only one component of the spin can be measured at a time. The fact that the experimental arrangements needed for measuring components of the spin are mutually exclusive is in keeping with the fact that the quantum operators representing the components of the spin in each direction do not commute. Just as successive position and momentum measurements cannot be combined to violate the uncertainty relations when a quantum state is assigned to a system, successive spin measurements cannot be combined in violation of the corresponding spin uncertainty relations.

The "spin" measured in the Stern-Gerlach experiment is really the magnetic moment of atoms that have an unpaired electron. The notion of a magnetic moment is classically well defined. This means that the notion of complementarity can be extended to the description and measurement of components of the electron magnetic moment or spin, if we choose to do so, but only when the electron is bound to an atom or some larger entity.

In assessing this experiment, the general failure of the disturbance theory of measurement should not obscure the legitimate application of the notion of a disturbance under certain conditions. Bohr and Heisenberg repeatedly made the point that if we are going to localize a particle by constraining it with forces or if we are going to make successive position measurements of it, these measurements will disturb the path of the particle, disturb the momentum, and the conservation laws will not apply. Bohr spoke of this particular situation in terms of establishing a connection between the entity under observation and the rods and clocks that "serve to define the reference frame."[33]

---

used group theory in 1927 to characterize the general case with N particles. These results and principles were soon applied to show the connection between spin and statistics in a restricted case, which Pauli [1950] subsequently did for the general case, and to demonstrate the importance of particle statistics in collision processes. Philosophical aspects of the exclusion principle were discussed by Margenau [1944] and the history of the exclusion principle was the subject of Pauli [1946] and John L. Heilbron [1983].

[33]See Bohr [1929a], pp. 95, 98, [1930], p. 375, [1937a], pp. 291–292, [1938b], p. 22, [1961], p. 62.

The requirement that a reference frame be defined by physical interaction between the entity and the apparatus in some experiments is determined by a classical analysis of the measurement of the kinematic variables in the description to be applied. The possibilities of observation must be investigated in each particular experiment to ascertain whether such a connection can be made without violating the integrity of the system or assuming that more information is available than is allowed by possible descriptions of the system.

Duality and Complementarity.

The wave and particle descriptions are the two descriptions that Bohr discussed in reference to complementarity in atomic physics. However, he never explicitly limited the possibility of complementarity to 'particle versus wave' terms. The kinematic variables: position, time, azimuthal angle (of a particle in an orbit), are part of the particle description, while the dynamic variables conjugate to these: momentum, energy, angular momentum are part of the wave description. For each of these pairs of conjugate quantities, an uncertainty relation may be written—if due regard is paid to the caveats raised above with respect to difficulties with the time-energy relation and the azimuthal angle-angular momentum relation.

For those quantities without classical analogs, the question arises as to whether they can play a role in complementarity descriptions. Bohr did not explicitly address the question in this form, but the answer is implicit in his writings. Because electron spin does not play a role in classical descriptions, there is no a classical Hamiltonian interaction term that uses the electron spin. However, there is a classical Hamiltonian interaction term that couples the electron intrinsic magnetic moment to the gradient of the magnetic field. Because of the proportionality of the electron spin and its magnetic moment, the classical definition of the magnetic moment can be used to give a meaning to the description of the interaction between the electron spin and the gradient of the magnetic field. In this sense, the components of the electron spin moment can play a role in descriptions that meet all three requirements for being complementary stated above in Section 7.1.

From a more general perspective, the question can be raised whether nonclassical quantities such as isospin, strangeness, or charm, etc., associated with elementary particle descriptions and their mutual interactions can participate in complementary relationships. The important issue is whether a Hamiltonian term can be written in which these parameters play a role in the interaction energy between particles and the measuring instrument. The quantity determined by the measuring instrument in this Hamiltonian interaction term must be described as a macroscopic quantity that is the expectation value obtained by averaging it over the particles in the instrument. It must also have a conjugate quantity associated with it such that together they meet the requirements on quantities in complementary descriptions stated above. Bohr's implicit thesis is that any quantity that can be obtained in macroscopic form as an expectation value in this way is already described in classical terms as required and will likely already play a role, perhaps in another form, in some previous classical theory such as classical electrodynamics. Under these circumstances, the quantities may be deemed complementary.

Von Neumann [1932], pp. 241–247, made scant use of the concept of complementarity as such. He did not really make the logical status of complementarity within his theory clear, although he hints at its necessity in his requirement (p. 238) that a classical analysis must be given of various measurement processes as a matter of principle. Bub [1969] has maintained that the content of Bohr's principle of complementarity is embodied in the theorem of Kochen and Specker [1967]. This theorem states that different phase spaces and associated probability measures for non-coherent sets of associated probability measures cannot be reduced to a single phase space and associated probability measures. According to Bub, this theorem forms the mathematical counterpart to von Neumann's physical thesis (originally stated by Bohr) that a classical analysis of the measurement system must be used as a matter of principle.

Measuring Instruments.

To justify his view that the instruments used for making measurements should be described quantum mechanically when they are the objects of measurement but must be described classically if they are being used as measuring instruments, it is necessary that quantum effects are negligible in its operation as a measuring instrument. Bohr stated this compatibility requirement in the form: "In actual experimental arrangements, the fulfillment of such requirements is secured by the use, as measuring instruments, of rigid bodies sufficiently heavy to allow a completely classical account of their relative positions and velocities."[34] Also [1949], pp. 49–50, " ... a clock is a piece of machinery, the working of which can be completely accounted for by ordinary mechanics and will be effected neither by reading the position of its hands nor by the interaction between its accessories and an atomic particle." The distinction that Bohr was drawing between a measuring instrument and an atomic system is not that between macroscopic matter and microscopic matter, as he is often interpreted as maintaining,[35] but rather a statement concerning the epistemological requirements underlying the use of quantum theory.

The justification for Bohr's requirement that the measuring instrument be described classically is epistemological. In accord with his requirement that an experimental arrangement is in essence part of the definition of the

---

[34]Bohr [1949], p. 51. See also Bohr and Rosenfeld [1933], pp. 4–5, 8, and Bohr [1948], p. 13, [1958b], p. 3, [1960a], p. 11, [1961], p. 59.

[35]See Grünbaum [1957], p. 717, for this view.

quantum state of a system, it follows that a quantum state cannot be attributed to a measuring instrument unless there is an instrument to observe it. If the first measuring instrument $M1$ is included in a larger experiment $M2$ that provides an experimental context for the combination of the system k with $M1$ as $k + M1$, the potentials due to $M1$ that act on particles in k may be obtained by marginalizing the joint state into separate states for k and $M1$ and then averaging the interaction potentials between particles in k and particles in $M1$ over this $M1$ state. However, the situation is still not completely determinate, and cannot be, because the interaction of $M2$ with $k+M1$ is not itself subject to quantum determination. To do so would require measuring instrument $M3$ and would lead to an infinite regress. At some point we must simply use the description of the classical model of $M2$ or $M1$ to compute the potential and use that in making Schrödinger's equation for the system $k + M1$ or the system k definite. This situation differs significantly from the classical case, where a state can be attributed to an unobserved instrument.

The classical description of the measuring instrument is an idealization to which actual measuring instruments roughly correspond. We do not have the freedom to push this description too far. An experiment requiring the localization of the atoms of the measuring instrument and the control of their momentum to a degree that violates the uncertainty relations cannot be performed. Further, an investigation of the use of the proposed instrument when its atoms are localized and its momentum controlled to that degree shows that the measurement desired is "washed out" as a consequence. In this case, we would need to consider the instrument as part of the observed system.

The requirement by Bohr that measuring instruments be analyzed classically does reflect the actual practice of physicists. Born [**1969**], p. 144, for example, concurred with Bohr on the need for a classical description of instruments and their functioning on the grounds that "One cannot give up such an interpretation without paralyzing intuition which is the source of research and rendering communication between scientists difficult." It is sufficient to describe the operation of the magnet in the Stern-Gerlach experiment, for example, classically because the undesired small-scale inhomogeneities of the field, caused by the uncertainties in the precise locations of the atoms in its pole pieces, are of no consequence in the experiment itself. These deviations from the classical description could be investigated by making precise observations on the field; but, in keeping with the results of Bohr and Rosenfeld [**1933**], these observations would themselves distort the original field to the point where the classical description would no longer be satisfactory and the atoms in the beam would no longer be separated according to their spins.

Measurement and Observation.

There are a number of indications that Bohr did not accept the theory of measurement developed by von Neumann. According to Bohr [**1938b**], p. 19,

"In the first place, we must recognize that a measurement can mean nothing else than the unambiguous comparison of some property of the entity under investigation with a corresponding property of another system, serving as a measuring instrument, and for which this property is directly determinable according to its definition in everyday language or in the terminology of classical physics." There is nothing in this approach involving reductions of wavepackets by an observer looking at a macroscopic instrument or pictures of wavepackets moving through space and dividing. Bohr explicitly rejected the particle picture proposed by Einstein for a photon and Dirac's discussion of a photon wavepacket striking a half-silvered mirror and dividing in half. This misleading picture leads us into difficulties, Bohr [**1949**], p. 51, maintained, because "In any attempt of a pictorial representation of the behavior of the photon we would, thus, meet with the difficulty: to be obliged to say, on the one hand, that the photon always chooses *one* of the two ways and, on the other hand, that it behaves as if it had passed *both* ways. It is just arguments of this kind which recall the impossibility of subdividing quantum phenomena and reveal the ambiguity in ascribing customary physical attributes to atomic objects." For Bohr, the results of an experiment are defined as soon as the phenomenon involved is "fixed into the descriptive framework of daily life" whether concerned with measuring the place where an electron entered a photographic plate or observing a flash of light with the eye. And [**1938b**], p. 45: "Any question of observation beyond these limits was ... a philosophical problem common to all domains of knowledge, and for which atomic theory was in no way distinct from classical physics."

From the standpoint of Bohr's theory, the concept of measurement is coordinated with that of a phenomenon. Bohr [**1938b**], p. 20, expressed this point as: "Any measurement in quantum theory can in fact only refer either to a fixation of the initial state or to the test of such predictions (of subsequent observable properties of the system), and it is ... the combination of measurements of both kinds which constitutes a well defined phenomenon." Bohr's version of measurement gives the same predictions as von Neumann's in that the descriptions of the system given in each case can be translated into each other. The 'interaction' between the system and the measuring apparatus (von Neumann) can be translated into the 'definition' of the situation by the experimental arrangement (Bohr). The final 'state' of the system (von Neumann) and the final 'description' of the system (Bohr), with regard to the wavefunction used to make predictions of the outcome of the experiment, are both represented by the same vector (or ray) in Hilbert space in both theories. The probability of each outcome is computed in both theories as the inner product of this wavefunction with each of the members of the set of eigenfunctions of the operator that was measured. The thrusts of the two approaches, and the conceptual viewpoint that each embodies, are quite different, however. I shall return to this in Chapter 15.

Fock [**1957**], p. 208, took Bohr to task for his views on measurement and, in particular, for maintaining that the formalism of quantum mechanics was purely symbolic. Fock's grounds were that "The task of physical theory is always to describe the properties of physical objects in their relation to the external world." Fock also objected to Bohr's insistence on completed experiments (phenomena). But it is just these points, where Fock felt that Bohr was being "careless", that contain the essence of the distinction between Bohr's thought and that of traditional physics—and Bohr was fully aware of this. The real issue, which Fock does not analyze, is the difference in physical perspective between Fock and Bohr. Bohr developed his position after a painstaking analysis of the adequacy of the position from which Fock was speaking. Fock was trying to maintain a realist viewpoint with respect to quantum theory in the traditional sense of attributing properties to objects. But, as indicated above in reference to the EPR experiment and in the discussion of Bell's theorem, no realistic interpretation of quantum mechanics in the traditional sense is possible. This provides a significant difficulty for those who are trying to reconcile quantum theory to Marxist materialism and Lenin's principles of empiro-criticism.[36]

One of the important differences between Bohr and von Neumann is on the issue of what "properties" could be ascribed to atomic objects. Bohr objected to saying an atomic entity "has" a state partly because the state depends on the macroscopic context in which the entity finds itself (the experimental arrangement), and partly because we cannot consistently attribute properties to objects on an atomic scale—though Bohr spoke once, in a quote given above, of comparing properties of the entity with a corresponding property of the measuring instrument. Bohr's difference with von Neumann is really with respect to von Neumann's picture of a state function representing an entity developing and splitting in time (either continuously via Schrödinger's equation or discontinuously in a measurement) versus Bohr's view that the quantum state cannot be "observed" doing these things. Bohr spoke only of completed observations interpreted through the use of quantum state descriptions of the entity in reference to the whole experimental arrangement.

As far as the operation of Bohr's quantum theory goes, that is, as far as the experimental verification of its predictions are concerned, Bohr's theory is operationally equivalent to von Neumann's. Both are quantum theories, as opposed to some version of a statistical theory or hidden variable theory, and both share complementarity in some form. The choice between von Neumann's theory and that of Bohr must be made on grounds other than experimental adequacy if a choice is to be made at all.

---

[36]See the discussion in Heisenberg [**1958a**], pp. 129–137. See also the discussion of realism in D'Espagnat [**1965**], [**1971a**], [**1971b**].

CHAPTER 8

Bohr's Epistemological Theory

A number of elements that Bohr employed in his theory of knowledge have been introduced and delineated in the preceding chapters. These will be gathered now into a systematic exposition of Bohr's epistemological theory. This systematization is a "rational reconstruction" of his ideas and, as such, suffers from all the difficulties and excitement of inductive work.

8.1 The Components of Bohr's Epistemology

Bringing together the elements that Bohr introduced as basic to his theory involves combining ideas that Bohr developed almost forty years apart. As remarked on above, Bohr was careful and consistent in the development of his ideas, so the later ones are elaborated versions of his earlier ones. I shall accept the later ones as the final version of his theory.

Bohr introduced some novel aspects in his theory of knowledge. The first is the contextualization of knowledge embodied in his principle of complementarity. The second is the argument he gave for why the means of acquiring knowledge and statements of our experience cannot transcend the limits of ordinary experience. The third is the requirement of the explicit separation of subject and object in physical descriptions.

Because Bohr was responding to the conceptual dislocations associated with quantum mechanics, the relation of theory and experiment was a central concern for him. In the last few chapters, Bohr's views on certain questions concerning theory and observation were examined. His responses to these questions are summarized in this list:

1. What is the root of the coordination of possibilities of description and observation? Ans: They reflect each other in the experimental arrangements, are themselves classically described; the experimental arrangement warrants the use of specific theoretical descriptions and determines what it is possible to observe.
2. What are the conditions for the definite attribution of a description to a system? Ans: Descriptions are based on and require reference to both the system measured and the whole experimental arrangement; this implies that the appropriate description is the system wavefunction, which is a solution of Schrödinger's equation for the system with definite macroscopic initial and boundary conditions determined by the experimental arrangement; the experimental arrangement also determines the Hamiltonian used in Schrödinger's equation and which observable quantities can be measured by the experiment.
3. What can we say about observations on a system? Ans: Predicted quantities are expressed as expectation values for observables computed using the description appropriate to the experiment; observed results and their interpretation are justified by reference to the experimental arrangement.
4. When is an observable is definite for a system? When an experiment measuring the observable is complete and the results have been irreversibly recorded.

While these questions and Bohr's answers form the centerpiece of Bohr's epistemology, there are a number of other fundamental components that are needed and play a role in his theory.

8.1 THE COMPONENTS OF BOHR'S EPISTEMOLOGY

Bohr grounded his epistemology on the notion of a conceptual framework. Within a conceptual framework, there are primitive concepts concerning the reference frame (e.g., location, time), basic physical concepts (e.g., position, momentum), certain metaphysical conceptions as requirements on descriptions (e.g., causality, determinism, continuity, symmetry), methods for selecting acceptable theories (e.g., experimental confirmation, mathematical consistency), definitions of some concepts in terms others (e.g., $v = \dot{q}$, $\mathbf{v} = m^{-1}\nabla$), and a collection of currently accepted theories. Descriptions are fashioned within a conceptual framework and the interpretation of observations must also be done within a conceptual framework.

In some of the passages discussed above, Bohr maintained that the conceptual framework provided by ordinary experience and classical physics has a special role in epistemology. His statements that measuring instruments must be described using the concepts of classical physics and that observations must be expressed within the framework of ordinary experience both fall in this category.

Let us begin by systematizing Bohr's notion of what is required of a description. Expanding on the summary above and collecting the ideas stated by Bohr in quoted passages and others, the results of his inquiry into theoretical descriptions can be stated as a set of requirements that an adequate description in Bohr's sense must meet:[1]

Bohr's Description Thesis: The theoretical description of an entity provides a state function, an evolution equation, and a measurement formalism. It rests on a conceptual framework that provides it with needed concepts and procedures not defined within the description itself. A description is made definite by fixing the macroscopic initial and boundary conditions. These conditions are associated with the experimental arrangement used to make the measurements on the system. The description of the experimental arrangement itself must be given in terms of the conceptual framework of classical physics. A description is unambiguous with respect to a given physical variable in a given experimental setting if this variable does not depend on microscopic variables referring to particles outside the system.

The wavefunction used to compute the probabilities of the various outcomes of a completed experiment is the description of the system in that setting. As the solution of Schrödinger's equation, it is usually required to be single-valued and unique.

Bohr also presented a systematic view of the requirements on observation. His ideas on observation can be collected and summarized as a set of requirements on observation:

---

[1] Honner [**1987**] has provided some distillations of Bohr's ideas that are similar in some respects to the ones presented here. I will discuss these in connection with his contention that there is a transcendental aspect to Bohr's thought in Chapter 10.

Bohr's Observation Thesis: The observation of an entity requires a classical conceptual framework for the expression of both the results of the experiment and the description of the experimental arrangement. All observations are closed, i.e., have resulted in an irreversible macroscopic change. The interpretation of an observation requires that the subject making the observation and the object of the observation have separate descriptions in which the microscopic quantity measured and its macroscopic indicator have an unambiguous relation.

The requirement that the subject and object have separate descriptions and an unambiguous relation means that the variables describing the subject and those describing the object are not shared. In Chapter 14, I will show what this requirement means with respect to physics.

These formulations preserve explicitly the great degree of symmetry in Bohr's concepts of description and observation. It is to be emphasized that nowhere did Bohr make such summaries of his ideas. These theses are, however, very closely based on the many statements Bohr made concerning observation and description that have been quoted above. Moreover, as they are stated here, they are consistent with Bohr's other ideas on quantum theory and language. I shall rely on them heavily in what follows.

8.2 Bohr's Main Argument

The heart of Bohr's theory of knowledge is an argument that connects his ideas on the relations between observation, description, and language. This argument will be referred to as Bohr's *main argument*.

Beginning with ideas he had mentioned in his Como lecture, Bohr developed a complete justification for his version of quantum theory. He addressed himself to the problem of why classical descriptions of the experimental arrangement must be retained, worked out a rationale for why complementarity is a general feature of epistemology, and altered the nature of physical explanation for the new context provided by quantum theory. In particular, Bohr's main argument ties together the components of his epistemology into a coherent whole and shows why they are permanent features of the epistemology of physics.

Bohr [1949], pp. 39–40, expressed his *main argument* succinctly as follows:

"... *however far the phenomena transcend the scope of classical physical explanation, the account of all evidence must be expressed in classical terms.* The argument is simply that by the word "experiment" we refer to a situation where we can tell others what we have learned and that, therefore, the account of the experimental arrangement and the results of observation must be expressed in unambiguous language with suitable application of the terminology of classical physics. This crucial point ... implies the *impossibility of any sharp separation between the behavior of atomic entities and the interaction with the measuring instrument which serves to define the conditions under which the phenomena appear.*"

This particular quotation, published in 1949, is representative of the argument that Bohr stated and restated from 1938 through 1962.[2] The point of the main argument is to justify Bohr's Observation Thesis. While allowing complete freedom for physical explanation (as allowed by the Description Thesis), the statement of the results of an observation—indeed, the very interpretation of what that observation is an observation of—requires more. It demands both an account of the experimental arrangement and statement of the results of the observation in a form in which the measuring instrument and the measured system are independent. Because we cannot separate the quantum descriptions of the measuring instrument and the measured system (they must interact), there is an ambiguity in the values of the system variables we are measuring in the context of the quantum description of the combined system. To evade this problem, Bohr stated that it is necessary to use an appropriate classical description of the measuring instrument. Using a classical description of the measuring instrument disengages its variables from the quantum variables describing the measured system and removes the ambiguity.

This argument is clearly the core of Bohr's epistemological theory and the justification of his version of quantum theory. The disengagement of the variables describing the measuring instrument from those of the measured system by using a classical description of the measuring instrument enforces the subject/object distinction on the combined system. As support for his view that this is the central issue in epistemology, Bohr examined the part that language and the subject/object distinction play in these issues.

Bohr's concern with language in connection with epistemology stemmed from his attempt to find the most general context and justification for his concept of complementarity and other aspects of his theory. He, [**1927**], p. 91, was concerned about concepts and language already in his Como lecture "... every word in the language refers to our ordinary perceptions." And in 1929: "... all our ordinary verbal expressions bear the stamp of our customary forms of perception, from the point of view of which the existence of the quantum of action is an irrationality."[3] In 1937, Bohr [**1937a**], p. 293, restated his concern with language and sharpened it by focusing on "unambiguous communication." The argument given in connection with this notion and its restatement in [**1938b**], p. 26, formed the prototype for the quotation of the *main argument* given above. He [**1938a**], p. 27, [**1954**], pp. 80–81,

---

[2]Bohr [**1938b**] pp. 25–26, [**1948**] p. 11, [**1954**] p. 72, [**1955**] p. 89, [**1956**] p. 87, [**1958b**] p. 3, [**1960a**] p. 11, [**1961**] p. 59, [**1962a**] p. 78, [**1962c**], p. 24.

[3]Bohr [**1929c**], p. 19. Compare this with Wittgenstein [**1953**], p. 48.

highlighted its importance to human inquiry: "In emphasizing the necessity in unambiguous communication of paying proper attention to the placing of the subject-object separation, modern development of science has, however, created a new basis for the use of such words as knowledge and belief." Bohr then fused his concerns with observation and language into the main argument quoted above. He also made statements like [**1962a**], p. 78: "Just the requirement that it be possible to communicate experimental findings in an unambiguous manner implies that the experimental arrangement and the results of observation must be expressed in the common language adapted to our orientation in the environment." Many other authors have subsequently approved and restated Bohr's views on the need for unambiguous communication and the conditions necessary to achieve it.[4]

In summary, Bohr's argument is: To do objective scientific work implies that we can communicate our experimental procedures, our theoretical description of the experimental situation, and the results of our observations. Because we have a unique language oriented to our environment, we have no choice but to make use of the conceptual framework and unambiguous concepts provided by this language as extended by classical physics. We must also keep in mind the limitations on the valid statements we can make due to the interaction between the subject and the object of measurement.

The various elements discussed above can be expressed in terms of the following thesis as to the requirements involved in communication and consequences of the need for it:

> *Bohr's Communication Thesis:* Knowledge is communicable unambiguously if and only if the communicating subject is sharply distinguished from the object communicated about and the statement of the knowledge of the object contains only well-defined concepts within a familiar conceptual framework. This implies that every communicable statement of knowledge must use the concepts and relations of ordinary language supplemented by classical physics.

For Bohr, an objective statement is a communicable one. Any acceptable statement of an observation must meet the requirements of communicability; it is then *ipso facto* an objective observation. The requirement of the separation of the subject and object is in fact automatically satisfied for statements meeting the conditions of the Observation Thesis. Thus all statements that may count as observation statements must be communicable, while not all communicable statements meet the conditions of the Observation Thesis. Descriptions are not limited by the Description Thesis to statements of communicable knowledge, but the Description Thesis does require that

---

[4]See Petersen [**1963**], pp. 10, 11, Heisenberg [**1958a**], pp. 44, 56, 144, 171, Rosenfeld [**1967**], pp. 116, 122, [**1961a**], p. 386, Weizsäcker [**1952**], pp. 75, 94, Weisskopf [**1958**], p. 215, and many others. It is clear that not everyone understood what Bohr was saying in the same way Bohr did, however.

the description of the experimental arrangement, required for a well-defined description, be given in classical terms.

Bohr's Observation and Description Theses can be restated using Bohr's concept of communication:

Observation: Only those statements that are communicable statements of knowledge concerning phenomena (closed experiments) are observations. Raw observational data is interpreted by reference to the experimental arrangement under which the data was obtained. The description of the experimental arrangement and the analysis of its functioning must be made using communicable statements.

and:

Description: Only those statements concerning an object that are valid in the context of the whole experimental arrangement in which the object is observed can be part of well-defined descriptions. The description of the experimental arrangement must be made using communicable statements.

8.3 Bohr's Theory of Knowledge

I shall now make explicit the relationships between the elements of Bohr's theory in reference to their role in what I shall expand as his theory of knowledge. For Bohr, every major component in his theory of knowledge concerned with description is linked to a parallel component concerned with observation. That is, there are links between (1) complementarity and mutually exclusive experimental arrangements, (2) the Description Thesis and the Observation Thesis, (3) the Subject/Object Distinction and the Communication Thesis and, (4) Language and the Forms of Perception. Underlying and uniting all of these is a Conceptual Framework.

The hierarchy of these relationships is established in Bohr's *main argument*. In order to reveal its full import to his theory, I will structure it now. It begins with the statement: "... however far the phenomena transcend the scope of classical physical explanation ...." Bohr is here intimating that there is no limit on the form and scope of potential descriptions. We are free to employ any concepts and any relations between them that are found to be useful; we are not limited in this undertaking by preconceptions as to the form that a theory must take or to the elements that must appear in it. Moving to the conclusion of the argument, however, we find that there are limitations on observation: "... the account of all evidence must be expressed in classical terms." This shows that the argument is intended as a justification of Bohr's Observation Thesis.

Bohr's support for this conclusion followed: "The argument is simply that by the word "experiment" we refer to a situation in which we can tell others what we have done and what we have learned ...." In other words, when we are doing an experiment, it is necessary that we be able to describe in communicable terms both the experimental arrangement and the results of the experiment. Bohr continued: "... and that, therefore, the account of the experimental arrangement must be expressed in unambiguous language with suitable application of the terminology of classical physics." Bohr is using here the Communication Thesis as a suppressed premise.

According to the Communication Thesis, the possibility of communication requires that the subject and the object be sharply distinguished and that statements concerning knowledge of the object be expressed in a familiar conceptual framework that makes use only of well-defined concepts taken from this conceptual framework. This in turn requires, in Bohr's theory, the use of just those concepts and relations that appear in ordinary language supplemented by classical physics. If this is accepted, we have the result that Bohr was seeking: "... the account of all evidence must be expressed in classical terms." If the Subject/Object Distinction is included as an inseparable part of the Communication Thesis, then Bohr's argument could, if valid, serve as a full justification of the Observation Thesis, which itself forms one cornerstone of his quantum theory.

The final aspect of Bohr's *main argument* is the statement that the necessity of using a classical statement of the results of measurement "... implies the impossibility of any sharp separation between the behavior of atomic objects and the measuring instruments which serve to define the conditions under which the phenomena appear." This statement must be interpreted, in order to preserve consistency with Bohr's overall theory, to mean that in *this* experiment we are renouncing any inquiry into and control over the interaction between what is designated as the subject and what is designated as the object of this measurement. In another experiment, we could concern ourselves with this interaction. But that would simply move the cut between the original object, the measured system, and the original subject, the measuring system, to a cut between the combined measured system and measuring instrument as the new object and the second measuring instrument as the new subject.[5] The other implication of the statement that a sharp separation between the object and measuring instrument is impossible is a consequence of using an interaction between the object and the measuring instrument to make the observation. In order to evade quantum ambiguity that results from doing this, we must use a classical description of the measuring instrument so that this sharp separation of subject from object will be true.

In this epistemological situation, Bohr [**Arch**], 21:1, 7/20/54, p. 5–6, referred in unpublished notes to what he called a "section line" between what

---

[5]This is clearly stated by Bohr [**1949**], pp. 39–40. This is a statement about experimental procedures. It is not equivalent to the claim that every state or interaction is further analyzable either theoretically or experimentally. As far as we know, transitions between stationary quantum states are not, so setting up an experiment to capture further details of an atomic transition would not be successful.

we are conscious of and can communicate and what forms the subjective background for our discourse, i.e., the circumstances under which this discourse is judged. He stated that psychic experiences, corresponding to different section lines between "object" and "subject", appear as complementary phenomena to us. He claimed a deep analogy in this regard to the need for complementary descriptions in physics. Applying these ideas to the relation between instinct and reason, Bohr made the joke that "some of the marvelous and surprising feats which certain animals can do are only possible for them because they do not know why they do it and how they do it."

With regard to descriptions, Bohr looked upon mathematical and logical terms and relations as part of extended ordinary language. By employing symbolic methods, the relations between the concepts in mathematics and logic can be clear and unequivocal. Bohr viewed the concepts available in mathematics and logic as refinements of ordinary concepts and dealt with them within the same general framework as any other concepts. The application of concepts from mathematics and logic to experience must meet the same epistemological conditions as the application of any others; for this reason, they play the same role in Bohr's theory of knowledge. The relation between the forms of perception and language was taken note of above, where Bohr was quoted as saying that "... every word in the language refers to our ordinary perception." And that "... all our ordinary verbal expressions bear the stamp of our customary forms of perception ...." These statements should not be interpreted too literally, but they do mean that, from Bohr's point of view, all perceptions function within the conceptual framework of everyday life, which is itself essentially like that of classical physics.

Viewed as physical principles, the Observation and Description Theses regulate what statements can count as observations and descriptions in physics. As such, they are justified in part by the fact that these are the forms that statements of experimental results actually take in physics. Bohr was also concerned with the further question of whether his epistemological perspective should be understood as referring only to physics in the current era or whether it offers a longer lasting solution to a broader set of epistemological problems. There is no necessity that it should be more general. The use of these theses in physics may also depend on the nature of physics itself and one can raise the question of whether the they must remain in their current form. Bohr was clearly trying to do more than develop his theses as principles of contemporary physics. The above justification he gave for the Observation Thesis shows that he felt that his account of observation is the only possible one. One of the purposes for his epistemological analysis was to justify the form he gave the concepts of observation and description and state why they are, and will remain, important elements of the theory of knowledge.

Table 8.1: Bohr's Theory of Knowledge

Conditions on Description	Conditions on Knowledge
Complementary Descriptions	Mutually Exclusive Experimental Arrangements
Description Thesis	Observation Thesis
Communication Thesis	Subject/Object Distinction
Language (Mathematics & Logic)	Forms of Perception (Classical Concepts)
Conceptual Framework	

The dualistic form in which Bohr presented his epistemological notions has been discussed above. In addition to this, there is a hierarchy of elements in his theory of knowledge. Each set of conditions on a higher level allows us to choose from a set of statements that meet the conditions imposed on the lower levels those statements that can play a significant role in the description of a given experiment and the interpretation of its results. The Observation Thesis, for example, designates which of the statements meeting the conditions of the subject/object distinction can count as part of the statement of an observation. This scheme is represented diagrammatically in Table 8.1. The relation between the Bohr's Communication Thesis and the Subject/Object Distinction and between Language and the Forms of Perception will be analyzed in the next two sections.

As indicated by the hierarchy of elements in the above diagram of the structure of Bohr's epistemology, the fact that certain experimental arrangements are mutually exclusive limits the possibilities for making and interpreting observations; this regulates what we can hope to measure and the statements that can be made about measurements. The Observation Thesis requires that statements concerning observations be accepted only if the observations are made under conditions that meet the requirement that the subject and object be distinct. The Subject/Object Distinction in turn sets conditions on the situation in which raw data may be unambiguously recorded and interpreted intelligibly. The raw data appears, in Bohr's theory, as dots on a photographic plate or traces in a cloud chamber within our ordinary (classical) forms of perception. This scheme will be discussed further in Chapter 10 when it is compared to Kant's theory of knowledge.

All of the facets of Bohr's theory of knowledge I have discussed here are distinct and all of them play an important role in his theory. Furthermore, both the hierarchical structure and the correlative structure outlined in Table 8.1 are important to his theory. This dualism grew out of Bohr's original concern with comparing the possibilities of observation in the laboratory with the possibilities of description within quantum theory. This concern crystallized in Bohr's 1927 Como lecture and was important in every major essay involving the interpretation of experience afterward.

On the upper two levels of Bohr's theory of knowledge are the concepts important to quantum theory. The application of complementarity, experimental arrangements, description and observation in the function of Bohr's quantum theory has already been discussed. I shall only add here that the mutually exclusive character of some experimental arrangements is a necessary condition for complementarity—but complementarity is not a necessary condition for two particular experimental arrangements to exclude each other. The two concepts are quite distinct and should not be amalgamated.

Bohr's requirement that an observation be closed is both a key feature and a problematic feature of his theory. Closure, when characterized as an irreversible macroscopic change, is not irreversible from the microscopic point of view—in spite of the attempts of the quantum ergodic theorists and decoherence theorists to show that the final state of a quantum system after a measurement is indistinguishable from a mixture of closed results.[6] Closure operates at the juncture between the macroscopic description of the results of an experiment and the microscopic description of the evolution of the system leading to this result. It therefore plays the same role in Bohr's approach to measurement that consciousness does in von Neumann's theory of measurement. However, Bohr's association of closure with irreversibility requires further explanation in light of the reversible evolution of the microscopic quantum description. I will examine this issue and complete the discussion of closure in Chapter 15.

Bohr rarely spoke of attributing properties to atomic entities. When he did, it was usually with respect to the need to give up prior viewpoints concerning them. In [**1937a**], he viewed these attributes as an aspect of the idealizations of classical physics and stated that the situation in atomic physics deprives such attributes of all meaning. He also, [**1938b**], stated that experiments concerning phenomena that lie outside the range of classical physics cannot be interpreted as ascribing independent properties to objects. Later, in a letter to Born, Bohr [**Arch**] BSC 27, 3/2/53, stated that his concept of "closed phenomena" removes the obscurity concerning the degree to which we can ascribe properties to atomic objects. He referred to the context of a completed experiment, including the whole experiment arrangement, as setting the conditions concerning to what degree we can make this ascription.

---

[6]The claims of quantum ergodic theory and decoherence theory that the macroscopic world is a consequence of the operation of physical factors at the microscopic level will be discussed in detail in Part IV.

He observed that the properties we attribute to an electron in one experiment may be very different from those we can attribute to it in the environment of a more complex experiment.

The scope of Bohr's concerns in his theory of knowledge is much greater than that of most contemporary scientists who have addressed these issues. While most of them assumed that the nature of perception is not an issue requiring discussion, Bohr turned his attention to it. It is true that he did not discuss the traditional issues concerning sense data or the relation between sensation and the "external world"; nor did he deal with the traditional problems concerning memory and other minds; but he was very much concerned with the relation of language and our everyday concepts to what we can perceive, describe and communicate. His discussion of the need for classical concepts and of the classical nature of what he called our forms of perception preceded by many years the reawakened philosophical discussion of the question of the degree to which observation is 'theory laden,' that is, how much of what we perceive is determined by what we know, by what we expect, by our language, and by our conception of the nature of reality.[7]

The unique feature of Bohr's theory of knowledge lies in its systematic concern with how knowledge can depend on the circumstances under which it is obtained coupled with the possibility that full knowledge of a physical object, in the sense of a simultaneous specification of all its properties, may be impossible in principle. As an epistemological theory, Bohr's work is worthy of more concern than it has received to date. It has also been seriously misunderstood by many of those discussing his views. This no doubt stems from the meagerness of his account of it and the difficulty in getting a grasp on it. It is hoped that this work will contribute to making it more accessible and better understood.

8.4 Communication and the Subject/Object Distinction

Bohr's views can be roughly summarized as follows: Communicable sets of interpreted perceptions are data. Communicable sets of interpreted data are information. Communicable sets of interpreted information are knowledge. Theoretical and contextual issues are involved at every step—but different theories are often involved at the different levels.

Bohr's Communication Thesis, stated in terms of necessary and sufficient conditions for achieving unambiguous communication of knowledge about an entity, rests on two ideas: the need for a distinct subject and object, and the need to use only well-defined concepts from a familiar conceptual framework. With reference to experience, Bohr [**1954**], p. 67, identified objective descriptions of experience, i.e., statements of our knowledge concerning it, with

---

[7] Bohr's view that every observation appears in the context of our 'forms of perception' will be analyzed in Chapter 12 after the discussion of the relationship of Bohr's views to those of Kant.

statements that can be unambiguously communicated: "Every scientist ... is constantly faced with the problem of objective description of experience, by which we mean unambiguous communication." This problem concerning the kinds of knowledge we can have of entities in the atomic domain is forced upon us, in Bohr's view, by the unanalyzable link between the measuring instrument and the object under investigation. Indeed, Bohr [**1938a**], p. 25, stated this directly: "As soon as we are dealing, however, with individual atomic processes which, due to their very nature, are essentially determined by the interaction between the objects in question and the measuring instruments necessary for the definition of the experimental arrangements, we are, therefore, forced to examine more closely the question of what kind of knowledge can be obtained concerning the objects." Bohr followed this statement immediately by: "In this respect, we must, on the one hand, realize that the aim of every physical experiment—to gain knowledge under reproducible and communicable conditions—leaves us no choice but the use of everyday concepts, perhaps refined by the terminology of classical physics, not only in all accounts of the construction and manipulation of the measuring instruments but also in the description of the actual experimental results." Bohr [**1949**], p. 40, also stated directly his claim that the interaction or relation between the measuring instrument and the object of measurement is unanalyzable: "In fact, the individuality of the typical quantum effects finds its proper expression in the circumstances that any attempt at subdividing the phenomena will demand a change in the experimental arrangement introducing new possibilities of interaction between objects and measuring instruments which in principle cannot be controlled." In some places, Bohr referred to this latter "circumstance" as the quantum postulate.

In an early essay, Bohr [**1929a**], pp. 96–97, related objectivity to the "... attempt to attain uniqueness by avoiding all reference to the perceiving subject." I have discussed this in terms of the separation of the variables used to describe the perceiving subject or measuring instrument from the object measured. This can be extended by an additional requirement that the influence of the measuring instrument on the information obtained concerning an atomic entity be negligible or at least predictable. The problem here is familiar in physical terms in a situation, for example, in which the "back radiation" produced by a measuring instrument during the measurement of an electromagnetic field quantity must be taken into account of in order that an accurate measurement of the field be made.[8] In cases in which the influence of the measuring instrument is not completely controllable or predictable, we are faced with the problem of how to obtain a unique and definite description of the object.

---

[8]This is an important consideration in Bohr and Rosenfeld [**1933**]. See also Bohr [**1930**], p. 7.

Bohr looked for a deeper explanation of the problem of obtaining an objective description. In 1929 he [**1929a**], p. 96, presented a philosophical discussion of the difficulty in distinguishing subject and object and of maintaining a sharp separation between them:

"The epistemological problem under discussion may be characterized briefly as follows: For describing our mental activity, we require on the one hand, an objectively given content to be placed in opposition to a perceiving subject, while, on the other hand, as is already implied in such an assertion, no sharp separation can be maintained, since the perceiving subject also belongs to our mental content. From these circumstances follows not only the relative meaning of every concept, or rather of every word, the meaning depending upon our arbitrary choice of view point, but also that we must, in general be prepared to accept the fact that a complete elucidation of one and the same object may require diverse points of view which defy an unique description."

The wave-particle duality in atomic physics and Bohr's discussion of complementarity in relation to it make a strong case for the last point in the above quotation in reference to atomic physics. As a general epistemological position, however, it is more problematic. It is clear in Bohr's essays that he was trying to establish the universality of the subject/object distinction in reference to all human inquiry and our everyday life—not just simply warn us that the possibility exists that our usual assumption (that we may give a unique and full description of an entity valid under all circumstances) may be mistaken. It is to this end that he discussed examples of alleged complementarity in several fields outside physics.

Bohr's general position can be reconstructed as follows: When engaged in the operation and discourse of everyday life, we do not need to pay attention to problems connected with the subject/object distinction because these are built into our language. (Bohr [**1938a**], p. 25: "... all experiences have so far been based on the assumption, already inherent in ordinary conventions of language, that it is possible to distinguish sharply between the behavior of objects and the means of observation.")[9] By "ordinary conventions" here, Bohr obviously means those underlying communication. When, however, we move into domains in which the concepts and descriptions of everyday life are not sufficient, we must deal with whatever consequences may come from maintaining a sharp distinction between subject and object in this new domain.

---

[9]Contrast this, however, with Bohr [**1954**], p. 68: "In this connection, it may be stressed that, just by avoiding the reference to the conscious subject which infiltrates daily language, the use of mathematical symbols secures the unambiguity of definition required for objective description."

8.4 COMMUNICATION AND THE SUBJECT/OBJECT DISTINCTION 189

Given that Bohr said "must be prepared to face problems" in the longer quotation above from [**1929a**] rather than "must face problems" that arise from the need for the subject/object separation, his point is sound. But there are places in his writings where he speaks as if a stronger point had been made. More is required for the conclusion that the subject/object distinction cannot be maintained in a unique manner, and that complementarity must be invoked, than just pointing out that the observer has an important effect on the situation. For example, when surveying opinions in a population, we might well be able to avoid phenomena like 'self-fulfilling prophecies' or the 'bandwagon effect', which are cases in which the observer influences the opinions being observed, by redesigning the instruments used (i.e., the questionnaire) or by developing a new way to make this investigation (e.g., a semantic differential method). Similarly, there does not seem to be any in principle reason at this time why we could not provide as part of our mental content a model of some of our mental activity. Such a model might require a recursive formulation to account for our ability to think about our ability to think and so on. This characterization would not be complete in the sense of a closed formulation that cuts off this reflective faculty at some point, but any chosen level of such activity could possibly be described in this way. And there is no reason now why this description could not be given objectively. Such a reason may, of course, ultimately be found.

For the above reasons, I shall reexpress the part of Bohr's *main argument* concerned with the subject/object distinction in terms of atomic physics in order to make clear its role in Bohr's *physical* theory. I call this *Bohr's Extended Main Argument:*

It has not proved possible in the domain of atomic physics to give a description of the behavior of objects within one unique picture in the classical sense. Furthermore, the possibilities of description provided by quantum mechanics are in accord with the possibilities of observation, which means that no experiment has yet come into conflict with quantum mechanics. In this situation, the requirement that an observation be definite and unambiguous, i.e., that the observed quantity is well defined, means that the observation must be closed. Furthermore, the requirement that the measuring instrument must be described objectively implies that it cannot be included in the quantum description of the system. This is because the quantum description of the combined system does not allow of a unique decomposition into a description of the measuring instrument and of the object of measurement. Any attempt to pursue or control the variables representing the measuring instrument further, in order to make this decomposition or separation, will, as an examination of the possibilities of description and the possibilities of observation will show, introduce a new situation in which some of the information previously available regarding the initial experimental arrangement is no longer available to us (while new information may have become available). The consequence of this situation is that the part of the 'experimental arrangement plus atomic system' designated as the measuring instrument must meet the conditions of the classical approximation and must be classically described with definite values assumed for each of its variables.

The quantum postulate, and the concepts of individuality and wholeness, are consequences of the situation regarding the failure of the classical mode of analysis in atomic physics and the necessity for adopting quantum mechanics in this domain. I will investigate in Chapters 12 and 13 whether they are a consequence of a universal theory of knowledge, as Bohr maintained, or only an aspect of atomic physics. Raising this question does emphasize the point that what we can know with regard to a discipline must depend in many ways upon the actual structure of the world and cannot be given an *a priori* formulation. It is very much in accord with the point of view Bohr expressed in his reply to Einstein, Podolsky and Rosen: We must draw philosophical conclusions from nature, not impose them on it.[10]

Although one is not forced to adopt Bohr's epistemological analysis to account for the appearance of complementarity and the problems concerning the subject/object distinction, the possibility remains that some of these features of Bohr's theory are forced on us, so to speak, by the underlying structure of our intellectual-perceptual apparatus. Bohr believed this and made it part of his theory. He outlined a theory of language and perception as a justification for his position. I shall now look into this part of Bohr's theory to lay the groundwork for the inquiry into this matter in Part III.

8.5 Subjectivity and Objectivity

Bohr placed particular emphasis on "the character of objective description, independent of subjective judgment, in any field of experience where unambiguous communication essentially involves regard to the circumstances in which evidence is obtained."[11] Bohr has placed the opposition between objective description and subjective judgment. The question is what is he contrasting here and why is it important.

An objective description as Bohr put it has no reference to a given subject. As such, an objective statement is one that can be understood and tested by more than one person. Its truth does not depend on the history or current state of mind any one person. Objective knowledge can be communicated to others either directly through some sense modality (e.g., verbally or visually) or stored in books or other devices. It is also essential for objective knowledge

---

[10] This is a paraphrase of the quotation form Bohr [**1935**], p. 696, given in the first section of this chapter.

[11] Bohr [**1961**], p. 60.

that there be substantial agreement within a given group on the truth or falsity of statements made about it. This leaves open the question of whether there is superordinate knowledge that we can almost all agree upon. This characterization of objectivity is purposefully vague, bending language to what it does best, and allows a wide latitude for what may currently be characterized as knowledge in different disciplines and room for what has been or what may someday be called objective knowledge.

The social and intellectual context is clearly important in judging whether a claim of knowledge is objective or not. Various disciplines have guidelines, which are usually implicit but appear in discussions of methodology within the discipline, regarding the kinds of tests, proofs and arguments that are accepted when gathering and reasoning about objective knowledge in their areas of interest. They also impose guidelines on how various results are to be interpreted as supporting or contradicting a claim of knowledge. These are the "rules of the game" at a given time in a given discipline as Wittgenstein might say. This contextual component should warn us against braying too loudly the truth as presented by some current worldview. On the other hand, many disciplines change slowly and some are unlikely to change much during a human lifetime.

Bohr's remarks, however, do not seem directed at pursuing definitions such as these concerning the nature of objective descriptions. Rather, one has the feeling that he is positioning his chess pieces. He perhaps has in mind the unpleasant aspects of von Neumann's theory of measurement and the possible involvement of the observer in determining the experimental outcome. Von Neumann's theory seems like such an obvious extension of the quantum formalism itself, the question for Bohr is how to evade either its formal expression or the conclusions it leads to.

In support of the point concerning situations in which we are operating outside of the domain familiar in everyday life, Bohr often brought up the example of the Danish student in Poul Møller's story who is unable to decide which "I," in the sequence of "I's" looking at themselves, to attend to.[12] In addition, Bohr's concern with the conditions of objective knowledge was stimulated by the fact that in his view of quantum theory you cannot even state the possibilities for description until you have defined the context (the experimental arrangement) in which the observation is to be made (the possibilities of observation).

The requirement that there be a sharp distinction between the knower and the known has physical implications that will play an important role in Part IV. We will see there that Bohr's requirement that the measuring instruments be described classically, while acknowledging that these instruments

---

[12] Poul Møller was a Danish philosopher and novelist who was also a teacher and friend of Kierkegaard. Relevant excerpts from his book appear in English in an article by Holton [**1970**] and in Favrholdt [**1976**], pp. 215–216.

are to be described quantum mechanically when not used for measurement, forces the subject/object distinction at the price of placing what appears to be an artificial boundary in the physical world.

Bohr identified subjectivity and objectivity with the distinction between subject and object. The issue of subject and object for Bohr are associated with, and in juxtaposition to, the concepts of wholeness and individuality. Bohr was aware that his concern with issues such as the place of the knower in relation to the object of knowledge and the treatment of the universe as either the 'one' or a collection of the 'many' reflects some very old issues in epistemology that were discussed in the ancient texts of Hindu, Buddhist, Taoist, and Greek thinkers. I will return to these issues in Chapter 9 when the subject/object distinction is probed historically and in subsequent chapters when Bohr's theory of knowledge is compared to standard epistemologies.

8.6 The Replacement of Concepts

Let us now consider the question of whether classical concepts can be replaced by new ones in quantum theory. Feyerabend [**1962**], pp. 228, 231, has argued that Bohr's contention that classical physics must be retained could equally well have been applied to Aristotelian physics before Galileo. However, the situations are not analogous. The change from Aristotelian dynamics to Galilean dynamics came about in part because the two theories differed on concrete predictions concerning the behavior of falling bodies. It was not the basic descriptive concepts of Aristotelian physics that were under attack by Galileo but rather the theoretical relationships between them.[13] To be sure, the attack on the Aristotelian system involves an attack on aspects of the way Aristotle characterized motion, e.g., in terms of natural place, the need for a body to move through some resistance, or the Aristotelian notion of "causes," but this is not equivalent to attacking Aristotle's notions of what position, to be in a place, and uniform motion mean. In other words, Aristotle's kinematic concepts were not challenged by the new mechanics but some of his dynamical concepts were. Aristotle's analysis of motion in terms of a spacetime picture was not itself called into question.

Wittgenstein [**1953**] felt that concepts do develop in time and that we could have concepts other than the ones we have now.[14] Heisenberg replied to this possibility by saying that we simply do use classical concepts and there

---

[13] Kuhn [**1962**], p. 118, has also discussed this.

[14] Wittgenstein [**1953**], p. 230: "I am saying: if such-and-such facts of nature were different people would have different concepts (in the sense of a hypothesis). But: if anyone believes that certain concepts are absolutely the correct ones, and that having different ones would mean not realizing something that we realize—then let him imagine certain very general facts of nature to be different from what we are used to and the formation of concepts different from the usual ones will become intelligible to him. Compare a concept with a style of painting. For is even our style of painting arbitrary? Can we choose one at pleasure? (The Egyptian, for instance.) Is it a mere question of pleasing and ugly?"

8.6 THE REPLACEMENT OF CONCEPTS

is no use in discussing what could be done if we were other beings than we are.[15] Weizsäcker [1952], p. 128, spoke in a similar vein. Born [1969], p. 144, was closer to Bohr in his statement that we cannot give up the notions of particle and wave in the interpretation of cloud chamber data and periodic blackening of a photographic plate without paralyzing intuition and rendering communication more difficult. Bohr [1929c], pp. 15–16, made his position explicit:

"However, we can no more hope to attain a clear understanding in physics without facing the difficulties arising in the shaping of our concepts and in the use of the medium of expression than we can in other fields of human inquiry. Thus, according to the view of the author, it would be a misconception to believe that the difficulties in the atomic theory may be evaded by new conceptual forms. Indeed, ... recognition of the limitations in our forms of perception by no means implies that we can dispense with our customary ideas or their direct verbal expressions when reducing our sense impressions to order. No more is it likely that the fundamental concepts of the classical theories will ever become superfluous for the description of physical experience."

As pointed out before in connection with a discussion of conceptual frameworks, this statement should not be interpreted as meaning that no new concepts can be added to the ones we have. Bohr was claiming instead that all those concepts without a classical analog, such as electron spin, must rest for their interpretation on those, such as the electron magnetic moment, that do. And Bohr would not object to statements like "the atom was observed in such-and-such a stationary state," if it was understood that this is an interpretation of the data, which is itself described in classical terms.

Arguments limiting the future of physics in some way and placing limitations on the employment of concepts are very risky indeed. But, as indicated in a previous discussion of Feyerabend's rejection of Bohr's views, there is something different in the situation faced by physics with the advent of quantum theory. While theories have disagreed on the interpretation of observations, and perhaps people holding two such theories actually saw things differently, there has never been a situation previously in which pairs of concepts in incompatible descriptions are required for a full description of a single entity. Within any given theory in the past, it was at least assumed that a full unique description could be given of the entities playing a role in it. The fact that electromagnetic theory does not have a mechanical interpretation was not a problem within electromagnetic theory but it did count against it at first. Thus, in the current situation, extra-ordinary considerations are in

---

[15]Heisenberg [1958b], p. 56. See also p. 44, where Heisenberg states: "We cannot and should not try to replace these concepts by any others .... We cannot and should not try to improve them."

order, which may have a bearing, for ontological or epistemological reasons, on the future of physics.

8.7 Reflection 16

It is my contention that those up to now who have tried to interpret or criticize Bohr within the framework of the epistemological terms Bohr used to frame his theory have missed Bohr's point with respect physics (and therefore with respect to epistemology). What is needed first is a clear analysis of how the elements of Bohr's theory of knowledge function with respect to his physics. My interpretation, admittedly a reconstruction, maintains that Bohr's major points can be expressed in terms familiar to physics. The question of whether, in contrast to Bohr's view, the situation we face is currently peculiar to physics will resurface after an evaluation of complementarity in Chapters 13 and 14.

Support for Bohr's statement about the data of the laboratory is provided by an examination of what is recorded as data and what is published in journals: the positions of spots on photographic plates, pictures of oscilloscope traces, pictures of light and dark bands, graphs of measured points, relative counter rates at various angles, etc. The point is established by examining how an experimenter would retreat from her statement that she had observed a wave. Upon having it pointed out to her that the pattern might be an artifact of her instrumentation, or that there might be a complicated underlying mechanism providing particle correlations (as in a hidden variable theory), the experimenter could retreat from saying that she had observed a wave to saying that she had seen and photographed light and dark bands. If pressed, she could retreat even further and say that she had simply recorded a collection of specks on the photographic plate. I shall agree with Bohr then that there is nothing in the raw, macroscopic laboratory data that cannot be adequately and completely described and communicated (and reproduced in a picture or a table of data) by concepts based on everyday language supplemented by the terminology of classical physics.

The second, equally important, point—that the interpretation of measurement requires a physical model and that the model must be classical—is more difficult.[16] The argument is that in order to know precisely what we are measuring, we must have a model for it. This model is related to how we understand the functioning of the instrument we are using and how we understand its interactions with other entities. The model, in fact, helps us design

---

[16]This point was emphasized, as a point of principle, by von Neumann [**1932**], p. 238, in accord, he claimed, with Bohr [**1927**]. Bohr never spoke explicitly in terms of a model. But this interpretation seems to be the only one consistent with Bohr's discussion of causality as underlying the interpretation of observations and his discussions of how we analyze the possibilities of observation. See, in reference to this, the accounts in Bohr [**1927**], pp. 62–63, [**1949**], pp. 41–47, 52–56.

our instruments and serves to define the range of experimental results we expect and look for. Kuhn [**1962**], p. 39, emphasized this point in his discussion of the circumstances surrounding the Davisson-Germer experiment:

"The man who builds an instrument to determine optical wave lengths must not be satisfied with a piece of equipment that merely attributes particular numbers to particular spectral lines. He is not just an explorer or measurer. On the contrary, he must show, by analyzing his apparatus in terms of the established body of optical theory, that the numbers his instrument produces are the ones that enter the theory as wavelengths. If some residual vagueness in the theory or some unanalyzed component of his apparatus prevents his completing that demonstration, his colleagues may well conclude that he has measured nothing at all. For example, the electron-scattering maxima that were later diagnosed as indices of electron wavelength had no apparent significance when first observed and recorded. Before they became measures of anything, they had to be related to a theory that predicted wave-like behavior of matter in motion. And even after that relation was pointed out, the apparatus had to be redesigned so that the experimental results might be correlated unequivocally with the theory."

Quantum theory itself, in Bohr's view, does not provide us with a model in the sense needed for the interpretation of measurements. When we concern ourselves with the functioning of the instrument and its interaction with the object of the measurement, Bohr pointed out that we must analyze this situation with regard to a causal account of the behavior of the instrument and the response of the system. Without some sort of model here, we cannot even get started in an analysis at all.

The von Neumann version of quantum mechanics often does provide a model in its visualizations of moving wave packets and their divisions and reduction. And this model plays a role, as in Bohr's theory, in the analysis of measurement. At some times, it is convenient to view this as a moving particle contained within this "probability envelope", and at other times it is convenient to emphasize the physical aspects of the wavefunction itself. When we wish to deal with forces external to the system, e.g., forces exerted by instruments on the "particle", the wavepacket solutions of the Schrödinger equation exhibit a change in shape, a change in their direction of motion, and changes in their time development. These changes all reflect the effects of the force on the particle. It is important that the force is treated as operating on the particle located at some point, although we do not (and cannot) know where in the wavepacket the particle is located. In many cases these external forces are described by a classical potential and the particle is assumed to have a negligible effect on the sources of the potential. In the analysis of measurement, the classical features of which were emphasized by von Neumann

[**1932**], pp. 237–297, one may choose to emphasize the particle or wave aspects (and make use of the appropriate idealizations), but an analysis along one classical line or another must be made if the concepts of quantum theory are to be connected with the operation of measuring instruments. It follows that von Neumann's theory, interpreted as it often is in terms of measurements involving wavepackets moving in space, still rests to some degree on conceptions from classical mechanics such as that of a particle on a path.

I shall now collect the major tenets of Bohr's approach to physics in my version of his epistemology of physics:
1. Science must be objective, i.e., there is to be no intervention of the observer in the course of the events with which we have no direct physical connection;
2. The concepts of everyday life supplemented by classical physics are adequate for expressing the raw data of completed experiments;
3. The description of the part of the apparatus designated as the measuring instrument and of its functioning must be classical;
4. The interpretation of a measurement must be based on a model that rests essentially on the classical description of the measuring instrument.

Except for the last item that was just discussed, each of these items will be subjected to detailed scrutiny in the succeeding chapters.

Part III

The Foundations of Bohr's Thought

"What's the good of Mercator's North Poles and Equators,
Tropics, Zones, and Meridian Lines?"
So the Bellman would cry: and the crew would reply
"They are merely conventional signs!"

Lewis Carroll, *Fit the Second, The Hunting of the Snark;
an Agony in Eight Fits*, 1876

CHAPTER 9

The Natural History of Subject and Object

While Bohr did not acknowledge any specific philosophical viewpoints as the source of his ideas, it will be shown in Part III that the concepts he used are rooted in past work. This inquiry is begun with a brief review of the more than 6000 year history of the subject/object distinction and viewpoints on reality in both Eastern and Western thought. Kant's theory of knowledge is studied next because of its importance to European thought in the nineteenth and early twentieth century. The investigation then widens into a review of nineteenth century work on several themes concerning philosophy, biology, social sciences, physics, and language that Bohr wove into his work. Work on these themes in the early twentieth century by several professors, including some at University of Copenhagen, are examined to show the intellectual milieu surrounding Bohr when he was formulating complementarity and its justification. The result of this extended investigation is the basis for a critical evaluation of Bohr's concept of complementarity, his justification of it by an appeal to the epistemological role of language and perception, and his employment of it outside of physics.

9.1 Bohr's Philosophical Themes

Bohr did not do his epistemological work in a vacuum, but neither he nor his colleagues were aware of just what influence traditional philosophical concerns and concepts had on his thinking. As discussed in Chapter 1, Bohr and those around him have remarked that philosophy was not important in the development of his ideas. It is true that philosophical systems were of little interest to him and he did not study philosophy outside of his university work as a student. However, I will present evidence that Bohr's epistemological vocabulary, that he drew on when he fashioned his concept of complementarity and then its justification, was in fact strongly influenced by a number of philosophical ideas and theories. This is not equivalent to adopting anyone's philosophical system and working from that vantage point. I have argued on the contrary that it was the needs of physics and not philosophy that set the requirements for the concepts he needed and shaped the epistemology he fashioned.

There are a number of traditional philosophical issues that are important to Bohr's approach to epistemology:
- perception, forms of perception
- experience
- causality, claim of causality
- knowledge
- subject and object
- reality

He made reference to each of these, and, either explicitly or implicitly, each plays a central role in his theory of knowledge. In weaving these issues together, and developing a theory of knowledge broad enough to deal with modern physics, Bohr adapted a number of other philosophical concepts and themes:
- observation
- description
- irrationality
- individuality
- whole versus part
- ambiguity and sharpness
- role of language

Each of the topics in the two sets above has a long philosophical history. One of my major contentions is that Bohr's philosophical perspective on these concepts was determined by direct and indirect exposure to philosophical thinking in which they were employed. This will be made plausible by comparing the locutions Bohr used for the concepts he was trying to convey and similar statements by other thinkers on these subjects. I will also show that the way Bohr fit some of these concepts together had precursors in the work of other thinkers.

9.2 Wisdom of the East

Bohr was aware of the significance of Eastern thought in the history of philosophy and in particular with regard to the subject/object distinction. He phrased himself characteristically in the statement: "We are here confronted with complementary relationships inherent in the human position, and unforgettably expressed in old Chinese philosophy, reminding us that in the great drama of existence, we are ourselves both actors and spectators." [1] Translations of some Chinese and Japanese philosophical and religious texts had appeared in the seventeenth century and were well known in European intellectual circles. These texts included the works of Confucius, Lao Tse, other works on Taoism, and some Buddhist works. Translations of ancient Sanskrit texts of Indian philosophical thinking also began to appear in Europe at the end of the eighteenth century.[2] Before the mid nineteenth century, many Vedic works and translations of Buddhist texts had also appeared in Europe.[3]

It should be mentioned that one of the major philosophical concerns in Eastern traditions has to do with understanding the human condition, including an analysis of suffering in Buddhism and the role of citizens in a society in Confucianism. Many of the views expressed in Eastern philosophies stem from these inquiries. The "ways to knowledge" recommended in relation to the concern with suffering are aimed at the goal of emancipation from attachment to that which is the source of suffering. Because of certain misconceptions in western thought, it should be emphasized, however, that the philosophical work of Eastern philosophers concerning issues of perception, knowledge, and reality, is no more "mystical" than the work of Western philosophers on these subjects.[4] Because of my narrow focus, I will mention only briefly these concerns with human suffering and the meditative methods

---

[1] See Bohr [**1960a**], p. 15.

[2] See Herbert Gowen [**1931**], Chapter 1, for a discussion of the discovery and translation of Sanskrit texts in India and their introduction into Europe beginning in the late 18th century. See Joseph Needham [**1956**], Vol. 2, on the introduction of Chinese works into Europe in the 18th century.

[3] See Max Müller's 1862 article on Buddhism, in [**1869**], pp. 184–197, where he discussed the information available in the mid nineteenth century concerning the Vedic works and Buddhism. He mentioned the works of Lao Tse and Confucius and discussed the scholarship that had produced translations of Buddhist works and some of its impact on Europe.

[4] For this reason, I disagree with the emphasis in Fritjof Capra's [**1975**] ground breaking work *The Tao of Physics,* because he conflated the meditative "ways to knowledge", which he characterized as mystical, with the logical philosophical positions in Hindu, Buddhist, and Chinese thought. Nevertheless, he showed many striking parallels between the conception of the behavior of matter in modern quantum and high-energy physics and the views of reality in various ancient Eastern philosophies.

associated with them. I simply state that much of Eastern thought is missing in this treatment of the subject.[5]

Let us begin with a discussion of Vedic philosophy and then look at the Buddhist and Taoist offshoots.

Vedic Philosophies.

Some traditions claim great antiquity for the views expressed in their teachings. As examples, there are the Vaiseshika system (the study of objective reality) and the Nyaya system (the study knowledge in relation to reality) that were formulated as sutras by Gautama Akshapada.[6] These philosophies are considered to be more than 6000 years old. The Nyaya philosophy was the science of logic in ancient Indian philosophy that concerned itself with a "critical examination of the objects of knowledge by the means of the canons of logical proof". Both the Vaiseshika and the Nyaya assumed the existence of an objective reality independent of the knowing subject, which can be characterized as a plural realism. Both also assumed an atomic theory in which the universe was constructed by the mere action and interaction of atoms. These atoms were independent of the mind and existed as unalterable, causeless, eternal, minute particles. Both the Vaiseshika and Nyaya were originally materialist philosophies with no place for theism or deism. Their focus on objective reality placed them in opposition to idealist doctrines that also appeared very early. The idealist viewpoint downplayed or rejected the reality of external objects and focused on the mind of the knowing subject.

It was the goal of the Nyaya system to explain human existence in terms of the laws of nature. Reality was viewed as a combination of the conscious (chetana) and the unconscious (achetana), which existed as independent, but related, elements. The mental realities were inseparably connected with the independent objective external realities, which were necessary for the phenomena of mental life. The Nyaya philosophy was based on five eternal elements: earth, water, fire, air, and ether. In addition to the five elements, the Nyaya system recognized time, space, mind, and self or soul (âtman). The self could not function without the body, which was the seat of action and of the senses, through which the self came into contact with the outside world and gained knowledge. The mind orders the sense impressions and participates in the acquisition of knowledge and reasoning about it. With regard to knowledge acquired by perception, the Nyaya school held that direct interaction between the observer and the observed was required for truth to be perceived. Correspondence with the object was the criterion of truth. Valid

---

[5] For a good précis of the philosophical thinking of these schools, including a discussion of their concern with human suffering and its philosophical consequences, see John Koller [**1970**].

[6] I am relying on K. Damodaran [**1967**], pp. 159–165, for information on the Vaiseshika and Nyaya systems. See also Koller [**1970**].

knowledge leads to successful activity and invalid knowledge does not. Other sources of knowledge included inference, analogy and the testimony of others.

Gautama Akshapada taught that finding right knowledge was the key to avoiding suffering and disappointment. He also taught that to know a thing as measured means knowing the measure. Perception was analyzed into four factors: sense experience, the object sensed, contact of the senses with the object, and cognition derived from this contact. The perceptual knowledge obtained by these steps is determinate (well-defined), expressible in words and without error. The realization of true knowledge requires the external object, satisfaction of external conditions (sufficient light, etc.), the organs of the senses (to do the sensing), the mind (which helps these organs function), and the observer. A problem with any one of these elements can lead to error and mistakes.

Simultaneous to these schools of thought were the non-dualistic Vedânta schools that emphasized the knowing subject and de-emphasized external reality. The teachings of these idealist schools exploited weaknesses in the Vaiseshika and Nyaya doctrines and led later thinkers in these traditions to compromise their empiricist basis—opening the door to theism. The idealist doctrines were taught in the ancient Vedas followed by the Upanishads.

The primary concern here is the Upanishads because of the strong impact they had on European thought. I am interested most in the ideas that appeared in European thought by the end of the nineteenth century, so I will rely primarily on the 1899 work of Paul Deussen for these connections. He was concerned both with understanding the Upanishads in their own right and showing the strong parallels to idealistic European philosophy.[7]

As Deussen [**1899**], p. 38, pointed out, all thought of the Upanishads revolves around two fundamental ideas: the Brahman and the âtman. These are usually treated identically, but he observes that the Brahman appears to be the older, less intelligible concept, and âtman is the later more significant concept. Brahman is the unknown cosmological principle that needs to be explained. Âtman explains it and finds its place in so far as it is known as the inner self of man. The universe is Brahman and the Brahman is the âtman within us. Then, p. 39, "If for our present purpose we hold fast to this distinction of the Brahman as the cosmological principle of the universe, the âtman as the psychical, the fundamental thought of the entire Upanishad philosophy may be expressed by the simple equation:—

$$\text{Brahman} = \text{âtman}.$$

That is to say—the Brahman, the power that represents itself to us as materialized in all existing things, which creates, sustains, preserves and receives back into itself again all worlds, this eternal infinite divine power is identical with the âtman, with that which, after stripping off everything external, we

---

[7]Deussen's work was chosen for its reflection of European thought at the end of the nineteenth century. It does not necessarily represent current views on the Upanishads.

discover in ourselves as our real most essential being, our individual self, the soul. This identity of the Brahman and the âtman, of God and the soul, is the fundamental thought of the entire Upanishads. It is briefly expressed in the "great saying" ... "that art thou". It is also expressed in equivalent forms as "I am Brahman ..." and in the compound word *brahma-âtma-aikyam,* "unity of the Brahman and the âtman". Deussen characterized these statements as the fundamental dogma of the Vedânta system.

Deussen, p. 40, drew an immediate parallel between this idea and Kant's philosophy: the universe is only appearance and not reality. In other words,

"the entire external universe, with its infinite ramifications in space and time, as also the involved and intricate sum of our inner perceptions, is all merely the form under which the essential reality presents itself to a consciousness such as ours, but it is not the form in which it may subsist outside our consciousness and independent of it; that, in other words, the sum-total of external and internal experience always and only tells us how things are constituted for us, and for our intellectual capacities, not how they are apart from intelligences such as ours."

Deussen considered this idea to be the basis for all philosophy—at least as far as the term philosophy is not being used as a "cloak for the empirical sciences". He saw the difference between the goals of philosophy and the empirical sciences as a concern with the nature of things versus simple knowledge of objects in their circumstances, surroundings, and causal connections. His reason is that the totality of empirical reality, which is all the empirical sciences can give us, itself requires further explanation. This explanation is provided by the principle set forth by philosophy from which one can infer the real nature of things and their relations. Deussen found powerful support for this view in the fact that the work in the ancient texts concerning man's early attempts to understand the universe fit with this idea: "This fact, then, that philosophy has from the earliest times sought to determine the first principle of the universe, proves that it started from a more or less clear consciousness that the entire empirical reality is not the true essence of things, that, in Kant's words, it is only appearance and not the thing-in-itself."

Deussen, pp. 41–42, went on to wax philosophical: "There have been three occasions, as far as we know, on which philosophy has advanced to a clearer comprehension of its recurring task, and of the solution demanded: first in India in the Upanishads, again in Greece in the philosophy of Parmenides and Plato, and finally, at a more recent time, in the philosophy of Kant and Schopenhauer. ... Greek philosophy reached its climax in the teaching of Parmenides and Plato, that this entire universe of change is, as Parmenides describes it, merely phenomenal, or in Plato's words, a world of shadows; and how both philosophers endeavored through it to grasp the essential reality, ..., that which Plato, in an expression that recalls the doctrine of the

Upanishads no less than the phraseology of Kant, describes as the αὐτώ (âtman) καθαιτό (an sich [in itself]).”
As far as the objects we see around us in the universe are concerned, they are only appearances. This corresponds to the doctrine of the Upanishads in that they are not âtman, the real self of things, but mere mâyâ, which is illusion or self-deception. From this perspective, all change is word play—just as Parmenides asserted that what is regarded as real is merely a name. This point of view is stated clearly in the Brihadâranyaka, 4. 4. 19, sutra in the verse:[8]

In the spirit should this be perceived,
Here there is no plurality anywhere.
From death to death again he rushes blindly
Who fancies that he here sees difference.

Deussen felt a marvelous agreement between these doctrines: "It is clear from the foregoing:—... that this fundamental doctrine of the Upanishads is seen to be in marvelous agreement with the philosophies of Parmenides and Plato, and of Kant and Schopenhauer. So fully indeed is this true, that all three, originating from different modes of thought entirely independent, mutually complete, elucidate, and confirm one another."

The conclusion that Deussen, pp. 226–227, drew from the philosophy of the Upanishads is "When Kant in his inquiry into the capability of the human intellect drew the conclusion that the entire universe, as we know it, is only appearance and not reality, he said nothing absolutely new, but only in more intelligible demonstrated form uttered a truth which in less intelligible shape had been in existence long before him; which indeed as intuitive half-unconscious knowledge had from the very beginning formed the basis of all philosophy."

The idealistic doctrines were stated clearly in the Upanishads. As Yâjña-valkhya pointed out in his dialog with his wife Maitreyi, "In truth, not for the husband's sake is the husband dear, but for the self's sake is the husband dear." By the self is to be understood the knowing subject within us. The thought is that all objects and relations of the universe exist for us, and are known and loved by us, only in so far as they enter into our consciousness, which comprehends in itself all the objects of the universe, and has nothing outside of itself. Yâjña-valkhya went on: "The self in truth we should comprehend, should reflect upon, O Maitreyi. He who has seen, heard, comprehended and known the self, by him this entire universe is known. As the notes of a drum, a conch-shell, or a lute have no existence in themselves, and can only be received when the instrument that produces them is struck, so all objects and relations of the universe are known by him who knows the âtman."[9]

---

[8]Deussen [**1899**], p. 44.
[9]See Deussen [**1899**], pp. 229–231.

Deussen [1899], pp. 235–236, summarized the philosophy of Yâjña-valkhya as 'The âtman is the knowing subject in us'. From this it follows that the âtman as the knowing subject is always itself unknowable. It also follows that there can be no reality outside our consciousness. Deussen noted that Yâjña-valkhya recognizes and states both consequences. This is the climactic point of the philosophical conceptions of the Upanishads, "and together they seem to bar any further progress in philosophical thought". The identification of the Brahman and the âtman solved the immediate problem for the Indian thinkers of identifying what we can know. However, there is a problem involved in stating that all we can know is the âtman. Yâjña-valkhya stated in the Brihadâranyaka Upanishad that "Thou canst not see the seer of seeing, thou canst not hear the hearer of hearing, thou canst not comprehend the comprehender of comprehending, thou canst not know the knower of knowing."[10] This solution therefore contained within itself the seeds of its own destruction. If the âtman is to be known, there must be a knowing subject to know it as an object of knowledge and the unity becomes a dualism. But the âtman is all there is, an absolute unity.

The realization of this paradox led the thinkers in the Upanishads to further thought on the issues. As Deussen observed, "The inquiring mind of man could not rest here." Succeeding works of the Upanishads ignore the unreality of the universe outside of the âtman and discuss the universe as though it were real. These later sutras move from the idealism expressed in the Brihadâranyaka through a succession of stages consisting of pantheism, cosmogonism, theism, atheism and deism.

The broader viewpoint that came about through these inquiries implied, as Deussen [1899], p. 201, pointed out, "We know (and the Indians knew also as early as Brihadâranyaka, 2. 4. 5) that the entire objective universe is possible only in so far as it is sustained by a knowing subject. This subject as sustainer of the objective universe is manifested in all individual subjects, but it is by no means identical with them." This led to the conception that there are 3 different âtmans: (1) the corporeal (material) self, the body; (2) the individual soul, free from the body, which as knowing subject is contrasted with and distinct from the object; and (3) the supreme soul in which subject and object are no longer distinguished from one another, or which, according to Indian conception, is the objectless knowing subject.[11]

The pantheistic stage arrives when the empirical reality of the universe is identified with the âtman as its soul. This stage occupies most of the sutras. It reconciles the empirical reality of the universe with the assertion that the âtman is the sole reality. The incomprehensible assertion of the identity of the âtman with the empirical universe is then given meaning in the cosmogonistic stage when the empirical notion of causation is added and the âtman is seen

---

[10]This abridged statement appears in Deussen [1899], p. 79.
[11]Deussen [1899], p. 94.

as the cause of the universe, which it then enters as soul. The growing opposition between âtman as creator and soul of the universe and âtman as the knowing subject leads to the theism of the S'vetâs'vatara Upanishad. The distinction between God, as creator of the universe, and individual souls then opens the way to atheism by allowing God to be removed and attributing the creative powers of God to matter. This leads to the dualism of souls (*purusha*), burdened with their actions and receiving recompense from birth to birth, and the primitive matter (*prakriti*), which renews itself. This move represents the transition from the Vedânta doctrine to the Sâṅkhya system. This is the dualism of nature and spirit, of the knowing subject, separate from all that is objective, and the rest of the universe, that which is merely objective.

One of the most important concerns of the Vedic philosophies is the analysis of causation. These analyses were used in understanding the relation between the empirical self and the self that is pure subject. I will return to these questions below when we examine those aspects that are relevant to Bohr's statement of the role of causation in his theory of knowledge.

We leave the Upanishads and Vedic philosophy at this point. The succeeding sutras do not add to the part of the philosophical picture we are concerned with. For those engaged in European philosophy from the standpoint of Kantian idealism, the views expressed in the Upanishads were a striking precursor and a confirmation of their point of view.

Buddhist Philosophies.

Although not conforming to the Vedas, Buddhist philosophies share many conceptions with the Vedic philosophies I have summarized. Buddhism began with the historical Buddha, who lived from 563 to 483 BC. Buddhist thought analyzed a person into the (1) physical self, (2) activities of sensing, (3) activities of perceiving, (4) impulses to action, (5) activities of consciousness—and nothing else. The mental conception of self, to which all these activities belong, is held to be a fiction. Because the craving for this fictitious self leads to suffering, it is the goal of Buddhism to extinguish this craving. One can extinguish this craving by achieving perfect enlightenment or *Nirvana*.

The analysis of the origin of this self and its ills led to the *theory of dependent origination*. The theory of dependent origination holds that "whatever is, is dependent on something else", and is the root of all Buddhist thought.[12] All beings and objects are mutually self-creating. Reality, in this view, is of the nature of process. Space, time and objects are all abstractions rather than reality. There are only becomings that are never completed so being is never reached. Thus the existence of independent objects is denied.

---

[12] See Koller [**1970**], pp. 112, 127. I will be relying in good part on Koller's summaries of the philosophical commitments of various Eastern schools. See Koller also for references to translations of the original sources.

Following this basic insight, Buddhist thought, some time after the death of Buddha, divided into the realist (Theravada) and idealist (Mahayana) groups of schools as Vedic thought had done. There were further divisions into absolutist and relative positions. But, as Koller [1970], p. 146, emphasized, there was an underlying unity in their thought:

"As a consequence of the common principle of dependent origination, Buddhist theories of the world and self have certain features in common. (1) Neither selves nor external things are of the nature of substance. (2) Both are constituted as processes of elemental forces. (3) Permanence is not found in either things or selves. (4) Space and time are not determining characteristics of either things or selves, since space and time are relative to the processes (which are already relative to each other)."

The denial of the reality of the world as substance was not a denial of the reality of the world. It was the source of this reality that was at issue and differences in the interpretation of the principle of dependent origination with regard to reality led to the differences in the Buddhist schools. Some schools were realistic. They found ultimate reality in things external to ourselves and viewed consciousness as relative to that. Other schools were idealistic and took consciousness as the ultimate reality and viewed external things as relative to consciousness.

There are four major Buddhist philosophical schools of concern to us. The first is the *Vaibhashika* school that taught a form of plural realism. This school held that the ultimate elements of reality are dharmas, brief entities that act as forces. Reality is the constant flux of these dharmas. They come into being and replace previous dharmas until they pass away and are replaced by subsequent dharmas. This is not a causal relationship between the dharmas, which act too briefly to be causes, but a law of connectedness between moments in accord with the principle of dependent origination. These dharmas are spaceless and timeless forces, which arise and fall in dependence on each other. All things, and living things in particular, change, so we cannot identify a thing in terms of some permanent substance comprising it. The Vaibhashika philosophy also denied the existence of universals, such as 'redness' or 'chairness' because we can perceive only particulars.

The *Sautrantika* school taught a pluralistic conditioned realism. Many of their doctrines are close to those of the Vaibhashika school. They also subscribed to a view of external reality as flux instead of substance. But the Sautrantikas viewed the experienced in terms of both the experiencer and other non-experienced elements. These non-experienced elements are representations of the things we experience expressed by the fleeting flux of dharmas. They are therefore the fundamental elements of reality and give rise to the content of experience. The Sautrantika school, along with the Vaibhashika, rejected idealism on the grounds that we cannot distinguish consciousness from its contents and we cannot distinguish valid from erroneous decisions if we do not have external standards against which to measure them. The Vaibhashika followers disagreed with the Sautrantika representational view of reality on the same grounds. The Sautrantikas, in turn, felt that the Vaibhashikas could not explain perceptual error and that the dharmas did not last long enough to be directly perceived.

The *Yogacarin* school was idealistic. The Yogacarins argued against the Vaibhashika and Sautrantika schools by saying that reality is of the nature of consciousness and that we cannot experience anything outside of consciousness. They felt that dreams show us the difference between the consciousness of an object and the object itself. They used the fact that in dreams we are mistaken when we feel that we are experiencing objects outside of our own consciousness to conclude that having this feeling does not imply its truth. They denied that consciousness requires external objects. They also argued that we cannot separate objects from our knowledge of them. From this point of view, the Yogacarins viewed the subject/object distinction as a distinction within consciousness. Consciousness was considered to be self-revealing and self-existent.

The *Madhyamika* school taught complete relativism (*shunyata*). This is one of the most interesting schools and we shall discuss some of its doctrines in more detail in a later chapter. This school tolerated no conceptual absolutes. The major philosopher of this school was Nagarjuna who lived around the second century AD. He held that the most exciting fact about man is his quest to be. This quest led man to the activity of creating the world out of the fundamental elements of reality. Knowledge of this world unites man with the self. However, we mistake the world that we have created with reality.

Nagarjuna's goal was to unite all the Buddhist schools, so he criticized the doctrines of each of them. He claimed that their views were self-contradictory and proceeded to examine the assumptions on which each of them was based. He developed a dialectic method for this examination, but realized that this dialectic, which could only give a negative result, must itself be abandoned afterward. Finally, the relative position itself must be abandoned. The Madhyamika philosophy taught that both the realists and idealists confuse the conditioned with the unconditioned in their analysis of causality. This doctrine recognized an absolute, unconditioned reality, but did not mistake their conceptual grasp of this for the unconditioned itself. For Nagarjuna, the unconditioned is beyond all views. It cannot be grasped intellectually, but only through direct insight.

Underlying each of the other Buddhist schools was a doctrine concerning causality. As Koller [**1970**], pp. 171–175, put it, "Every attempt to explain the nature of reality rests upon an assumption about the causal connectedness of reality." This includes both philosophical and scientific thinking.

With causal connections, we can make inferences between one observed fact and another and organize our observations. However, these connections assumed between the elements of the theory and reality cannot themselves be demonstrated. In the *Madhyamika Karika*, Nagarjuna began his critique of the other schools by trying to show that the assumptions about causality at the base of each of their theories are inconsistent. He also criticized the weaker theory of the *Candrakirti* school that the relation of cause and effect is one of coordination rather than the production of effects by causes. In short, the Madhyamika school denied that reality is constituted of causes and effects. The Madhyamikas also distinguished the world we conceptualize from reality.

The details of the arguments of the Madhyamika school against the conceptions of causality of the other schools are not important to this discussion.[13] The Madhyamika discussion of causality and reality led to certain points of view concerning the world and what we can know about it. Koller [**1970**], p. 179, summarized this viewpoint:

"The items in this world are constructed by the mind and analyzed by the mind. Mind is by itself incapable of dealing with anything other than what is mind-made. And what is mind-made is relational, for the nature of mental construct requires that one thing be in relation to another. ... The dialectic, whereby the essential relativity of the mind-constructed world is demonstrated, reveals the non-ultimacy of the various views about this world, shows the conditionedness and dependent character of the entities of this world, and thus paves the way for going beyond mere views of reality to a direct realization. But it does not, by itself, provide such a realization. Such a realization is necessarily beyond the world of conceptualization."

The conclusion the Madhyamika philosophers drew from this analysis is that *samsara* (ordinary existence) = *Nirvana* (enlightenment).

There were several non-Vedic Indian philosophies that were not Buddhist. One of these is Jainism. The last major Jainist teacher was Mahavira, who was mentioned under the name Nataputta as a contemporary of Buddha in several early Buddhist writings. The philosophical views of the Jainists also seem to antedate the ancient Vedic texts and the subsequent Upanishads. The Jainist texts present a simple atomistic theory of matter in addition to the standard Indian concerns with the place and role of a person in the universe. Jainists feel that the views represented in their texts are at least 4000 years old and probably much older.

---

[13] See the account in Koller [**1970**], pp. 171–179, for details.

Chinese Philosophies.

The two major Chinese philosophies are *Confucianism* and *Taoism*. Both began more than 6000 years ago and were likely based on earlier doctrines. Confucianism, created by Confucius at a time of war and turmoil, was primarily concerned with the role of persons and government in society and less concerned with the analysis and understanding of the material world. The focus was on cultivating the activities that would make a person good. This notion was extended to an analysis of the purpose of government in acting for the good of its people.

The Taoist doctrines were more metaphysical, but were also primarily concerned with the role of persons in society. The basic doctrines were collected by Lao Tse in the *Tao Te Ching*. It held that our knowledge transcends perception and concepts. It rejects the duality of subject and object as false. The principles of life are those of nature. The purpose of Taoism is to illuminate the *Tao* or Way, which means the source of whatever exists and its principle of functioning. Chang Tzu, who lived in the 4th century BC, illustrated Taoist thought by considering questions of perspective. He asked which of our perceptions of a thing from different points of view was the correct one. He also asked if what a worm or a cat perceives is the same as what a person perceives and whether what I am perceiving now is the same as what I perceived a minute ago. He said that these questions could not be answered and concluded that we cannot, therefore, know a thing in itself because there is no absolute standard to use when attempting to answer these questions.

When Buddhism entered China about 1200 years ago, its philosophical doctrines challenged those of Confucianism and Taoism. It was modified by Chinese thinkers, who had been shaped by Confucianism and Taoism. These thinkers extended and transformed the ideas of Yoga and the Madhyamika school into *Zen Buddhism*. Zen Buddhists denied the subject/object division as an arbitrary and misleading division of reality because it sets the individual apart from the reality in which he or she lives. Their goal was direct enlightenment, which means going beyond mental conceptualizations and seeing reality directly. This reality is without division. The importance of Madhyamika philosophy to Zen was due to the fact that it rejected all absolutes. Since no philosophical analysis or justification of this reality can be given, all that remains is Zen practice, *koans* and meditation, in the quest for enlightenment.

Chinese philosophers also responded to this challenge by making a synthesis of the Confucian and Taoist doctrines and created Neo-Confucianism. This synthesis was based on the Ultimate Principle as the root of all things. All things participate in it and it gives them their essence. To this is added the material force that gives the material form to all things. Finally, the physical form is added which gives to all things their existence. The Ultimate principle was identified with the Tao and the Confucian concern with humanity (jen) was identified with the mind in this system.

9.3 Reflection 17

This brief survey of Eastern thought has shown that it provided an ongoing, deep, and sophisticated analysis of reality, perception, causality, and mankind's place in the universe for more than 6000 years. The issues connected with subject and object, reality, and causation were considered by these philosophies from the beginning and received a diverse treatment in the various schools of thought that arose out of the early doctrines.

The fallibility of perception has been a central concern of philosophy. Everyone has been deceived at one time or another by something that appeared to be one thing and later turned out to be another. The existence of illusions and dreams, and the consequences of injury and madness, added to the conviction that perception could not be trusted to show us a true view of reality. If our methods of experiencing the world are not trustworthy, the question becomes how can we acquire knowledge and free ourselves from deception and error.

The issue of what is "in the mind" and what is external to us has also been a persistent theme for many centuries. It was known long before written texts that the seat of the mind is the brain. When the brain is damaged in certain ways, even if the perceptual apparatus is intact, our ability to perceive, know, and interact with the world is impaired. The brain is therefore essential to experience and knowledge. This in turn raises the question of whether all experience and knowledge are in the mind in the brain. The answer to this question depends in part on the attitude of the thinker toward what the mind is made of, if anything, and what it means for something to be "in" it.

The set of relationships between one thing and another, expressed as a theory of causation, is one of the basic elements in most theories of the world. Any attempt at a further analysis of how our perceptual apparatus can give us information about an external world depends on some causal theory connecting the outer world with the inner experience. The theories of causation expressed in the various schools discussed above were determined in great part by an attempt to make the answer to this question intelligible in the context of the fundamental assumptions on which the school was based.

The basic alternatives in Eastern thought revolved around the question of how we acquire experience of reality—either by direct intuitive or meditative experience (enlightenment) or indirectly through our senses. In the latter case, the question moved to that of how to understand and correct our knowledge of the experience we have. The approach to this problem was subdivided into the various realist and idealist camps. The realists generally believed in an external reality, which was either substance based or consisted of a mutually dependent collection of competing forces. The knowing subject was often discussed realist thought in terms of consciousness. This was seen in Eastern thought either as a substance in its own right or a particular collection of these forces. Idealists denied the existence of a directly knowable external reality. One group of idealists viewed the subject and object as both aspects of the internal soul or âtman. Another group denied the subject/object distinction altogether.

Vedantic thought has exerted a quiet influence on European thinking for some time. It offered an alternative to the materialistic and Christian viewpoints that were held by the majority of thinkers. In the twentieth century, the novels of the author Hermann Hesse reflected the presence and influence of these ideas. The philosophical standpoint of Erwin Schrödinger concerning reality, the unity of consciousness, and our relation to the world were shaped by these ideas as well.

9.4 Wisdom of the West

There is much in early Greek thought that reflects issues of importance to the earlier thinkers in India, but I will resist the temptation to conjecture some connection between them before the fifth century BC.[14] Differences between Greek and Indian thought were also numerous. Greek thinkers developed mathematics, rationalist thought and empirical science to a much greater degree than Indian thinkers had. The emphasis of the Indian thinkers on suffering and release from suffering was not a central feature of Greek thought. Both sets of thinkers, including the Chinese, were concerned with moral and ethical issues. Again, because of my narrow focus, I will neglect moral philosophy and concentrate on those issues important to natural science and Bohr's work.

Greek thinkers raised the question of what the world is made of early in the development of Greek philosophy. About 600 BC, the Greek thinker Thales reacted against the anthropomorphic polytheism of his time, which explained natural phenomena in terms of the actions of intelligent Gods, by attempting a naturalistic explanation. Early attempts at a naturalistic conception viewed the world as a living organism. The stars in one example of this approach were considered to be the world's "breathing holes". More sophisticated later work in this direction propounded the four elements theory that explained natural phenomena and their evolution in terms of the fundamental elements earth, air, water, and fire. Explanations of natural phenomena based on these ideas replaced the polytheistic ones with components that were at once simpler and had the potential of being observed.

---

[14]There were definite connections by the third century BC. Alexander the Great had pushed into northwest India and the Selucid dynasty that followed after Alexander founded Greek cities in that area.

The work of Anaxamander followed that of Thales and represented the beginning of an evolution away from the conception of the universe as alive. He saw in elementary contraries, such moist and dry or heat and cold, the seeds of conflict that had a dynamical consequence in the form of eternal motion. The interactions of these elements led to the formation of land out of a primordial ocean and the evolution of living creatures on this land. These ideas were extended by Heraclitus and Empedocles who attributed the initial motion of matter to a certain living will that inheres in matter. This viewpoint saw forces between components of matter, by analogy with the causes of the actions of living animals, in terms of animistic forces such as "strife" and "love" proposed by Empedocles. The subsequent transformations of this matter because of these forces were viewed to be due to inanimate and impersonal causes. The view that everything is in flux, taught by Heraclitus, is expressed in the view that nothing is, everything is becoming. This is similar to the views expressed in the Vaibhashika and Sautrantika schools, and found unity in the world only in the combination of opposites.

Soon afterward, about 500 BC, Anaxagoras removed the animistic aspect of the theory and separated the concepts of matter and force. He sowed the seeds of materialism by presenting a new analysis of matter in terms of minute particles of many different kinds and treated the observed world as the result of a process of these particles cohering in various ways. The world Mind, as the last vestige of the anthropomorphic theory, played an original role in setting these particles in motion, but afterward they interacted through the blind forces between them and evolved into the universe we see.

The school of Democritus, at about 450 BC, and the work of Leucippus removed the last remnants of animism from these theories of the world and presented a full-fledged atomic theory. They gave an account of matter and the changes we see in it by supposing that matter is composed of minute, infinitely hard, indivisible bodies called atoms. In order to get at the essential qualities of these atoms, and remove from them those properties that appear only in connection with an observer with particular kinds of sensory organs, they removed most of the qualities we associate with matter, such as color and hardness, from them. From this viewpoint, information about a thing is a consequence of an interaction between our senses and the atoms composing the thing in which both components participate and contribute to the result. We can gain knowledge of the atoms composing things if we can show successfully how the atomic assumption can give rise to what we have observed.

While there was growing recognition of the importance of knowledge obtained from the senses in distinguishing between competing theories about the world, there was also a growing recognition of how they can deceive us. Parmenides, for example, taught that the senses are deceptive and believed that the change we experience is a delusion. This led to an increasing sophistication on the part of rationalist thinkers who tried to get past the possibility of sense deception and develop knowledge of the essential nature of things.

Plato, writing in the fifth century BC, drew on the Orphic tradition to illustrate the point that our sense experience is not a direct representation of what is. In *The Republic,* Book VII, he presented the analogy of the cave. He likened perception to the situation of someone who is chained with his back to the door of a cave and can only see the moving shadows of things passing by the entrance. He used this to illustrate the fact that our senses do not give us a direct and complete representation of reality. He concluded that our concepts do not arise from experience because experience can never give us a truthful representation of reality. Experience can, however, excite in us the archetypical ideas that are or become our concepts. While no triangle we have seen is a perfect exemplar of the concept of a triangle, we can nonetheless recognize the example as a triangle and reason about it.

This distinction between appearance and reality is fundamental to Plato's views. As part of his inquiry into this distinction, Plato investigated the difference between knowledge and opinion in the second half of his *Republic.*[15] Plato divided the world of the senses from the world of the intellect. He further divided the intellect into reason and understanding. Reason is above the understanding in its concern with pure ideas and its dialectical method. The understanding is used to reason with hypotheses it cannot test. For example, we may assume that all men are mortal, state that Socrates is a man, and the understanding concludes that he is mortal; but the understanding only uses and cannot test the hypothesis that all men are mortal. Thus, knowledge gained by the understanding is hypothetical and depends on other sources for the knowledge of the premises.

Plato, following Parmenides, claimed that knowledge must be of something that exists or it is not knowledge of anything and therefore not knowledge at all. In this sense it is infallible and cannot be mistaken. Opinion, which can be mistaken, cannot be opinion of what is not, because that is impossible; it cannot be opinion of what is, because then it would be knowledge. Therefore opinion participates in both what is and what is not. Plato makes this intelligible by observing that particular things participate in their opposites. Things of perception, in particular, have this character. He concluded that opinion is of the world of the senses while knowledge must be of some non-sensible world. The statement that 'Opinion is concerned with beautiful things but knowledge is concerned with beauty' illustrates this difference.

Plato extended the distinction between opinion and knowledge into a view concerning the nature of universals. We can have opinions of many real cats, but they all participate in an ideal notion of 'catness', which allows us to identify them all as cats. It is only by means of this ideal notion, called

---

[15] For more details, see Bertrand Russell [**1945**], pp. 119–132.

an *idea* by Plato, that we can have knowledge of a triangle or cat in Plato's view.[16]

Plato discussed knowledge and perception further in the dialog *Theaetetus*. The dialog begins with Euclid recalling to Terpsion the notes he had taken on a discussion between Socrates, Theodorus, who was a former disciple of Protagoras, and a young Theaetetus on the subject of knowledge. Socrates asks 'What is knowledge?' and eventually Theaetetus answers that knowledge is perception. Socrates declares that this is the doctrine of Protagoras: "Man, he says, is the measure of all things, of the existence of things that are, and of the nonexistence of things that are not." However, Socrates observes that a cold wind is perceived differently by different people and that when we are ill, things taste differently. Furthermore, because perception is due to an interaction between the object and the sense organ and, as Heraclitus teaches, all things are in a constant state of flux, our perceptions will also change. Thus, there is no unchanging element in perception that we can call knowledge of something because perception does not tell us of the existence of some unchanging thing. We also have dreams and illusions that seem real to us at the time. Because we cannot have knowledge of things that do not exist, knowledge for Plato implied knowing the existence of the thing known. Since we can be deceived by our perceptions, it follows again that perception is not the source of knowledge. This supported Plato's conclusion that we can only have knowledge of objects of reason such as mathematics.

Aristotle, writing soon after Plato, based his philosophy on an analysis of logic. In extending these ideas to the understanding of universals, ideas that express abstract concepts, Aristotle stated that it is impossible to grasp a universal without induction from particulars provided by sense experience.[17] In a proof, Aristotle allowed definitions and intuitions to act as premises. Definitions for Aristotle are stipulative statements (this is a dog) or statements of a thing's essential nature, which means knowing the cause of its existence. Intuition of what something is is necessarily true and that, along with scientific demonstration (syllogistic deduction), provided Aristotle with the pillars on which to construct infallible reasoning. In his discussion of reasoning, Aristotle also introduced a principle of simplicity.[18]

---

[16] The notion of ideas is pursued further in the dialogue *Parmenides*.

[17] Posterior Analytics I, 18, $81^b(5)$. But sense experience alone is not enough. See Posterior Analytics I, Ch. 31.

[18] See Posterior Analytics I, 25, $86^a(34)$. This notion of simplicity is based on the principle stated in Physics I, 5, $188^a(32)$, that nothing acts on anything else at random and nothing may come from anything else except by means of a concomitant attribute. Compare this to Newton's [**1687**], p. 398, words: "Rule I. We are to admit no more causes of natural things than such as are both true and sufficient to explain their appearance. To this purpose the philosophers say that Nature does nothing in vain when less will serve; for Nature is pleased with simplicity and affects not the pomp of superfluous causes."

Aristotle discussed knowledge in his *Metaphysics*. He too felt that the senses give us experience but not wisdom. Wisdom for him is knowledge of first principles, which are themselves universals. These principles are distinct from the four causes referred to below that appear in his *Physics*. With respect to objects, he made a distinction between 'form' and 'matter'. In its simplest aspect, the form of some matter is its shape in the ordinary sense. However, Aristotle also used form in the sense of essence and primary substance. Essence is the ultimate definition of what a thing is. It is what remains in something, as its *sine qua non*, after you remove everything that is accidental. The substance of something is that in which its properties reside.[19] The notions of essence and substance have played an important role in metaphysics ever since.

Aristotle stated in the *Posterior Analytics* that not all knowledge is demonstrative because knowledge of the immediate premises is independent of demonstration. Furthermore, he also maintained that scientific knowledge of these immediate premises is not possible through perception—even if this perception were exact. To have knowledge of a particular, we must know the universal under which it falls. Aristotle concluded that intuition and induction, which can lead from particulars to universals, are the sources of scientific knowledge. Although these universals, as primary premises, are the sources of the scientific knowledge obtained by deductions from them, there can be no scientific knowledge of them because otherwise we have an endless regress. Aristotle defined ten ontological categories in our intuition which are the unchanging characteristics of an absolute objectivity and the basis of reality.

Knowledge itself Aristotle defined as the answer to four kinds of questions: (1) whether the connection of an attribute with a thing is a fact; (2) what is the reason for the connection; (3) whether a thing exists; and (4) what is the nature of the thing. Scientific knowledge of something requires answers to these questions concerning the four types of causes of it. These causes are called the *material, efficient, formal,* and *final cause* of the thing. The answer to a request for a scientific explanation of something for Aristotle must be with respect to one or more of these causes. The material cause answers the question of what something is made of; the efficient cause answers how it was formed or constructed or what it came from; the formal cause is the plan of its construction or its archetype; the final cause is the reason why it was made. Aristotle [**Physics**], Book II, does allow chance and spontaneity to be causes.

In *On Generation and Corruption,* Aristotle rejected atomism because he felt that the concept of particles moving in a vacuum was logically absurd.

---

[19]See the critical discussion of Aristotle's metaphysics and logic in Russell [**1945**], pp. 159–172, 195–202. Russell concluded that these notions are based on reifications, the conversion of mental entities into objects, of grammatical forms.

Aristotle also rejected 'action at a distance' and maintained that immediate contact is required for a force to act.

Aristotle applied his logical and explanatory structure in his *Physics* to the analysis of certain observations. He distinguished between natural and violent motion of objects and stated that if the cause of motion is in the thing itself, then the motion is natural. He accounted for the motion of light things and heavy things to their proper locations by calling it their natural tendency to do so. This tendency contains the essence of their lightness and heaviness, the former leading to upward motion and the latter leading to downward motion. At this point the argument rests—just as it did for Newton about 2000 years later when he described the action of gravity in the *Principia* and stated that he would feign no hypotheses concerning its cause.

In parallel with the explanations of Aristotle and others of the phenomenal world in essentially continuum terms, there was also a concern with explaining this world in terms of simpler elements. At about 350 BC, Epicurus codified the work of the atomists into a comprehensive philosophy of nature. The work of Epicurus was summarized by the Roman poet Lucretius and applied to the explanation of natural phenomena in his poem *De Rerum Naturum* written about 60 BC.[20] One of the goals of Lucretius in this poem was to emancipate people from their fear of death that he associated with supernatural religious thought. In this way his work parallels the earlier concerns of the Indian Buddhist philosophers.

Lucretius began with the assumption that all knowledge is derived from sense experience and that sense experience is the sole arbiter of the truth of statements about the world. He observed, in a pre-echo of the anthropic principle, that the fixed seasons of sun and rain are necessary for the production of food and that food is necessary for life. Furthermore, nature is uniform in that similar events occur in different places. In observing the round of birth, life, and death, Lucretius noted that things change their appearance, but nothing is created or destroyed in the changes of form that matter undergoes. These facts were explained by the underlying assumption is that there is nothing but minute atoms and the void:[21]

> But now again to weave my task in words,
> The whole of Nature is of two things built,
> Atoms and the Void.

The only properties the atoms have in this system are solidity, indestructibility, weight, and shape. They are infinite in number and move incessantly in infinite space. Everything observed in nature, including life, is to be explained in terms of atoms, their properties, and their motions.

---

[20]See the W. H. Mallock 1895 translation of Lucretius [**DRN**] and his notes on Lucretius' philosophy and its precursors.

[21]This translation is from A. D. Winspear [**1956**], p. 20.

Lucretius maintained further that there is no way to gain knowledge other than by sense experience. Reasoning about the hidden atoms can only be done by comparing the consequences of assumptions about them with the behavior of matter that we can experience directly.

The assumption of atomism allowed an easy explanation of motion and changes in density and form. The assumption of a variety of atoms, either smooth or with various hooks on them, was used to explain the ways in which particular forms of matter come together and interact to form substances. Lucretius argued for the existence of void spaces, even in hard, solid items such as bone, as necessary to explain how food can enter into and nourish them. Although the number of atoms is infinite, the number of different shapes the atoms can take is finite because an object of limited size can have only a limited number of distinct shapes. Moreover, these atoms do not have color or other sensible qualities such as odor, heat, or sound. Finally, Lucretius stated that time is a consequence of the fact that events happen and things evolve.

All sensation for Lucretius is a mode of touch. Particles are assailing us continually as part of the swarm of atoms in constant motion. In our sense organs, specific particles lead to various tastes, smells, and sounds. Vision is treated similarly in that objects are considered to continually give off films of particles that give rise in the eye to sight of the object. Lucretius stated that light and shadow are the only things we see. Distance and solidity are inferred properties. The source of optical illusions in this view is due to the mental suppositions concerning what we have seen that we add to the thing perceived.

Because all things come into being as a collection of particles, these things will eventually decay and dissolve into their constituent particles and be recycled into other things. This includes minds as well as bodies and even the universe itself. Furthermore, Lucretius argued that there are many universes that have arisen from collections of these particles in boundless space in the same way as our own and at the same time. Finally, because he was aware of no history earlier than the destruction of Troy, Lucretius felt that the origin of the universe may have been fairly recent and its dissolution may take place in a matter of a few centuries.

More than a thousand years later, the Persian poet Omar Khayyám presented a materialist worldview in a very different setting.[22] He was known for his accomplishments in astronomy and mathematics and did important work on the Persian calendar. He, as Lucretius, eschewed religion and was viewed

---

[22] Omar Khayyám's verses are still celebrated today in Persian culture for their music and lyricism. Khayyám's collection of quatrains, The *Rubáiyát*, was introduced to the English speaking world primarily by Edward Fitzgerald's 1859 translation and subsequent editions. There is an important English prose version by Friedrich Rosen as well as German and French versions. For the translations of Fitzgerald and Rosen, along with some of the French and German versions of some quatrains, see Omar Khayyám [**Rub2**].

by many with suspicion because of this. While Lucretius celebrated this as an emancipation from suffering imposed by religion, Khayyám mourned the loss of comfort that religion could provide.

Because of their poetry and similarities in their philosophies, the works of Lucretius and Khayyám are often mentioned together. The nineteenth century understanding their worldviews is illustrated by Fitzgerald's discussion comparing them:[23]

> "Lucretius, indeed, with such material as Epicurus furnished, consoled himself with the construction of a Machine that needed no Constructor, and acting by a Law that implied no Lawgiver; and so composing himself into a Stoical rather than Epicurean severity of Attitude, sat down to contemplate the mechanical Drama of the Universe of which he was part Actor; himself and all about him, (as in his own sublime Description of the Roman Theatre,) coloured with the lurid reflex of the Curtain that was suspended between them and the outer Sun. Omar, more desperate, or more careless, of any such laborious System as resulted in nothing more than hopeless Necessity, flung his own Genius and Learning with a bitter jest into the general Ruin which their insufficient glimpses only served to reveal; and, yielding his Senses to the actual Rose and Vine, only *diverted* his thoughts by balancing ideal possibilities of Fate, Freewill, Existence and Annihilation;"

While Fitzgerald's religious worldview is clearly in marked contrast with that of Khayyám, he nonetheless recognized Khayyám's genius.

In his *Rubáiyát*, Khayyám presented the world as a predestined show governed by blind necessity. He observed that we are alive for a brief moment and argued against alternative worldviews that reflected the religious beliefs common in his day. He [**Rub1**], p. 167, recommended focusing on today rather than looking to tomorrow or to the past to give meaning to one's life:

> Ah, make the most of what we yet may spend,
> Before we too into the Dust descend;
> Dust into Dust, and under Dust to lie,
> Sans Wine, sans Song, sans Singer, and—sans End!

While he did not explicitly expound a detailed materialist philosophy in the *Rubáiyát*, such an interpretation is consistent with the point of view expressed in the poem.[24]

---

[23]This discussion appears as pp. xi–xii in the preface to one of Fitzgerald's editions (See Arberry [**1959**], pp. 159–160). See also Mallock's discussion of the philosophy of Khayyám in relation to that of Lucretius in [**DRN**].

[24]Information about Khayyám and his philosophy is sketchy and controversial—in part because of the bigotry of his day. For more information on his philosophy and verse, see the "Preface to TARANEHAYE KHAYYAM" by Sadegh Hedayat, who was a well-known

Between the time of Lucretius and the seventeenth century, Western philosophical thought came to be dominated by the Catholic church. After a round of neo-Platonism, Aristotelian ideas became dominant in philosophy. A notable exception was the work of William of Occam in the fourteenth century, who allowed the possibility of action at a distance forces and had a more empirical orientation than his colleagues. His ideas had little influence, however.

The slow progress of physics accelerated after Nicolaus Copernicus and Galileo Galilei [**1638**] began to shake the foundations of the worldview supported by the renaissance church. Their work also contributed to shaking off the hold of Aristotelian ideas on Western thinking. Empirical research by Galileo on moving bodies and their mathematical description laid the groundwork for the systematic study of the laws of motion and their mathematization.

The astronomical work of Tycho Brahe helped Johannes Kepler to discover the elliptical orbits of the planets and to formulate his laws of planetary motion. There was work on pressure by the Bernoullis and on the collision of bodies by a number of thinkers. René Descartes, in particular, helped in the middle of the seventeenth century to clarify the laws of motion and the notion of momentum and its role in mechanics. He also contributed the Cartesian coordinate system that allowed the algebraization of geometrical thinking and the geometrization of mechanics. This had a profound and lasting influence on the development of science and physics in particular. Leibniz was another thinker who contributed to the discussion of physical issues at this time. His concept of vis viva (living force) is what we now call energy. He used observations on the collisions of bodies in debates with the Cartesians over whether the 'quantity of motion', mv or the 'vis viva', mv^2 is the appropriate measure of force.[25]

The general study of the impact of bodies played an important role in these discussions. Huyghens showed at the end of the seventeenth century that the vis viva of the bodies is conserved in a collision.[26] Huyghens believed that atoms composing bodies are inelastic—which made this conservation of vis viva in the impact of two bodies difficult to understand. Leibniz, on the other hand, believed that they are elastic. While this allowed him to understand the conservation of vis viva in the collision experiments, the existence of inelastic collisions required explanation. To explain inelastic collisions, Leibniz maintained that they can only happen between macroscopic bodies and contended that the rest of the vis viva is dissipated among the microscopic constituents without being created or destroyed.

Persian writer of the early twentieth century. It is reprinted as pp. 23–53 in Khayyám [**Rub2**].

[25]The concepts of energy, momentum, and force, were not yet clearly distinct.

[26]See Jammer [**1957**], Chapters 6 and 9, for more details on the work of Huyghens and Leibniz.

The concept of force was one of the issues that scholars were trying to clarify, and remove the occult and deistic aspects of, in the wake of medieval scholastic philosophy. The issue of action at a distance was still not considered acceptable to Descartes, Huyghens, and others who struggled to understand how terrestrial gravity worked and what determined the motion in the heavens. Both Descartes and Huyghens subscribed to a vortex theory of gravity and gave qualitative descriptions of how these vortices pressed planets toward each other. The decisive step was made by Isaac Newton, who ignored the true cause of gravity and fashioned a mathematical description of how it determines the structure of the solar system. In spite of this, he did not feel that action at a distance forces were acceptable, and allowed himself in his *Optiks* [**1704**] to speculate on the causes of gravity.[27] Newton's mechanics dominated physics for the next two hundred years.

Returning to epistemological issues, let us begin again with the work of the rationalists in the seventeenth and eighteenth centuries.[28] Represented in the seventeenth century primarily by Descartes and then in the early eighteenth century by Leibniz, the rationalists believed that all scientific knowledge of things in the world is comprehensible in rationalist terms. Scientific knowledge of something in the rationalist sense is complete, systematic, a priori, and dogmatic. It is a priori in that it can be obtained by direct insight and is dogmatic because it is 'without critical analysis of its scope and limits'.

Descartes felt that extension is the defining attribute of both matter and space. He concluded that a vacuum, space without matter, is impossible. He held a continuum view of matter and opposed atomism. Descartes also showed, although this point has often been forgotten, that all perceptual knowledge must be symbolic in character. Thomas Huxley [**1874**], p. 209, reminded us, in his appreciation of Descartes as a physiologist, that Descartes stated clearly in his *Principles de la Philosophie* that our sense organs do not provide us with little images in the brain. Huxley, p. 211, expressed one consequence of Descartes' discoveries in the statement: "The nervous system stands between consciousness and the assumed external world, as an interpreter who can talk with his fingers stands between a hidden speaker and a man who is stone deaf—and Realism is equivalent to a belief on the part of the deaf man, that the speaker must also be talking with his fingers." Descartes went further and claimed that motion of a living body is impossible unless all the elements required for a machine to move are present. He viewed the mind or soul itself as a distinct substance in which reasoning and the will

---

[27] Action at a distance was one of the issues disputed between Leibniz and Samuel Clarke, who was Newton's surrogate in the debate over Newton's theory and priority in inventing the calculus. See the Leibniz-Clarke correspondence in Henry Alexander [**1956**]. For a discussion of Newton's conception of force, see Jammer [**1957**], Chapter 7.

[28] For a very useful discussion of philosophy from the late renaissance through the nineteenth century from a unified perspective, and much more information on the philosophical ideas summarized here, see Høffding [**1882b**], Vols. 1 and 2.

inhere. This left him with the problem of how the soul and body can interact to change events in the physical world. His view has been characterized as the 'ghost in the machine'.

Leibniz also made contributions to philosophy and epistemology in addition to his work in logic, mathematics, and physics. He was in active correspondence with Jesuits in China. Needham [1956], Vol. 2, pp. 496–505, discussed the manuscripts that Leibniz received from them. Needham also speculated that the myth of Indra's net was discussed in this correspondence. This is the story of a net with a jewel at each node suspended over the palace of the God Indra. Each jewel in the net reflects every other jewel and is in turn reflected by them, which illustrates the interconnectedness of all things. Needham felt that this may a have been a direct influence on Leibniz's theory of monads.[29]

Leibniz held that perception occurs by means of sensoria or internal images of external scenes. He agreed with Descartes that the mind or soul is a nonmaterial substance and reconciled Descartes' problem of the connection between material and nonmaterial by denying it. The actions of our will in changing the outcome of events does not change the physical world directly, nor do physical changes effect the soul. Rather, he proposed a theory of pre-established harmony, or psychophysical parallelism, in which the impressions of the soul parallel the changes in the physical world. He argued with the Newtonians concerning Newton's conception of the role of God as watchmaker, who must from time to time set the solar system right. He accepted Descartes conception of matter as a continuum and argued against the existence of a vacuum. From the perspective of physics, he engaged those who believed in atoms, as Newton, Clarke and others certainly did, with contradictions based on the energy (vis viva) lost in the inelastic collisions of infinitely hard bodies.

Leibniz introduced the 'Principle of Sufficient Reason', and stated that one aspect of it is the causal principle that 'nothing happens without a cause'. He then drew as another consequence the 'Principle of the Identity of Indiscernibles'. He tried to use these principles to refute Newton's conception of real, distinct, but indiscernible points in space and time and replace it with the relational view of space as coextensive phenomena and time as successive phenomena. The Newtonians were not convinced by Leibniz's reasoning.

The notion of individuality, which Bohr put to significant use, appeared first in the philosophy of Leibniz. Leibniz had introduced it as part of his theory that each individual substance has its own law of change. For Leibniz, only absolutely simple, indivisible individual substances, which are true unities, had reality. Matter is only a phenomenon and does not meet this criterion. The absolute individual was called a monad by Leibniz and was viewed

---

[29]See the Avatamsaka Sutra in Mahayana Buddhism or the ideas of the Japanese Kegon School of Buddhism for this metaphor of the universe.

as analogous to a "soul or a substantial form similar to that which we call 'I'". Leibniz maintained that there is a law of continuity for all things and that by virtue of this law every part of the universe is in reciprocal action. Each monad, in a darker or clearer manner, represents the whole universe and feels the changes in all the others. Because monads have no windows to let anything in or out, Leibniz made it the task of God to maintain this pre-established harmony in the multiplicity of independent representations of the universe.[30]

Meanwhile, in England, John Locke reawakened critical thinking about knowledge by discussing the relation of empirical perception to knowledge and the origin of knowledge. He criticized the scholastic theory of innate ideas and asserted that all ideas are gained from experience. This includes the content of our consciousness, which arises from both external sources (sensation) and internal sources (reflection). He considered the properties attributed to objects and, following Galileo, Hobbes, Descartes, and Robert Boyle, distinguished between the primary qualities, such as extension and hardness, which inhere in the objects themselves, and the secondary qualities, such as smell, color or taste, which depend on both the object and our sensory apparatus. In his *Human Understanding,* Book II, Chapter viii, he used the account of perception given by Descartes, in which nerves connect the sensory organs to the brain and transmit information to it, to show that our ideas and sensations are not like anything outside us. Knowledge for Locke resides in the agreement or disagreement of ideas with perception. Immediate perception, or intuition, is for Locke its simplest form. The principle of causality arises from experience, but its validity is proved by intuition.

George Berkeley made a penetrating critique of this approach to knowledge at this time. In his *Theory of Vision,* [**1709**], he took up issues of perception and abstract ideas in relation to knowledge. He discussed the fact that we "see" distance, texture, pain, and sorrow just as we see objects. Locating these objects in space with surfaces and feelings is to combine more than one kind of sensation. These associations are constant, a matter of habit, but they are arbitrary. In his *Principles of Knowledge,* [**1710**], Berkeley stated that he wished to find clear meanings for philosophical concepts such as 'matter', 'material object', 'thing', 'reality', and 'existence'. He was also concerned with concepts in science and common language such as 'force', 'gravity', 'mass', 'extension', 'color', and others. He began with 'thing', 'reality', and 'existence' as fundamental concepts. His method was to ask the reader to imagine what a word means, or, even better, to imagine what it signifies. He [**1710**], p. 39, made clear his distrust of words themselves.

As part of this inquiry, Berkeley took on Locke's view that we have a "faculty of abstraction" and promoted the idea that while we can speak of redness as an abstraction, whenever we think about it, we always think

---

[30] See Høffding [**1882b**], Vol. 1, pp. 343–356.

in concrete terms of red things as its exemplars. He denied that primary qualities of a thing can be perceived apart from its secondary qualities. Thus, he assigned reality to things seen, felt and heard, but he denied reality to the abstract notion of matter created by philosophers when they removed all perceptible (secondary) qualities from it. For Berkeley, then, knowledge consists of perceived particulars. In addition, we can both be conscious of this fact and reason about the relations of the ideas that represent these particulars.[31] Furthermore, in an echo of Descartes, Berkeley, p. 39, claimed that these ideas are incorrigible in that he could not be mistaken about his own clearly conceived thoughts.[32] His, [1710], p. 42, analysis of the concept of existence illustrates his ideas in action. He discussed as an example perceiving his writing table: seeing it, touching it, smelling it, and hearing the sound of it. He maintained that statements about the absolute existence of this table apart from mentioning these actual sensations is unintelligible: "There *esse* is *percipi*, nor is it possible they should have any existence apart from the minds of thinking things which perceive them."

In *De Motu*, Berkeley [1721] criticized the employment of the concept of force in mechanics as a holdover from scholastic philosophy. He stated that if forces are a quality of a body in the same way that extension or hardness are considered to be, then they too must be removed along with the other qualities that Galileo and Locke had removed from objects. Anticipating Hume, he remarked on our tendency to find causes and forces in the succession of sensations that appear in a regular pattern. However, in spite of a universal human tendency to do this, Berkeley maintained that it is not legitimate to do so. He observed that the only way to measure forces are by their effects on the motion of bodies. It is therefore the motion of the bodies that is primary from an epistemological standpoint and the concept of force is a metaphysical construction based on this. As Jammer [1957], p. 206, pointed out, Berkeley clearly realized that the modification of the motion of two bodies by contact has the same interpretational problems that explaining it in terms of action at a distance has.

Berkeley's claim, with regard to the theory of knowledge, that objects of knowledge exist only in so far as they are perceived leads to some immediate difficulties. Berkeley was aware of these and answered the question concerning the existence of objects when no person is perceiving them by stating that God always perceives them. Berkeley emphasized that he is not denying the reality of nature—only the reality of abstract matter. In keeping with this, he [1709], p. 231, felt that nature, comprised of the objects of vision, is an expression of the universal language of the Author of Nature. Moreover, he

---

[31]Berkeley [1710], p. 89. See also Berkeley [1713].
[32]See also, for example, Berkeley [1709], p. 173: "Everyone is the best judge of what he perceives and what not", and [1710], p. 238: "Some truths are so near and obvious to the mind, that a man need only to open his eyes to see them."

did not object to the use of the word "object" for a constant conjunction of ideas as long as we are clear that this is all the word object means. Physics for him is the explanation of phenomena in terms of other phenomena. The concept of causality, which is obtained from experience, is used to link these phenomena. He rejected the idea that cause is something apart from a constant conjunction of observable effects. For him, physics is concerned only with observable phenomena and not with abstract notions of force, gravity, or matter.[33]

Although his critique of abstract ideas was insightful, not many were prepared to follow in Berkeley's footsteps. He had in effect made visualization primary to knowledge and converted intentional definitions into extensional ones by equating abstract ideas to the set of objects they can be applied to. To prove the Pythagorean theorem in this situation requires verifying that it applies to all the possible triangle objects of perception that contain a 90° angle. And he had blurred the distinction between 'seeing' and 'seeing that'. By identifying a statement with its verification, Berkeley was left without a way to deal with the problems of dreams, hallucinations, or Plato's example that when we are ill, our perception of a given object can change. At this point Berkeley invoked the help of God. These difficulties and others made it hard to see the validity of the part of his critique of the analysis of abstract ideas pursued by Locke.

David Hume continued down the path that Locke had blazed. His greatest undertaking was the reexamination of the concept of causality. He [**1748**], pp. 41, 87, observed that "All reasonings concerning matters of fact seem to be founded on the relation of cause and effect." Hume rejected this procedure and believed that while experience is the only source of our knowledge of causes, it can provide us with no guarantees that inferences we make from effects to causes will always be true. We infer the cause and effect relation inductively from experience of invariant succession. Because Hume rejected the rationalist conception that causality is founded on reason alone, he stated clearly that we cannot prove the validity of the principle of causality. We apprehend causality in our imagination. The concept of causality in turn serves as the source of our belief in an external world that is independent of consciousness.

Hume denied that the concept of the self, of 'I' or the soul, requires any special substance in which it inheres. This was his second attack on the elements upon which speculative and rational metaphysics was based. Hume, p. 164, also considered the nature of our knowledge of objects in the world and removed not only the secondary qualities from them, but also their primary qualities: "Bereave matter of all its intelligible qualities, both primary and secondary, you in a manner annihilate it and leave only a certain unknown

---

[33]Berkeley [**1710**], p. 69, 88; [**1709**], pp. 264–265; [**1721**], p. 40, 49, 51.

inexplicable *something* as the cause of our perceptions—a notion so imperfect that no skeptic will think it worthwhile to contend against it."

By successively demoting things to things-in-themselves, Galileo and Descartes, followed later by Locke and then Hume, fixed attention on the perceiving subject as opposed to Aristotle's unchanging characteristics of objectivity and paved the way for the idealism of Berkeley and for Kant's theory of knowledge.

9.5 Reflection 18

One of the differences between the approaches of the Eastern and Western philosophers to the basic themes I have been discussing is the emphasis in the East on the human questions, the alleviation of suffering and choice of right social action, versus the emphasis in the West on the explanatory questions and the mechanisms underlying matter and perception. Their attitude toward the acquisition of knowledge was correspondingly different as well. On the other hand, there are many parallels between the two traditions regarding subject and object, knowledge, perception, and causality.

It is remarkable that two separate philosophical traditions, developed independently over many centuries, should parallel each other so much with respect to notions of knowledge, reality, causality, and perception. This suggests that we are seeing some universal aspects of the human mind as a knowledge gatherer and problem solver. Parallels of this sort with respect to learning language led Noam Chomsky to suggest that the language learning and production facilities of the human mind can be understood in terms of the rationalist conception of innate ideas.[34]

The concept of causality also plays a central role in the theory of knowledge in both the Eastern and Western traditions. It has been claimed by many, including Bohr, that the concept of cause lies at the root of any attempt to understand knowledge and its limits. Part of the strong impact that the development of quantum theory had on researchers was because certain events appear not to be caused within quantum mechanics. Because of this tension, I will follow the notion of cause, and its putative role in the theory of knowledge, in the work of a number of philosophers and scientists. These thoughts on its role in the theory of knowledge will be pulled together in Chapter 18.

---

[34]See Chomsky [**1959**], [**1966**], [**1968**] for more on this.

CHAPTER 10

Bohr and Kant

We have come to the end of the eighteenth century. From the standpoint of the theory of knowledge, and European philosophy in general, the publication of Kant's monumental work on the theory of knowledge at this time was the important event. Kant's influence extended throughout the nineteenth century, and although philosophical fashions waxed and waned, his work remained the most important. From a scientific perspective, Kant's work formed part of the conceptual framework of the time, and those in the various sciences who reflected on fundamental issues usually expressed them within the framework of Kantian epistemology. Because of the unique stature of Kant in this regard, I will present a focused summary of his work and an analysis of his theory of knowledge and a comparison with Bohr's.

10.1 Kant's Theory of Knowledge

Immanuel Kant was dissatisfied with the speculative systems of philosophy that were popular when he began his work.[1] He came to see that the issue was how to understand the limits of knowledge and reason. He credited Hume with shaking him out of his rationalistic dogmatic slumber and teaching him the importance of the critical analysis of the scope and limits of knowledge. In spite of this rude awakening, Kant did not lose his taste for the a priori.

Kant was engaged in what he called critical philosophy. His purpose was two-fold. He was concerned with metaphysics, which is a collection of propositions about the world that can contain nothing empirical and consists exclusively of a priori propositions that express only possibilities. He was opposed to speculative metaphysics, which uses the logical possibility of a substance or thing as the sole requirement for its admissibility, and wanted to remove it as an acceptable method of doing philosophy. He took as his task to show, in terms of a priori principles governing the employment of reason on the objects of experience, how knowledge and science were possible. This philosophy has been characterized by Robert Butts [**1986a**], p. 4, as "a philosophy that ... condemns classical substantive metaphysics as a texture of fictions, but then revitalizes the fictions as ingredient ideas in regulative principles of reason ...."

In his analysis of thought during the period before he began work on the *Critique of Pure Reason,* Kant found that thought consists in comparing and analyzing. Every judgment for him is a comparison of an attribute with an object. The object either does or does not have the attribute. In this way we always operate according to the principles of identity and contradiction and can move from one concept to another only when the identity of the two is shown. The concept of causality must then be like a deduction if the effect is to follow from the cause. But, as Hume had emphasized, there is no logically necessary relation of cause and effect in nature itself that would support this view. Kant finally came to realize, in a turning point that he compared to that of Copernicus, that our axioms of knowledge and causality are in fact subjective and express the sole conditions under which we can understand or apprehend an object. The laws of space, time, and causality become the laws of our perception. Everything we perceive must be in accord with these laws determined by the forms of our perceptive faculty.[2] It follows that we can only perceive phenomena, which are part of our experience of things, and not the noumena, or things-in-themselves. Kant believed that the things-in-themselves exist and are the causes (by some means) of our experiences. In

---

[1] For more details on Kant, his life and thought, see Høffding [**1882b**], Vol. 2, pp. 41–109.

[2] By *form* Kant refers to the properties of the faculty itself. By *matter* he refers to effects in this faculty produced by external influences.

this way Kant had explained the distinction made by Plato between what we perceive and what is real in terms of the difference between phenomena and noumena.

Causality requires more than this as Kant realized after publishing this work in his *Dissertation* of 1769. It requires a synthesis as well as an analysis if we are to connect separate perceptions as required by causality. He then extended to the understanding or consciousness the ability to connect and combine perceptions in certain relations. He set up Categories of the understanding and stated that we are able to understand things only when they are united in accord with these Categories. In extending his insight about the nature of perception to the understanding, he had extended his basic idea to both components of knowledge. In each component, the human mind acts to unite separate entities, which means, as Høffding [1902], pp. 48–49, observed, Kant has identified "synthesis in general as the fundamental form of the activity of consciousness." This extension was consistent with the rules for doing metaphysics, which Butts [1986a], p. 6, extracted from Kant's early work of 1764 in the form: "1) in metaphysics, one should not begin with definitions (as in mathematics ...), but with what one's analysis picks out as "immediately certain"; and 2) having noted various propositions whose claims are immediately certain, one should separate those not contained in others, and make them the basis of inferences to other derived properties; in short, one should look for immediate certainties that can act as axioms." Butts noted the similarity between this approach and that of René Descartes. From Kant's point of view, this procedure in metaphysics is the same that Newton used in his *Principia:* we begin with experiences that are certain and use geometry, which is a deductive science, to aid us in the discovery of laws governing the behavior of the appearances of nature. We do not require the ultimate causes of these appearances but only that our account of them is empirically adequate.

In 1781, Kant published his masterwork, the *Critique of Pure Reason,* in which he proposed his completed epistemological theory of the world as the object of knowledge. His task was to show how the succession of what he called appearances are organized in the way they are independent of the nature of the things-in-themselves. In other words, the occurrence of certain features in a succession of appearances, to which others would attribute the existence of an object with certain properties, must be explained in Kantian terms in a way independent of what one might want to call the properties of the thing-in-itself.[3] As a consequence of his previous analysis, the attribution of properties to things-in-themselves does not make sense because the

---

[3]Høffding [1902], pp. 112–113, discussed the thing-in-itself: "The justification of Kant's setting up the notion of the 'thing-in-itself' lay in the fact that a transcendental concept is needed in order to express the irrational relation between what he called the 'form' and the 'matter' of our knowledge." The term irrational means 'unanalyzable' here.

concepts employed in doing so are not meaningful outside of their application to appearances which, by definition, are all we can have experience of. Kant went on to show how the properties of the mind and our perceptual apparatus (that which provides us with the appearances) must be such that the descriptions (which would ordinarily be interpreted as ascribing properties to objects) are really modes of organizing the succession of appearances. I will follow his argument in some detail.

Kant recommended the following procedure for examining the scope and limits of knowledge in the *Prolegomena* [**1783**], p. 70:

"To search in our common knowledge for concepts which do not rest upon particular experience and yet occur in all knowledge from experience, of which they as it were constitute the mere form of connection, presupposes neither greater reflection nor deeper insight than to detect in a language the rules of the actual use of words generally and thus to collect elements for a grammar (in fact both researches are very nearly related), even though we are not able to give a reason why each language has just this and no other formal constitution, and still less why any precise number of determinations in general, neither more nor less, can be found in it."

Language in this weak sense is thus a repository of philosophy, a notion that goes back to the ancient Greeks.

Knowledge, for Kant [**1781**], p. 41, begins with experience but does not all come from experience. We gain knowledge beyond that provided by experience by analyzing the "faculty of knowledge" in terms of the strictures that it puts on both what we can observe and how we can reason. Those of Kant's principles that are not based on, or derived from, experience (though they are perhaps suggested by experience) are called *a priori*. A pure a priori proposition contains no aspect of sense experience or, to use Kant's terminology, of *sensation*. As a necessary condition for a proposition to be pure a priori, Kant [**1781**], pp. 43–44, imposed the requirement that the proposition expresses a necessary property of a class of appearances or, equivalently (for Kant), that it be used with respect to these appearances with strict universality. This means that a pure a priori proposition must not allow of conceivable alternative possibilities with respect to those appearances it is to be applied to.

Kant defined an *appearance* as involving both a perception and its form. The term *form* in this case refers to those concepts under which all perceptions are subsumed. An investigation of the a priori possible forms of perception comprises the basis for the Transcendental Aesthetic of the Critique [**1781**], pp. 65–66. Kant distinguished two such forms: space and time. Neither space nor time are properties of "things-in-themselves," but rather are properties of our perceptions of them [**1781**], pp. 71, 74, 76, 257, 275. As a further terminological point, Kant called "transcendental" those considerations dealing with the a priori possibilities of knowledge or of its employment [**1781**], p. 96.

Høffding [**1882b**], 2, pp. 51–52, pointed out a weakness in this part of the Kantian program. Kant cannot guarantee that the forms and Categories discovered by his analysis are a complete set. Kant promised to fill in the gap with a proof, but never did. Høffding [**1917**], [**1922**] offered a new Category of his own that he called 'Of Totality' and wrote on the Category 'Of Relation'.

Kant characterized the Transcendental Logic in the following famous passage [**1781**], p. 93:

"Thoughts without contents are empty, intuitions without concepts are blind. It is, therefore, just as necessary to make our concepts sensible, that is, to add the object to them in intuition, as to make our intuitions intelligible, that is, to bring them under concepts.... The understanding can intuit nothing, the sense can think nothing."

Kant [**1781**], p. 65, defined intuitions as being immediately related to the objects of sensation presented in the mind (i.e., in the understanding). He was arguing that in order to avoid the errors that reason can lead into, e.g., speculative metaphysics [**1781**], pp. 327–383, our ordinary concepts must be related to (possible) experience [**1781**], pp. 174, 286. And in order that intuitions of sensation be recognized and understood, i.e., that we *know* what they are, it is necessary that they be expressed in concepts [**1781**], p. 286. In any statement of what we have perceived, this requirement has already been satisfied. In other words, Kant [**1783**], p. 48–56, maintained that for a perception to become an experience, it must be subsumed under a concept. Thus experience has a dual nature: "Experience consists of intuitions, which belong to the sensibility, and of judgments, which are entirely the work of the understanding." Following this to its conclusion, Kant maintained that "the principles of experience are the very laws of nature."

Concepts and intuitions are manipulated, that is, thought about and reasoned with, in the *understanding*. By an analysis of the a priori requirements of knowledge in the Transcendental Analytic, Kant, [**1781**], pp. 104–110, hoped to discover the elements of the pure understanding that organize and systematize our concepts and intuitions of sense, and thereby essentially to determine the forms of our possible experience. Out of this analysis, [**1781**], p. 112, came the *pure concepts of the understanding* that apply a priori to objects. Kant called these pure concepts of the understanding 'Categories,' similar to those of Aristotle, and distinguished four main types: Of Quantity, Of Quality, Of Relation, and Of Modality [**1781**], p. 113. The Categories are the forms of thought [**1781**], pp. 164, 173, and express laws prescribed a priori on appearances and the sum of all appearances.

Nature in general, which was what Kant called the sum of all appearances, is analyzable according to these concepts of the pure understanding because appearances must conform to them.[4] The analysis of appearances includes the analysis according to the concept of causality, which itself appears in the Category of Relation. Special laws of nature concerning the behavior of specific objects in relation to each other cannot be derived from the Categories but must be discovered empirically. Nevertheless, these particular laws are still subject to the general overall requirements of the Categories [**1781**], pp. 173–174, 205–208. The Category of Relation was further used for the derivation of the forms underlying all laws of nature. Such a form was called by Kant an Analogy of Experience in the following passage [**1781**], pp. 243–244; see also p. 173:

"For the existence of the thing being thus bound up with our perception in a possible experience, we are able in a series of possible perceptions and under the guidance of the analogies to make the transition from our actual perception to the thing in question. Thus from the perception of the attracted iron filings we know of the existence of magnetic matter pervading all bodies, although the constitution of our organs cuts us off from immediate perception of this medium. For in accordance with the laws of sensibility, and the context of our perceptions, we should, were our senses more refined, come also in an experience upon the immediate empirical intuition of it. The grossness of our sense does not in any way decide the form of our possible experience in general. Our knowledge of the existence of things reaches, then, only so far as perception and its advance according to empirical laws can extend. If we do not start from experience or do not proceed in accordance with the laws of the empirical connection of appearance, our guessing or enquiring into the existence of anything will only be an idle pretense."

As this passage indicates, Kant's strictures on possible experience cannot be too narrowly related to actual experience or structural properties of the world. Thus, for example, to call Weizsäcker's [**1952**], p. 94, statement: "... the propositions of classical physics mirror the structure of the world given by perception ..." a Kantian one is risky unless one can establish that the basic propositions of classical physics express the only ways possible for experiencing the world. In point of fact, Aristotelian physics is closer to mirroring the phenomenal world of our experience in which, for example, bodies come to rest when they are no longer pushed, than classical physics is.

A similar case would have to be made with respect to the Analogies of Experience in order to justify Weizsäcker's [**1952**], p. 94, statement: "In this way classical physics has a peculiar middle position between the world of sensation and the world of things." It is true that Kant himself misjudged

---

[4]In his *Prolegomena*, Kant, [**1783**], p. 67, stated this in the form: *"The understanding does not derive its laws* (a priori) *from, but prescribes them to, nature.*

the scope and application of his theory in attempting to derive Newtonian mechanics a priori (*Metaphysical Foundations of Natural Science* [**1786**] and later writings), but his general theory does not fall with this overextension. Kant [**1781**], p. 205, in fact, explicitly warned against the errors of applying transcendental philosophy outside its proper realm:

> "Since all appearances, alike in the extensive and in their intensive aspect, are thus continuous magnitudes, it might seem to be an easy matter to prove with mathematical conclusiveness the proposition that all alteration (transition of a thing from one state to another), is continuous. But the causality of an alteration in general, presupposing, as it does, empirical principles, lies altogether outside the limits of a transcendental philosophy .... Since in our present enquiry we have no data of which we can make use save only the pure fundamental concepts of all possible experience, in which there must be absolutely nothing that is empirical, we cannot, without destroying the unity of our system, anticipate general natural science, which is based on certain primary experiences."

The explanation of how pure concepts of the understanding could have pure a priori application to objects not arising in experience was called by Kant [**1781**], pp. 120–128, 170–175, the Transcendental Deduction. The transcendental deduction of the Categories follows from the analysis of the "possible ways in which synthetic representations and their objects can establish connection, obtain necessary relation to each other, and, as it were, meet one another."[5] It is only through the representation of the object that it can be known as an object [**1781**], pp. 126–137, and thus the possibilities for experience and our understanding of experience determine what is to count in the world as an object or thing.

The general rules governing experience do not refer directly to objects of experience and are not deducible from experience. To account for them, Kant introduced in his Transcendental Dialectic the notion of a transcendental idea. A transcendental idea is an a priori pure concept of reason [**1781**], pp. 318, 315–322. Ideas have no empirical content [**1781**], p. 320: "For even if they cannot determine any object, they may yet, in a fundamental and unobserved fashion, be of service to the understanding as a canon for its extended and consistent employment." Kant [**1781**], pp. 322–323, characterized the transcendental ideas as follows:

> "From the natural relation which the transcendental employment of our knowledge, alike in reference and in judgments, must bear to its logical employment, we have gathered that there can be only three kinds of dialectical inference through which reason can arrive at knowledge by means of principles, and that in all of these, its business

---

[5] Kant [**1781**], p. 125.

10.1 KANT'S THEORY OF KNOWLEDGE

is to ascend from the conditioned synthesis, to which understanding always remains restricted, to the unconditioned, which understanding can never reach."

There is more than one echo of Plato's Ideas and his distinction between reason and the understanding here.

The conditioned synthesis is the synthesis of the relations of objects of possible experience into a general principle, universal concept, or law. Kant continued by spelling out the relations within our representations:

"The relations which are to be universally found in all our representations are (1) relation to the subject; (2) relation to objects, either as appearance or as objects of thought in general .... All transcendental ideas can therefore be arranged in three classes, the *first* containing the absolute (unconditioned) *unity of the thinking subject,* the *second* the absolute *unity of the series of conditions of appearance,* the *third* the absolute *unity of the condition of all objects of thought in general.*"

Each proposition in the understanding can be derived from a more general one by means of inference according to the pattern of a syllogism. This shows the relation of the *conditioned* synthesis, i.e., judgments involving concepts that are related to (possible) objects of experience, to the *unconditioned,* i.e., to a synthetic a priori proposition from which the conditioned propositions follow (as well as other unconditioned synthetic propositions). Kant [**1781**], p. 306, went on to state that in reference to the transcendental ideas, "the pure understanding—inasmuch as it has to deal with objects of a possible experience, the knowledge and synthesis of which is always conditioned—knows nothing."

Two examples Kant [**1781**], p. 54, gave of synthetic a priori principles in physics are the conservation of the quantity of matter, and the equality of action and reaction. In addition, he [**1781**], pp. 52–54, considered all mathematical judgments to be synthetic a priori.[6]

With regard to the fact that no objects of possible experience correspond to the transcendental ideas, Kant [**1781**], pp. 327–338, warned against their misapplication and misuse:

"The transcendental (subjective) reality of the pure concepts of reason depend on our having been led to such ideas by a necessary syllogism. There will therefore be syllogisms that contain no empirical premises, and by means of which we conclude from something that we know to something else of which we have no concept, and to which, owing to an inevitable illusion, we yet ascribe objective reality .... They are sophistications not of men but of pure reason

---

[6]For various discussions of the a priori in the twentieth century, see Clarence I. Lewis [**1923**], Alfred J. Ayer [**1936**], Cooper H. Langford [**1949**] and Wilfrid Sellars [**1953**].

itself. Even the wisest of men cannot free themselves from them. After long effort he perhaps succeeds in guarding himself against actual error; but he will never be able to free himself from the illusion, which unceasingly mocks and torments him."

These illusions form the subject matter of metaphysics for Kant and lead into the various blind alleys and errors of metaphysical thinking that he wrote the *Critique* to help destroy.

Kant's *Metaphysical Foundations of Natural Science* was published in 1786. In this book, Kant examined the relation between his critical philosophy and Newtonian mechanics, which he saw as a paradigm of science. Kant's goal was to provide an epistemological foundation for the speculative science of pure physics and show the role of empirical observations in conjunction with the a priori principles. This relation took the form of a "special metaphysics" which includes the empirical concept of matter in addition to the a priori principles regulating reason.

Recently the *Metaphysical Foundations* and the relation of Kant's philosophy to Newtonian mechanics have been freshly reexamined. In a collection of articles exploring some new viewpoints on Kant, Butts [**1986a**] has discussed the fact that the *Metaphysical Foundations* was being prepared by Kant at the same time as the second edition of the *Critique*.[7] He, p. 14, argued that this work extended and completed the *Critique* by supplying it with a concrete application in the form of a philosophical foundation for Newtonian physics. Natural science is the science of matter and motion because it is solely concerned with matter that is subject to motion in the outer sense (external experience). In accord with the categories of the *Critique,* it is studied under the headings of (1) kinematics, subsumed under the Category of Quantity as the pure geometry of motion, (2) dynamics, subsumed under the Category of Quality, and refers to the moving force, (3) mechanics, subsumed under the Category of Relation, which studies the relations of external moving bodies, and (4) phenomenology, subsumed under the Category of Modality, which is concerned with the motion or rest of the matter. Part of what is at issue in these new readings of Kant is the question of whether the a priori principles are seen to have a constitutive character, which means they shape our experience by determining its form, or a regulative character, which means they have a methodological status and govern how we express it.[8]

An illustrative difference between Kant and Newton on unobservable entities was presented by Kathleen Okruhlik [**1986**] in a discussion of Kant's methodology and realism. She noted that Newton, in his methodological rule stated in the Third Rule of Reasoning in Philosophy, "allows us to attribute to the observable just those properties that characterize all bodies in experience and that neither intensify or remit." To support this, Newton appealed

---

[7]See other references to new work on Kant given in C. A. Hooker [**1994**].
[8]See Butts [**1986b**], p. 181.

to nature, as a unified whole, which is something given antecedent to experience. Kant on the other hand, stated that the unity of nature flows from the scientific taxonomies that involve these theoretical concepts, which are "posited in order to *bring about* the unity of nature." In other words, reason "projects" this unity. She, p. 327, observed that it follows from this for Kant that the projected unity of nature is our only criterion for scientific truth.

The publication of the *Critique of Judgment* in 1790 completed Kant's method for metaphysics and provided a foundation for pure physics, which is a speculative science in the absence of experience. This "metaphysics of nature," as Butts [**1986a**], pp. 18–19, summarized it, consists of three parts: "First, there is the essential "general or universal metaphysics of experience" provided by the pure principles of the understanding. Second, there is the "special metaphysics" of natural science, with one empirical ingredient—the concept of matter—but with all the rest following on purely a priori grounds. This also includes the metaphysical and mathematical constructions of possible concepts. Third, there is the methodology of the regulative employment of ideas of reason ...." In addition, an object must be given in the outer sense, and subject to the conditions of space and time, in order to be substantial.

The central tenets of Kant's program were summarized by Butts [**1986b**], p. 165:[9]

1. Knowledge has a dual source in sensibility and understanding: To know is to conceptualize sense-contentful intuitions of objects in space and time under the categories.
2. That which we know about space and time, the categories, pure schemata or rules of meaning, mathematical constructions, and pure principles instancing categories, is what we can know a priori in the domain of the theoretical: "We can know *a priori* of things only what we put into them". (Bxviii)
3. Objects of possible experience (knowables) are just those objects structured by the schematized categories; "experience" is categorically idealized sense-contentful intuition.
4. Concepts natively apply only to evident sense-contents (or to constructs, in the case of mathematics); thus no conceptualization of that which transcends the realm of possible experience (the phenomenal) is possible.
5. Ideas are sense-contentless forms having application in logic (in thinking, not in knowing); ideas do not present objects of possible experience (knowables).
6. Traditional metaphysics separates ideas from the dual sources of knowledge, relying solely upon appeal to logical possibility; it follows that

---

[9]This passage was discussed by Hooker [**1994**], pp. 191, 192, who has also discussed the other passages by Butts mentioned just below.

there can be no metaphysical knowledge that derives from ideas—there can be no knowledge of *an sich* reality; no knowledge of things as they are in themselves.

7. Metaphysical ideas thus have a merely regulative employment; they guide research and condition systematic expectations; their proper employment encourages us to stay within the bounds of possible experience—in effect, to settle for the kind of knowledge that positive science yields.

The way the components of Kant's theory are to be used together was also nicely summarized by Butts [1986b], p. 189, and the characterization from Kant's point of view of the relation between Nature, as given a priori in our understanding, and nature, given as experience in the outer senses, was summarized by Butts [1986b], p. 165, as well.

The power and coherence of Kant's thought had a major impact on European philosophy for well over a hundred years.[10] In Chapter 11 some aspects of Kantian thinking through the nineteenth century and its influence on thought in every other discipline will be traced.

10.2 Bohr and Kant

Both Bohr and Kant were interested in examining the possibilities of (or conditions under which we may have) objective knowledge. To do this, they both engaged in an examination of the scope and limits of knowledge.[11] Some similarities in their modes of expression and several parallels between their epistemologies have been remarked on a number of authors.[12] However, most of the treatments of Bohr and Kant in the literature are concerned with Bohr's use of Kantian terminology without examining and comparing their epistemological structures as a whole. The results obtained by this approach are equivocal and unilluminating. There are a few, on the other hand, who have probed more deeply into the question of exactly what the connections are and how far-reaching Bohr's commitment to a Kantian framework was.[13]

There are a number of parallels that suggest themselves immediately in a comparison of the enterprises of Kant and Bohr: (1) Kant's objective was to overturn the speculative metaphysics that dominated philosophy and to give a philosophically acceptable account for the possibility of science as a

---

[10] For a discussion of the value of Kant's conceptions and some problems with them, see Høffding [1882b], volume 2, Chapter III.

[11] See Kant [1781], pp. 9–10, 25, 32–33, [1783], p. ix. For Bohr's program see Bohr [1929a], pp. 96–97, [1937a], pp. 289–290, [1954], pp. 68–69, 78–79.

[12] Weizsäcker [1952], pp. 92, 115–120, Heisenberg [1958a], pp. 88–91, Heelan [1965], pp. 81–82, 141, 143, Meyer-Abich [1965], p. 176, Einstein [1949], p. 647, Folse [1978], Folse [1985], Honner [1987], E. MacKinnon [1982], Hooker [1972], [1994], and others.

[13] These exceptions are Weizsäcker [1952], pp. 115–126, MacKinnon [1982], pp. 370–376, Folse [1978], and Hooker [1972], [1994]. For further references to those who have discussed Kantian aspects of Bohr's work, see Folse [1978].

consequence of experience. Bohr's objective was to answer the objections to quantum theory by those who felt that it violated some deeply held principles concerning the reality, continuity, and intelligibility of nature. (2) Both Bohr and Kant were concerned with the possibilities of experience and the forms of perception associated with that. (3) Both Bohr and Kant were concerned with what concepts we could use in a theoretical description of objects and the rules regulating the employment of these descriptions. (4) Both looked to specific experiments or observations in science to provide paradigms to illustrate their views. (5) Both were concerned that the practice of science not be held back by an outmoded metaphysics. Finally, (6) some have suggested that Bohr's *main argument* is actually a transcendental deduction.

In spite of these parallels, there is no evidence that Bohr was substantially influenced by the particulars of either Kant's epistemological theory or his methodology. Bohr did use some terminology associated with Kant in ways that are reminiscent of how Kant and others used them. But, given the pervasive influence of Kantian ideas at the time, these modes of expression were common and their use was not limited to philosophical circles. In spite of these similarities, a comparison of their philosophical commitments and the structures of their epistemologies will show that Bohr and Kant were quite different. To demonstrate this, I will make a point-by-point comparison of Kant's theory of knowledge to Bohr's.

In an early essay, Bohr [**1927**], pp. 54–55, called the "spacetime coordination" of an atomic process a symbolization of the "idealization of observation." In this essay and subsequent ones, Bohr made clear the importance of the concepts of space and time with respect to the interpretation of observations. But, in accord with his observation thesis, Bohr also emphasized that the statement and interpretation of experimental data involves reference to the experimental arrangement that is described using everyday language and the machinery of classical physics. Kant's forms of perception, on the other hand, refer only to space and time and do not require a further contextual reference external to the observer.

In Kant's theory, appearances are apprehended in the intuition and knowledge of them is expressed in concepts. These concepts and those relating to the succession of appearances are regulated by the Categories. Bohr's theory of observation involves the classical description of macroscopic instruments operating in space and time. The employment of these instruments in a particular experimental arrangement, which is suitable for measuring a particular quantity, determines the concepts that are appropriate for describing what is observed. Bohr's theory thus combines elements that correspond to those appearing in Kant's Transcendental Aesthetic and Transcendental Analytic.

A 'phenomenon' in Bohr's theory is a completed (or closed) observation for which the results have been made permanent and recorded. In Bohr's Observation Thesis, any statement of a phenomenon must be made in classical terms accompanied by a reference to the type of experimental arrangement used to obtain it. Bohr justified the requirements in his Observation Thesis by means of his *main argument*. Kant, on the other hand, justified the application of the Categories as conditions for possible experience by means of a transcendental deduction.

Kant's "deduction" of causality will be reviewed next with an eye to the general question of the possibilities of experience in relation to Bohr's use and justification of his Observation Thesis that regulates the application of concepts to experience.

Transcendental Deduction.

In Kant's treatment of causality as an a priori pure concept of the understanding, he had to face the problem of how this concept would apply a priori to objects and not just turn out to be empty of application. With regard to the a priori knowledge of objects, Kant [**1781**], p. 112, distinguished three factors: the manifold of pure intuition (within which representations of objects are given to us), the synthesis of this manifold by means of the imagination (making the connection between individual representations), and the concepts that give unity to this pure synthesis (which consists solely in the representation of the necessary synthetic unity). We can view this manifold as analogous to a stack of sheets of paper each containing a single representation of an object at a different point in time. As Kant [**1781**], p. 124, pointed out, it is not obvious why this manifold of appearances should necessarily contain connections like causality. It could happen that all appearances are given to us in confusion, so that we are unable to place these pages in a meaningful order, and that nothing in the series of appearances presents itself from which we could draw a rule of synthesis like that of the (in Kant's terminology) necessary connection of cause and effect. No empirical investigation could give us this information, since the empirical induction could not establish the necessity inherent in the rule of causality [**1781**], p. 125: "For this concept makes strict demands that something, A, should be such that something else, B, follows from it *necessarily and in accordance with an absolutely universal rule.*" To establish that the concept of causality is not empty, requires therefore, in Kant's theory, a transcendental deduction.

The purpose of the transcendental deduction is to show how the [**1781**], p. 124, "subjective conditions of thought" can have objective validity. The proof that causality is a necessary feature of the succession of appearances is given in the Second Analogy of Experience; it is based on the notion of *apperception*, which refers to an act of attention. Pure apperception [**1781**], p. 153, generates the representation '*I think*,' that must be capable of accompanying all other representations, and which in all consciousness is one and the same and cannot itself be accompanied by any further representation.[14]

---

[14]This excludes Poul Møller's regression of the 'I's.

The unity of this apperception is titled the Transcendental Unity of Self-consciousness, which indicates the possibility of a priori knowledge arising from it. Since, according to Kant, only in so far as I can grasp the manifold of the representations in one consciousness, can I call them mine, it follows that [**1781**], p. 154, "... the synthetic unity of the manifold of intuitions, as generated *a priori*, is thus the ground of the identity of apperception itself, which precedes *a priori* all *my* determinate thought." This is an affair of the understanding alone; and the principle of the necessary unity of apperception [**1781**], pp. 154, 194, is the highest principle in the whole sphere of human knowledge. It is also an analytic (necessary) proposition. Kant continued:

"... it is the unity of consciousness that alone constitutes the relation of representations to an object, and therefore their objective validity and the fact that they are modes of knowledge .... The synthetic unity of consciousness is, therefore, an objective condition of all knowledge. It is not merely a condition that I myself require in knowing an object, but is a condition under which every intuition must stand in order to *become an object for me.*"

This peculiarity of our understanding [**1781**], p. 161, that it can produce the a priori unity of apperception solely by means of the Categories, and only by such and so many, is not capable of further explanation. And the Categories, as yielding knowledge of things, have no application than to things that may be objects of possible experience.

Honner [**1987**] investigated the transcendental aspects of Bohr's philosophy. He, p. 73, stated that Bohr's thought must be viewed more as circular than axiomatic, by which he meant that Bohr's approach acknowledges "the hermeneutic circle of language and reality". This refers to Heidegger's circle of words taking their meanings from sentences and sentences taking their meanings from words. He, p. 74, went on to maintain that Bohr's approach to philosophy reflects the transcendental approach. By this he, p. 77, meant that Bohr's concern with "the necessary conditions governing the formation of concepts and the possibility of giving a precise description." To support this point Honner quoted from a 1927 letter from Bohr to Einstein in which Bohr discussed the notion of visualizability. Bohr stated that the concept of a field is essential to quantum theory and that a simple presentation of the quantum theory will elude us unless it is "based on a reference to the essential limitation in the possibilities of observation." Bohr connected this with the impossibility of a "detached description" of the properties of particles of light when using the wave description.

The transcendental aspects of Bohr's philosophy are associated with his justification of the conditions required for unambiguous communication. This requires, Honner, p. 88, claimed, a combination of a priori and synthetic judgments in the form of a statement of the 'simple logical demand' that we meet the necessary conditions for unambiguous communication by using only suitably refined everyday concepts "no matter how far the processes concerned transcend the range of ordinary experience." Honner, p. 91, observed that Bohr [**1929c**], pp. 15, 20, appealed not only to quantum physics but also to general epistemological considerations concerning the nature of human consciousness in his justification of complementarity. He, p. 97, then referred to the distinction between conceptual relativism, which he maintained is equivalent to a complete holism, and transcendental arguments that try to answer skeptics by stating that certain conceptual or linguistic frameworks have a special status. The use of these particular frameworks is then claimed to be necessary for knowledge or intelligible experience. Based on his reading of Bohr and this criterion, Honner, p. 98, maintained that Bohr has much more in common with the transcendentalists than with the pragmatic relativists. Bohr's argument was summarized by Honner as a circular sequence of ten steps, which both begins and ends with the statement that "all knowledge presents itself within a suitable conceptual framework which is adapted to our previous experience". He boiled this down into three basic propositions that he felt Bohr based his theory on. He characterized these as a transcendental claim, a version of the correspondence principle, and the prescription of complementarity:

(B1) Some kind of conceptual framework is a necessary condition of the possibility of ordering experience.

(B2) It is a necessary condition of the possibility of objective description of processes at the boundaries of human experience that concepts related to more normal experience be employed.

(B3) Our position as observers in a domain of experience where unambiguous application of concepts depends essentially on the conditions of observation demands the use of complementary descriptions if the description is to be exhaustive.

Honner noted that no mention of either quantum theory or the subject/object distinction appears in these statements.

This series of statements summarizing Bohr's views was used by Honner to pursue what he viewed as Bohr's transcendental argument. He, p. 199, observed that transcendental arguments do have an element of circularity. Honner, p. 203–205, stated further that Bohr had defined a conceptual framework as "an unambiguous logical representation of relations between experience." Replacing the term 'conceptual framework' in (B1) with this phrase yields "Some kind of unambiguous logical representation of relations between experiences is a necessary condition of the possibility of ordering experiences." He noted that this is nearly a tautology and remarked that, as in all transcendental arguments, its purpose is "laying bare the general features of our use of concepts". Approaching the analysis from the standpoint of Strawson's descriptive metaphysics, Honner also considered (B2) to be another indispensability claim.

Honner, p. 207–208, then argued that because the apparatus-object interaction cannot be divided, the system must be treated as an unanalyzable whole, which means that the object cannot be identified as separate from the apparatus and cannot be assigned a path. He went on to identify what he called the most difficult aspect of Bohr's vision:

"The source of much vexation in coming to understand his position is that there is so little to be understood. He makes a reasonable claim rather than elaborating an inexorable argument. His critics imply that something like a leap of faith is required if one is to enter into his camp. Such criticisms, while not always charitably couched, are not inaccurate. Transcendental argument entails reflection on given capabilities and then the articulation of the necessary conditions of such capacities 'to which we can conceive no alternatives'. The argument only works when we engage in it ourselves."

Based on his analysis of the transcendental aspects of Bohr's philosophy, Honner, p. 222, called Bohr's approach "performative and self-referential." Further, in reference to Bohr's lack of knowledge of traditional philosophical concerns and lack of attention to them, Honner, p. 214, stated that his "amateurish instincts" are tied closely to the way physics works.

In Honner's, pp. 216–224, conclusions concerning Bohr's work, he stated that Bohr's fundamental arguments hint at a relation between "the given character of ordinary language and a deterministic-mechanistic view of the workings of nature." He justified this view, of an "intriguing and covert connection between ordinary language and mechanistic descriptive concepts", by stating that Bohr was engaged in a form of descriptive metaphysics when he characterized the workings of language in the way he did.

I will return to the question of whether Bohr used a transcendental argument in his philosophy and draw a conclusion after the structures of the epistemologies of Bohr and Kant have been compared below.

Einstein and Kant.

In Chapter 5, I discussed what Einstein [1949], pp. 673–674, referred to as his "Kantian" categories. These Categories are free conventions rather than being fixed and determined by the understanding. They are selected for their usefulness in grasping experience and their objectivity is secured by identifying as Categories only those that are independent of particular sense experience. It is through the help of these Categories that Einstein felt we can have knowledge of the real. Einstein did not specify how these free conventions are established and how one would resolve a controversy over which convention to choose for a given category. Presumably some aspects of experience would apply and guide us in the fashioning of these Categories, but Einstein did not say which. Clearly, much more is required if Einstein's viewpoint is to be extended into an epistemology.

If these Categories are identified with certain elements of the conceptual framework underlying classical physics and ordinary experience, Einstein's views resemble Bohr's views to some degree. When Einstein spoke of obtaining "knowledge of the real" by means of these Categories, however, he clearly felt that the reality obtained must meet certain conditions that have traditionally been part of our conception of reality, but are not compatible in any straightforward way with quantum mechanics. At this point, he and Bohr parted ways. Bohr would not allow the notion of reality to be used outside of what he considered its proper range of application, which is encompassed by our ordinary (macroscopic) experience and the results of our experiments. Thus Einstein's view that the reality of microscopic particles requires that they exhibit causal relations with each other, for example, would be rejected by Bohr as being outside the proper application of the concepts of reality and causality. Both experience and experimental results are, and for Bohr must be, expressed in our common language which does not include direct reference to microscopic particles and their behavior. Moreover, as mentioned in Chapter 5, Bohr argued that the classical view of reality does not take account of the subject/object interaction and the failure of the classical ideal of causality.

Compared to Bohr, Einstein spent little time on epistemological issues and probably saw little need to do so. His view of the one-to-one relation of concepts to 'objects of reality' lacks a philosophical grounding and an epistemological justification. Bohr, on the other hand, was driven by what he saw as contradictions in using a classical conceptual framework with quantum mechanics into providing a complete epistemology.

Subject and Object.

Kant did not say much about the nature of the connection between subject and object. His concern was primarily the framework within which the subject interpreted the sensations caused by the object. His work was taken up and modified by Arthur Schopenhauer, who believed that subject and object are inextricably entwined.[15] This is actually the crux of the issue for the theory of knowledge in that, if Schopenhauer is right, objective science would not be possible because we could not know that we had separated ourselves from the object observed sufficiently to make an objective statement about it. In opposition to Schopenhauer's view, Bohr felt that a clear distinction between subject and object is a necessary prerequisite for knowledge and held that the physical variables characterizing the object would be ambiguous without a clear separation between subject and object.

Bohr considered the subject/object distinction to be a general aspect of the theory of knowledge in all fields of human inquiry. He often spoke of the movability of the dividing line between the subject and object in terms

---

[15]See Schopenhauer, [**1847**], pp. 41, 51, 207–208, [**1859**]. See also P. Gardiner [**1963**], pp. 80, 84.

of an analogy. He told several stories to illustrate this point. In one story, he imagines using a stick to investigate things in a dark room. When held tightly the stick is perceived to be an extension of the hand and is thus part of the subject. But when it is held lightly, so it can move in the hand, it is perceived as part of the object being touched.[16] Bohr [**1929c**], p. 96, also spoke once of the requirement of an 'objectively given content' and a 'perceiving subject' as a condition for knowledge: "The epistemological problem under discussion may be characterized briefly as follows: For describing our mental activity, we require, on the one hand, an objectively given content to be placed in opposition to a perceiving subject, while, on the other hand, as is already implied in such an assertion, no sharp separation between subject and object can be maintained since the perceiving subject also belongs to our mental content." In the same essay Bohr [**1929a**], pp. 99–100, made use of Kantian ideas (similar also to those of Høffding) in his general discussion of the epistemological problem:

"On the whole, the analysis of our sense impressions discloses a remarkable independence of the psychological foundations of space and time, on the one hand, and the conceptions of energy and momentum, based upon actions of force, on the other hand. Above all, however, this domain ... is distinguished by reciprocal relationships that depend upon the unity of our consciousness and which exhibit a striking similarity with the physical consequences of the quantum of action. We are thinking here of the well-known characteristics of emotion and volition that are quite incapable of being represented by visualizable pictures. In particular, the apparent thinking and the preservation of the unity of the personality exhibits a suggestive analogy with the relation between the wave description of the motions of material particles, governed by the superposition principle, and their indestructible individuality."

Bohr did not, however, pursue this line of thought further in any of his later essays.

Folse [**1978**], p. 63, has characterized Kant's view of the subject/object boundary as an immovable and unbridgeable chasm whereas for Bohr it is movable. He noted also that Bohr does not need to show how concepts supply form to our sensible intuitions and Kant does. He contrasted Bohr's use of (space, time) and (momentum, energy) as concepts with Kant's view of space and time alone as forms of intuition required for the representation of experience. By "proper use of concepts" Folse noted that Bohr meant meeting the requirements of objectivity, but Kant meant that they are used in the understanding to provide objective features to experienced representations. Folse, pp. 64–65, discussed Bohr's [**1958a**], p. 74, reference to our role as

---

[16]See Oscar Klein [**1964**], p. 93, for this story; several others have recounted it as well.

Table 10.1: The Structure of Kant's Theory of Knowledge

Form	Content
Ideas	Categories
Concepts	Intuition
Apperception	Appearance

"detached observers of nature". He also mentioned that Bohr reiterated, in a letter from Bohr to Pauli, 2/15/55, his belief that subjectivity had been eliminated in science by use of complementarity and following the requirements for objective communication using the detached observer concept. Folse, p. 65, observed that the measuring instrument must be interacting with the measured system for a measurement to occur, but that we must represent this situation in unambiguous terms using a criterion of objectivity which warrants the characterization "detached observer" in this situation.

Structures of the Theories of Knowledge of Kant and Bohr.
The elements of Kant's theory have a hierarchical structure similar to those we have discerned in Bohr's Theory. The structure of Kant's theory is presented in Table 10.1. In this table the element on the left regulates the element on the right and the result of the two working together is presented to the element on the right that is above them. Thus, the unity of apperception, as an act of attention focusing consciousness, governs how the appearances are presented to the intuition. The intuition interprets and identifies the components of these unified appearances by means of the concepts. The subsumption of an intuition under a concept makes it into an object of knowledge. These objects of knowledge are then passed to the Categories which convert them in accord with the forms of experience into a description of the flow of experience in accord with causality and other applicable laws. The operation of the Categories in this activity is regulated by the Ideas. The ideas include the schemata or rules of meaning, the constructions of mathematics, and other aspects. In accord with Butts' summary of Kant's theory given above, the result of this activity is knowledge. This structure can be compared to the structure of Bohr's theory of knowledge given in Table 8.1.

A comparison of Tables 8.1 and 10.1 shows that the structures of the two epistemologies are quite different. For Kant, the a priori nature of the ideas and the categories means that they are imposed on experience from the top down in the process of converting experience into knowledge. For Bohr, the conceptual framework underlies the operation of his epistemology and provides the stock of concepts that can be drawn on to characterize experience. His forms of perception include wave and particle concepts and descriptions (wave patterns; particle coincidences) expressed in common language supplemented by physics. The proper experimental setup is regulated by the requirements of the subject/object distinction which has its parallel on the theoretical side in the form of requirements for communicability. When the requirements at the lower levels are met, the Observation Thesis allows the statements of the experimental results to count as an observation and the Description Thesis regulates what can be said about these results. Finally, the consistency of all this must be maintained in the face of the possibility that a single viewpoint may not be sufficient to characterize all of experience. This consistency follows from the connection between a viewpoint and an experimental arrangement and the realization that, as long as the theory is valid, incompatible viewpoints are supported by incompatible experimental arrangements. Viewpoints related to each other in this way were called complementary by Bohr.

The examples Kant used in his discussion in the Second Analogy of Experience show that what he had in mind by 'appearance' corresponds to our ordinary idea of experience (a ship moving in a river; a hot stove; a ball on a cushion), and this corresponds to organized experience (observation) in Bohr's Theory (spots on a photographic plate; Geiger counter clicks). Apperception in Kant's theory functions on the same level as the Subject/Object Distinction in terms of the conflict between the flow of thought (succession of appearances) and the unity of the personality (the unity of apperception). In the theory that Bohr developed, the synthetic unity in the ordering and succession of experiences, which Kant found in the unity of apperception, Bohr could find in the requirement that the functioning of the measuring instrument and its interaction with the object must be described using a classical model. This classical model provides the ordering of the succession of appearances in Bohr's Theory, in the sense, for example, that the continuous motion of the hands of a clock can be understood in the classical way as measuring the progression of time, and a particle passes sequentially through the slits of a slit system before impinging on a screen. Thus Bohr's requirement that the "frame of reference" be classically described functions in the way Kant's unity of apperception does.

Proceeding to Kant's Intuition, we see that it corresponds to other aspects of observation in Bohr's theory. Bohr sometimes referred to experience as appearing within one of the forms of perception that are then interpreted by means of a classical description of the results of observation. Kant's term Concept, which he uses in the interpretation of experience, will be understood narrowly here as applying to (macroscopic) objects. To Kant's Concepts corresponds Bohr's set of classical descriptive terms for macroscopic objects, which includes the concepts of ordinary language and classical physics. Finally, to Kant's Ideas corresponds Bohr's Descriptions. While there are some limitations on what can count as a theory and a theoretical statement, Bohr does not have a set of rules for forming descriptions that would correspond to Kant's Categories. Issues such as causality for Bohr are aspects of the descriptions (theories) in which they play a role, but they are not required of all descriptions and are not aspects, as they are for Kant, of our conceptual apparatus concerned with perception. There is nothing in Kant's theory corresponding to Bohr's complementarity and mutually exclusive experimental arrangements.

Kant used his unity of apperception to account for the necessary appearance of causal relations in the succession of appearances. He followed Hume in stating that the objective relation of these appearances cannot be established by mere perception [**1781**], p. 219: "In order that this relation be known as determined, the relation between the two states must be so thought that it is thereby determined as necessary which of them must be placed in the reverse relation." A principle that does carry with it a necessity of synthetic unity can only be a pure concept of the understanding. Thus, if there is a genuine parallel between Bohr's theory and Kant's, it is necessary to show that Bohr's requirement that the measuring instruments be classically described is a pure a priori concept of the understanding. And this must be reconciled with Kant's [**1781**], p. 219, view of causality: "Experience itself—in other words, empirical knowledge of appearances—is thus possible only in so far as we subject the succession of appearances, and therefore all alteration, to the law of causality; and, as likewise follows, the appearances as objects of experience, are themselves possible only in conformity with the law." One possibility for making this reconciliation, hinted at above, would be to limit the application of the concept of an object in Kant's theory to those appearances dealing with a succession of events involving macroscopic objects. In other words, the succession of appearances in experiments dealing with entities on the atomic level does not allow of these entities being understood as objects in the sense of Kant's view of them; therefore there is no need to apply the concept of causality to the succession of appearances concerning them.[17] But one does need the concept of an object, its persistence in time, and its causal relations to other things to make sense of cloud or bubble chamber photographs. We cannot relinquish causality here, and Bohr said as much, without making the situation unintelligible and leaving us with no way to apply theory to the explanation of these observations.

The differences between Kant and Bohr can be summarized so far as follows: Kant obtains causality from the succession of appearances through a transcendental deduction based on the unity of apperception. Bohr finds

---

[17] See Meyer-Abich's view above that Bohr was concerned with 'objects as the subject of physics.'

causality to be an aspect of the theoretical description of entities between the successive observations on them. Kant feels that various unities in the thinking subject are sufficient to derive certain a priori laws and concepts. In his later theory, Bohr rarely refers to the thinking subject. His concern with the necessity of a sharp separation between subject and object is expressed as a requirement that the description of the measuring instrument be given in classical terms. When this is the case, the measuring instrument acts as and is described as a "detached observer".

Another deep problem in the attempt to understand Bohr's Theory in a priori Kantian terms is that of finding an a priori justification for the need to refer to the circumstances in which knowledge is obtained in order that this knowledge be fully specified and determinate. In other words, is it possible to give an a priori justification of the appearance of complementarity as a principle regulating the application of certain descriptive concepts to certain kinds of objects or things in certain circumstances? While one might make an a priori case for the possibility of complementarity, it does not seem possible to give an a priori argument for its necessity without phrasing it, as Bohr occasionally did, in terms of an "objectively perceiving subject" and the "object of perception." But in the discussion in Chapter 8, I rejected Bohr's analysis of complementarity in these terms. If it turns out that complementarity is of significance only to quantum physics, an explanation of why it is important only under such peculiar circumstances must be given. That is, if complementarity is seen to be an a priori and necessary feature of the appearances or their succession, the question is why it seems to be of significance only to a very limited set of appearances. An answer must be given in terms of the appearances alone.

In his *main argument,* Bohr appealed to the need for communicability and the Subject/Object Distinction as the justification for his conclusions. As pointed out above, this is similar in some ways to Kant's transcendental deduction, given in the Analogies of Experience, of the necessity that appearances conform to the concepts of the Categories. But Bohr had no basic principle, like Kant's unity of apperception, suitable for a transcendental proof. Bohr's discussion of the necessity of maintaining a distinction between subject and object as the basis for unambiguous description and observation will not suffice for an a priori proof, since, as above, I reject the characterization of the situation in terms of "an objectively given perceiving subject" and the "object of perception." And there is nothing in the appearances themselves that will suffice to single out a particular set of concepts as having epistemological priority. We do in fact use classical concepts to describe what we have done and what we have observed in the laboratory; and they are fully adequate to this task. But this justification is a posteriori. The question is whether we can have an adequate a priori guarantee that just this set of concepts is both complete (or extensible to a complete set) and adequate for the task of characterizing fully the raw data of the laboratory. In addition, the failure of Kant's program with respect to the necessity of causality—in that certain events are not, as far as we can tell, causally determined—throws doubt on the status of any synthetic a priori principles in science.

In this regard, Bohr made very clear that, in spite of his requirement that all observations must be stated in classical terms, he was not being aprioristic with respect to the concepts that can play a role in his theory. He [1960a], pp. 9–10, rejected the idea that "... space and time as well as cause and effect had to be taken as *a priori* categories for the comprehension of all knowledge .... Indeed, from our present standpoint, physics is to be regarded not so much as the study of something *a priori* given, but rather as the development of methods of ordering and surveying human experience." Weizsäcker [1952], p. 128, viewed this situation as one in which the "a priori" is a methodological or relative concept. Thus, not: every experimental arrangement *must* be classically described, but: every experimental arrangement *is* classically described. Weizsäcker concluded that classical mechanics is neither purely empirical nor purely a priori.[18] Because Weizsäcker did not give a justification or explanation of why the use of classical concepts is an epistemological requirement, as Bohr did, he has not made his case with respect to Bohr's ideas.

Bohr was trying to give an account of why we *must* use classical concepts and not simply restate the fact that we *do* use them or to make a methodological point. Bohr's justification in terms of language and communication was an appeal to a deeper level of experience embodied in our language. I will begin the discussion of nineteenth century theories concerning the philosophical import of language in the next chapter along with other nineteenth century views on issues of philosophy and physics in relation to the adequate description and interpretation of physical and biological phenomena. We must wait until after these discussions to complete the analysis of Bohr's work.

10.3 Reflection 19

At the end of the eighteenth century, there was some general agreement on how issues of knowledge were to be approached. The dualism between subject and object was unchallenged. Rationalism, idealism, empiricism, and various other approaches to philosophical problems, were being vigorously pursued. This continued well into the nineteenth century. Another philosophical stream, romanticism, became ascendant in philosophy for a while and then waned. Scientific work, stimulated by successes in physics, chemistry, biology and astronomy during the eighteenth century, continued and expanded

---

[18]Heisenberg [1958a], p. 56, maintained a similar position. Feyerabend [1962], p. 229, footnote 148, however, indicated that the position of Heisenberg and Weizsäcker on the methodological a priori status of classical concepts, cannot really be distinguished from maintaining that they are logically a priori.

its sphere into language, psychology, geology and other fields. Philosophical discussions of the role of God, as a participant in the world and in explanations of events, continued for some time into the nineteenth century and then began to fade.

As we shall see, the influence of Kant on the subsequent development of philosophy and on the analysis of the philosophical foundations of science was very strong during the whole nineteenth century. This was particularly true in continental European thought and less so in England and the United States.

CHAPTER 11

Nineteenth Century Philosophy and Science

The question of where Bohr obtained the philosophical ideas he worked with has been raised by a number of authors. That issue is approached in this chapter by surveying the introduction and development in the nineteenth century of particular philosophical ideas in several of the disciplines that were important to Bohr's thought and looking at the meanings that were attached to these ideas at the time.

11.1 European Philosophy

In the investigation of the sources of Bohr's ideas, the philosophical milieu in Europe up to the beginning of the twentieth century, and at the University of Copenhagen in particular, is the major concern. Because the most important philosophers at the university worked in the Kantian tradition, a primary interest is the further development and criticism of Kant's ideas in continental Europe during the nineteenth century.

Kant's philosophy was pervasive in nineteenth century thought. Many scientists in various disciplines adopted some form of Kantianism as the epistemological foundation for their subject area. Kant's views were widely accepted and offered a ready-made framework for approaching issues concerned with empiricism and knowledge. The newly emerging field of psychology, for example, was seen by European workers as the study of human consciousness and behavior as Kantian structures relating to the subject side of the subject/object distinction, while the Kantian aspects of biological and physical science were concerned in different ways with the object side of Kant's philosophy. As the popular lectures by a number of European scientists readily indicate, Kant's approach to the fundamental philosophical ideas associated with knowledge—including perception, time and space, holism in biological systems, and the analysis of causality—was considered to be well-established.

Kantian ideas were not the only survivors from the eighteenth century. Leibniz's conception of individuality was important to the philosophy of Høffding [1917], p. 106, who gave an account of it's philosophical role: "The concept of individuality in Leibniz invites us to discover the property of a given totality and simultaneously to find its essence in the law that expresses the experimental connection there must be between its different states and its different transformations." As a given totality, something that possesses individuality is not further analyzable, at least within the current framework. We grasp what it is by means of the law based on experience that describes the transformations it undergoes from one state to another.

After Kant's death, the center of gravity for philosophy in continental Europe moved toward romanticism. The great metaphysical systems of the eighteenth century had given way to more directly personal concerns with spiritual and esthetic issues and systems built on them. The dominant themes in academic philosophical thinking in German countries at the beginning of the nineteenth century were those of the romantic philosophers, primarily Johann Gottlieb Ficte, Friedrich Wilhelm Joseph Schelling, and Georg Wilhelm Friedrich Hegel. These philosophers read Oriental and Arabic texts, as well as Medieval ones, which reflected the thought of other times and places. The teachings of Lao Tse, Confucius, and the Bhagavad-Gita were also well known by this time. Part of the concern of the romantics was to heal the separation of subject and object by investing the world with spirit. Hegel was one of the great practitioners of romantic philosophy in the form of speculative idealism. Speculative idealism modeled on the work of Hegel was in ascendancy at German universities until Hegel's death in 1831.

In spite of the popularity of romanticism in German thought at the time, Schopenhauer [1847] took up Kant's theory and fought against this tide.[1] He was an original thinker who approached Kant's ideas from an independent and critical perspective. He supported the attack Kant had made on transcendent metaphysics and felt that Kant's greatest idea was the distinction of the phenomenon from the thing itself by showing that the intellect always stands between them. He was highly critical, on the other hand, of Kant's view of things-in-themselves, which he felt violated Kant's own prescription on populating the world with things not subject to experience. He was also critical of what he considered to be Kant's failure to distinguish clearly abstract thought from perception when he subsumed perceptual processes under the Categories. Eastern thought, in the form of Hindu and Buddhist thought, was also a significant influence on him and he pointed out analogies between ideas in his own work and ideas in those works. His work rose to prominence and by the late the nineteenth century he was one of the best-known philosophers in the world. In the twentieth century his influence rapidly waned.

One of Schopenhauer's major concerns was the subject/object distinction, and the inseparable relation between them, which he discussed at length. He viewed the subject/object relation as fundamental to all epistemology. His [1847], p. 104, perspective was that we have double knowledge of our own body as both actor and object—as will and representation. He maintained that there is no causal connection between subject and object because cause operates only in the phenomenal world. In Gardiner's [1963], pp. 87–88, discussion of Schopenhauer's thought, he emphasized that this view of objective reality is that it is not simply "out there" to be discovered, but: "Instead, it must be realized that it is we who contribute the standards of objectivity and subjectivity, of reality and unreality, implicit in our judgments of what we are aware of, and who supply the conditions of valid explanation and inference in terms of which we render experience intelligible; and that is it upon common employment and acceptance of such criteria that all customary knowledge and communication finally rest." Furthermore, Schopenhauer saw science as simply an extension of ordinary modes of apprehension and emphasized the role of language in the communication of experience.

Schopenhauer maintained that the issues connected with subject and object are not two sets of issues, one for the subject and one for the object, but must be seen as parts of one set of issues. Subject and object limit each other in a common and reciprocal way in that the universal form for all objects is an a priori aspect of consciousness. To say that an object is determinate

---

[1] For information on Schopenhauer and his work, see Patrick Gardiner [1963].

in certain ways is exactly the same as saying that the subject knows the object in certain ways.² Gardiner, p. 86, summarized Schopenhauer's view of empirical reality by saying that empirical reality is definable by reference to a certain framework. It follows from this view that because we, as knowing subjects, participate in this framework, it is possible a priori to determine the forms in which experience of reality will appear. Moreover, pp. 109–110, "Our awareness of empirical reality consists in the apprehension of ideas or representations, these having as their basis the data provided by the senses and being structured in accordance with the universal framework imposed by the perceiving subject." This reality does not appear as a seamless whole, but is differentiated into individual objects. It follows that this cannot lead to "a complete all-embracing comprehension of reality." Finally, Schopenhauer was aware of what he considered to be essential limitations in language and its employment. The abstractness of some concepts and inferences from them supported by language is separated from its other purpose of practical communication. This, Schopenhauer felt, has led to errors on the part of philosophers concerning how the world is to be represented and understood.

There is no direct evidence that Bohr studied the works of either Schopenhauer or Kant in any detail and certainly no evidence that either one directly influenced the philosophical position he constructed. Nevertheless, as pointed out before, these ideas were common in intellectual thought at the end of the nineteenth century and in works on epistemology in particular. Høffding was certainly very familiar with the work of both Kant and Schopenhauer. Whether Bohr had read Kant or Schopenhauer or not, the strong possibility of indirect influence from a number of secondary sources is sufficient to account for the similarities in Bohr's modes of expression concerning a number of concepts he employed. Thus, Bohr's statement concerning Eastern thought, that we are both actors and spectators in the great drama of existence, is more than a little reminiscent of Schopenhauer's concern with the double knowledge of our bodies as actor and object and his references to the prior concerns with these issues in Eastern thought. Further, Bohr's concern with the conceptual framework and communicability as a necessary context for knowledge reflects Schopenhauer's references to the conceptual framework and language underlying all knowledge. In contrast with these philosophers, on the other hand, Bohr did not attempt to assign a priori status to any of his conceptions.

When Bohr spoke of the quantum of action as an "irrationality," he was also employing a venerable philosophical concept. As explained by the French philosopher Emile Meyerson, the term irrational is applied, for example, to

---

²See Gardiner [**1963**], pp. 84–85. Gardiner also pointed out that Schopenhauer was a formative influence on Wittgenstein and referred to passages in the Tractatus concerning the individual self as a limit of the world that reflect Schopenhauer's influence.

the unanalyzable relation between a perceived sensation, which cannot be explained mechanically, and the sensibility (irritability) of certain tissues in our sense organs, which can.[3] He designated connections of this type, between the aspects of a particular human experience that can be mechanically described and the aspects that cannot, as irrational because "It has the advantage of clearly indicating that it is a question of *fact,* which we believe to be certain, but which remains and always will remain incomprehensible, inaccessible to our reason, irreducible to purely rational elements." Høffding also used the term irrational in many of his writings to refer to this unanalyzable relation. It is this same relation between sensitivity and sensation that Descartes had discussed as the symbolic connection between the stimulation of our nerves caused by objects and our perception of them.

Another aspect of the philosophical concept of the irrational that played an important role in nineteenth century thinking was expressed as the statement of the 'irrational relation of the whole to the parts' of an entity. In biological systems in particular, a living whole is composed of parts, but none of these can be separately alive. The idea behind the use of the term irrational in this way was to emphasize a limit to rational inquiry in that the issue under discussion is at or beyond the limit of those things accessible to rational analysis. In scientific inquiries, rational analysis had, for the most part, come to mean giving a mechanical explanation.

In the 1840s, at the same time the German philosophers were shaking off the romantic movement, English philosophy was enjoying a revival. William Whewell and John Stuart Mill were the most important contributors in the mid-nineteenth century to a resurgent concern with science and epistemology that had received relatively little attention since the time of Hume. Soon afterward, the work of Charles Darwin on evolution and parallel work in philosophy from a similar perspective by Herbert Spencer created a stir. In spite of these factors, English academic philosophy acquired a Kantian flavor as well.

After the middle of the century, the philosophy of materialism received a significant stimulus due to the successes in chemistry, physics and biology. Scientific work, which had increased in the late eighteenth century, picked up speed during the nineteenth century as old fields more clearly defined their boundaries and new disciplines such as linguistics and experimental psychology were founded. Materialist explanations, which usually meant explanations in terms of physics and chemistry, slowly became the ideal for science when they were available.

One of the areas of philosophical importance was the theory of probability. This was formalized in the great work of Pierre Simon Laplace at the end of the eighteenth and beginning of the nineteenth centuries. The concepts of probability, which are now central to the conceptual foundations of modern

---

[3]See Meyerson [**1930**], Chapter IX: "The Irrational"

thermodynamics, classical statistical mechanics, and quantum physics, will be discussed briefly in Chapters 14 and 15.

The German academic philosophers, however, were not the only ones engaged in philosophizing in German speaking countries. Natural scientists in a number of disciplines began to examine the philosophical foundations of work in their respective areas with a focus that was distinct from the general epistemological and ontological concerns of philosophy itself. I will present specific philosophical ideas that were put forward by workers in the areas of language, biology, and physics.

11.2 Views of Language

The view that language has an important role in the theory of knowledge dates back to ancient times. It was seen as a bond between people and a source from which our common reality emerges. Heraclitus, for example, felt that speech, which the Greeks called *lógos,* is the divine law on which all human laws are nourished. It represents for us when awake the common cosmos, but when asleep we are in a world of our own. This private world of the sleeper is *idiocy* to the Greeks because the sleeper is shut off from the common meanings of the words and ideas encountered there. As to meaning itself, Heraclitus stated: "The lord to whom belongs the oracle at Delphi neither speaks out, nor covers up, but gives an indicator." Here Heraclitus is playing with words in that the ambiguity of an indicator (*sēmaínei,* root word of semantics), as either a sign or as a theory of language, reflects the ambiguity of an oracle. As James H. Stam pointed out, those who take the oracle too literally, such as Oedipus and Croesus, miss the point, as do those who ignore the oracle altogether. Thus language does not directly reveal what is, or conceal it, but only gives us guideposts to it.[4]

In the *Cratylus,* Plato made fun of those who argued over the correctness of names, that is, those who claim either that words have a natural meaning or that they are completely conventional. Socrates proves there that the (Greek) word for 'famous' implies, by its etymological derivation, that "that is real for which there is a search." One of the points of this dialog is to raise the question of how we judge the better and worse use of language. At issue for Cratylus and Hermogenes in their discussion with Socrates is whether one can know the truth of something from possession of the right word for it.

The scope of language includes the mathematical and physical works of Euclid and Archimedes and the poetry of Homer. Aristotle defined it in his *De Anima* as "sound with meaning." He associated language with society because he felt that life outside society was possible only for animals or gods, and beasts have no languages and gods have no need of one. He also

---

[4]See Stam [**1976**], pp. 139–140, for a discussion of these fragments of Heraclitus and for many of the other topics covered in this section.

emphasized the importance of social intercourse to the understanding and employment of language.

These Greek texts and arguments, which had raised basic philosophical questions concerning the nature of language and its role in epistemology, played an important part in the discussion of the origin of language and its philosophical aspects in the seventeenth and eighteenth centuries and were quite familiar to writers at the beginning of the nineteenth century. Marin Mersenne, a contemporary of Descartes in France, was a strong supporter of the mechanical philosophy in the first half of the seventeenth century. He argued against cabalistic doctrines and against the notion that we can know the internal constitution or essences of things. He felt that language is purely conventional and that the knowledge available to us of things must be based on external manifestations. He rejected the then popular notion of the original language of Adam as a natural language. Subsequently Locke developed similar ideas and combined certain elements of empiricism with some rationalist ideas on the associations of ideas in our consciousness. The French philosopher Condillac, writing in the middle of the eighteenth century, had strong empiricist leanings and followed Locke's point of view on many topics. Leibniz held up the possibility that a universal language or a philosophical language might be useful in understanding the world and resolving philosophical disputes. Many others, less well known, also wrote on these issues at the end of the eighteenth century.[5]

The nineteenth century saw an explosion of interest in the philosophical aspects, scientific study, and origins of language. In this brief account of some of the dominant nineteenth century ideas on language, the goal is to search for the 'turns of a phrase' and concepts that Bohr may have drawn on for his conception of language and its role in epistemology.

Wilhelm von Humboldt, the brother of the more famous Alexander von Humboldt, was one of the most important early nineteenth century thinkers on this subject.[6] He contended [**1836**], p. 18, that "... language is at once a way of comprehending the total process of thinking and feeling." He further explained that, pp. 20–21, "Inasmuch as languages are inseparably interlaced with the innermost nature of man and far more automatically erupt from it than they are arbitrarily engendered by it, the intellectual peculiarity of peoples could equally be termed its effect. The truth is that both emerge spontaneously and in reciprocal coincidence from the unfathomable depths of the mind. ... For language is related to everything contained in it, to the totality and the individual."

---

[5] See Aarsleff [**1976**] for a brief discussion and references.

[6] Chevalley [**1994**], and in the references given there to her earlier work, has independently identified Wilhelm von Humboldt as a likely source for Bohr's philosophical ideas on these matters and given examples from Humboldt's writing.

Humboldt went on to point out the importance of language to our intellectual activity, in the "transformation of the world into ideas." In fact, he stated, p. 25, "In reality there is no such arbitrary distinction between intellectuality and language. If language correctly appears to us as something possessing divine characteristics, unlike other intellectual creations, the relationship between language and human intellectual power might be a different one if it did not confront us in the form of isolated phenomena, but instead were to transmit its very nature to us from unfathomable depths, and we were capable of perceiving the connections within the human individuality, since language too transcends the estrangement inherent in individuals."

Humboldt identified language as the "structural organ of ideas," and approached the possibility and form of knowledge through that perspective. He, p. 39, identified concepts with objects and went on: "Man lives principally, or even exclusively with objects, since his feelings and actions depend upon his concepts as language presents them to his attention. By the same act through which he spins out the thread of language he weaves himself into its tissues." We cannot see very far into the past of language. He spoke of it as flowing forth from the past containing untold wealth, which we can still recognize some of today, and then veering off and becoming inaccessible to us "leaving behind only the sensation of its unfathomableness." The intellect can draw material from language in proportion to what it has mastered in language (p. 125): "For the intellect hovers over language as over an unfathomable abyss from which it is capable of drawing material in proportion to what has already been exhausted from the source."

If each of us hovers over our language in this way, the question of how we, as "estranged individuals" separated from each other by the abyss, can communicate. This also calls the possibility of objective knowledge into question. Humboldt's response, p. 130, was that communication is possible and humans understand each other by striking corresponding "keys" in their intellects. He went on to emphasize the social aspects of language in a discussion of the interplay of language with art, music, and character in Greek thinking. This connection between language and culture implies that there is more to language than what is said. In other words, p. 145, "It may therefore be quite definitively stated that in each word there reposes something not again to be distinguished by words, and that the words of numerous languages, even if they designate the same ideas on the whole, are never true synonyms."

The idea that language is the repository of ancient theories about the world was important in the eighteenth century thought about language and shows up in a number of nineteenth century thinkers including Mill [1846], p. 413.[7]

---

[7]See also L. Geiger [1868].

Max Müller, the translator of Kant into English, moved to England in the mid nineteenth century to work for the East India company on its collection of Sanskrit manuscripts. He was influential and wrote extensively on language into the early twentieth century. He viewed the identification of *lógos* with both language and reason by the Greeks as evidence that thought and language are inseparable. He opposed Locke's theory of thought without speech and Locke's view that there was some prelinguistic era in human development where there were concepts before words for them. Because animals do not speak, Müller felt, they do not reason. From this perspective, he also felt that deaf and dumb people do not reason except indirectly through the signs in their sign languages. He agreed with Leibniz's view that language is the best mirror of the human mind and "that an exact analysis of the significance of words would make us better acquainted than anything else with the operations of the understanding."[8] He then went on to discuss Leibniz's ideas on a universal language and a philosophical language as devices for resolving philosophical disputes and clarifying our understanding of reality. The problem in using these tools, Müller felt, is that we cannot "take off the spectacles of language."[9]

The view that language is an organism existed during this time as well. Among the proponents was Ludwig Noiré [1885]. He objected to Kant's view of the relation of concepts to objects and felt that the clarification of the origin of language will show us the proper relation. In Noiré's view, language grows from a single seed and specific parts, i.e., different kinds of concepts, grow out of this seed in an organized manner. In this way, language expresses the same individuality and totality that an organism does. The organismic view of language was shared by few others and did not outlast the nineteenth century.

There were several important Danish linguists and philologists who wrote during the nineteenth century. The earliest was Rasmus Rask who formulated a law of sound change in language in his work on Icelandic in 1818. By his comparative work on the Baltic and Slavic languages, he showed they have a common root, and that the Finnish and Lap languages have a different source. His analysis had thus given him a vague glimpse of the Indo-European language. Because his work was published in Danish, he did not receive much recognition at the time.

The linguistic work of the Danish philologist Johan Nicolai Madvig was written in Danish and met a similar fate. In spite of his lack of international influence, however, Madvig is important for the great influence he had on several generations of Danish philologists, linguists, and students. In particular

---

[8]Müller [1864], p. 42–47. In Müller [1887], Vol. II, p. 510, he stated "... language is the autobiography of the human mind, and that all and every secret of philosophy is to be studied in the world-old diary of language." See also Müller [1864], pp. 70–72, 336–337, for his arguments against Locke and Müller [1861].

[9]Müller [1887], Vol. II, pp. 542–543.

he influenced Vilhelm Thomsen, Holger Pedersen, and Louis Hjelmslev. His most important influence was on a few generations of Danish Gymnasium students who studied from his lectures in the Encyclopedia of Philology.[10] This makes it very likely that Bohr was exposed to Madvig's ideas on language.

Madvig's main starting point was that language is the medium of communication. He felt that language should not be studied from a psychological, philosophical, or historical viewpoint, but should be studied empirically. He opposed the notion of a "general grammar" having both linguistic and philosophical import. This conception of a general grammar had an a priori character, and was popular in rationalist philosophy when Madvig wrote about it. He also felt that it was an inadmissible mixing of categories to view the life conception of a culture or a people as being built into their language or the conception of language as an organism. He believed that all concepts in language stem from meaningful representations. This means that nonsense can only be defined by analogy to the meaningful. It also follows that language is a system of relations that does not consist of concepts, but is used to stand for concepts.

Madvig's empiricist approach to language was shared by others primarily outside the circles in which Kant's influence was large. There were also a number of other thinkers, such as the American William Dwight Whitney, who emphasized communication as the primary function of language. Madvig felt that his theories had been stolen by Whitney and the German philosopher Hermann Lotze, but this was not the case.[11]

Whitney [**1867**], p. 404, emphasized that language must be understood in terms of the community—although individuals initiate aspects of it. He rejected the theory that language is necessary for thought. Rather, he stated that man speaks in order to impart his thought. Speech is a product of his social needs and his social instincts force him to express them. He concluded: "Language, then, is the spoken means whereby thought is communicated, and it is only that. Language is not thought, nor is thought language; nor is there a mysterious and indissoluble connection between the two, as there is between soul and body, so that the one cannot exist without the other."[12] He went on to outline an extended argument against the equivalence of language and thought. His main points were:

1. Language does not give a full representation of thought, except, perhaps in the most objective scientific reasoning. In other cases, meaning must be inferred from the totality of intercourse and expression;
2. Language is impotent to express our feelings;
3. The variety of expressions of the same thought argues against the identification of them;

---

[10] See Karsten Johansen's [**1971**], "Einleitung" to Madvig's works, p. 39.
[11] See Johansen [**1971**], p. 39.
[12] See Whitney [**1867**], p. 405.

4. The sign language of the deaf and dumb show how arbitrary and conventional language is.

As part of his justification of these points, Whitney talked about thought and judgment that go beyond or precede linguistic formulation. He discussed in detail the sign language of the deaf from this perspective. He also observed that dogs can engage in fairly complex reasoning based on experience and can respond to commands. He viewed words as signs and stated that they are merely the instruments of thought and are created by it. He used the analogy that "Language ... is the instrument of thought, the machinery with which the mind works." But just as a loom does not equal the weaving on it, language does not equal thought.[13] Because his views were so different from those of the continental linguists, he engaged in an ongoing exchange with Max Müller that turned rather bitter.

Histories of some of these issues, with an emphasis on the development of linguistics have been written by the Danish linguists Thomsen [**1927**] (first published in 1902) and Otto Jespersen [**1922**]. In these histories, the work of W. von Humboldt was discussed in detail. The work of Madvig was approved by both and the controversy between Müller and Whitney was discussed. Both Thomsen and Jespersen sided with Whitney in his controversy with Müller. These books trace how empiricism had supplanted rationalism in the discussion of issues connected with language and give a general feeling for the philosophical perspective of science and the studies of language in the early twentieth century in Copenhagen.

Fritz Mauthner, who wrote on language in the 1900–1910 era, maintained the primacy of conventional language in scientific work. Language cannot put us in touch with the truth according to Mauthner, but it is our chief means of seeking the truth. Gershon Weiler [**1970**], p. 133, expressed Mauthner's argument in the form: "Scientific language is not separate and different from ordinary language but is part of it. The purpose of creating a refined and precise terminology is to enable those who use it to identify certain features of reality not identifiable by using everyday language. But since reality is ultimately all that we experience or can experience and is nothing beyond possible experience, scientific language is but a variant of ordinary language which grew out of experience." The explicit assumption here is that all our experiences and all possible experiences are expressible in terms of extended ordinary language and that this language gives us an adequate account of reality. The argument continues with the assertion that we cannot dispense with ordinary language in science because when two theories are competing, and both claim to be an adequate account of the same set of phenomena, we need a common, agreed upon, neutral ground on which to compare them. It is reasonable to presume that ordinary language is that ground.[14]

---

[13] For the details of this argument, see Whitney [**1867**], pp. 404–420, [**1892**].
[14] See Weiler [**1970**], pp. 133–134.

Mauthner felt that communication is the only criterion for judging a language. He also subscribed to a "meaning is use" view of the meaning of words much like that adopted by Wittgenstein later.[15] Furthermore, Weiler [1970], p. 135, pointed out that "For Mauthner, ordinary language neither incorporates nor is capable of expressing truth. It is but a set of conventions of speaking about certain situations and these conventions prescribe, in a way, a view or a cluster of possible views about matters that are spoken of. ... Ordinary language is misleading since no refinement of terminology can dispose of its basic features, namely that it assumes a sharing of what is fundamentally unshareable, i.e. sense-experiences. So all improvements in precision will have only marginal value in approaching truth."

Weiler felt that German academic philosophers never took Mauthner very seriously because Edmund Husserl's phenomenology by that time held sway.[16] Nevertheless, his ideas reflect a significant aspect of the thought on language at the time.

11.3 The Study of Perception

Perception plays a central role in philosophy because it is the source of our experience of the world. The issues of perception and experience have been the subjects of philosophical speculation for millennia. The existence of dreams, illusions, injury, and madness have been known for centuries to deceive us into thinking we have perceived what we have not and that we have not perceived something we have. In the nineteenth century, the study of perception by scientific means was begun and rapid progress was made. The older phenomena were subjected to experimental investigation and new phenomena of perception, which illustrated aspects of the perceptual process, were added.[17]

By the mid-nineteenth century, conceptions of perception in the work of the physiologists were detailed and relatively sophisticated. The physiologist and anatomist Johannes Müller [1840] analyzed the relation of the excitation of the nerves of the sensory apparatus, or sensorium, to the sensations we feel. As part of this inquiry, he used empirical information to establish a number of principles concerning the relation of stimulation to sensation. These principles were: (1) external agencies cannot produce any sensation that cannot be produced by internal causes by stimulating the proper nerves in the right way. (2) the same internal causes acting on nerves associated with the different senses can give rise to different sensations. (3) the same external cause gives rise to different sensations in each sense in accord with the special endowment

---

[15] See Weiler [1970], pp. 125. See also the account of Mauthner in Allan Janik and Stephen Toulmin's [1973] discussion of Wittgenstein's work.

[16] Weiler [1970], pp. 319.

[17] The nineteenth century essays on perception collected in the book by W. N. Dember [1964] were sources for much of this information.

of its nerves. (4) "... the peculiar sensations of each nerve of sense can be excited by several distinct causes internal and external." To establish these points, Müller discussed various experiments, listed a number different agents that caused sensations when used to excite nerves, and cataloged their results with respect to various organs of sense.

Continuing with Müller's list, the next was (5) "Sensation consists in the sensorium receiving through the medium of the nerves, and as the result of the action of an external cause, a knowledge of certain qualities or conditions, not of external bodies, but of the nerves themselves; and these qualities of the nerves of sense are in all different, the nerve of each sense having its own peculiar quality or energy." This point of view implies that the nerves are not mere conductors of the properties of external bodies to our sensorium. "We are made acquainted with external objects merely by virtue of certain properties of our nerves, and of their faculty of being affected in a greater or less degree by external bodies. Even the sensation of touch in our hands makes us acquainted, not absolutely with the state of the surfaces of the body touched, but with changes produced in the parts of our body affected by the act of touch." He went on to discuss the experiments of Alessandro Volta who connected a battery by wires to each ear, forming a circuit through the head, and wrote about the sounds he perceived when a current was flowing between his ears. Müller also summarized the effects of chemicals and mechanical blows on the nerves in generating sensations.

Müller's list of principles also included (6) the nerves of each sense are unique to that sense. (7) "It is not known whether the essential cause of the peculiar "energy" of each nerve of sense is seated in the nerve itself, or in parts of the brain and spinal cord with which it is connected." Müller referred to a number of experiments in patients who had lost an eye and perceived, when stimulated by electricity or other agents, sensations of light associated with the missing eye. (8) "The immediate objects of the perception of our senses are merely particular states induced in the nerves, and felt as sensations either by the nerves themselves or by the sensorium." Because these nerves are themselves physical bodies and participate in the properties of matter generally, changes in them due to stimulation by external causes convey to the sensorium information not only about themselves but also about properties and changes in external bodies as well.

(9) Ideas derived from experience cause us to interpret the sensation in terms of the external objects. Müller discussed the example of an operation that gave sight to a boy who was born blind who then saw all objects two-dimensionally as if they were flat and located in a given plane. He also discussed the constancies in our perceptions of things as we move around them. (10) The mind both perceives sensations and has a direct influence on them. Examples of this occur when we are occupied with something else and do not notice a particular stimulus. He also discussed blind people whose

sense of touch is greatly enhanced and are able to feel the denominations of paper money by the slightly raised ink on the bills. Another example is our ability to follow a particular instrument in an orchestra even though it may be playing more softly than the others and is less distinct. There are many other examples of the influence of the mind on perception and a number of experiments demonstrating these effects.

Other work in the nineteenth century included Neckar's discovery of the Neckar cube illusion, Helmholtz's theory of color vision, and studies of binocular vision, illusions of motion, spatial orientation, inverted images on the retina, perceptual integration, and unconscious processes.

Perception and observation and the distinction between them are problematic in philosophical work. In spite of all the scientific activity in the nineteenth and twentieth centuries on this topic, it seems as if philosophy for the most part has remained ignorant of the progress in this area and its practitioners often rely even today on introspection or the accounts of other philosophers for their information on perception. Sense data theorists, logical positivists, and phenomenologists regularly deny the importance of the scientific study of the mechanism of perception and then offer theories of their own concerning how it works. The philosophical moral is that when Weizsäcker [**1952**], p. 94, stated, for example, that a wave or particle picture is simply "what is seen" or that classical physics mirrors our perceptions, he ignored work on understanding perception that dates back at least to Descartes.

11.4 The Foundations of Biology

Niels Bohr's father, Christian Bohr, was a physiologist at the University of Copenhagen in the late nineteenth and early twentieth centuries. He had studied with the German physiologist Carl Ludwig and worked on issues of respiration. Niels Bohr has recalled listening to many discussions at his home between friends of his father's. It is reasonable to conclude that Niels received an early and detailed exposure to biological issues and theories.[18]

John Scott Haldane, a well-known biologist and a former student of Christian Bohr's, discussed and critiqued Christian Bohr's work at a meeting in Cape Town, South Africa, early in the twentieth century.[19] He mentioned that Christian Bohr had handed on to him two of Ludwig's ideas on respiration, which had been used by Christian Bohr and served as the basis for his own work. He recounted the results Bohr obtained on the association and dissociation curves of oxygen and blood oxyhemoglobin in the lungs and tissues. He observed that both Christian Bohr and Ludwig had approached the study of life from the biological standpoint rather than the perspective of a "mere physicist or chemist" when faced with complex issues of blood

---

[18]For more details on Christian Bohr and Niels Bohr's exposure to biological ideas, see Favrholdt [**1992**].

[19]See Haldane [**1931**], pp. 126–131.

chemistry. Haldane felt that this was the reason why they both did so much for physiology.

From a historical perspective, Aristotle was the father of biological studies. He wrote extensively on various biological phenomena that he and others had observed and tried to explain and systematize what he had learned. He emphasized that an organism is a unified whole. Aristotle's concept of *entelechy* was later applied to biological theory—in the explanation of reproduction and embryo development, in particular. Aristotle had introduced the concept of entelechy in his *Physics,* when he made a distinction between the agent and the patient in some activity. Thus, in Book III, he contrasted the mover, or agent, as being in a state of energia and the moved, or patient, as being in a state of entelechia. In Book VII, he used the example of a teacher and student. He was, however, not consistent in his application of this terminology. Roughly, we can understand these terms if we view energia as a reference to dynamic activity and entelechia as a reference to the beginning and endpoints of these activities.

Skipping to the seventeenth century, William Harvey's work on the circulation of the blood was the first important demonstration that mechanical principles and explanations could be applied to biological phenomena. Descartes, as mentioned above, was another significant contributor to physiological studies at that time. Descartes recognized, for example, that the brain was the organ of sensation, thought, and emotion, and viewed the operation of the body in terms of its mechanical aspects.[20] He also recognized that (1) pain felt in the heart or foot requires the brain to be felt, (2) a change in the nerves in muscles is required for movement, and (3) sensations are due to the motion of a substance in the nerves that connect the sensory organs to the brain.

While the work of Harvey and Descartes had shown that mechanical principles could account for some of the behavior of biological organisms in terms of machines, there were many phenomena that seemed to be inexplicable from this perspective. Chief among these were the problems of reproduction and growth. The theories and speculations inherited from the renaissance, which attempted to explain reproduction from the physical and chemical perspective, were clearly inadequate to account for the accumulating information concerning the development of the embryo. Another difference between organisms and machines was the obvious dependence of the organism on its parts, which are not separately alive, and on its environment for the maintenance of its integrity and the continuation of life.

In Kant's *Critique of Judgment,* [**1790**], he remarked that the opposition between teleology and mechanism concerning the origin of life may only be an apparent one. Mechanism in a biological organism, seen as the blind

---

[20]For more information on Descartes' physiological work, see his *Principles de la Philosophie* and Huxley [**1874**], Chapter V.

cooperation of its parts, and teleology, as the purposeful cooperation of the parts, may only be aspects of a single deeper reality. If so, their opposition is just a limitation in the nature of our knowledge. He, p. 220, was concerned with how the whole can reciprocally determine the form and combination of all the parts. From his perspective, p. 225, the "internal form of a mere blade of grass is sufficient to show that, for our human faculty of judgment, its origin is possible only according to the rule of purposes." However, p. 226, it is clear that "this is not a principle for the determinant but only for the reflective judgment." This means that it does not have the same status as those aspects of the understanding in the *Critique of Pure Reason* that determine the possibilities of knowledge. We do not "observe the purposes in nature as designed," because they are not given to us through the object. We can therefore only use these principles to guide our judgment when we reflect on the object. Thus, p. 254, "Certain natural products, *must be considered by us*, in regard to their possibility, as if produced designedly and as purposes." This is "merely a consequence of the particular constitution of our understanding."

From Kant's perspective, the analysis of a living organism by building the whole from its parts, as mechanism would do, or by understanding the parts in terms of the whole as biology does, may thus reflect a single hidden principle that our reason may be unable to formulate.[21] However, p. 261–262, the union of both principles cannot rest upon a ground of explanation in a determinant judgment but only in a reflective judgment. "Mechanism, then, and the teleological (designed) technique of nature, in respect to the same product and its possibility, may stand under a common supreme principle of nature in particular laws. But since this principle is *transcendent*, we cannot, because of the limitation of our understanding, unite both principles *in the explanation* of the same production of nature ...." Ideas of this sort were subsequently reflected in some of the thought of Hegel and were central to the thinking of many who worked in biology during the nineteenth century. This provided a philosophical framework for accepting both the mechanical approach to biological phenomena, studied by the methods of physics and chemistry, and the organismal point of view, in which organisms were viewed *sui generis* within their own framework.

Along these lines, Johannes Müller taught early in the nineteenth century that organic structure and function could never be explained by physical laws alone and that special laws would always be necessary. He felt that the origin of these laws and how matter came to obey them were "beyond the compass of our experience and knowledge to determine."[22] Carl Ludwig relegated issues

---

[21] See the discussion in Høffding [**1882b**], Volume 2, pp. 108–109.
[22] See E. Mendelsohn [**1965**] for further details. The references are to Müller's *Handbüch der Physiologie des Menchens*, published in two volumes in 1835 and 1837, and translated into English in 1838 and 1842. These quotes from the *Handbüch* appear on p.

of this sort to philosophy and not physiology. The proper role for physiology is "to know the forces which give life to organic bodies in particular, and then to examine more closely their properties." He approved of Kant's view that the cause of the existence of living bodies resides in the whole, while in ordinary matter each part contains the cause within itself. Müller's student, Theodore Schwan, asserted in 1839 that teleological explanations were acceptable when the physical explanations can be shown to be impossible.

Carl Ludwig was the student of Ludwig Fick. Emil du Bois-Reymond, Ernst von Brücke, and Hermann von Helmholtz were students of Johannes Müller's . Together, Ludwig, du Bois-Reymond, von Brücke, and Helmholtz formed the "1847 Group" that rejected the romanticism of the Naturphilosophie school that was popular in biological circles at the time. They wanted to reduce all physiology to a physical and chemical foundation.[23] Helmholtz began his work as a physiologist, but later became a well-known physicist.

The biologist Xavier Bichat dominated French biology in the early 1800s. Bichat maintained that there are special processes in living matter that are not in accord with the laws of physics and chemistry. He passed his ideas to Francois Magendie who taught Claude Bernard. Bernard made full use of the tools of physics and chemistry, but was concerned with the relation between the organismic approach and that of physics and chemistry to physiological questions. He emphasized the importance of both the special properties of the living cell and its environment in supporting life and observed that without either component there is no life. He contrasted the outer environment with the special inner environment of living things that is the true physiological environment. He concluded that "vital phenomena are the result of contact between the organic units of a body with the *inner physiological environment.*"[24] He rejected the contention of most German physiologists by that time that all organic phenomena can be reduced to physical and chemical laws. He felt that there should be special biological laws that reflected the complexity of biological phenomena. Although the same substances and physical and chemical processes can be found in cells as in non-living matter, cells have a special type of organization such that when we "analyze them chemically, we destroy their vital properties."[25]

Bernard argued for the importance of a "force vitale," but, in contrast to Bichat, one that acts only by means of ordinary physical and chemical processes in matter. It has only a legislative importance, not an executive one: *"The vital force directs the phenomena it does not produce; physical agents produce the phenomena they do not direct."* He felt strongly that

---

206 of Mendelsohn's article. See this article also for further information on Schwan and Bernard.

[23]See P. Cranefield [**1957**] for more information. E. Nordenskiöld [**1920**], p. 286, indicated that Naturphilosophie was not long a factor in Scandinavia.

[24]Bernard [**1864**], pp. 75–76, [**1866**], p. 55.

[25]See Bernard [**1866**], pp. 22, 23.

"Life cannot be characterized exclusively by either a vitalistic or materialistic conception."[26]

Thomas Huxley in England was a strong proponent of Darwin's theory of natural selection. He also championed the application of mechanical principles from physics and chemistry to the study biological phenomena and the exclusion of psychic concerns from biology. Somewhat later the physiologist J. S. Haldane, also English, presented another point of view. He felt that mechanism is inadequate to explain biological phenomena. He maintained, as one example, that the homeostatic aspect of biological systems under changing internal and external conditions is a function of the organism as a whole that cannot be comprehended in terms of its parts. He acknowledged that this is a teleological point of view but contended that without it physiology would lose itself in a mass of details. Haldane argued for a biological physiology and not merely a biochemistry. Haldane did reject vitalism and its modification of mechanistic causality by entelechy and psyche.

Max Verworn was a professor of physiology at Göttingen in the late nineteenth and early twentieth centuries.[27] He developed a theory called conditionalism in which a state or process is determined by the totality of its conditions. It held that (1) similar states or processes are always the result of similar conditions and (2) a state or process is identical to the totality of its conditions. Thus to know a state or process, it is sufficient to establish the totality of its conditions. This conception lent a contextual flavor to causality and broadened it into a polyvalent interpretation of causal relations. The goal was to broaden causality so that many-sided living material could be understood within its framework.

Another influential biologist who wrote on philosophical matters was Hans Driesch. His biological and philosophical work was influential in Europe in the late nineteenth and early twentieth centuries. In the two volumes of his Gifford Lectures at the University of Aberdeen in 1907 and 1908, he presented an extended and comprehensive review of the philosophical aspects of biology at the beginning of the twentieth century. He [**1907**], 1, p. 11, began by noting that biology is special in that some experiments needed to provide detailed information and answer questions about an organism may kill it. In his lecture on the limits of pure description in science, he, 1, p. 50, reviewed Kirchhoff's famous statement, which will be discussed in the next section, that the task of mechanics is to describe as completely and simply as possible all the motions that occur in nature. But Driesch maintained that it means something different in physics than it does in biology. He observed that by the use of experiments and hypothetical constructions, physicists have located what is truly elemental and described that. The more complex phenomena have then been explained in terms of these elemental descriptions.

---

[26]See Bernard [**1885**], pp. 38–39, 48–52.
[27]Verworn is mentioned in Nordenskiöld [**1920**], p. 589.

Driesch, 1, pp. 99–102, reviewed the concept of cause and concluded that the restricted view of cause held by physicists may not be an adequate one for biology because of the ambiguities in applying it there. As an example, he discussed morphogenic processes, such as embryo growth, and remarked that the location of an element that causes the development and differentiation of tissues in the embryo is a presumably nonphysical factor in determining what happens. He, 1, p. 137, noted that specificity of organic form does not go hand in hand with specificity of chemical composition, so the organic form cannot depend on the chemical composition in the morphogenic setting.

Driesch, 1, p. 138–143, next considered the possibility that some kind of real physical and chemical machine in the system, once set going, could be responsible for the localization of tissue differentiation observed in the embryo. Location determines what a particular set of undifferentiated cells in the embryo will become. But, if cells in the embryo are moved to a new location before differentiation, they will become the type of tissue appropriate to the new location and not to the prior location. This implies that the "machine", or mechanical process, that directs differentiation would have to be present in any volume of cells in the embryo, whatever size, which can play a role in morphogenesis. He argued that it would be a strange machine indeed that is present in every part of a differentiating harmonious-equipotential system such as the flattened ectoderm of the gastrula of a starfish. Because this is absurd in his view, he concluded that it is not possible to explain differentiation in terms of any sort of machine or causal mechanism based upon the constellation of components in such a system. This in turn implies that biology is not some sort of applied physics and chemistry, but is an independent science. He observed that what he has just proved has always been called *vitalism*. He, 1, p. 226–228, adopted Aristotle's term *entelechy* for "that which lies at the beginning of all individual morphogenesis and lies at the root of inheritance." But, he went on to state, this does not imply that there is a conflict between entelechy and the material basis of inheritance.

In his second volume of lectures, Driesch mentioned the issues of part and whole in biology. He [**1907**], 2, p. 26, noted that for methodological reasons we always hold onto the machine theory as long as possible even though it may not be correct in even the simplest phenomena in an organism. As an example, he, 2, p. 43, discussed instinct as a limiting notion for the possibility of a mechanical explanation and, 2, pp. 66–81, reasoned that if we were to become aware of a specific individualized stimulus of an instinct, then the limits of a mechanical explanation ("same causes have same effects") would be exceeded on the grounds that it cannot be understood how the specifically combined or "individualized" stimulus could give rise to a specific and fixed series of motions by the organism. By a specifically combined or individualized stimulus, Driesch meant an object such as a table or a dog. We can be trained (conditioned) to react to some individualized stimulus in some specific way *or* some other quite different way. This correspondence between the individualized stimulus and the individualized effect, both of which are totalities, cannot be understood in terms of the operation of a machine for which the same causes always have the same effect. Machines lack this historical aspect that biological organisms have.

Driesch, 2, pp. 169–199, went on to discuss the concept of entelechy further. He stated that it lacks all characteristics of a quantity. It is an order relation and absolutely nothing else. It is able to suspend ordinary physical and chemical processes in specific, arbitrary, and reversible ways, but it cannot create new chemical processes. He stated that it acts to increase diversity in the same way that Maxwell's demon does. Driesch, 2, pp. 235–236, claimed further that entelechy modifies spatial causality as if it came from some ultra-spatial dimension. It does not act in space, it acts into space and may have a direct individualizing action upon electrons. Finally, he, 2, p. 258, stated that entelechy always manifests itself individually.

An extended criticism of the mechanical philosophy and its misapplication was one way that Driesch, 2, pp. 209–218, "made room" for special biological laws. He went on to offer another proof of vitalism based on subjective or introspective analysis. He, 2, p. 282, concluded from the evidence presented that he had shown the necessity of vitalism as far as "my body" can be considered as an object of biology. He did not extend this analysis to phenomena of consciousness, however, because he felt that the terms "mechanism" and "vitalism" lose their meanings in that setting.

The concept of individuality in biology was emphasized by Driesch as a distinguishing characteristic.[28] He, 2, p. 335, further associated teleology with individuality. He completed his work by stating that morality requires the presence of entelechy. He asked how one could feel morally toward other individuals if he knew that they are machines and nothing more—machines that someday he might construct himself like a steam engine. Morality could not emerge from a mechanical system because wholeness never appears out of a mere mechanical aggregation.

11.5 Philosophical Aspects of Physics

The work of Galileo, Copernicus, Kepler, Newton, and others began to turn attention from both divine and natural causes as explanations of processes and events to dynamical laws stated as mathematical descriptions of the quantitative interactions of well-defined parts with each other. Newton explicitly chose this path for the *Principia*. Although he allowed himself to speculate in the Queries appended to his *Optiks* as to what mechanism might

---

[28]This concept also played a role in Ernst Mach's philosophy regarding life. See Mach [**1910**], p. 236, where he stated, from an epistemological perspective, that only psychological matters depend on the individuality of life. He also mentioned Driesch's work.

be responsible for gravity, these speculations were not part of his theory of the world. Newton retained some aspects of the prior perspectives when he left the long-term working of world machine (e.g., stability of the solar system) in supernatural hands.

The success of Newton's dynamical theory gave strong support to the mechanical worldview. This view was expressed in Christian Huyghens' *Traité de la Lumière* (1678) in terms of: "... the *true philosophy*, in which the causes of all natural effects are conceived of as *mechanical* causes. Which in my judgment must be accomplished or all hope of ever understanding physics renounced." This statement shows that, by the end of the seventeenth century, the mechanical philosophy had been clearly enunciated. Even more important for the subsequent development of thought concerning the understanding of the natural world, the proper mode of scientific analysis and theorizing began to be associated with mechanical explanations.

At the beginning of the eighteenth century, the innovations of Newton's theory of the world—and priority for the invention of the calculus—were debated by Leibniz and Samuel Clarke. Leibniz supported a continuum view of matter inherited from Descartes in opposition to the explicit and implicit atomism in much of Newton's thought. He was critical of what he felt was Newton's reintroduction of action at a distance into physics and Newton's views on atoms in a vacuum. He also debated Newton's conception of absolute space and time with Clarke in ways that parallel some of the modern thought about relativity theory. Leibniz felt that Newton's treatment of gravity and force, in particular, retained some of the scholastic occult qualities associated with it in the middle ages. Part of the debate centered on the issue of whether gravity must be conceived of as acting at a distance in Newton's theory.[29]

Work in the late eighteenth century, primarily the *Mécanique analytique* of Joseph Lagrange in 1788 and the *Mécanique céleste* of Pierre Laplace in the early nineteenth century, increased the mathematical tools available for the study of physical phenomena and many successes were recorded in the application of Newton's physics to the study of nature. The notion of a force became associated with relations between bodies because all forces in the macroscopic theories of Lagrange and Laplace were central forces associated with bodies. The observed phenomena in the areas of electricity, magnetism, heat and light were explained in terms of the Laplacian corpuscular system. This system consists of seven types of particles: positive and negative electricity, boreal and astral magnetism, ponderable matter, light, and caloric. The first five types obeyed a Newtonian inverse square law. The force laws for light and caloric particles were unknown.[30] One consequence of this corpuscular system is that almost every substance is required to have an atmosphere of

---

[29] For this correspondence and a useful commentary by the editor on these issues, see the Leibniz-Clarke correspondence in H. G. Alexander [1956].

[30] See L. P. Williams [1967] for more information on these issues.

each kind of particle because many substances can be decomposed into positively and negatively charged components in solution, many exhibit magnetic forces, metals give off light and heat when pounded long enough, and so forth.

An alternative view, that there were no particles but just centers of force, appeared in the mid eighteenth century. Roger Boscovich had proposed in 1753 a point atom based on these views. It had alternating zones of attractive and repulsive forces surrounding it. Associations between Boscovich atoms were postulated as an explanation of chemical transformations. A similar idea was discussed in the work of Leibniz and became influential in continental Europe in the late eighteenth century. Kant [**1786**] also contributed to it with his dynamic theory of forces that replaced matter in mechanics. It was brought to England from the continent by Samuel Coleridge, the poet and critic, at the beginning of the nineteenth century. For him, this step removed the dualism of matter and spirit, evaded the strict materialism of the continental physicists, and made room for God as an active agent in the world. The conversion of particles into each other was not contemplated in the Laplacian corpuscular theory, but was natural in the force theory if the strength of the forces depended on the conditions. This led to a successful search for the conversion of electricity into magnetism by Hans Christian Ørsted. The English chemist Humphry Davy, and initially his assistant Michael Faraday, also subscribed to these views.

The work of Kant, and his attempt to provide a philosophical foundation for Newtonian mechanics, had an important effect on physics in continental Europe in the nineteenth century, primarily in Germany and Scandinavia. The combination of Kantian epistemology and mathematical physics in particular seemed to account for both how we can know the world and how it works. The search for causes was still important to this picture, but was being shaken off. Whewell [**1847**], 2, p. 103, for example, mentioned August Compte's rejection of the search for causes or "modes of production" for phenomena. However Whewell, 2, p. 105, also recommended that we search for both the laws of phenomena and their causes. Helmholtz [**1847**], p. 90, in his groundbreaking paper on the conservation of energy, stated that the purpose of science is to "seek the laws by which the particular processes of nature may be referred to, and deduced from, general rules." The empirical portion of science finds laws like the gas law or the law of reflection and refraction. He, p. 91, went on to state the aim of science:

"The final aim of the theoretical natural sciences is therefore to discover the ultimate and unchangeable causes of natural phenomena. Whether all the processes of nature are referable to such,—whether nature is capable of being completely comprehended or whether changes occur that are not subject to the laws of necessary causation, but spring from spontaneity or freedom, this is not the place to decide; it is in all events clear that the science whose subject it is to comprehend nature must proceed from the assumption that it is comprehensible, and in accordance with this assumption investigate and conclude, until, perhaps, she is at length admonished by irrefrangible facts that there are limits beyond which she cannot proceed. ... Finally, therefore, we discover the problem of physical natural science to be, to refer natural phenomena back to unchangeable attractive and repulsive forces, whose intensity depends solely upon distance. The solvability of this problem is the condition of the complete comprehensibility of nature."

This relationship between the conservation of energy and causality foreshadows Bohr's later association of the conservation of energy with the "claim of causality."

The perspective in England and the United States was somewhat different. While Whewell [1847] considered theoretical statements, such as Kepler's statement that 'Mars moves in an ellipse' to be inductions from experience, Mill [1846], writing at about the same time, adopted a more modern perspective. Mill, pp. 384–385, affirmed the dual nature of perception, involving both sensation and judgment. He [1846], p. 386, went on to claim that every observation includes a description. He disagreed with Whewell on the nature of theoretical statements, which he called 'general descriptions' rather than inductions, and maintained, p. 387, that the statement 'The planet mars moves in an ellipse' is a description and not an induction. This distinction was elaborated by William John Macquorn Rankine [1855], in his "Outline of the Science of Energetics." Rankine identified two stages in the process of advancing our knowledge of physical laws. The first stage is observing the relations between things as they occur in the course of nature or in experiments and expressing these relations in formal laws. The second step is the reduction of these laws to a science, by which he meant "discovering the most simple system of principles, from which all the formal laws of the class of phenomena can be deduced as consequences." He went on to distinguish two ways of creating physical theories and called them the Abstractive and Hypothetical methods. The former is the inductive method and the latter is now called the hypothetico-deductive method.

Helmholtz [1873] took up the issue again in his Popular Lectures. He repeated the view that the search for the ultimate forces as the causes of phenomena was the goal of science. These causes are the source of the connection represented in physical laws that are independent of our thought and will. He argued against vitalism. His examination of the functions of the ear and eye impressed him with the idea that sensations are only *signs* of external objects and are not *images* of these objects.[31] He concluded that the sensations, which are signs of the changes taking place in the exterior

---

[31] Høffding [1904], p. 125, discussed the statements Helmholtz's made in his *Physiologishe Optik* that sensations are signs that are in no way a copy of the external influence

world, can only be regarded as pictures in that they represent succession in time. In a later paper, Helmholtz [1878], p. 372, emphasized that even if our sensations are only signs whose specific nature depends on our makeup, they are nevertheless signs of something and are not to be discarded as empty appearances. He, pp. 387–388, referred to F. Schiller's poem *Die Spaziergang* in this regard that 'The wise man:[32]

Seeks the familiar law
amidst the multiplicity of accidental occurrences,
Seeks for the eternal Pole Star
amidst the constant flight of appearances.

and to Goethe's Faust, Part II,[33]

Everything that passes,
Is only a symbol

Helmholtz drew the conclusion that if we are to comprehend and understand this flux of appearances, we must use causality as a regulative principle. He concluded, p. 390, that our belief in causality "expresses our belief in the comprehensibility of the world."

Gustav Kirchhoff [1874], p.1, opened his book *Lectures on Mathematical Physics* with the famous words "Mechanics is the science of motion; its task is to describe natural motion *completely and in the simplest way.*" By complete, he meant that no question dealing with motion remains unanswered. With regard to the simplest description, he recognized the contextual and historical component and that the answer could change in some future development of science.[34] In this statement, Kirchhoff completed the transformation begun much earlier and explicitly stated the independence of physical theory from the search for causal explanations. In doing this, he removed all notions he considered metaphysical, such as those maintaining that force is the cause of motion, and spoke only of accelerations. He also sidestepped the question of whether a theory, or a component of a theory, represents an independent element of reality discovered in nature.

Ernst Mach took up these issues in the mid to late nineteenth century. He made a critical and historical inquiry into matter, mechanics, and the theory of heat. His purpose was "to take up a standpoint which he would

---

arousing them. The relation between the object and the sign is that a similar object under similar circumstances will call up a similar sign.

[32] "Sucht das vertraute Gesetz in der Zufalls grausenden wundern, Sucht das ruhenden Pol in der Erscheinungen." This was translated by Russell Kahl.

[33] "Alles vergängliche, Ist nur ein Gleichnis." It is interesting to note that both of these poems were also favorites of Bohr's.

[34] See John T. Merz [1914], Vol. III, p. 578, for a discussion of the impact of Kirchhoff's introduction to his mechanics as marking the beginning of a new era in scientific thought.

not abandon when he passed from physics to psychology."[35] Using the ideas developed in his study of physiology and from the science of energetics as a basis, Mach [1883], p. 579, claimed that nature is composed of sensations as its elements and that things are constructed out of these elements. He thus viewed the concepts of things and theories about them as representing economical methods of representing actual empirical data. Because atoms are not accessible through direct sensation, Mach accorded them only a logical significance in organizing our thinking economically, but did not accord them a reality. He accorded the same status to the causal relation, which is the closest a description comes to connecting two elements of experience. Mach thus felt that the concept of causality helps us organize our experience, but does not express a real connection between experiences.

Mach was hurt that his own ideas on the role of description in theory, which had preceded those of Kirchhoff, were neglected at the time. He [1883], p. 325, lamented the fact that Kirchhoff had caused "universal astonishment" and received all the attention for his theory of "description" while his own analogous views on description in physics, and the replacement of the concept of cause by function, introduced in 1871 and 1872 before Kirchhoff's work was published, were ignored. Mach [1905], pp. 308–309, also took note of the fact that the concept of description had played a role in the philosophical analyses of science by Mill and Whewell before Kirchhoff published his work. In addition, in a passage of interest for us regarding Bohr, Mach [1905], p. 445, anticipated to some degree the way in which Bohr would use complementarity: "If one finds at some time that a law ceases to be valid under circumstances in which it had always been found as valid, then we are compelled to search for a *still unknown* complementarity relation of laws."

Maxwell [1877] began his treatise on *Matter and Motion* with a statement of the perspective of physical science. In the Preface he noted that mechanics had moved from the era in which we were forming a conception of natural phenomena in terms of the forces between bodies into the era of computing the energy of a system in terms of the configuration of bodies and their forces and motions, which are themselves generalized to the maximum extent possible. He, p. 2, made the observation that "In all scientific procedure we begin by marking out a certain region or subject as the field of our investigations. To this we must confine our attention, leaving the rest of the universe out of account till we have completed the investigation in which we are engaged." This important statement reflects the standard practice of scientists and, as we shall see in Chapter 14, its implications are seldom investigated or understood.[36]

---

[35] See the discussion of Mach in Høffding [1904], pp. 115–121. See also Høffding's interesting discussions of Maxwell, Heinrich Hertz and Wilhelm Ostwald in the same chapter.

[36] He also enunciated the viewpoint that the fixed stars of the universe must furnish the frame of reference for mechanics. This had an important influence on the theory of relativity and has come to be called Mach's Principle.

Maxwell discussed the absolute space and time of Newton's mechanics. He took Descartes to task for identifying matter with extension and thereby confounding matter with space. He went on to quote a general maxim underlying science that "The same causes will always produce the same effects." He explained that this means that if the causes differ only with respect to their absolute time or absolute place, they will produce the same effects. He distinguished this statement about causes from the statement that "like causes produce like effects", which is true only under limited conditions. He, pp. 89–90, also used the principle that energy can only exist in connection with matter to conclude that the matter that transmits light and thermal energy, later called the ether, extends throughout the universe.

In 1878 du Bois-Reymond wrote an article on the limits of scientific knowledge in which he criticized the concepts underlying atomism. He asked that if the atom is indivisible, why is this so, and if it is infinitely hard, then how do forces effect it. He located the source of our difficulties in the fact that we are limited in our concepts. The problem arises in our inability to visualize something other than with our external senses or with our internal sense experience. He went on to say that "No one who has thought through the issue somewhat more deeply can fail to recognize the transcendent nature of the obstacles we face."[37] He was battling what he considered to be two errors. The first is the belief that the nature of things, such as matter and consciousness, can be clarified by reference to mechanical conceptions. He went on to discuss the mind-body problem in Leibniz and Descartes. He pointed out in reference to this that there is an indissoluble contradiction between the mechanical worldview and freedom of the will, and thereby ethics. For more than two thousand years mankind has been unable to explain mental activity in mechanical terms and, on the basis of his argument, du Bois-Reymond concluded that it never will.

Bois-Reymond went on in a second article to discuss the "Seven Puzzles of the World." He stated that the intention behind the first paper was to present the problems with the conceptions of force and matter and with the explanation of consciousness in mechanical terms. In this paper, he extended those concerns to seven fundamental puzzles:

1. The existence of matter and force (first limit of natural knowledge);
2. The origin of motion;
3. The first development of life;
4. The purposefulness of nature (not transcendental);
5. The origin of simple sense experience (second limit of natural knowledge);
6. The origin of thought and language (not transcendental);
7. The freedom of the will.

---

[37]See Bois-Reymond [**1882**], pp. 7–57, for this paper and references to contemporary literature of the time on these issues.

With regard to giving a mechanical explanation of these problems, he stated that we must once and for all proclaim our 'Ignorabimus.' The idea that we can never proceed on these issues excited severe condemnation from several groups of thinkers.

In the meantime, the English scientist P. G. Tait [1877] expressed at the beginning of his mechanics a set of *a priori* axioms that he felt underlie science:
(i) the universe has an objective existence;
(ii) we know it only by our senses;
(iii) our senses are imperfect;
(iv) reason allows us to control this.

For the concepts of space and time, Tait quoted Kant's discussion of their a priori nature. Tait distinguished two kinds of "things" in the universe: matter and energy. He rejected action at a distance and claimed that force is not something objective. He also expressed a Kantian perspective in stating that matter is not like what our senses tell us. Tait's point of view seems to reflect that of many non-continental scientists at that time concerning how to view reality, space and time, and the role of science in helping reason control the imperfection of our senses.

Hertz [1894] took a fresh approach to the principles of mechanics. He had been a student of Helmholtz and acknowledged debts to Helmholtz, J. J. Thomson, and especially Mach. Mach [1883] stated that his goal is to give a complete and definitive presentation of mechanics, which is not too restrictive or too inclusive. It must include all natural motions and exclude all that do not occur in nature. He affirmed a Kantian form of causality in which we form symbolic pictures of internal objects and the necessary consequences of the form we give them are always the necessary consequences in nature of the things pictured. He required that these images be logically permissible, correct so that they do not contradict known facts, appropriate and simple. His mechanics is a rational mechanics along Kantian lines.

One of the goals of Kirchhoff, Hertz and Mach was to remove causality and force, which they viewed as the last occult quantities in physics, from our theories. To this end, force was defined in terms of the accelerative component in motion. Hertz, in particular, tried to express everything in mechanics as mass in motion. To this end, he invented invisible masses that move in accord with the laws of motion so that he could account for all accelerations in terms of some body associated with the body that was accelerated.[38]

The concept of force that emerges from these considerations is a functional one that no longer rests on the anthropomorphic notions of a push

---

[38] For further details on this program, see Jammer [1957], Chapter 11. The employment of invisible masses in Hertz's mechanics foreshadows the approach taken by the hidden variable theorists with respect to quantum mechanics.

or a pull or contact. This perspective was continued in the development of relativity theory and quantum theory.

11.6 Reflection 20

During the nineteenth century, the epistemological analysis of Kant provided a foundation for the development and understanding of science and philosophy for most practitioners in continental Europe. The plausibility of the way Kant approached the subject/object distinction and his own work on applying these ideas to physics and biology made it a natural choice. It avoided the problem of attributing properties to objects, which Locke had excised, and neatly explained the role of causality in a way that evaded Hume's criticism. It also provided an explanatory framework that assured the intelligibility of human inquiry in that this inquiry must be made with respect to the appearances and these must fall under the Categories in order to be intelligible at all. The Kantian concern with appearances was also compatible with the materialism that had emerged triumphant in mechanical philosophy after the work of Newton.

Empiricism continued to make headway against rationalist conceptions. In physics, biology and the study of language, the increasingly rapid development of empiricist techniques and methods made great strides in reducing the subject matter to order and systematizing it. Simultaneously, the explanation of phenomena became more strongly associated with giving a mechanical explanation. This was almost universally agreed to be the best choice when it was available. Other conceptions, such as those associated with individuality and whole versus part, offered much less in the way of avenues to follow experimentally and came to play the role of boundaries for mechanical explanations.

Important progress away from the scholastic conceptions of force and explanations, inherited in part from Aristotle, was made during the nineteenth century. The reconception of theories as descriptions, rather than requiring them to provide causal explanations in the traditional (scholastic) sense, was an important step in freeing them from the old requirements of what a physical theory should do and the form it must take. Bohr honored this evolution with his choice of the term 'description' to represent a theory.

An important factor not touched on yet was the growth of mathematics during this period. There was a rapid expansion of mathematical ideas and theories following the introduction of the calculus in the late seventeenth century. This led to the development of increasingly powerful mathematical tools for expressing mechanical theories. These theories in turn stimulated mathematics still further. There was also a parallel development of technology and experimental technique during this period that was equally important. As a number of thinkers have pointed out, the descriptions we can make of natural phenomena are limited to the tools we have for studying them.

Consequently, as the supply of these technological and mathematical tools increased, so did the sophistication and depth of their applications to science. Most of our current theories in physics and other sciences at the end of the twentieth century could not even have been formulated in a usable way in the nineteenth century.

CHAPTER 12

Copenhagen: 1902–1935

When Bohr entered the University of Copenhagen in 1902, the issues associated with blackbody radiation and specific heats had not yet been seen as an insoluble crisis for classical theory. When he completed his theory of the hydrogen atom in 1913, he joined with Planck and Einstein in setting in motion progress along a path that would profoundly alter physics and our conception of the world. The period between 1913 and 1935, when the Einstein, Podolsky and Rosen paper and Bohr's reply to it were published, marked the emergence of Bohr's correspondence principle, complementarity, and his most fundamental epistemological ideas.

12.1 Bohr and Høffding

At the beginning of the twentieth century, Kant was the dominant influence on Danish and German philosophy and on the philosophical foundations of the sciences. Both Harald Høffding and Kristian Kroman, who together taught philosophy at the university of Copenhagen for more than 30 years beginning around 1883, worked within the Kantian mold. Similarly, Kantian ideas were important to some of the biologists with a philosophical bent, such as C. Joh. Petersen, who did work on the geographical distribution of biological organisms and physiology at the University.

Harald Høffding was an important factor in European philosophy during the late nineteenth and early twentieth centuries. He was admired for the thoroughness of his study of philosophy and its history, his work in Kantian philosophy, his interest in science and its problems, and his prolific work on behalf of philosophy itself. He reviewed the work of previous philosophers from a unified standpoint in his *A History of Modern Philosophy*. Høffding showed considerable insight into the workings of these theories and gave a useful treatment of the themes and the main ideas. His own work was firmly within the Kantian traditions, but he differed with Kant on a number of points concerning things-in-themselves and the Categories. Høffding was also known for his open mind and for emphasizing the philosophical problems in science and philosophy rather than specific solutions to them.

The question of influences on Bohr and the controversy over the degree of Høffding's influence on Bohr, primarily between Jan Faye and David Favrholdt, was reviewed in Chapter 1. As mentioned there, Bohr had been taught by Høffding when he entered the university and Høffding was a friend of Bohr's family. Bohr credited Høffding with emphasizing in his work and teaching how much the nature of an explanation has changed in the history of physics.[1] I will discuss Høffding's ideas now, looking for ideas and phrases that Bohr may have adopted.

Høffding was at the peak of his career as a professor at the University of Copenhagen when Bohr entered it. Because of the importance of precision in looking for precursors to the concepts, phrases, ideas, and examples Bohr introduced in his epistemological thinking, I will let Høffding speak in his own words as much as possible.[2] I will show that all of the major philosophical elements that Bohr employed in his theory, except, perhaps, complementarity, are discussed in the writings of Høffding. This is not to say that Høffding anticipated Bohr's application of these ideas when Bohr created his epistemology. However, Høffding did feel that he had anticipated complementarity in the field of social phenomena.

A comparison of the epistemological elements of Høffding's writing and those that play a role in Bohr's theory shows that Bohr did not employ any of

---

[1] Bohr [**Arch**], 13:2, August 1932.
[2] For Høffding on Høffding, see Høffding [**1923b**].

Høffding's philosophical positions in his own work or show signs of Høffding's influence on the shape of the epistemology he developed. While there are some tantalizing similarities, there are a number of aspects of Høffding's philosophy brought out in the discussion below that are opposed to the position Bohr took on the same matters. There are similarities, for example, in how the two of them expressed their understanding of the position of humor in life.[3] Two immediate examples of the differences are their attitudes to causality and individuality.

The passages below will illustrate the fact that in continental Europe at the end of the nineteenth century, much of the thinking in psychology was still very closely connected with philosophy. This component of psychology concerned itself with the thinking subject aspect of the subject/object distinction. Although Wilhelm Wundt, Hermann von Helmholtz, Gustav Theodor Fechner, Ernst Mach and others were beginning to employ experimental techniques in the study of perception, rationalist introspection was still the main tool used to discern internal psychological structures and study them.

William James [1881] wrote his *Outline of Psychology* from the perspective of introspective psychology. James was well known to Danish scholars because he and a Danish physiologist Carl Georg Lange independently proposed the theory, now called the James-Lange theory, that emotions are first created by a bodily response to a situation and then experienced by us as an emotion. As part of his concern with psychological issues, Høffding developed an acquaintance with James. He was responsible for translating some of James' works into Danish and met with James when he traveled to the United States.

In his *Outlines of Psychology*, Høffding [1882a] spoke of the individuality of the elements of our mental content in juxtaposition to their union in consciousness. He, p. 66–67, began by maintaining that "the material world shows us no real individualities." He, p. 139, located individuality in the unity of consciousness and, p. 343, observed that "the central point of individuality does not coincide with the central point of consciousness. When it becomes a question of action, therefore, it is not to be wondered at if something happens which astonishes both the spectator and actor." Finally, he, p. 353, said "Research may and must admit that, as regards the individual, it does not succeed in giving every detail, that there is always something which escapes it,—that the individuality appears in consequence an irrational whole, which admits of only approximate determination."

He, p. 129, went on to discuss the idea, which also appeared in James [1890], that there is an inverse ratio between the current of free ideas and the course of the actual percepts in our minds, just as between the elements of perception, that is, the uninterpreted sensation and the implicate idea. They endeavor to check and suppress each other so that the more energy one

---

[3]See Høffding [1918] for his view of the philosophical aspects of humor.

element claims the less there is for the other. Both elements and currents are present in every state of consciousness, but with different strengths. They do battle for the attention, but they cannot be in equilibrium because the attention can only be focused in one place at a time. Along these same lines, Høffding, p. 218, spoke of the "reciprocal play of our ideas and sensations," and, p. 277, of "complementary colors" that pass into one another just as opposing feelings can pass into one another.

His viewpoint toward psychology and physics was dualistic, which he expressed in the statement that "Mind and matter form an irreducible duality, just as subject and object." He, p. 345, also spoke of causality in psychology and stated that "If there are limits to this assumption, they will coincide with the limits to psychology."

In the *Problems of Philosophy*, Høffding [**1902**], turned his attention to philosophical issues of interest to science. With regard to biological issues, he, p. 20, wrote of the "irrational relation of the whole to the elements ...," and used the phrases, p. 21, "biology recognizes the individuality of the living organism" and "the irrational here as elsewhere not only places the limit, but also sets us the task, the ever new task."

With regard to issues of psychology, Høffding contrasted descriptive psychology with experimental psychology and then, pp. 47–48, restated his previous viewpoint on sequences of mental states and correlated sequences of sensations: "In psychical and physiological phenomena we have two serial forms of states, which experience shows us to vary in certain reciprocal relations .... The close interrelationship of the two series of states makes it impossible to trace them back to two different 'beings' or 'things'; it comes entirely natural to conceive them as different manifestations of one and the same 'being'." He goes on, p. 65, "It is, however, not only the intellectual necessity of finding a connection between experiences that has led to giving such prominence to the concept of causality, but also the necessity of distinguishing sharply between the subjective ideas and objective reality."

With regard to epistemology, Høffding [**1902**], pp. 71–72, spoke of four theories that conceive of the principles of knowledge as intuitions, postulates, generalizations, and economic tools of thought. In each of these cases, Høffding claimed that Kant's approach to understanding knowledge is presupposed in that we can only find the entity by beginning with experience and finding the presuppositions on which the understanding is based. With this he, pp. 99–100, challenged the view of Richard Avenarius and Mach that "... it is the aim of science to give an exact, methodological *description* of all relations and transitions."

Høffding felt that we cannot simply accept Kant's theory as it is because there are aspects of Kant's theory of knowledge that are obscure. To illustrate this, he, pp. 112–113, discussed subject and object in relation to Kant's thing-in-itself: "... if we wish to hold on to the 'thing-in-itself,' we can use it in the spirit of Kant and still avoid the contradictions which cling to it in Kant's philosophy. The issue is where does a Subject get its objective contents. We can do this by employing it to express the fact that the difference between Subject and Object always springs up anew whenever we think we have found an objective analysis of the character of the Subject or a subjective explanation of the character of the object. Each refers to the other indefinitely, and the irrational crops out in the fact that an infinite series (of the type: $S_1\{O_1\{S_2\{O_2\ldots\}$) is both possible and necessary." [4]

On the issue of reality, Høffding [1902], p. 115, stated: "The reality which we recognize is, however, only a part of a greater whole,—and here we are not in a position to determine the relation between the parts and the whole. An exhaustive concept of reality is not given us to create." [5] He followed this in Høffding [1910], p. 260, with "The truth cannot be defined as an accord of our thoughts with existence. We know existence only thanks to incessant toil having for its end the appropriation of the objects to our forms of thought. Reality, the truth of objects consists practically, even for common sense, in the narrow connection between as much of the subject exactly understood as possible. ... Kant has committed the fatal error of supposing that the "matter," which I have called the subject, was recognized passively." [6] Furthermore, this active involvement with reality means (Høffding [1910], p. 292) that: "When one places a totality in opposition to its elements, for example, the organism in opposition to its parts, the mind in opposition to its thoughts, its sentiments or its desires, society in opposition to the individuals, that signifies only that outside of the action that we discover in particular cases in the parts, there is yet a world of possibilities, a storehouse of potential energy, which, under certain conditions, may be engaged and may change the effect on the part. And there is a continual reciprocal action between them." [7] Høffding [1922], p. 217, maintained that relations between objects are part of the determination of reality: "That criterion of reality is made deeper and more exact in science by a finer examination and more exact determination of the relations which create the connections between objects." He [1925], pp. 488, 492, then explained further: "A certain structure of reality appears through

---

[4] Høffding's has written extensively on the relation of Subject and Object in nineteenth century philosophical and psychological thought. For further information, see Høffding [1902], p. 113, and Høffding [1910], pp. 298–308.

[5] In relation to this, I mention footnote 48 on page 107 in Høffding [1902] in which he refers to a work by a Danish author Partus Wilner who tries to show that the highest completeness can only be reached by the successive unfolding of qualities that would mutually exclude one another if simultaneous.

[6] Høffding [1917], p. 159, stated similarly that truth is only attained by incessant toil that never comes to an end. All new experiences force us to reexamine our previous truths.

[7] This reciprocal action includes the personality as well: Høffding [1910], p. 366: "I add that, in the personality itself, the different interests and different desires are opposed to each other. These oppositions are in a mutual dependence and are subordinate to a reciprocal action."

the theories of science. The physicist is and remains a metaphysician." He attributed this conception to Emile Meyerson.

In spite of Høffding's acquaintance with William James, he did not follow the paths that James [**1890**] was pursuing in his *The Principles of Psychology*. James presented both a broader view of both psychology and associated philosophical issues than would fit within Høffding's Kantian perspective. James proposed that with respect to sensation *esse est sentiri*, i.e., that the existence of a sensation is in the experiencing of it. James was also concerned with the nature of reality and his philosophical concerns evolved into his later works *Pragmatism,* James [**1907**] and *Essays in Radical Empiricism,* James [**1911**]. In the *Principles,* James discussed subject and object and their relation. He opposed the "dualistic discontinuity" implicit in associationism with its "atomism" of sensation that was popular in European thought at that time. In his later philosophical work, he moved from dualism to pluralism and maintained [**1907**] that we make reality for ourselves. There is no evidence in the work of either Bohr or Høffding that these ideas of James were important to their thinking.

Høffding [**1917**], pp. 107-114, discussed vitalism and mechanism and mentioned the work of Driesch and Haldane. Continuing in this vein, Høffding [**1923a**], p. 122, contrasted the approach of mechanics in physics, which begins with the elements and builds the whole, and the approach of biology, which begins with the whole and decomposes it into the elements. He went on, in a work presenting his own conceptual development, [**1923b**], p. 87, to discuss Kant's error in assuming that the categories are fixed and valid for all time. He pointed out that he had added a category of his own, Of Totality, and extended the category Of Relation. Høffding maintained that the two principal sources of the doctrine of the categories are the psychological study of common sense and the study of the history of the sciences.[8] These sources continually react to each other: science stems from common sense and common sense changes over time due to science.

Høffding kept somewhat abreast of the developments in physics though his contact with Bohr and others at the University of Copenhagen. In his 1923 work on analogy and symbol, he [**1923a**], p. 41, stated that "The concepts such as "analogy" and "symbol" are correlative and express a reciprocal relation." He, pp. 114–115, then applied these ideas to Bohr's 1922 paper "On the Constitution of Atoms": "That which is of interest to the theory of knowledge, if one abstracts the results important for objective science, is the manner in which these results are expressed. And Bohr's use of the expression "this means that" (and not "this is that") reminds us constantly of analogies and not of identities between the qualitative series which constitutes the onset of research and the quantitative series which leads to a definite idea concerning atomic structure." He felt that the careful locutions of Bohr in

---

[8] Høffding [**1922**], p. 166.

relation to the interpretation of certain experimental results in atomic physics in 1922 supported the perspective on analogies that he had developed in his own work. However, Favrholdt [**1992**] has shown clearly that Høffding did not really have a good grasp of the physics.

By 1930, Høffding [**1930a**], [**1930b**], had become apprised of Bohr's philosophical work and of complementarity in particular. He [**1930a**], pp. 489–490, referred explicitly to Bohr in this regard: "When this connection was designated as "complementary," no new thought content was expressed thereby, and Bohr himself referred to the relation between the consciousness of the will and the causal order and thereby also to the relation between ethical and psychological conceptions of one and the same action, which I have pointed out above, and which come forward at all times when psychic concentration and the search for understanding are both active.—When Bohr further cautions us about the use of the word "free will," because the strict causal concept cannot be applied, such a warning is very well founded because the word "freedom" has been used with six different meanings (see my Ethics, Ch. 5)." Høffding, p. 490, went on to restate his claim that complementarity is not new: "As already stated before, "complementarism" is no stranger to philosophy. The analogies, which cannot be analyzed further by thought, do not have so simple a character as they previously may have appeared to have where pure natural science was concerned."

Høffding [**1930a**], p. 491, continued with a discussion of the concept of individuality when applied to the realm of atomic theory in terms of a limit on our viewpoint: "If atomic particles, for which research ends at the physical limit, have an "individuality," one designates by this the boundary of a general viewpoint; "individuality" is therefore also a negative concept, and not, as for other boundaries, the expression of such deep and rich relations, that research cannot exhaust it. Moreover, one must be satisfied to picture those things that express such individuality by typical representations and only with the help of analogies can anchor their preceding and succeeding states. Such an anchoring is even not possible for an atomic particle. One can form from such things no typical conception of individuality. Only single opposed isolated states can be known." These statements contradict his earlier position on individuality stated above.

A review of the issues discussed by both Høffding and Bohr, and of the very language in which they expressed themselves, shows a strong relation between the modes of expression both used. An examination of Bohr [**1929b**], in which he mentions analogy, reciprocal modes of expression, forms of perception, subject and object in epistemology, objectivity, unity of consciousness, and free will, shows this connection. Bohr, p. 100, stated explicitly that in the relation of causality to free-will, it has "not eluded philosophers that we may be concerned here with an unvisualizable relation of complementarity."

This reference is clearly to Høffding's work. In other places Bohr makes reference to humor and its role in life in a way that reflects Høffding's thinking and writings on the subject. In sum, Bohr's choice of the same philosophical terms that played a central role in Høffding's writings and the locutions Bohr used to characterize the concepts he was presenting all make it probable that Bohr absorbed some of his philosophical knowledge from Høffding's work.

Høffding's claim that complementarity is no stranger to philosophy, however, is more problematic. Høffding wrote extensively in the late nineteenth century on reciprocal relations between concepts used to describe our mental states and social situations. And it is true, as Høffding maintained, that most of the examples Bohr used to illustrate complementarity outside of physics are taken from or suggested by Høffding's work. In particular, Høffding's review of holism in biology illustrates the simultaneous need for alternative incompatible descriptions (physical versus holistic) of biological phenomena. On the other hand, Høffding never suggested that these ideas would apply to physics or chemistry.

Mere reciprocity is not equivalent to complementarity as Bohr understood it. It is a necessary feature, but not a sufficient one. In biology, for example, the reasons stated for why a unifying explanation that respects both the whole and the part cannot be given were not compelling even in Høffding's day. There was no reason, other than philosophical, to believe at that time that experiments in biology could not overcome their current restrictions and investigate these issues more deeply.

Overall, Høffding, and other philosophers and psychologists who agreed with him, did not pursue the implications of the reciprocity they saw in the 'current of free ideas' and the 'flow of actual percepts' in psychology. Nor did they pursue more deeply an explanation for the opposition of individuality or wholeness to analysis they saw in biology. Høffding in particular did not search for an explanation for why a unifying theory in these cases could not eventually be found. By the time experiments in psychology and biology began testing some of these issues, the theory and practice had moved far beyond the introspective psychology and nineteenth century biology he was familiar with and his perspective no longer represented a significant school of thought.

Let us return now to the discussion of influences on Bohr between Faye and Favrholdt initiated in Chapter 1. Faye has given a useful précis of Høffding's work in Part I of Faye [**1991**]. Faye maintained that Høffding was a substantial influence on Bohr and that Bohr absorbed whole philosophical positions from him and fashioned these into his own philosophy. The contrary position was maintained by Favrholdt [**1992**], who gave a summary and criticism of Høffding's work and exhaustively discussed the various claims of influence of Høffding, and others, on Bohr. Favrholdt observed that epistemology was not a specialty for Høffding, whose first published book on epistemology was *Human Thought*, which was published in 1910 when Høffding was 67 years old. Favrholdt presented a number of philosophical commitments that Høffding had, such as a strong commitment to determinism, that Bohr opposed in his own work. Favrholdt also argued that Bohr used some philosophical terms, such as *Anschauung*, in a sense that is closer to ordinary language than to philosophical discourse.

In spite of all this, Favrholdt did acknowledge that Bohr's philosophical training had to come from somewhere. My own conclusion is that some of Høffding's philosophical vocabulary, as opposed to his philosophy, was used by Bohr in his work. Bohr did not necessarily obtain this vocabulary from Høffding, but all I need is to show that these ideas were in the air in Copenhagen at the time. I think that both Faye and Favrholdt could agree on this.

12.2 Bohr on Language

The role of language in Bohr's epistemology has been delineated above. He expressed himself informally on many occasions to the effect that language and communication are necessary for objective knowledge, but that it also places limitations on us. Hans Bohr, Niels Bohr's son, has recounted his father's views with respect to the use of words in our lives: "They were tools and their limitations had to be recognized. ... The eternal question of life's meaning was freely summed up when in his particular way he said that in any case there is no meaning in saying that life has no meaning, and to Kierkegaard's remark on finding 70,000 fathoms of water underneath him, he used to add with a twinkle in his eyes: "It is much worse—we are suspended over a bottomless pit, caught in our own words." " [9]

Bohr first mentioned language in connection with the problems of atomic physics in [**1927**], p. 91. He [**1929c**], pp. 15–16, followed this by drawing a connection between them: "... we can no more hope to attain a clear understanding in physics without facing the difficulties arising in the shaping or our concepts and in the use of the media of expression than we can in other fields of human inquiry." Bohr [**1929c**], p. 16, then argued that we cannot evade the difficulties in atomic physics by replacing the concepts of classical physics by new conceptual forms:

"Indeed, ... the recognition of the limitation of our forms of perception by no means implies that we can dispense with our customary ideas or their direct verbal expressions when reducing our sense impressions to order. No more is it likely that the fundamental concepts of the classical theories will ever become superfluous for the description of physical experience."

---

[9]See Hans Bohr [**1964**], pp. 327–328.

The argument that Bohr gave for this conclusion was two-fold: "the recognition of the indivisibility of the quantum of action, and the determination of its magnitude, ... depend on an analysis of measurements based on classical concepts ...; and, "... it continues to be the application of these concepts alone which makes it possible to relate the symbolism of the quantum theory to the data of experience."

The question of how to understand Bohr's statements on perception and language is not an easy one. At some points, it appears as if Bohr was making a statement of how perception determines what can be "seen." At other times, he speaks of organizing perceptions within the forms of perception, e.g., by the use of the concept of causality, by which we reduce them to order. Bohr generally used the term sensation to mean raw experience and perception to mean organized experience, which involves an element of interpretation and the possibility of communication. Perception, in other words, will be taken here to mean a sensation or group of sensations about which we can make a statement, such as, 'The particle made a spot on the photographic plate at this position.' Weizsäcker [**1955**], pp. 75, 94, 122, and Rosenfeld [**1961b**], p. 386, have stated that our perceptions themselves are classical, namely, that a wave is a 'simple description of what is seen in experiments', and claimed that these ideas represent Bohr's view.[10] I shall hold in abeyance for now the question of whether this is an accurate characterization of Bohr's point of view or not, and turn to a comparison of Bohr's epistemological ideas with respect to language with those of Wittgenstein. In the next chapter, I will examine whether Bohr's view on language and its role in his epistemology can be maintained in the light of current investigations into language and perception.

12.3 Bohr and Wittgenstein

There is little likelihood that Bohr was directly influenced by Ludwig Wittgenstein's views, but there are many striking parallels between the views expressed by Bohr and those of the early and late Wittgenstein. One of the central issues, for the philosophical work of both Bohr and Wittgenstein, is the role of language in epistemology and its influence on us.

Wittgenstein [**1922**] stated in the *Tractatus* that the connection between the world and elements of our language is not itself subject to logical analysis. We can only show it.[11] This perspective is consistent with Wittgenstein's [**1953**] later concern in the *Philosophical Investigations* with how language functions to accomplish its task. Wittgenstein maintained that elements of language are given meaning by the context in which they are employed. He emphasized that the ways in which we use language in various social contexts allow us to attach intersubjective meaning to its components. Wittgenstein

---

[10] See also Weizsäcker [**1952**], p. 75.
[11] See, for example, the discussion of this in Janik and Toulmin [**1973**], pp. 218–223.

observed that this behavior is on the one hand conventional and on the other hand governed by rules. He highlighted these facts in his later work by speaking of the employment of language for various purposes as engaging in *language games*.

Wittgenstein [1953] approached philosophical analysis via an inquiry into how words or language are being used and maintained that this is the proper way to make a philosophical analysis. He rejected the traditional inquiry into the supposed "essence" behind the words. Because of the connection between the use of language in social situations and the meanings we can attach to what was expressed, Wittgenstein [1953], p. 48, was concerned with our *everyday*, working language.

Bohr expressed on several occasions the view that language has a transcendent aspect. A typical example of this type is the statement by Bohr quoted by his son above or the one quoted by Petersen [1963], p. 10:

"We are suspended in language. Our task is to communicate experience and ideas to others. We must strive continually to extend the scope of our description, but in such a way that our messages do not lose their objective or unambiguous character."

Compare this to Wittgenstein [1922], in the *Tractatus*, p. 115: *"The limits of my language mean the limits of my world."* Along similar lines, Wittgenstein [1922], pp. 139, 143, rejected the idea that the possibility of describing the world by Newtonian mechanics tells us something about the world:

"... the possibility of describing the world by means of Newtonian mechanics tells us nothing about the world: but what does tell us something about it is the precise *way* in which it is possible to describe it by these means. We are also told something about the world by the fact that it can be described more simply with one system of mechanics than with another .... The whole modern conception of the world is founded on the illusion that the so-called laws of nature are the explanations of natural phenomena."

It was around the time Wittgenstein published this passage that Bohr was progressively giving up the hope of finding an explanation of spectral lines in terms of motions within atoms, and was looking for other kinds of laws to reduce the spectra to order. Wittgenstein's attack on the illusion of what a physical theory is supposed to provide, and his emphasis on the form a description can take, presage Bohr's growing concern with descriptions and the instrumental interpretation of physical theory.

In Bohr's investigation of the ways in which our conceptual framework may be extended, he clearly felt that language, and the basic concepts of our experience must remain primary, while those concepts used in making theoretical connections within this experience could take a more wide-ranging form. This is in keeping with the discussion of his views by Petersen [1963], p. 12, who indicated that Bohr felt that to attempt to replace these basic concepts with others is incompatible with our fundamental situation, in which we have a unique language adapted to everyday life. Petersen [1963], p. 12, quoted Bohr further on this: "But our problem is not that we do not have adequate concepts. What we lack is a sufficient understanding of the unambiguous applicability of the concepts we have." This point of view is very much like that adopted by Wittgenstein [1953], p. 14, in his investigation of philosophical problems.

As I have noted before, Bohr rejected the introduction of a system of three-valued logic for the solution of the problem of quantum indeterminacy. He felt that logic and mathematics are part of our ordinary language—albeit a part with particularly clear relationships between the components—and, therefore, still subject to the same limitations as any other part of language when used for the purpose of communication. A logic with a category covering statements that cannot be said to be either true or false would simply have a category for Bohr's ambiguous descriptions without illuminating their status.

Both Bohr and Wittgenstein rejected the possibility of an ideal language as a solution to the problems that face us. Wittgenstein's [1953], p. 38, reason for rejecting ideal languages was that he did not feel that they somehow serve their purposes "better" than ordinary language. On the contrary, [1953], pp. 46–47, the vagueness of some sentences is the root of their usefulness at times. What we must do, Wittgenstein [1953], pp. 38, 49, 51, went on, is develop a clear understanding of how our language actually operates.

Wittgenstein [1953], p. 48, also cautioned against the difficulties that we can get into when we use words outside of their everyday language context:

"When philosophers use a word—"knowledge", "being", "object", "I", "name"—and try to grasp the *essence* of the thing, one must always ask oneself: is the word ever actually used this way in the language-game which is its original home?"

Bohr [1949], p. 64, was also wary of using terms outside the range of their use in "common language and practical definition." One way of avoiding this issue of words, as Wittgenstein [1953], p. 42, pointed out, is to analyze what we can properly say about things:

"We feel as if we had to *penetrate* phenomena: our investigation, however, is directed towards phenomena, but, as one might say, towards the *'possibilities'* of phenomena. We remind ourselves, that is to say, of the *kind of statement* that we make about phenomena."

This is the tack Bohr took with his emphasis on the need to investigate the possibilities of observation and description in atomic physics. The outcome of Bohr's investigation was his statement of the need for classical descriptions with classical concepts for the proper characterization of what we observe in experiments. Bohr's investigation, with its emphasis on everyday language and reference to definite experimental contexts, would probably have met Wittgenstein's approval.

Another conception, in which several distinct levels of description appear, is that attributed to Bohr by Rosenfeld [**1946**], pp. 12–13, [**1963a**], p. 49, and Petersen [**1963**], p. 11. Rosenfeld said that Bohr was guided in his early thought on the description of mental activity by what Rosenfeld called a beautiful analogy with the concept of a multivalued function on a Riemannian surface. An example of such a function is the logarithm, $\ln z$, of the complex number z. This function has a singularity at $z = 0$ and is not single-valued on the complex plane. If one begins at a certain point on this plane and takes a path that eventually returns to the original point, the value of the function at that point will depend on whether or not the loop contains the singularity at the origin. If it does not, the function will have the same value it did originally. If the loop does contain the singularity, the value of the function will depend on how many times the singularity was circled by the path. However, the function may be made single valued by viewing it as taking values on many copies of the complex plane, called the Riemann sheets of the function, which can be visualized as stacked above one another. You can move from one sheet to another only on a path that circles the singularity at the origin.

Rosenfeld [**1963a**], p. 44, stated Bohr's idea as follows:

"The ambiguity of every word referring to our mental activity may be expressed by saying that it belongs to different "planes of objectivity," just as the values of a multiform function are distributed on a different Riemann plane. The use of words in everyday life must be subject to the condition that they be kept within the same plane of objectivity; and as soon as we deal with words referring to our own thinking, we are exposed to the danger of gliding onto another plane."

Rosenfeld [**1946**], pp. 12–13, had also cautioned us that whenever we use words that refer to our own thinking, we run the risk of gliding to a different plane of objectivity: "For instance, in the seemingly innocuous remark "One might imagine beings on some other planet whose logic would be different from ours", a fatal danger is hidden in the word "imagine"." Rosenfeld noted that self-reference is forbidden in the theory of sets in mathematics because of the paradoxes it engenders. But, just as Riemann considers these planes all part of one function, we use the word 'will' to refer both to voluntary behavior and to refer to a conscious feeling of volition. To believe that we can remove this fundamental ambiguity by "new" concepts is an illusion. "The complementary relations of the planes of objectivity to each other cannot be but primitive, irreducible ones, corresponding to an essential property of our very use of language to describe and communicate our experiences."

Meyer-Abich [**1965**], p. 175, used the metaphor that "I" is a "singularity in consciousness," reference to which must be made, in establishing which plane a statement about an object is on. This he then associated with Bohr's view of the difficulties caused by the subject/object distinction when we are trying to understand mental states.

The idea of "planes of objectivity" should be distinguished from the "planes of discourse" discussed briefly by Wittgenstein.[12] He considered a situation in which person A pushes person B into a river. A says to B, "I was pointing something out to you." A's psychoanalyst says "A subconsciously hates B." Wittgenstein went on:

> "Both explanations may be correct. ... Here are two motives—conscious and unconscious. The games played with the two motives are utterly different. The explanations could in a sense be contradictory, and yet both correct."[13]

For Wittgenstein, the two explanations, while contradictory if we try to unite them within one framework, function simultaneously on the two levels—each within its own language game context. But we are not forbidden from combining the two. It is possible that A's psychoanalyst can convince A that he hates B and that the "lesson" he was pointing out to B was just that. Thus Wittgenstein's levels differ from the "planes of objectivity" model above because for Bohr's notion of complementary descriptions, the descriptions are operating on only one level at a time with respect to a given situation and are required to be mutually exclusive.

It is difficult to judge either Bohr's idea or Wittgenstein's because neither of them is formulated with full reference to a theory or a set of criteria that would allow us to delineate the levels to which they refer, or at least to be sure that at some times we are operating on distinct levels that cannot be amalgamated. Wittgenstein's conception is closer to contact with contemporary ideas of the levels of operation of the mind. Bohr's idea is another of many suggestive examples, but does not contribute anything more to our understanding of his views, or to their justification, than the examples discussed previously. It also appears that Bohr rejected this characterization of his views in a late essay. In a passage in which he seems to be replying to a position he held in the past, he [**1954**], p. 79, stated; "Since, in the philosophical literature, reference is sometimes made to different levels of objectivity or even of reality, it may be stressed that the notion of the ultimate subject as well as conceptions like realism and idealism find no place in objective description as we have defined it; but this circumstance of course does not imply an limitation of the scope of enquiry with which we are concerned." From Bohr's own point of view, then, the notion of simultaneously existing planes of objectivity with regard to mental states runs counter to his

---

[12]See the discussion in Wittgenstein [**1967**], p. 53.

[13]See Wittgenstein [**1967**], pp. 22–23. Compare this to James' [**1890**], p. 206, discussion of hysterical patients whose consciousness contains mutually exclusive parts that he called 'complementary.' He was probably referring to patients that would be diagnosed as exhibiting a multiple personality syndrome today.

conception of complementarity. As Bohr has emphasized in connection with complementarity, one description of a situation is appropriate *or* another one is. He was careful not to use elements from a particle description, for example, when discussing the interference effects in a wave experiment. He rejected on many occasions the attribution of properties to objects when the conditions necessary for their appearance had not been met. In sum then, I reject the idea of "planes of objectivity" as a characterization of Bohr's fully developed ideas related to his conceptions of theoretical descriptions and complementarity.

Bohr and Wittgenstein had similar versions of the conditions necessary in order that communication be possible. According to Wittgenstein [**1953**], p. 88:

"If language is to be a means of communication there must be agreement not only in definitions but also (queer as it may sound) in judgments. This seems to abolish logic, but it does not do so.—It is one thing to describe the methods of measurement and another to obtain and state the results of measurement. But what we call "measuring" is partly determined by a certain consistency in the results of measurements."

Bohr stressed the need for well-defined concepts from a familiar conceptual framework and a sharp distinction between the subject and object. From Bohr's point of view, the situation in von Neumann's theory where there can be superpositions of the states of the measuring instruments, is one in which no consistent judgments can be made until after an observation is completed and the superposition is resolved. A completed observation provides definite results that can be described and recorded. For this reason, Bohr limited his theory to dealing with completed observations (phenomena), and did not allow it to be applied to situations involving superpositions of the (quantum) states of a macroscopic measuring instrument *during the measurement*. On the other hand, he would allow superpositions of the (quantum) states of these macroscopic objects when they are considered as physical systems and are not being used for a measurement. This distinction, if it can be supported, allows a consistent judgment regarding what happened and when in a measurement—as required by Wittgenstein in order that communication be possible. It is not clear how Wittgenstein would have reacted to Bohr's general requirement that the subject and object be distinct. In so far as this renders our judgments independent of the peculiarities of our internal mental states or processes, Wittgenstein would probably agree—especially since he had grave reservations about bringing references to our mental states or processes into things.

One thing Bohr and Wittgenstein did not agree on is the characterization of mental activity. While Bohr spoke on occasion of the unity of consciousness, or the unity of the personality, or of the perceiving subject and the psychological object (e.g., an emotion), as all part of our mental content, Wittgenstein had strong objections to this kind of characterization. He [1953], p. 103, indicated how we can be taken in:

"How does the philosophical problem about mental processes and states and about behaviorism arise?—The first step is the one that altogether escapes notice. We talk of processes and states and leave their nature undecided. Sometime perhaps we shall know more about them—we think. But this is just what commits us to a particular way of looking at the matter. For we have a definite concept of what it means to learn to know a process better. (The decisive move in the conjuring trick has been made, and it was the one that we thought quite innocent.) And now the analogy which was to make us understand our thought falls to pieces. So we have to deny the yet uncomprehended process in the yet unexplored medium." [14]

Wittgenstein would probably also be very reluctant accept von Neumann's interpretation of quantum mechanics, in which the observer's consciousness reduces the quantum wavefunction, because he [1953], p. 153, felt that "an inner process stands in need of outer criteria."

12.4 Fundamental Issues in Biology

Bohr wrote on biological matters during a period of profound change in biology that began in an era in which the concept vitalism still had some currency and ended after the discovery of the DNA double helix and the beginnings of molecular biology. An examination of his writings shows that his ideas on biological matters evolved somewhat between the late 1920s and the late 1950s as biology itself went through these radical changes.

I have spoken of the influences on Bohr because his father, Christian Bohr, was a professor of physiology at the University of Copenhagen. Favrholdt [1992] pp. 10–12, discussed the fact that Christian Bohr attended lectures of Rasmus Nielsen on the clash between mechanism and vitalism. Niels' interest in mechanism versus vitalism was stimulated in childhood when Christian Bohr and guests spoke on these matters at their home. These guests often included the physiologists Carl Lange, I. H. Chievitz, and others.

The various conceptions of biology presented in the last chapter were very much present at the University of Copenhagen at the turn of the twentieth century. In a 1928 review article by C. G. Joh. Petersen, a professor at the University, he discussed the perspectives that were current in biology at that time. His purpose was to "elucidate the principles that should be used as the basis for biology." I will present his ideas in some detail as a good indication

---

[14]See Wittgenstein [1953], pp. 61, 73, 153, 196, 204, for a further elaboration of this point.

of the prevailing thought in Copenhagen on fundamental issues in biology at the beginning of the twentieth century.[15]

Petersen [**1928**], p. 4, began his review by stating that most philosophers were too abstruse for him, but that he relied on the work of Kant and Høffding in his elucidation of the principles of biology considered as a natural science. He reviewed Thomas Huxley's ideas that biological systems must be studied in mechanical terms and that psychical elements must be banished. He pointed out that Huxley would be the first to admit that the laws of nature we establish are not the causes of order in nature but only an expression of what we have grasped of this order. Our knowledge is not absolute, but relative and limited. Moreover, he felt that Huxley had overstated his case and had not shown that mechanism is the only way to properly interpret biological phenomena. Petersen felt that adopting such a position would "paralyze the powers of the mind and wreck the beauty of life." In spite of this, he felt that a review of Huxley's ideas is useful considering the attitude of many biologists toward mechanical explanations in biology.

The issue of allowing psychic elements and consciousness into biology was one that biologists also disagreed about. Petersen presented Huxley's ideas as an "antidote to the psychobiological tendencies in biology, which have, also recently, been cultivated." Using Huxley's examples, Petersen discussed the controversy surrounding the application of the concept of consciousness to non-human living beings. We often say that the crayfish swims away from our hand or a dog runs from us because it feels fear. But this raises the question of whether it is meaningful to say that a crayfish, a dog, or any non-human species, feels fear. However we answer that question for the crayfish and the dog, there are many species to which we would not attribute feelings and consciousness. Petersen concluded that consciousness is not necessary for the existence of life. The issue lurking behind these discussions was the question of whether psychic activities, such as making a decision and acting on it, could alter the mechanically determined causal course of events. Whether we treat psychic activity as mere epiphenomena that simply accompany the mechanical unfolding of events or we adopt the mechanical approach simply as a methodological strategy, Petersen felt that mechanical explanations, while scientifically desirable, had not been completely successful. The study of living organisms is simply so complex that approaching it from a single point of view is not sufficient.

Petersen, pp. 12–13, recalled that Kant stated that even if another Newton were born, he would not be able to explain the coming into existence of a single blade of grass on the sole basis of mechanistic principles. On

---

[15]There is much indirect evidence of Bohr's familiarity with biological writing. In his notes recorded in the Bohr Archive, thinking about biology plays a prominent role. The thought of C. Joh. Petersen and Hans Driesch are explicitly mentioned. See, for example, Bohr [**Arch**], 21:1 and 22:2.

the other hand, Kant felt that mechanistic principles are the only ones that can give any real explanation of the organism—even if it cannot be carried through completely.[16] With regard to purposiveness, biological organisms are regarded as individual, indissoluble wholes: "This principle of totality need never conflict with the causal principle; where it is possible to carry through the latter, the former is superfluous." Petersen then pointed out, in agreement with Huxley, that we cannot use the concept of a whole as a biological explanation without introducing vitalism. And we do not have a mechanical explanation for the whole until the mechanically explained parts can be mechanically reassembled into the working whole as we do with a steam engine.

On the issues of description and explanation, Petersen stated that a mechanical explanation or a holistic description are really not so different. They are both descriptions that begin with different principles. Thus, "In reality all science is only description, since we "know" only our own subjective conceptions and we observe only their contemporaneity or consecutive order." This observation is done after the fact, *post hoc,* and not before the fact, *propter hoc,* in accord with Kant's viewpoint that we cannot see the ultimate causes (things in themselves). Petersen discussed the idea of the Norwegian professor Johan Hjort [**1920**] that we must associate the use of the concept of the whole in biology with teleological explanations. Hjort was strongly influenced by Kant and Høffding and also reviewed in his book ideas concerning the philosophical aspects of biology current at the time. He included the works of Johannes Müller , Huxley, Haldane, Darwin, and Whitehead in this review. He equated the viewpoint of an organism as a whole, composed of parts, in biology with the perspective of a mechanical system as a whole, composed of a collection of particles, in physics and chemistry. The organization itself has infinite complexity in his view, as the thing in itself, and can never be the object of investigation.

Petersen mentioned that his discussion of these fundamental matters did not imply that most biologists in Denmark at the time had a taste for philosophy. He, pp. 15–16, admitted that "Biologists in this country have as a rule shown but little interest in philosophy, at least in my apprentice days it was almost a crime to talk about philosophy." However, he went on to point out that "our knowledge of animals and plants and everything else is only derived from the contents of our own consciousness and is a phenomenon of consciousness." Our hope, as he put it, is that the phenomena in our consciousness are at least roughly in accord with what we naively regard as the external, the real, world; if this is true we can construct science about the phenomena. He felt that Kant is probably correct concerning the possibilities of biological knowledge and that "Therefore, if we take Kant's viewpoint as a base, it will confer the following advantage, that on principle there is no

---

[16]See Kant [**1790**], Section 75.

cause for conflict between the mechanistic principles and the principle of the whole."

Petersen, p. 24, felt that his presentation of the concept of wholeness in biology was in accord with Høffding's philosophical treatment of totality. He mentioned, on the other hand, that as D'Arcy Thompson has emphasized, *"The principle of the whole can not, however, be used as an explanation but only as a description and orientation.* This description cannot attain to scientific objectiveness, but suffices for an orientation which, though subjectively colored, is nevertheless for the present indispensable." We have to recognize, Petersen says, p. 29, that the mystery of life has not been solved by physiology and this will probably always be the case. One's worldview is a matter of perspective. As an example, p. 31, he recounted Jakob Johann Uexküll's concern in *Umwelt und Innenwelt der Tiere* with the worldview of different animals: "For a gnat the world has another aspect than for a human being; a gnat has only gnat-interests; it is up to biologists and physiologists to examine what these interests are."

Petersen stated in a number of places that biologists must assert their right to work with their own methods independent of the theories of other sciences as long as these sciences do not give biology something positive and better. The strongest objection to vitalism, p. 45, is that "it is of no help as a working hypothesis; on the contrary, it tends to check the search for causal explanations; on the other hand, vitalism is of importance inasmuch as it indicates a great number of unsolved problems that we should otherwise be apt to miss." Petersen left open the question of whether vitalism is actually needed by biology.

In reviewing the perspectives he had presented, Petersen maintained that to employ science in its strictest sense, the mechanical methods of physics and chemistry should be used. He observed that at that time the domain of mechanical explanations in biology was very limited, so there was plenty of room for other conceptions. He warned against mixing conceptions within one explanation or falling into the trap of anthropomorphism. Although a biologist cannot state what life really is, neither can a physicist or chemist show what matter really is nor can a psychologist show what psyche really is. Petersen concluded, for the biology of his time, mechanical explanations were not sufficient to encompass all biological phenomena and other types of explanation must be used.

During the era between 1900 and the 1930's, the discussion of the question of whether the laws of chemistry and physics could fully account for the nature of biological systems or not was carried on by a number of prominent biologists.[17] By 1929, Bohr [**1931**], pp. 22–23, had formulated his version of the idea that those concepts suited for use in chemistry and physics may not

---

[17] See Lancelot Thomas Hogben [**1930**], Joseph Henry Woodger [**1929**], Edward Stuart Russell [**1930**], and J. S. Haldane [**1931**].

be suitable for describing laws related to the phenomena of life. More precisely, he [**1931**], p. 23, contrasted the 'ideal of causal spacetime description' with the 'domain of biology that is characterized by teleological arguments." Some biologists of the time, notably J. S. Haldane [**1931**], p. 29, expressed views quite similar to Bohr's:

> "If in biological interpretation, the parts and actions with which we are concerned cannot be separated from one another in perception, it is impossible to combine physical with biological interpretation. Thus when we interpret biologically any observation which we had previously tried to interpret in physical or chemical terms, we have radically transformed our mode of perception. We are no longer perceiving in terms of how matter and energy are influenced, but in terms of life and its maintenance. Nothing but confusion can result if we do not realize this."

Underlying this statement is the position that Haldane maintained to the effect that, since an organism cannot be separated from its environment, it cannot be observed as isolated and the influence of its environment on it cannot be separated from its activity. This mode of argumentation is very similar to that of Bohr when he was discussing the subject/object distinction as an underlying presupposition to the notion of observation.

Haldane [**1931**], p. 31, also discussed the stability of atoms from a biological point of view in terms of a tendency "... to maintain intense coordinated internal specific activity, which does not become dissipated in its environment ...." Haldane concluded that

> "Thus the assumed basic conceptions of the Newtonian physics have been shown not to be in reality basic; and we are presented instead with what seems to resemble in essential respects the facts which biological study forces on us." [18]

Haldane has drawn attention to an analogy between life in its homeostatic aspects and the stability of atoms; he was also expressing a biological holism akin to Bohr's "individuality" or "wholeness" in atomic processes: "We are dealing with an indivisible whole when we are dealing with life." [19] Haldane and Woodger believed that biology and biological laws could not be reduced to those of physics and chemistry. Woodger [**1929**], p. 83, even went so far as to maintain that if biology had developed before physics then physics might perhaps have borrowed concepts from biology rather than vice versa.

---

[18]Haldane [**1931**], p. 31. Compare this with Bohr [**1930**], p. 9.
[19]Haldane [**1931**], p. 14. See also p. 20 and Bohr [**1955**], p. 92. Høffding [**1902**], pp. 21–22, stated "But just as biology, in spite of its recognition of the individuality of the living organism, knows no other method than to seek by means of observation, experiment and analysis, to understand the complex processes through the simpler; ... But the irrational here as everywhere not only places the limit, but also sets us the task, the ever new task."

Bohr, along with Haldane, rejected vitalism, the doctrine that some nonphysical "force" directs the operation of biological systems.[20] Bohr did not expect that in the analysis of living organisms by physical means one would find any features foreign to inorganic matter. Nevertheless, biological systems possess features that inorganic systems do not possess:

"In this dilemma it must be kept in mind, however, that the conditions in biological and physical research are not directly comparable, since the necessity of keeping the object of investigation alive imposes restrictions on the former which finds no counterpart in the latter. Thus we should doubtless kill an animal if we tried to carry the investigation of its organs so far that we could tell the part played by the single atoms in vital functions. In every experiment on living organisms there must remain some uncertainty as regards the physical conditions to which they are subjected, and the idea suggests itself that the minimal freedom which we must allow the organism will be just large enough to permit it, so to say, to hide its ultimate secrets from us. On this view, the very existence of life must in biology be considered as an elementary fact, just as the existence of the quantum of action has to be taken as a basic fact that cannot be derived from ordinary mechanical physics."[21]

As mentioned, Bohr's ideas on biology changed somewhat over the years as biology itself changed. In the 1950s he recognized that advances of molecular biology, and the discovery of the structure of DNA in particular, had rendered some of his earlier ideas obsolete. He [**Arch**], 21:1, p. 3, acknowledged these facts, but still maintained that biologists must be prepared for the possibility that biological analysis may not be able to give a full mechanical explanation of biological phenomena. In a letter to Elsasser, Bohr [**Arch**], 24:2, May 1960, located the complementarity in biological systems in their "inexhaustible complexity" and "historical development."[22]

12.5 The Maturation of Classical Physics

Just after the end of the nineteenth century, Boltzmann summarized the perspective that had been developing since Kirchhoff's mechanics. "The task of our thinking," he stated, "is to use and connect concepts in such a way that with their help we always and most easily perform the right actions and also guide others to the right actions." He raised the questions of whether

---

[20]See Haldane [**1931**] and Bohr [**1930**], p. 9. See also Bohr [**1937a**], p. 296, and [**1937b**], pp. 20–21.
[21]Bohr [**1930**], p. 9. It should be noted that this same argument *mutatis mutandis* applies to any attempt to follow individual atoms in any macroscopic classical chemical reaction. To do so would blow up the experiment.
[22]See also Bohr [**Arch**], 24:3, p. 7. A later discussion by P. T. Landsberg [**1964**] raised the question of whether quantum mechanics excludes life.

only matter exists and force is one of its properties or does the latter exist independently of matter or, conversely, is matter a product of force. He dismissed these questions as devoid of meaning "since all of these concepts are merely thought-pictures that have the purpose of consistently representing appearances."[23] He went on to agree with Hertz's point of view that these inner pictures must conform to the "laws of thought." Although innate, these laws of thought can undergo modification due to upbringing, instruction, and personal experience. The final and sole decision concerning the usefulness of a picture is in its representation of experience as simply and accurately as possible. He concluded that, since there can be more than one representation of certain facts, the choice between them is a "matter of taste, truth is not unique." He compared what he called the Euclidean method of deriving consequences from a priori axioms with Hertz's view that the correctness of a general theory rests on correct inferences of known appearances. Finally, to search for what may be hidden behind the world of appearances and propelling it along, so to speak, is not the task of natural science.

H. A. Lorentz's *Theory of Electrons* was referred to by Bohr in his 1911 doctoral thesis at the University of Copenhagen. In it Lorentz [**1909**], pp. 1–2, set out his perspective on physical theory. He recounted the attempts by Maxwell and others to build mechanical models of the electric and magnetic fields. But, he observed, this is not necessary and the theme in recent years had been to avoid models of this sort altogether and establish a theory on a few assumptions of a more general nature. From this perspective, he affirmed Hertz's statement that the (electromagnetic) theory of Maxwell is Maxwell's equations.

Bohr also referred to Gibbs' [**1902**] *Elementary Principles in Statistical Mechanics* in his thesis when he was examining the statistical mechanical aspects of the behavior of electrons in matter. As a number of authors, including Heisenberg, have stated, Gibbs' work was very important to Bohr and he asked those visiting Copenhagen to read it. Bohr felt that Gibbs had understood the relation of thermodynamics and statistical mechanics at the proper level of abstraction. Even more important was Bohr's feeling that the characterization of a particle system in terms of either a canonical distribution or a microcanonical distribution had a strong relation to his own conception of complementarity. I will discuss these issues in great detail in Chapter 14.

Planck [**1909**], p. 1–2, contrasted the approach of rational mechanics, which sets a philosophical principle at the center of the theory and tries to derive the physical facts from it, with the descriptive approach that Kirchhoff recommended. He, p. 22, asked: "Is the physical world simply a more or less arbitrary creation of the intellect, or are we forced to the opposite conclusion that it reflects phenomena which are real and quite independent of us?

---

[23]See Boltzmann [**1905**], pp. 245–252.

Expressed in concrete form, can we rationally assert that the principle of conservation of energy was true, even when nobody could think about it, or that the heavenly bodies will move according to the law of universal gravitation when our earth and all that is therein is in ruins?" Planck answered yes, in opposition to Mach and some other scientists.[24]

These ideas were expressed in popular form by leading European scientists in the late nineteenth and early twentieth centuries. Although there is direct evidence that Bohr was familiar with Lorentz and Gibbs, it is not unreasonable to suppose that he was familiar, either directly or indirectly through Høffding or others, with the positions and perspectives on the foundations of physics presented by Kirchhoff, Helmholtz, Hertz, Mach, Boltzmann, Planck and likely many others as well.

12.6 Reflection 21

I have traced the major elements that Bohr employed in his philosophy of physics to their sources. It is time now to sort through the issues in the theory of knowledge that I have presented and identify the elements of Bohr's theory that fit within the previous frameworks and those that do not. I will focus primarily on the sources of Bohr's views on (i) issues connected with irrationality, individuality, and wholeness, (ii) the role of language in knowledge and epistemological theory, and (iii) the subject/object distinction.

Irrationality.

The concept of the irrational is used to delimit the scope of rational analysis. The irrational sets a limit to what either physical or philosophical analysis can accomplish; but it does not impose a particular location as to where this boundary must go. The location of the boundary depends on the question under investigation and the currently accepted theories that are part of the conceptual framework. Traditionally, this limit was with respect to the possibility of a mechanical explanation, which Høffding and others, identified as paradigmatic of explanations in science. The relation of the part to the whole in biological systems and of sensation to perception are standard examples of this irrationality.

We encounter these limits to our understanding when we examine the connection, such as that between sensation and perception, that cannot itself be analyzed in rational (mechanical) terms. The standard philosophical explanation for this is that we may give a mechanical description of the effect of some stimulus on a sensory organ, in terms of changing nerve potentials, on the one hand, or we may speak of perceiving an object, on the other. We may even speak of these mechanical stimuli "causing" our conscious perceptions in some sense, but we may not speak of how the mental entity is created by

---

[24]See also Planck [**1913**], p. 54, where he discussed the prospect of finding a comprehensive world picture that meets all the claims put upon it.

the physical stimulus. Depending on the theory, these limits may be due to an unknowable, transcendent relation between matter stuff and mind stuff or between matter and perception. Similar limits were claimed in our attempts to understand the relation between the parts and the whole of a biological organism. As Høffding put it, the irrational in this context sets us the never-ending task of pushing the limits further as our understanding of processes in biological systems in terms of physics and chemistry develops.

Bohr also used the term irrational in the biological arena somewhat after these ideas were no longer in vogue. During the 1930s and 1940s, mechanical explanations in biology continued their rapid successes in one area after another. The concept of vitalism faded quickly. As biological science continued development during the second half of the twentieth century, and in particular after the double helix molecular structure of DNA was discovered in 1953, the perspectives expressed by Haldane and Driesch on the foundations of biology disappeared completely. Thus Bohr's use of biological terms such as teleology, vitalism and holism lost what philosophical justification they had earlier in the century.

Individuality.

The concept of individuality, inherited originally from Leibniz, is also a boundary concept. It was used primarily in biology to capture the specialness of life as a historical phenomenon for which the relation of the part to the whole at a given time could not be given in terms of a mechanical analysis. While an individual phenomenon or process may not be subdivided, it nevertheless can follow regular laws that express changes in its state in terms of its transformations. It seems clear that Bohr was using the concept of individuality in the sense introduced by Leibniz and discussed by Bernard, Høffding, Meyerson, Driesch, and many others.

Bohr employed the notion of individuality first to characterize the change of electron orbit in a atom accompanied by the emission or absorption of electromagnetic radiation and then to any atomic component undergoing general transitions involving the emission or absorption of quanta. Such an atomic transition is not itself further analyzable. All attempts to apply classical electrodynamic theory to describing the change of an electron in an atom from one orbit to another failed. In quantum theory, there is no description that gives a causal, spacetime account of this transition either. The concept of individuality captures well what we face in this situation.

Bohr characterized the limits to analysis implicit in the individuality or wholeness of an atomic processes as an 'irrationality'.[25] Bohr's use of the term individuality represents an interesting extension of the term compared to the way Høffding used it. Recall that Høffding [**1882a**], p. 66, reserved the term 'individuality' for mental entities or processes and stated explicitly: "the material world shows us no real individualities." He, p. 67, also spoke

---

[25]See Bohr [**1927**], pp. 54, 75; [**1929c**], p. 7.

of mind and matter as an irreducible duality, just as subject and object. He, p. 353, went on "Research may and must admit that, as regards the individuals, it does not succeed in giving every detail, that there is always something which escapes it,—that the individuality appears in consequence an irrational whole, which admits of only an approximate determination." In reference to the personality, Høffding [1902], p. 20, 123, stated that analysis is justified, but went on to say that the irrational relation of the whole to the elements remains.

Bohr's use of the terms individuality and irrationality in reference to state transitions in quantum theory is consistent with their core meanings as limits on both the possibility of further analysis and on rational knowledge as a consequence of the fact that state transitions cannot be further analyzed within quantum theory itself or any other theory currently available.

Forms of Perception.

With respect to the forms of perception, Bohr developed the constellation of ideas that I have collected and called his Observation Thesis. These ideas summarize his views on the essential elements of observation in connection with knowledge. Bohr drew on the nineteenth century conceptions of language and its relation to knowledge as the justification for his requirements on observation, which he expressed in terms of requirements for communication. He described the limits imposed by the uncertainty relations as an essential ambiguity in the expression of the values of the variables involved that must be resolved before we can communicate the results of our experiments to others. He gave various justifications for the role he assigned language and for our inability to step outside it.

In the operation of his theory, Bohr was concerned with showing that the forms of perception, as far as they can be used to provide us with objective knowledge, are unavoidably classical in nature. This is turn would provide the foundation for his Observation Thesis, since observations stated as exemplars of those forms of perception would then already meet the requirements of the subject/object distinction and communicability. Bohr characterized the forms of perception in several different ways. In his first statement of the connection between language and perception, he [1927], p. 91, said that: "... every word in the language refers to our ordinary perceptions." He followed this in 1929 with the phrase "... the forms of perception are adapted to our ordinary sense impressions." Bohr in this essay also drew a parallel between the forms of perception as related to the subject/object distinction: "... a close connection exists between the failure of our forms of perception, which is founded on the impossibility of a strict separation of phenomena and means of observation, and the general limits of man's capacity to create concepts, which have their roots in our differentiation between subject and object." For Bohr [1929a], p. 99, there is a deep connection between the ordinary forms of perception and the subject/object distinction: "it would scarcely be an exaggeration to maintain, purely from psychological experience, that the concepts of space and time by their very nature acquire a meaning only because of the possibility of neglecting the interaction with the means of measurement." The interaction between subject and object forms a (Bohr [**1929b**], pp. 103, 108) "... natural limitation of our forms of perception."

When speaking of the forms of perception, Bohr was concerned with a great deal more than statement like 'I saw a flash of light at point X.' He [**1929b**], p. 111, spoke of forms of perception in connection with things like "matter waves" and said that these "... lie outside the domain where it is possible to carry out a causal description corresponding to our customary forms of perception ...." In discussing observations of phenomena in the domain of quantum theory or relativity theory, where we are concerned with physical laws that also lie outside the domain of our ordinary experience, Bohr [**1929c**], p. 6, stated:

"We learn that these forms of perception are *idealizations*, the suitability of which for reducing our ordinary sense impressions to order depends upon the practically infinite velocity of light and upon the smallness of the quantum of action. In appraising this situation, however, we must not forget that, in spite of their limitation, we can by no means dispense with these forms of perception which color our whole language and in terms of which all experience must ultimately be expressed. It is just this state of affairs which primarily gives to the problems in question their general philosophical interest."

Bohr [**1927**], p. 77, spoke of the interpretation of data in terms of abstractions: "... the interpretation of experimental facts ultimately depends on the abstractions of radiation in free space, and free material particles." He [**1930**], p. 370, called the wave and particle descriptions 'analogies.' And, in 1938, Bohr [**1938b**], p. 23, called them "limiting cases of special simplicity." From an examination of these characterizations of the forms of perception, Bohr was talking about organized experience that we describe verbally using these analogies, abstractions and limiting cases. The concept of causality also plays a role in the forms of perception: "... causality may be considered as a mode of perception by which we reduce our sense impressions to order." And [**1937a**], p. 293: "In particular it should not be forgotten that the concept of causality underlies the interpretation of each result of experiment, and that even in the coordination of experience one can never, in the nature of things, have to do with well-defined breaks in the causal chains." Finally, [**1958b**], p. 1, [**1960a**], p. 14, "... all account of physical experience is, of course, ultimately based on common language adapted to orientation in our surroundings and to tracing relationships between cause and effect." Bohr did not use the phrase 'forms of perception' after his initial essays in 1927–1930. He spoke in terms of classical descriptions and classical concepts. For this reason, I adopted 'classical description' in Chapter 6 as capturing his meaning. It is clear that Bohr intended the full conceptual machinery of classical physics to be included in either 'forms of perception' or 'classical description.'

In this early work, Bohr made several claims concerning the relation of perception to the world. These are:
1. every word in our language refers to perceptions
2. the forms of perception are adapted to our ordinary sense perceptions
3. man's capacity to create concepts requires the subject/object distinction
4. space and time acquire a meaning only when the interaction between an object and a measuring instrument may be neglected
5. the subject and object interaction forms a natural limitation on the forms of perception
6. the concept of causality underlies every interpretation

These statements may be viewed as claims concerning the nature of perception, concept formation, and the requirements of objectivity in making observations. While Bohr did not use 'forms of perception' after his initial essays, his general claims concerning language and perception, the subject/object distinction, and the role of causality were retained. Empirical evidence concerning the relation of perception to the world will be discussed in the next chapter as part of our evaluation of Bohr's justification for his epistemology.

Observation.
The idealizations involved in describing measuring instruments and the associated physical abstraction of the instrument were discussed by Pierre Duhem [**1906**]. As Ernst Cassirer [**1923a**], p. 144, 280–281, put it "In truth, no physicist experiments and measures with the particular instrument that he has sensibly before his eyes; but he substitutes for it an ideal instrument in thought, from which all accidental defects, such as necessarily belong to the particular instrument, are excluded." Given that the theoretical descriptions of our measuring instruments are idealizations, and we use these idealizations to compute predictions of the consequences to be expected in an actual experiment, what is the relation of theory to experiment and what is the status of what we observe in this experiment? We are fortunate that quantum mechanics is a linear theory in this regard. Small accidental variations in the configuration of the components of the instrument wash out when superimposed at a sufficient distance from the instrument so that we can use it as if it were the idealized instrument of our calculations. We are not forbidden from including these small variations in our calculations; we just show, when it is true, that it is not necessary to do so.

I have described in detail Bohr's view that the concepts of classical physics will never be replaced in statements of what we have observed. Others have also supported this conception. Heisenberg [**1952**], pp. 44–45, for example, stated this in a paper written in 1935. He gave two reasons why classical concepts must always be retained: (i) any progress in physics must rest on already existing concepts, and (ii) "Classical physics represents, in a sense, the clearest expression of matter (Dingbegriff), in that it attempts to make the description of the world as independent as possible of our subjective experience. Because of this, the concepts of classical physics will always remain the basis for any exact and objective science." And, in 1941, p. 93, "... all perception must, so to speak, be suspended over an unfathomable depth. When we talk about reality, we never start at the beginning and we use concepts that become more accurately defined only by their application. Even the most concise system of concepts satisfying all demands of logical and mathematical precision can only be tentative efforts of finding our way in limited fields of reality."

Description.

Bohr's use of the word 'description' instead of 'theory' was a deliberate one. Aristotle introduced causes as the explanations of how and why things work the way they do. For many years, this was the paradigm of theory making. But, building on the work of Galileo, Copernicus, and Kepler, Newton had a clear view that the description of how gravity acts is a separate issue from the explanation of how it works in terms of some mechanism. Kirchhoff took the next step in the nineteenth century in removing explanation, expressed in terms of causes or forces as it had been understood in Aristotelian and scholastic terms, as goal of physical theory. The impact of Kirchhoff's statement that it is the task of mechanics is to describe as completely and simply as possible all the motions that occur in nature was discussed in the last chapter. This was an important step in liberating physicists from the past as the reactions of other physicists in the nineteenth century, even years after Kirchhoff's work, shows. Somewhat before Kirchhoff's work, Le Compte and Avenarius sought to free physics from metaphysics. Rankine, Mach, Ostwald and others took up the cause and stated that theories simply summarize potential or actual experimental data and, as such, simply provide economies of thought.

Bohr's use of description in this context is consistent with the view that theories are not required to provide explanations within some predetermined framework like mechanism, but, as Einstein put it, are free creations of the human mind. However, Cassirer [**1923a**], p. 138, observed that the term description is itself ambiguous in that it unites investigators who oppose speculative metaphysics, but otherwise disagree on the logical structure of physics. Nevertheless, the term is well chosen in that it reflects this historical thrust in a situation in which quantum theory has challenged materialist metaphysics.

Language.

As I have shown, Bohr's views on language reflect those of many who wrote on the epistemological aspects of language during the nineteenth century. One common perspective was stated by Meyerson [**1930**], p. 378, when he maintained that science and common sense have much in common: "... all language has been made in view of the "realities" created by common sense and scientific theories." I have also discussed the views of Madvig and others concerning the importance of viewing language as the medium of communication and therefore as an arbiter of objectivity. Finally, I have mentioned statements in the work of nineteenth century writers and the early Wittgenstein to the effect that the "limits of my language are the limits of my world." I will evaluate statements like this by looking at recent studies of the effects of language on perception and knowledge in the next chapter.

Challenges to Subject and Object.
The issue of subject and object predates written history and at the beginning of the twentieth century was a central issue in European epistemology. It is clear that Bohr was drawing on this philosophical legacy when he used the idea of subject and object as the centerpiece for his epistemology. The view that the subject/object distinction is fundamental for epistemology was challenged, however, early in the twentieth century by William James. He [1911] argued in two essays, "Does 'Consciousness' exist?" and "A World of Pure Experience," against his earlier view that consciousness is an independent 'thing' that is set in opposition to experience as the recipient of this experience. He characterized consciousness as a function and not an entity. He stated his belief "that 'Consciousness,' when once it has evaporated to this estate of pure diaphaneity, is on the point of disappearing altogether." He presented an argument against the need for a Cartesian dualism of mind and matter as two kinds of stuff. The subject/object distinction in his view is a relationship between two aspects of our experience that he considered to be the "immediate flux of life." As such, it is not an entity, but a function; that is, the entity of consciousness is a fiction; consciousness is simply an awareness of content. This means that it is a relation between two aspects of experience. He argued, p. 5, that the subject/object distinction is separate from the other dualisms, based on notions of substance, of mind/matter and soul/body. He, pp. 52–53, denied the need for a representation of reality in consciousness to transcend the gap. Similarly, he rejected a transcendent relation between subject and object or the need for the Absolute to unite them.

As I mentioned above, neither Høffding nor Bohr seemed to pay much attention to these ideas or others that were beginning to challenge the traditional conception of subject and object in epistemology. From the standpoint of philosophy, however, they had a great impact. I will return to these issues in Part IV.

CHAPTER 13

Complementarity, Observation, and Language

The two important remaining aspects of Bohr's theory to be discussed are complementarity and his claim that we must use ordinary language supplemented by classical physics to describe measuring instruments and the results of experiments. For this reason, the main concern of this chapter is the justification Bohr gave for his *main argument* that ties these components together. As part of the discussion, I will assess Bohr's appeal to language and communication, and their role in observation, as the justification for his epistemological theory.

13.1 Quantum Theory and Views of Reality

Bohr stated at some points in his work that atoms are real—and stated at other places that what we mean by 'real' may require revision. His was not the only voice on this issue, and a number of other approaches to understanding the nature of reality were advanced by those who accepted quantum theory itself. Other authors have made statements to the effect that the "amount" of reality can vary, or that it is "multifaceted", or that it has many distinct "levels".

The first point of view was adopted by Walter Elsasser, who felt that the amount of physical reality in a system depends on the amount of quantitative information we have concerning the system. The amount of physical reality, on this view, can vary in time and from system to system. Elsasser [**1951**], p. 304, identified reality with the connections between the microscopic world and the macroscopic world: "Reality, then, in the microscopic world is but an expression of the ascertainable relationships with the macroscopic realm." This is a variant of a position that the properties measured in a system are "created" in part by the process of measurement itself.[1]

Heisenberg adopted a somewhat similar notion of partial or intermediate reality. He [**1958a**], p. 50, stated, with Schrödinger [**1933**], p. 316, [**1928b**], p. 154, that we cannot describe what "really" happens in an atomic event. He, p. 55, followed this with the statement that the wavefunction exhibits an Aristotelian "potentia"—halfway between the idea of a thing and the thing itself. Weisskopf, on the other hand, in a review of Heisenberg's [**1958a**] book, preferred a "multifaceted" view of reality. For Weisskopf, the notion of reality for atomic systems (consequent on quantum mechanics) and for macroscopic systems (related to the classical viewpoint) are both equally valid and equally important aspects of the concepts of reality both of which "exist in nature."

Weizsäcker [**1952**], p. 97, called the failure of causality a failure of determinism that follows from "the failure of the objective reification of the processes of nature." We can answer every question of the sensible world but "we cannot weave these together these isolated segments together into the web of perceptible and causal relations which alone constitutes the permanent objective nature of the scientific world view." A similar statement was made by David Bohm and Jeffrey Bub [**1966**], p. 457.

Born [**1964**], pp. 103–109, connected the notion of reality with our emotions and pointed out that the reality of an artist is not comparable with that of a prophet, a businessperson, or a scientist. He considered invariants in our sense impressions of the independently existing physical world as representations of reality for us. An object such as a chair is such an invariant and we create words to represent these objects in our thought and speech. On these grounds, an electron is real because whenever we measure its mass, charge

---

[1] See Elsasser [**1953**], p. 98, and Weizsäcker [**1952**], p. 58. See also H. Mehlberg [**1967**].

and spin, we find the same values. The issue of the reality of the "waves" used to describe matter, Born left as a "matter of taste." He raised the question of what the probabilistic statements of statistical mechanics or quantum theory tell us if they are not based on an objective underlying reality. He answered that in the case of quantum mechanics, the view of reality is not that of an objectively given external world independent of us, but rather we have a relational view that ascribes reality depending on the experimental arrangement. He stated that if we accept this view, "the fundamental indeterminacy in physical predictions becomes natural, as no experimental arrangement can ever be absolutely precise."

After an extended discussion of issues connected with the concept of reality and the papers written on it, Bernard D'Espagnat [1965] concluded that no realistic interpretation of quantum mechanics exists. The criteria D'Espagnat applied in making this judgment were concerned with the localization of quantum systems and the question of whether quantum entities have properties in the same way that classical entities do.[2]

An examination of the attempts to give a "realistic interpretation of quantum mechanics", as D'Espagnat called it, shows that these attempts are based on treating the wavefunction itself as a physical entity or, at the very least, of maintaining a particle based interpretation of the wavefunction even when the experimental arrangement does not warrant the observation of particles. Quantum mechanics practiced in this way is primarily a particle theory. This view of quantum mechanics does not fit with Bohr's viewpoint because it is not compatible with Bohr's full commitment to the wave-particle duality.

The primary problems for those making a "realistic interpretation" of this sort are explaining the reduction of the wavefunction in a measurement and the division of the wavefunction at half-silvered mirrors or at the boundaries of a system into transmitted and reflected components. It is clear that the wavefunction itself is the "real object" in these investigations. These problems show that the attempts at what are called realistic interpretations of the wavefunction are really attempts to treat it either as a substance or as representing a substance. For accuracy, therefore, I will use the term 'substantialist interpretation' instead of 'realistic interpretation' below when discussing these issues.

Theories are interpreted by identifying elements of the theory with aspects of the world and comparing the predictions of the theory with experimental observations. The underlying question is what this procedure tells us about the entities postulated by the theory. Realistic views of theories treat the elements of the theory as real entities that are independent of both

---

[2]The difficult issue of localization in quantum mechanics requires a deeper inquiry than is appropriate here. It will be taken up in detail in QIS.

the observer and the theory. By contrast, the instrumentalist view of theories treats the components of the theory as parts of a calculating device for predicting experimental results and does not assign further meaning to them as independent aspects of the world. Ernest Nagel [1961], pp. 131–151, has pointed out that the difference between those who adopt a realist position and those who prefer an instrumentalist position regarding theories is mostly a difference in their views of the status of theories. The realists regard a theory as either true or false and the instrumentalists view it as either adequate or not. Nagel makes the point that there seems to be no actual difference in behavior between the two groups when faced with scientific questions. This lends weight to the view that the differences are over "preferred modes of speech."[3]

While discussions of reality by physicists were focused on interpretations of the quantum formalism in analyses published during the 1960s and 1970s, the focus has changed in recent years. Rather than trying to find how a conception of reality can be reconciled with the quantum formalism, current theorists have resuscitated attempts to use the quantum formalism to show that the quantum situation approximates the classical one at the end of an experiment.

Recent discussions by philosophers of quantum mechanics of the concept of reality in Bohr's work and in quantum mechanics have focused, naturally enough, on the concept of reality from a philosophical perspective. This has helped make the discussions more sophisticated regarding the analysis of the concept of reality itself; but this has happened at the expense, as Hooker [1994] and Honner [1987] have noticed, of reduced sophistication with regard to the physics and the concerns of physicists.

To get a sense of some of the philosophical views, let us first examine the assessment of Bohr's approach to reality by Faye [1991], Chapter VIII. He argued that Bohr's position on reality can be characterized as 'objective antirealism.' He, p. 198, based his analysis on a definition of realism given by Michael Dummett, who proposed that those subscribing to realism hold the following tenets: "(1) the world exists independently of our minds; and (2) truth is a non-epistemic notion; that is, a proposition is not true because it is provable or knowable." Faye observed that in Dummett's view knowing the circumstances in which a statement is true or false is equivalent to understanding the meaning of the statement. This means that every substantive statement about the world is true or false depending on an objective state of affairs "independently of our power to establish which of these values it is (the principle of the transcendence of truth conditions), and according to

---

[3]See the discussion of the reality of theoretical entities in Ernst Nagel [1944], B. Mayo [1954], [1956], R. Traill [1955], J. J. C. Smart [1956], and Feyerabend [1958b]. See also related issues in the studies of the logic of explanation by Hempel [1942], [1958], [1962], Dray [1957], Hempel and Oppenheim [1948], Michael Scriven [1962], and G. Maxwell [1962a], [1962b].

which any declarative statement is either determinately true or determinately false (the principle of bivalence)."

An antirealist, on the other hand, subscribes to an epistemic notion of truth, that the truth of a statement is determinate only if it can be established, and that the principle of bivalence is not universally valid. Faye stated that the antirealist position is not equivalent to idealism because the world is not considered merely as a product of the mind and the existence of the external world is not being denied. An objective antirealist from this point of view asserts that "(1) there is an objective, mind-independent world, and (2) truth is related to our cognitive powers." According to Dummett then, the issue between realists and antirealists is primarily with respect to the notion of the truth-value of statements. Faye considered the objective antirealist perspective on the world to be Bohr's legacy.

In another approach to the issue of realism, Folse [**1994**] discussed realism in classical theory as a conjunction of what he called ontic realism, e.g., atoms exist independent of circumstances, and epistemic realism, e.g., atoms have knowable properties. These work in alliance with the epistemic concept of mechanistic representationalism, which he referred to as the 'ideal of visualizability', mechanistic materialism, which is a doctrine of substance, and a doctrine of primary properties, which asserts that the substance possess the properties needed to satisfy the requirements of the other concepts. Folse maintained that Bohr believed in ontic realism but not necessarily epistemic realism with regard to atoms. Bohr on this account also rejected mechanistic representationalism, mechanistic materialism, and the doctrine of primary properties. With regard to quantum theory, Folse argued that Bohr adopted ontic realism, because the latter is required for asserting the reality of atoms, and rejected materialism and primary properties. He went on to observe that the rejection of materialism and primary properties implies that Bohr did not subscribe to the correspondence theory of truth.

By contrast with these views on Bohr's realism, John Honner [**1987**], felt that Bohr was a realist and subscribed to the type of critical realism that physicists usually subscribe to. Honner viewed Bohr's work as that of a physicist and not of someone trying to provide a philosophical position regarding realism. In agreement with Honner, I have argued more than once above that it is necessary to approach Bohr as a physicist and in the context of the times in which he worked if he is to be understood correctly.

I do not intend at this point to either raise objection or make a contribution to these discussions of realism for Bohr. The subject will be taken up again in Chapter 18 from a fresh perspective. I will only remark that the philosophical viewpoints on reality presented here are far from what Bohr was thinking when he spoke of the reality of atoms. Bohr was using the term 'real' as a physicist would to refer to entities that he believed existed apart from him.

Bohr certainly made clear his rejection of concepts that are associated with the philosophical notions of materialist metaphysics and metaphysical, or "God's eye", realism.[4] He also rejected arguments that attributed properties to atomic entities in situations in which these properties could not in principle be displayed. At any rate, nothing in Bohr's theory hinges on his viewpoint on this matter, so I shall leave it at this point.

Bohr also avoided assigning a role to consciousness in his approach to quantum mechanics. This contrasts with the use of consciousness in von Neumann's theory of measurement, which requires the participation of the consciousness of the observer in reducing the wave packet in a measurement. Bohr consistently and carefully avoided what he felt were subjective components, so his quantum theory does not need anything like consciousness in order to function.

13.2 Complementarity in Biology

Because Bohr felt that complementarity is a general feature of epistemology, he considered a number of analogies that were suggestive of complementarity outside of physics.[5] Let us begin a critical evaluation of the central ideas in his epistemological work by examining his claim that there are situations in biology in which complementarity may be required.

Bohr's views on the need for complementarity in biology and the form it might take underwent a subtle evolution over the years. In part this evolution was stimulated by the rapid advances in biology during this period and in part it was due to changes in Bohr's own conception of complementarity. In each case, Bohr was searching for the circumstances in the biological context that might open the door for complementarity.

In the last chapter, Bohr's statement that it is not possible to give a complete mechanical description of a living organism was examined. His argument was based on the idea that a complete mechanical description of a system k with $\mathcal{N}_k$ particles at some time t is a full and exact spacetime description of its classical mechanical state (Q_k, P_k), where the phase space variables $Q_k = q_1, q_2, \ldots, q_\mathcal{N} = \times_{i \in k} q_i$ and $P_k = \times_{i \in k} p_i$ are the direct products of the locations and momenta of each particle belonging to k. It is true that using an experiment to define the locations and momenta of all the atoms in an organism closely enough to determine its classical mechanical state would kill it. Approaching an organism from this perspective fits with Bohr's concern with the opposition in physics between the 'space-time coordination', which

---

[4]The 'God's eye view' conception of reality, its problems, and Bohr's thoughts about it are discussed in Favrholdt [**1994**], pp. 86–94.

[5]See Bohr [**Arch**], 17:1, p.2, for a list of these in the notes for a lecture "Epistemological Problems in Science" given at Lund on 6/11/46. As Favrholdt [**1976**], pp. 219–220, has recalled, this meeting (which he places in 1947) was a great disappointment for Bohr because the social scientists there were not interested in his epistemological ideas.

attaches each particle in a system to the reference frame, and the 'claim of causality' that is concerned with the conservation laws for this collection as a whole. These formulations play an important role in many of his discussions of complementarity.

Although Bohr moved away from this formulation in his later writing on biology, I shall inquire below as to whether this description is what workers in biology ever had in mind when they discussed a mechanical description of an organism.

Bohr went on to point out a particular 'complementarity' (an "obvious exclusiveness") between a focus on the self preservation and self generation of individuals and a focus on the physical and chemical analysis of them:

"I shall not enter further into such purely terminological points but only add that the essence of the analogy being considered is the obvious exclusiveness between such typical aspects of life as the self-preservation and the self-generation of individuals, one the one hand, and the sub-division necessary for any physical analysis on the other hand. Owing to this essential feature of complementarity, the concept of purpose, which is foreign to mechanical analysis, finds a certain application in biology. Indeed, in this sense teleological argumentation may be regarded as a legitimate feature of physiological description that takes due regard to the characteristics of life in a way analogous to the recognition of the quantum of action in the correspondence argument of atomic physics."[6]

The statement concerning "the subdivision necessary for any physical analysis" is a reference to the part versus whole issue in biology. Taken to its extreme, this subdivision leads to a complete mechanical description of the type discussed above.[7]

Bohr's view on biological issues and complete mechanical descriptions began to evolve in the late 1930s. In 1937, Bohr suggested that the reason that we could not hope to give a mechanical description of a biological system even in classical terms lay in the fact that an organism could not be considered a well-defined system of particles since an organism cannot be isolated from its environment: "The incessant exchange of matter which is inseparably connected with life will even imply the impossibility of regarding an organism as a well-defined system of material particles like the systems considered in any account of the ordinary physical and chemical properties of matter."[8] This is the physics version of the view expressed by many biologists of that era to the effect that an organism and its environment cannot be effectively

---

[6] Bohr [**1930**], p. 9. See also Bohr [**1955**], p. 92.

[7] See also the discussion in Høffding [**1923a**], p. 122, on the application of the concepts of physics and chemistry to the analysis of living organisms.

[8] Bohr [**1937b**], pp. 20–21. Bohr [**1954**], p. 76, stated that biological processes are not "closed" as are those studied in quantum physics. See also Elsasser [**1958**] and [**1961**].

separated. In addition, Bohr [**1938b**], p. 20, stated that the "holistic" and "finalistic" aspects of biological phenomena are not explainable directly in terms of the individuality of quantum processes but rather should be sought on the statistical level. In this progression, Bohr is moving from a conception of the mechanical description of an organism in terms of its mechanical state to one that is akin to his views on the relation between thermodynamics and statistical mechanics based on Gibbs' [**1902**] theory.

Bohr's ideas on the possibility of complementarity in biology and the corresponding possibility that in biological systems one might find new biological laws influenced the physicist Max Delbrück to take up the study of biological systems. Delbrück focused on the replication system used by organisms as one place in which such laws might be found.[9] Along these lines, Delbrück [**1949**] emphasized the historical nature of a biological organism. He considered how we might analyze an organism in the same way we would analyze a physical system. We could try, for example, to consider a group of organisms as an ensemble in quantum statistical mechanics and then work out laws that would make predictions on the average behavior of the organisms in the ensemble. But, to take a cell as an example, the historical nature of the organism means that what the cell does at this point in time depends on what has happened to it previously. Its size, likelihood of division, sensitivity to irritants, and other things depend greatly on the environment the cell has developed in. This situation, however, contrasts greatly with that in physics in which the history of the system beyond its last preparation or measurement is usually (but not always) irrelevant to its current behavior. The resulting essential uniqueness of the cell as the unit of living biological organization, Delbrück argued, implies that one cannot consider biological systems in terms of ensembles.[10] Delbrück concluded that it follows that quantum mechanics cannot be applied to an ensemble of cells in this sense, and furthermore, he, p. 188, went on

"To make structural observations on an individual cell with the accuracy required to fix all of its constituents so that a quantum mechanical calculation of its development could be made would require a practically infinite number of cells in *identical quantum states*. This seems possible neither in principle nor practice."

Delbrück concluded on the basis of these considerations that certain features of the living cell, e.g., replication, "stand in a mutually exclusive relationship

---

[9] See Stent [**1968**] for a discussion of Delbrück's work and Bohr's influence on it. See also M. Polyani [**1968**] and D. Fleming [**1969**].

[10] A. Shimony has pointed out (private communication) that the historical nature of a cell *per se* does not imply Delbrück's conclusion. One would simply need to make the phase space sufficiently detailed. It should also be noted that large ensembles of macroscopic systems like this are never actually used for measurements on physical systems.

to the strict application of quantum mechanics, and that a new conceptual language has to be developed to embrace this situation."

Elsasser incorporated this idea into his notion of the principle of finite classes in reference to biological systems.[11] He noted that "Classes of organisms are immensely small as compared to the number of microscopic configurations that members of the class may assume." The point of this principle is that the dynamics of these biological systems is such that uniquely biological laws can exist that are compatible with any possible physical predictions for the class. The membership of the class would be exhausted long before a statistical proof of a contradiction between the physical and biological laws could be achieved. Elsasser has in effect incorporated into his theory Bohr's notion, quoted above, that the freedom we must allow an organism is just great enough so that it can hide any contradiction between the requirements of biological laws and physical laws from us. Elsasser [**1953**], pp. 201, 208–209, felt that the possibility of the appearance of new, specifically biological laws did not rest on the falsity of quantum mechanics for biological systems, but on a lack of operational verifiability of the details of microscopic structure and dynamics. His [**1968**], pp. 739–740, general claim is that the "question of what the exact state of a complex physical (or biological qua physical) system *is* has no operational meaning." We have only a 'total descriptor' for the system, i.e., the set of all wavefunctions that could describe the system and the conservation laws that are valid for it. In the case of biological systems, Elsasser went on, we cannot hope to reduce this set to a single wavefunction by making experiments. Moreover, according to his notion of the 'total descriptor', it does not make sense to describe a biological system by a pure state anyway.

In 1960, Bohr incorporated the notion of complexity into his conception of the origin of complementarity in biological systems. Apparently drawing on the work of Delbrück and Elsasser, Bohr [**1960a**], p. 21, noted that due to the immense complexity of organisms as entities, non-physical notions such as purposefulness and self-preservation have found a place in biology. The complexity involved, as is evident in the examples Bohr chose to illustrate his meaning, is not simply that of the large numbers of atoms in each organism because this is already taken into account by thermodynamics or kinetic theory:

> "Even though we are here concerned with typical complementary relationships as regards the use of appropriate terminology, it must be stressed that the argument differs in essential aspects from that concerning exhaustive physical objective description in quantum physics. Indeed, the distinction demanded by this description between the

---

[11] Elsasser [**1968**], pp. 150–160. See also Elsasser [**1966**], [**1969**], and R. Rosen [**1968**].

measuring apparatus and the object under investigation, which implies a mutual exclusion of the strict application of spacetime coordination and energy-momentum laws in the account of individual atomic processes, is already ... taken into account in the use of chemical kinetics and thermodynamics. The complementary approach to biology is rather required by the practically inexhaustible potentialities of living organisms entailed by the immense complexity of their structures and functions."[12]

The specifically biological complexity must be that of the levels of biological organization in the cell and the interaction of these biological structures with each other.

This argument lacks force because we can now mimic a cell's behavior, albeit a bit crudely, with machines involving feedback or by computers. Significant progress in understanding the operation of living cells has also been made in the last half century by taking account of the physical principles operating at each level of the organization of the cell and then taking account of the interaction of these levels with each other. The great strides in molecular biology have demonstrated the fruitfulness of this approach.

In summary, Bohr abandoned his earlier concerns with teleology and came to view the origin of complementarity in biological systems as residing partially in the fact that living organisms cannot be isolated from their environment (as physical systems to a good approximation often can be) and partially in the complexity of the organization of the organisms. The ideas of Delbrück and Elsasser on the 'principle of finite classes' were attempts to make notions such as these precise.

Biologists in the 1930s paid some attention to the statements by Bohr and the more direct ones by Pascual Jordan concerning the implications of the new physics for biology. In an address to the Berlin Akademie, the biologist Max Hartmann [**1936**] discussed the concept of causality in physics and biology in a thoughtful and informed review of the application of the new ideas in physics to biology. He, p. XXXIX, began by stating that judging the correctness of the application of the acausal ideas of physics to the principal questions of life, which includes psychology, philosophy, and the solution of the problem of the freedom of the will, requires a thoroughgoing epistemological analysis to see if they are correct or not.

Hartmann felt that the concept of causality had acquired an extreme ontological-metaphysical character in the nineteenth century. He, p. XL, attributed this fact to the influence of Laplace's fiction of a spirit who can see the entire future and past in the context of Newton's deterministic mechanics. He also attributed it to Kant who, under the influence of Newtonian mechanics, had extended the meaning of causality into a concrete category in which truth in science was narrowly connected with the possibility of mathematical

---

[12]Bohr [**1960c**], p. 5.

representation. This had the result that "All of classical physics had adopted this over-stated "over-determined" causal concept and identified the causal relations of an event with their exact mathematical expressibility."

In reviewing the new physics, he observed that the concept of a "wave" had lost its immediate phenomenological character in quantum theory and had become only a symbol for a mathematically formulated construction. He also mentioned that the statistical character of quantum theory was distinct from that of thermodynamics. Finally, he, p. XLV, maintained that a future theory might have a different character concerning these matters.

Hartmann, p. XLVIII, felt that both vitalists and mechanists alike had made an important error in their understanding of causality. This is the assumption that all causal laws can be reduced to those of physics and chemistry. He argued that biology is an independent discipline with causal laws of its own. He acknowledged that he did not know whether the relentless reduction of biological phenomena to physical and chemical events in the sense of extreme mechanism is possible or not. But this is not relevant in the macrophysical biological realm in which there are causal laws, which may have a qualitative character, that function in that context. On these grounds, Hartmann objected to the statements made by Bohr and Jordan that living processes are "acausal".[13] He contrasted the help that quantum theory and physicists provided to biology in unraveling the problem of photosynthesis with the "hypothetical possibilities" of Bohr and Jordan. He chided Bohr for not extending to biology the viewpoint that Bohr maintained in physics that new realms may require new systems of concepts.

Returning to the question of complementarity in biological systems, recall that to establish complementarity in biological systems requires meeting the conditions for complementary established in Chapter 7. It must be shown that the descriptions involved in accounting for biological phenomena in both the physical-chemical domain and the biological domain are incompatible with each other. Furthermore, it must be shown that both descriptions are necessary. This means in effect showing that the biological laws are not in some way reducible to those of physics and chemistry.

Suppose, in order to make the issues clear, we were interested in the question of whether or not complementarity between a biological approach and a physical-chemical approach is a factor in a particular biological case. Let us examine the kind of analysis needed to answer this question in terms of a simple biological example. Consider the tendency of bacterial cells to avoid a chemical irritant. This behavior could be given a physical-chemical explanation in terms of the reaction of the cell wall to the irritant such that it

---

[13]The reference to Jordan is probably to Jordan [**1933**], where it was argued, p. 101, that an organism is not a machine that operates exclusively in accord with the laws of macrophysics, or to Jordan [**1936**], where Bohr's ideas are discussed in Chapter 5, "Atome und Organismem".

triggers a general avoidance mechanism based on physical structures within the cell. This mechanism operates selectively according to the differing degrees of irritation over the whole cell wall. The general avoidance mechanism could be studied by looking for the cell structures involved, investigating the way in which the different irritants trigger this mechanism, establishing how the physical structures change their shape on triggering, and so on. Such an explanation would make sense, and is not too far from the realm of possibility at the present time. Recent progress in untangling the complexities of what is happening during various phases of cell operation and division provide further examples.

The force of the chemical irritant example is that it reflects how research in biology is actually carried out. In case after case, physical-chemical-molecular explanations have been given of biological processes that were long thought to be too complex or inaccessible to these techniques. No in principle barrier to continuing in this fashion has been found and no limit has been set on laboratory technique or human ingenuity such that this procedure will end. In sum, the claim that complexity can permanently hide cell behavior and allow the possibility of complementary laws cannot be maintained at this time. Moreover, the recent work on the molecular level in biology demonstrates that the continuing reduction of biological behavior to physical and chemical laws is the most likely outcome of research.

The major difficulty in Bohr's conception of the problem of reconciling the biological description of a system with its physical-chemical description lies in his characterization of what a physical-chemical description is. To require that a description of a system of many atoms, whether it is an organic system or not, be a given in terms of the trajectories of each of the atoms in spacetime misses the point. Bohr is correct in saying that making a measurement of each of these trajectories is would kill an organism. A similar point is in fact true for any large and complicated physical system in the sense that localizing each of its components precisely would likely destroy it. But, as in the example above, this is not what is meant by a physical-chemical description of a biological system or an explanation of its operation. Rather, in the case of the cell, for example, we look for a set of chemical reactions that is controlled in some ways by proteins obtained from the cell DNA or by some feedback mechanisms that are subject to the laws of chemical kinetics. The attempt to treat the cell as a member of an ensemble in the quantum mechanical sense is neither relevant nor appropriate to the kind of explanation sought. And Bohr's 'ideal of spacetime description' would be useless to a biologist trying to understand the workings of a biological system.

There are similar arguments against the quantum mechanical examples used in attempts to establish that there is room for complementarity in biology. What is needed is not an ensemble of biological systems that would serve to distinguish all the quantum microstates of the particles comprising the biological system. It is a quantum explanation of the behavior of specific macromolecules, i.e., enzymes, in controlling reactions in certain chemical environments, etc. The quantum mechanical ensemble approach of Delbrück and Elsasser thus suffers from the same problem as Bohr's spacetime coordination approach.

The problem in these attempts to establish room for complementarity in biology is that they view a physical-chemical explanation in biology as a calculation based on the physical laws of motion for the microscopic particles in the biological system. While in principle this could solve the problem and allow prediction of the future behavior of the organism under fixed initial and boundary conditions, the answer would be far more complex than the problem itself and not at all useful to biologists. It has already been established that this is not the paradigm of physical-chemical explanation in biology, and it seems extremely unlikely that a plausible argument could be made as to why biology should require the spacetime coordination approach instead.

The arguments based on complexity by Bohr and others have not shown that the descriptions given in biology and those in physics and chemistry are, or need to be, incompatible. Elsasser has not proved that the alleged incompatibility between the description of a system using his total descriptor and the description using a wavefunction is of significance to biology. When we are dealing with systems that exhibit volition, and operate on a level above that of stimulus-response, the situation becomes admittedly more complex. But the existence of volition by itself does not seem to call for the exclusion of a physical-chemical description. At this time, its is likely that these levels will be meshed without conflict.

13.3 Complementarity in the Social Sciences

Bohr felt that complementarity is a general aspect of the theory of knowledge and not restricted to physics or biology. He proposed several examples in the fields of psychology, sociology, anthropology and philosophy that he felt were at least suggestive of the existence of complementary aspects of descriptions in these fields. The degree of Bohr's feelings as to whether these examples were genuine examples of complementarity or not is hard to assess. At one point he speaks of these examples as merely being "more or less appropriate analogies."[14] Yet, he went on to say, that behind these analogies may lie a kinship between physics, the social sciences and biological sciences with regard to epistemological aspects. At other times it seems as though Bohr ([**1958b**], p. 7) is proposing these examples seriously as genuine examples of complementarity outside the realm of physics: "However, the gradual development of an appropriate terminology for the description of the simpler situation in physical science indicates that we are not dealing with vague

---

[14]Bohr [**1929c**], p. 20, [**1929b**], p. 101. The way in which Bohr expressed himself in terms of analogies reflects the terminology used by Høffding in several of his books.

analogies, but with clear examples of logical relations which, in different contexts, are met with in wider fields." Some examples will be analyzed here to see if they really meet the criteria stated in the Chapter 7 for being genuine examples of complementarity; if not, I shall investigate that circumstances under which they could meet these criteria.

Bohr's first example of complementarity outside the natural sciences, proposed in 1929, was in connection with the controversy over free will versus determinism in human actions.[15] The feeling of free-will according to Bohr "governs the psychic life." On the other hand, there is the "apparently uninterrupted causal chain of the accompanying physiological processes." Bohr analyzed this issue in terms of the possibility of establishing through a detailed investigation of the processes of the brain a unique representation of the emotional mental experiences in some physical-physiological causal chain.[16] While such a possibility is visualizable, the experiment involved in actually verifying the association of sensation to a particular "brain state," if such makes sense at all, would probably bring about an essential alteration of the situation. Recall in reference to this the warning of Wittgenstein against accepting an argument of this kind without having the account of such a brain state in hand.

The primary direction in Bohr's thinking on psychological and mental factors is embodied in this example. Bohr offered it almost conversationally as an example of complementarity. A deeper analysis would, however, require a considerable tightening of the notions Bohr employed such as "volition", "emotional mental experience", "awareness", and what it means to represent a mental experience of emotion in terms of a causal chain on the psychological level. For this reason, let us go on to a more sharply defined example.

Bohr proposed examples based on the idea that one can exhibit complementary descriptions in the problem of 'having a thought' versus 'having an emotion'. He also mentioned the example of the Danish student in Poul Møller's tale who felt confusion due to the fact that when he considered the 'I' who experienced things he then considered the 'I' that considered this 'I' and so on into an infinite regress. Other ideas along this line included the 'stream of thought' versus 'introspection' example of William James or 'using a word'

---

[15]Bohr [**1929c**], pp. 100–101, 116–117. See also Bohr [**1954**], p. 78. Faye [**1991**], pp. 146–148, has tried to make the case that statements concerning psychic phenomena in Bohr [**1929a**], [**1929b**], and [**1929c**] were directly influenced by a series of discussions in 1928 and 1929 with Høffding. This claim does not seem to be well supported.

[16]Bohr [**1931**], p. 24, called this "... an essential refinement of our interpretation, originally based on physical causality, of the psycho-physical parallelism ...." See also Bohr [**1930**], p. 11, [**1937a**], p. 297, [**1949**], p. 62. In addition, Rosenfeld [**1961b**], pp. 120–121, has given an account of Bohr's views on this example in terms of a complementarity between the experience of an emotion and the accompanying complex of physiological sensations.

versus 'defining or analyzing it'.[17] William James also discussed "hysterical" patients with split, coexisting consciousnesses that James designated as 'complementary' to each other. Pascual Jordan [**1948**], p. 77, has suggested in reference to this example that people with 'split personalities' might be exhibiting a complementary condition. Jordan [**1948**] then extended this into an analysis of the Freudian concept of the unconscious and repression, including hysteria and split personalities, as examples of complementary. In addition, there is the infinite series of knowing subjects and objects of knowledge that was discussed in Høffding [**1910**], pp. 298–308.

Another example Bohr [**1938a**], p. 27, presented was the complementarity he saw in having feelings versus thinking about them:[18]

> "We all know the old saying that, if we try to analyze our own emotions, we hardly possess them any longer, and in that sense we recognize between psychical experiences, for the description of which words such as "thoughts" and "feelings" are adequately used, a complementary relationship similar to that between the experiences regarding the behavior of atoms obtained under different experimental arrangements described by means of different analogies taken from our usual ideas."

Even in this example, which is typical of many that Bohr proposed, the "complementary core" is not clearly indicated. It is often possible, for instance, to think, plan, and carry out complicated maneuvers even when very emotionally involved or upset with the situation. It is true that the emotional involvement may be distracting, but it does not always prevent us from accomplishing our ends. On the other hand, there is some sort of incompatibility involved in situations in which we would characterize someone as 'coldly rational' versus those in which we would say that he or she was 'hysterically upset,' 'in a blind rage,' 'prejudiced' or 'emotionally biased'.

If we take, for example, the state of 'being happy' and contrast that with the state of analyzing or reflecting on our happiness, we might allow Bohr an incompatibility of some sort. Similarly the opposition of justice and mercy can tug at us in some cases. But to make the case that these incompatibilities or conflicting desires are not merely operational incompatibilities, Bohr would have to show that they fit the criteria for being genuine examples of complementarity. This would mean that both descriptions of

---

[17] See Bohr [**1937a**], pp. 297–298, [**1938a**], pp. 27, 28, 30, [**1954**], pp. 77–81, [**1955**], p. 93, [**1960a**], pp. 14, 15.

[18] See also Høffding [**1882a**], Chapter VI, "The Psychology of Feelings." There he discussed states of mixed and conflicting emotions, e.g., joy/sorrow, laughter/tears, in terms of an analogy to complementary colors. He also mentioned humor in this regard. However, Høffding [**1910**], p. 267, stated "The battle between the "head" and the "heart" is in reality the conflict between two interests." See also Jordan [**1948**], who connected aspects of Freud's theory of the unconscious, including repression, hysteria, and split personality, with complementarity.

someone's state would be (i) necessary for a complete account of someone's state of mind, (ii) operating on the same level, i.e., both referring to mental states, and (iii) logically incompatible if one attempts to apply them simultaneously. To make the case that 'being happy' and 'reflecting on our emotional state' are complementary descriptions requires a psychological theory in which both descriptions would play a part. Then one would need to show that within this theory 'being happy' and reflecting on our emotional states' would imply logically contradictory properties of the mental apparatus entertaining these states. Without meeting these conditions we cannot distinguish complementary descriptions from operationally incompatible ones. Thus, while "I am sleeping" and "I am riding a bicycle" are in fact mutually exclusive descriptions of part of my potential behavior in the sense that they will never be applied simultaneously to me, they are nowhere near being complementary. One could even envision the state of sleep riding by analogy to sleep walking as a possible kind of behavior that could be induced in someone.

Even if one could show that the two descriptions under consideration above were both logically incompatible, the further case would have to be made that they were both necessary. This would require again either a comprehensive theory of mental processes or a situation in which certain aspects of the behavior or experience associated with both of these processes be deemed paradigmatic for the attribution of the descriptions in question to the behavior. In the realm of psychology, philosophy, anthropology, sociology, and other areas involving human behavior, this requirement is very hard to meet. Only the most radical of behaviorists would make such a close connection between these inner processes and certain kinds of exhibited activity or reports of internal states. With respect to the domain of 'inner experience', there are also Wittgenstein's objections to establishing private paradigms.[19]

It should also be kept in mind that if two descriptions of some phenomenon did turn out to be both necessary but contradictory, this would initially be good grounds for claiming that one or both is likely to be wrong or that the conceptual framework within which they operate is improperly constructed. The standard procedure would be to examine the theoretical and experimental status of these descriptions for mistakes or unwarranted assumptions. Such a procedure of attempting to reconcile or replace the descriptions could go on indefinitely. Seldom, if ever, would we expect to find ourselves in the position that atomic physics has put us in; the force of complementarity lies in the direct and simple connections between the experimental results involving interference patterns or Geiger counter clicks and the wave and particle paradigms.

---

[19]See Wittgenstein [**1953**], pp. 61, 89–104.

Another kind of example that Bohr proposed, this time from sociology, is related to an incompatibility between things valuable to an individual and to the welfare of society as a whole:

"With respect to the organization of human societies we may particularly stress that description of the position of the individual within his community presents typically complementary aspects related to the shifting border between the appreciation of values and the background on which they are judged. Surely, every stable human society demands fair play specified in judicial rules, but at the same time, life without attachment to family and friends would obviously be deprived of its most precious values. Still, though the closest possible combination of justice and charity presents a common goal in all cultures, it must be recognized that any occasion that calls for the strict application of the law has no room for the display of charity and that, conversely, benevolence and compassion may conflict with all ideas of justice."[20]

A careful examination of this example shows the same features as the last example. While the desire not to inflict pain on a transgressor because of charitable feelings does conflict with the desire that he or she be punished or forced to make restitution to those who were wronged, it is not necessarily the case that a satisfying compromise could not be worked out. Thus the requirements of the law on the one hand could be balanced against our knowledge and intuition of the individual on the other and that "justice" would be done if we tempered the law to some degree with mercy in some cases. In cases in which one is emotionally involved with the defendant, the desire to free him or her may outweigh the usual desire that the law be upheld. And it may be true that no good balance between these two deeply held and conflicting desires can be struck. This may lead one to vacillate from one side to the other, to be unable to make up one's mind, or to be paralyzed with respect to action on the issue of whether to free the defendant or to punish him or her according to the law. But to hold conflicting desires or interests as in this case is not the same as being described by complementary descriptions. An individual experiencing these conflicting desires may reduce the cognitive dissonance associated with them by some unconscious change in his or her opinions, perception of the situation, or values.[21]

One must conclude that Bohr's suggestions of complementarity outside of the realm of physics are not compelling. Such a position could only be adopted after an exhaustive examination of alternative hypotheses and theories in psychology and sociology. This sort of examination did in fact occur in atomic physics for a number of years before Bohr finally felt compelled to

---

[20]Bohr [**1954**], p. 81.

[21]See the discussion of cognitive dissonance in Festinger [**1962**] and the references cited there.

accept complementary descriptions of atomic phenomena. From our present standpoint it does not appear likely that Bohr's position on complementarity in the social sciences will be upheld. This point counts heavily against his feeling that complementarity is a general epistemological feature of the world.[22]

13.4 An Assessment of Complementarity

Bohr's ideas on complementarity influenced a number of scientists in various disciplines outside of physics.[23] One of these was the Danish linguist Viggo Brøndal, who had attended the university with Bohr and was a member at that time, along with Niels and Harald Bohr, of Ekliptika. In a series of essays from the late 1930s to the mid 1940s, Brøndal wrote of the complementarity in language between what he called the systematic elements (phonemes, words) and the rhythmic set (syllable, phrase). He termed this a complementarity between language and speech.[24] However, he never followed up these ideas nor did anyone else pick them up afterward.

While Bohr rejected the possibility of an underlying causal mechanism in atomic physics, i.e., a hidden variable theory, he did not present an analysis of this position and state what aspects would be unacceptable to him. Considering the unquestioned acceptance of von Neumann's proof of the non-existence of dispersion free states before Bohm's papers [**1952a**], [**1952b**], this is understandable. The situation was not really clarified until the papers by Bell [**1964**] and [**1966**]. Clearly, no current hidden variable theory would have been acceptable to Bohr.

The acceptance of complementarity as a physical principle does not imply that this conception is without serious philosophical difficulties. Bohr's conviction of its inevitability is a separate issue. I simply mention here that most difficulties (e.g., with ontology, locality, separability) connected with the concept of complementarity are shared by the von Neumann version of quantum mechanics in which complementarity does not play as central a role.

It is clear that Bohr's brief sketch of mental processes in psychology and the need for complementary descriptions in the proper characterization of them would not stand up well to a Wittgensteinian inquiry. This does not prove that such a characterization is impossible and that complementarity will never find a role in psychology. But, as argued above, for this to happen would require meeting the requirements of a sensible theory of mental states and processes and then establishing that the descriptions needed meet the criteria for complementarity.

---

[22]Others have attempted to extended Bohr's ideas further. As one example, see the discussion of the idea that science and religion might be complementary in P. Alexander [**1956**] and D. M. MacKay [**1957**], [**1958**].

[23]See Rosenfeld [**1953**].

[24]Brøndal [**1943**], pp. 41–48, 60, 71, 135. For more on Ekliptika and its members in various years, see Faye [**1991**], Part I, and Favrholdt [**1992**].

Arguments in favor of Bohr's extension of complementarity outside of atomic physics have been given by Menas Kafatos and Robert Nadeau [**1990**]. They approached Bohr's work from the standpoint of the relation of part and whole. Their approach to Bohr, by way of a concern with the metaphysics underlying our physical concepts, has led them to a number of conclusions parallel to some of those drawn in this book. However, their central theme, p. 128, is based on the idea that "complementarity is the fundamental structuring principle in our conscious constructions of reality in both ordinary and mathematical languages." This is opposite to the point of view developed here. The analysis in this chapter indicates that the conclusions in Chapters 7 and 8 of their book concerning the status of complementarity in sciences outside of physics, and speculations on how it might function there, cannot be supported.

One general justification Bohr [**1960a**], p. 12, gave for the expected appearance of complementarity in every field of human inquiry was that complementary descriptions are rooted in our language: "It is evident that words like thoughts and sentiments, referring to mutually exclusive experiences, have been used in a typically complementary manner since the very origin of language." This argument and questions of language will be taken up in the next section.

Bohr's failure to make a good case for complementarity outside of physics casts doubt on his general thesis that complementarity is an unavoidable feature of descriptions in every field of human inquiry. It follows that complementarity is a principle regulating the application of particular descriptions within quantum mechanics; it is even further removed from direct experimental significance than the theoretical terms of quantum theory itself. Its direct significance to atomic physics lies in the position towards physical theory that it exemplifies: current atomic physics is not incomplete and is not inadequate. This viewpoint is opposed to one that would have to be adopted under the circumstances from the standpoint of classical theory. Part of what Bohr was doing in proposing complementarity, and providing for it the philosophical justification he did, must be seen as an argument for a change in those things that we expect of, if not require of, physical theory.[25] Bohr, of course, was aware of this and that is why he discussed conceptual frameworks and a need for a change in physical explanation as he did. The question of whether to accept complementarity or not does not just rest on the experimental adequacy of quantum mechanics, although this is important, but just as importantly on the cogency of the point of view behind it.

Within quantum mechanics the concept of complementarity is independent, to a great degree, of the particular formulation of observation and description in Bohr's own theory. Given the validity of quantum mechanics, complementarity as a physical principle allows us to keep separate those

---

[25]This scenario follows a pattern suggested by Kuhn [**1962**].

elements of the description of atomic entities which, if applied simultaneously, would contradict each other. If we accept with Bohr the equal footing of both the wave and particle concepts, and acknowledge the necessity of both descriptions in accounting for observations in the atomic domain, then complementarity is inescapable. For quantum theory, under any version of the Copenhagen Interpretation, this is the case. The question of whether complementarity will continue to play a central role in physics in the future, and is an unavoidable aspect of physical epistemology (as Bohr believed it was) is another issue.

Bohr tried to answer the question of whether complementarity would have a role as a part of future physics in the affirmative by making use of the elements he incorporated into his *main argument* discussed in Chapter 8. His claims concerning the necessity of using classical concepts to describe observations and the connection he posited between descriptions, observations, and experimental arrangements are part of the physical theory Bohr was proposing. His *main argument* links the Observation and Description Theses with his notions of a conceptual framework and what I called in Chapter 8 his Communication Thesis. This is the philosophical core of Bohr's theory and an assessment of the strength of his position concerning the inevitability of complementarity in physics will rest in part on an evaluation of this philosophical position. It should be emphasized that this inquiry does not bring into question the position of complementarity within current quantum physics.

The discipline outside quantum physics in which Bohr felt complementarity might play a role that remains to be discussed is classical physics. I shall hold in abeyance the question of whether there are cases of complementarity in classical physics, as Bohr [1930] had suggested might be the case, and discuss it in detail Part IV.

13.5 Perception and Observation

In the previous chapter, a number of claims that Bohr had made in connection with perception and language, concept formation, causality, and the subject/object distinction were summarized. Although some of these formulations were not repeated in his later work, he consistently referred to the relation between perception and language as one of the foundations of what I have called his Observation Thesis. The work on perception in the nineteenth century was summarized in Chapter 11. This will be carried forward through the twentieth century and some conclusions concerning the adequacy of Bohr's claims will be drawn.

Beginning with Descartes and again with the nineteenth century physiologists, there was the recognition of the inevitably symbolic of nature of the transportation and representation of information within the nervous system and the brain. Because of the transformations of information in the course of perception, the question arises of how well perception informs us about the world. Modern research on perception has gone beyond the work of the nineteenth century and extended our understanding of the mechanisms of perception and the role of nerve clusters and the brain. It has been established in psychological experiments that perception is not independent of what we know and of our past experience. It is also clear that perception is "never a sure thing" or an "absolute revelation of what is." These studies characterize what we see, for example, as being more in the nature of a prediction, "the best possible bet for carrying out our purposes in action," based on our past experience.[26] The extent of the role of experience in perception is a matter of continuing investigation.

The next point is that perception is never a complete representation of an object—even within a limited domain, such as the visual aspect of the object. Indian philosophers long ago realized that every perception of an object involves a point of view and that not all points of view can be experienced simultaneously. In addition, again considering the visual field, we do not see all the detail an object has to offer at any one time even from a fixed perspective. As we get closer, we see details that we could not resolve before, and lose sight of other larger scale details. Changes in our state of motion or in the available light all contribute to modifying the conditions under which we do our seeing. In spite of these quite different situations, we still see objects that retain their identity as we move and the light changes with respect to them. These facts imply that even if perception were represented internally just as we "see" the external objects, in what was called a *sensorium* in the seventeenth through nineteenth centuries, we never see at any one time everything that there is to see of an object. I conclude that perception can never offer us a complete "picture" of "what is" no matter what internal form is used to represent it.

From this point of view, a scientific observation in Bohr's sense is a schematized, interpreted perception. When we say that something is exhibiting wave-like properties, we are focusing on some particular elements of the situation, schematizing the relationship of the components, and identifying the result as matching a wave pattern or as showing wave-like interference patterns. There is no harm in saying that we are observing a wave, that is, saying that what we see is the thing-in-itself, as long as it is understood that this is not an absolute or certain statement of any kind.

In the interpretation of the meaning of Bohr's 'forms of perception' and of his later views on the relation of perception to language in the last chapter, it was concluded that he was not concerned with sensation but was emphasizing the subsumption of an observation under some theoretical concept, e.g.,

---

[26]W. N. Dember [**1960**], pp. 268, 290–293. See Chapters 7 and 8 for data on learning and perception. See also J. A. Fishman [**1960**]. These points confirm Laplace's insight, to be discussed in Chapter 14, that probability plays and essential role in epistemology.

when we identify a collection of spots on a photographic plate as a 'wave pattern'. When we do this, we are operating at a higher level than we are with the statement 'a spot appears here'. Moreover, the characterization of a collection of spots as a wave pattern is not a final characterization either. The wave pattern itself may be identified as a component in a still higher order observation involving patterns of wave patterns or a whole wave pattern may function as a relatively localized activity from some other perspective. Thus the statement of 'what is seen' depends in large part on what you are and what you are looking for.

It is with regard to the theoretical component of observation, the subsumption of observations under concepts, that Bohr invoked the epistemological role of language. He tried to show that some elements of how we interpret observations are prompted by and limited to the concepts in our common language supplemented by classical physics. In that sense, the claim is that language shapes some aspects of our reality. This claim will be investigated next.

13.6 Language and Epistemology

Studies of language in relation to concepts, words, and communication were begun in the late nineteenth century and flourished in the twentieth century. The philosophical perspective on the epistemological aspects of this relation were discussed by Cassirer [**1923b**], [**1923c**]. This approach to language evolved into analytic schools of philosophy and the study of language itself continued the path blazed by the empirical studies of the late nineteenth century.

Empirical studies of concept formation in children began before the 1930s in the work of Jean Piaget. Questions of the relation of word and object, sensation and thought, understanding and communication were all studied. Questions with epistemological import slowly became less important but did not die away all at once. One typical investigation, which had one foot in the past and one in the future, was the work of L. S. Vygotsky [**1934**], who tried to study the "inner workings of thought and speech". He, p. 153, characterized the perspective that his work had opened up with the statement: "Thought and language, which reflect reality in a way different from that of perception, are the key to the nature of human consciousness. ... A word is a microcosm of human consciousness."

The characterization of thought and speech in these studies gives a different feel for the nature of language than that conveyed by Bohr, and others after him, who spoke of being 'suspended in language.' Bohr's view seems to be that language has a transcendent aspect and, if this is the case, it is not clear how it could be studied empirically. The early Wittgenstein stated that 'the limits of my language mean the limits of my world'. One interpretation of this statement is that there are limits, either imposed by language or exemplified by it, on what we can know or express because language itself is finite in some sense. Another interpretation is that language must be extended to encompass new experiences. Both interpretations are similar in some respects to statements made by Bohr. Neither represents the views expressed by those currently studying language acquisition empirically. Because of the importance of language to Bohr's justification of his epistemology, these ideas will be examined in detail.

In looking for the limits associated with language, for example, one could maintain that the distinctions and boundaries drawn by language cut through some unitary reality and we are forced by language to characterize this reality in artificially delimited terms. The subject/object distinction would then be viewed as an example of one such boundary. Other limits are encountered when we wish to convey some subjective experience, such as a taste, smell, or feeling. In dealing with the quantum situation, we would like to say what "really" happens during an atomic transition, but we cannot. Is this a limitation of our language?

Wittgenstein's statement in the *Tractatus* concerning the limits of our language and the limits of our world implies that our conceptual structure and our ability of understand and reason is coextensive with the shared stock of concepts and theories we can express with our language. However, the later Wittgenstein [**1953**], pp. 48–49, replied to the possibility he had raised earlier by asking if the limits are real:

> "When I talk about language (words, sentences, etc.) I must speak the language of everyday. It this language somehow too coarse and material for what we need to say? *Then how is another one to be constructed?*"

Where is the limit and what determines it? It is clear that sensations caused by the same object are experienced differently by different people—taste is an excellent example of this. This means that we cannot convey the subjective experience of sensing to someone else. Nevertheless, there are objective ways of studying taste and providing some objective measures of the differences between our experiences.

The linguists Edward Sapir [**1928**], p. 69, and Benjamin Lee Whorf [**1939**] hypothesized even further that language and culture have an especially significant influence on perception and the organization of reality. Whorf went further: "We are thus introduced to a new principle of relativity which holds that all observers are not led by the same physical evidence to the same picture of the universe unless their linguistic backgrounds are similar, or can in some way be calibrated."[27] Based on his investigation of the Hopi Indian language, Whorf pointed out that the concept of time expressed in English

---

[27]Whorf [**1939**], p. 152, [**1940**], p. 214. See also Whorf [**1941**], pp. 239, 244, and [**1942**], p. 263.

13.6 LANGUAGE AND EPISTEMOLOGY

differs markedly from that in the Hopi language. This led him to the suggestion that the "ways of analyzing and reporting experience, which have become fixed in the language as integrated "fashions of speaking," lead to differences in the analysis of reality that can be made using different languages." Whorf [**1939**], p. 158, [**1940**], pp. 213–214, has made one of the most explicit claims of this type:[28]

"We dissect nature along lines laid down by our native languages. The categories and types that we isolate from the world of phenomena we do not find there because they stare every observer in the face; on the contrary, the world is presented in a kaleidoscopic flux of impressions which has to be organized by our minds—and this means largely by the linguistic systems in our minds. We cut nature up, organize it into concepts, and ascribe significance as we do, largely because we are parties to an agreement to organize it in this way— an agreement that holds throughout our speech community and is codified in the patterns of our language. The agreement is, of course, an implicit and unstated one, *but its terms are absolutely obligatory;* we cannot talk at all except by subscribing to the organization and classification of data which the agreement decrees."

Whorf [**1956**], p. 217, went on to hypothesize that Hopi physics might be different from our own. In a similar vein, Norwood Russell Hanson [**1958a**], p. 19, has given an accessible discussion of the role of language in the recurrent idea that "seeing" is 'theory laden', that is, it depends on prior knowledge, language and the notation in which the perception is expressed. He [**1958a**], p. 25, concluded that there is a linguistic element in seeing due to or need to express what we have seen in a fashion suitable for it to be an object of knowledge and *a fortiori* communicable.

The evidence from studies of the influence of language on perception, along with the philosophical points of Wittgenstein, Hanson and many others before them, lend weight to the viewpoint that the justification of Bohr's position cannot be made simply by saying that our perceptions are "classical". Whorf has further criticized the position implicit in claims like "the propositions of classical physics mirror the structure of the worlds given by perception" (Weizsäcker [**1952**], p. 94) or the above characterization of the results of a double-slit experiment in which Bohr seems to be saying that "a wave is simply what is seen." Whorf [**1956**], p. 262, said in this regard:

"We say 'see that wave'—the same pattern as 'see that house.' But without the projection of language no one ever saw a single wave. We see a surface in ever changing undulating motions. Some languages cannot say 'a wave'; they are closer to reality in this respect. Hopi say *walalata*, 'plural waving occurs', and can call attention to one

---

[28]See also Wittgenstein [**1953**], pp. 90, 121ff, 167, 184, 226, 230, on this matter.

place in the waving just as we can. But, since actually a wave cannot exist by itself, the form that corresponds to our singular, *wala*, is not the equivalent of English 'a wave', but means 'a slosh occurs', as when a vessel of liquid is suddenly jarred."

The abstract character of attributing the action of a wave to the interpretation of the pattern of spots on a photographic plate or attributing the passage of a particle to a Geiger counter click is even clearer if one considers that in neither case is a wave or a particle actually seen, but rather, through a series of inferences based on the behavior of our instruments and the experimental arrangement, the conclusion is drawn that the theoretical concepts wave or particle may be properly applied to describe what is observed.[29]

As the above discussion of Bohr's use of the term 'wave' and 'particle' as 'abstractions', 'analogies', and 'limiting cases' when applied to the interpretation of experiments shows, Bohr was usually careful when he was using the phrase 'form of perception' to make clear that he was not talking about sensation or direct perception. Rather, he concerned himself primarily with the interpretation of data within the conceptual framework in which observations are made. For this reason, the 'direct perception' thesis of Weizsäcker and Rosenfeld ("a wave is just what is seen") does not represent Bohr's point of view and was rejected in a previous discussion. The question of the relation of a language to a conceptual framework is deeper than the question of whether we can have direct perception of some event or collection of events as an exemplar of a concept.

Bohr's statement that we are 'suspended in language' reflects the mode of expression of a number of nineteenth century writers on language and its epistemological status that were discussed in Chapter 11. It seems likely that the terminology Bohr used and his viewpoint stem from these sources. This view of language is also similar in many respects to the views of Sapir and Whorf. After quoting Bohr's statement, Petersen [**1963**], p. 10, continued, we may at times extend the form of our communication (the "conceptual framework"), "Yet logical possibilities for extending or generalizing any frame lie like seeds in the pre-suppositions for using our concepts." The emphasis is on extending and generalizing the conceptual framework—not the concepts within it. Petersen [**1963**], p. 12, also quoted Bohr to the effect that it is not new concepts that we lack in this situation: "But our problem is not that we do not have adequate concepts. What we may lack is a sufficient understanding of the unambiguous applicability of the concepts we have." Bohr's position is that we may widen the scope of the relations allowed within a conceptual framework but we may not substantially alter those concepts

---

[29] An attempt to characterize the factual content of theoretical concepts was made by W. Rozeboom [**1962**].

13.6 LANGUAGE AND EPISTEMOLOGY

related to experience that we use in expressing these relations.[30] I shall argue in Part IV that he needs a less restrictive point of view to make his theory operate.

L. S. Feuer [1953] and Max Black [1959a], [1959b], disagreed with the close connection between language and the analysis of reality drawn by Sapir and Whorf. Feuer argued that the translation of philosophical and literary works into other languages does not seem to be hampered by a different 'metaphysics' in each language. In particular, Feuer mentioned that the statement 'God exists' can be expressed adequately in Hebrew even though Hebrew does not contain a word with the direct force of 'to exist'. Feuer's main point is that language is flexible and can be made to serve a variety of purposes that could not properly be characterized, to extend his argument, as having the metaphysics underlying classical physics built into it.

Black maintained that there is no clear evidence that language limits the ability of people to perceive differences in things to which they attach the same word. In the Navaho language the colors we call green and blue are covered by one word. But there is no evidence that Navaho people cannot distinguish different colors as well as anyone else. Further, as Black [1959a], p. 232, pointed out, "... inferences from vocabulary to cognitive capacities are always precarious." Black examined several other aspects of Whorf's view and concluded that Whorf's contention that language contains an implicit metaphysics, in terms of which our worldview is fashioned, cannot be upheld. In particular, Black took Whorf to task over the metaphysics of space and time as Whorf has characterized them. Whorf gave no demonstration that an English pattern of analyzing space and time could not be made meaningful in the Hopi language even though the Hopi language does not contain words for the passage of time that correspond directly to the English words.

The issue does not turn on the question of what a Hopi might, by virtue of his language or culture, choose to observe and look for relations in, but on whether or not Hopi physics could be translated into standard physics and vice versa. An inquiry into some of these issues was made by Eleanor Rosch [1973] in which she studied the color remembering abilities of people from New Guinea who have only two names for color: $mola$ = bright, warm and $mili$ = dark, cold. She has shown that New Guineans can remember as many different colors as English speaking people and that "they made the same kinds of correct answers and mistakes that a group of English-speaking people made on a similar test."

Solving the translation problem so that the same theory could be expressed in two very different languages may require the introduction of new

---

[30] In several places Bohr rejected a proposed approach to a quantum problem on the grounds that it departed from the "basic conventions of language" or from "common language and practical definitions." See Bohr [1938a], p. 24, [1958b], p. 6. Bohr's point of view here is in keeping with what I called his Communication Thesis.

concepts in both languages, which would be definable in terms of other concepts in each language (Whorf does describe the Hopi view of time in English); and there seems to be no reason why this cannot be done in general. While an argument may be made that in the translation of literary works, the translation misses the nimbus of associations a native speaker would have, this does not impute the possibility of translating scientific works in which this nimbus is not (or should not be) a component. The weight of the above argumentation is therefore against the view that language and culture provide us with a metaphysical framework within which we *must* operate. Thus Bohr's reference to language *per se* as a foundation for his theory cannot be upheld. Apart from the role of language in the demonstration of his *main argument,* it is possible to view his comments on the need for "plain language" and "practical definition" as a statement of a desire to avoid fruitless philosophical discussions of models or mechanistic metaphysics inappropriate to his point of view.

Joshua Fishman [**1960**] has provided a detailed analysis of different levels of the Whorfian perspective, which support the conclusions drawn here. In addition, Eric Lenneberg [**1960**] has given a modern view of the role of language in the formation of concepts. Hans Furth [**1966**], pp. 37–39, raised the same points as those made by Whitney [**1867**]. He, pp. 145, 149, 155, discredited Whorf's hypothesis by mentioning studies of the abilities of deaf people to conceptualize and think logically without language and, pp. 194–195, blind people to think without pictures. He, p. 197, found fault with this view of thinking: "The basic flaw of any theory which attempts to explain thinking in terms of verbal or other symbolic units lies in three false assumptions. One is that concepts are real units of thinking, the other, that concept and symbol, particularly verbal symbol, are identical, and the third, that symbols are transmitted and function like signals or substitute stimuli." This led him, pp. 198–199, to conclude: "The evidence for conceptual thinking in the linguistically deficient deaf has been presented and leads to the direct conclusion that thinking develops through living contact with the environment regardless of the presence or absence of a ready linguistic symbol system."

Jacob Bronowski and Ursula Bellugi [**1970**] studied how language influences our worldview. They, p. 673, maintained:

"For humans, the environment consists of objects, properties and actions, and we are tempted to assume that these exist ready-made in the outside world, and present themselves simply and directly to the senses. But this is a naive simplification of the complex of interlocking processes by which we are persuaded of the existence and the persistence of even so unitary a natural object as a tree or a bird. Most of what we regard as objects in our environment, however, are far more sophisticated concepts than these. Thus the logic by which a child unravels the sentences he hears and his experience of the environment together is much more than a capacity for language and expresses in miniature a deeper human capacity for analyzing and manipulating the environment in the mind by subdividing it into units that persist when they are moved from one mental context into another. ... What language expresses specifically in this scheme is the reification by the human mind of its experience, that is, an analysis into parts (including actions and properties) which, as concepts, can be manipulated as if they were objects. The meaning that these concepts have derives from their construction (as parts of reality) and cannot be displayed by a direct appeal to the senses, singly or in combination. ... If the reification of the environment serves to manipulate its parts in the mind, then the laws which distinguish admissible from inadmissible rearrangements round out and complete the same mental process as a necessary part—as the addition of *one* and *one* belongs to the concept *two*. That is, we cannot separate the naming of concepts (objects, actions and properties) from the rules which govern their permissible arrangements—the two form an interlocking whole."

Finally, they, p. 673, concluded

"In short, we must not think of sentences as assembled from words which have an independent existence already, separate from any kind of sentence. This puts the matter in linguistic terms; in more philosophical terms, we must not think of the external world as already existing in our consciousness as a previously analyzed assembly of conceptual units, such as things, actions, and qualities. The experience of learning about the world consists of an inner analysis and subsequent synthesis. In this way, human language expresses a specifically human way of analyzing our experience of the external world. This analysis is as much a part of learning language as is the more obvious synthesis of sentences from a vocabulary of words. In short, language expresses not a specific linguistic faculty but a constellation of general faculties of the human mind."

This means that "When we watch the way a child learns to speak from his point of view, we become aware of his mental activity in finding for himself inductive rules of usage which constitute both a grammar of language and a philosophy of the structure of reality."

The weight of the evidence clearly rejects a view that language holds us back or suspends us in some way over an inarticulate abyss. The conclusion drawn from this is that the properties of language and the requirements of communication cannot be used to justify the claim that classical concepts must be retained in any future physics. Nor are we obligated to retain the current meanings and associations for the concepts we do retain.

Bohr's *main argument*, as presented in Section 8.2, requires the description of the experiment and the experimental results to be expressed in unambiguous language suitable for communication. The argument begins with the requirement that the results of experiments be communicable and concludes "therefore, the account of the experimental arrangement and the results of observation must be expressed in unambiguous language with suitable application of the terminology of classical physics." The requirement that the concepts not be ambiguous refer to the subject/object distinction which is not under discussion here and will be accepted for now. Bohr has made clear that the reference to unambiguous language is to ordinary language supplemented by the concepts of classical physics. It is this part of the argument that breaks down in the face of the empirical studies marshaled here. In sum, research on language and its role in human existence shows that the epistemological claims Bohr has made for it cannot be supported. This conclusion cuts the heart out of Bohr's *main argument* and leaves his epistemological theory hanging.

13.7 Reflection 22

I have completed the discussion of the development of Bohr's ideas in the context of his physics, collected and sorted his philosophical thought, presented the structure of his epistemological theory, and suggested the sources for his ideas. In this chapter, most of the evaluation of Bohr's work has also been completed and some conclusions were drawn about it. Up to now, I have tried to stay close to Bohr's point of view and provide a reliable analysis of what he said and why. This will change in Part IV when I begin to offer some revisions of the components of his epistemology based on the problems discussed in this chapter and in prior ones.

There are still some issues left unresolved at this point. In spite of my rejection of Bohr's justification for his *main argument,* I claim the core of what Bohr is trying to get at in presenting this argument is correct. One goal for Part IV is to prepare a revised version of Bohr's *main argument* that will preserve his epistemology and meet the objections that have been raised regarding the justification he gave for it.

There are a number of other things left undone that will also be addressed in Part IV. First, there is the question of whether complementarity can be supported in classical physics. Next, the account of Bohr's theory of measurement requires completion so that a detailed comparison with von Neumann's theory can be made. I will proceed to examine a number of important epistemological issues in quantum theory that are not addressed or not resolved by Bohr's work. Finally, there is the question of why Bohr introduced the subject/object distinction as a matter of physics and the implications this has for physics and therefore for philosophy.

Part IV

Reflections

The purpose of playing, whose end, both at first and now, was and is, to hold, as 'twere, the mirror up to nature.

William Shakespeare, *Hamlet*, 1623

CHAPTER 14

Epistemological Issues in Classical Physics

The broader implications of Bohr's epistemological work for both physics and philosophy are the concerns of Part IV. While the focus in this century has been on the conceptual challenges and dislocations in our understanding of reality due to quantum theory, this investigation shows that classical theory has its own conceptual problems. Bohr also left important aspects of his theory unfinished. These gaps, including a theory of measurement and an account of closure, need to be filled in order to complete his theory. To adequately address these issues and concerns, the framework that Bohr provided will be extended in a direction consistent with his viewpoint. A final review of the issues concerned with subject and object leaves us with an echo of where we began.

14.1 Probability in Classical Physics

Bohr's conviction that complementarity is an important aspect of the theory of knowledge in general, which led him to look beyond quantum theory to biology, sociology, and other areas, extended also to classical physics. Several physicists responded to his suggestion in 1930 that complementarity would be found in the relation of thermodynamics to statistical mechanics and published calculations to support this conjecture. Understanding these examples and the critique of them from the perspective of the Theory of Interacting Systems requires a little background in thermodynamics, statistical mechanics, and the connection between them. A suitable formalism, which encapsulates the relation of thermodynamics to statistical mechanics, is introduced and discussed briefly for this purpose. This discussion of thermodynamics and statistical mechanics will prove useful in the next chapter when I evaluate Bohr's suggestion that an increase in entropy may play a role in the irreversible recording of an observation and thereby satisfy the requirements of his concept of closure.

The relationship between thermodynamics and statistical mechanics is based on particle probability distributions, so the introduction of probability into physics is discussed first to provide a foundation for understanding the conceptual tension between the mechanical and the statistical mechanical views of particle mechanics.

Probability was originally concerned with computing the likelihood a given macroscopic event will occur. It first entered physics in pressure and mean free path calculations in elementary kinetic theory. Probability played a fundamental role in the subsequent work of Maxwell and Boltzmann, which represented a significant step for both physics and probability theory. The consequence of introducing probabilities in these particle theories was a loosening of the connection between the exact mechanical description of the evolution of a system of particles in time and the values of the physical quantities calculated for that system. Probability became central to physics with the advent of quantum theory. An additional epistemological role was acquired by probability when it was mentioned in connection with perception in the last chapter. Finally, probability is important to the Theory of Interacting Systems in connection with the subject/object relation in both classical and quantum physics.

The theory of probability began with the study of games of chance and the analysis of errors. Early investigations were summarized in the eighteenth century in works such as Jacob Bernoulli's *Ars Conjectanti*, published posthumously in 1713. This was followed by a number of authors who added to a growing corpus of work. Pierre Simon Laplace contributed significantly to this literature in the last quarter of the 18th century and the early 19th century. Laplace [**1819**] wrote a nonmathematical précis of probability theory titled *A Philosophical Essay on Probabilities* in which he introduced the

14.1 PROBABILITY IN CLASSICAL PHYSICS

principles behind the developing theory. He stated that the most important questions of life are for the most part problems of probability. This is because of human ignorance of all the relevant details behind the occurrence of an event and our inability to process all those details. He went on:

"Strictly speaking it may even be said that nearly all our knowledge is problematical; and in the small number of things we are able to know with certainty, even in the mathematical sciences themselves, the principal means of ascertaining truth—induction and analogy—are based on probabilities; so that the entire system of human knowledge is connected with the theory set forth in this essay. ... I hope that the reflections given in this essay may merit the attention of philosophers and direct it to a subject so worthy of engaging their minds." [1]

This challenge did not seem to be taken very seriously by philosophers writing on the theory of knowledge afterward.

Laplace went on to present the principle of causality in the form 'all events are produced by a cause' and claimed that this is a consequence of the 'principle of sufficient reason'. In one of his most striking passages, based on a statement he first made in 1776 and quoted innumerable times thereafter, he imagines an intelligence so vast that it can comprehend the past and future at once as determined by these causal relations. To this intelligence, everything would be known and no recourse to probabilities would ever be needed. This image, reexpressed in the form of a contrast between deterministic particle mechanics and probabilistic statistical mechanics, was later used in reference to the second law of thermodynamics by Maxwell and Gibbs. Maxwell observed that a being who could watch each particle in its course would have no need of the concept of entropy. Gibbs remarked that the status of the second law had been reduced from that of a statement of the impossibility of a decrease in entropy to a statement of the improbability of a decrease in entropy.

Laplace stated several principles that underlie the theory of probability. His first principle is that probabilities are determined at a given time by relative frequencies, that is, the ratio of the number of possible favorable outcomes to the number of all possible outcomes. He immediately amended it, in the second principle, by saying that the assumption underlying the first principle is that the *a priori probability* of each outcome is the same. If this is not true, then a modified version of the relative frequency calculation, which reflects this, is to be used.[2]

His discussion of applications of the theory of probability to natural phenomena included an account of calculations of the likelihood that particular irregularities in planetary motions were due to chance errors in the observations. These computations showed that certain laborious calculations, to

---

[1] See Laplace [**1819**], pp. 1–2.
[2] Laplace did not say how *a priori* probabilities are to be obtained or computed.

verify that the causes of these irregularities are the gravitational effects of other planets, were justified because the probability that the irregularities are due to observational errors was so slight. He also discussed applying probability to the calculation of the effects of the sun and moon on the tides and to choosing an effective treatment for diseases.

In more recent times, the relative frequency interpretation of probability has received a number of challenges.[3] It would take us too far afield to go into these fundamental questions here, but some related issues of significance to this inquiry into classical statistical mechanics and thermodynamics will be raised. There are, to begin with, many cases in which probability theory is used, but the conditions for an appropriate application of relative frequency ideas are not met. In other cases, discrete combinatorial calculations are used to justify conclusions about calculations expressed in terms of continuous probability distribution densities. There are also questions concerning when probabilistic calculations are justified in connection with a deterministic theory. Finally, there are issues connected with the relation of observed experimental outcomes to the probabilistic representation of these outcomes in a theoretical calculation.

The original concern with errors in measurement in the seventeenth century by DeMoivre and Laplace led to the normal law of errors when the number of independent terms approaches infinity. The original asymptotic theorem was concerned only with what are now called Bernoulli trials in which each term has the integral value 0 or 1. Extending this law to general outcomes required more sophisticated mathematical tools and was not done until the nineteenth century work of Chebyshev, who showed that the behavior of sums of large numbers of mutually independent random variables follows the law of large numbers. The Central Limit Theorem, which is the general result that supports this statement, was proved after Chebyshev's death first by Liapunov and then in a different form by Markov. Liapunov's work showed for probability laws expressed as continuous distributions that the normal distribution is the limit under certain general conditions of the behavior of independent random variables as their number grows. These theorems were considerably strengthened and generalized in the twentieth century.

The methods of statistics and probability turned out to be powerful tools when used in physics to deal with situations in which many agents are acting. The employment of statistical methods in conjunction with kinetic theory by August Krönig and their use in the mean free path calculations of Rudolph Clausius in the middle of the nineteenth century gave them the power to extract information from large collections of particles. They employed distributions of microscopic particles that were simple enough and specialized

---

[3]See, for example, Leonard J. Savage [**1972**], and the references cited there, for a critique of the relative frequency view of probability and an account of several other approaches to the foundations of probability—including his own personalistic approach.

enough to make calculations possible. This extended the use of probability beyond standard calculations of the chance that a given macroscopic event will occur. Statistical methods were used with microscopic particles in a more sophisticated way very soon afterward by Maxwell [**1860**], [**1866**] in his work on transport equations. Maxwell introduced the concept of a general statistical distribution of particle velocities in his theory and showed how to compute the rate of transport of physical quantities with it. By analogy to Gauss' mean square law of errors, Maxwell found a steady state solution, in the form of a particle distribution in which there is no net transport of physical quantities, and identified it as the equilibrium distribution.

For systems with more than a few particles, solving the dynamical equations for each particle is out of the question. To make progress requires the use of more powerful methods in which the contributions of individual particles can be subsumed under laws concerning their behavior in aggregate. Maxwell approached this problem by using a one-particle velocity distribution function, which represents an average particle in the system. Maxwell computed his velocity distribution for a collection of $\mathcal{N}$ particles by dividing the velocity range into a set of "buckets", where the range $(v_x - \frac{1}{2}dv_x, v_x + \frac{1}{2}dv_x)$, for example, represents the x component of the velocity bucket of width dv_x centered at the velocity v_x. He let $\mathcal{N}f(v)dv = \mathcal{N}f(v_x, v_y, v_z)d^3v$ represent the number of particles whose velocities fall into the 3-dimensional bucket of volume dv centered on the velocity v. Maxwell found that the steady state or equilibrium distribution for his transport equations is proportional, in modern notation, to $e^{-mv^2/2k_BT}$, where k_B is Boltzmann's constant, m is the particle mass, $v^2 = v_x^2 + v_y^2 + v_z^2$, and T is the absolute temperature.

In addition to the equilibrium distribution for the system, Maxwell also identified various microscopic analog functions of macroscopic thermodynamic quantities. These analogs, defined in terms of the microscopic particle velocity coordinate, included the particle density, momentum, and kinetic energy. He used these analog functions to compute the microscopic flux of various physical quantities, such as the mass, momentum, and energy flows, passing through a boundary. This microscopic flux was then averaged in his transport equations over the boundary surface to obtain the macroscopic flux.

Boltzmann [**1872**] extended Maxwell's transport theory into a dynamical theory. Boltzmann used a one-particle probability distribution density, which represents an average particle, as the basis for his theory. Formally, the one-particle probability distribution density $f(q,p,t)$ is the probability density of finding a particle in the mechanical state (q,p) at time t. The particle mechanical states are points in 6-dimensional *phase space*, which is the direct product of the 3-dimensional coordinate space and 3-dimensional momentum space. Boltzmann developed an evolution equation for the one-particle probability distribution density called the *Boltzmann equation*. In this equation,

Boltzmann computed the rate of change of the one-particle distribution using Maxwell's formula for the number of collisions between the particles in a unit time to define a "collision term". Boltzmann also extended Maxwell's equilibrium solution into the Maxwell-Boltzmann equilibrium distribution by replacing the kinetic energy $mv^2/2$ with the total energy $\mathcal{H}$ in the exponent of Maxwell's equilibrium distribution density.

In the early twentieth century, Gibbs [1902] began with an $\mathcal{N}$ particle probability density distribution and extended these ideas into a general account of the relation of equilibrium thermodynamics to statistical mechanics. Gibbs worked in the $6\mathcal{N}$-dimensional particle *phase space,* which is the direct product space of all the individual particle phase spaces. Gibbs worked out the equilibrium thermodynamics and statistical mechanics of a system of $\mathcal{N}$ particles using the $\mathcal{N}$ particle canonical distribution that is the equilibrium version of this general time-dependent probability distribution function. The system probability distribution density represents the probability that the system is in a particular $6\mathcal{N}$-dimensional mechanical state $(Q, P) = \times_{i=1}^{\mathcal{N}}(q_i, p_i)$. As part of his work, Gibbs concerned himself with finding the proper analog functions, expressed in terms of particle variables, to represent macroscopic physical quantities. These thermodynamic quantities were computed as averages of the corresponding analog functions over the $6\mathcal{N}$-dimensional phase space weighted by the system probability distribution density. This procedure for computing the expectation values of these analog functions is usually called *phase averaging* in statistical mechanics.

The use of probability distributions by Boltzmann and then Gibbs in this domain was significantly different from the statistical distributions used previously by Maxwell. Maxwell defined $\mathcal{N}f(v)dv$ as the *actual* number of particles with velocities in the volume dv centered on v. Boltzmann's one-particle probability distribution $f(q, p, t)dqdp$, on the other hand, represents the *probability* that the particle state will fall at time t within the phase volume $dqdp$ centered on the state (q, p). The differences in meanings of $f(v)$ and $f(q, p, t)$ in these two theories implies that these quantities should not be viewed as the same.[4] As an additional mathematical requirement, Boltzmann's state $f(q, p, t)$ is assumed to be at least once continuously differentiable in its arguments because Boltzmann's equation and his mathematical proof of the H theorem are based on this fact.

Maxwell and Boltzmann were aware of some of the conceptual problems associated with using a probability measure in the context of a deterministic particle theory. They were uncomfortable with the implications of doing so and felt the need to justify it. The question was how to justify the identification of the value of a thermodynamic quantity at some given time as an expectation value, which is a weighted average over a distribution of many mechanical states, when we know that the value of the thermodynamic quantity

---

[4]These differences are discussed in more detail in EIS, Chapter 2.

is determined by the unique mechanical state of the system at this particular time.

Initially, both Maxwell and Boltzmann interpreted the value of the one-particle probability distribution $f(q,p,t)$ at a given phase point (q,p) as the relative frequency with which a representative particle of the system will be in the neighborhood of that point. Subsequently, they looked for a more precise notion and considered time averages of the values of physical quantities. The time average of a physical quantity is computed as the integral over a particular time interval of the value of that quantity as a function of time divided by the length of the time interval.

For the justification of the replacement of the time average of a physical quantity over the path of the phase point representing the system by a phase average, Maxwell and Boltzmann turned to ergodic theory. Ergodic theory assumes that the system trajectory over sufficient time covers most or all of the phase space available to the system. It was introduced in similar forms by both Maxwell and Boltzmann and sets the value of a physical quantity obtained during a measurement to its time average of this quantity in the limit of a measurement with an infinite duration, i.e., the limit $T \to \infty$. The use of ergodic theory in practical cases rests on the assumption that the system visits an appreciable portion of its phase space during the time a measurement lasts. This assumption provides the justification for both setting the infinite time average of a physical analog equal to the phase average of that analog and using the result to represent the macroscopic value of that physical quantity.[5]

C. G. Darwin and R. H. Fowler extended the application of mathematical methods to physical descriptions in 1922 with their asymptotic formulas for thermodynamics. Aleksandr Khinchin subsequently understood their work to be a crude form of an application of the Central Limit Theorem of probability and used the mathematical methods of probability theory in 1943 to simplify their work and put it on a better mathematical footing.[6]

14.2 Thermodynamics in Bohr's Thought

Bohr was a great admirer of Gibbs and felt that in Gibbs' [1902] version of the relation of statistical mechanics to thermodynamics we might find an aspect of classical theory that resembles complementarity in atomic physics. It was in his lecture to the Faraday Society in England that he [1930], pp. 376–377, made the suggestion that complementarity might appear in the classical physics of many particle systems in the form of a complementary

---

[5] For a discussion of ergodic theory and its problems in justifying phase averaging as the mapping between statistical mechanical analogs and thermodynamic quantities, see EIS, Chapter 2.

[6] See R. H. Fowler [1936] for a discussion of the asymptotic methods and references to the papers of Darwin and Fowler. See also the discussion of these matters in QTS, Part III. Various aspects of the work of Khinchin are discussed in CIS, EIS, and QTS.

relation between a 'complete dynamical description' of a system and a 'statistical description' of the system in terms of the equilibrium distribution. In contrasting these descriptions, he, p. 377, referred to "the incompatibility of such a detailed account with the definition of temperature". For an isolated system, the total energy is fixed and the temperature of the system plays no role in the dynamical description. A system at equilibrium, on the other hand, is embedded in a heat bath with rigid walls to fix its temperature and volume. In this situation, the energy is indeterminate.

In an interview, Heisenberg recalled how important Gibbs was to Bohr.[7] Heisenberg had studied Boltzmann at Göttingen, but Bohr insisted that he read Gibbs:

"As I say today, Bohr emphasized the complementarity between temperature and energy to the extreme. He said, "As soon as I know the temperature, the energy has no meaning. I mean this is just one example of a canonical ensemble which means that I do not know the energy. So either I can know the energy or I can know the temperature, but I can never know the energy and the temperature." So that temperature came in some way to be a concept of our knowledge of the things, because a canonical ensemble defines our knowledge. And the great paradox, both for Bohr and all of us in this discussion was always how can a concept, which means in some way our knowledge of something, be an objective property of the thing. ... So one cannot really understand Bohr unless one really understands this deep liking for Gibbs."

Gibbs' Thermodynamics.

The two fundamental ideas that underlie Gibbs' [1902] equilibrium thermodynamics are the description of a particle system by a system probability distribution density and the concept of an analog function to represent physical quantities. Gibbs spoke of the probability distribution density in terms of what he called an ensemble of systems. In statistics, an ensemble is an unlimited set of copies of the same system such that each fixed quantity has the same value in each system, while the free variables take on random values.[8] An ensemble for Gibbs was defined equivalently as a collection of identical systems prepared in all possible different initial states. An ensemble of classical systems with a fixed energy E is represented as a collection of phase

---

[7]See Heisenberg [**Arch**], Set I: Interview #12, 7/12/63.

[8]Laszlo Tisza and Paul M. Quay [**1963**], p. 53, characterize the ensemble approach to the description of the system in terms of distributions as follows: "A quantitative description of values of the free variables can be given in terms of statistical distribution functions the nature of which depends on the type of physical situation considered, and exhibits, in general, an interplay of randomness with correlations arising as a consequence of molecular dynamics." Compare this to the macroscopic viewpoint in Tisza [**1951**]. See also Tisza [**1966**].

points, representing system mechanical states, distributed on the $(6\mathcal{N} - 1)$-dimensional surface in phase space with energy E. The microcanonical distribution is the ensemble of states that is uniformly distributed on this surface. The canonical distribution, on the other hand, is an ensemble conditioned by the temperature that gives equal weight to phase points that represent mechanical states with the same energy.

Boltzmann's Thermodynamics.
Other aspects of thermodynamics of importance to Bohr are the concepts of entropy and irreversibility. Bohr had expressed an interest in the arrow of time and aspects of observation with regard to thermodynamics in a letter to Dirac in 1928,[9] and remarked then that he was interested in the unidirectional aspect of time, but that this had no meaning for an isolated system. He also stated in this letter the idea that permanent results, marks on a photographic plate or memories, are inherent in the very idea of an observation.[10]

In the same letter to Dirac, Bohr was critical of Boltzmann's attempt to deal with the recurrence and reversibility objections to the H theorem by claiming that the universe is basically at equilibrium, but just happened to start as a cosmological fluctuation in a low entropy state. He felt that Boltzmann's assumption is not very plausible. He followed this by expressing the feeling that the whole epistemology of mechanism is untenable and needs to be replaced by one "embodying a deeper relation between the description of the phenomena and their observation." Bohr's later answer to the question of "time's arrow" was to refer to closed observations that have registered a permanent mark.

Another of Bohr's unpublished notes, written in 1959, mentioned Boltzmann's work again in connection with the "arrow of time" and work by Rosenfeld on the relation between classical statistical mechanics and thermodynamics.[11] He also discussed again the idea that an irreversible registration of an observation involves an increase in entropy and expressed the hope that this could be used to justify his concept of closure.

Some of the formalism associated with thermodynamics and statistical mechanics is required so that we can submit Bohr's speculations to a precise analysis and evaluate them. The representation of entropy in statistical mechanics and thermodynamics will be considered in Section 14.4 below and that formalism will be used to evaluate Bohr's ideas in the discussion of the concepts of observation, entropy, and closure in the next chapter.

Although Bohr was not aware of it, there is a third aspect of thermodynamics that is important to his approach to epistemology. This is concerned

---

[9] See Bohr [**Arch**], BSC 10, letter to Dirac, 3/24/28.
[10] He mentioned the idea of a unidirectional aspect of time shortly afterward in a letter to Ralph H. Fowler, 5/19/28. As will emerge in later volumes in this series, the arrow of time in quantum mechanics is just as problematic as it is in classical mechanics.
[11] See Bohr [**Arch**], 23:4, pp. 2–3, 11/22/59. Rosenfeld's work will be examined below.

with the thermodynamic consequences of establishing the subject/object distinction in experiments. This will be taken up from a thermodynamic perspective in Section 14.6.

14.3 The Relation of Thermodynamics to Statistical Mechanics

The central issue in the connection between statistical mechanics and thermodynamics is how the microscopic and macroscopic levels of description are related. The statistical mechanical formalism is expressed in terms of a particle probability distribution density function. The relation between the macroscopic and microscopic levels is established by assigning a microscopic analog function to each macroscopic physical quantity and designating the macroscopic physical quantity as the expectation value or phase average of this analog.

In the $\mathcal{N}$ particle equilibrium theory of Gibbs, physical quantities are computed in this way and thermodynamics is built out of these physical quantities. The temperature derivative of these physical quantities is defined using the fact that the derivative of the equilibrium distribution with respect to the inverse absolute temperature places a factor of the form $-\mathcal{H}$, where $\mathcal{H}$ is the system Hamiltonian energy, in the integrand of that quantity.

This approach can be extended to general nonequilibrium theory by replacing the equilibrium particle distribution with a general $\mathcal{N}$ particle probability distribution density. This change allows thermodynamic quantities to be defined as local time-dependent functions representing the values of the macroscopic physical quantities associated with the system. As the particle distribution evolves in time in accord with Hamiltonian statistical mechanics, these phase averages will also evolve in time. This parallel behavior between the microscopic and macroscopic levels is used in TIS as the basis for computing time derivatives of the macroscopic quantities in terms of time derivatives of the system distribution function and the analog functions. The movement of the boundaries of a system of particles also has physical implications that are captured in the formalism. In summary, this formalism is concerned with parallel microscopic and macroscopic descriptions of the behavior of a collection of matter. The descriptions on the two levels are connected by the phase averaging procedure that maps microscopic analog functions to macroscopic physical quantities.

For definiteness, let us consider a system k of $\mathcal{N}_k$ interacting particles described by classical Hamiltonian mechanics. The mechanical state of system k in this phase space is written (Q_k, P_k), where the $3\mathcal{N}_k$-dimensional system coordinate and momentum vectors are the direct products $Q_k = (q_1, q_2, \ldots, q_{\mathcal{N}_k}) = \times_{i \in k} q_i$ and $P_k = \times_{i \in k} p_i$, and where $i \in k$ refers to particle i in system k. The $\mathcal{N}_k$ particle probability distribution density is written $F_k(Q_k, P_k, t)$ and represents the probability density that the system will be

14.3 THE RELATION OF THERMODYNAMICS TO STATISTICAL MECHANICS 351

found in the mechanical state (Q_k, P_k) at time t. As a probability density, it is required to be normalized so that $\int dQ_k \int dP_k\, F_k(Q_k, P_k, t) = 1$.

Both Maxwell and Gibbs represented physical quantities microscopically as particular analog functions defined in terms of the microscopic particle coordinates and momenta. Examples of analogs are the particle Hamiltonian energy $\mathcal{H}_k(Q_k, P_k, t)$ and the total momentum function $\mathcal{P}_k = \sum_{i \in k} p_i$, where the sum is over all particles in system k.[12]

There is considerable latitude inherent in the application of the statistical mechanical formalism to a given system of particles. The standard procedure for representing a particular system in statistical mechanics is to attribute some specific probability distribution density to the collection of particles in the system as an initial condition. This initial condition is used in conjunction with an evolution equation for the system probability distribution density and the boundary conditions to determine the distribution $F_k(Q_k, P_k, t)$ at all subsequent times. The usual requirement for choosing an initial probability distribution density $F_k(Q_k, P_k, t_0)$ at time t_0 is that bounds and expectation values of physical quantities must be consistent with the empirical information we have concerning the system. In most cases this information amounts to a few macroscopic parameters, so a wide range of system probability distributions, representing quite different microscopic configurations, will satisfy this requirement.

When macroscopic thermodynamic quantities, such as temperature or pressure, are measured in a system, the values obtained can be used to limit the set of possible probability descriptions that can be applied to the system. This in turn limits the set of probability descriptions that the system can evolve into afterward. Consider in this regard a general probability distribution density $F_k(Q_k, P_k, t_0)$ that is consistent with some set of measured macroscopic data for a system. Using this as an initial condition, the solution $F_k(Q_k, P_k, t)$ of the system evolution equation for future times can be computed. The physical system evolves and, at time t_1, some more measurements are made. Based on this new information, a new, also not uniquely determined, state $F'_k(Q_k, P_k, t_1)$ is assigned to the system at time t_1. This will "reduce" the system distribution $F_k(Q_k, P_k, t_1)$ to $F'(Q_k, P_k, t_1)$ by eliminating possible microscopic trajectories from states starting at t_0 that have led to states at t_1 for which the macroscopic values of the system parameters contradict the results of the new measurement.

In this situation, there is a reduction problem similar to the one von Neumann faced regarding wavefunctions in quantum mechanics. We do not feel the same pull in this case as we do with quantum mechanics because the classical distribution is assumed to be a purely mathematical device. In spite of this feeling, the system state has changed by this procedure in a way that

---

[12] All of the formalism introduced in this chapter is explained in much more detail in CIS where it is extended into a complete and general thermodynamics.

is not determined by the evolution equation. Because the entropy is defined below in terms of the system distribution, the entropy will also undergo a change when this reduction occurs. Without going into details at this point, this "ambiguity" in the entropy makes the epistemological situation for thermodynamics and classical statistical mechanics rather similar in some ways to that of quantum mechanics.

14.4 The Theory of Interacting Systems

To discuss both the subject/object distinction in classical physics and Bohr's speculations concerning observations, entropy, and closure, I will need to introduce some more elements of thermodynamics, statistical mechanics, and the theory that connects them. Existing theories by Boltzmann and Gibbs refer to single systems and do not address the description of the interaction between distinct macroscopic systems that is needed for the formal representation of the subject/object distinction. Moreover, Boltzmann's equation is part of a one-particle theory that uses a particle collision term that is not compatible with Hamiltonian mechanics. Gibbs theory, on the other hand, is compatible with Hamiltonian mechanics and successfully connects $\mathcal{N}_k$ particle equilibrium thermodynamics to equilibrium statistical mechanics, but his equilibrium theory does not answer the general question of how the thermodynamic description and the statistical mechanical description of a system are related in the general nonequilibrium case. For these reasons, TIS was developed to describe the thermodynamics of collections of these interacting systems. TIS is a formalism for a local time-dependent thermodynamics that is compatible with Hamiltonian mechanics. It is based on a set of time-dependent probability distribution densities $\{\, F_k(Q_k, P_k, t)\, \}$ that represent a collection of particle systems sharing some common boundaries as interacting macroscopic systems.

Enough of the interacting systems formalism will be presented so that what Bohr called a 'complete dynamical description' can be compared to what he called a 'statistical description'. The complete dynamical description is made concrete by interpreting it as a reference to the detailed particle trajectories embodied in the description of the particle system as a microscopic Hamiltonian flow. The 'statistical description' is interpreted in this context as the equilibrium distribution of the particle system with the system temperature and volume as parameters. To compare these two descriptions and make judgments concerning their potential for a complementary relation, a single mathematical formalism is required that is broad enough to include the representations of both cases. Without a unified formalism of this sort, Bohr's questions concerning the relation of the dynamical description of a system to its description in terms of equilibrium thermodynamics cannot be answered with confidence.

14.4 THE THEORY OF INTERACTING SYSTEMS

For the discussion of Bohr's ideas concerning entropy and observation, the aspects of the formalism associated with the entropy are introduced also. The formalism to be presented is therefore limited to just those elements that will be sufficient for the discussion of the possibility of complementarity in a thermodynamics based on statistical mechanics and an evaluation in the next chapter of Bohr's claim concerning the role of entropy in observation. Consult CIS and EIS for more detailed information on these topics and for the full theory.

The basic formalism of the TIS approach, including the calculation of expectation values, is similar to the $\mathcal{N}_k$ particle formalism of Gibbs. For every macroscopic physical quantity, a microscopic analog function defined in terms of the particle positions and momenta is required. One of the major extensions to the existing theories provided by TIS is a formalism for representing simultaneously the dynamical evolution of a collection of interacting systems and an account of the conserved quantities exchanged between them. It is shown in CIS that this extension in both formalism and conceptualization is necessary to allow for an adequate treatment of the entropy.

For simplicity, a system described by nonrelativistic classical Hamiltonian mechanics defined in an inertial frame that is composed of spinless particles that interact with each other via central forces will be used. The particles have mass and the interactions between them are described by the usual action at a distance potentials. Radiation, charge, and electrodynamics are neglected.

To formalize these considerations, consider again a system k containing $\mathcal{N}_k$ particles. For simplicity, let k be a closed system, which means that no particles enter or leave it. Let k be endowed with a non-intersecting smooth boundary and a bounded volume. The symbol k is also used to represent the collection of particles in the k system, so the notation $i \in k$ refers to particle i in system k. The system mechanical state is the direct product of its particle mechanical states: $(Q_k, P_k) = \times_{i \in k} (q_i, p_i)$. The space of system states is the $6\mathcal{N}_k$-dimensional system phase space $\mathbf{R}^{6\mathcal{N}_k}$, where $\mathbf{R}$ refers to the real numbers. For any given system, the set of possible system states is assumed to be a bounded subset in this phase space. As before, the quantity $F_k(Q_k, P_k, t)$ represents the $\mathcal{N}_k$ particle probability distribution density for system k at time t. It is normalized so that $\int dQ_k \int dP_k \, F_k(Q_k, P_k, t) = 1$.

There are several specialized system states that are useful in specific contexts. The first is the singular *exact state* $F_k^\delta(Q_k, P_k, t)$, which is defined as

(14.1) $\qquad F_k^\delta(Q_k, P_k, t) = \delta(Q_k - Q_k(t))\delta(P_k - P_k(t)),$

It fixes the value of the phase space point (Q_k, P_k) at time t at the single point $(Q_k(t), P_k(t))$ on the system trajectory and is equivalent to a solution of Hamilton's equations. The next specialized state is the time-independent *equilibrium state* $F_k^\epsilon(Q_k, P_k)$, which is defined by

(14.2a) $$F_k^\epsilon(Q_k, P_k) = [Z_k^\epsilon]^{-1} e^{-\beta_k \mathcal{H}_k^\epsilon(Q_k, P_k)},$$

where $\mathcal{H}_k^\epsilon(Q_k, P_k)$ is the system equilibrium Hamiltonian function, $\beta_k = 1/k_B T_k$, and the normalization factor Z_k^ϵ, called the *partition function*, is defined by

(14.2b) $$Z_k^\epsilon = \int dQ_k \int dP_k\, e^{-\beta_k \mathcal{H}_k^\epsilon(Q_k, P_k)}.$$

The equilibrium state is the familiar equilibrium probability distribution density, or canonical distribution density in Gibbs' terminology, based on the Maxwell-Boltzmann equilibrium distribution. The third specialized state is Gibbs' *microcanonical state* $F_k^\gamma(Q_k, P_k)$ that assigns equal probability to all mechanical states (Q_k, P_k) with a given total energy, momentum, and angular momentum. Taken together, the elements of this formalism meet our requirements because the time-dependent exact state distribution and the time-independent equilibrium distribution can be used in the formalism to compute phase averages, time derivatives, and other thermodynamic derivatives in the same way as the time-dependent general probability distribution density $F_k(Q_k, P_k, t)$.

The Hamiltonian mechanics of an isolated system t with $\mathcal{N}_t$ particles is based, for $1 \leq i, j \leq \mathcal{N}_t$, on the set of particle masses $\{m_i\}$, the set of particle mechanical states $\{(q_i, p_i)\}$, and the set of particle interaction potentials $\{\phi_{ij}(q_i - q_j)\}$. The evolution equation for this system depends only on combinations of these quantities, their derivatives, and the time. A thermodynamic physical quantity G associated with system k is represented by the microscopic analog quantity $G_k(Q_k, P_k, t)$ and the macroscopic thermodynamic function $G_k(t)$. The *expectation value* or *phase average* of $G_k(Q_k, P_k, t)$ is

(14.3)
$$G_k(t) = \int dQ_k \int dP_k\, F_k(Q_k, P_k, t) G_k(Q_k, P_k, t) = \langle G_k(Q_k, P_k, t) \rangle_{kt},$$

where a convenient bracket notation was introduced to represent phase averaging. As a specific example, the Hamiltonian energy analog $\mathcal{H}_k(Q_k, P_k, t)$ is used to compute time-dependent macroscopic k system Hamiltonian energy as $\mathcal{H}_k(t) = \langle \mathcal{H}_k(Q_k, P_k, t) \rangle_{kt}$.

The rate of change of a phase function $G_k(Q_k, P_k, t)$ due to the interactions of the particles and their motion is obtained from Hamiltonian statistical mechanics. It is expressed in terms of the total time derivative d/dt in the form

(14.4) $$\frac{dG_k(Q_k, P_k, t)}{dt} = \frac{\partial G_k(Q_k, P_k, t)}{\partial t} + \{\mathcal{H}_k(Q_k, P_k, t), G_k(Q_k, P_k, t)\}_{PB},$$

where $\{\mathcal{H}_k(Q_k, P_k, t), F_k(Q_k, P_k, t)\}_{PB}$ is the classical Poisson bracket operator. Using this formula with the k system probability distribution density $F_k(Q_k, P_k, t)$ yields the k system *evolution equation*

$$(14.5) \quad \frac{dF_k(Q_k, P_k, t)}{dt} = \frac{\partial F_k(Q_k, P_k, t)}{\partial t} + \{\mathcal{H}_k(Q_k, P_k, t), F_k(Q_k, P_k, t)\}_{PB}.$$

For an isolated system t, the total time derivative of the system probability distribution density vanishes in accord with what is called Liouville's theorem and so that $dF_t(Q_t, P_t, t)/dt = 0$. For systems that are interacting with each other across a shared boundary, this is not the case. The evolution of the thermodynamic quantities of the theory follows from the evolution of the microscopic distribution representing the system, and the time derivative of any thermodynamic function $G_k(t)$ can be computed easily with this formalism.

The Hamiltonian function for a system at equilibrium $H^e(Q_k, P_k)$ is independent of the time and it is easy to see that the Poisson bracket of the equilibrium Hamiltonian with the equilibrium distribution vanishes. By (14.5), this implies immediately that $dF_k^e(Q_k, P_k)/dt = 0$ as required. The equilibrium state $F_k^e(Q_k, P_k)$ fits smoothly within this formalism and phase averages of analog quantities are computed in the same way as with the general state $F_k(Q_k, P_k, t)$.

The only non-mathematical requirement on choosing a probability distribution density $F_k(Q_k, P_k, t)$ to represent a system is consistency with the information we have about that system. In practice, the information we typically have is the temperature, pressure, and volume of the system. As mentioned above, there is usually a very large collection of microscopic system particle states (Q_k, P_k) consistent with any particular set of values for these parameters. This means that there is a very wide range in acceptable choices for the system probability distribution density to represent a system that is consistent with this macroscopic information at any given time.

Let us next divide an isolated particle system t exhaustively into a finite set $[t] = \{k, l, \ldots\}$ of subsystems. For the particle interactions, let $\phi_{ij}(q_i - q_j)$ represent the interaction potential for $i \in t$ and $j \in t$, where particles i and j may belong to any subsystems of $[t]$. Next, let $k \in [t]$ be one of these subsystems. Because all interactions are between particles, the *i-particle external potential* and the k system *external potential* are defined for $i \in k$ by

$$(14.6a) \quad \Phi_{i,x}(q_i, t) = \sum_{l \in [t]-k} \sum_{j \in l} \langle \phi_{ij}(q_i - q_j) \rangle_{lt},$$

$$(14.6b) \quad \Phi_{k,x}(Q_k, t) = \sum_{i \in k} \Phi_{i,x}(q_i, t),$$

where the sum over $j \in l$ means to sum j over all particles in the l system and the sum over $l \in [t] - k$ means to sum l over all the systems in $[t]$ except

k. The quantity $\langle \phi_{ij}(q_i - q_j)\rangle_{lt}$ is the phase average of $\phi_{ij}(q_i - q_j)$ over the l system particle coordinates and momenta at time t. This definition of the k external potential respects the Hamiltonian particle dynamics of the other subsystems that belong to $[t]$.

The system Hamiltonian energy is defined in terms of the particle momenta and the individual particle interaction potentials $\phi_{ij}(q_i - q_j)$ by

(14.7) $$\mathcal{H}_k(Q_k, P_k, t) = \mathcal{K}_k(P_k) + \Phi_k(Q_k, t).$$

In this definition, the system kinetic energy is

(14.8) $$\mathcal{K}_k(P_k) = \sum_{i \in k} \frac{p_i^2}{2m_i}$$

and the system potential energy $\Phi_k(Q_k, t)$ is defined as the sum of the internal and external k system potentials by

(14.9) $$\Phi_k(Q_k, t) = \Phi_{k,n}(Q_k, t) + \Phi_{k,x}(Q_k, t),$$

where the k internal potential $\Phi_{k,n}$ is defined by

(14.10) $$\Phi_{k,n}(Q_k) = \tfrac{1}{2} \sum_{i \in k} \sum_{j \in k-i} \phi_{ij}(q_i - q_j).$$

The $1/2$ in this definition compensates for the double counting of particles.

Let us step back a moment and review our progress. For a classically described system, the system is always assumed to be in some classical mechanical state which at time t_0 can be represented as a point $(Q_k(t_0), P_k(t_0))$ on a unique trajectory $(Q_k(t), P_k(t))$ in $6\mathcal{N}_k$-dimensional phase space. If the system passes through point (Q_k^0, P_k^0) at $t = 0$, then this trajectory is the unique solution to Hamilton's equations that satisfies the initial condition $(Q_k^0, P_k^0) = (Q_k(0), P_k(0))$. The system state associated with this trajectory is the exact state $F^\delta(Q_k, P_k, t)$. When there is not sufficient information to fix this trajectory at some point (Q_k^0, P_k^0) at time $t = 0$, a general probability distribution density $F_k(Q_k, P_k, t)$ is used to describe the system. For systems at equilibrium, the state $F_k^\epsilon(Q_k, P_k)$ is used.

14.5 Entropy

Historically, the second law of thermodynamics, the entropy, and their relation were important concerns in the reduction of thermodynamics to statistical mechanics. Boltzmann introduced a quantity that served as a microscopic entropy analog that took the form (TIS notation) $S^{(B2)}(q, p, t) = -k_B \ln f(q, p, t)$, where k_B is Boltzmann's constant.[13] The phase average of

---

[13]Boltzmann's original definition was $H(q, p, t) = \ln f(q, p, t)$. For consistency, the TIS versions of the entropies introduced by various authors use the TIS sign convention and include Boltzmann's constant as a factor. The TIS versions of these entropies are

this is $H(t) = \int d^3q \int d^3p\, f(q,p,t) S^{(B2)}(q,p,t) = \left\langle S^{(B2)}(q,p,t) \right\rangle_{kt}$. Boltzmann identified $H(t)$ as the thermodynamic entropy and showed in his H theorem that the macroscopic quantity $H(t)$ always increases (TIS sign) as $f(q,p,t)$ evolves in time unless the system is at equilibrium. He initially associated the fact that $H(t)$ never decreases in time with the irreversibility of thermodynamics.[14]

Gibbs introduced in 1902 a quantity called the "index of probability", which he used as an entropy analog. It took the form (TIS notation)

(14.11a) $\qquad S_k^{(G1)}(Q_k, P_k, t) = -k_B \ln F_k(Q_k, P_k, t).$

The phase average of this quantity is the thermodynamic entropy

(14.11b) $\qquad S_k^{(G1)}(t) = \left\langle S_k^{(G1)}(Q_k, P_k, t) \right\rangle_{kt}.$

When the equilibrium distribution F_k^ϵ is used in place of the general system distribution F_k, the equilibrium entropy analog function results

(14.12a) $\quad S_k^{(G1)\epsilon}(Q_k, P_k) = -k_B \ln F_k^\epsilon(Q_k, P_k) = k_B[\beta_k H_k^\epsilon(Q_k, P_k) + \ln Z_k^\epsilon].$

Phase averaging this over the equilibrium distribution using (14.3) gives the thermodynamic equilibrium entropy

(14.12b) $\qquad S_k^{(G1)\epsilon} = k_B[\beta_k H_k^\epsilon + \ln Z_k^\epsilon],$

where $H_k^\epsilon = \left\langle H_k^\epsilon(Q_k, P_k) \right\rangle_{k\epsilon}$ is the phase average of the equilibrium Hamiltonian energy over the equilibrium state.

When Gibbs' computed the time derivative of the general time-dependent thermodynamic entropy, $S_k^{(G1)}(t)$, he obtained the result $dS_k^{(G1)}(t)/dt = 0$. This was unacceptable to him because he believed that the entropy should be increasing, so he then substituted a quantity, later called the "coarse-grained entropy", for this one. Gibbs was able to show that the coarse-grained entropy increases in time.

In the quantum mechanical case, von Neumann [**1932**], Chapter V, defined the quantum entropy analog in terms of the statistical matrix U_k representing a system k by $S_k^{(vN)} = -k_B \ln U_k$. The thermodynamic entropy is computed using the standard trace formalism as $S_k^{(vN)}(t) = \text{Tr}(U_k S_k^{(vN)})$. The statistical matrix U_k can represent the system as a pure state or as a

---

therefore proportional to the original definitions. Each distinct version of the entropy that is discussed is designated by a unique superscript that is preserved across this series of volumes. This will reduce confusion and facilitate comparisons. See CIS, for example, for a discussion of two of Boltzmann's entropies and Gibbs' version of the entropy and QIS for many more.

[14] After criticisms based on the reversibility and recurrence paradoxes, Boltzmann changed his characterization of $H(t)$ significantly. See CIS and EIS for details.

mixture of various pure quantum states with respect to some basis of quantum states. Computing the time derivative of $S_k^{(vN)}(t)$, von Neumann showed that the change in time of this definition of the entropy is 0 when U_k evolves in accord with Schrödinger's equation.

For the definition of the classical entropy analog, Gibbs' phase analog $S_k^{(G1)}(Q_k, P_k, t)$ will be adopted here. Before using this formalism, however, the implications of this choice in the physical situation we are concerned with must be examined. Because a microscopic classical system is always assumed to be pursuing a unique trajectory in phase space and occupies a unique point in phase space at a given time, the question of what it means to represent this physical situation by a probability distribution, which ranges over a set of possible system mechanical states, is significant. The issue takes on added importance because the phase entropy in this form cannot be defined for a system represented as a moving point on a unique trajectory. The reason for this is that the moving point is represented by the singular exact state $F_k^\delta(Q_k, P_k, t)$ and the phase average of the singular exact state phase entropy $S_k^\delta(Q_k, P_k, t) = -k_B \ln F_k^\delta(Q_k, P_k, t)$ is not defined mathematically. This implies that the use of nonsingular probability distribution densities is essential in the development of thermodynamics out of statistical mechanics if we wish to obtain the thermodynamic entropy as a phase average of a microscopic analog quantity over the system probability distribution density.

To recapitulate, Bohr's 'complete dynamical description' of an isolated system t in this setting is interpreted as the classical spacetime description of a system represented by $F_t^\delta(Q_t, P_t, t)$. The total system energy is fixed in this case. Bohr's 'statistical description' of a system at a definite temperature is interpreted as a reference to the asymptotic description of a small system embedded in a much larger system, which plays the role of a "heat bath" for the smaller system. In this situation, the energy is a random variable and the system is represented by the equilibrium probability distribution density $F_k^\epsilon(Q_k, P_k)$.

With these definitions, it is easy to see that the descriptions $F_k^\delta(Q_k, P_k, t)$ and $F_k^\epsilon(Q_k, P_k)$ cannot both be applied simultaneously to a given system because a system cannot be simultaneously described as both isolated and embedded in a larger system. This means that the conditions appropriate for the attribution of one or the other of these descriptions cannot be satisfied simultaneously. There is a *prima facie* match between Bohr's claim of complementarity that mandates that both descriptions are needed for a complete description of a thermodynamic system and requires that they cannot both be applied simultaneously to a given system.

In this example we are dealing with a logical and not an operational incompatibility because being isolated and being a small part of a larger system are logically incompatible experimental arrangements. The next question is whether these descriptions are both needed for a complete description of a given system. An examination of the situation from the microscopic point of view shows that the answer is no. We have all the information we can have about a classical system of interacting particles when we have a phase space trajectory $(Q_k(t), P_k(t))$ that is equivalent to the corresponding exact state $F_k^\delta(Q_k, P_k, t)$. To show that we have this microscopic information, consider a small system k embedded in a large system l and assume that the combined system $t = k + l$ is isolated. Let $F_t^\delta(Q_t, P_t, t)$ be an exact state solution of Hamilton's equations for the trajectory of the combined t system. The properties of the delta measure are used to marginalize this solution by integrating over the variables representing the particles in the large system l to obtain the solution $F_k^\delta(Q_k, P_k, t)$ for the collection of trajectories of the particles contained in the small system k. Thus, even though the small system is described by the equilibrium state from one perspective, it can still be described in microscopic terms as the k component of the unique solution to Hamilton's equations for the isolated combined system t.

Because the microscopic system distribution $F_k(Q_k, P_k, t)$ is not fixed uniquely by the macroscopic boundary conditions that can be imposed on the system, the value of the system entropy will also have an arbitrary aspect as well. This, as with the reduction problem outlined above, can be construed as an essential "ambiguity", to use Bohr's term, in the interpretation of thermodynamic quantities in terms of the underlying particle system.

14.6 Attempts to Find Complementarity in Classical Physics

Because fixing the system temperature precisely, from the standpoint of the ensemble metaphor, would require measuring the energy of each member of the infinite ensemble, the measurement of the temperature of a system by a finite system (the thermometer) or the assignment of a temperature to an isolated system are considered to be examples of "parameter estimation" in the sense of statistics. The energy is assumed to be a sufficient statistic for these estimations. In the usual case of a small system attached to a large system (the heat bath), the requirement that the energy be a non-trivial sufficient statistic determines, in great part, the form of the canonical distribution function.[15] In Gibbs' canonical ensemble, the (normalized) equilibrium distribution is $F_k^\epsilon(Q_k, P_k) = [Z_k^\epsilon]^{-1} e^{-\beta_k \mathcal{H}_k^\epsilon(Q_k, P_k)}$ and the equilibrium Hamiltonian energy is treated as the random variable. These statements capture what it means for the temperature to be a parameter of the equilibrium probability distribution density describing the canonical ensemble.[16]

When the theory is developed in this way, the specification of the value of the temperature designates a particular infinite ensemble, with the energy as a free variable, from the range of possible ensembles. As mentioned, a complete

---

[15]Benoit Mandelbrot [**1962**], pp. 1025, 1027–1028, Tisza and Quay [**1963**], pp. 72–78.

[16]For a further discussion of some of these points, see Edwin T. Jaynes [**1957a**], [**1957b**], [**1967**], and especially Mandelbrot [**1962**].

energy measurement in this infinite ensemble provides sufficient information to determine the temperature exactly for that ensemble. This approach is compatible with the idea that a thermometer is an instrument for energy measurements that is marked in units of temperature only for convenience. Consequently, the only limitation on this measurement is that of having to deal with an infinite number of systems—not any incompatibility between the measurements of energy and of temperature. On the other hand, the specification of a definite energy rather than the temperature picks from each ensemble, in the infinite collection of ensembles with different temperatures, the one member of that ensemble with that energy without determining an ensemble itself. This means, given a single measurement of the energy, we cannot specify the temperature exactly.

Calculations of Classical Uncertainty Relations.

A number of workers discussed Bohr's ideas in this domain. Heisenberg [**1955**], pp. 25–27, for one, considered the description of a piece of metal emitting thermal electrons. Heisenberg's ideas were then expanded upon by Rosenfeld [**1961a**], pp. 5–7.[17]

For a precise example, consider a volume of gas in a box. A complete dynamical description consists of the microscopic Hamiltonian equations of motion, the detailed particle initial conditions, and the microscopic boundary conditions for the system. A statistical description (in Bohr's sense of the term), on the other hand, consists of the specification of the volume and temperature as the macroscopic boundary conditions for the system. The temperature is used as a parameter of the equilibrium distribution for the particles in the system and the volume determines the boundaries of the system.

Rosenfeld [**1961a**] considered a small sample of a larger system and stated for the phase average of the variances (also known as dispersions or fluctuations) of the temperature T and the energy E the following relations:

$$(14.13) \qquad \langle (\Delta T)^2 \rangle = \frac{k_B T^2}{C_V}; \qquad \langle (\Delta E)^2 \rangle = C_V k_B T^2,$$

where C_V is the heat capacity at the temperature T at constant volume.[18] Combining these relations, Rosenfeld obtained

$$(14.14) \qquad \langle (\Delta T)^2 \rangle^{\frac{1}{2}} \langle (\Delta E)^2 \rangle^{\frac{1}{2}} = k_B T^2.$$

---

[17]Bungé [**1956**], pp. 147–148, also briefly discussed an example like this.

[18]Formulas of this type date back to Brownian motion and blackbody radiation fluctuation calculations in the early twentieth century. See, for example, Lorentz [**1912**], pp. 42, and the calculations leading up to it. For more recent derivations, see Lev Landau and E. H. Lifshitz [**1958**], pp. 352, 355–356, or Goodstein [**1975**], pp. 76–78. The particle volumes are assumed to be fixed so $\Delta V = 0$ in these calculations.

Since this relation does not depend on the heat capacity, it is independent of the size of the system. Rosenfeld argued further that because

(14.15) $$k_B \propto \mathcal{A}^{-1},$$

where $\mathcal{A}$ is Avogadro's number, the quantity k_B is an atomistic parameter similar to h.[19] Rosenfeld proposed these relations as an example of classical limitations similar to the quantum uncertainty relations. In reference to this work, Rosenfeld [**1961b**], p. 387, spoke of a complementarity between the microscopic description of matter, given in terms of energy relationships, and the macroscopic description expressed in terms of the temperature.

An examination of the steps Rosenfeld used to establish the connection between the "fluctuations" of temperature and heat in the above sequence of calculations shows that his derivation is misleading and does not support his conclusion. To see this, let us use the definition of the average equilibrium energy $\mathcal{H}_k^\epsilon = \langle \mathcal{H}_k^\epsilon(Q_k, P_k) \rangle_{k\epsilon}$ and the facts that the derivative of the partition function with respect to β_k is $\partial Z_k^\epsilon / \partial \beta_k = -\mathcal{H}_k^\epsilon$ and the heat capacity is $C_V = \partial \mathcal{H}_k^\epsilon / \partial T_k$. Using these definitions with Gibbs' definition of $F_k^\epsilon(Q_k, P_k)$ gives

(14.16)
$$\langle (\Delta E_k)^2 \rangle = \frac{1}{Z_k^\epsilon} \int dQ_k \int dP_k \, F_k^\epsilon(Q_k, P_k)(\mathcal{H}_k^\epsilon(Q_k, P_k) - \mathcal{H}_k^\epsilon)^2$$
$$= -\frac{\partial \mathcal{H}_k^\epsilon}{\partial \beta_k} = k_B T_k^2 \frac{\partial \mathcal{H}_k^\epsilon}{\partial T_k}$$
$$= C_V k_B T_k^2.$$

For the variance of the temperature, the phase average of the square of the formula

(14.17) $$\Delta T_k = \left(\frac{\partial T_k}{\partial \mathcal{H}_k^\epsilon} \right)_{V, \mathcal{N}_k} \Delta E_k$$

yields

(14.18) $$\langle (\Delta T_k)^2 \rangle_{k\epsilon} = \frac{1}{C_V^2} \langle (\Delta E_k)^2 \rangle_{k\epsilon} = \frac{k_B T_k^2}{C_V}.$$

This means in fact that the variance of the energy and that of the temperature are proportional and not reciprocal; as a consequence, these quantities cannot

---

[19]k_B can be defined using the mass, m, average velocity, $\bar{v}$, and the temperature of the particles of a gas by making use of the following formula

$$\tfrac{1}{2} m \overline{v^2} = \tfrac{3}{2} k_B T^2.$$

If M is the mass of one mole of the gas, then $m = M/\mathcal{A}$ and the proportion (14.15) follows. The numerical value of k_B is $1.38 \times 10^{-16} ergs/\deg K$.

be related in the same way that $\langle(\Delta x)^2\rangle$ and $\langle(\Delta p_x)^2\rangle$ are related in the uncertainty relations.[20]

The variance of the temperature calculated for an isolated system is usually interpreted, as Rosenfeld did, as a fluctuation in the temperature. If the definition of temperature in terms of the average energy is adopted, as was done above, it is hard to see how this can be real for isolated systems for which the energy is fixed and definite. Mandelbrot [**1962**], pp. 1035–1036, has argued convincingly that the variance of the temperature of an isolated system should rather be viewed as the measure of the goodness of the estimate for the temperature of the system. I adopt Mandelbrot's suggestion, which is consistent with (14.18), and conclude finally that Rosenfeld has not demonstrated a genuine case of complementarity here.

Another important point is that this example is not of the type that Bohr envisioned. Rosenfeld used calculations for the variances of both the temperature and the energy that are in fact consequences of equilibrium theory and do not represent a juxtaposition of the 'statistical description', conditioned by the temperature, and the 'complete dynamical description' as Bohr was proposing. This means that the attempts by Heisenberg, Rosenfeld, and other authors to exhibit a classical form of complementarity do not represent what Bohr had in mind in his 1930 lecture. It follows that Bohr's claim of complementarity in classical physics cannot be supported by this example and the calculations made in conjunction with it. The analysis above indicates that it is not likely that there are other situations in classical physics in which we would be inclined to attribute a complementary relationship to two descriptions.

In spite of the failure of these attempts to demonstrate complementarity in classical physics, Bohr's intuition that something in this situation has epistemological implications was correct. To pursue the question further it is necessary to go on to a deeper analysis of the underlying issues in this branch of classical physics and to some old and new work on the relation of the macroscopic and microscopic modes of description.

14.7 Subject and Object in Classical Physics

Maxwell [**1877**], p. 2, observed that the standard procedure of physical science is to select a system for study and neglect the rest of the universe. Without explicit notice, the subject/object distinction is maintained by this procedure in that the knowing subject is not included in the system studied. A division such as this of the world into distinct systems or macroscopic

---

[20] J. Lindhard [**1985**], pp. 101–102, has independently come to the same conclusion. He went on to develop another approach to a temperature/energy complementarity based on fluctuation theory in equilibrium thermodynamics. This attempt fails also for reasons similar to those that are brought to bear in this section.

objects—and the consequent replacement of the microscopic Hamiltonian evolution equation of an isolated system (the universe) by a collection of the Hamiltonian evolution equations of its subsystems (the system under study and the rest of the universe)—is a situation that the formalism of the Theory of Interacting Systems is designed to describe.

Bohr made the subject/object distinction the basis for his analysis of the possibilities of knowledge. The central question for Bohr's approach to epistemology, then, is to give a justification for why the subject/object distinction is required at all. The obvious philosophical answer—that there must be something independent that observes something else in order that knowledge can be acquired—is unilluminating. The underlying question is whether this distinction is just a philosophical matter or has implications for the representation of the system in terms of physics. Even if it is required in quantum mechanics, the question remains whether this distinction is required in the classical case.

Bohr's answer to this question, framed in TIS terminology, is that for one system to observe and acquire knowledge of another system, their variables must be separated. Because we can view two systems of particles, which may include the observer as one of the systems, together as one large system, we can always give in principle a microscopic description of both together. In this case each particle in one system can potentially interact with each particle in the other system. An instrument reading in this case is at least implicitly a function of both systems and we cannot unambiguously separate the contribution of either system in the outcome of an experiment.

In TIS, the separation of the variables belonging to different systems is achieved by expressing the influence of other systems on a given system exclusively in terms of the system external potential. As illustrated in the definition (14.6), the k system external potential $\Phi_{k,x}(Q_k, t)$ is expressed as a function only of the locations of the set of particles at positions $Q_k = \times_{i \in k} q_i$, for $i \in k$, and the time. It does not refer to the locations of the particles in any other system because they have been averaged over. The same is true for the l system external potential that does not depend on the locations of the k particles. This method of achieving the separation is compatible with the standard procedure mentioned by Maxwell. With this separation, the probability distribution representing a system depends only on the variables associated with that system and is independent of the distributions representing the other systems. The separation of interacting systems in this way is called the *independence approximation* in TIS. In this approximation, independent Schrödinger equations are set up for each individual system that belongs to the collection of subsystems. It follows that this procedure is needed in both the classical and quantum cases to achieve the independence of systems and thereby the subject/object separation.

The TIS approach to dividing the world can be summarized as follows: First, an isolated system is described by its Hamiltonian formalism. This system is then subdivided into a collection of interacting subsystems and a Hamiltonian formalism is defined for each of the subsystems so that they can be studied separately. When a system k is selected for study, the others form the environment of that system and influence the k system only though its external potential $\Phi_{k,x}(Q_k, t)$. The use of these average external potentials allows us to represent the subsystems as independent of each other in the sense of probability—even though they may be exchanging energy, momentum, and angular momentum through their boundaries. When the subsystems are described as independent in this way, the probability distribution density for the collection of subsystems as a whole can be written as the product of the subsystem probability distribution densities. This 'independent systems' assumption is the physical correlative of the philosophical subject/object distinction.[21]

How a large system is divided into subsystems is a matter of choice and is not forced on us in any particular way except for maintaining a few formal requirements. Some ways are more convenient than others are and some divisions respect the surfaces of macroscopic objects, but this is not a requirement.

14.8 Microscopic and Macroscopic

The terms 'microscopic' and 'macroscopic' have been used without defining them very closely. For the most part, microscopic considerations are important when we are dealing with lengths that are a few Ångstrøms (10^{-8} cm) and below. Macroscopic considerations are important for lengths a few microns (10^{-4} cm) and above. These lengths correspond roughly to atom-sized entities and to the limit of resolution of a light microscope, respectively. The radius of a typical nucleus is on the order of 10^{-12} cm, which is about the size of the classical electron radius ($e^2/m_e c^2$), where e is the electron charge, m_e is the electron mass, and c is the velocity of light. The Compton wavelength of the electron, defined by $\hbar/m_e c$, is 10^{-11} cm.[22]

The notions of size and complexity have often been invoked to explain entropy, complementarity, or the non-classical behavior observed in quantum situations. Rosenfeld [**1961a**], p. 384, for example, quoted Protagoras' statement that 'man is the measure of all things' and claimed that complementarity is related to size. Although no details supporting this claim were given, there is a germ of truth in his idea. Quantum effects are seldom encountered in a macroscopic setting. Furthermore, and this is the important point, the fact

---

[21]The classical version of the TIS formalism outlined here is given in more detail in CIS and the quantum version appears in QIS.

[22]h is Planck's constant and $\hbar = h/2\pi = 1.05450 \times 10^{-27}$ erg-seconds.

that we are composed of macroscopic collections of heterogeneous microscopic elements is crucial for what we can do.

The starting point for the argument supporting this claim is that life is necessarily a macroscopic affair—even though it is constructed on a molecular substrate. All life is based essentially on some form of information processing. Even the parasitic forms of DNA and proteins such as viruses, phages, and prions, require a macroscopic living host whose information systems they tap into. For those sentient life forms that can hunt for prey, find shelter, and reproduce sexually, much more is required.

Our concerns are also macroscopic. We have no interest in the activities of individual molecules, per se. On the most basic level, we are interested in our own homeostasis and acquiring the information we need for survival. From that point of view, when we encounter a tiger unexpectedly in the jungle, we are not concerned with what the tiger's molecules are doing. We only want to know if the tiger is aware of us. Similarly, we eat food, not molecules. While these observations seem trivial, they actually represent a significant epistemological point.

Size also has an influence on the reality an organism will encounter. What counts as an object depends on what you are. This means, as Indian philosophers realized many thousands of years ago and Uexküll pointed out much later, that the objects of interest to a gnat, with its corresponding "gnat consciousness", and those objects of interest to a person are likely to be quite different. But that does not make one view of the universe better than the other. The reality we experience is adapted to our needs. Indeed, it may not be possible to coordinate all the realities of sentient beings into one superordinate view.

Objects are the currency of the world. We hang concepts on them and use them to fulfill our desires. We attach properties to objects and fill our imagination with them. We associate reality with the set of objects we allow into our consciousness and our world. This collection is not static. Things thought to be very real by most people in the past have faded from the consciousness of most people in the present and other things have similarly come into being. As measuring instruments and theories have changed and become more refined, the set of entities that can count as objects has changed and become more refined as well. One can rephrase the old joke, which states that when you have a hammer everything looks like a nail, and say that the creation of new hammers has led to the discovery of new nails and vice versa.

The concept of an object has been the subject of some philosophical attention. Objects for Kant, as pointed out in Chapter 10, are those components of the appearances that we are tempted to ascribe properties to. He concluded that what it means to be an object depends on us: "the possibilities for experience and our understanding of experience determine what is to count in the world as an object or thing."

Object-oriented computer theorists are currently doing some of the most interesting work on objects. For them, objects are conceptual models of reality. They have, in a sense, dematerialized our reifications and used the results to represent the world. The objects of the computer theorist play roles in dynamical sequences of states, transitions, ongoing activities, and events. A specific model of the behavior of the system is called a *use case*. Each use case can be expressed in one or more *scenarios*, which are specific sequences of states, transitions, activities and events for a specific collection of objects in a given context. Use cases are employed to represent system requirements in terms of the functions or processes that the software needs to provide. The point of these comments is that the notion of an object vis á vis a theory of knowledge is not obvious and requires elucidation.

I contend that the concept of an object is properly macroscopic, although it is used loosely for microscopic entities such as atoms. I am therefore recommending that the philosophical notion of an object be limited to things that can, at least in principle, be named, identified, examined, tracked, and accounted for. Except in rare circumstances, such as experiments using scanning tunneling microscopes and their successors in which individual atoms are being viewed or manipulated, this recommendation limits the notion of an object to macroscopic entities. Moreover, it is not possible, even in principle, for a sentient object composed of atoms to name and track each atom it is made of.[23] The point is that knowledge itself is macroscopic in character. It is limited in quantity and scope to the bandwidth available for receiving information and the mechanisms available to process and store it. To function, a knowing subject must meet the requirements stated above and have sensory organs, a memory, an associator, a comparator, and a planner. Because atoms have no pockets, so to speak, they cannot individually have memory except in an elliptical sense when they are in a metastable excited state. Nor can they have a comparator or a planner. This implies that knowledge, its acquisition and employment are all macroscopic affairs.

The issues of size or objecthood are also important in physics. In the Theory of Interacting Systems a sharp distinction is made between those concepts that function at the microscopic level and those that function on the macroscopic level. The microscopic concepts are those associated with the Hamiltonian mechanics of particles. The macroscopic concepts are those of thermodynamics and macroscopic mechanics, which includes the system volume, temperature, entropy, and pressure, as well as any other macroscopic boundary conditions that may be imposed on the system. The concepts of time, position, momentum, angular momentum, and energy function at both levels. The distinction between macroscopic and microscopic in this context

---

[23] Aside from the storage, memory and data processing problems, for the knowing subject to know itself in complete microscopic detail would likely lead to a serious problem with self reference and paradox.

14.8 MICROSCOPIC AND MACROSCOPIC

is reflected in how the concepts are used. In the microscopic particle world, there are no surfaces or volumes defined in any intrinsic or natural way. This means that volume, and the associated concept of a boundary, are clearly macroscopic concepts. The temperature and entropy reflect their macroscopic origins in the dependence of their definitions on the system distribution as a whole.[24]

The data provided as the raw results of experiments is macroscopic from Bohr's point of view in that it is always described and communicated using concepts suited to the conceptual framework of macroscopic beings. The description of the instruments used to make the measurements, which is the theoretical model of these instruments, is also macroscopic in that a macroscopic collection of matter is being used to define the experimental context, often in the form of providing an external potential, that is experienced by the system under observation. The results themselves, as spots on a photographic plate or some other signs in some other medium, are accessible to us as macroscopic beings with limited powers of resolution.

In spite of the resonance between these points and the position Bohr was stating in his *main argument,* it was shown in Chapter 13 that his justification of that position in terms of requirements on communication and the use of language do not work. I have also made the point in this section that the knowing subject is necessarily macroscopic in nature and concerns. In the light of these results, let us reconsider Bohr's *main argument* that was presented in Section 8.2. To begin with, in spite of the objections presented here to the justifications he used in the *main argument,* the thrust of Bohr's epistemological point is sound. The purpose of the *main argument* was to show how the subject/object distinction works with regard to observation and theory in physics and establish that it is essential in quantum mechanics and perhaps elsewhere. His justification failed because the concept of communication and the nature of language do not fit the roles in which he cast them.

With these ideas in mind, and some trepidation, I will make some replacements in Bohr's *main argument* to fix these flaws. I will replace 'classical terms' with 'macroscopic terms', 'unambiguous language' with 'macroscopic concepts'. I will also turn the phrase "implies the impossibility of any sharp separation between the behavior of atomic objects and the interaction with the measuring instrument which serves to define the conditions under which the phenomena appear" into "is a consequence of the requirement of a sharp separation between the variables describing the observed system and those describing the measuring instrument that serves to define the conditions under which the macroscopic results of the experiment appear". With these changes, I write the *Revised Main Argument* in the form:

---

[24]See CIS for the definition of the temperature analog.

"... *however far the phenomena transcend the scope of classical physical explanation, the account of all evidence must be expressed in macroscopic terms*. The argument is simply that by the word "experiment" we refer to a situation where we can tell others what we have learned and that, therefore, the account of the experimental arrangement and the results of observation must be expressed in macroscopic concepts with suitable application of the terminology of physics. This crucial point is a consequence of the *requirement of a sharp separation between the variables describing the observed system and those describing the measuring instrument that serves to define the conditions under which the macroscopic results of the experiment appear.*"

This argument expresses the need for the subject/object separation in the description of experiments and interpretation of the results. Macroscopic concepts, when used for the expression of experimental results, meet this requirement *ipso facto*.

Let us examine next the other requirements that Bohr imposed on experiments. First, an experiment must be closed so that observations will be definite, unambiguous, and well defined (in Bohr's terminology). The measuring instrument may be analyzed using quantum mechanical concepts and methods, but the requirement that the description is macroscopic—in both the design of the experiment and the account of its results—means that quantum superpositions of its measuring components (meter pointer, spot locator) must not be observable in this experiment. We in fact determine that a particular macroscopic object is suitable as a measuring instrument for this experiment by demonstrating that quantum mechanical ambiguities do not vitiate its use for that purpose in this setting. The connection between the measuring instrument and the system measured is described by a classical potential computed using a macroscopic model of the measuring instrument. This maintains the proper subject/object distinction because the variables describing the subject (i.e., the "detached subject" or measuring instrument for Bohr) and those describing the object are separated. These requirements on measurement will be examined in the next chapter in which a theory of measurement compatible with Bohr's views will be introduced and compared with von Neumann's.

CHAPTER 15

Bohr's Approach to Quantum Measurement

The outcome of a valid measurement is an observation. Behind this simple statement lies a sea of interpretation and controversy. The main question at stake in this chapter is whether a purely epistemological solution to the problem of measurement in quantum mechanics can be provided. The overall success of Bohr's program for understanding and interpreting quantum mechanics in epistemological terms rests on it.

15.1 Measuring Instruments

The theory of measurement is where quantum mechanics intersects the macroscopic world. Macroscopic instruments are set up to interact with microscopic systems to make this connection for us. It is appropriate, therefore, to begin with a discussion of what is required for something to be a measuring instrument. This is followed by an analysis of the differences between Bohr and von Neumann concerning how measurements are to be expressed formally and results computed.

In the Revised Main Argument that was presented in the last chapter, I rephrased Bohr's requirement that a measuring instrument be described by suitable classical concepts as the requirement that it be described by suitable macroscopic concepts. It is true that statements of classical mechanics are part of a conceptual framework that is consistent with our ordinary macroscopic experience when applied to the description of macroscopic objects and their dynamics. However, from the TIS perspective, concepts of classical mechanics are neither macroscopic nor microscopic *per se* because this distinction rests on how the concepts are being used, that is, on which concepts are part of the microscopic dynamical description and which are concerned with the macroscopic boundary conditions and the description of the measuring instrument. Some concepts, such as the energy, momentum, or angular momentum, can play a role in both contexts. Some, like the system volume, are purely macroscopic. Moreover, the set of physical concepts that can have macroscopic significance is much larger than the small set of concepts that play a role in classical or quantum Hamiltonian mechanics.

Considerations of language are not allowed in the Revised Main Argument as a justification for requirements or limitations on measuring instruments, experimental arrangements, theoretical descriptions, or anything else. The requirement is that only those concepts that are being used in a macroscopic sense are allowed for the characterization of instruments and data. These modifications of Bohr's principles are important because they remove a significant obscurity in his thought. They also reflect how Bohr actually used classical concepts to characterize measuring instruments and state the results of the measurement.

Bohr observed that a macroscopic measuring instrument is obviously composed of many particles and certainly requires a quantum mechanical description to account for its structure and stability. To use it successfully as a measuring instrument therefore requires that we can show that quantum fluctuations and superpositions in the instrument will not mask the effects being measured. This means computing theoretically how the measuring instrument will react to various inputs of the quantity to be measured in a microscopic system and showing that the value of the microscopic quantity in the range under consideration can be reliably measured. In practice, meeting the requirement for a macroscopic description of the instrument's behavior usually means representing the connection between the instrument and the measured system by a classical, possibly time-dependent, instrument potential $\Phi_M(Q_k, t)$ that is used in the Schrödinger equation of the observed system k.

A case in point is the Stern-Gerlach experiment in which the magnetic field gradients in the measuring instrument are described by a classical computation based on the macroscopic geometry of the pole pieces and the currents through them. Another example is an experiment in which an incoming beam of particles encounters a target and the behavior of the scattered beam is observed. The incoming beam is usually described in idealized macroscopic terms as a planewave incoming state and various types of instruments at various locations are used to detect the scattered beam. Alternatively, in experiments such as Compton's experiment, the photon projectile and the electron target are both treated quantum mechanically and the detection of the scattered particles is by means of macroscopically described instruments.

To make an observation requires both a measuring instrument and an idealized model of it. One does the work; the other plays the role of the instrument in theoretical calculations and interpretations of the results.[1] When an actual piece of equipment used for measurements is examined closely, we see that the sharp boundaries and volumes employed in our calculations are gross idealizations. In a double slit experiment, for example, real slits are rough over very small, but macroscopic, distances. These imperfections do not matter because the linearity of Schrödinger's equation implies that superpositions of solutions of are also solutions. This means that the imperfections will be generally be too small to measure or will cancel by destructive interference at a sufficient (macroscopic) distance from the slit. An explicit example of an investigation of the suitability of the model for the double slit experiment was the demonstration by G. Beck and H. M. Nussenzveig [**1958**] that the properties assigned to the double slit arrangement by the model are consistent with quantum mechanics. They, pp. 1075–1076, computed the results expected for slits of various widths and showed that certain aspects of the description diverge for very narrow slits, but the uncertainty relations are never violated.

Macroscopic Operators.

There are a number of other issues associated with measurement that have been raised in the literature. The question of the association between a given instrumental arrangement and a microscopic quantum mechanical operator that acts only on the system state, and the related question of how to associate a microscopic operator for a given physical quantity with some

---

[1]The idealized nature of the measuring instrument in theoretical calculations was emphasized by Duhem [**1906**] and Cassirer [**1923a**]. See also the statement by Kuhn concerning the need for a physical model of the instrument quoted in Reflection 16 in Section 8.7.

instrument to measure it, have both been mentioned as issues for quantum mechanics. As discussed above, this lack of a prescriptive connection between operators and instruments is at the root of some of the complaints that quantum mechanics is incomplete.[2] One version of this objection was brought up by Schrödinger [**1954**], although it was little noticed at the time or since. He argued that quantum mechanics is incomplete because it does not contain operators for measuring the (macroscopic) angles between crystal faces. The basic question Schrödinger was considering is how macroscopic objects, as collections of microscopic particles, are to be represented in the quantum mechanical formalism. This issue is central to our understanding of how the macroscopic world emerges from its microscopic substrate and to the justification of the use of macroscopic collections of particles as measuring instruments.

Von Neumann [**1932**], pp. 354–357, reviewed the requirements on a successful measurement in nonrelativistic cases in which it is not assumed that the measurement is instantaneous. As examples, he considered the processes of the emission of light, the emission of a particle, and bringing a particle to rest in a potential. In each case, he showed that the experimental arrangement should be set up so that the evolution of the measured component of the system during the measurement is small, i.e., so that the operator $\mathbf{A}$ being measured commutes with the Hamiltonian operator $\mathcal{H}$ as much as possible. He showed that this is the case for measurement of the momentum or location in the three examples above when the light quantum is not reabsorbed, the particle has a large mass, or the potential is constant. When these conditions hold, the momentum operator $\mathbf{p}$ or the position operator $\mathbf{q}$ effectively commutes with the Hamiltonian operator $\mathcal{H}$.

These ideas were extended by von Neumann [**1932**], pp. 398–416, into a demonstration that the operators associated with a macroscopic measuring instrument commute in what he called the *macroscopic approximation*. In considering the approximation of operators, he noted that questions concerning whether the measurement of an operator falls within a given interval can be reframed as yes/no questions, which are the same as 1/0 projection operators. He began with a discussion of the entropy in quantum thermodynamics and showed, in agreement with Gibbs' classical result, that the calculated entropy is constant for a system undergoing evolution in accord with Schrödinger's equation. This led him to investigate measurements of macroscopic quantities in which we have very limited information on the microscopic state of the system. Using an idea of E. P. Wigner's, he worked out the example of an observer who can measure the pressure and temperature in each cubic centimeter of a gas and nothing else.

---

[2]This incompleteness claim is not the same as those that are based on the fact that properties cannot be assigned to atomic entities in the same way they are for macroscopic objects.

The main issue of concern to von Neumann was the simultaneous measurability of the macroscopic operators approximating microscopic operators. For the simultaneous measurement of the coordinate **q** and momentum **p** for a given particle, two observations are needed. These are represented by two different and independently generated spots on one or more photographic plates. Let us represent the macroscopic operators by $\mathbf{Q}'$, $\mathbf{P}'$ and their corresponding measured results by q', p'. Von Neumann argued that q' and p' are the quantities that we actually measure. He set as a general procedure for macroscopic observations that: (1) the set $\mathbf{A}, \mathbf{B}, \ldots$ of microscopic operators, which generally do not commute with each other, should be replaced with a corresponding set $\mathbf{A}', \mathbf{B}', \ldots$ of macroscopic operators that do commute with each other. He then observed that (2) if $\epsilon_A, \epsilon_B, \ldots$ are the magnitudes of the operators $\mathbf{A}' - \mathbf{A}, \mathbf{B}' - \mathbf{B}, \ldots$, then the quantity $\epsilon_A \epsilon_B$ is of the order of magnitude of $[\mathbf{A}, \mathbf{B}]$. He placed as a condition on the macroscopic operators that they reproduce a given microscopic result with a small variance. That is, if a'_n is the result of measuring $\mathbf{A}'$ for the system in state ϕ_n, then it is required that $\langle \phi_n | (\mathbf{A} - a'_n \mathbf{1})^2 | \phi_n \rangle \leq \epsilon_A^2$ for some small ϵ_A.

After working out the details, von Neumann showed that a set of commuting macroscopic operators can be constructed that answers all the macroscopic questions we can ask about the system for any given experimental arrangement. As part of this, he showed that the Hamiltonian energy $\mathcal{H}$ cannot be one of these macroscopic operators, which is generally plausible because the energy cannot be measured with complete accuracy in a macroscopic measurement due to the interaction between the measuring instrument and the system needed for the measurement. Von Neumann, p. 409, observed that the outcome of his procedure of constructing a complete set of commuting macroscopic observables is analogous to the division of phase space into cells in the classical coarse-graining procedure. Using this formalism as a basis, he went on to show that the macroscopic coarse-grained entropy increases in time as the system evolves in accord with the Schrödinger equation.

Size Requirements on the Measuring Instrument.
Calculations making precise the size of the instrument needed for making a given measurement, and related questions concerned with ascertaining that the instrument is suitable for the purpose, were performed in the 1950s and 1960s. These calculations extended the statements of Bohr, quoted in Section 7.3, and others on the need for instruments that are sufficiently heavy so that we can give a completely classical account of their relative positions and velocities, and Bohr's later example of an ordinary clock as an instrument that meets this criterion. Estimates of the size and mass of the measuring instrument needed were discussed by Wigner [**1952**], Huzihiro Araki and Mutsuo M. Yanase [**1960**] and Yanase [**1961**].[3] Part of the concern of these authors

---

[3] See also the review and discussion of this work in H. Stein and A. Shimony [**1970**].

was to show that an operator that does not commute with an additive conserved operator cannot be measured exactly. They went on to show that this operator could be measured approximately by a measuring instrument that is large enough to be in a superposition of many quantum states of the conserved quantity. Yanase also computed the probability that the measurement could fail. Wigner [**1963**] subsequently reviewed these issues.

While a complete set of commuting operators represents the maximal set of values that can be fixed in a given experimental arrangement in quantum mechanics, the issue of concern now is how the quantum mechanical description of atomic processes meshes with the observed events in the macroscopic world. The question is whether we have to deal with superpositions of macroscopic states that are "ambiguous", to use Bohr's terminology, for which there is the possibility that they will be resolved suddenly by observers into very different definite macroscopic outcomes.

The question of setting up and observing macroscopic quantum mechanical states is significant and independent to some degree of the interpretation of the wavefunction adopted. Work in this area has been reviewed by A. J. Leggett [**1980**], [**1985**], [**1998**]. He [**1985**] considered an experiment in which there are two possible microscopic states, ψ_1 and ψ_2.[4] Leggett gave the example of a double slit experiment, which he described in terms of the wavefunction for photons passing through slit 1, ψ_1, the wavefunction for photons passing through slit 2, ψ_2, and $\psi_1 + \psi_2$ is the combined wavefunction for the experiment when both slits are open.[5] Leggett let the wavefunctions Ψ_a and Ψ_b represent the "macroscopic wavefunctions" of two photon detectors located behind the slits. When the experiment is in operation, a detector is triggered when a photon enters it. Leggett concluded from this arrangement that the superposition $\psi_1 + \psi_2$ of the photon wavefunctions for the two slits leads to the superposition $\Psi_a + \Psi_b$ of the macroscopic detector wavefunctions. In his, pp. 46–47, discussion of measurement, he mentioned two steps. The first step, which he claimed is noncontroversial and accepted by most physicists, requires that the detector or measuring instrument exhibit a great deal of irreversibility in to order to "stabilize the result of the measurement". When this is the case, one can proceed to the second step and assign a definite macrostate (not a superposition) to the combination of detectors. Otherwise,

---

[4]I will present the experiment in the form Leggett presented it. It is clear that Bohr would not have agreed with some of the ways in which Leggett has characterized the experiment and the "macroscopic quantum states" of the detectors in particular.

[5]The state ψ_1 describes a situation in which slit 1 is open and slit 2 is closed. The state ψ_2 describes the reverse situation. The state ψ_3 is defined as the description of the situation when both slits are open. M. D. Semon and J. R. Taylor [**1987**], I, p. 28, footnote 6, discussed this situation and observed that many texts state that $\psi_3 = \psi_1 + \psi_2$ because of the superposition principle. However, ψ_3 is different from $\psi_1 + \psi_2$ because these three states satisfy different boundary conditions. Nevertheless, Semon and Taylor observed that $\psi_1 + \psi_2$ may be a good approximation for ψ_3 if ψ_1 is 0 in the neighborhood of slit 2 and ψ_2 is 0 in the neighborhood of slit 1.

as Leggett put it, if we are faced with a superposition of the macroscopic detector wavefunctions at the end of the measurement, the question is how we get any definite result at all.

To get at this question, Leggett observed that a macroscopic superposition of states has not yet been shown experimentally. His discussion of how this might be accomplished showed how difficult it actually is to see such an effect. Leggett considered the possibility that macroscopic objects may always be in a definite pure state. He introduced a set of postulates for this case that define what he called *macrorealism*. According to macrorealism, a macroscopic body is (1) always in one of these states and not a superposition of them, (2) the state can be determined noninvasively, (i.e., measured without modifying it), and (3) the results of the measurement of a finite subset of these states holds true for an infinite ensemble of them. Leggett then showed that these assumptions lead to predictions that contradict quantum mechanics.[6]

The existence of quantum superpositions per se in macroscopic collections of matter is not the major issue as Leggett realized in his later work. Araki and Yanase in fact made the existence of many possible superpositions of the state of an instrument with respect to a conserved quantity one of the criteria for its suitability as a measuring instrument in certain cases. The question is whether a superposition of quantum states can be set up in which the center of mass of a system, or some other macroscopically measurable feature, occupies two macroscopically distinguishable locations.[7]

Bohr did not divide the world into macroscopic and microscopic aspects with separate and incompatible descriptions. He clearly felt that quantum mechanics is adequate to describe all collections of matter. Thus, regardless of whether macroscopic superpositions can be demonstrated experimentally or not, the use of an aggregate of matter as a measuring instrument and describing it macroscopically rests on a logical and epistemological distinction, not a physical one. From Bohr's point of view, we need only show that the quantum aspects of the instrument will not interfere with its use in the measurement. The possibility of macroscopic superpositions and the question of how we can get any experimental results at all rest on the question of what the quantum state represents. In the substantialistic interpretations of the wavefunction, we are faced with the prospect that the world is continually piling superpositions of possibilities on possibilities as quantum events occur. Since individual microscopic events, such as the absorption of a photon or particle, can be made to trigger macroscopic events, this implies that the macroscopic world would also be infected by the essential ambiguity at its

---

[6]See also Leggett [**1980**], [**1998**], and Wigner [**1963**].

[7]See the recent measurement in the experiment by H. C. Manoharan, C. P. Lutz, and D. M. Eigler [**2000**] that is interpreted by its authors as a 'quantum mirage' in which a Cobalt atom resonance is observed at two distinct locations. Many other such experiments with photons and particles are underway.

root. An observer in this world could destroy a large building with a glance. However, we never see anything like this.

There is a tendency to write down symbols for the wavefunctions assigned to macroscopic collections of matter, including sentient beings, and discuss the situation as if these symbols were just like those for single particles or small collections of particles in quantum mechanics. It seems to be assumed that the treatment of macroscopic collections of particles in quantum mechanics is a trivial extension of the existing formalism. However, this is not obvious and must be established. That was part of the point behind the objection raised in Schrödinger [**1954**] concerning the lack of a characterization of macroscopic objects in quantum mechanics and part of my objection to the conclusions drawn from Schrödinger's cat example. A related point is that the assignment of properties to macroscopic objects is a different issue than assigning them to microscopic entities. While we may be forbidden by quantum mechanics from assigning microscopic properties to atomic entities in the mechanistic sense, this may not apply to the assignment of properties to macroscopic objects—even though the microscopic laws govern all the microscopic constituents of the object. Properties, in this sense, may be macroscopically "emergent". These properties would not "inhere" in the object as part of its "essence" in the sense of materialist metaphysics. They would be of microscopic origin in that they would be a consequence of the quantum description of the collection of particles composing the macroscopic object in the context of the experiment in which these properties appear. This would justify ascribing them to objects of sufficient size under usual conditions in the sense that macroscopic measurements would exhibit them consistently and reproducibly for that object. Support for this conjecture can be found in the version of quantum thermodynamics that appears in QTS.

Let us turn now to the question of the association of a given operator with a particular measuring instrument. When making a measurement it is necessary to show that a particular macroscopic configuration of matter is appropriate for the measurement of the values for a particular quantum mechanical operator. As Bell has pointed out clearly, the measurement of operators, such as the spin operators σ_x and σ_y in the x and y directions for a system consisting of a single particle or atom, is independent of the measurement of the operator $\sigma_x + \sigma_y$ in that each requires a separate configuration of the measuring instrument. The operator $\sigma_x + \sigma_y$ may not even make sense within quantum mechanics when written in this form. We may interpret it, of course, as the operator σ_w, where w is an axis at a 45° angle to the x-axis in the positive quadrant of the (x, y) plane, but this interpretation is neither a consequence of quantum mechanics nor required by it. Similarly, the measurement of the operator $\sigma_y \sigma_x$ is usually interpreted as a measurement of σ_x followed some time later by a measurement of σ_y, but this is not a required interpretation either.

Consider next a complete set of eigenfunctions $\{\,|s^2, s_z\rangle\,\}$ for the operator $\mathbf{s}^2$ representing the square of the total spin and the operator $\mathbf{s}_z$ representing the z component of the spin. Any spin function can be represented in terms of eigenfunctions taken from this complete set. This implies that the eigenfunctions of the operator $\boldsymbol{\sigma}_x + \boldsymbol{\sigma}_y$ may be represented as an infinite sum of terms using eigenfunctions taken from this set. But this mathematical representation does not require or imply a corresponding experimental arrangement for measuring these functions. Nor does it imply that a measurement of each term of the sum in turn will leave the system in the state represented by the eigenfunction of $\boldsymbol{\sigma}_x + \boldsymbol{\sigma}_y$. At present, we must use our classical imagination to fashion a potential that will effect the measurement of the quantity sought, construct a measuring instrument that will present the observed system with this potential, and show for both that they are adequate to the task.[8]

I have raised, without resolving, a number of points that are important to the application of quantum mechanics to the world. Let us go on now to juxtapose the viewpoints of Bohr and von Neumann on measurement as one of the central issues in quantum mechanics and one that crosses the microscopic/macroscopic boundary.

15.2 Bohr and von Neumann

It should be stated from the outset that Bohr did not create a mathematical formalism for quantum measurement. Nor did he consider in detail how von Neumann's formalism should be applied. In Chapters 7 and 8, I observed that Bohr did not accept von Neumann's version of measurement theory. Moreover, Bohr's version of the quantum state, presented in Chapter 8, is not compatible with the way in which von Neumann approached the quantum state. Nevertheless, it appears that he deferred to what he [**1938b**] called "the elegant axiomatic exposition of von Neumann" for describing experiments and calculating probabilities, but imposed on this formalism restrictions on how it can be used and understood. These restrictions are key to understanding the differences between Bohr's point of view and the views of von Neumann and others. They also indicate what Bohr felt was important in a measurement and were used to develop of a version of quantum measurement compatible with his views.

In Chapter 3, some of the issues connected with the theory of measurement in quantum mechanics were examined: (1) the expression of the

---

[8]The general question of associating quantum mechanical operators with observables based on classical observables was addressed by von Neumann and used in his proof of the impossibility of hidden variable theories. These rules were presented in Chapter 5. Over the years since von Neumann proposed them, there have been a number of critiques pointing out inconsistencies in the application of von Neumann's rules and proposing alternatives. See J. R. Shewell [**1959**], QIS, and QTS, for a review of these issues and references to the literature. It would take us too far afield to discuss these questions further here.

subject/object distinction in quantum mechanics; (2) the question of choosing what is to count as part of the system to be observed, the measuring instrument, the observer, everything else, and whether these boundaries matter; (3) the lack of a rule specifying how a particular classical quantity used in the description of a measuring instrument is to be represented as an operator in quantum mechanics (discussed in the last section); (4) the role of the observer in quantum mechanical measurements; and (5) the question of what counts as a completed experiment.

Murdoch is one of the first philosophers to discuss in detail the significant differences between Bohr and others on the issue of measurement. He [1985], Chapter 6, presented a comparison between Bohr's approach to measurement in quantum mechanics and von Neumann's. He characterized measurement for Bohr as involving the recognition that the measuring instrument and measured object form an indissoluble whole and evolve together during the measurement. After the measurement, the pointer of the measuring instrument is simply "read-off". By this means, Murdoch, p. 114, contended that Bohr had given a "brilliantly simple" solution to the measurement problem for which the reduction of the wavefunction is not an issue. However, this solution, according to Murdoch, comes at the expense of a new problem of explaining the definiteness of the state of the combined system after the measurement that corresponds to a definite pointer reading. The important issues for Murdoch were primarily those connected with the question of an intrinsic-values theory of measurement versus his objective-values theory and the question of Bohr's approach to the concept of meaning in these theories.

To explain why the measuring instrument + observed system can yield a pointer reading after the measurement, Murdoch invoked the work of quantum ergodic theorists who claim that the final pure state of the measuring instrument "pointer" is indistinguishable from a mixture of distinct pure states of the pointer. Quantum ergodic theory, and the newer version in the form of decoherence theory, are often interpreted as physical solutions of the measurement problem that show how superpositions are converted into mixtures. These theories actually show that under the proper circumstances final states evolve into approximations of mixtures. From either viewpoint, it is claimed that the outcome of a quantum measurement is equivalent or almost equivalent to one of the alternative outcomes of a classical measurement.

Murdoch, p. 126–128, rejected both von Neumann's theory of measurement and his projection postulate on the grounds that most measurements are not 'ideal', which means that the system is not left in a state that is an eigenfunction of the operator measured. He pp. 128–133, also gave a cogent argument that the usual distinction between pure states and mixtures should be rejected. He supported this argument by analyzing the employment of the wavefunction in several experiments. However, his rejection of the distinction between pure states and mixtures undercuts his previous view that quantum ergodic theory resolves Bohr's measurement problem.

Murdoch's discussion of the intrinsic-values (microscopic properties) versus objective-values (reproducible measurements) view of the quantum state engages Bohr's views from a philosophical perspective. His account of measurement for Bohr is not adequate, however. First, and foremost, it is not a complete, or completely accurate, rendition of Bohr's characterization of measurement in quantum mechanics. This is shown in an alternative analysis of the relation between von Neumann's theory of measurement and Bohr's that will be presented in this section. Second, the discussion of aspects of quantum ergodic theory and decoherence theory in this chapter and the next shows that Murdoch's resolution the problem of the definiteness of the final instrument state after the measurement using this theory does not work.[9] It is not compatible with Bohr's views either.

Let us return to von Neumann's theory of measurement, introduced in Chapter 3, and critique it step by step using Bohr's perspective.[10] Von Neumann [**1932**], pp. 417–421, expressed Bohr's subject/object distinction as a "cut" between the observer and the observed system. Von Neumann's cut is not identical to Bohr's subject/object distinction, but it is closely related. Consider a measuring instrument M that measures some quantity A in system k. Let x represent the variables of the observed system and y represent the variables of the measuring system. We have the option of representing the interaction between M and k by the Schrödinger equation for the evolution of either the combined system $\Psi(x, y, t)$ or the observed system $\psi(x, t)$ alone. In the former case, M and k are treated as a single system, the particle interactions between the instrument and the system are considered as internal microscopic interactions, and $\Psi(x, y, t)$ is the solution of Schrödinger's equation for the combined system. In the latter case, Schrödinger's equation for the system k is used and the interaction between M and k is represented by a possibly time-dependent potential $\Phi_M(x, t)$ that is obtained theoretically from a macroscopic model of the instrument.[11]

In the double slit case, for example, the potential is a consequence of the physical configuration of the instrument and determines the locations for which $\psi(x, t)$ can propagate and have non-zero values. For the Stern-Gerlach experiment, the potential consists of the inhomogeneous magnetic

---

[9] As mentioned, his (correct) rejection of the distinction between pure states and mixtures also counts against this solution. The issue of pure states and mixtures and its previous scientific literature are discussed in detail in QIS.

[10] For an account of some of the philosophical aspects of von Neumann's theory of measurement and other theories, see Jammer [**1974**], Chapter 11.

[11] Observe that $\Phi_M(x, t)$ is defined only in terms of the macroscopic instrumental arrangement and expresses the value of the instrument potential at the locations x within the measured system. It does not include variables associated with the state of particles in the measuring instrument itself.

field strength that couples to the net spin on the atoms, projected into an up or down state, and guides the atoms into separate channels.

During the measurement of an operator **A** with eigenfunctions $\{\phi_n\}$ and eigenvalues $\{a_n\}$, the combined system evolves from $\Psi(x,y,t_0)$ to $\Psi(x,y,t_1)$, as a Type 2 von Neumann process, in accord with Schrödinger's equation. When the instrument is read, the wavefunction is reduced, in a Type 1 von Neumann process, to the final state wavefunction $\Psi_i(x,y,t_1)$. A measurement according to von Neumann is represented diagrammatically in the form:

$$\Psi(x,y,t_0) \xrightarrow{2} \quad \Psi(x,y,t_1) \quad \xrightarrow{1} \quad \Psi_i(x,y,t_1)$$
$$\downarrow \qquad\qquad \downarrow \qquad\qquad \downarrow$$
$$\psi_0(x)\phi_0(y) \to \sum_n a_n c_n \psi_n(x)\phi_n(y) \to a_i c_i \psi_i(x)\phi_i(y)$$

FIGURE 15.1. Von Neumann's Account of Measurement

The upper row of this diagram represents the evolution of the combined system followed by a reduction of the wavefunction. Von Neumann's interpretation of the sequence of states during the measurement is that the probability of the outcome i with value a_i is $|c_i|^2$ and the system is left in the state ϕ_i.

When the steps involved here are looked at carefully, it is clear that von Neumann had already implicitly made the separation of variables required by Bohr's subject/object distinction when he represented in (4.20) the state $\Psi(x,y,t_0)$ of the combined measuring instrument and system at time t_0 before a measurement as a product, $\Psi(x,y,t_0) = \psi_0(x)\phi_0(y)$, of the separate states of the observed system, $\psi_0(x)$, and the measuring instrument, $\phi_0(y)$. The factored form means that states $\psi(x)$ and $\phi(y)$ are independent of each other in the sense that the state ψ does not depend on the variables of the measuring system and the state ϕ does not depend on the variables of the observed system. Before the measurement, then, von Neumann assumes that the statistical correlation between these states is 0 so the initial probability $|\Psi(x,y,t_0)|^2$ decomposes into the product $|\psi_0(x)|^2|\phi_0(y)|^2$.

Before a measurement, there is usually not much detailed information about a system—perhaps the number of particles involved, their masses, charges, and a physical description of the measuring instrument as the experimental environment. This means that an initial state may be chosen and assigned to the system that is of the form $\psi_0(x)\phi_0(y)$ as long as it is consistent with the experimental arrangement and with the macroscopic information we do have concerning the measuring instrument and the system. This initial assumption of a separable state is not pernicious. From Bohr's point of view, any assignment of a state to the joint system $k+M$ before the beginning of the measurement is arbitrary to this degree because there is no experimental arrangement before the measurement to warrant assigning any other state. In fact, in the absence of an experimental arrangement and a measurement before this one, there are simply no grounds for assigning a state at all from Bohr's perspective. In this sense, the system does not have a state before the measurement in Bohr's quantum mechanics. Bohr does allow an initial state, such as that represented by the planewave approximation of an incoming particle beam, to be prepared, of course, and used as the initial state of a measurement. On the other hand, for those maintaining the point of view that the system is always in some quantum state, von Neumann's claim is that the state assigned initially to a system before a measurement is a formal 'place-holder', so to speak, and does not matter.

From either von Neumann's point of view or Bohr's, assigning the state $\psi_0(x)\phi_0(y)$ at time t_0 to the combined system $k + M$ means that we cannot even pretend that this step is part of the normal evolution of some description of the joint system from prior times under Schrödinger's equation. Having assigned this product state to $k + M$ at time t_0, an interaction between particles in M and k, as is required for most measurements, implies that this product representation will not be valid after time t_0.[12]

If information is needed about either the system or the instrument before the measurement under consideration, a prior measurement on the system can be made. However, at some point this regress must simply be ended and a description given of the operation of the measuring instrument and its interaction with the measured system in terms of a macroscopic model of both the measuring instrument and its operation that is expressed in terms of macroscopic (classical) mechanics and electrodynamics.

Let us now contrast von Neumann's approach to measurement with what I will call *Bohr's theory of measurement*. Although Bohr did not explicitly work out a separate version of the theory of measurement, and as noted seemed to defer to von Neumann's version, I contend, nevertheless, that Bohr had a very different idea in mind when he discussed measurement than von Neumann did.

Von Neumann discussed the issue of measurement in terms of an abstract measuring instrument that displays the result of a measurement by a meter. In discussing the physical aspects of measurement, he spoke of wavepackets, representing particles in motion that move through space and sequentially interact with components of the measuring instrument. For the most part, von Neumann's approach was abstract and mathematical. His goal was to illustrate the proper application of the mathematical formalism of quantum mechanics in his discussion of abstract meter readings in undefined experiments.

Bohr, on the other hand, was very careful from the beginning about what he said about entities and issues encountered in atomic physics. Høffding spoke with approval of the fact that Bohr [**1922**] spoke in terms of "This means that" rather than "This is that." Bohr was equally careful with respect

---

[12] See the discussion in Messiah [**1961**], pp. 126–129.

to measurement. In comparing von Neumann's view of measurement with Bohr's, the distinction between the locutions 'the state of a system' and 'the state assigned to a system' is important. Moreover, Bohr did not discuss measurement in the same abstract terms that von Neumann did. He did assume that the instrument provides us with a macroscopically readable result but he did not assume that the instrument is in some state before or after the measurement. Finally, he did not assume that the state is a property of the entity under discussion or that a system must always be in some state.

Bohr focused on a few concrete experiments that were paradigmatic for him. He discussed the double slit experiment and diffraction gratings, versions of which can be used to compute the wavelengths of light or matter, the gamma ray microscope for measuring the position of a particle, the Stern-Gerlach experiment, which separates a beam of atoms into different discrete channels depending on their net spin, scattering experiments, and atomic transitions. Bohr's goal was to extract from these experiments and their quantum mechanical representation a working knowledge of how to properly apply quantum mechanics to the analysis of other experiments and to the interpretation of their results.

For Bohr, the macroscopic physical model of the measuring instrument serves to define the component of the potential $\Phi_M(x,t)$ contributed by the measuring instrument in the Hamiltonian of the Schrödinger equation. This potential determines a state $\psi(x,t)$ for a quantum system as a solution of Schrödinger's equation for the system with the initial state and macroscopic boundary conditions provided by the measuring instrument. Suppose the set of eigenvalues $\{a_n\}$ and associated set of normalized and mutually orthogonal eigenstates $\{\psi_n(x)\}$ belong to the operator $\mathbf{A}$. Bohr's procedure for the measurement of a quantity represented by the operator $\mathbf{A}$ can be diagrammed as the sequence of steps:

$$\psi(x,t) \to \sum_n a_n c_n(t) \psi_n(x) \to a_i,$$

$$\mathcal{P}(a_i,t) = c_i(t) \int dx\, \psi_i^\dagger(x)\psi(x,t) = |c_i(t)|^2,$$

$$\mathcal{E}_{\psi_i}(\mathbf{A}) = \mathcal{P}(a_i,t)a_i = |c_i(t)|^2 a_i.$$

FIGURE 15.2. Bohr's Account of Measurement

After the experiment is completed at time t, the normalized wavefunction $\psi(x,t)$ is expanded in terms of the set of eigenfunctions of the operator $\mathbf{A}$ with the set $\{c_i(t)\}$ of time-dependent complex coefficients. In light of the normalization of $\psi(x,t)$ and mutual orthogonality of the normalized eigenfunctions of $\mathbf{A}$, it follows that $|c_i(t)| \leq 1$ for each i and that $\sum_i |c_i(t)|^2 = 1$. The measurement itself results in one recorded outcome i with value a_i. The probability $\mathcal{P}(a_i,t)$ of the result a_i at time t is $|c_i(t)|^2$ and the expected value of this result is $|c_i(t)|^2 a_i$. No statement is made about the state of the system at the end the measurement or afterward.

A measurement ends for Bohr when the experiment is closed and the results are recorded. This step corresponds to recording the result a_i for the measurement described above. It has been characterized as the most problematic aspect of Bohr's approach because it replaces von Neumann's wavefunction reduction with his concept of closure. Bohr gave no criterion for judging when an experiment is closed and no explanation of what closes it. He spoke of an irreversible recording of results, but this begs the question of how the evolution of the system in accord with the reversible Schrödinger equation can lead to irreversible results. I will return to these issues in Section 15.4.

Let us compare these two approaches to measurement. When the diagram in Figure 15.1 of von Neumann's theory of measurement is examined, several problems appear. Because a product of independent states is assigned to the combined systems at the beginning of a measurement, a tensor product of the system and measuring instrument Hilbert spaces may be used to represent them. Let us designate the Hilbert space for the system by $\mathcal{H}_k$ and the measuring instrument by $\mathcal{H}_M$. Initially then, the Hilbert space for the combined system can be represented by the tensor product space $\mathcal{H} = \mathcal{H}_k \otimes \mathcal{H}_M$. To get at the first problem, consider the measurement of an operator $\mathbf{A} = \mathbf{A}_k \otimes 1 + 1 \otimes \mathbf{A}_M$ in system k using the measuring instrument M. Assume next for the operator $1 \otimes \mathbf{A}_M$ that $\{\phi_\nu^{(M)}\}$ is a complete set of orthonormal vectors indexed by ν in $\mathcal{H}_M$ that are eigenvalues of $1 \otimes \mathbf{A}_M$ in that space. Similarly, assume for $\mathbf{A}_k \otimes 1$ that $\psi_\mu^{(k)}$ is a complete set of orthonormal vectors in $\mathcal{H}_k$ that are eigenvalues of $\mathbf{A}_k \otimes 1$ in the system space. Let us assign the instrument the state $\chi^{(M)}$ before the measurement and the system the state ψ_μ. According to von Neumann's theory of measurement, the measuring instrument and system are allowed to interact for a short time and the system evolves according to the scheme[13]

(15.1) $$U(t,t_0)(\psi_\mu^{(k)} \otimes \chi^{(M)}) = \psi_\mu^{(k)} \otimes \chi_\mu^{(M)},$$

where $U(t,t_0)$ is the unitary operator that represents the action of Schrödinger's equation in carrying the combined system forward from time t_0 to time t. It is the correlation of the instrument state $\chi_\mu^{(M)}$ with the system state $\psi_\mu^{(k)}$ by the interaction and our ability to ascertain the state $\chi_\mu^{(M)}$ of the instrument that allows the measurement to work.

Following the lead of von Neumann and Wigner, H. Araki and M. M. Yanase [**1960**] went on to show that the scheme (15.1) will not hold and that a measurement of the operator $\mathbf{A}$ for the system k cannot be exact if

---

[13]Degeneracies and other details have been ignored. This formalism is taken from Araki and Yanase [**1960**], p. 622, and Yanase [**1961**], [**1964**].

there is a universal conserved additive quantity for the combined system that does not commute with $\mathbf{A}$. Let us represent the conserved operator in the combined system by $\mathbf{L} = \mathbf{L}_k \otimes 1 + 1 \otimes \mathbf{L}_M$. By a universal conserved quantity they meant that it satisfies the commutation relation $[U(t,t_0), \mathbf{L}] = 0$. The claim of Araki and Yanase is that an exact measurement is impossible unless $[\mathbf{L}_k, \mathbf{A}] = 0$. This result shows already that many measurements, such as those of energy, are often approximations and that von Neumann's formalism is not exact for these cases. For the sake of argument, let us assume that $[\mathbf{L}_k, \mathbf{A}] = 0$ and focus on the other underlying issues.

The Assignment of Quantum States.

To highlight the differences between von Neumann's point of view concerning quantum states and Bohr's, let us examine the popular assumptions that (1) quantum mechanics can be applied to the description of the universe as a whole and (2) a system is always in some quantum state. To make these considerations concrete, assume that there are $\mathcal{N}_t$ particles in the universe. Let us index these particles by i and let $i \in t$ represent particle i out of the set t of the $\mathcal{N}_t$ particles in the universe. The locations of these particles are given by the $3\mathcal{N}_t$-dimensional variable Q_t, where $Q_t = \times_{i \in t} q_i$. With this notation, the set of interparticle interactions $\{\phi_{ij}(q_i - q_j)\}$ for $i,j \in t$, can be used to write a wavefunction for everything, $\Psi_t(Q_t, t)$, as the solution of the Schrödinger equation for the universe. Assuming the initial conditions are known, this state could serve as the "master state" for the universe from which the states of all the subsystems of the universe are derived. Even if the initial conditions were not known, various initial conditions could still be postulated and Schrödinger's equation used to calculate the succeeding states of the universe.

Suppose next that it is decided to divide this isolated universe $U = t$ into components: a system k, a measuring instrument M, and their environment E consisting of everything else, so that $t = k+M+E$. Suppose further M is to be used to make a measurement on k in the context of E. At this point, the problem arises of how to obtain the states $\Psi_k(Q_k, t)$, $\Psi_M(Q_M, t)$, and $\Psi_E(Q_E, t)$ to assign to each of these components and the relation between these states and $\Psi_t(Q_t, t)$. Given the state of the universe $\Psi_t(Q_t, t)$, one method of doing this is to first marginalize Ψ_t for each system at $t = 0$ by integrating in each case over the variables belonging to the other systems and then representing k, M, and E, as independent systems. Under this assumption, the state approximating $\Psi_t(Q_t, t)$ at $t = 0$ is $\Psi_{[t]}(Q_t, 0) = \Psi_k(Q_k, 0)\Psi_M(Q_M, 0)\Psi_E(Q_E, 0)$. In accord with what was called the *independent system approximation* in the last chapter, the particle variables Q_k, Q_M, and Q_E, used in the Schrödinger equations for each of these subsystems are independent of the others. This means that the evolution of the initial state $\Psi_t(Q_t, 0)$, in accord with the Schrödinger equation of the universe, to $\Psi_t(Q_t, t)$ and then marginalizing it to the product form $\Psi_{[t]}^t(Q_t, t)$ is in general distinct from the product state

$\Psi_{[t]}(Q_t, t)$ that evolves from the state $\Psi_{[t]}(Q_t, 0)$ in accord with the separate solutions of the Schrödinger equations of k, M, and E.

A consistent quantum formalism for the universe cannot be based on the assumption that systems are always in quantum states and that these are independent of the designation of some macroscopic collections of matter as experimental arrangements. In any particular case, we have the choice of attempting a wave or a particle experiment on a given system. Since we cannot ever set up or solve the Schrödinger equation for the universe with the appropriate initial conditions, the wavefunction $\Psi_t(Q_t, t)$ is unavailable and the point is moot. In the face of this, von Neumann's theory of measurement sensibly assigns arbitrary wavefunctions to the system, the measuring instrument, and the environment, at the beginning of a measurement.

Under the assumption that particle systems are always in some quantum state, the procedure of dividing the world into parts described above and assigning arbitrary initial wavefunctions to these parts represents a noncausal disjuncture in the state attributed to the components of the universe at the time the experiment begins that is similar to von Neumann's Type 1 change of the wavefunction. It is not hard to show, in the same way von Neumann does for a Type 1 change in a measurement, that the change $\Psi_t(Q_t, t) \to \Psi_{[t]}(Q_t, t)$ never decreases the entropy computed for the universe and usually increases it. In terms of the relation proposed between entropy and information, the increase in entropy is due to discarding information about these correlations in moving from a presumed original state to a product of marginalized states. These steps are implicit in the representation of the situation by the sequence given in Figure 15.1.

The argument is not that quantum mechanics is misapplied in von Neumann's account of the measuring process. His approach to measurement does not require the assumption that quantum systems are always in some quantum state or that there is a wavefunction of the universe. Moreover, the decomposition of the wavefunction Ψ_{k+M} is necessary to meet the requirements of Bohr's subject/object distinction. I am simply pointing out that this decomposition represents an approximation, needed for epistemological reasons, that has an associated cost in the form of an increase in the entropy assigned to the system. This increase in the entropy is an artifact of our choice of representation and not a consequence of a physical process. Because this decomposition of the world into parts is not unique, a different entropy cost will be associated with the choice of a different decomposition into a system, measuring instrument, and environment. It follows that whenever a measurement is made, we step outside the assumed unitary flow of events describable by the formalism and introduce epistemological boundaries into the situation. This is simply an act of choice in how to describe the situation and does not represent a physical or dynamical change in the microscopic description of these systems.

By contrast, Bohr's approach is to impose the subject/object distinction from the outset and use the potentials defined by a classical model of the measuring system to define the Schrödinger equation for the evolution of the measured system. This equation is solved for the system wavefunction and it is used to compute the probabilities of the various outcomes of the experiment.

The Role of Consciousness in Quantum Mechanics.

The second major problem in von Neumann's theory is his use of the observer to 'reduce' the wavefunction and determine a particular outcome for a quantum mechanical measurement. This led to a long series of discussions in the literature concerning the role of consciousness in quantum mechanics. Attempts were made to account for the role of the observer delineated by von Neumann by including the observer in the formalism for a quantum mechanical measurement. The theory presented by Fritz London and Edmond Bauer [**1939**], which included the observer's consciousness in the quantum mechanical formalism, was summarized and critiqued by Abner Shimony [**1963**]. In these approaches, the wavefunction $\psi_O(z)$ of the observer refers to the observer's conscious mind. It is included in the quantum formalism along with the measured system and the measuring system, so that before a measurement the combined quantum state is $\psi_{k,0}(x)\psi_{M,0}(y)\psi_{O,0}(z)$, where the 0 designates the initial wavefunctions. After a measurement of the operator **A**, it is assumed that the measured system k can be represented by a linear combination of the eigenfunctions of the operator **A**. The states of the measuring instrument and the observer are correlated with this as before, so the combined system is in a state that can be represented in the form $\Psi(x,y,z) = \sum_n a_n c_n \psi_{k,n}(x)\psi_{M,n}(y)\psi_{O,n}(z)$. In this version of von Neumann's theory of quantum measurement, the observer decides by introspection what state he or she is in and thereby reduces the wave packet by selecting a particular value for n.

Shimony raised the question of how the observer state $\psi_O(z)$ fits within the formalism of quantum mechanics, that is, whether a Hamiltonian $\mathcal{H}_0$ can be defined for a 'state of mind' so that Schrödinger's equation would apply to it. After reviewing psychological evidence, Shimony argued that superpositions do not seem to be features of mental states or required to explain them. Shimony rightly criticized these extensions of quantum mechanics to 'states of mind' as well as the explicit psychophysical parallelism in von Neumann's point of view. He also raised the question in this regard as to why two different observers will resolve a superposition of the wavefunction into the same result. Shimony [**1963**] rejected this characterization of the mind as requiring a form of "pre-established harmony." [14]

---

[14]It is interesting to note that the pre-established harmony between the observers in von Neumann's theory of measurement plays a role similar to the pre-established harmony between the monads in Leibniz's work.

The issue of consciousness in measurement was also discussed by Wigner [1962]. He introduced two observers. The first observer watches the experiment and the second later questions the first. If the account of London and Bauer is correct, both observers are in a state that is a linear superposition of states at the end of the experiment until each becomes conscious of the result. Suppose the second observer asks the first what the result was and receives an answer. At this point the state of the second observer is reduced to the final state. Then the second observer asks the first observer what she felt before she was asked the result. The first observer tells the second that she knew the result to be what was observed. That is, the first observer had already reduced the resulting state of the instrument. Wigner concluded that this is an example of the influence of consciousness on the physical and chemical conditions on living systems. He felt that these physical and chemical conditions in turn influence the sensations these observers have.[15]

The logical consequence of London and Bauer's approach as extended by Wigner is that everyone's consciousness is involved in every experiment ever performed anywhere in the universe at any time. Each person's mind remains in a superposition of all the possible outcomes of all these experiments. Only those superpositions are resolved for which the observer somehow gains knowledge of the outcome. On the other hand, if one observer resolves the superposition for everyone everywhere, Shimony's criticism concerning a preestablished harmony between the observers applies. Moreover, the fact that simultaneity is not preserved under all relativistic transformations of coordinate frames indicates that some observers will see others in a superposition of outcome states before they see the experiment being performed.

The issue of what qualifies as an observer is another problem for von Neumann's theory of measurement and other theories that interpret the wavefunction in substantivist or "realistic" terms and require consciousness to play a role in changing the wavefunction. D'Espagnat [1995], pp. 328–329, quoted Bell as asking whether a one-celled system or a better-qualified system with a Ph.D. is required for a measurement.

Another objection to the employment of consciousness to project the outcome of the experiment into a specific physical result is concerned with the possibility of error. Suppose photographic plates are exposed in a double slit experiment, but are not developed and read for some time. Are we to assume that the physical systems in the photographic plate remain in a superposition of quantum mechanical states for years and that this superposition is not resolved even when the plates are developed, but only when a conscious observer reads the plates and *understands* the result? Given the observer's role in von Neumann's measurement theory in keeping the quantum mechanical books straight, can an observer reading the plates make a mistake? If the first observer does make a mistake, what is the status of a second observer

---

[15]See the discussion in Jauch [1968], Chapter 11.

reading the plates correctly? The view that the projection of a wavefunction associated with someone's consciousness is a physical process due to that person becoming aware at some point in time of someone else's statement about a prior experiment, and further that these projections have an effect on the physical process measured in the experiment, is therefore not acceptable on many physical and philosophical grounds. Problems of interpretation such as these cast strong doubts on the validity of this approach.

Other Differences Between Bohr and Von Neumann.
The final step in von Neumann's account of measurement leaves the instrument plus system represented as a weighted sum of products of system and instrument states. Each element in this sum represents a possible outcome of the measurement expressed as the product of an eigenvalue and an eigenstate of **A** with an associated instrument state. Von Neumann's view is that the system is now in one of these eigenstates of **A** (the Projection Postulate), but we cannot know which one until the state of the measuring instrument is "measured" in the elliptical sense of an observer taking notice of its result. Here we see that the notion of state is applied to an instrument in a way that Bohr's approach forbids. There is no experimental arrangement to measure the state of the instrument, so Bohr's criterion for being able to assign a definite one to it is not met.

Another difference between Bohr and von Neumann lies in the perspective of each toward the concept of causality. Von Neumann considered the evolution of a system in accord with Schrödinger's equation to be causal and the change in a system due to a measurement to be acausal. He [**1932**], pp. 326–327, also observed that in the macroscopic case there is no experiment that supports causality in the standard sense of classical physics. He maintained that the apparent causality with respect to macroscopic objects is completely independent of the microscopic issue of causality. He attributed the apparent sharpness of the variables characterizing macroscopic objects as one consequence of the law of large numbers, which states that as the number of independent elements in a system becomes infinitely large, the variance of the mean of a set of measurements for quantities summed over these elements tends to zero.[16]

Turning to atomic systems, von Neumann stated that quantum mechanics is our only successful theory in this domain, given the failure of the hidden variable theories, and this militates against the validity of the principle of causality in the microscopic domain. He noted that causal thinking is an age-old way of thinking, but maintained that it is not logically necessary to think in this way. From this perspective, he, p. 328, did not accept those who would reject quantum mechanics because it is not causal in the same

---

[16]See also Schrödinger [**1928a**] on this and the discussion of causality in physics by A. P. Ushenko [**1953**].

way classical mechanics is and asked if "it is sensible to sacrifice a reasonable physical theory for its sake."

From Bohr's point of view, causality refers to theoretical connections between elements of a description. Neither he nor von Neumann subscribed to any of the metaphysical conceptions based on doctrines such as the 'principle of sufficient reason' or 'everything has a cause'. For Bohr, attributing causality to a system requires satisfying the 'claim of causality' by our choice of a description of the system and a compatible experimental arrangement to measure the system. He [**1937a**], p. 293, felt that the concept of causality underlies the interpretation of every experiment, and that we can never have to do with what he called "well defined breaks in the causal chain".[17]

A major difference between Bohr and von Neumann, that has been mentioned above, concerns how they understand and use the wavefunction itself. Bohr stated quite clearly that the wave and particle aspects of matter have equal weight. From his point of view, quantum theory should not be interpreted as a peculiar form of particle mechanics. For von Neumann, on the other hand, quantum mechanics seems to be a variant of particle mechanics. Thus, von Neumann's account of some experiments in terms of particles in flight, which are described by moving and dividing wavepackets, violates Bohr's requirement that the wave function describe the system in the context of the whole experimental arrangement and not attribute a separate identity to individual components of it at various points in time without a separate measurement to warrant it.

In light of the significant differences between Bohr's point of view toward measurement and von Neumann's, it is ironic that some of those arguing against von Neumann's interpretation of measurement in quantum mechanics express it as an argument against the Copenhagen Interpretation of quantum mechanics and assume that they are arguing against Bohr. It is hard to say how many of those who worked with Bohr, and were loosely associated with the standard view of quantum mechanics titled the Copenhagen Interpretation, would have agreed with Bohr or with von Neumann. Given that so many see von Neumann's account of measurement as part of the Copenhagen Interpretation, it might just as well be said that Bohr did not subscribe to the Copenhagen Interpretation.

Before making a choice between Bohr's approach and von Neumann's to quantum measurement, it is necessary to examine Bohr's concept of closure, which has been held in abeyance pending further investigation. This will be done in Sections 15.4 and 15.5.

---

[17]The issues associated with causality will resurface in Chapters 16 and 17.

15.3 Reflection 23

Let us consider where this discussion has led us concerning Bohr's views on the interpretation of classical and quantum states. In Section 5.8, I discussed the close coupling between the conditions needed for a definite solution to Schrödinger's equation and Bohr's philosophical position. When an experiment on a quantum system is prepared, the equipment is set up and serves to define the initial state and macroscopic boundary conditions on the system. The potentials used in the Schrödinger equation for the system are those defined by a macroscopic model of the measuring instrument. The Schrödinger equation is solved with the given initial and boundary conditions to obtain a state that is assigned to the system under investigation. At the end of the experiment, this state is used to compute expected results. Bohr therefore connected the procedures we in fact follow in using quantum theory with a reflection on what it means in the broader senses of the physical, mathematical, and philosophical consequences of following them.

Bohr next faced the problem that the macroscopic boundary conditions and potentials produced by the measuring instrument as part of the experiment must themselves be computable and made definite without entering into an infinite regress. Bohr's answer, given in Section 7.3, was to define an epistemological role for an instrument used for this purpose and step outside quantum theory to compute the potentials associated with the instrument. This point was reframed as a concern with the macroscopic description of the instrument when used for these purposes. Moreover, for consistency, it must be demonstrable in a separate inquiry that the quantum description of the instrument itself does not rule out using it for its intended purpose and that the macroscopic approximation of its potentials is consistent with this.

By this time, von Neumann's account of the theory of measurement in quantum mechanics has taken on an almost paradigmatic quality because it has seldom been seriously challenged from within the framework of standard quantum theory. It is hard to remember that his account of measurement is not imposed or required by quantum mechanics itself. Moreover, it is seldom mentioned that von Neummann's formalism is not sufficient to encompass all the kinds of measurements that can be made on quantum systems. This was pointed out clearly in an important but neglected paper by G. R. Allcock [1969]. Allcock had set out originally to examine the employment of the particle concept in quantum mechanics by calculating the probable time of arrival of particles at detectors, but ended up criticizing the conceptual framework in which, as Bohr might put it, the particle idealization is the only component of the conceptual framework used for interpreting the measurement of the particle time of arrival. Allcock noted that there is no Hermitian operator that represents the time of arrival and that the measuring instrument significantly distorts the wavefunction of the particle in the experiment—thereby significantly distorting the result. His detailed calculations and critique of measurement theory led him to reject von Neumann's particle-centric approach to quantum mechanics.[18]

15.4 Entropy and Observation

The concepts of measurement and observation lie at the juncture between quantum theory and knowledge. For Bohr, the closure of a phenomenon represented this juncture. Bohr did not discuss how closure works in a quantum experiment to make the results macroscopic and definite. He simply used it as one of the primitive terms of his theory. Several authors have recently pointed to this as a gap in his work. I have mentioned his private speculations that closure might be related to an irreversible macroscopic change that is associated with an increase in entropy when the results of an experiment are recorded macroscopically. The possibility of a role for entropy in observation will be examined first and then the concept of closure.

Von Neumann [**1932**], Chapter V, Section 4, computed the change in entropy associated with a reversible expansion from a volume $\mathcal{V}/2$ to a volume $\mathcal{V}$ by making the particles do work against a movable piston. He contrasted this with a free expansion from the volume $\mathcal{V}/2$ into the other half of $\mathcal{V}$ with no piston. In accord with standard equilibrium thermodynamics, he labeled the first expansion reversible and the second irreversible. Using the version of thermodynamics published by Leo Szilard in 1929 as a basis, he showed that the difference in these two cases has to do with our knowledge of the system in each setting.[19] He stated that if an observer could know all the coordinates and momenta, there would be no change in the entropy. He, p. 401, concluded that the variations of the entropy in time are associated with our partial knowledge of the system.

This conclusion was consistent with the result he found for the change in the thermodynamic or macroscopic entropy during the ordinary evolution of the system in accord with Schrödinger's equation. Von Neumann's definition of the macroscopic or thermodynamic quantum mechanical entropy for system k was introduced in the last chapter in the form $S_k^{(vN)}(t) = -k_B \text{Tr}(U_k(t) \ln U_k(t))$, where k_B is Boltzmann's constant, $U_k(t)$ is the time-dependent quantum statistical matrix representing the system, and Tr is the trace operator. It is the expectation value of the quantum entropy analog written $S_k^{(vN)} = -k_B \ln U_k(t)$. Von Neumann showed mathematically that $S_k^{(vN)}(t)$ it constant in time for a statistical matrix representing a wavefunction undergoing a Type 2 evolution described by Schrödinger's equation.

---

[18]To do justice to Allcock's work requires a more detailed treatment than is appropriate to the discussion of the differences between ideas of Bohr and von Neumann presented here. It will be deferred until QIS.

[19]The works of Szilard on thermodynamics, which were published in 1925 and 1929, are reviewed briefly in CIS and in much more detail in QTS.

He, p. 387, also showed that there is an "irreversible" increase in entropy when a measurement is made and the wavefunction undergoes a Type 1 change and the quantum mechanical wavefunction is reduced from the post-measurement superposition of the form $\sum_n a_n \phi_n(y)\psi_n(x)$ to a particular outcome $a_i\phi_i(x)\psi_i(y)$. This claim of an irreversible change in the entropy due to an observation had a powerful influence on thought about observations.

Bohr's first public discussion of closure in association with an observation that is made in a specific experimental context, i.e., a phenomenon, was in [**1949**] and in subsequent books. He had raised the issue of understanding an observation in terms of an entropy increase earlier in an exchange of letters with Pauli in 1947. Bohr [**Arch**], Set III, Letter to Pauli, 1/15/47, said that the idea that any observation involves an increase in entropy had been discussed already in 1928. He related it to the operation of the measuring device. Pauli [**Arch**], Set III, Letter to Bohr, 1/28/47, asked in reply if there is a *minimum* increase in entropy independent of the particular experimental arrangement. Bohr [**Arch**], Set III, Letter to Pauli, 5/16/47, stated that he thought that the irreversibility is a purely epistemological and qualitative effect of the situation and is not quantitative. He went on to consider capturing a particle in a box and measuring its presence there when we wish. Somewhat later, Bohr [**Arch**], Set III, Letter to G. S. Stent (unsent), 11/13/47, said "Of course, it is also my opinion that the problem of observation is inseparably connected with the question of entropy, or in particular that any decrease in the attitude of knowledge of position and momentum coordination of a mechanical system will entail an increase in its entropy."

Because von Neumann had associated a Type 1 change in the wavefunction in a measurement with an increase in entropy, it is possible that this may have been what Bohr had in mind. However, the entropy increase associated with Bohr's concept of closure cannot be a Type 1 von Neumann change in the system wavefunction because that would explain the entropy increase in an observation in terms of a change of the quantum wavefunction due to an observation. It therefore does not explain how an observation results in the change in the wavefunction. If we want to explain an observation in terms of an increase in entropy, it is necessary to show that a measurement in some way causes the entropy change that triggers the specific outcome of the observation and then, in von Neumann's case, somehow causes the Type 1 change in the wavefunction. This imagined sequence would not make sense from the point of view of either von Neumann or Bohr.

Because the mechanical aspect of making an observation for Bohr is merely a physical process taking place in an experimental setting, a Type 2 change in the wavefunction is the only other possibility. However, an entropy increase cannot be explained in terms of a Type 2 change of the wavefunction in accord with Schrödinger's equation because a Type 2 change does not change the quantum entropy. This point and the one above imply that an attempt to give a quantum mechanical account of an increase in entropy in an observation, and thereby explain closure, would render Bohr's account of the observation of a system by a measuring instrument either circular or pointless. Moreover, his reference to the *macroscopic* registration of the observation implies that he had something else in mind.

Let us move on to the possibility that Bohr was referring to a change in the macroscopic classical entropy in a successful observation. This immediately raises the question of whether the notion of entropy in classical physics can support this view and whether we can separate the role of a change in the macroscopic classical entropy in an observation, as Bohr would have it, from the fact that the macroscopic system is itself composed of particles that are subject to quantum mechanics.

The first question is whether there really is an irreversible increase in the classical entropy when a macroscopic change occurs, such as the blackening of a spot on a photographic plate. As pointed out in the last chapter, Gibbs [**1902**] had discovered that the classical entropy he defined is constant in time for an isolated system. His response to this fact was to coarse-grain the system distribution to obtain an entropy that increases in time. This parallel between the results for the classical and quantum entropies, for both the standard and coarse-grained cases, are not hard to understand when one examines the mathematics involved. Without going into the mathematical details, I will just state that (i) whenever a particle encounters a boundary that is described in terms of a stochastic transition probability, or (ii) there is a discontinuous reduction in the set of options available to a system, such as that caused by the action of a projection operator used to coarse-grain the particle distribution or reduce the wavefunction after a measurement, there will be an increase in the entropy (TIS sign convention). Otherwise the entropy will not change. The increase in entropy in the coarse-grained case, for both classical and quantum mechanics, depends on the size of the cells selected for the coarse-graining and is therefore a mathematical artifact of the way in which we have chosen to represent the system. The value computed for the increase does not have either an absolute or a dynamical significance.[20]

Let us investigate the implications of these points for Bohr's conjecture. Assume that the measuring instrument, including a photographic plate for recording the results, and a system being measured are together isolated from the rest of the universe. Let us describe the combined system microscopically in terms of classical Hamiltonian mechanics and consider the change of entropy in an observation. When a photon encounters a grain of silver halide in this case, the exact laws of motion are reversible and the entropy will not change. The blackening of a spot on a photographic plate will be reversed if the trajectories of all the particles involved, including photons, are reversed.

---

[20]See CIS, EIS, and QTS, for the formalism and calculations that support these assertions.

The initial change in the silver halide grain, caused by the photon striking it, and the subsequent amplification effects due to a cascade of chemical bond changes are therefore microscopically reversible. The concept of entropy has no role in these transformations, which are determined only by the microscopic equations of motion. In support of this statement is the fact pointed out in the last chapter that the entropy is not defined when the exact equations of motion are used, so an "irreversible change in the entropy" cannot be computed or used as a criterion for a successful measurement. Bohr's conjecture that an increase in entropy on the macroscopic level is responsible for closing an observation must therefore be rejected.

While Bohr was not aware of these points concerning the unsuitability of the entropy for enforcing closure, he did indicate discomfort with using the entropy in this role in his letter of 5/16/47 to Pauli in which he stated that this is a qualitative effect and not a quantitative one. In his unsent letter of 11/13/47 to Stent on this, he correctly stated that a loss of knowledge will entail an increase in entropy.[21]

My rejection of Bohr's conjecture that a mechanical change reflected in either the quantum or classical entropy can provide a physical explanation for his concept of closure requires that we search elsewhere for its interpretation and evaluation.

15.5 Bohr's Concept of Closure

Although macroscopic ideas may be adequate to the task of fully describing the results obtained by a macroscopic measuring instrument acting on a quantum system, the standard question of how that information becomes available macroscopically still needs to be resolved. It has already been established that an attempt by the quantum ergodic theorists to view measurement as a physical process that reduces the wavefunction to a set of alternatives similar to classical alternatives, i.e., from a superposition to a mixture, followed by the selection of one outcome, does not work. There is also no evidence that Bohr considered such a mechanism. Since the attempt to use the classical or quantum entropy as the mechanism of closing an observation does not work either, there is no physical solution to the problem of closure. This means that at least an epistemological account of why quantum coherences are not a factor in our observations must be given if closure is to be explained at all.

An epistemological account of closure that is consistent with quantum mechanics is obtained by showing that we cannot obtain from a measurement more information than the quantum mechanical description of the measured system allows us. Thus the notion of closure implies at the very least that we cannot undo the quantum evolution of the system and recover the previous states from which the system has evolved. The significance of this can be

---

[21]This statement is based on the formalism presented in CIS.

understood by considering as an example a photon or particle striking a screen in a double-slit interference experiment demonstrating wave aspects of light or matter. Because correlation information persists as the particle interacts with other particles in the instrument, the possibility exists that we could find a way to extract this information by a sequence of further interactions in a subsequent experiment. If the details of the motion of the photon or particle just before impact could be reconstructed using this information, it would be possible to show which slit it passed through without destroying the interference pattern. This outcome would violate wave-particle duality and complementarity as Bohr had understood and presented them.

Bohr allowed a measuring instrument to be considered suitable for a given measurement only if it could be shown that quantum superpositions would not interfere significantly with its operation in this role. Since he did not attribute quantum states to systems that are not the subject of a measurement, such superpositions are not a logical problem for his approach if they cannot be used to extract more information than is provided by the quantum account of the measurement. This means that the significant question for Bohr's epistemological approach is whether information, in the form of quantum correlations in the system + measuring instrument viewed as a single quantum system, could be used after the fact in another experiment to determine the quantum state that gave rise to them.

The work of Asher Peres [**1980**] addressed this question. He was not concerned with reducing the wavefunction but with what is required to "undo" a quantum measurement. By this he meant recovering the information needed to reconstruct the state of the observed system from the state of the united system consisting of the observed system and measuring instrument: $k + M$. To do this means measuring the phase relationships between superimposed states of the united system after the measurement and using this information to establish the phase relationships of the observed system. Peres assumed in his analysis that the united system is isolated. Otherwise, information may leak into the environment or from the environment and the situation will be trivially irreversible.

Peres presented a simple experiment to make his ideas plausible. He recalled the well-known result that a pure quantum state will not be transformed into a mixture by Schrödinger's equation. He demonstrated in a spin measurement example that the coupling between the system and the instrument results in a state that is a superposition of two outcomes. He showed that the phase relation between these outcomes just after the measurement could be obtained by measuring an operator $\mathbf{A}$. He then reviewed the work of the quantum ergodic theorists who claimed that phase relations will physically removed by the evolution of the system after the measurement. Their calculations, based on the state of $k + M$ after a measurement and its evolution via Schrödinger's equation, show that $< \mathbf{A} > \rightarrow 0$ as $t \rightarrow \infty$ as the united system subsequently evolves and the many other degrees of freedom of the measuring instrument (or the environment) make their influence felt. This calculation and similar ones are the basis of the claims by quantum ergodic theorists that the phase information in a measurement is lost. Peres indicated that the time needed to erase $<\mathbf{A}>$ is inversely proportional to the strength of the interaction between the degrees of freedom of the instrument associated with the measurement and all its other degrees of freedom.

Peres objected to the interpretation that the phase information is lost on the grounds that it could be obtained by measuring another operator $\mathbf{A}^t = e^{-itH}\mathbf{A}e^{itH}$, where $\mathbf{A}^t$ is the operator $\mathbf{A}$ in the Heisenberg representation, instead of the operator $\mathbf{A}$ defined in the Schrödinger representation. He showed that $<\mathbf{A}^t>$ is constant in time and retains the value that $<\mathbf{A}>$ had at the end of the measurement and before the subsequent evolution of the system. He observed that this means that $\mathbf{A}^t$ is both explicitly time-dependent and a constant of the motion. Peres pointed out that this is a familiar situation in classical mechanics where, for a system with $\mathcal{N}_k$ particles, there are $6\mathcal{N}_k$ degrees of freedom and $6\mathcal{N}_k$ constants of the motion. A few of these, such as the total energy, momentum, and angular momentum, are constant in time and the rest are time-dependent. The explicit meaning of the rest of the constants of the motion is to give the $6\mathcal{N}_k$ initial particle positions and momenta at $t = 0$ as explicit functions of the positions, momenta, and time at time t.[22] For $\mathcal{N}_k$ large and t finite, these constants are extremely complicated. When an observed system interacts with a macroscopic instrument, and the results become macroscopically available, information has dissipated into the $6\mathcal{N}_k$ degrees of freedom of the instrument. From a microscopic point of view, we still have full information and the situation is reversible.

The next step in Peres' argument was to show that we are unable to make use of these microscopic constants of the motion. He argued that in the classical case the situation is so complicated that we are forced to move from classical mechanics to classical statistical mechanics. This implies that the measurement of the operator $\mathbf{A}^t$ is too complex to do classically so the classical dynamical quantity corresponding to this operator is not an observable. This means that the quantum mechanical operator is not an observable either because we do not have a macroscopic model of an experiment that can measure it. He associated the complexity in this situation with classical irreversibility, which he characterized as an aspect of the transition from describing the situation by classical mechanics to describing it by classical statistical mechanics. He then concluded that it is the classical irreversibility in this situation that leads us to interpret these complicated quantum states of $k + M$ as a mixture of states of the combined system.

---

[22]There are other ways to define these invariants. Liouville's theorem in physics is itself a consequence of one of the $3\mathcal{N}_k$ Poincaré integral invariants of a system with $6\mathcal{N}_k$ degrees of freedom.

Peres has put his finger on the core issue of macroscopic irreversibility in a microscopically reversible world. His work differed from those that viewed the problem as that of providing a physical explanation of the collapse of the wavefunction. The difference between his approach and that of the collapse theorists was his recognition that we need an epistemological solution of the problem of connecting the microscopic and macroscopic worlds and not a physical one. His solution took the form of a demonstration that the information we can obtain and use in an experiment cannot violate quantum mechanics. However, Peres' statement that classical irreversibility, based on either microscopic mechanical or macroscopic entropy arguments, is the explanation for this quantum irreversibility was rejected in the last section.

The issue of classical irreversibility in thermodynamics is addressed in CIS and EIS. The analysis of the second law of thermodynamics and the entropy presented there indicates that macroscopic irreversibility and microscopic irreversibility are distinct concepts and should not be amalgamated. This led to the introduction of a concept called *macroscopic unreturnability* in EIS, Chapter 10, that is useful in this situation.[23] As many authors have remarked, the large number of microscopic states that correspond to each member of a set of macroscopically distinct observables implies that the concept of irreversibility in macroscopic thermodynamics should be treated differently than the concept of microscopic irreversibility. In the latter case, the reference is to the equations of motion and these are fully reversible. At the macroscopic level, the procedures discussed in the various versions of the second law of thermodynamics are concerned with returning a system to the same macroscopic state it once occupied. The macroscopic methods available to do this are changing its boundary conditions, such as temperature, volume, or pressure. In some cases, this will return a system to a previous macroscopic thermodynamic state. This does not mean that the particles are returned to their former microscopic state.

Let us apply this idea to the post-measurement of the $k+M$ system after the evolution of the combined system during a measurement. If the concept of unreturnability is applied to the post-measurement system, it is being asserted that there is no macroscopic way of preparing an experiment for the combined $k+M$ system and no quantum operator that can be measured in this new experiment that will have the effect of reversing the evolution of the post-measurement system so that it returns to the joint $k+M$ quantum state it occupied prior to the measurement. This means that information cannot be extracted from the macroscopic observations obtained in an experiment concerning the state of $k+M$ in the original experiment over and above what is provided by the result measured in the original experiment. This is all that is asserted by Bohr's concept of closure.

---

[23] This is related to the old thermodynamic notion of *unrecoverability*.

With these results, the definition of the closure of an experiment can be restated in the form:

An experiment is *closed* when the combination of the measuring instrument and observed system is in an *unreturnable* state, so that it cannot be returned to its initial quantum state by macroscopic means in a new experiment.

The concept of unreturnability is weaker than the standard concept of macroscopic irreversibility in thermodynamics that was itself assumed to be enforced by an increase in entropy. But the thermodynamic entropy does not change for a closed and isolated system in either the classical or quantum case, so there is nothing like the entropy to enforce a genuine macroscopic irreversibility. This is consistent with the fact that a reversal of the microscopic system will return the macroscopic system to a previous macroscopic state. I conclude that it is unreturnability that determines the epistemological situation for a macroscopic sentient system studying microscopic entities from either the classical or quantum point of view.

15.6 Reflection 24

With the discussion of closure given in the last section, my account of Bohr's theory of measurement is complete. The epistemological solution of the issues associated with Bohr's theory of measurement is consistent with his general principles. On the weight of the evidence gathered and the successful completion of his theory of measurement, my conclusion is that Bohr's theory of measurement is clearly superior to von Neumann's for both physical and philosophical reasons.

There is no way to know if Bohr would have approved the approach to completing his concept of closure taken here. Nor can we be sure of his reaction to the theory of measurement presented in his name or the revision of his main argument. With these disclaimers, let us take a moment to sum up the perspective that has emerged concerning Bohr's views of the epistemological foundations of physics. This is the final update of the theses concerning physics attributed to Bohr in Chapter 8.

Possibilities of Description.

A macroscopic knowing subject must use a measuring instrument that is described macroscopically to perform experiments on other systems. The suitability of the instrument is established by showing that the quantum ambiguities inherent in using it for this purpose will not exceed the error limits allowed for the quantity to be observed. The measuring instrument, its operation, and its boundary conditions, define the quantum description that is appropriate for the observed system. Knowledge of microscopic entities can only be obtained in a setting that is consistent with the appropriate quantum description of the observed system. The descriptions of the observed system and the measuring instrument must meet the requirement of independence so that subject and object, instrument and system, are represented by separate variables. The physical interpretation of the theoretical components used to describe the observed system, and the possibility of combining several components in one description, must also meet the requirements of the principle of complementarity.

Possibilities of Observation.

The information that can be obtained from experiments is determined by the operation of the measuring instrument in conjunction with the observed system. The interpretation of this information must be consistent with the quantum description of the observed system and the model of the measurement provided by the macroscopic description of the instrument. It must also be expressed in a macroscopic form suitable for communication. The macroscopic information representing observations contains no detailed quantum information concerning the interaction between the particles in the measuring instrument and the observed system that is not measured as part of the experiment.

Requirements of Communication.

Information is communicable if it has been obtained in accord with the possibilities of description and the possibilities of observation. These requirements on descriptions and observations do not place limitations on the macroscopic questions that can be asked in an experiment. They are concerned with how definitive results are obtained from experiments and do place a limit on how we can interpret the macroscopic results of experiments in terms of microscopic entities, their properties, and their behavior. The macroscopic information obtained by a valid experiment becomes knowledge within the conceptual framework associated with the macroscopic viewpoint supplemented by quantum mechanics when it is shown that this macroscopic outcome is consistent with the interpretation of the quantum mechanical account of the observed system. This viewpoint does not explain how a particular macroscopic outcome, obtained from a range of microscopically determined possibilities, is selected physically. In fact, no physical explanation of this fact may be possible. This approach simply recognizes our place as macroscopic knowing beings living in a macroscopic world with a microscopic substrate.

The reformulation of Bohr's fundamental principles in this chapter is required by the need to replace unacceptable aspects of the justification he gave for his epistemology and extend his views in a manner that is consistent with his overall perspective. The completeness and consistency of his original analysis, which pointed the way to these extensions, is a tribute to his epistemological intuition and philosophical skills.

CHAPTER 16

Questions of Interpretation

Bohr's viewpoints are tested next against some of the other approaches to the foundations and interpretation of quantum mechanics. The discussion is limited to a brief review of selected works that are representative of ways in which these problems have been addressed.

16.1 Dynamical Theories of Wavefunction Reduction

The ontological approach to the interpretation of quantum mechanics assigns a measure of 'reality' to the wavefunction itself.[1] The goal of these theories is to show that the wavefunction can be interpreted as a real substance of some kind and that all changes in the wavefunction arise from its quantum dynamics and not from some extraphysical interventions by consciousness or anything else. The problem is to reconcile this stance with the behavior of the wavefunction that seems to contradict it. In other words, the ontological approach wants to avoid Type 1 von Neumann reductions of the wavefunction, and show that when there is a superposition of states after a measurement, it evolves spontaneously into a mixture soon afterward.

Ontological interpretations of quantum theory are often called "realistic interpretations" because they give the wavefunction the status of a substance which has properties that are compatible with those assigned to substances by materialism and metaphysical realism. However, the issue is not whether quantum theory refers to reality, but whether the wavefunction itself is a substance. To call this a "realistic" interpretation of the whole of quantum mechanics is therefore a misnomer because it carries a misleading nimbus of meaning. Similar issues of interpretation also play a role when one examines the status of the system particle distribution in classical statistical mechanics. An investigation in EIS of various interpretations of the equilibrium distribution showed that the equilibrium canonical distribution is often assigned many characteristics of a substance, and therefore a "reality", that goes beyond its role in the theory. This step, called 'reification of the distribution', leads to errors in judging when and why systems go to equilibrium and what it means when they do. For these reasons, the ontological approaches to quantum theory will be discussed here, as suggested above, using the term 'substantiality' in place of the term 'reality' and the ontological versions of quantum mechanics will be referred to more precisely as "substantialistic interpretations".

Bohr was clearly opposed to a substantialistic interpretation of the quantum wavefunction as attested to by numerous quotations given above. For him, these interpretations are holdovers from the materialist interpretation of Newtonian mechanics. He felt that they do not recognize or do justice to the new situation we have found ourselves in with quantum mechanics. The purpose of this chapter is to juxtapose the perspectives of the substantialistic interpretations with Bohr's views so that the relative merits of each position can be assessed.

---

[1] More detail on the theories discussed here, and an analysis of some theories not discussed, can be found in the exhaustive and balanced study, with extensive references, by D'Espagnat [**1995**]. D'Espagnat discussed many of the questions that are important to this chapter and the next one.

The general perspective of many concerned with the relation between the microscopic world described by quantum mechanics and the macroscopic world we live in was shaped by the works of Schrödinger [1927], [1935a], [1935b], [1936]. Schrödinger [1935a] spoke of the states of two systems coming together and then separating as becoming "entangled" or "entwined" with each other so that individual components in the two systems lose their individual identities. He postulated that when quantum systems are separated after an interaction, their states will spontaneously evolve into a mixture. He recognized that this is a violation of quantum mechanics, but felt that quantum mechanical correlations may not apply to systems that are sufficiently far apart. After the appearance of the EPR paper, Schrödinger [1935b], [1936], acknowledged that these long distance entanglements persist. Since that time, Schrödinger's concept of quantum entanglement has dominated discussions of these issues.

A number of theories have been proposed that purport to show that a quantum superposition, which represents possible outcomes of the measurement that can interfere with each other, is spontaneously converted into a mixture of noninterfering outcomes during the evolution of the quantum system after a measurement. These theories try to show that this is a consequence of ordinary quantum dynamics in conjunction with the environment or other factors. The goal of this work is to obtain from quantum mechanics a set of outcomes that can be interpreted as classical alternatives. Accomplishing this would allow the demonstration of why quantum superpositions do not infect the macroscopic world we occupy and provide an explanation of the classical world of our experience as a direct consequence of quantum dynamics.

Early work in the 1960s based on this approach was called *quantum ergodic theory*. More recent work is represented by variants of *decoherence theory*. While all of these theories differ in a number of details, they are essentially variations on a theme.[2]

16.2 Quantum Ergodic Theory and Decoherence Theory

The conversion of quantum superpositions into mixtures of alternatives is considered to be important because superpositions of the states of macroscopic objects are not observed. Quantum ergodic theorists have employed

---

[2]Fine [1970] presented a pessimistic view of the possibility of solving the measurement problem. Recent theories have been treated in some detail in the book by D'Espagnat [1995] and the review paper and book by Roland Omnès [1993], [1994]. I will briefly discuss the perspectives presented in Omnès' paper and in the books by Penrose [1994] and Murray Gell-Mann [1994]. It would take us too far afield to deal in more detail here with the consistent histories theory or make a more detailed response to the theories of Omnès, Wojcieck Żurek, Gell-Mann and James Hartle, and others, that are summarized in these books. Some of these topics are discussed further from the physical point of view in QIS.

two main tools to demonstrate that this spontaneous conversion always occurs. The first tool an infinite time averaging procedure and the second is the thermodynamic limit. The infinite time average method is the same as that used by classical ergodic theorists and one variant of the thermodynamic limit lets the number of particles and the total energy in a system approach infinity while keeping the energy per particle fixed. These devices are used to demonstrate mathematically that the probabilities associated with nonclassical phase relationships in superpositions, also called the interference or "cross-terms", vanish asymptotically.[3] In spite of a strong motivation and a great deal of effort, these theories have not been successful. The essential problem is that attempts to provide an account of the loss of coherence based on standard quantum dynamics founder on the fact that the Schrödinger equation is linear and reversible in time. There is simply no physical mechanism that will accomplish the required reduction of the wavefunction.

It was pointed out in the last chapter that the quantum interferences may diffuse into a very large number of degrees of freedom and become practically unobservable, which is part of what the quantum ergodic theorists are claiming. But this is not equivalent to a reduction of the wavefunction and does not remove the logical problems connected with a substantialistic interpretation of the wavefunction or allow a materialist notion of reality to prevail.

The main objection to using limits of this sort is that there is no physical justification in either case for using an infinite time average or an infinite number of particles to describe actual experiments. The usual justification for an infinite time average is that systems visit a good portion of their accessible phase spaces during a measurement, so the value obtained by the measurement is almost equal to that obtained over an infinite time interval. The justification for the thermodynamic limit is that a collection of 10^{23} particles is infinite from a practical perspective. In actual fact, however, systems visit only a minuscule portion of their available phase spaces during a measurement, or a human lifetime, and 10^{23} particles in a system does not mathematically justify taking the $\mathcal{N}_k \to \infty$ limit. Moreover, for a system in a closed bounded volume, the results obtained at these limits contradict Poincaré's recurrence theorem—which is another indication that the limits are mathematically illegitimate.[4]

A second, equally telling objection to these theories, is that there is no way to distinguish a mixture from a pure state. As discussed in detail in QIS,

---

[3] See, for example, the papers on quantum ergodic theory by A. Danieri, A. Loinger and G. M. Prosperi [1962], [1966]. See also the critical review by J. Bub [1968].

[4] The unsuitability of ergodic theory as a justification of phase averaging in obtaining thermodynamic functions from classical statistical mechanical analogs is discussed in EIS, Chapter 2.

for each situation in which we would be tempted to assign a mixture to a system there is a pure state that could be assigned.

In the last chapter, the objections of Peres to the assumptions underlying these points of view were summarized. The dissipation of phase information into 10^{23} degrees of freedom after the measurement of a particular operator does make it hard to recover this quantum phase information, and any particular degree of freedom will ultimately contain a vanishingly small amount of information on these phase relations. Peres showed, on the other hand, that a change in which operator is measured can in principle give this dissipation a different form and change the possibility of capturing this information. In addition, the dissipation of information into many degrees of freedom may make it difficult for us to capture the information, but it does not solve the logical and philosophical problem associated with the dissipation of the quantum substance of the wavefunction among these degrees of freedom and does not show us how that substance becomes concentrated on a single outcome or a set of classically distinct outcomes.

Decoherence theorists have a more sophisticated approach. They begin with an examination of various experiments that have resulted in quantum superpositions. In these experiments, as Bohr and others had long emphasized, the wave aspects that give rise to superposition effects would disappear if the particle aspects, embodied in the path, could be measured. Decoherence theorists examined the possibility that an interaction between the system and its environment would have the effect of removing quantum superpositions.[5]

In one of the original papers on decoherence theory Żurek [**1981**], p. 1521, claimed that for a quantum system considered to be a measuring apparatus there is a component we can identify and call the "pointer". It has the task of measuring and recording the experimental results. He observed that for this component to function properly, the environment must not disturb it appreciably during the course of the experiment. He postulated that there is a quantum representation of the pointer component, and a basis of states for this representation called the "pointer basis", which is not appreciably perturbed by interaction of the apparatus with the environment. He, p. 1524, claimed to have shown that the interaction between the apparatus and the environment "may single out a preferred pointer basis of the apparatus." This was later viewed as a "measurement" of the pointer by the environment.

As with quantum ergodic theory, the objective of decoherence theory is to show that the phase correlations between the alternatives in a superposition at the end of a measurement are lost. To accomplish this goal, decoherence theories have relied variously on (1) the complexity of the interaction between the system and the measuring instrument, with the resulting "entanglement"

---

[5]Decoherence theory is discussed in Żurek [**1991**]. Letters responding to this article and Żurek's reply appear in *Physics Today*, April 1993, pp. 13, 15, 81–90. See also Żurek [**1981**] and the references cited in these papers.

16.2 QUANTUM ERGODIC THEORY AND DECOHERENCE THEORY

of the state of the instrument with that of the measured system leading to the loss of detailed phase information, or (2) superselection rules for system observables when measured by the instrument, or (3) leakage of information into the environment.

Recent experimental work has explored the transfer of information between the system, the measuring instrument, and the environment.[6] In describing these experiments, the experimenters make a number of assertions about what is happening during the course of the experiment. Many of these statements are unacceptable from Bohr's point of view, but rather than bog the discussion down with excess detail, most of the characterization of the experiment by the experimenters will be accepted so that we can focus on the main points at issue and their conclusions.

One experiment investigates the effects of attempting to detect which slit an atom passes through in a double slit interference experiment. Using sodium atoms and a laser detector for the atom paths, the experimenters showed that when the laser was set up to be able to detect which slit an atom had passed through, the interference pattern on the screen was destroyed. But when the separation of the paths of the atoms through the apparatus was adjusted to a quarter of the laser wavelength, so that the information on which slit the atom passed through could not be measured by the laser, the interference pattern returned.

In another experiment, an atom is placed in a superposition of two states. This atom passes through an electromagnetic field trapped in a cavity and transfers the superposition of states to the field. A second atom passes through the cavity after some time delay, absorbs the superposition of states from the field, and reemerges. Measurements on the second atom are used to test the effects of both the delay and differences in the number of photons in the electromagnetic field of the cavity (the field density) on the transfer of information from the first atom to the field and then to the second atom. Increasing the time delay or increasing the number of photons in the trapped electromagnetic field decreased the coherence of the state of the final atom.

Quantum decoherence theorists point to the results of experiments like this to show a general leakage of coherence information into the environment. In this sense, they claim that the environment is acting as a measuring device that can detect or influence the properties of the atom. Żurek went so far as to say that decoherence theory represents both a confirmation of Bohr's intuition and an explanation of how a particular outcome of the experiment

---

[6] See the recent summary article by Philip Yarn, [**1997**].

is selected.[7] He explained that the environment selects, by means of an environmentally induced superselection rule, only that outcome that is macroscopically (classically) viable in terms of the connection of the system to the measuring instrument. Żurek expressed the feeling that, while decoherence answers the physical questions concerning a measurement, a full explanation of what he called the metaphysical question of how the conscious mind perceives an outcome in an experiment must await a better understanding of how the brain and mind are related.[8]

Decoherence theorists refer to the enormous complexity resulting from an interaction of the atomic system with a macroscopic number of particles in the measuring instrument to explain their expectation that a superposition will "decohere" as time goes by. The purported superselection rule that is supposed to be acting in this case is never identified, but if it exists, it simply means that a measurement can only be approximate. However, this by itself does not mean that the quantum superposition itself has in some sense "decohered".[9]

If we simply assume that there is random leakage of particles into or out of the environment or random interactions between particles and the environment, the resulting theory is a variant of the random phase theories proposed long ago and decoherence follows as a matter of course due to the randomization of phase relations between components of the original system.[10] A problem for this group of decoherence theories is to explain what happens if there is no environment to do the decohering. Because of the arbitrariness in quantum theory, which stems from the choice of what to call the system, the measuring instrument, and the environment, the system can

---

[7] Żurek is quoted in Yarn, loc. cit., pp. 125, 127. Anthony Leggett, also quoted in this article, disagrees that decoherence theory can provide an explanation of how a particular outcome is selected.

[8] Yarn, ibid., p. 128.

[9] A similar point is made in Bell's discussion of a theory, which he called the Coleman-Hepp model, that claims to show a "rigorous reduction of the wave packet" for all local observables. Computing the system evolution in this model requires taking the limits of an infinite time average and an infinitely large instrument. Bell [**1987**], Chapter 6, shows that these limits are not legitimate.

[10] A prequantum grandparent of theories of this type is Planck's late nineteenth century theory of "natural radiation", which postulated that there is a random background or environment of radiation present in all exchanges of radiation with matter. He used this to show that the entropy of a system of particles interacting with radiation increases in time as a mathematical consequence. Although Planck abandoned this theory in the face of Boltzmann's proof that Maxwell's equations are time reversible, random interactions between a system and its environment were later invoked by many other authors to explain the evolution of a closed system to equilibrium in both the classical and quantum cases. In classical mechanics, Boltzmann invoked "molecular chaos" for essentially the same purpose. This 'randomization of phases' mechanism has also been used in many textbooks on quantum mechanics as a *deus ex machina* to remove superpositions in discussions of particular quantum phenomena.

be closed by including the environment as part of the (now isolated) system. This means that we are back where we were because there is no external environment providing a physical mechanism to remove the coherence.

Decoherence theory has been used as one of the fundamental building blocks in the study of quantum computation and the theory of what has been called "quantum teleportation". As one example out of many, I mention M. A. Nielsen, E. Knill, and R. Laflamme [**1998**] who studied quantum teleportation using nuclear magnetic resonance with the molecule trichloroethelene, C_2Cl_3H. The goal of these authors was to teleport state information from one of the carbon atoms to the hydrogen atom in these molecules. They prepared the state of the molecule using Nuclear Magnetic Resonance (NMR) gradient pulse methods and phase cycling. These unitary operations were implemented by nonselective radio frequency pulses tuned to the nuclear spins with delays to allow entanglement to form by the interaction of neighboring nuclei. After the delay, a new NMR pulse, based on the natural spin-spin coupling of the carbon nuclei, was used to create a superposition of four states represented in what was called the "experimental wavefunction basis". At this point, a measurement would be required to decide which of the four states actually obtains. However, there is a problem:

"We cannot directly implement the second step in NMR. Instead, we exploit the natural phase decoherence occurring on the carbon nuclei to achieve the same effect. We note that phase decoherence completely randomizes the phase information of these nuclei and thus will destroy the coherence between the elements of the above basis. Its effect on the state of the carbon nuclei is to diagonalize the state in the computational basis. ... As emphasized by Żurek, the decoherence process is indistinguishable from a measurement in the computational basis for the carbons accomplished by the environment. We do not observe the result of this measurement explicitly, but the state of the nuclei selected by the decoherence process contains the measurement result, and therefore we can do the final transformation conditional on the particular state the environment has selected."

After consideration of the various time delays in the decoherence of the relation between different components of the molecule, they concluded that "for delays of the order of 1 s, we can approximate the total evolution by the exact phase decoherence on the carbon nuclei. The total scheme therefore implements a measurement in the Bell basis, with the result of the measurement stored as classical data on the carbon nuclei following the measurement."

To draw their conclusion, Nielsen, Knill, and Laflamme invoked what they called "the natural phase decoherence occurring on the carbon nuclei" as a "measurement". They based this approach on Żurek's view that "the decoherence process is indistinguishable from a measurement ... accomplished by the environment." This is claimed to have the effect of completely randomizing the phase information of these nuclei and destroying the coherence between them.

In response to this interpretation, I observe immediately that this account of a measuring process facilitated by microscopic particles whose phases are randomized by the environment has little in common with the theories of measurement expressed either by von Neumann or Bohr. It assumes the validity of the interpretation of a measurement offered by decoherence theory and assumes, in the absence of an actual measurement to verify it, that what they have said about the carbon nuclei is true, accurate, and makes sense physically. Furthermore, the so-called "experimental wavefunction basis" and the "Bell basis", referred to in the discussion of this experiment, are presumably a set of eigenfunctions of some complete set of commuting operators that function in the same way a basis does in von Neumann's measurement theory. No set of operators was given, so it is not clear that this set of eigenfunctions exists and has the properties assigned to them. Moreover, this purported basis is not rooted in any macroscopic measuring instrument, so there is no justification for using them in the way von Neumann employed a basis in his theory of measurement and drawing conclusions about their role in a "measurement". Finally, there is no intervention of either consciousness or closure, which is required in the measurement theories of von Neumann and Bohr, respectively, to reduce the wavefunction to a final form.

The notion of the environment providing us with measurements in any sense, and the further claim that it causes events we can count on as having happened without verifying that they have, runs contrary to the thrust of the work in the previous 70 years in which it was emphasized that we cannot take for granted in quantum mechanics what we have not verified and we cannot use quantum states as representations of physical systems apart from an effective experimental apparatus for measuring them. Bohr's point was that we cannot assign a state to a system, and assume that this assignment is appropriate, apart from this context of an experimental arrangement. In reference to the experiment discussed above, the problems with the interpretation of its authors are (1) we cannot assume that the carbon nuclei are in any definite state; (2) any action of the environment must be represented in the Schrödinger equation for this experiment in the form of an external potential; (3) the evolution of the states of these atoms requires a suitable Schrödinger equation with a definite experimental arrangement that is suitable for measuring the quantities that are to be made definite; and (4) a measurement requires an interaction with a macroscopic instrument.

Finally, I observe that even if a measurement of the carbon atom spins seemed to support the claimed decoherence of these nuclei, the situation may in fact be an example of the old spin-echo experiments of Otto Hahn who used the recurrence of coherence in a field of spins as an argument against the assumption that the spin systems had decohered and gone to equilibrium.[11] Thus the claim of the authors that the unmeasured "state of the nuclei selected by the decoherence process contains the measurement result" is hard to understand and certainly does not measure up to the standards of von Neumann or Bohr. For these reasons, I reject the interpretation of the role of the environment suggested by the decoherence theorists and the use of decoherence theory to interpret the results of experiments like that of Nielsen, Knill, and Laflamme.

16.3 Relative State Theories

Von Neumann's introduction of consciousness into the measurement process was difficult for many to accept. A theory created to avoid this was the 'relative state' or 'many worlds' interpretation of quantum mechanics proposed by Hugh Everett.[12] This interpretation does not make use of a separate subject and object. Everything evolves in accord with Schrödinger's equation at all times. In terms of von Neumann's types, the wavefunction in Everett's theory always evolves as a Type 2 process and never undergoes a Type 1 discontinuous change corresponding to a measurement. The observer is part of the total system envisioned by Everett. When an observation is made by this internal observing system, the wavefunction to splits into parts corresponding to each of the possible outcomes. Each of these branches is assigned equal reality. This implies that the universe is constantly splitting into separate real components that have no access to each other.

A major flaw in the relative state theory is that it is not clear what counts as an observer, what counts as an observation in the absence of a formal experiment, and when these observers can split the universe. This solution, like some of those proposed by the hidden variable theorists, cries out for William of Occam's razor. The idea that there is a continuum of simultaneously real worlds, each having the same total energy, each occupying the same space, and none being accessible to the others, is completely unverifiable and much less palatable philosophically and physically than giving up the conception of the "reality" of the wavefunction that leads to it.

An interesting variant of Everett's theory has been formulated by Gell-Mann and Hartle. They have reframed Everett's theory by combining a form of Richard Feynman's representation of quantum probability calculations in the form of a sum over particle histories with decoherence theory.[13]

---

[11] See the discussion of Hahn's spin-echo experiment and its impact on thinking about equilibrium in J. M. Blatt [**1959**].

[12] For more information, see Everett [**1957**], Wheeler [**1957**], DeWitt [**1968**], and D'Espagnat [**1971a**], Chapter 20. For a critique, see D'Espagnat [**1995**].

[13] See the nontechnical summary of this theory in Gell-Mann [**1994**], Chapter 11. Technical references are Feynman and Hibbs [**1965**], Omnès [**1994**] and D'Espagnat [**1995**].

Feynman's insight was that the current probability of a certain quantum mechanical outcome can be viewed as the "sum" (in the form of an integral equation) over all the possible ways in which this outcome could have come about from a given initial state. It depends on the fact that the evolution of the wavefunction in accord with Schrödinger's equation is a unitary transformation of the wavefunction in time, which means that the particles are conserved. An initial pure state or mixture, represented by the statistical matrix, will evolve between time t_0 and time t by means of the unitary time shift operator $U(t, t_0)$ into a current pure state or mixture. During this evolution, some of the possible paths may interfere with other possible paths due to a superposition of components of the wavefunction representing the collection of different paths.

The role of the observer in Gell-Mann and Hartle's system is to prune the untaken branches from the tree of possibilities.[14] An observer is an information gathering and utilizing system (IGUS), which is a special case of a complex adaptive system. The actions of the IGUS in pruning the tree of possible sequences of events is interpreted by von Neumann as the 'collapse of the wavefunction' and by Gell-Mann and Hartle as the "recognition that one or another of a set of *decohering* alternatives has occurred." Observers live in a world described (in Gell-Mann's terminology) by macroscopic quasiclassical states that have decohered, so they do not have problems with quantum superpositions. Gell-Mann does raise some issues concerning the possibility of inequivalent quasiclassical domains and whether independent observers will share a single domain. By contrast with Everett, Gell-Mann and Hartle are not explicit concerning the reality of the branches that go forward versus those that are "pruned by observation".

Gell-Mann and Hartle replaced Everett's 'branches of reality' formulation of his theory with probabilistically described 'sets of possible histories' for a given event. They then extended this viewpoint by using the ideas developed by Hartle and Steven Hawking in a paper called the "Wave Function of the Universe".[15] In presenting these ideas, Gell-Mann used the examples of a one and a two electron atom. In the one electron case, such as a hydrogen atom, Gell-Mann claimed that it is legitimate to say that the electron is in a definite quantum state. He contrasted this with a two electron case, using the helium atom as an example, and noted that individual electrons cannot be said to be in a definite quantum state because their states are "entwined", "entangled",

---

[14] See Gell-Mann [**1994**], pp. 155–165.

[15] The 'wave function of the universe' is defined as a solution to the Wheeler-DeWitt equation and not the Schrödinger equation. A brief and accessible summary of the Wheeler-DeWitt equation, with references, is given in David Atkatz [**1994**]. He discussed some of the conceptual and interpretational problems involved with the idea of a wave function of the universe. The problems involved in treating quantum theory as universally valid, and in obtaining the Schrödinger equation from the Wheeler-DeWitt equation, are discussed by Claus Kiefer [**1994**].

16.3 RELATIVE STATE THEORIES

or "correlated", due to the interaction. Gell-Mann then maintained that when you sum over the histories of the joint wavefunction representing the pair of electrons, you obtain a mixture of states of a single electron. He applied this idea to the wavefunction for the whole universe and stated that summing over the histories of part of the universe gives you a mixture for the states of the remaining particles.

After acknowledging that fine-grained histories will have quantum interference terms, Gell-Mann then "coarse-grained" these histories by dividing the fine-grained histories into disjoint sets and treating each set of fine-grained histories as a single coarse-grained history. Gell-Mann stated that this has the effect of "decohering" the coarse-grained histories due to marginalization of the wavefunction of the universe over all variables associated with particles in the environment. It is those particles in the environment that are "entangled" with particles in the system under study that lead to the decoherence:

"In practice, quantum mechanics is always applied to sets of decohering coarse-grained histories, and that is why it is able to predict probabilities. ... What is the underlying explanation for decoherence, the mechanism that makes interference terms sum to zero and permits the assignment of probabilities? It is the entanglement of what is followed in coarse-grained histories with what is ignored or summed over. ... and quantum mechanics tells us that in the summation, under suitable conditions, interference terms vanish between histories involving different fates for what is ignored."

As an example of a non-decohering experiment, Gell-Mann mentioned the double slit experiment and stated that the two histories for the photon, passing through one slit or the other on its way to the screen, interfere and cannot be assigned probabilities. He maintained that it is meaningless in this case to say which slit the photon has come through.

As a justification for the introduction of coarse-graining, Gell-Mann made the claim that we perceive the elements of the universe in the form of mutually exclusive coarse-grained histories. He views these perceived elements as representatives of equivalence classes of fine-grained histories and stated that we treat each fine-grained member of the equivalence class we encounter as if it were the coarse-grained class itself. He then argued that interference terms between alternative fine-grained histories within a single coarse-grained history are "washed out" because they represent the sum of many terms with different signs.

Let us summarize some of the problems that have been pointed out in connection with the various versions of decoherence theory. The first is that the division of the world into object + measuring instrument + environment is an arbitrary choice. Any conclusions drawn based on properties of the environmental component of this division will therefore also share this arbitrariness. Second, as shown above, the marginalization of the wavefunction of an isolated system t into components that are labeled as the k system, which is the measured object system, the M system, which is the measuring instrument, and the E system, which is the environment, involves throwing away detailed information. It is not hard to show, using von Neumann's formula to compute the entropy and the convexity of the entropy function, that this replacement of the t system wavefunction by the product of the k, M and E system wavefunctions by itself leads to an increase in the calculated value of the entropy as mentioned in the last chapter. Third, decoherence theory cannot be applied to an isolated system because there is no external environment to make the system superpositions decohere. Because we can always choose to embed the system plus its whole environment in a larger isolated system, it is not clear that the decoherence point of view can ever lead to any definite result.

Another problem with this theory is that decoherence does not act on all quantum systems to remove superpositions. Gell-Mann [**1994**], p. 147, admitted that there are systems such as the double slit system to which decoherence does not apply at all. Why decoherence does not apply in the double slit experiment case is not clearly explained. On the other hand, he, pp. 148–149, considered the classical character of the trajectory of the planet Mars to be a consequence of the decoherence of the quantum interference terms due to the *physical* effect of many photons, such as those left over from the big bang, striking the planet. Contrary to his statements that decoherence is a consequence of marginalizing the wavefunction over the variables representing the environment, this seems to be a physical decoherence mechanism that operates whether there is a human observer involved or not. Gell-Mann stated that the physical decoherence envisioned in this case is due to the fact the photon distribution is a nearly random environment for the planet. In other words, we attribute a random distribution to these photons in interaction with the planet and then sum over them. In this way, these photons cancel out (most of) the planetary superpositions by the magic of decoherence.

There are a number of flaws in the claim that random environmental influences decohere our perceived world. First, we presume that nature is not doing the summing over the environment because nature does not need to. This means that decoherence does not occur simply because something is immersed in a bath of photons. Thus, unless there are humans or other macroscopic knowing subjects who need to average over the environment in accounting for their observations of the trajectory of Mars, there is no decoherence at all. Second, we could try to sum only the photons striking one side of the planet and account for the others exactly or block them in an eclipse. Gell-Mann does not tell us whether the planet state will fail to decohere in these cases. Third, the properties assumed for the environment are magically just what we need for decoherence. In all cases, the environment is treated as the *deus ex machina* referred to above that randomly interacts with systems in just the right way to decohere them. We might as well skip the story and simply average mathematically over the quantum phases in our representations of experiments and be done with it.

The introduction of coarse-graining by Gell-Mann and Hartle also increases the entropy of the system in an arbitrary way that depends on choices by the experimenter. No physical conclusions can be drawn from a representation of the system by this procedure. In addition, the various superselection schemes invoked have not been made definite and it has not been shown that the system is forced either into a mixture at the end of a measurement or into a given result. Attempts such as these to extract from quantum mechanics a definite result in the face of many possible outcomes and quantum superpositions are similar to the attempt to extract the second law of thermodynamics from the laws of mechanics. Trying to carrying the argument through in both of these cases leads to circularities.

These problems with decoherence theory and other substantialistic theories support the perspective that Bohr's concept of closure needs to be viewed as an epistemological step, and not assign it a physical role, in establishing a connection between a macroscopic subject or measuring instrument and a microscopic system under investigation. Closure represents the fact that at some point a transition must be made from a detailed microscopic account of an event to a macroscopic account of it. To compute the probability of a particular outcome in an experiment, we throw away, so to speak, the information on the coherence of various possible outcomes and treat the result of the measurement and its probability as if it were one outcome selected from a mixture of possibilities. This is a purely epistemological step, reflecting the fact that we are macroscopic objects who cannot obtain or use this information, even in principle, and not a physical or ontological one.

To approach the problem in this way does not explain why we do not see a macroscopic superpositions of the center of mass of an instrument pointer, for example, because such an explanation is not needed in the epistemological view of the quantum state. If such a macroscopic superposition could be achieved, observing it would likely give a particular result for the location of the center of mass or the experiment might fail. It is unlikely that we would see the instrument in two places at once.

16.4 The Transactional Interpretation

John G. Cramer [**1986**] approached the problem of the reduction of the wavefunction, interpreted in substantial terms as a real physical wave, from a different perspective. He presented what he called the *transactional interpretation* of quantum mechanics.[16] Cramer emphasized that his theory provides

---

[16] See Cramer's paper for references to the work of authors mentioned but not cited directly in this section.

an interpretation of the elements of the quantum formalism that does not modify any of the predictions of quantum mechanics.

Although the transactional interpretation has not as yet secured a wide following, it is interesting because it is quite different from the other approaches to interpretation and because of Cramer's critique of the Copenhagen Interpretation.

The Transactional Interpretation is modeled on the Wheeler-Feynman Absorber Theory. The Wheeler-Feynman Absorber Theory is a version of electrodynamics that uses both retarded and advanced potentials in the description of an interaction between charged particles. Wheeler and Feynman originally hoped that it would resolve the problem of the infinite self-energy of the electron and the runaway solutions of the electron equation of motion in standard electrodynamics. In determining the probability that a photon will be emitted by some atom and absorbed by another, the theory uses advanced potential waves moving backward in time from the possible future absorbers of photons and retarded potential waves moving forward in time from potential emitters of photons. The probability of an exchange of a photon between electrons in two specific atoms is computed by means of a superposition of the retarded electromagnetic wave from the emitter atom moving into the future and the advanced wave from the absorber atom moving into the past. The probability of an exchange is at a maximum when these waves interfere constructively. Cramer called the exchange of a particle or photon between atoms a *transaction*, which is a completed interaction that requires both the emission and absorption (in either time direction) of some particle.

Cramer made use of Feynman's 1949 visualization of the time sense of quantum processes and Feynman's interpretation of the positron as an electron traveling backward in time with Wigner's time reversal operator to associate the adjoint wavefunction $\Psi_k^\dagger(Q_k, t)$ with a time-reversed wave. From this point of view, we can interpret the wavefunction $\Psi_k^\dagger(Q_k, t)$ as an advanced particle wave from the future and the wavefunction $\Psi_k(Q_k, t)$ as a retarded particle wave from the past. The real part of Ψ_k is therefore even under time reversal and the imaginary part is odd under time reversal. The basic idea behind the transactional interpretation, then, is that $\Psi_k^\dagger(Q_k, t)$ and $\Psi_k(Q_k, t)$ are both required to define a completed quantum transaction. This fact is reflected in the formula $G_k(t) = \int dQ_k\, \Psi_k^\dagger \mathbf{G} \Psi_k$ for the expectation function $G_k(t)$ of any observable operator $\mathbf{G}$.

Cramer saw the Copenhagen interpretation of quantum mechanics as his chief opponent and provided a critique of the basic tenets of the Copenhagen interpretation. As part of this, he examined the reactions in the literature to Bell's [**1964**], [**1966**], and [**1987**], work on locality and hidden variables in quantum mechanics. Cramer also reviewed the experiments that followed from it. Bell had showed that we cannot maintain simultaneously the assertions that physical quantities have definite values in a physical system and that the quantum state description is local. The former statement concerns unmeasured quantities and has been called *contrafactual definiteness* by Henry Stapp. Cramer mentioned a similar assumption of "an objective external reality independent of the knowledge of observers" by D'Espagnat and the assumption of "realism," i.e., that external reality exists and has definite objective properties whether we measure them or not, in Clauser and Shimony [**1978**]. Cramer characterized the concept of *locality* as the assumption that "the separated parts of the system described are assumed to remain correlated only so long as they retain the possibility of speed-of-light contact and that when isolated from this contact the separated parts can retain correlations only through "memory" of previous contact." He also distinguished the nonlocal enforcement of correlations, the concern here, from nonlocal communication—a much stronger concept.

Cramer mentioned that most physicists, when they considered these issues at all, would probably abandon contrafactual definiteness rather than locality on the grounds that nonlocality may conflict with special relativity in some way. Cramer's transactional interpretation takes the other tack and retains contrafactual definiteness and rejects locality. He explicitly demonstrated that the manifestly nonlocal transactional interpretation that results is "relativistically invariant and fully causal." With reference to an interpretation, Cramer stated "The interpretation must not only relate the formalism to physical observables. It must also define the domain of applicability of the formalism and must interpret the nonobservables in such a way as to avoid paradoxes and contradictions."

A detailed critique of the Copenhagen interpretation was provided by Cramer. He, pp. 649–650, began by stating that it is based on the principles:
C1 The uncertainty principle of Heisenberg;
C2 The statistical interpretation of Born;
C3 The complementarity concept of Bohr;
C4 The identification of the state vector with knowledge by Heisenberg;
C5 The positivism of Heisenberg.
By the "positivism of Heisenberg," Cramer was referring to the statements Heisenberg made that "physics must confine itself to the description of relationships between perceptions." Thus, quantities such as the momentum of a particle between measurements, are not 'objects of physics' as Meyer-Abich would put it. Cramer also noted that this element of the Copenhagen interpretation is the most detachable and that several authors have softened it since Heisenberg first enunciated it in 1927. Cramer maintained that (C1) and (C2) are concerned with the relation of the formalism to experiment and (C3), (C4), and (C5), are concerned with avoiding paradoxes associated with the collapse of the state vector and nonlocality. He asserted that (C1) and (C2) are the only ones used by working physicists and are represented in textbooks as the Copenhagen interpretation.

While Cramer's list of the defining characteristics of the Copenhagen does not match the structure of Bohr's quantum theory, and may not match well the views of Heisenberg, von Neumann, and Pauli, it has some interest in its own right as the basis for his criticism of some elements of standard quantum theory. To avoid confusion, I will express Cramer's criticisms in terms of Cramer's definitions and advise the reader that what he calls the Copenhagen Interpretation does not match the way it has been treated in this book.

The nature of the wavefunction from the Copenhagen perspective was discussed by Cramer in terms of (C2) and (C4). He noted that (C2) does not require that there is a unique wavefunction representing the current and evolving state of a system and claimed that (C4) and (C5) were devised by Heisenberg to avoid the nonlocality problem inherent in interpreting the wavefunction as a real wave in the sense of an electromagnetic wave. The critique of (C4) in particular was a chief concern of Cramer's. He raised the issues of "whose knowledge" the wavefunction refers to and "when" that knowledge may change. He also observed that this interpretation requires an observer that is both conscious and intelligent and noted that observers with these "extra degrees of freedom," which are not present in the quantum formalism itself, are not required for interpretation of the formalism of special relativity.

Cramer objected to many aspects of (C4), but I will restrict my remarks to the most pertinent here. He, p. 652, stated that (C4) requires that the macroscopic observer have a memory and that this implies a direction of time that "is quite alien to and inconsistent with the even-handedness with which microphysics deals with the flow of time." Furthermore, because (C4) requires an observer that is outside the system, (C4) does not apply to the wavefunction of the universe as a whole. Cramer viewed this as a serious defect and stated that it calls into question the identification of the wavefunction with knowledge in (C4). He also noted the objections of Wigner, discussed above, who introduced a second observer into the situation and questioned what happens when one observer makes an observation and then tells the other about the result. Cramer voiced his suspicion that the broad acceptance of (C4) is due more to "the lack of a satisfactory alternative than to its compelling logic."

In Cramer's view, the collapse of the wavefunction in a measurement is one of the most difficult issues to deal with in substantialistic (realistic) interpretations of the wavefunction and one of the chief motivating factors in the adoption of (C4). Various authors have remarked that a substantialistic interpretation requires a role for consciousness in physics,[17] the permanent recording of the results of an experiment,[18] or thermodynamic irreversibility.[19] Cramer, p. 654, observed that most of the efforts to replace the Copenhagen interpretation focused on the problem of the collapse of the wavefunction.

The nonlocality of the wavefunction is another factor that causes difficulties for the substantialistic interpretation of the wavefunction. In a discussion of the Freedman-Clauser experiment, a cascade decay in Calcium that emits two correlated photons, Cramer showed that the experimental results do not support Furry's [**1936a**] idea that the photons were in definite, but random states after they left the region of interaction. They are in states that Cramer called *connected,* but not *specified.* He presented this connectedness as a difficulty for those who claim that the quantum wavefunction reflects our knowledge of the system. He distinguished two variants of principle (C4) above: (C4a) There is a unique wavefunction that describes our knowledge of the system that changes in a measurement; (C4b) Each possible observer ascribes a nonunique wavefunction to the system that changes when his or her knowledge changes. He showed that applying alternative (C4a) to the Freedman-Clauser experiment leads to a problem with relativity or causality in that the collapse of the wavefunction, triggered by measurements of the polarization of each of the photons, will be seen to be triggered by one or the other measurement depending on the frame of reference. This is because distant events in relativity, when a spacelike distance separates them, will occur in either time order depending on the motion of the frame of reference relative to these events. The most serious criticism of (C4b) Cramer could muster was that it "bears little resemblance to the SV [state vector] most physicists *think* they are calculating ...." Cramer, p. 657, concluded that "Nonlocality is dealt with by (C4b) in an airtight but counterintuitive way."

Cramer completed his critique of his version of the Copenhagen interpretation by observing that the greatest weakness in (C2) is that it provides us with no insight into the means by which the probabilistic interpretation comes about in quantum mechanics. It provides us with no insight into the "gaming apparatus" used by nature to chose an outcome. He also objected that (C1) in conjunction with (C4b) weakens the ontological status of (C1) because (C4b) does not locate the uncertainty relations in physical aspects of the particle but seems to locate them in the wavefunction itself.

An ideal interpretation according to Cramer would (1) permit the operation of the microcosm to be separated from the macrocosm and in particular from "knowledge, intelligent observers, consciousness, irreversibility, and measurement;" (2) "it should account for the nonlocal correlations of

---

[17] See Von Neumann [**1932**], London and Bauer [**1939**], and Wigner [**1962**].
[18] See Schrödinger [**1935b**].
[19] See Heisenberg [**1960**].

the Bell inequality tests in a way consistent with relativity and causality;" (3) it should account for the collapse of the wavefunction without the intervention of consciousness; and (4) it should give added insight into the nature of the wavefunction. Based on his analysis, Cramer claimed that the time-symmetric Wheeler-Feynman Absorber theory satisfies these goals. In operation, the Wheeler-Feynman theory of the exchange of energy between electrons requires averaging over all possible future absorbers to calculate the current probability of the emission of a photon by a given electron. Cramer sought to turn this fact to advantage by extending the theory to matter as well as photons with his identification of $\Psi_k^\dagger(Q_k, t)$ as the advanced wavefunction and $\Psi_k(Q_k, t)$ as the retarded wavefunction in quantum mechanical calculations.

In support of his approach, Cramer noted that a classical nonrelativistic approximation of the relativistic Klein-Gordon equation leads to two equations of motion. One is the Schrödinger equation for wavefunction $\Psi_k(Q_k, t)$ and the other is the time-reversed Schrödinger equation for the adjoint wavefunction $\Psi_k^\dagger(Q_k, t)$. Both of these equations are required for a full description of a physical system in quantum mechanics. The adjoint wavefunction involves negative energy components and is usually discarded. Negative energy components also appear when we try to localize a particle too closely. The negative energy components have been interpreted as the onset of particle pair production due to the large amount the energy required by the precise localization procedure.[20]

The transactional interpretation is based on the following principles presented by Cramer, p. 665–666:

T1 The uncertainty principle of Heisenberg (same as (C1));

T2 The statistical interpretation of Born (same as (C2));

T3 All physical processes, including observers, consciousness, and the like, have equal status and none serves in a special role in measurement; both the "wholeness" and "complementary" aspects of (C3) are retained but are reinterpreted in the light of action of the combined advanced and retarded waves;

T4 "The fundamental quantum-mechanical interaction is taken to be the transaction, ... The state vector of the quantum mechanical formalism is a real physical wave with spatial extent and is identical with the initial retarded "offer wave" of the transaction." A transaction is only complete when the appropriate quantum boundary conditions are satisfied at all loci of admission and absorption. "The correspondence of the state vector with "knowledge of the system" of (C4) is a fortuitous but deceptive consequence of the transaction, in that such knowledge must follow and describe the transaction."

---

[20]Issues of localization and negative energy states of Dirac electrons are considered in QIS.

T5 "A distinction must be made between observable and inferred quantities. The former are firm predictions of the overall theory and may be subjected to experimental verification. The latter ... are not verifiable and are useful only for interpretational and pedagogical purposes. It is assumed that both kinds of quantities must obey conservation laws, macroscopic causality conditions, relativistic invariance, etc. Resorting to the positivism of (C5) is unnecessary and undesirable."

Cramer went on to show that the transactional interpretation is able to explain the elements of standard quantum mechanics. He discussed the failure of Schrödinger's interpretation of $\Psi_k(Q_k, t)$ as a real wave in terms of the nonlocal interaction at a distance aspect of correlated quantum states, the fact that $\Psi_k(Q_k, t)$ is complex, and the fact that particles cannot be interpreted as wavepackets. He observed that these problems do not affect the transactional interpretation because the superposition of advanced and retarded waves is real ($\Psi_k + \Psi_k^\dagger = 2\mathrm{Re}\Psi_k$), and both the nonlocal and particle aspects of the wavefunction are taken account of by the requirements placed on a completed transaction. He then presented a number of experiments, including the Freedman-Clauser experiment, which were interpreted in accord with the transactional interpretation.

The compatibility of the transactional interpretation with some of the thought experiments that test the conceptual situation in quantum mechanics were the next subjects of Cramer's analysis. For Renninger's [**1960**] negative-result thought experiment, Cramer noted that the absence of an observable result when one is expected is also a measurement and leads to a reduction of the wavefunction.[21] This fact calls into question Schrödinger's [**1935b**] distinguishable states interpretation of a measurement, which claims that two macroscopically distinguishable states are distinct whether observed or not. Similar considerations were applied to Heisenberg's [**1960**], pp. 60–62, requirement of the registration of an irreversible thermodynamic (or macroscopic) change.

Another experiment, devised by Wigner, consisted of a modified version of the two-slit experiment. This experiment is called Wigner's delayed choice experiment because the choice of what to measure is made at random while the photons are in flight from their source toward several possible targets to be chosen. The choices are to measure the interference pattern on a screen, raised for that purpose during the experiment, or to use one of two telescopes instead of the screen. Each telescope is concerned with one slit and is aimed in a way that can ascertain whether the photon passed through that slit. Cramer showed that the transactional interpretation works in this setting because no transaction is complete until a photon is exchanged so the delay in choosing

---

[21] See also the conceptual discussion of modern versions of "interaction free measurements", previously referred to as "negative measurements" in the literature, in Paul Kwait, Harald Weinfurter, and Anton Zeilinger [**1996**] and the references cited there.

which version of the experiment to perform does not affect the fact that it is the successful observation of the photon by some device that determines what the transaction was. Cramer, p. 674, noted that this experiment, along with those called *Schrödinger's cat* and *Wigner's friend,* are all concerned with *when* an experiment is complete and the collapse of the wavefunction occurs. There are no guideposts in the behavior of the microscopic particles to tell us, so this is a matter of choice on our part. From Cramer's point of view, the question is not when but *how* the wavefunction collapses and he offered an account of this in terms of a transactional view of the experiment.

A thought experiment was devised by Herbert in 1982 to allow faster than light communication by making measurements of the polarizations of distant correlated photons. Cramer blamed the Copenhagen Interpretation for misleading Herbert into thinking that the measurement of the state of polarization of one photon would lead immediately to the collapse of the wavefunction and that the second photon would be in a particular polarization state before it was measured. If this is true, a third photon in the same state can be cloned from the second photon and local correlation measurements on these two photons would allow us to decide the state measured for the first photon at a location that may be light years away. A careful analysis shows that this interpretation cannot be maintained and that faster than light communication is not possible with this method. Cramer argued in his interpretation of this experiment, echoing Bohr, that it is only a completed observation, involving all the components, that can be analyzed properly. Conclusions of the sort Herbert wanted cannot be drawn from a change due to measurement in one part of a correlated system.

In a discussion from the transactional perspective of the Hanbury-Brown-Twiss long baseline interferometry experiment in astronomy, Cramer, p. 676, noted that "particles like photons and electrons cannot consistently be described as blobs that travel from point 1 or 2 to point A or B." He also noted that we cannot state unequivocally that the photons observed originated uniquely in one source or the other. This point is relevant to (T4) which states that transferred particles have no separate identity apart from that enforced by the appropriate boundary conditions. He also discussed the Albert-Aharonov-D'Amato thought experiment in this regard.

The transactional interpretation offered by Cramer is both thoughtful and interesting. I will limit my critical remarks to a few observations. The weakest point is the reliance on the Wheeler-Feynman Absorber theory and its use to account for the observed results in some of the experiments Cramer discusses. There are problems with this alternative interpretation of electrodynamics as Cramer acknowledges. In addition, his extension of the electromagnetic transaction perspective to a duality between the "retarded" quantum wavefunction and its "advanced" adjoint for material particles is intriguing as an explanation of this duality, but this has not been thoroughly investigated.

In many ways, Cramer's position is close to Bohr's position in that both maintain that only completed experiments can be analyzed. Putting aside the proposed transactional mechanism and the ascription of reality to the quantum wavefunction as a physical wave, many of Cramer's viewpoints are compatible with those of Bohr.

16.5 Quantum Entanglement

The ubiquitous role of Schrödinger's concept of entanglement in discussions of quantum phenomena has been noted above. Many of the papers using entanglement assign special properties to entangled states and draw conclusions about what can be obtained from these states. This is particularly true of papers on what is called quantum teleportation, quantum computation, and quantum communication. There has been a proliferation of new concepts, e.g., 'quantum information theory', a distinction between 'classical channels' and 'quantum channels' for the transmission of information, and claims of an 'entanglement assisted channel capacity' and increased capacity using quantum 'superdense coding',[22] a distinction between 'classical strategies' and 'quantum strategies' in an extension to quantum theory of the theory of games introduced by John von Neumann and Oskar Morgenstern,[23] 'quantum cryptography', and many others.

Although statements about entanglement by authors of experiments discussed previously were accepted for the sake of argument to get at the issue under discussion, many of the ways in which it has been employed are suspect. Schrödinger introduced entanglement to characterize two independent systems that come into interaction, entangle their states, and then leave the interaction and become independent again. He assumed initially that quantum systems spontaneously convert their entangled superpositions into mixtures with the passage of time. In moving from this earlier conception to his post EPR conception, he retained his definition of entanglement but gave up the idea that quantum systems would spontaneously convert their superpositions into mixtures.

To use the concept of entanglement in the description of an experiment presumes that it is legitimate to assign separate states to the components of a system before they have interacted and again after they have ceased interacting. The notion of inseparability, i.e., the situation in which the state of a system cannot be factored into a product of the states of individual components in the system, was discussed above. As far as the concept of entanglement is used in a way equivalent to the inseparability of a state,

---

[22]See, for example, Charles H. Bennett, Peter W. Shor, John A. Smolin and Ashish Thaplial [**1999**] and the references cited there.

[23]See David A. Meyer [**1999**] and Jens Eisert, Martin Wilkens and Maciej Lewenstein [**1999**] and their references. The quantum theory of games is discussed briefly in QIS in an examination of the status and proper application of the concept of a quantum mixture.

it is not controversial and fits with Bohr's ideas. However, the discussions of entangled states in the recent literature referred to go far beyond this viewpoint.

The concept of entanglement is most often used in contexts in which it is assumed, at least implicitly, that a quantum system and its components are always in some quantum state whether or not there is an experimental arrangement to define it. The discussion then proceeds to draw conclusions about how this entanglement will affect other states as the experiment proceeds. A good example is Gell-Mann's [1994] distinction between the ground state of a hydrogen atom, which he characterized as a definite one electron state that is unentangled, and the ground state of a helium atom, which he characterized as consisting of two entangled electron states. The presumption in this characterization of the ground state of the helium atom is that it makes sense to assign states to individual electrons in an atom. As noted above, this implies that these individual states are properties of the electrons. This point of view is typical of many, if not most, of the discussions of quantum experiments, whether thought experiments or real ones, and is clearly at odds with Bohr's thinking.[24]

The assignment of states to individual components of a quantum system is appropriate for a substantival interpretation of the wavefunction because the states of quantum entities are assumed to be properties of the entities. However, the many objections to this view presented above in discussions of the quantum state, its arbitrary aspects, and its dependence on the choices of the experimenter, shows that this perspective cannot be held consistently. If the quantum state is seen to depend on the experimental context as Bohr concluded it must be, many of the discussions of entanglement in particular experiments make invalid or unwarranted assumptions about what information is available or how states can be represented in a given context. The concept of entanglement also relies on a presumed fundamental distinction between pure states and mixtures to draw its conclusions.[25] These points raise serious questions concerning the interpretations given for quantum teleportation, quantum communication, and many similar experiments and thought experiments, that have appeared in the recent literature.

From Bohr's perspective, particles are brought together and come apart in the context of a given experimental arrangement in which observations are made. The experimental arrangement, with definite initial and boundary conditions, determines what we can say about a system and how we should represent it during the whole course of the experiment. This also determines

---

[24]Other recent analyses of the picture of the sequence of events provided by Schrödinger's entanglement model have complained that it is too rooted in classical conceptions and is not framed properly for quantum mechanics. See Alexander Bach [1988], pp. 639–640, and Park [1991].

[25]Longstanding objections to the distinction between pure states and mixtures are discussed in QIS.

what state is appropriate to assign to the system and whether or not individual components of the system can be assigned their own states. It is easy to show that the representation of two systems or two components of one system by a joint wavefunction versus their representation by the product of two independent wavefunctions in the course of an experiment are not equivalent either mathematically or physically. From Bohr's point of view, the experimental arrangement defines which representation is appropriate and therefore whether correlations are significant in a given experiment.[26]

While the problem in using the concept of entanglement follows from the implicit assumption that individual components have separate states that have become entangled, it is important to note that not all papers using nonseparable states are subject to this criticism. In some papers on quantum computation, for example, a nonseparable state of a collection of ions is used as a register for a quantum computer gate that can provide, as the state evolves, parallel computations of different solutions for a problem. The answer is obtained at the end by measuring a quantity associated with one of the components of the quantum system. Another example is the recent use of the Bose-Einstein condensate of a gas to slow the speed of light. The proposed and actual experiments of these types prepare the system in a nonseparable quantum state, but they do not assume or require that the subcomponents have definite individual states. Bohr would have no objection to this.

16.6 Reflection 25

There are many experiments, in addition to the ones Cramer cited, that illustrate seemingly paradoxical aspects of quantum mechanics. One type of experiment depends on a concrete physical model of the entity having an independent existence as the experimental arrangement is changed, sometimes randomly, during the course of the experiment. The analysis of experiments such as these get at the issues of how much we can trust our conceptual models of the microscopic world. These models are useful in investigating the questions associated with the intermediate reduction of the wavefunction in the course of an experiment or the attribution of a definite state to an entity in the middle of an experiment. In each case, quantum mechanics can successfully make predictions even if the author is complaining about its interpretational problems.

The various substantival interpretations of the wavefunction are faced with too many problems to be serious contenders for a role in a conceptual framework that supports quantum mechanics. It was problems such as these that Bohr was trying to avoid by focusing on the epistemological issues. He had embraced the wave-particle duality as a consequence of various wave and particle experiments for both electromagnetic radiation and matter

---

[26]These issues are discussed in much more detail in QIS, Chapter 3.

that he considered paradigmatic for attributing the wave and particle concepts. He realized that the wave-particle duality by itself makes a reasonable substantival interpretation impossible.

The complaints raised here about the interpretation of the wavefunction are not new. The problems faced by this view, which were present from Schrödinger's first attempts to interpret the wavefunction as the density of charge or matter, have to do with how to interpret the division of the wavefunction into parts in a double slit experiment or in explaining the interaction between a particle and a whole diffraction grating followed by the subsequent observation of the particle when it strikes a screen. The dissipation of particle wavepackets over time or the splitting of the energy of particles at half-silvered mirrors are also problems for this view. Schrödinger [**1935a**], pp. 161–167, long ago raised similar objections to the effect that ψ is not a model of reality because one cannot assume that the system can always be described by some state. He also stated that in a measurement ψ disappears and is replaced by another.

In the discussion of the recent attempts by Gell-Mann, Żurek, and other decoherence theorists, to invoke the environment as a randomizing feature, a parallel was noted between this strategy and that of Boltzmann with the molecular chaos assumption, Planck with the assumption of "natural radiation", and with other theories that simply invoke randomization without explanation. There is little formally that distinguishes these recent theories from those that preceded them by many years. In each of the substantival interpretations except Everett's relative state interpretation, this randomization step has the effect of triggering an averaging procedure that separates the variables of one system from another and makes them independent of each other. This has the result of making the subject/object distinction without providing an understanding or acknowledgment of why it is important. In that sense these interpretations achieve functional equivalence to quantum theory at the cost of introducing procedures, mechanisms, and justifications, which are less plausible physically and philosophically than Bohr's no nonsense epistemological approach. Saving materialist particle metaphysics seems hardly worth the trouble.

CHAPTER 17

Epistemological Issues in Quantum Physics

Electromagnetic radiation plays a central and inescapable role in our interactions with the world. As with the particle theories examined in the last chapter, the quantum theory of electromagnetic radiation has conceptual problems associated with localization, superposition, and the separation of states. The discussion includes these and other outstanding questions in the theory of electromagnetic radiation and quantum mechanics.

17.1 Conceptual Issues in Electrodynamics

Almost all of our empirical information about the world comes to us via electromagnetic radiation. Internally, information is transmitted along our nerves by waves of membrane depolarization. It is stored in our brains by means that we do not yet fully understand. The ubiquity of electromagnetic radiation and electric charge in the capturing, transmission, and storing of knowledge, has important implications. In an analysis of the possibilities of knowledge, for example, there is the question of how the finite bandwidth, slow signal transmission, and limited capacity of our internal information processing and storage system influences what we can know. It certainly limits the amount of information that any one person can personally acquire and store. But it does not prevent us from creating books and machines to do much more. Nor is it likely that the fact that our internal "symbolic" representation of objects and our ability to manage complexity by creating layers of abstraction depends on the electro-chemical substrate provided by the brain. Nevertheless, the possibility remains that a Kantian case could be made that a system such as this is inherently limited in certain ways.

Electromagnetic radiation plays an important role in the physics of both the large and small. The special and general theories of relativity attribute some special properties to electromagnetic radiation and depend on it to define a connection between distant parts of the universe. Reconciling the transformation properties of the electromagnetic field with the transformation properties of mechanics by means of Lorentz transformations was the one of the great triumphs of the special theory of relativity. Quantum electrodynamics united special relativity and quantum mechanics to give an astoundingly accurate account of the behavior of electromagnetic radiation and its interactions with matter.

Among the issues that were not resolved in classical electrodynamics is the relation between the electromagnetic field and charged particles. Although they interact, the mathematics of that interaction is paradoxical. These problems include the "preacceleration" of charged particles in a classical electromagnetic field and runaway solutions that predict a particle will continue to accelerate indefinitely.[1] One mathematically cogent response to these problems was the Wheeler-Feynman Absorber Theory, discussed briefly in the last chapter, which used ideas that seemed to violate causality by employing both advanced and retarded fields in the equations of motion of the charged particle.[2] The solutions obtained with advanced potentials and fields by several workers imply that there is something important at the root. I also mentioned briefly above the view of the quantum state proposed by Feynman [1948] in his seminal work on quantum electrodynamics. He considered the

---
[1] See Fritz Rohrlich [1965], pp. 147–152, 176–179.
[2] Wheeler and Feynman [1945]. See also the discussion of their work in Silvan Schweber [1994], pp. 380–389, and the related work of Dirac [1938].

relationship of the description of the electron in terms of a wavefunction $\psi(x)$ and the description of the positron in terms of the Hermitian conjugate function $\psi^\dagger(x)$. Wheeler advanced at this time the idea that there is only one electron in the universe. This electron seems like many electrons at many different places because it is on complex a trajectory weaving forward and backward in time. Feynman used this idea to view the positron state as the same as the electron state with the time reversed. Preserving the notion of causality in these theories may be difficult—but it is not a reason for rejecting them.

Aharonov-Bohm Effect.

In Chapter 4, a brief review was given of the work of Aharonov and Bohm on the question of locality with regard to an electromagnetic potential. They challenged the usual conception in physics that potentials are convenient fictions and that only their gradients, the forces, are real physical entities with dynamic consequences. Aharonov and Bohm showed theoretically that, if locality is a requirement on quantum theory, the potential itself has an important role in modifying the wavefunction and the behavior of objects it describes.[3] Because this work calls into question our notions concerning the fictional status of potentials on the one hand and our conception of locality on the other, it deserves further discussion. In four-dimensional notation, the electromagnetic field strengths, $F_{rs}(x^t)$, are obtained from the electromagnetic potential, $A_r(x^t)$ by

$$(17.1) \qquad F_{rs}(x^t) = \frac{\partial A_r(x^t)}{\partial x^s} - \frac{\partial A_s(x^t)}{\partial x^r}.$$

In this equation $x^t = (ct, x^\mu)$ and $1 \leq r, s, t \leq 4$. In three-dimensional notation, the electric field components are $\mathfrak{E}^\mu(x^t) = F^{0,\mu}(x^t)$ for $1 \leq \mu, \nu, \xi \leq 3$, and the magnetic field components are $\mathfrak{H}^\mu(x^t) = \epsilon^{\mu\nu\xi} F_{\nu\xi}(x^t)$ (no summation over ν and ξ). The quantity $\epsilon^{\mu\nu\xi}$ is the completely antisymmetric 3-dimensional unit tensor with value +1 for even permutations of the indices and -1 for odd permutations of the indices.

The electromagnetic Lorentz force on a particle with charge q and three-velocity v_ν is

$$(17.2) \qquad \mathfrak{F}^\mu(x^t) = \mathsf{q}\left[\mathfrak{E}^\mu(x^t) + \epsilon^{\mu\nu\xi} v_\nu \mathfrak{H}_\xi(x^t)\right],$$

---

[3] For more information, see Aharonov and Bohm [**1959**], [**1961b**], [**1962**], [**1963**]. See also the different manifestations and aspects of the Aharonov-Bohm effect presented in W. H. Furry and N. F. Ramsey [**1960**], R. G. Chambers [**1960**], H. Boersch, H. Hamish, D. Wholleben and K. Grobmann [**1960**], Henri Mitler [**1961**], L. J. Tassie and M. Peshkin [**1961**], Peshkin, I. Talmi and Tassie [**1961**], F. G. Werner and D. R. Brill [**1960**], Stanley Mandelstam [**1962**], B. DeWitt [**1962**], F. Lenz [**1962**], G. Mollenstedt and W. Bayh [**1962**], G. T. Trammel [**1964**], Martin Kretzschmar [**1965b**], B. Liebowitz [**1968**], and Herman Erlichson [**1970**].

where repeated contravariant and covariant indices are summed over as usual. It is easy to show by (17.1) that the field strengths and Lorentz forces acting on a charged particle are unchanged if the electromagnetic potential is altered by a four-dimensional gauge transformation

$$(17.3) \qquad A_r(x^t) \to A'_r(x^t) = A_r(x^t) + \frac{\partial \Lambda(x^t)}{\partial x^r},$$

where the gauge function $\Lambda(x^t)$ is an arbitrary continuously differentiable function of x^t. It is this arbitrariness that led to the view in classical theory that potentials are calculational aids devoid of primary physical significance. Aharonov and Bohm suggested experiments that could show interference effects due to the different phases of electrons passing through a field-free region on one side of a domain containing a magnetic flux compared to those passing through a field-free region on the other side.

The Aharonov-Bohm effect was validated experimentally in a number of papers soon after it was proposed. The experiment by R. C. Jaklevic, J. J. Lambe, A. H. Silver, and J. E. Mercereau [**1964**], for example, used the modulation of the conduction through a pair of parallel Josephson junctions located at opposite sides of a circular conductor to show that the conduction was proportional to the flux Φ within the circle regardless of whether this flux was produced by an external magnetic field or by a completely enclosed solenoid within the circle. In the latter case, the field strength at the junctions was negligible. The authors concluded that there is a physically observable effect produced by a static vector potential under conditions in which the field effects are absent. The observed effect was in accord with quantum mechanical calculations and the authors stated that "This observation seems to promote the vector potential [A^r] to a position of experimental reality long enjoyed by its derivatives, the electric and magnetic fields." A number of other experimenters have also observed the effect.

In response to the Aharonov-Bohm work, Stanley Mandelstam [**1962**] showed that attempts to remove the potential from quantum mechanics and replace it everywhere with field strengths leads to nonlocalities in the wave equations. He replaced the potential $A^r(x^t)$ by a path integral of the field strength $F_{rs}(x^t)$ from infinity to the four-dimensional point x^t. A similar result was obtained by P. D. Noerdlinger [**1962**], Bryce S. DeWitt [**1962**], Frederik J. Belinfante [**1962**], and V. I. Ogievestskii and I. V. Polubarinov [**1962**]. In response, Aharonov and Bohm [**1963**], p. 1625–1626, observed that the potential $A_r(x^t)$ had been replaced in these papers by one of the nonlocal forms

$$(17.4) \qquad A'_r(x^t) = \int_{-\infty}^{0} d\chi \, F_{rs}(z^\lambda) \frac{\partial z^s(x^t, \chi)}{\partial \chi}$$

or

$$(17.5) \qquad A_r''(x^t) = \int d^3z \, F_{rs}(z^t) \frac{(x^s - z^s)}{4\pi r^3}.$$

This is the trade-off: either we accept the potentials and the canonical way in which Schrödinger's equation, a complete set of commuting observables, and the field equations are developed from them, or we are faced with nonlocal equations expressed in terms of forces and an uglier formalism such as that developed by Mandelstam.

In the final paper in their series, Aharonov and Bohm [**1963**] focused on the conceptual issues that they felt followed from their work. They emphasized that when quantum electrodynamics is expressed in terms of potentials, a complete local set of commuting observable operators and a set of purely local equations of motion follow. They also stated that the *principle of localizability* plays a role in the current formulation of mathematical theories in this domain and that there is no "clear and natural" way to express this in terms of the field strengths. It was in this sense that they viewed the potentials as playing an "essential" role in quantum mechanics. Aharonov and Bohm acknowledged that the formulations (17.4) and (17.5) can be used in place of the potentials, but maintained that this is not *mere* a matter of convenience or taste because it ignores the importance of the *unasserted* physical-geometrical assumptions that underlie the development of theories. They emphasized the topological and structural form of these theories as an important consideration. They answered the objections of DeWitt and Belinfante that the potentials were not observables by stressing that a number of quantities that are not directly observable play an important role in physics. Finally, they stated that they did not consider the current form of quantum mechanics to be its final form.

Recent discussions of the interference patterns in the Aharonov-Bohm effect attribute these patterns to the fact that the constant potential in a region has the effect of changing the phase of the particle wavefunction as a function of position in the force-free region. This differential phase change is the cause of the light and dark bands of the interference pattern. It is not due to changes in the particle paths because of forces acting on them.

It seems that the 'action at a distance' potential, which we thought had been replaced by the field concept, has reared it head again in the Aharonov-Bohm effect. It appears that the nonlocality of quantum mechanics in EPR type experiments has a deep physical counterpart in the domain of the quantum electromagnetic field that had previously been seen as analogous to the local classical field.[4]

---

[4]It should be mentioned that the treatment given here does not exhaust either the physical or philosophical consequences of the Aharonov-Bohm effect. These will be discussed further in QIS in relation to more recent work on gauge theories.

17.2 Locality and Superposition in Quantum Mechanics

One of the most striking result concerning locality is that obtained by R. L. Pfleegor and Leonard Mandel [1967]. They were engaged in testing Dirac's [1930], p. 9, statement that the wavefunction of a photon interferes only with itself. Using beams from two independent, i.e., not coherent, lasers, and limiting the number of photons in the system at a time to one, they, p. 1088, showed that Dirac appears to be right. Their conclusion is of some interest:

"In terms of photons, the experiment raises one or two interesting questions of interpretation. Whereas, in a conventional interferometer with a half-silvered mirror it is possible (if undesirable) to think of each photon as going partly into each beam, this point of view is even less valid here, since the beams originate in two separate sources. It seems better to associate the interference with the detection process itself, in the sense that the localization of a photon at the detector makes it intrinsically uncertain from which of the two sources it came. For, in order that the appearance of interference fringes be identifiable, it is necessary that the position of each absorbed photon be recognizable to within $\Delta x < l = \lambda/\theta$ (λ is the wavelength) in the direction normal to the fringe and to $\vec{k}$. This implies that the component of the photon momentum in this direction is necessarily uncertain by an amount $\Delta p_x \geq \hbar\theta/\lambda = \hbar k\theta$ which is just enough to rule out any identification of the source. No measurement of the sources will yield this information without at the same time destroying the fringes."

Commenting on this, R. J. Sciamanda [1969] stated that we could have anticipated this result long ago by using a full analysis of certain ordinary interference experiments involving mirrors (Lloyd's mirror; interferometers). Every theory of reflection involves the absorption of incident photons and the subsequent emission of the reflected photons. No photon preserves its "identity" in such processes (though phase and direction relations are preserved) unlike the double-slit experiment case. As Sciamanda, p. 1129, observed, "The basic difficulty seems to stem from an intuitive temptation to view spatially separated sources as necessarily producing physically different photons ...." He maintained that we must write a wavefunction as a superposition of amplitudes for all the possible photon sources since "in the general situation an observed photon carries with it no label identifying its previous path or the location of its source." Only under special experimental conditions can one associate a definite source location with an observed photon. In other words, p. 1130, it makes no sense to say that a photon originated in a definite location if it is in principle impossible to determine that location. The same

17.2 LOCALITY AND SUPERPOSITION IN QUANTUM MECHANICS

principle applies to the question of how many photons we are dealing with at a given time.

Mandel [**1999**] reviewed the theoretical descriptions of a number of single photon interference optical experiments that have been performed in recent years. These interference experiments, and some of those with other particles such as neutrons, are arranged so that only a single photon or particle is present in the apparatus at a time and there was a long delay, by microscopic standards, before the arrival of the next one. Mandel calculated the interference to be expected in some configurations of an experiment and not in others and showed the strong agreement of the calculated curves with experiment. He, p. S275, then stated that "interference is the physical manifestation of the intrinsic indistiguishability of the sources of the photon paths. If the different photon paths from source to detector are indistinguishable, then we have to add the corresponding probability amplitudes before squaring to obtain the probability. On the other hand, if there is some way, even in principle, of distinguishing the photon paths, then the corresponding probabilities have to be added and there is no interference." He again reiterated the conclusion of Pfleegor and Mandel that one photon does not interfere with another. It is only the two probability amplitudes of the same photon that can interfere with each other.

The results of Pfleegor and Mandel, the commentary of Sciamanda, and the subsequent reflections of Mandel, add strong support to Bohr's point of view concerning the inapplicability of spacetime pictures to photons. I interpret the association of the interference with the "detection process itself", as Pfleegor and Mandel suggested, from Bohr's point of view as a consequence of our choice of the whole experimental arrangement in this case—including the lasers and the detection equipment as Sciamanda mentioned. Even though one photon was in the system at a time, interference effects were observed. This implies that a photon is not interfering with other distinct photons. Bohr's wholehearted acceptance of the wave-particle duality and its consequences has no difficulty here. But those who try to hold the particle picture of the photon as primary and "attribute" the wavefunction to it in the form of a wavepacket, and then speak of the unfolding picture of the moving wavepacket as representing in some blurred way the behavior of the particle, which breaks into pieces at a half-silvered mirror, etc., have great difficulty with these results. Similarly, those who hold the field as primary have trouble with the photoelectric effect.

Not everyone agrees with the interpretation given by Pfleegor and Mandel of their experiment. While accepting their experimental results, Harry Paul [**1986**], for example, has presented an extended argument based on an analysis of modern optical experiments that claims independent photons can interfere with each other. There has also been an explosion of papers in the 1990s using modern experimental techniques that allow working with beams consisting of single atoms at a time and making these beams interfere. In some of these papers, the question was debated as to whether Bohr's concept of complementarity is simply a consequence of Heisenberg's uncertainty relations or has an independent basis. The controversy was rooted in the disturbance theory of measurement, discussed in Chapter 5, which some current textbooks still present as one of the underpinnings for the uncertainty relations and complementarity. The question under investigation in the recent papers was whether momentum transfers, which supposedly occur in the process of measuring which path a photon or particle takes in an interference experiment, are always responsible for washing out interference phenomena when the path is measured. Because new optical and resonance cavity techniques have minimized the amount of energy and associated momentum transfer needed to ascertain the presence of a particle in a volume, the momentum transfers were claimed to be much smaller than those required to destroy the interference fringes.

While I support the perspective on the role of the detector presented by Pfleegor and Mandel, a complete discussion will require an analysis of the theory of interference phenomena in quantum mechanics and the associated formalism and methods for demonstrating interference. The detailed discussion will therefore be postponed and taken up again in QIS.

17.3 Outstanding Issues in Quantum Physics

Let us consider now a number of concepts that play a role in both classical and quantum physics. The goal is to raise questions associated with the use and interpretation of these concepts and, where appropriate, show what Bohr's perspective was on them. The concern is strictly with the issues associated with these concepts in standard quantum mechanics and not with their expression in relativistic quantum theory, field theory, or elsewhere. Many of the concepts below are associated with the employment of what I call macroscopic concepts in conjunction with the microscopic description provided by quantum mechanics. I will not try to resolve the issues associated with them here. Sorting out these issues in quantum mechanics, and the proposed solutions of the problems associated with them, is the focus of the work in QIS and QTS.

Volume.

The system volume has been virtually ignored in quantum mechanical texts and papers. If it is considered at all, the volume is often a "throwaway" normalization factor in the definition of the electromagnetic field or in a 'particle in a box' calculation used to define solutions of Schrödinger's equation with discrete energy levels. At the end of a calculation in these cases, the volume normalization is usually discarded by taking the limit Vol $\to \infty$. The lack of interest in the system volume is understandable in that the focus of most quantum mechanical calculations has been on a few particles interacting with each other or with planewave states representing a beam of particles that is scattered by a fixed classical potential representing a target. With this focus, most of the attention has been on computing scattering cross-sections, approximation methods, using various special potentials such as the coulomb potential, and working out special cases such as the harmonic oscillator. The system volume in these cases appears only indirectly, and usually not explicitly, in the normalization of the wavefunctions.

There is a second reason why the volume of a system of particles has been neglected. This is because many quantum operators are no longer Hermitian when they are computed in a bounded domain in coordinate space. For this reason, most workers have shied away from computations in finite volumes and others have spoken of "unwanted surface terms". However, almost all systems of interest to us are located in bounded volumes, so the representation of macroscopic bodies, and their treatment as separate objects in thermodynamics makes a formalism expressed in terms of volumes and boundaries desirable. Some of the issues along these lines have been discussed by W. L. Clinton [1962].[5]

Von Neumann did use the system volume in his discussion of entropy in quantum thermodynamics, but these calculations were based on the standard equilibrium thermodynamics available to him. The definition of a general quantum thermodynamics requires an interacting systems point of view so that the thermodynamic volume derivative of the system can be defined and issues concerning the temperature and entropy in the nonequilibrium case can be resolved.

Time.
Time is clearly treated differently from space in quantum mechanics. In Chapter 3, in connection with the uncertainty relations, the difference between the association of time and energy and the association of position and momentum as conjugate variables in quantum mechanics was mentioned. This difference is puzzling in the light of the association between time-space and energy-momentum, and their corresponding transformation properties, in relativity theory. In spite of this, attempts to define time as a dynamical variable in quantum mechanics have all failed. In addition, the failure of an attempt by Allcock [1969] to define the 'time of arrival' for quantum particles in the standard formalism led him to propose an alternative to von Neumann's characterization of measurement.

Localization.
Although quantum mechanics is usually treated as a mechanics of particles that show certain wave properties, the use of the particle concept in

---
[5]See also the discussion of macroscopic bodies and measurement by a classical apparatus in A. Peres and N. Rosen [1964a], [1964b].

quantum calculations encounters difficulties. These difficulties are easiest to see in connection with attempts to represent particles localized in a volume or to compute the probability of their arrival at a detector within a particular time interval.

An illustration of these problems is the mathematical result that a particle in a localized state at one moment in time immediately spreads to all space in the following instant. Several versions of this spreading theorem, based in nonrelativistic quantum mechanics, relativistic quantum mechanics, and quantum field theory, respectively, were proved by a number of authors. These results present a serious challenge to the construction of macroscopic objects out of a quantum particle foundation and they threaten to undermine the possibility of a local thermodynamics in the quantum domain.

Energy.

In classical theory, entities cannot enter regions from which they are energetically forbidden. In quantum mechanics, states are not strictly limited to regions that are energetically allowed. There is a small, but finite probability of finding a particle in a region of a potential that would be energetically forbidden to it in classical theory. This fact allows particles to "tunnel" through small volumes that are energetically forbidden to them and emerge into another allowed volume.

Energy plays a central role in classical mechanics as does the symplectic structure of the coordinate and momentum aspects of classical Hamiltonian mechanics. This symplectic structure results from the fact that the particle i momentum $p_i(t)$ is a function of the vector $\dot{q}_i(t)$ that is tangent to the coordinate trajectory $q_i(t)$. The energy retains its central role in quantum mechanics and the symplectic aspects of the classical mechanical state (q, p) are preserved by the dual $(q, -i\hbar \partial/\partial q)$ structure of quantum mechanics.[6] Because potential energy in the classical sense is expressed in units of energy and can be converted to kinetic energy of particles under suitable circumstances, it is plausible that these potentials have an independent significance in quantum mechanics as suggested by Aharonov and Bohm.

Spin.

The classical concept of the spin of a macroscopic body is generalized in quantum mechanics to that of particle spin, which was discussed in terms of Pauli's characterization as a nonclassical two-valuedness. Electron spin is needed, for example, in the theory of the hydrogen atom to preserve the conservation of angular momentum of the electron stationary state when the charged electron circulates in the electrostatic field around the proton. The classical and quantum mechanical separation of the angular momentum into orbital angular momentum and particle spin is not preserved under relativistic

---

[6] See the discussion of these topics for classical and quantum mechanics in Mackey [**1963**].

transformations. The notion of spin still has more surprises in store for us as illustrated in the discussion of the 'spin crisis' in Robert Jaffe [**1995**].

Symmetry.
Another decidedly nonclassical aspect of the quantum state function for multiparticle systems is the symmetry requirement on the wavefunction. The joint wavefunction for a collection of identical particles is required in quantum mechanics to satisfy either symmetric or antisymmetric statistics under interchange of particles.

Symmetry issues, expressed as the requirement that electrons be exchanged in calculations of multielectron atoms, appeared in 1926 in the work of Heisenberg on the many-body problem in quantum mechanics.[7] This was followed shortly by the work of Heitler and London who calculated chemical bonds in terms of exchange forces. The model was an actual exchange of identical particles at different locations in a molecule. At this time, the Born interpretation of the square of the quantum wavefunction as a probability had not been fully accepted and issues of superposition and symmetry were not well understood. Heisenberg went on in 1928 to use the notion of exchange forces to explain ferromagnetism, which had been mysterious because the spin-spin interaction forces in iron atoms were too weak by themselves to line electron spins up at room temperature and account for it. Other applications of exchange forces were used to explain the spectra of multielectron atoms and electron collisions.

The notion of exchange forces was extended to nuclear forces implicitly in work of Heisenberg in 1932 and more explicitly in the work of Majorana in 1933. It quickly became the dominant view of nuclear forces. As Carson has shown, the concept of an exchange of identical particles between locations eventually evolved into the concept of a force due to an exchange of particles between particles. The initial model for this was the exchange of photons between charged particles that finally emerged clearly in QED calculations of the 1940s.[8] Modern theories of forces due to particle exchanges were based on these ideas.

From a philosophical perspective, there is a long history concerning how identical entities are to be understood. Leibniz proclaimed the identity of indiscernibles. Subsequently, identical particles were rendered distinct in classical Hamiltonian mechanics by their unique trajectories. However, quantum

---

[7] See Cathryn Carson [**1996a**], I, [**1996b**], II, for a discussion of the introduction of the concept of exchange forces in early quantum mechanics and its subsequent evolution into a modern conception of force in terms of particle exchanges. References to the works cited here can be found in this paper.

[8] Quantum electrodynamics had been initially developed by Heisenberg and Pauli in 1929 and was developed rapidly thereafter. The slowness with which the photon exchange viewpoint developed during the 1930s and 1940s has been examined in detail by Carson [**1996b**].

mechanics turned Leibniz on his head in that the quantum symmetry requirements express the indiscernibility of identicals. The physical consequences of these symmetry requirements are the particular statistics they obey: Bose-Einstein statistics for particle with integral spin and Fermi-Dirac statistics for particles with half-integral spin.

Symmetry has also played a role in distinguishing physically meaningful quantum operators from those that are not. The study of how observables in quantum mechanics are separated from mathematical objects that are self-adjoint Hermitian operators but not observables was taken up by Wick, Wightman and Wigner [1952]. They considered symmetry operations for which we want to say that the result of the symmetry operation is the same situation with which we started. As an example, they considered the mathematical consequences in the quantum mechanical formalism of a rotation by 2π radians around an axis. Because for us the situation is the same as before the rotation, we want the quantum mechanical calculations to reflect this. This is the origin of certain 'superselection rules' that single out operators representing *physical observables* from the set of all self-adjoint Hermitian operators.[9]

Force.

In the discussion of the Aharonov-Bohm effect, the replacement of a local potential by a nonlocal force in the Schrödinger equation, while mathematically equivalent with regard to the solutions determined by the equation, faces us with an alternative that is perhaps less palatable physically than giving the local potential itself a more significant status. The notion of force in quantum theory is complicated by the fact that there are requirements on the wavefunction such as symmetry that would be interpreted in classical terms as forces acting at a distance because they seem to cause the particle to deviate from a Newtonian path. These "forces", such as the exchange force mentioned above, are not local. Furthermore, the quantum kinetic energy is the divergence of a gradient operator, which means that it can act on potentials. This implies that there is a deep connection between kinetic energy, potentials, and the symmetry requirements on the wavefunction, which are connected with locality and the superposition of wavefunctions. Put another way, the wave-particle duality is deeply embedded in quantum mechanics and it cannot be interpreted as either primarily a wave theory or primarily a particle theory. These facts lend support to Bohr's view that this duality is central.

Causality.

The question of causality on the microscopic level has not been resolved. Although most quantum field theories support microscopic causality as a

---

[9]See Messiah [1961], pp. 534–536, for more details.

fundamental feature, Robert Pugh [1963] has presented a version of the S-Matrix version of quantum field theory that does not assume microscopic causality.

The One and the Many.
In Chapter 14, the standard operating procedure of physics as stated by Maxwell was introduced. This procedure neglects the rest of the universe when we are analyzing a physical system and computing values for it. While the consequences of doing this are seldom noticed or remarked on, it is even rarer that there is a calculation of when it is valid to do this and what the consequences are. This issue with respect to quantum symmetry was addressed by Messiah [1961], Vol. II, pp. 600–603. He discussed the consequences of ignoring the symmetry requirements on a system wavefunction with respect to particles outside the system. He concerned himself with the question of when the dynamical properties of a system of $\mathcal{N}$ electrons, say, are not affected by the other electrons in the universe. He claimed that when the wavefunctions of the particles in the two systems do not overlap, we can treat them as independent and are not required to maintain the symmetry requirement between the systems.[10] However, calculations of this sort were criticized by Bach [1988], pp. 639–640, on the grounds that if the two identical particles are represented jointly by a wavefunction in a pure state, their individual one-particle states are not defined. Furthermore, Bach used the well-known property of symmetric or antisymmetric wavefunctions—that their one-particle marginal probability distribution densities not only overlap, but are identical—to support his case that we cannot separate them theoretically. Both Messiah and Bach have their points. This difference raises the central question of how we theoretically separate systems into subsystems and when it is justified to do so.

From Bohr's point of view, we are free to assign a state to a system when we have provided an experimental context within which to observe it. The state assigned must be appropriate to the intended measurement, the existing initial conditions, and the boundary conditions provided by the experiment. This means that the experimental context and its intended purpose will largely determine the appropriate way to represent the system and the state to assign to it. The question under consideration here is when this is proper in the light of the symmetry requirements of quantum mechanics that link the experimental arrangement to the system.[11]

Quantum Thermodynamics and the Approach to Equilibrium.
Several mechanisms that have been postulated by various authors to be at work in converting wavefunctions from pure states into mixtures were

---
[10] This point of view is probably held by the majority of physicists. See, for example, Jauch [1968], p. 276.

[11] This topic is subtle and deserves a more detailed treatment. I will return to it in QIS as part of a discussion of the representation of particle systems in quantum mechanics.

discussed in previous chapters. Each of these employs a device similar to Boltzmann's molecular chaos assumption. For two particles i and j, the molecular chaos assumption amounts to setting $f_{ij} = f_i f_j$ for the relation of the joint ij probability distribution density to the individual i and j particle probability distribution densities. It is used to justify the collision term in the Boltzmann equation and this in turn is used to prove Boltzmann's classical H theorem for the evolution in time of the one-particle probability distribution density.

From the standpoint of thermodynamics, von Neumann [1932] felt that the advent of quantum theory had removed the need for a molecular chaos assumption by assigning the increase in entropy to measurement of the state of the system. However, this was not satisfactory as an explanation of thermodynamic processes and was not applicable to unmeasured systems. Boltzmann's molecular chaos assumption soon entered quantum theory in the form of the "random phases" assumption. These random phases were periodically averaged over to obtain the predicted evolution of the system. This device was widely used in the calculation of quantum transport equations and was used by Pauli in his 1928 demonstration of the quantum H theorem.[12] When applied to thermodynamics, the procedure of averaging over the random phases at various times leads to the entropy increase sought by the authors of these theories.

Another assumption that often plays a role in the calculation of the evolution of quantum systems from the thermodynamic perspective is that the thermodynamic limit is required. When the thermodynamic limit is taken, the number of particles or the density of discrete energy levels is allowed to approach ∞. Leaving aside mathematical problems connected with taking this limit, using the thermodynamic limit usually results in an increase in the entropy and evades Poincaré's recurrence theorem. However, there is no physical justification for this limit and it leads to a violation of the proper representation of the quantum state and its evolution.

Quantum H theorems are supposed to show that a system will evolve to equilibrium. These proofs suffer from the need to employ random phases in the calculations and the fact that the assumptions needed to support the proofs severely limit the scope of their application. In Pauli's case, perturbation theory was used and the transitions he employed in his analog to Boltzmann's collision term took place between eigenstates of the unperturbed part of the Hamiltonian. Needless to say, these assumptions mean that this proof is not satisfactory or very useful as a guide to the behavior of a quantity such as the entropy.[13]

---

[12]See the discussion of random phases in van Hove [1955], pp. 517–520, and their use in the references cited there.

[13]Oscar Klein provided in 1931 a better proof. This will be taken up in QIS.

Probability in Quantum Mechanics.

The treatment of probability within quantum theory has been severely criticized by Suppes [**1963**]. He contended that "there is a large logical gap" involved in viewing the uncertainty relations as a product of the variances of a probability measure for two noncommuting operators. In standard probability theory, the variances of each quantity in a joint probability measure are independent of each other. In quantum mechanics, the uncertainty relations connect certain quantities such as the position and momentum of a particle. In a discussion of joint probabilities, Suppes [**1963**], pp. 331–335, used Wigner's joint distribution on the phase space representation of the particle mechanical state (q, p) to show in the case of the quantum harmonic oscillator that there is a joint probability density for the location **q** and momentum **p** operators when the system is in its ground state, but not for the excited states. He concluded that genuine joint probabilities are rare in quantum mechanics. Similar uses of Wigner's distribution have been made by some of the decoherence theorists.[14] There are questions concerning how this perspective on probability dovetails with the work on noncommutative probability theory that has been done by V. S. Varadarajan and others since.[15]

Ontology and the Quantum State.

In Shimony's [**1963**] discussion of consciousness in quantum mechanics, he stated that there are two distinct problems in the relationship between physical objects and consciousness. He considered the first to be the ontological problem of how two kinds of things, physical objects and consciousness, can exist and interact with each other. The second is the epistemological problem of how we can justify physical theories by reference to experience. He felt that Bohr had bypassed the ontological problem and therefore could not solve the epistemological problem. He argued that the quantum state could not simply represent our knowledge of a system on the grounds that statistical mechanical calculations of the entropy, using the Sakur-Tetrode equation for a Boltzmann gas, assigns to each physical state a volume $h^\mathcal{N}$ in phase space, where $\mathcal{N}$ is the number of classical degrees of freedom. He does not find this comprehensible unless the uncertainty relations $\Delta p \Delta q \sim h$ represent an ontological limitation on ψ.

In response to Shimony, I refer to the brief discussion of entropy in Chapters 14 and 15, and the extended ones in various theoretical contexts in CIS, EIS, and QIS. I maintain that these analyses show that an appeal to entropy theory or to entropy calculations cannot be used as the justification of an ontological claim.

---

[14] See D'Espagnat [**1995**], Chapter 6, for a discussion of Wigner's phase space distribution and Chapter 14 for a discussion of its use by decoherence theorists. See also Feynman [**1961**].

[15] See the discussions and references in Mackey [**1963**], Jauch [**1968**], and by other authors after them.

Shimony's discussion of Bohr's position is carefully done. He observed the strengths of Bohr's epistemological stance vis á vis that of von Neumann and of London and Bauer. For Shimony, however, the sticking point is the ontological issue of what intrinsic properties we can attribute to entities—whether they are microscopic or macroscopic. Shimony considered Bohr's refusal to speak on ontological matters to be defect in Bohr's approach. He [1963], p. 771, referred to Bohr's statement that 'we are both onlookers and actors in the spectacle of existence' and chided Bohr for not providing us an account that includes our experience as onlookers in the world. He objected to what seems to be "the renunciation of an ontological framework for locating the activity of knowing." The subject/object separation cannot then be understood as "a natural event, but only as a mode of organizing experience." He found both this and Bohr's account of the theory of measurement unacceptable because they do not deal with the issue of the reduction of the wave packet as a natural process.

In reply to this point of Shimony's, recall that in Chapter 12 there is an account of William James' rejection of the characterization of consciousness as a substance in his defense of what he called radical empiricism. Consciousness is precisely a "mode of organizing experience" and is as much a natural event as any other. It has been subjected to scientific scrutiny and analysis just as physical events have.

Shimony's point of view towards the wavefunction is that of many, if not most, physicists. This viewpoint reflects a strong pull to view changes in the wavefunction as real aspects of the world itself. The reality that was attributed to the particles, each represented by the trajectory of its mechanical state $(q(t), p(t))$ in 6-dimensional phase space, has been transferred to the wavefunction. When the wavefunction represents a pure momentum planewave state, it is often interpreted as reflecting the wave aspect of matter; when it is highly localized as a wavepacket it is often interpreted as reflecting the particle aspect of matter. I contend that the wavefunction is not the entity it represents and that attributing reality to it is an example of what I have called 'reification of the state'. The classical equilibrium probability distribution density in thermodynamics and statistical mechanics (the canonical distribution) is often treated this way as well. I argue further that identifying the state description of an entity with the entity itself is a fundamental error that has been the source of many problems in understanding both theories.

An Evaluation of Bohr's Quantum Physics.

Bohr was very careful not to place more into his characterization of quantum phenomena and their measurement than could be associated with a definite experimental arrangement. He was reluctant to discuss either particles or waves except as they could be expressed in terms of a wavefunction defined within a definite experimental context. He repeatedly returned to experiments to test the ideas he was using to characterize the epistemological situation. While he discussed the difficulties of giving a physical characterization of biological systems, and life in particular, in quantum mechanical terms, he did not participate in discussions, such as those of Schrödinger's cat, in which conclusions based on quantum mechanical considerations are expressed in terms such as "alive" or "dead" that are foreign to quantum mechanics.

As a differential equation, solutions of Schrödinger's equation are determined mathematically when a suitable function space has been chosen and the appropriate initial and boundary conditions are determined. Only when all these factors are specified and definite can we compute an actual solution $\psi(x,t)$ of Schrödinger's equation and thereby the probability distribution density $|\psi(x,t)|^2$. This is true even in the so-called "delayed choice" experiments in which the boundary conditions, such as the orientation of the measuring instrument, are changed during the experiment. To decompose a wavefunction $\Psi(x,y,t)$, which, say, describes a positron-electron annihilation in which two photons of equal energy are emitted in opposite directions with correlated momentum and angular momentum, into the components $\psi(x,t)$ and $\phi(y,t)$ and treat them as separate particles as in the EPR experiment, is to do violence to the quantum formalism. In this case, materialist intuition, which views distant particles as independent entities with separate properties, misleads us. To perform this separation is to commit the sin of reification in a place where it is forbidden. The issues are subtle in that the dependence of $\Psi(x,y,t)$ on the future conditions at some distant boundary, the totality of which serve to define it, is sharply at odds with our concepts of causality and locality as expressed in the formalism and practice of classical mechanics. From a purely mathematical perspective, we have no definite solution $\Psi(x,y,t)$ of Schrödinger's equation until we have defined the initial conditions and all the boundary conditions in effect during the course of the experiment that was actually performed. I must therefore agree with Bohr when he emphasized that an experiment depends on the whole experimental arrangement and that the components of the experiment can only be interpreted after it is completed. Furthermore, Bohr's realization that a description of the whole experimental arrangement is necessary for a well-defined application of the quantum formalism excludes the possibility, mentioned above, of applying the formalism to the whole universe.

Bohr was the most willing of those who worked at developing quantum mechanics to reexamine the philosophical presumptions the underlie our approach to science. His approach to quantum physics was always based on this underlying inquiry, which he understood to be a reexamination of the foundations of our knowledge of the world. This has given his theory a deep consistency that cannot be found in those who have tried to fit quantum theory into a patched up version of standard materialist metaphysics.

CHAPTER 18

What Do Theories Tell Us?

In Chapter 13 several philosophical analyses of Bohr's conception of reality were rejected on the grounds that they did not capture what Bohr intended and that they missed the point of his view that reality is not presented to us "ready-made" so the we must devise theories and use them to learn about it. The question of what reality means from Bohr's point of view is examined from the standpoint of what theory can tell us about it.

18.1 Issues in the Theory of Knowledge

How do we divide truth from error, reality from dreams? These questions have been raised by both poets and philosophers for thousands of years. Is it true that

> ... We are such stuff
> As dreams are made on, ...

as William Shakespeare told us in the *Tempest*? Does the nursery rhyme

> Row, row, row your boat
> Gently down the stream.
> Merrily, merrily,
> Merrily, merrily,
> Life is but a dream.

teach children epistemology? Are we the play? Is the medium the message? Will the sleeper awaken?

Knowledge has been associated in different ways with the concepts of perception, description, explanation, prediction, understanding, hypothesis, information, finding causes, discovering essences, identifying qualities, naming things, other minds, objectivity, subjectivity, certainty, faith, error, truth, falsehood, and many others. For the purposes of this discussion, the primary concern is with issues related to the acquisition and justification of knowledge in scientific settings.

Most of the theories of knowledge that were discussed in the historical summary in Part III agreed that perception has an essential role, but that it does not provide us with a true picture of "what is". We are told that perception distorts reality, provides only a shadow of the external world, is limited to appearances, can give us no knowledge of the thing-in-itself, and so on. Descartes' discovery of the symbolic nature of the internal representation of our sensations contributed to this trend. Attacks on this view were mounted by the phenomenologists, logical positivists, and the sense data theorists, in the late nineteenth and early twentieth centuries. Each group claimed that in some way we could grasp the real out of the phenomenal and construct with certainty some picture of the world. None of these approaches is supported by recent research on perception.

In spite of the wide differences in the theories under discussion, there is actually a core of agreement concerning what is important. Perception and reasoning are almost always accorded an important role in the acquisition of knowledge and confirming it. The differences between these theories of knowledge tend to be with respect to the sources of knowledge, whether by introspection, induction, intuition, reification, or perception, and to the status of perception used in connection with it. Many of the differences in the theories reflect differences in what the author felt would guarantee the truth of a claim to knowledge. Other differences are concerned with conclusions concerning what it is possible to know based on an analysis of the ways we can acquire knowledge. Some are concerned simply with objective statements about the world and others are concerned with understanding our place in the world as emotional beings. Still others locate the source of knowledge in various introspective or meditative practices. Finally, there are various deistic theories that involve supernatural intelligent beings who care, for better or worse, about our knowledge and welfare.

The concern with the sources of knowledge and ways to acquire it implies that the procedures used to gain knowledge are important to understanding and assessing it. There is a natural division in this regard of knowledge into disciplines. A discipline consists of a delimited subject matter area, accepted methods (within the discipline) of studying this subject matter, and general agreement on what is known. Because of the importance that Bohr assigned to communication in conjunction with knowledge, the remark of Wittgenstein's, quoted in Chapter 11, that communication depends on agreement in both definitions and judgments, applies to Bohr's theory of knowledge as well. Bohr's unique contribution to the theory of knowledge was his understanding that information cannot be understood or validated as knowledge apart from the conditions under which it is obtained. This encompasses situations in which knowledge obtained in one set of circumstances seems to contradict knowledge obtained in another set of circumstances.

Other differences in theories of knowledge are concerned with what sorts of entities are allowed to play a role in them. Various Buddhist and Hindu theories, for example, differ on the nature of causation and its role in perception and knowledge. Within any one school, knowledge must be consonant with other accepted knowledge and expressed within the accepted metaphysical framework. It is at this point that a theory of knowledge meshes with what Bohr called the conceptual framework.

Based on the previous discussion, let us divide epistemological inquiries into three basic types: inquiries into the possibilities of knowledge, into the ways to knowledge, and into the metaphysical framework for knowledge. The justification of a claim to knowledge may involve a discussion at any of these levels—depending on the form of the challenge. To resolve a disagreement concerning a claim to knowledge requires sufficient common ground to allow a discussion to proceed. This includes agreement on what is at stake, agreement on what would resolve the issue, and agreement on the methods to be used to obtain the resolution. Without significant agreement on each of these areas, no resolution is possible.[1]

When the disagreement between the hidden variable theorists and the theorists who support standard quantum mechanics is examined, it turns out to be a disagreement concerning the metaphysical framework for knowledge

---

[1] A case in point is the controversy surrounding the work of Carlos Castañada [**1968**] and his subsequent books.

within physics. Both camps agree that the correspondence of theoretical predictions with experiment is a prime condition, if not a requirement, for an acceptable theory. Both camps also agree on the experimental procedures to be used to obtain information. They disagree on the metaphysical requirements that must be met in the theoretical interpretation of the information obtained by experiment. In the case of Bohm's hidden variable theory of the hydrogen atom, the deterministic causal structure of classical mechanics is preserved at the expense of a potential that is not local and can increase with distance. The standard quantum theorists, on the other hand, require locality and the local behavior of potentials at the expense of losing classical causality and determinism.

It has long been recognized that contingent information provided by sense experience can never be considered certain and infallible in spite of the efforts of phenomenologists, positivists, and sense data theorists to make it so. In fact, the quest for certainty has been an impediment to understanding the ways in which we actually use knowledge, the role of our perceptual apparatus and its information-managing component, and skewed much of the thinking on these issues. The work of the cognitive psychologists summarized in Chapter 13 shows that perception is at best an exercise in probabilistic decision making with imperfect information. This experimental and theoretic work has justified Laplace's view that considerations of probability are a pervasive aspect of knowledge.

In consonance with his concern with the circumstances under which knowledge may be obtained, Bohr rejected the requirement that this knowledge be consistent with the metaphysical framework of materialism. He widened our conception of the relation between knowledge and the world with his concept of closure, which recognizes the need for an epistemological cut in the account of the results of an experiment between the macroscopic knower and the microscopic substrate of the world. Bohr's view was distinct from von Neumann's in that Bohr's cut is an epistemological requirement imposed on knowing and not a physical consequence of the intervention of consciousness into the evolution of particle systems.

With these basic ideas concerning knowledge and how it works for us in mind, let us continue the pursuit of the elements of Bohr's epistemology.

18.2 Components of the Conceptual Framework

The question of why things behave as they do has been a concern from early on. Certainly in the matrix of human affairs, the questions of motive and means have been important to understanding and predicting the behavior of our neighbors. As agriculture developed and communities became settled, understanding the seasons and the weather became a matter of survival. The ancient Chinese developed algorithms for predicting eclipses to show the wisdom of the emperor and the harmony of his rule with the universe. The ancient Greeks went beyond this with their inquiries into the structure of the universe and their attempts to apply certain principles, such as that of circular motion, to understanding motions in the heavens. Aristotle presented a theory concerning the dynamics of objects within the sphere of the earth. He divided motions into natural motions, which require no further explanation, and violent motions, which are explained by pointing out the cause, a push or a pull, of the deviation from the natural motion. This distinction has been preserved in our dynamical theories ever since. Taken together, the collection of perspectives on the world common to most people in a culture at a given time form a conceptual framework for understanding the world and our place in it.

Bohr [**1954**], p. 68, characterized a conceptual framework in terms of the "... unambiguous logical representation of relations between experiences." This conception is broader than that of a theory in that the assessment of what an experience is an experience of may require more than one theory and some non-theoretical background knowledge as well. A theory works within a conceptual framework to explain relations between observations of a given type by showing that the observed relationships are to be expected in this experimental arrangement, to predict other relationships that can be investigated in other experimental arrangements, and to make quantitative predictions.

A conceptual framework is not a formalizable logical system and cannot be fully understood simply by cataloging its components and relations at a given time. It has a historical quality, as Bohr stated in several places. He recognized that the concepts available for the characterization of experience have some influence on what is experienced when he said the experiences manifest themselves within our customary forms of perception. For Bohr, everyday language and classical physics, needed to express our experience, are part of the conceptual framework. They establish the subject/object distinction, characterize the results of our observations, and allow us to connect quantum theory with the world of experience. Aspects of this crucial point and the role it plays in Bohr's epistemology have come up several times before.

Just as a theory functions within a conceptual framework, the conceptual framework is dependent on the theories that are accepted and function within it. When there is a significant change in one or more of the fundamental theories on which the framework rests, the framework itself must change to accommodate the new entities, their relations, and points of view that accompany the theory. Hard choices must be made in some cases of what to retain and what to let go. Bohr chose, sensibly, to preserve the macroscopic descriptive framework within which experimental data is expressed. He allowed the dynamical description of the microscopic world and our conception of our relation to it to shift. The greatest difficulties in accepting Bohr's version of this shift were a consequence of the severe challenge to the metaphysical

18.2 COMPONENTS OF THE CONCEPTUAL FRAMEWORK

underpinnings of our conception of mechanics that came into sharp relief at that time. We are no longer able to use what Bohr had called the classical 'pictures' that represent to our imagination the theoretical description of the evolution of a system of particles. These pictures allow us to visualize sequences of events in terms of components that meet the metaphysical requirements of the conceptual framework they function in. Their loss was deeply felt. To paraphrase Kuhn [**1962**], the paradigm of mechanics as an expression of mechanism had shifted in this change.

Modifications in a scientific theory take place in the context of the accepted scientific and philosophical commitments of those working on it at the time. Elements that have played a role in the conceptual frameworks of those working in physics over the ages have included a concept of God, demons, occult forces, natural motions and places, principles based on harmony and symmetry, and other things including kinematic and dynamical concepts. At each point in time, there are certain implicit views, shared by most, concerning what can play a role in a physical theory. The notion of locality, for example, which was discussed explicitly in the context of a debate over action at a distance in the Leibniz-Clarke correspondence, was an implicit requirement for physical theory at the end of the nineteenth century. It appears now not to be a necessary feature of our relation to the microscopic world. In addition, there are certain extra-theoretical, primitive elements, such as the notion of coincident events or of a point in space and time, which are used by all theories yet are not accounted for in any theory. This loose collection of basic metaphysical principles, accepted theories and knowledge, experimental procedures, and basic observational primitives, are all components of a conceptual framework.

For Bohr, classical physics—consisting primarily of Newtonian mechanics, electrodynamics, and thermodynamics, which are themselves consistent with a materialist metaphysics,—forms our usual conceptual framework in physics. It is the framework we use to formulate questions to test a given theory and guides us in putting these questions to nature. Thus, while Bohr challenged both the standard epistemological and ontological notions of an object as well as the form that relations between objects must take, he did not challenge the adequacy of our ordinary representation of the macroscopic world and its characterization of our observations. In other words, the concepts 'position' and 'wavelength' did not change. He used this representation of the macroscopic world as the foundation for developing his understanding of what quantum mechanics tells us.

I could not accept the justification that Bohr provided in his *main argument,* based on language, communication, and classical physical concepts, so I restated his argument to refer instead to macroscopic experience and macroscopic physical description. In support of my revision of Bohr's basic argument, I observe that even when we investigate macroscopic phenomena that are anomalous, such as spontaneous fountains of He^3 under certain circumstances, we still describe the observations using familiar time and space terminology while explaining them in very unfamiliar quantum terms.

In my revision of the *main argument* as the *Revised Main Argument*, I retained the core of Bohr's insight concerning the subject/object distinction and observations. The argument was reframed in terms of the fact that knowledge is necessarily macroscopic and it was suggested that this is the key distinction. With respect to the descriptions that are used to explain the observations, there are other requirements that were thought to be mandatory. It was these requirements that Bohr rejected in his attempt to widen the conceptual framework of physics to allow room for quantum mechanics.

The conceptual framework plays a role in the hierarchy of steps involved in converting perceptions into knowledge. Consider how we move from the data statement 'I saw bands of spots on a photographic plate' to the observation statement 'I saw an electron interference pattern on a photographic plate'. Consider also the sequence of steps we might use, and what we would give up first and what we would give up last, in a sequence of responses to the challenge that begins: 'Is that a globular cluster on this photographic plate or a fingerprint?' It is not possible to give a pat answer to questions like these that will cover every conceivable case, but we can recognize that some such hierarchy is always at work when we learn about the world and apply our theories to it or defend a claim to knowledge.

The notion of an interpretation, as in the interpretations of quantum mechanics discussed in Chapters 5 and 16, is a bit muddy and this has affected the precision of the arguments presented for the various viewpoints. There are at least three senses of interpretation at work here. The first sense is to give meaning to the components of a theory. This is the sense in which Born interpreted the square of the norm of the wavefunction as a probability density. Another sense of interpretation is that of an attempt to fit a theory into an existing conceptual framework. This is done by showing how each of the components in the new theory exemplifies an element or relation of the existing framework. The attempts of Maxwell and others to find an acceptable mechanical model of the ether to explain the noncentral force acting on a charged particle moving in a magnetic field in electrodynamics fits this form. Finally, there is the notion of interpretation as a complete reduction of one theory to another. In this case, each element in one theory is explained by some other set of components or relations in the other theory. Gibbs' reduction of equilibrium thermodynamics to equilibrium statistical mechanics is an example.

To clarify some of the basic ideas, let us make explicit the usual interpretation of Hamilton's particle mechanics within the conceptual framework of materialist metaphysics. In materialist metaphysics, entities are localized, can move in relation to each other, can interact with each other, and have intrinsic properties that persist as they move. By intrinsic properties, I mean properties that do not depend on the existence of entities that can perceive or experiment on them. In the nineteenth century atomistic version, the fundamental entities are the indivisible atoms, with intrinsic properties of mass and perhaps charge, and the ability to interact. These atoms are separated from each other by the void. All physical phenomena are to be explained in terms of these entities alone, their intrinsic properties, their spatial relations, their interactions, and their motions.

In this brief account of the interpretation of Hamiltonian physics, there is no reference to an observer although the application of Newton's dynamics does require a special reference frame in the form of an inertial system in absolute time and space. The solutions of the equations of motion in an inertial frame are unique for a given set of suitable initial and boundary conditions. The resulting theory is causal because future states are determined by current states and boundary conditions. It is deterministic in that the behavior of the particles for all time can be predicted in principle from their joint state at any time.

The development of Maxwell's electrodynamics seriously challenged the explanatory framework of mechanism in a number of ways. The concepts of a field and noncentral forces did not fit the usual mechanical conceptions in classical physics. After attempts to build mechanical models of Maxwell's equations failed,[2] electric and magnetic fields were accepted as additional basic elements of a larger explanatory framework. The notion of what counts as an object was expanded to include fields, but the mechanical notions of a particle and the role of forces in accelerating them were left untouched. The properties attributed to an object also expanded to include the possibility of charge as well as mass. The conceptual problem of understanding a field as a vibration in something simply disappeared without being resolved. As the sequence of theories associated with light from the time of Newton to the present shows, problems like this tend to return later in a different form as a discipline progresses.

Our notions of reality or realism are based on our choices of what is part of this ultimate grounding and are expressed in terms of the underlying metaphysics of choice. The Buddhists, Roger Boscovich, and Kant, for example, chose forces to be the underlying reality. For them realism = dynamism. For the materialists, on the other hand, realism = substantialism. Thus, in the EPR case, the criterion of reality used by EPR reflect their conception that certain intrinsic properties and the requirement of local interactions are

---

[2] One person's metaphysical meat is another's poison. In reference to Maxwell's models, Poincaré [1899], p. 5, stated that "The complicated structure he attributed to the ether rendered his system bizarre and repulsive." For more information on the attempts by Thomson, Maxwell, Helmholtz, Larmor, Fitzgerald, and others to build conceptual models of the ether on the basis of mechanical principles, see Edmund T. Whittaker [1910], Chapter IX, and Joseph Larmor [1900], Appendix E, pp. 323–340.

part of a complete description of a material system. Similarly the types of forces allowed, whether action at a distance or not, or central forces or not, are determined by the particular form of this metaphysics. Bohr was more aware than most of his contemporaries that the questions of interpretation are based in large part on metaphysical commitments rather than issues of physics.

Just as for any theory, there is a conventionalist aspect to our conceptual frameworks. The idea of "saving the phenomena", in which we modify a theory to improve its accuracy in specific ways that honor a metaphysical requirement, dates back to the ancient Greek thinkers and their attempts to explain the motions of the wandering stars (planets) in terms of circular motions alone by means of a hierarchy of epicycles.[3] Closer to home, the debate between Bohr and Einstein shows that there are strong elements of what we might call taste in our preference for one or another such framework. When faced with a serious enough challenge, we can choose to "save the framework", for example, as Bohm has done in developing a hidden variable theory based on the classical conceptual framework. Another example is the work of Edward A. Milne [**1948**], who developed his Kinematic Relativity theory because he was dissatisfied with the assignment of attributes to spacetime in standard relativity theory. Similarly, Robert H. Dicke [**1957**] developed an alternative to the general theory of relativity that employs a flat spacetime metric and can also explain the motion of the perihelion of Mercury. But there is a high price for each of these alternatives.

The different perspectives of the books by Murdoch [**1985**] and Folse [**1985**] and the paper by Honner [**1994**] on the adequacy of Bohr's philosophy of physics clearly illustrate some of these issues. Thus, while Bohr cannot compel us to adopt his conceptual framework, he can show us what the cost is if we do not. At some point the cost of an alternative framework, which saves certain metaphysical principles at the expense of violating other metaphysical principles, may be so high that it attracts few adherents.

These considerations also have some bearing on our notions of truth and reality in these domains, so they are not irrelevant to us—even though the "cash value", as William James would put it pragmatically, of two frameworks may be the same at a given point in time with respect to the experimental evidence. This is not to say that both of the frameworks have the same potential for development, the same fecundity, the same "pictures" behind them, the same adequacy with respect to other issues, etc. At any point in time, it is with respect to these other issues that the debate takes place.

Part of the issue in comparing conceptual frameworks is what is meant by an explanation. When the "realists" claim that a physical theory should

---

[3] Poincaré [**1905**], [**1912**], discussed this form of conventionalism in some detail. Conventionalism of this sort, with special reference to modern geometry and relativistic physics, was critiqued by Roberto Torretti [**1983**], Chapter 7.

explain the phenomena in terms of real underlying entities, we must ask what sort of an explanation they are looking for.[4] Does 'explain' mean "explain in terms of the elements and relations of some predetermined conceptual framework?" Is such a framework fixed for all time? Are we supposed to explain the "unfamiliar" in terms of the "familiar"?[5]

Since a theory and its conceptual reference framework together, the question arises as to how they make connection with the world and how we choose one theory over another. This is done by making use of certain primitive concepts that are not defined within the theory itself. The notion of a spacetime coincidence or event, where two entities meet, and the point through which an object passes at a given time, are used heavily within relativity theory but not defined there. These same concepts make sense in reference to the behavior of objects in Newtonian theory. This common set of primitives allows the results of experiments expressed in terms of spacetime coincidences to be used to compare the predictions and explanations of the two theories. This situation implies that some external primitives, which cannot be defined within the theory itself, are part of the foundation of every theory. In addition, a previously accepted theory may form part of the conceptual framework for investigating another theory that is in question.

18.3 What do Theories Tell Us?

The presence of both realist and idealist theories in ancient Eastern oral traditions shows that sophisticated views of the relation between the universe and us emerged early. In spite of this early start, the review of the recent philosophical literature on Bohr's conception of reality in Chapter 13 showed that there is still considerable disagreement on how to approach these ideas. The tenets of metaphysical realism were presented there and the categorization of Bohr's thinking in terms of these assumptions was examined in the work of several authors. These categories were ultimately rejected as proper characterizations of Bohr's thinking in agreement with the viewpoint of John Honner who said that Bohr's use of the concept of realism was in accord with that common to physicists and not to philosophers. Bohr stated explicitly in a number a places that metaphysical materialism and its associated worldview must be replaced. He showed that he felt theories are relevant to the assessment of what is real when he stated that the advances in physics may require that we reexamine the concepts of "to be" and "to know". He might also have reminded us, in parallel with Wittgenstein, that analyzing the word 'real' in philosophical discourse may place it too far from its use in "ordinary language suited to our experience". Let us take a fresh look at Bohr's views now from the standpoint of assessing what theories and perception can tell us about the world.

---

[4]See Murdoch [**1985**] on this in relation to Bohr.
[5]See Michael Scriven [**1962**] for the clarification of some of these issues.

When Bohr spoke of atoms or atomic particles themselves, as he did on occasion, he always spoke as if he thought them real. He [**1929b**], pp. 103, 104, [**1930**], p. 349, even stated as much in these two early essays. However, he also stated [**1927**], p. 54, that we cannot ascribe an independent reality to the phenomena and the agencies of observation. In his work on the proper application of concepts in quantum theory, i.e., his investigation of the possibilities of description, he avoided drawing any ontological conclusions from his descriptions. Complementarity was an important factor in this, as I have pointed out above. In an important later essay, he [**1954**], p. 79, made clear that the notions of realism and idealism have no place in objective description as he defined it. This, coupled with the many times he stated that the quantum formalism is a purely symbolic scheme useful in making predictions, seemed to undermine whatever realistic viewpoint he may have wished to maintain with respect to atomic systems, and opened his theory to an instrumentalistic interpretation. By banning these notions from his discussion, Bohr attempted to avoid unnecessary "philosophical" problems and remain on a purely epistemological level in his investigation into quantum theory. We are left, then, with the problem of finding a view of reality that is compatible with Bohr's views.

Any attempt to divide what is real from what is not immediately encounters serious problems. Early thinkers were well aware of the existence of illusions, delusions, and error, and that what we see may have little relation to what is. The fallibility of perception led to idealist schools that proclaimed that the world we perceive is *māyā*, illusion, and stated that we can have knowledge only of the *ātman*, or inner self. The realists focused on the independence of the world from individual observers and the fact that we have a shared view of it. The presumed reality of the spiritual world in Western thought during the dark ages and the middle ages, threw doubt on the reality, as well as the importance, of the perceived world. Stories of churchmen who refused to look through Galileo's telescope at the moons of Jupiter because they feared that it would weaken their faith show that other issues were more important than accord with the facts of perception.

In the historical summary of subject and object in Chapter 9, I observed that among the earliest philosophical concerns was the status of reality in relation of perception to knowledge. Various theories, most with ancient roots, attempted to fit the relation of reality and knowledge into some comprehensible form. Idealist theories focused primarily on the knower; realist theories focused on the rest of the universe. Some theories rooted matter in a general philosophical concept of substance; others denied this and rooted matter in evanescent forces. Still other theories viewed both matter and mind as substances. The striking fact is actually that these theories have so much in common. The human mind seems geared, as many philosophers have been more or less aware of and linguists and psychologists are currently studying, to inventing both substantial and relational categories as hooks to hang its conceptual components on. This makes sense when we consider that the original function of perception and knowledge was to enhance survival by organizing the world into comprehensible components that could be manipulated. It was paramount that the behavior of these components could be predicted in the quest for food, safety, shelter, and procreation.

The growth of science gave increasing support to the perspectives that analyzed the world in terms of substances and their interactions. These perspectives evolved with the evolution of science and increasingly identified realism with materialist philosophy. The successes of science offered the hope that eventually all scientific phenomena would be explained by materialist theories. By the beginning of the twentieth century, the clouds that Kelvin saw over classical theory had developed into a storm. The comfortable materialist metaphysics, with its kinship to our macroscopic view of the world was being washed away. Bohr was one of the first thinkers who felt strongly that the situation we find ourselves in with respect to quantum theory can no longer support the materialist viewpoint as a goal of physical theory. His response to the failure of classical physics to account for experimental data in atomic physics was to adopt an instrumental posture with respect to quantum theory and its possible successors while affirming the independent reality and existence of the external universe.

Einstein was not able to accept these changes. While this attitude, and those of Schrödinger, de Broglie, Bohm and others, has been viewed as dogmatism and conservatism on their part, it is actually a valuable stance to take. Their work tested and forced the clarification and refinement of the ideas that Bohr and other quantum theorists had proposed. A number of recent analyses of Bohr's work have noticed a change in Bohr's views concerning the disturbance theory of measurement after the work of Einstein, Podolsky and Rosen. Also, when EPR criticized quantum theory on the grounds that it allowed a property of one particle to be changed by measurements made on a distant particle without any physical connection between them, they stated that "no reasonable definition of reality could permit this". To bring out the meaning of a 'reasonable definition of reality,' we see that this statement still makes sense if we replace 'reality' by 'materialism' and reframe the statement as "no reasonable definition of materialism could permit this". This shows clearly the metaphysical assumptions underlying the statement. In the absence of a compelling alternative interpretation, it seems that EPR were equating reality with materialism.

Bohr's argument with Einstein was over whether the conceptual structure of materialism should be retained in spite of the evidence that it was no longer adequate to support the needs of current physics. At this point, barring further changes in physics that revoke the uncertainty relations and allow nineteenth century materialism to be reinstated as a viable interpretation of the equations, holding onto a version of realism that amounts to a "God's eye view" of matter implies that we are dealing with a form of metaphysical realism that is independent of current theory and experiment.

As a way of highlighting the significant issues from a physical perspective, consider the historical questions of whether the caloric was real in 1840 and whether quarks were real in 1980. The caloric was reasonably well established in 1840 as an explanation for heat related phenomena.[6] Whewell [1847], 2, pp. 103–104, stated that the doctrine of a fluid caloric may be false, but asked how the motion of heat could be conceived without such a fluid. Similarly, quarks were reasonably well established in 1980. The realists would have to say yes to the reality of both entities or run the risk of trivializing their position by being left without any way of establishing the reality of anything at any time. From a purely instrumentalist perspective, the answers to both historical questions must be no on the grounds that theories cannot tell us anything about reality.

Consider now the ahistorical questions of whether caloric was real in 1980 and quarks were real in 1840. In terms of current thinking, the realists must answer no and yes, respectively, and the instrumentalists still say no. In the light of this, consider the previously quoted statement of Wittgenstein [1922] from the *Tractatus* in which he states that "the possibility of describing the world by Newtonian mechanics tells us nothing about the world." What does tell us something about the world, in his view, is the precise way in which we can describe the world by Newtonian mechanics. And the fact that one system of mechanics describes it more simply than another also tells us something about the world. Wittgenstein was emphasizing the point that there is a conventional aspect to theories in that any one theory may be given ad hoc modifications to account for new observations. This means that other criteria, such as simplicity and fruitfulness, for example, must be used to distinguish two theories that give the same predictions. In the face of this, Wittgenstein rejected the idea that theories give us explanations of the phenomena in the traditional philosophical sense of displaying essences or absolutes.

If we look at these positions in more detail, we see that the realist view of physical theories maintains that they are substantive statements about the world, that they can be put in the form of statements that are either true or false, and they provide us with a conceptual model of the world.[7] The truth or falsity of a statement to a realist is determined by its correspondence to the

---

[6]Johannes Müller [1840], pp. 43–44, for example, discussed the action of caloric particles on the nerves to give rise to the sensation of heat.

[7]These ideas were discussed, for example, by Mach [1883], Duhem [1906], p. 21, and Poincaré [1912], pp. 28–29. There are many recent discussions of these issues in the philosophical literature. See the references to discussions of realism in the articles in Faye and Folse [1994] and other recent discussions of Bohr's work.

18.3 WHAT DO THEORIES TELL US?

world. The instrumentalist view, on the other hand, maintains that a theory is merely an algorithm for connecting sets of observations and without further import. Instrumental statements are not true or false, but are either useful or not in formulating a successful description and making predictions. Theories do not, on this view, provide us with pieces of one true picture of the world, but they do provide us with conceptual models of the world. The possibility that these pieces may conflict in their assumptions or conclusions is left open.

While it is possible to classify Bohr's thought according to philosophical criteria in a number of ways, the question arises as to what Bohr might have thought about these classifications. Based on the way in which he approached the subject in his writings, it seems clear that he would not have subscribed to most of these ways of analyzing his thinking. In his statements on reality mentioned in Chapter 4, reality has more of the flavor of a pragmatic concept. In other words, you can decide whether or not to attribute reality to a system once you have understood how to describe it. In that sense, it is unlikely he would have agreed to a philosophical analysis detached from the physics of the situation. Thus, while philosophers are free to label his thought as they will, the categories they employ may not be helpful for understanding Bohr better.

Other views have held that theories do not provide us with a view of reality, but are primarily for the purpose of providing an "economy of thought,"[8] or that theories provide us with a rational (or "natural") classification of the observed phenomena,[9] and that science does not provide explanations.[10] The conventionalist position was mentioned above that maintains that, because any theory may be saved by *ad hoc* modifications designed for that purpose, a theory cannot have deeper significance than as a computational or predictive tool. A related version of the conventionalist position holds that there are no laws in nature: *We* have selected and sorted out the regularities in the phenomena.[11]

There is a class of theories that does not pretend to reflect structures or entities in the world. These are the phenomenological theories that are created explicitly to express experimental regularities. There is no requirement on a phenomenological theory that the elements of the theory themselves have an interpretation that can be investigated experimentally in other contexts. Phenomenological theories are used when a deeper theory is unavailable or an exact theory based on presumed elements of reality is too complex to yield predictions. Current theories of the weather or macroscopic fluid dynamics, for example, fall into this category.

---

[8] See the discussions in Mach [**1883**]; Duhem [**1906**], pp. 23–27; Karl Pearson [**1892**], p. 110; Berkeley [**1721**], pp. 33, 35, 49.

[9] See Duhem [**1906**], pp. 8, 10, 18, 26 and Pearson [**1892**], p. 114.

[10] See Poincaré [**1905**], Chapter VI, and Berkeley [**1709**], pp. 69, 88, [**1710**], pp. 264–265.

[11] See, for instance, Pearson [**1892**], Sections 12 and 14.

The disagreement between the realists and the instrumentalists over the status of theories is not concerned with phenomenological theories. This disagreement is a philosophical difference over the epistemological status of non-phenomenological theories that are based on elements that can, and usually do, play a role in other theories.

Nagel [**1961**], pp. 131–152, gave a balanced discussion of these issues from the standard philosophical perspective. He felt that the argument between the realists and the instrumentalists as to whether theories ultimately tell us about reality or are simply calculating devices is a difference in preferred modes of speech and nothing more. In spite of the reasonableness of this resolution of the argument, it does not satisfy the protagonists. They maintain that the differences between their positions are real and that this resolution only papers over the differences. The realists are not satisfied with the view of science as an instrumental activity divorced from the world it is investigating and the implication that science is not advancing to a deeper understanding of matter, life and the universe. The instrumentalists are not satisfied with the claims of the realists that their current worldview is closer to the truth of 'what really is' because they recall the significant paradigm shifts science has gone through and will go through again.

D'Espagnat [**1995**] has exhaustively reviewed the issue of reality vis á vis quantum physics. He, pp. 21–22, first argued that, although there were paradigm changes in science in the past, they will not happen again because physics has "matured."[12] He conceded, p. 376, that there is no way to prove that we have reflected "independent reality" in our theories. He therefore looked to what he called "empirical reality", which is the collection of phenomena or "intersubjective appearances". As part of this approach, he introduced what he called empirical, as opposed to ontological, versions of the verbs "to have" and "to be." He followed a theory of Omnès and limited the employment of these terms to quantities obtained from measurements made on macroscopic objects for which the detailed quantum measurements are too hard or too tedious to do.

Bohr's statement that 'there is no quantum world' has been used by some to conclude that he is an instrumentalist regarding the microscopic world. Favrholdt [**1994**], p. 92, however, has given an interpretation that is consistent with how Bohr's expressed himself:

"Quantum mechanics does not deal with a reality which is independent of observation. It deals with the interaction between our means of observation and the reality that exists independent of observation. It is not a complete description of a mind-independent reality. But it is a complete description of our interaction with a mind-independent reality."

---

[12]This is reminiscent of the viewpoints of certain physicists in 1895.

Favrholdt, pp. 94–96, went on to conclude that one of the reasons that philosophers did not take Bohr seriously was that his views violated the correspondence theory of truth that states that true propositions mirror reality. From the correspondence theory perspective, theories in science are mappings of this truth in a close analogy to a map representing a country. Favrholdt associated this view with Bertrand Russell, Wittgenstein, and Einstein. He went on to make an interesting argument that a situation in which we must consider the context of concepts in order to determine their meaning is one in which the analytic/synthetic distinction breaks down.

In the face of the opposition between the realist and instrumentalist positions, a number of books have appeared that argue that the extremes are indefensible and seek a "middle way" between the positions of the realists and the instrumentalists. Eastern thought has been at the center of many of these discussions.[13]

A notable example of a discussion of reality in relation to physics framed along the lines of a middle way is in B. Allan Wallace [**1989**]. Wallace began by discussing some examples of experimental phenomena concerned with vacuum polarization in quantum field theory for which several incompatible theoretical explanations currently exist. He used this approach to loosen the tight connection that some realists would make between currently accepted theory and what is claimed to be real.[14]

Wallace [**1989**], pp. 47–52, discussed perception in terms of the 'theory laden' aspect of any observation.[15] His discussion has a kinship to Bohr's perspective that 'observations appear within the framework of our customary forms of perception'. Wallace pointed out that perspectives like this give credence to some forms of the anthropic principle that emphasize our contribution to making the universe intelligible by "discovering" what we can see in it. He, p. 91, expressed this in the form

"The anthropic principle reasserts the essential role of human beings in the universe that is experienced by human beings. This is not to say that the universe, including all other sentient beings will vanish when we disappear as a race; rather, only the world that we experience will vanish. The universes that are experienced by other

---

[13] The account by Capra [**1975**], detailing parallels between the theories of modern physics and the views expressed in Buddhist and Taoist thought, first brought some of these ideas to a wide audience. Many other books have appeared since then.

[14] As Wallace [**1989**], p. 85, pointed out "The more closely we examine the process of identifying physical objects, the more we encounter what are in fact theoretical entities. Nowhere do we find phenomena that are observed without any mediation of a system of detection and conceptual processing." See also Linda Roth's [**1986**] account of the middle way in Buddhist thought as a therapy for realist views.

[15] Statements of the theory laden aspect of observation, under various appellations, have a long history. See, for example, Høffding's [**1882b**], Vol. 2, pp. 16–17, discussion of Johann Nicolaus Tetens' treatment of this in the late eighteenth century, Mill [**1846**], or Hanson [**1958a**], [**1962**]. For other references, see Wallace [**1989**].

sentient beings will continue to exist in relation to them. From this perspective, living creatures play a participatory role in the worlds in which they dwell."

Although the name 'anthropic principle' is relatively new, Wallace noted that these ideas are not new.

Wallace proposed that we view knowledge and reality in terms of our participation in it. He, p. 99, went on to say that "The concept of a participatory universe is fundamentally incompatible, not with scientific knowledge of the cosmos, but with the mechanistic materialism that is still so prevalent in modern cosmology and science as a whole. ... Moreover, in failing to acknowledge its own metaphysical bearings, [natural science] proclaims its materialist biases as scientific conclusions and mistakes its ignorance of the nonphysical for knowledge that only the physical exists."

The idea behind a participatory universe is that we do not simply discover ready-made things, complete with their independent attributes, out there waiting for us. Before someone invented a chair, for example, there were no chairs to be discovered. Once invented or discovered, an item may become so much a part of our everyday world that we consider it a part of what is independently real and 'out there' on its own. However, encountering a chair without a concept for it, we would see an odd configuration of matter but we would not see a chair.[16]

Samuel Johnson felt, in reply to Berkeley's idealism, that kicking objects is a good test of their reality. And so it is—but the question is what view of reality is being affirmed. This is a question of the contrast class. The meaning of a statement that something is real depends on what is being claimed or explained or what question is being answered. To say that something is not real may mean that it is imaginary, ephemeral, illusory, evanescent, a prop in a play, etc. Until we know what the explicit or implicit contrast class is, we cannot interpret the statement and assess the claim. Framed in this form, and not as some over-arching context independent statement of existence, we can see how the notion of reality works. It often happens that the same object, such as a cloud, can be said to exist in one context and not in another. It is quite clear that there are real things that are not objects we can kick. As Wallace [**1989**], p. 101, put it

> "Theory, in the form of conceptual designation, permeates our experience. As theory is not determined by some intrinsic nature of reality, there is no one conceptual system that uniquely accounts for the myriad of natural phenomena. Objects exist relative to the theory-laden consciousness that experiences them."

Entities, then, are brought into existence by the act of designating them as conceptual elements in a description. If we do not do so, they do not exist.

---

[16] Some of these issues come into play when two cultures at very different technological levels encounter each other.

18.3 WHAT DO THEORIES TELL US?   459

That is, "we designate certain experimental phenomena as evidence for the existence of energy, quarks, and so on; and as that convention is accepted, the entity exists. But had that entity never been conceived, it would not exist at all."[17] Wallace went on to state that this is not a form of idealism in that the existence of the physical world itself is not being denied. The interactions we observe are manifestations of the behavior of a world apart from our mental processes. The issue is what we determine at any given time to be in this world and how we choose to explain the interactions we observe. This denies that physical and mental things have an intrinsic nature, but they do have a relative or conventional existence and can interact with each other. Neither physical nor mental events are more real than the other is and neither bears an absolute existence. In this way, both idealism and materialism are avoided in the centrist view.[18]

As the first step in this direction, consider an alternative to attempts to deal with the reduction of the wavefunction in substantivistic terms. Suppose we simply start from the position that macroscopic events happen. Let us call this the *macroscopic viewpoint*.[19] The job of the quantum mechanical formalism is then seen as mediating between the microscopic world and the macroscopic. If we adopt the macroscopic viewpoint, we must avoid the trap of supposing that a superposition of intermediate states in a measurement is equivalent either to a mixture of pure states or that one outcome has already occurred. That is, to avoid conflict with quantum mechanics, we may not apply the macroscopic viewpoint to intermediate states in a quantum measurement. The macroscopic viewpoint applies only to closed measurements in Bohr's sense.

The macroscopic viewpoint does not deny that quantum mechanics is applicable to all matter, including macroscopic collections of it. Rather, this position questions those interpretations of quantum mechanics that deny the truth that macroscopic events occur. It does not assume or require, on the

---

[17]Wallace [**1989**], p. 104. This position echoes that of W. v. O. Quine [**1953**] when he stated that we are ontologically committed to the entities that are represented by the bound variables in our theories.

[18]Wallace [**1989**], p. 110, stated that the emptiness of an intrinsic nature in all phenomena is itself not an absolute because it lacks an intrinsic nature of its own. The logical arguments used above to establish it are not grounded in absolute reality, but are authentic in a conventional sense. Wallace pointed out that these ideas are originally part of the centrist view of Buddhism, dating 2500 years back to the Sanskrit *Madhyamika* text. These ideas were reviewed briefly in Chapter 9. William James' radical empiricism echoed this denial of an intrinsic nature for things.

[19]This position is agnostic with respect to the representation and interpretation of the underlying microscopic theory. It is not an example of Heisenberg's potentia theory in which the wavefunction representing potential reality becomes real in one of its branches. It is also not an example of Leggett's macroscopic realism because the macroscopic viewpoint makes no assertions about the quantum state of anything. In particular, it does not assert that the *quantum state* associated with the macroscopic event is a pure state or a single member of a mixture of pure states.

other hand, that our theories can establish why a particular macroscopic event occurred. This viewpoint is not a contrast between macroscopic realism and microscopic idealism or other such. No division with physical import is being made between matter on one scale and another. We are simply beginning with what we know to be true and requiring that the interpretation of our theories concerning it fit this knowledge. This is not itself an absolute position and is open to revision if the cost of maintaining it is too high. However, this perspective seems to fit the situation best when we consider the multiplicity of problems that stem from attempts to give a substantivistic interpretation of the wavefunction. It is also in keeping with Bohr's requirement of the use of macroscopically described measuring instruments for the measurement and interpretation of microscopic events. Finally, the macroscopic viewpoint is consistent with Bohr's repeated emphasis that quantum mechanics is a purely formal calculating device. It is hard to say, of course, how Bohr would feel about this version of the macroscopic viewpoint.

If we reject the substantivistic interpretation of the wavefunction and adopt the participatory point of view that it is a mediating tool connecting the microscopic and macroscopic worlds, we must also be careful not to attribute properties to objects in ways that conflict with quantum mechanics. Thus, we cannot assume that an experiment has left a system in a situation that can be described by a particular pure state until we have completed the experiment and ascertained that the result is consistent with this attribution. Only at that point can we say what quantum mechanical representation is valid for the system afterwards. As I pointed out in the discussion of Peres' work in Section 15.3, the original wavefunction description is no longer valid for the system after the experiment is over. With regard to superpositions of states, we have the choice of continuing the experiment and using this superposition of states as an intermediate calculational tool or we can end the experiment by observing which outcome occurs. These are two different, and incompatible, choices representing different experiments. We must choose one experiment or the other—we cannot do both. I conclude that from Bohr's point of view we cannot successfully reify the state and associate it with the underlying system in the same way we are tempted to do in classical mechanics when we give a "substantivistic interpretation" of the state (q, p) of a particle.

In summary, the reality and existence of the material world is not being denied in the macroscopic participatory view—only the materialist conception of it. Our theories tell us about relations between the entities that have a role in them. These entities are real as long as there is a viable theory that includes them. A viable theory is one that makes predictions that are supported by empirical evidence and satisfies other requirements imposed by our conceptual framework. When a new theory replaces an older one, both the elements considered to be real and the metaphysical requirements on theories may need to change. However, because any set of observations can always be reproduced by a well-chosen set of theoretical entities and relations, we cannot conclude that our theories give us a vision of some absolute reality. There is no world of noumena hidden behind the phenomena. The world is simply what we make of it.

What we encounter in theories of how we can know the universe, when we examine views created many thousands of years apart, is the attempt to grapple with the essentially transcendent relation between our symbolic representation of entities in the world and the entities themselves. In one way or another, all attempts to form a causal chain from external reality to our perception and knowledge of it encounter this fact. Similarly, all attempts to assign certainty to particular perceptions and contingent facts about the world founder on our inability to control and analyze this connection. At some point, no matter where in our nervous system we attempt to track signals from the outside world, we must recognize that consciousness simply represents things as it will. Moreover, this representation is not one-to-one and is managed for us so that the objects we encounter in our various sense modalities retain their identity under a very wide range of external conditions.

William James has pointed out that this transcendent relation concerning the way in which the external world is represented within us is largely irrelevant. This is because the actual mode in which information is stored and retrieved is of no concern in most cases. Except when we are making a case that there are limitations on the possibilities of knowledge, we are only interested in connecting aspects of our experience, including our own consciousness, with each other.

The participatory view of reality is the perspective most compatible with views Bohr expressed over many years. He stated unequivocally that quantum theory had robbed microscopic objects of their classical attributes. With its ancient roots, the participatory universe is part of the wisdom of the ancients to which he referred. In the light of the lessons of quantum theory, I amend this to be a concern with a macroscopic participatory universe.

CHAPTER 19

Subject and Object

This final coda completes the circle and returns us to where we began. The role of subject and object in epistemology and in Bohr's work is examined one last time in the light of the information gathered above. The main concern is the reasoning behind the re-presentation of Bohr's *main argument* in the form of the *Revised Main Argument*. This examination leads to an assessment of subject and object in Bohr's theory of knowledge and of the directions he pointed us in. I will finally draw some conclusions concerning the enterprise that Bohr initiated and bring the inquiry to a close.

19.1 Subject and Object in Theories of Knowledge

Bohr [**1929b**], p. 117, stated explicitly that "... the relation between subject and object ... forms the core of the problem of knowledge."[1] This perception places him squarely in the philosophical tradition with respect to his epistemology. It is likely that none of the physicists who shared the Copenhagen perspective expressed themselves in this way or understood fully what he meant.

In certain respects Bohr's epistemology is an amalgam of the view that descriptions, as theories, are free creations and some components of the idealist views inherited from Kant perhaps by way of Høffding. The basic idea behind the idealist theories is that we, as the knowing subjects, have access only to the âtman, that which is inside us. On the face of it, idealist conceptions have a certain plausibility. But the early Indian idealists saw that they had painted themselves into a corner when they carried these ideas to their logical conclusion. They realized that if the appearances are all that we can know, then what is the "it" that we are knowing and "what" is doing the knowing. Everyone but a Berkeleyian idealist agrees that the internal representations of objects are not the objects themselves.

Consider next the arguments of the ancient atomists, followed by Galileo, Descartes, Locke, and Hume in which the properties of objects, also known as their qualities, were systematically removed from them. The reasoning of these thinkers was based on the fact that the sensations we receive from the object depend on both the object and on us. It is the combination of the incoming information and the functioning of our sensory apparatus that gives rise to our sensations. They were attempting with this procedure to remove all our contributions to the object and discover its immutable essence independent of any person and any mode of perception. But this leaves us in the end with the propertyless causes of our perceptions. And the question of how something without properties can be the cause of anything is left unanswered.

Consider color. Is a red ball not a red ball if someone lacks the ability to perceive its redness? Is a red ball still a red ball in the dark? The answer is that if no sentient being can perceive red things, then there are no red things in the universe. The question of the color of objects is certainly relative to the sensory apparatus available to a sentient being perceiving the object. But that is just the point. The question of what objects exist in the world of that being and the properties those objects possess depends on what aspects of the world that being can encounter. Thus, for some sighted beings, color is a property of objects and for others it is not. And some beings see nothing at all.

---

[1] See also Bohr [**1929a**], pp. 96–97.

Because of these facts, is it an illusion to say that there is a red ball here? No, if one adopts the participatory view of reality. However, it is clear that each kind of being may react to the presence of something we call a red ball differently than we do. It follows that the connection between knowledge and experience is what we agree it to be. That is, we can communicate only if we express ourselves in a way consistent with the implicit agreements that underlie the use of our shared concepts and the way we speak of things. We cannot prescribe or proscribe the interpretation of experience in terms of what we think reality must be without falling into error. If our views deviate from commonly accepted norms, as Bohr's critique of materialism did, we must be prepared to justify why. These points concerning knowledge, experience, and communication were never clearly stated by Bohr, but I believe they are consistent with Bohr's overall theory and are compatible with his views.

Given his statements about quantum theory as a purely calculating device, I have made a strong case that Bohr would disagree with the position of the metaphysical realist that our theories make true and false statements about the world and that the theories we adopt are moving closer to the truth as time goes on. It is not being denied that theories are becoming more accurate and encompass more phenomena. What is being denied is that the entities postulated by these new theories to accomplish the goal of representing the experimental data have moved further in some particular direction to be closer to a particular "truth" about the world. This view suffers from the fatal difficulty that no independent standpoint is available for judging truth or falsity here. If improved conformity to observational evidence is the only criterion, nothing is being asserted other than the fact that our theories have improved. If the entities in a new theory participate in more connections with entities in other theories and there are more kinds of experiments in which they play a role, an important gain has been made in understanding the world. This new or improved theory can show us more of what we can experience of the world and correct our previous ideas of what we thought we could find. But they do not give us any deeper ground for believing that the current conceptions will be preserved forever.

In the comparison of Kant's theory of knowledge to Bohr's I showed that the elements of Bohr's theory are quite different from those employed by Kant. However, both theories are rooted in experience and all experience is macroscopic. Bohr's Observation Thesis and Kant's critical philosophy both apply to the reified objects of this macroscopic representation of the world. But these objects are useful ones, not pernicious or deceitful ones. By contrast to Kant and in accord with Schopenhauer, it is not necessary to set up an opposition between a perceived object and the thing-in-itself that cannot be investigated. The objects we encounter have the properties we assign to them in the context of our macroscopic experience, but this does not mean that the particles they are constructed of have these properties. Bohr hinted at positions such as this one and at some of the viewpoints mentioned above at various times, but he never explicitly stated them.

Bohr never spoke of limits on our powers to represent the world in symbolic form with arbitrary relations between the symbols. But he did place limits on how knowledge gained by experiment must be expressed if it is to serve its purpose. These limits were concerned not with the internal structure of our modes of perception and the operations of the understanding, as Kant would have it, but with the necessity of using a common framework for expressing and communicating knowledge. Bohr would also not subscribe to the Kantian program of analyzing knowledge by introspection to discover those concepts "which do not rest upon particular experience and yet occur in all knowledge of experience" as a fruitful one for epistemology.

The ancient issue of monism versus pluralism, unity versus duality, has become unavoidable in the case of quantum theory. This issue was strikingly brought to the forefront with von Neumann's introduction of consciousness into quantum mechanics as some kind of entity participating in a physical process during a measurement. Bohr's view of the measurement process avoids this, but at the expense of making an epistemological distinction, during a measurement, between measuring instruments and the matter under investigation. However, this is not an intrinsic distinction between microscopic entities and macroscopic collections of them or between one collection of matter and another. Bohr himself did not say there is a distinction, and he mentioned at least once that quantum mechanics is required to account for the structure and stability of macroscopic instruments. In sum, there is no good evidence that he thought that an intrinsic distinction of this kind exists.[2] In my restatement of his *main argument* as the *Revised Main Argument* in Chapter 14 and Bohr's Observation, Description, and Communication theses in Chapter 15, I reframed Bohr's requirement that the measuring instrument be described by classical physics as the requirement that it be described macroscopically. Quantum mechanics does apply to the instrument, so a demonstration is required that the quantum aspects of the instrument will not interfere with its operation and the measurement to be made in the experiment. This is not a trivial requirement. In the case of electron spin, for example, this demonstration fails for unbound electrons. It was shown that no instrument can measure the spin of an electron unless that electron is bound to an atom or some larger structure. The new requirement of a *macroscopic* description, rather than Bohr's requirement of a *classical* description, of a measuring instrument is a slight extension of Bohr's ideas in terms of practice, but an important one conceptually.

---

[2] See the discussion in Honner [**1987**], p. 212, for a similar, but distinct, perspective on Bohr's views.

The unity sought by the writers of the Indian Sutras and many of the Greek philosophers can be found in the statement that the universe is composed only of interacting particles or only of interacting particles and fields or only of fields. While this may not be the unity these thinkers thought they were seeking, it is one nonetheless. It is only for particular macroscopic collections of these particles, which happen to have sentience and knowledge, that the world is split into parts. To have knowledge and possess information is not something individual atoms can do. Only macroscopic objects that are composed of large numbers of heterogeneous microscopic elements are capable of acquiring knowledge and storing it. This means that duality is a macroscopic concept and is an emergent byproduct of macroscopic sentience. Macroscopic sentience, sometimes dismissed as an epiphenomenon as though it were not real, emerges from the organization and dynamics of special collections of these particles. In this way unity and duality can coexist, each on its appropriate plane of existence, without coming into conflict. In this view, the mind is not a substance and does not have a separate existence. There is neither evidence for an immaterial substance of this sort that is the locus of our identity and mental powers nor is there a need for such a substance. The interaction of mind and body is an interaction between the controller in a conscious decision-making machine and its parts.

The question of the one versus the many in our account of the world is not just a philosophical conundrum. Consider the fact that the shared state of a pair of correlated distant photons implies that an observation of a quantity, such as the polarization, in either photon will result in attributing a particular correlated state to the other photon. Experiments of this type were discussed by EPR in 1935 and by many others afterward; demonstrations that the results of all such experiments conform to quantum mechanical predictions have appeared periodically since then. Nevertheless, each time a new experimental result is announced for some version of this experiment, the result is viewed with fresh awe and wonder and there are discussions concerning how photons or material particles can communicate with each other faster than the speed of light. This illustrates how deeply ingrained the view that the world is composed of independently existing objects that carry their properties around with them really is. In cases like this, Bohr's perspective can help us step outside macroscopic materialist metaphysics and engage the world with fresh eyes.

The ultimate issue of subject and object is how the object can be accounted for and known by the subject. Although previous thinkers had understood that an epistemological "cut" between the subject and object was needed for philosophical reasons, Bohr was the first to realize that understanding this cut is essential to physics. In TIS the subject/object distinction is played out in the mathematical representation of separate interacting physical systems.

19.2 Remaining Questions

Let us take up now the issues that remain outstanding in my account of Bohr's philosophy.

Causality.
Analysis of the concept of cause was central to ancient Indian philosophy. Differences in the conception of whether there are causes and how they work was one of the important distinctions between the Indian schools of thought. It played a similar role in Greek thought and, due to the influence of Greek thinkers, it became an important concern in Western philosophy. For much of its history, cause has been confused with force. There is a close conceptual relation in that both are concerned with how future events are related to current events and the early terminology reflected this confusion. The concept of force emerged into its own in the work of Newton. Building on the prior work of Galileo, Copernicus, and Kepler, Newton distinguished the functional description of the action of the force of gravity and its effects from its "true causes" (*vera causae*), the causal mechanism responsible for its action. This functional description freed physics from the Aristotelian legacy of the scholastic philosophers and paved the way for modern physics.[3] The functional conception of force is similar to the view expressed in the theory of dependent origination, which replaces the concept of causation in Buddhist thought.

While alternative viewpoints on the concept of cause were available for many thousands of years in Eastern thought, a single viewpoint attained a status of universality and necessity in Western thought. This was eventually challenged by Hume, who made clear that, while causality is essential in reasoning about matters of fact, one can have no guarantee of its validity and applicability in any given situation. Its usefulness lies in explaining and organizing our experience.

From a philosophical perspective, the concept of cause actually has two different aspects. Crudely put, the first aspect is that of a relation between two physical entities in which one is said to cause a change in the other. The changes in the second object are then explained by the actions of the first. The second aspect of causality has to do with the relation between our perceptions, conceptions, and the outside world. It is this aspect that plays a role in the theory of knowledge when thinkers try to show how our perceptions and interior experience are in some way determined, i.e., caused, by external objects or events.

In his early writings Bohr spoke of a "renunciation of the classical ideal of causality." He contrasted the 'claim of causality', in reference to the validity of the conservation laws, with the 'spacetime coordination', which requires

---

[3]For a historical account of the concept of force, see Jammer [**1957**].

measurements. Bohr also called causality a "mode of perception", presumably in relation to his view of what he called the forms of perception as indicated above: "... causality may be considered as a mode of perception by which we reduce our sense impressions to order." And [**1937a**], p. 293: "In particular it should not be forgotten that the concept of causality underlies the interpretation of each result of experiment, and that even in the coordination of experience one can never, in the nature of things, have to do with well-defined breaks in the causal chains." Finally, [**1958b**], p. 1, [**1960a**], p. 14, "... all account of physical experience is, of course, ultimately based on common language adapted to orientation in our surroundings and to tracing relationships between cause and effect."

Others working in quantum mechanics have expressed themselves quite differently. Heisenberg [**1927**], p. 197, and von Neumann [**1932**], pp. 326–327, for example, both rejected causality as an aspect of quantum theory and therefore as a requirement on physical theories. Many others have since repeated this position in various forms.[4] Von Neumann's reason for rejecting causality was that certain events, such as atomic transitions, seem to be undetermined in quantum theory and he considered the discontinuous change in the quantum wavefunction in a measurement to be a breach in the causal flow that he felt was described by Schrödinger's equation.

Numerous thinkers have stated over many thousands of years that the concept of causality lies at the root of all understanding of the world. This was true for Bohr as well. However, it plays a role in his epistemology only in the limited sense of the analyses of experiments and determining the suitability of measuring instruments. We determine causal relations in a situation by examining our theoretical description of that situation. However, from the mechanical perspective, cause does not play the role of an agent of change in the equations of motion independent of the mechanical concept of force.

The difference between the conception of Bohr and that of von Neumann concerning the issue of causality in quantum mechanics can be summarized as follows: While Bohr looked for the conditions under which the 'claim of causality' can be satisfied with regard to the entities under investigation, von Neumann and others were concerned with the conditions under which the evolution of the wavefunction follows Schrödinger's equation. For Bohr, the wavefunction is simply an aspect of the description of the system and not the system itself. He is closer to the classical point of view in this respect than von Neumann is. Even von Neumann must assume that the causal connections between the instrument and the system are valid, and the wavefunction does

---

[4]See, for example, a typical discussion in Messiah [**1961**], pp. 156–159. Messiah explained that we cannot verify causality because of the "unpredictable and uncontrollable interaction between the measuring instrument and the object." However, these claims of a causal disjunction are independent of Messiah's explanation, based on the disturbance theory of measurement, of why we cannot verify a causal chain.

not play a role in this analysis, if he is to establish that a particular measuring instrument is suitable for its task.

Wave and Particle.
Bohr was the first to embrace the wave and particle aspects of matter on an equal footing and to try to understand quantum mechanics from that point of view. There have been few others who have understood the need to do that as well as he did. Making one or the other aspect primary leads to serious difficulties with the experiments that are paradigmatic for the other aspect. The wave theory, for example, must deal with the photoelectric effect and the particle theory must deal with interference phenomena. Bohr understood that both viewpoints must be accepted and play a role if paradoxes are to be avoided.

Bohr's whole-hearted acceptance of the wave-particle duality gave him the perspective to understand just how radical a break must be made with our previous conceptions of substance, knowledge and reality. This viewpoint placed Bohr in a league by himself.

Macroscopic and Microscopic.
The roles of subject and object are basic to the epistemology Bohr fashioned to account for what we can know in a world in which quantum physics prevails. Bohr was right about the need for a distinction between subject and object. My investigation has shown that this distinction is more than an issue of philosophy in that it has consequences for physics. The subject/object distinction is due to the need to separate ourselves from the object under investigation—in order, as Bohr would put it, to obtain the sharp separation needed for an unambiguous interpretation of the results concerning the object. The physical consequences of this separation are expressed in the requirement that the variables describing the system are separate from those describing the measuring instrument. This is called the Independence Approximation in TIS.

What, then, is the role of subject and object in this version of Bohr's theory of knowledge? In sum, the difference between subject and object is a logical distinction, based on role, supported by the requirement that the description of the object under study must be independent of the subject and other objects. This epistemology is oriented to macroscopic sentient objects who need, as subjects, to know a world composed of other objects that is constructed on a microscopic substrate with its own dynamical laws.

19.3 The Possibility and Limits of Knowledge

Suppose there are some innate ideas as the rationalists supposed. Would this give support and credence to a Kantian view? Noam Chomsky, in several of his writings, has argued that the propensity for language in humans and the skills they attain with it at an early age with limited input must be viewed as reflecting a mental capacity that has the form of an innate idea. However, whether certain capacities are innate or not, the arguments of Whitney presented in Chapter 11—that thinking does not depend on language—indicate strongly that our capacity for symbolization and conceptualization is not limited by the physical form of our mental apparatus or its logical organization. We are working in effect with a very powerful symbolizing engine that does not seem to impose limits on what we can conceive of or investigate. If we were creatures other than we are, we might have different interests and different images and symbols to support these interests. The point is just that these limits, as far as we know now, are not built-in limits on the human capacity to abstract and understand relationships. In this way, we suppose that we could come to understand other entities with other interests just as we learn to understand other cultures and translate the languages of other humans.[5] However, this does not preclude the possibility that someday such limits might be recognized or found.

There is no doubt that what counts as knowledge depends on who and what you are. It is also possible to view different kinds of knowledge in terms of increasing levels of complexity and abstraction. This implies that there are certain minimal requirements for the possibility of knowledge on each level. We can measure the abilities of different kinds of animals to perform various tasks and exhibit various skills at different levels of proficiency. It seems that there are intrinsic limits to what a given type of animal can know and act on that depend on what it has available to it in terms of sensory input and brain processing power. In this regard, a creature with telepathic powers might someday find amusing our attempts to use language to express ourselves on matters of taste.

I have spoken of the attainment of certain physical skills as a form of knowledge. Other forms of knowledge in this sense include various abilities to perform scripts and remember information and to exhibit skills in mathematics and language. By analogy to our silicon cousins, I contend that the more complex and abstract forms of knowledge require, among other things, some kind of controller, a memory, an arithmetic unit, a comparator, an associator, and a communication unit. To this list, I might add units for emotions and attachment. It is not useful, however, to push this analogy too far. Humans have, up to now, a unique ability to extend their knowledge acquisition and storage capabilities by using machines to aid them. There seems to be no natural limit under these circumstances to the knowledge that can be attained as long as what we claim to know is consistent with what the world allows. Of course, extending what is to count as knowledge may require the extension of the theories we use to describe the world or the conceptual framework within

---

[5]Wittgenstein disagrees. He [**1953**], stated that if a lion could talk, we could not understand him. He may be pointing out that this translation thesis cannot be carried too far.

19.3 THE POSSIBILITY AND LIMITS OF KNOWLEDGE

which theories function. The statement of particular limits in this general setting, if there are any, is much more difficult and I will not hazard that here.[6]

Up to now knowledge and intelligence have been discussed in terms of living sentient beings. I have denied the mind-body dualism of Descartes and recommended understanding reality from a participatory standpoint. The substrate of all macroscopic objects, including us, is the microscopic matter that is described by quantum mechanics. Almost no theories of the world attribute consciousness and knowledge to the microscopic components of which they are made, so the question arises whether machines, whether living or not, can possess knowledge and exhibit intelligence. Historically, this has been denied for animals and non-living machines for various theological, philosophical, or scientific reasons. But these reasons have slowly lost their force and, with the dawning of the age of computers, the debate concerning whether machines will ever think and have knowledge already has a history.[7] I present some of the arguments for and against this idea because of their bearing on the overall perspective on the world that has been presented. Nevertheless, this topic will be treated briefly since it is tangential to the main concerns.

An interesting argument that only humans can be intelligent and possess knowledge was presented by John Searle [**1980**]. He considered a machine that is translating Chinese words, written in Chinese characters, into English words. Searle maintained that the machine does not understand what it is doing and cannot understand. He made his case by way of an analogy called the Chinese Room. In this room, a clerk who does not read Chinese makes translations from Chinese to English. As the requests for translation come in, the clerk uses the Chinese characters as a key to look up the corresponding English word in a dictionary and delivers the answer. This is a mechanical procedure, based on a simple lookup, in which no linguistic abilities of the clerk are used. Searle uses this analogy to show that a machine does not deal with the meanings of the words in making a translation. Searle then argued that this shows that machines cannot have intelligence or possess knowledge.

Penrose [**1989**] has also discussed whether machines, presumably computers, can have minds. He identified the operation of this kind of machine with the execution of an algorithm and argued, based on Searle's analogy, that they cannot. Even so, he, p. 23, objected when Searle claimed without explanation that humans have 'intentionality' and 'semantics' or 'meaning' whereas a machine cannot. Penrose himself, p. 447, later raised the question of whether his argument is directed at demolishing a straw man called 'strong AI' (the strongest form of the views of artificial intelligence theorists

---

[6]See also G. S. Stent [**1975**] on limits to understanding mankind.

[7]The computer is the intellectual equivalent of the wheel. As a machine to extend our intellectual capabilities, the computer is already, or will soon be, as important as the wheel has been to extending our physical capabilities.

concerning computation and intelligence), which he stated identifies intelligence with an algorithm that is executing in the brain. This is a claim that the processing of information by a computer is intrinsically algorithmic in nature, so Penrose directed his arguments against the possibility of algorithmic solutions to certain logical or mathematical problems. He also raised the question of whether our "conscious perceptions are merely the enacting of algorithms" and strongly suggested that "there is more to our feelings of awareness than mere algorithms".[8] Penrose, pp. 447–449, answered his own question concerning the straw man by appealing to the 'obviousness' of the fact that the mind cannot work the way a computer does. What he meant by this is that the mind does not work like a contemporary von Neumann sequential computer executing a fixed algorithmic program. He denied that a computer can have consciousness no matter what algorithm it may be executing. He justified this appeal to obviousness by showing that children are often not fooled by sophistications that adults succumb to.

The major difficulty with Penrose's view, even if his argument is valid for primitive serial von Neumann computers, is that it does not hold against computational machines that are not von Neumann serial computers. These machines may not be executing any algorithm at all. Neural nets of various types, genetic algorithms, newer heuristic methods, and even DNA based computations have already changed our ideas about computers and the problems they can solve. The failure of the predictions of the AI theorists in the 1960s that a chess playing program would soon defeat chess champions has often been presented as an example of the overreaching of these theorists and used to raise questions about the future of the artificial intelligence research program and its methods. But the methods used in AI in the 1960s and 1970s are already in the process of being replaced by better ones. Improvements in hardware and software have also helped, so much so that a computer recently defeated the world chess champion—who was himself widely considered to be the best chess player of all time. Computers have grown from monster vacuum tube calculating machines in the 1940s to miniature high-speed general information processing devices in less than 60 years. It seems risky to argue for an in principle limit on their abilities with regard to knowledge, intelligence, and sentience over the long run.[9]

---

[8]See the initial discussion of computers and minds in Penrose [**1989**], Chapter 2. The remarks quoted are an extension of this discussion and appear in Chapter 5, p. 149.

[9]There is strong evidence that, as a parallel neural net, the brain does not operate as a von Neumann computer. New theories, still somewhat speculative but reasonably well supported, have focused on the fact that communication in the brain can be modified and facilitated by hormones and neurotransmitters outside of neural synapses. In addition, these chemicals may link the mind and body in ways that we can only dimly see at present. See Stephen S. Hall [**1992**], Chapter 8, and the references cited there. See also John L. Casti [**1989**], Chapter 5, for a balanced discussion of these issues that reaches similar conclusions.

John Searle's statements that humans 'have intentionality' and 'understand meanings' and computers cannot, in the absence of objective definitions of what he means when he uses these terms in connection with humans, are not framed as scientific statements that can be tested. It seems that he assumes that we all know what he means by these terms and that they require no further justification or elucidation. He does not discuss adequately, for example, how children are able to acquire these capabilities and why computers cannot.

The case can also be made that our brains are simply very sophisticated Chinese rooms that make the proper connections, along with also retrieving a nimbus of associations, and that 'understanding meanings' means just this. I will not pursue the issue further here, but simply note that the use of terms such as meaning and intensionality in reference to humans is as obscure, unless explained, as any claim by artificial intelligence theorists that they can reproduce the behavior in a machine.

Let us finally turn to bodies of knowledge associated with a discipline and inquire as to what limits we might find there. Consider the knowledge in a discipline in terms of the symbolic representation of the information concerning what the commitments of that discipline are and its storage in memory or on paper. For most disciplines, and scientific and mathematical ones in particular, there are logical and mathematical relationships between sets of components—which may be theories or theorems, depending on the discipline. There are some statements that are not part of the discipline itself, but belong to the conceptual framework on which the discipline rests. The set of true statements in any one of these disciplines can be represented symbolically, by language or mathematics, and manipulated in accord with the rules of the discipline.

The implication of these considerations is that any discipline that includes at least arithmetic as part of its theoretical equipment must contend with the facts established by Gödel that certain questions concerning the completeness and consistency of statements that can be made within the discipline cannot be answered within the discipline itself. These matters can be investigated only by enclosing the original discipline within a larger, more powerful, discipline in which some of the axioms in the enclosed discipline are theorems in the enclosing discipline. However, there will still be statements in the new discipline for which we cannot answer the question of their truth or falsity or guarantee consistency for the same reason. We can therefore never have a guarantee that our knowledge is complete or consistent.

19.4 A Summing Up

In Part I, the problems that Bohr faced in physics were investigated to give us some idea of what he was trying to accomplish with his philosophical work. In particular, I observed in Section 5.8 the tight relation between what is needed in the quantum formalism for a determinate solution of Schrödinger's equation and Bohr's philosophical statement of the need for the subject/object distinction, the description of the measuring instrument in classical terms, and the requirement that only closed phenomena are suitable for computing probabilities of outcomes to compare with experiment.

The problem of Part II was to discern what Bohr's epistemological theory is and give it succinct expression so that it could be examined. This resulted in the Observation, Description, and Communication Theses. These theses then played a role in Bohr's *main argument* to produce the conclusion that measuring instruments and completed experiments must be described by ordinary language supplemented by concepts of classical physics and that the descriptions employed may be subject to restrictions of complementarity.

In Part III, the sources of the concepts Bohr employed were pursued in order to get at the meanings he intended for the terms in the philosophical vocabulary that he used. To establish the conceptual milieu in which Bohr worked, the subject/object distinction, the philosophy of Kant, nineteenth century thought in various disciplines, and the viewpoints of philosophers, biologists, and others based in Copenhagen were all considered. The information collected, along with new information concerning current work on concept formation and studies of the nature of language and what epistemological implications it may have, was then used to pass judgment on Bohr's claims concerning complementarity outside of physics and assess the cogency of his *main argument*. On the basis of this work, I rejected Bohr's application of complementarity outside of physics at this time and used the research on language and concept formation to establish that Bohr's justification for his epistemology given in the *main argument* will not work.

In Part IV, Bohr's epistemological theory was tested with regard to his idea that the in the relation of thermodynamics to statistical mechanics we will find a relation of complementarity in classical physics. This claim was accepted in part—with the understanding that the epistemological issues of classical thermodynamics and statistical mechanics are related to those associated with complementarity, but they take a different form than Bohr felt they would. Other epistemological issues in classical theory with a bearing on the relation of macroscopic subjects to a world of microscopic particles were discussed as well. I moved on to the construction of a theory of measurement based on Bohr's ideas that was then contrasted with von Neumann's theory of measurement. This was followed by providing an epistemological justification for Bohr's concept of closure, which completed his quantum theory. Various alternative interpretations were investigated next, including those I called the substantive interpretations of the quantum wavefunction, to see if they provided a viable alternative to Bohr's point of view. They did not. This inquiry was followed by a discussion of some important epistemological issues in quantum physics and viewpoints on reality. Finally, issues related to the subject/object distinction and the connection between theories and the world were examined.

Bohr has often been misunderstood by his critics and supporters alike. His analysis of the physical situation in quantum mechanics was not limited by narrow philosophical commitments. He did not, for example, limit the analysis of measuring instruments to the classical domain because of some form of "idealism".[10] Nor was he inconsistent in his philosophizing. On the contrary, as I have shown, Bohr maintained his position carefully—with some elaboration—over many years of development and investigation in quantum theory. A number of commentators have discussed how carefully he worked and the lengths he went to in his struggle over the precise way to put the concepts he was trying to express. Bohr [**1958b**], p. 1, and [**1957b**], p. 1, also felt that not only were philosophical considerations, in the form of epistemological analysis, appropriate to the doing of physics, but also that physics had something to offer philosophy: "The significance of physical science for philosophy does not merely lie in the steady increase of our experience of inanimate matter, but above all in the opportunity of testing the foundation and scope of some of our most elementary concepts."

Bohr did not see quantum mechanics as a final step in physics. He was well aware of possible difficulties in applying quantum mechanics at a level below the domain of atoms as a whole—even to the simplest of nuclei. In this domain, he [**1930**], p. 379, stated "... the present formulation of quantum mechanics fails essentially." From the fact that the helium nucleus is about the size of the classical electron diameter, he concluded that this region is "... entirely beyond the scope of any formalism based on the assumption of point electrons ...." And just this circumstance suggests that "... the stability of the helium nucleus itself is connected with the limitation imposed on classical electrodynamics by the existence and stability of the electron itself." On other occasions, Bohr spoke of the problems involved in understanding electron spin and the exclusion principle for which we have only the quantum formalism to guide us.

Bohr [**1937a**], p. 394, described his vision of the progress of physics:

"On closer consideration, the present formulation of quantum mechanics in spite of its great fruitfulness would yet seem to be no more than a first step in the necessary generalization of the classical mode of description, justified only by the possibility of disregarding in its domain of application the atomic structure of the instruments themselves in the interpretation of experiments. For a correlation of still deeper lying laws of nature involving not only the mutual interaction of the so-called elementary constituents of matter but also the stability of their existence, this last assumption can no longer

---

[10]Bungé [**1955**], pp. 8–9, believed that this is the case. See also Grünbaum [**1957**], pp. 717, 718.

be maintained, and we must be prepared for a more comprehensive generalization of the complementary mode of description that will demand a still more radical renunciation of the usual claims of so-called visualization."

Bohr was aware therefore that current quantum mechanics is only an approximation to some future mechanics. Moreover, in almost every application of quantum theory to describe some situation, approximations are made and information that is deemed unimportant to the calculation at hand is left out or averaged over. Thus, in most actual quantum mechanical calculations of the properties of multielectron atoms, say, the nucleus is treated as a point particle with a fixed total angular momentum, etc. The information we have discarded may not be important to the calculation at hand, but it shows that in most of our applications of quantum mechanics we are dealing with approximations. Although more information can usually be included when needed and calculations can be refined, the application of quantum mechanics to the world and the associated formalism should not be treated as a final representation of it.

This perspective is supported by the fact that standard quantum mechanics has not yet been successfully integrated with relativity theory, so it is not applicable to processes at high energies or with strong electromagnetic fields when there is particle creation. In fact, both the notion of a particle itself and the assumption that there are a determinate number of them at a given time have been called into question in quantum electrodynamics and quantum field theory. These facts should caution us against taking too seriously current ideas concerning the "reality" reflected by quantum mechanical descriptions or the 'wavefunction of the universe' and using this to draw conclusions about what things mean or how things must work. Bohr tried to warn us that further progress in both physics and our conceptual framework is needed if we are to go beyond our present understanding. His "renunciation" of visualization at the quantum level can in no way can be seen as leading scientific research into a dark age.[11]

Even with the severe tests provided by modern work in many domains of microscopic and elementary particle physics that were not envisioned when Bohr began his work on quantum mechanics, Bohr's concept of complementarity has survived and proved its fruitfulness. His careful attention to what could be said in a given situation has stood him in good stead over these years. Quantum mechanics itself has been able to meet every challenge in new microscopic domains (superconductivity, the Josephson Effect, the Mössbauer Effect). Considering the current pace of physics, this is a remarkable achievement.

---

[11]Popper [**1962**] expressed these feelings.

19.4 A SUMMING UP

The story is not over. We have only begun to explore how wave-particle duality fits into a new understanding of what localization, nonlocal interactions, and superposition mean in physics. The analysis of various experiments, such as that of Pfleegor and Mandel, indicates that complementarity is associated in some pervasive way with the possibilities of observation. And the root of complementarity seems to be very deeply tied up with the interplay of locality and nonlocality in quantum mechanics. In some cases, the kinematic variables seem to play the role of local variables, while the dynamic variables play a global role. The dynamic concepts do have a local significance, however, as can be seen in the local transfer of energy and momentum in the Compton effect and other experiments.

Bohr showed us how to understand both the importance of the conceptual framework we inhabit and its limitations. In the face of the challenges of reconciling the experimental results with theoretical calculations, he developed the principle of complementarity as a way of maintaining the unity of nature in the face of the wave-particle duality. With this step, he gave up materialist metaphysics, which had served physics well for over 200 years.

Bohr's analysis of the concepts of observation, description, and his requirement of the subject/object distinction, which I reformulated in my *Revised Main Argument* to replace the term 'classical concepts' with 'macroscopic concepts', provide guideposts to some of the "conceptual geography" of quantum theory, and show clearly the differences between the commitments of alternative approaches to quantum theory. Bohr also showed some ways of penetrating the difficult problem of understanding a situation as far removed from our ordinary experience and comprehension as we find in the domain of quantum theory. Bohr has made a contribution to philosophy in his theory of knowledge by showing that there are situations in which the statement of knowledge requires essential reference to the circumstances under which it was obtained.

Another aspect of concern to Bohr was the study of the relation between the microscopic description of the world and the macroscopic world we occupy. In classical theory, these issues are of fundamental importance when we look at the disjunction between the description provided by reversible microscopic Hamiltonian particle mechanics and irreversible macroscopic thermodynamics. In quantum theory, there is a corresponding disjunction between the description of microscopic entities provided by quantum mechanics and the results of experiments made with macroscopic measuring instruments. I have argued that these disjunctions are a necessary feature of the epistemology of sentient macroscopic beings constructed of microscopic particles. The reconciliation of the reversibility of classical and quantum microscopic particle mechanics with the irreversibility of thermodynamics will be discussed in the succeeding volumes in this series.

As a final note, it should be recognized that many of the ideas adopted by von Neumann in his version of quantum mechanics originated with Bohr, and that Bohr's influence on the development of quantum theory—and on its future—should not be minimized. The careful study of Bohr's science and Bohr's philosophy illuminates fundamental issues in both science and philosophy.

19.5 Epilogue

Any inquiry into epistemology involves digging up the ground you are standing on. In a situation like this, I am reminded of a pond deep in the forest I sat beside many years ago. The day was bright, but the waters were deep and dark. The darkness on the water was relieved by unexpected flashes of sunlight reflected off the ripples stirred up by a summer's breeze. It is unexpected flashes of illumination such as these that we slowly weave into the fabric of our understanding of the world around us. In this way many have contributed ideas and perspectives that are part of this understanding: Physicists have shown us how to describe things we cannot imagine; Niels Bohr reminded us of our role in knowing them; and poets have taught us how to participate in what they are.

The search for somewhere to stand has been part of human history since before recorded time. But, as Lao Tse reminded us long ago, one must know when to stop. In the end, as it was in the ancient beginnings, we are left with poetry:

> The more we seek, the more we find
> Until the very stars unwind
> The secrets of the celestial sphere.
>
> The more we find, the more we know
> Lies hidden in the worlds below
> The ones that we can see or hear.
>
> The more we know, the less seems real.
> The solid ground we think we feel
> Is gone and left its echo here.

Paul McEvoy, 1997

RSO Bibliography

Table of Contents
Bohr's Major Works 479
Bohr's Major Writings with Other Authors 481
The Bohr Archive 481
On Bohr 481
Philosophy 483
Physics 492
Mathematics 504
Language 504
Biology 505
History 506
Other 507
Supplement 507

Bohr's Major Works

[1913] N. Bohr, *On the Constitution of Atoms and Molecules, I, II, III*, Philosophical Magazine **26** (1913), 1–25, 476–502, 857–875; reprinted as pp. 159–271 in Bohr [**1986**], Vol. 2.
[1915] _____, *On the Quantum Theory of Radiation and the Structure of the Atom*, Philosophical Magazine **30** (1915), 394–415; reprinted as pp. 391–413 in Bohr [**1986**], Vol. 2.
[1918] _____, *On the Quantum Theory of Line Spectra*, D. Kgl. Danske Vidensk. Selsk. Skrifter Naturvidensk. of Mathem. Afd. (1918-1922), 1–118; reprinted as pp. 65–184 in Bohr [**1986**], Vol. 3. The Introduction and Part I are also reprinted as pp. 95–137 in van der Waerden [**1967**].
[1921] _____, *Atomic Structure*, (Letter), Nature **108** (1921), 208–209; reprinted as pp. 175–180 in Bohr [**1986**], Vol. 4.
[1922] _____, *On the Selection Principle of Quantum Theory*, (Letter), Philosophical Magazine **43** (1922), 1112–1116; reprinted as pp. 447–452 in Bohr [**1986**], Vol. 3.
[1923a] _____, *Über die Anwendung der Quantentheorie auf den Atombau. I. Die Grundpostulate der Quantentheorie*, Zeitschrift für Physik **13** (1923), 117–165; reprinted as pp. 455–499 in Bohr [**1986**], Vol. 3.
[1923b] _____, *The Structure of the Atom*, Nobel Prize Lecture, Nature **112** (1923), 29–49; reprinted as pp. 425–482 in Bohr [**1986**], Vol. 4.
[1925a] _____, *On the Law of Conservation of Energy*, (Letter), Nature **116** (1925), 262; reprinted as pp. 173–174 in Bohr [**1986**], Vol. 5.
[1925b] _____, *Atomic Theory and Mechanics*, Nature (Suppl.) **116** (1925), 845–852; reprinted as pp. 25–51 in Bohr [**1934**] and as pp. 241–248 in Bohr [**1986**], Vol. 5.
[1927] _____, *The Quantum Postulate and the Recent Development of Atomic Theory*, Nature (Suppl.) **121** (1927), 580–590; reprinted as pp. 52–91 in Bohr [**1934**] and as pp. 107–136 in Bohr [**1986**], Vol. 6.

[1929a] ———, *Wirkungsquantum und Naturbescreibung*, Die Naturwissenschaften **17** (1929), 483–486; reprinted in English translation as "The Quantum of Action and the Description of Nature" as pp. 92–101 in Bohr [**1934**] and as pp. 201–217 in Bohr [**1986**], Vol. 6.

[1929b] ———, *The Atomic Theory and the Fundamental Principles Underlying the Description of Nature* (1929); an address to the 18th Meeting of Scandinavian Scientists and printed in English translation as pp. 102–119 in Bohr [**1934**] and as pp. 219–253 in Bohr [**1986**], Vol. 6.

[1929c] ———, *Introductory Survey*, 1929, pp. 1–21 in Bohr [**1934**]; reprinted as pp. 255–303 in Bohr [**1986**], Vol. 6.

[1930] ———, *Faraday Lecture: Chemistry and the Quantum Theory of Atomic Constitution*, 1930, Journal of the Chemical Society **pt. I** (1932), 349–384; reprinted as pp. 371–408 in Bohr [**1986**], Vol. 6.

[1931] ———, *Addendum to the Introductory Survey*, 1931, pp. 21–24 in Bohr [**1934**]; reprinted as pp. 299–302 in Bohr [**1986**], Vol. 6.

[1932] ———, *Light and Life*, reprinted as pp. 3–12 in Bohr [**1958a**].

[1934] ———, *Atomic Theory and the Description of Nature*, Cambridge University Press, Cambridge, 1934; reprinted in 1961.

[1935] ———, *Can Quantum Mechanical Description of Reality be Considered Complete?*, Physical Review **48** (1935), 696–702; reprinted as pp. 291–298 in Bohr [**1986**], Vol. 7.

[1936a] ———, *Neutron Capture and Nuclear Constitution*, Nature **137** (1936), 344–348, 351; reprinted as pp. 151–156, 157–158, in Bohr [**1986**], Vol. 9.

[1936b] ———, *Conservation Laws in Quantum Theory*, Nature **138** (1936), 25–26; reprinted as pp. 213–216 in Bohr [**1986**], Vol. 5.

[1937a] ———, *Causality and Complementarity*, Philosophy of Science **4** (1937), 289–298.

[1937b] ———, *Biology and Atomic Physics*, pp. 13–22 in Bohr [**1958a**].

[1938a] ———, *Natural Philosophy and Human Cultures*, pp. 23–31 in Bohr [**1958a**].

[1938b] ———, *The Causality Problem in Physics*, (1938), pp. 11–30 in *New Theories in Physics* (1939), International Institut für geistige zusammenheit, Paris; reprinted as pp. 299–322 in Bohr [**1986**], Vol. 7.

[1948] ———, *On the Notions of Causality and Complementarity*, Dialectica **2** (1948), 312–319; reprinted as pp. 9–17 in Stogis [**1950**] and as pp. 325–338 in Bohr [**1986**], Vol. 7.

[1949] ———, *Discussion with Einstein on Epistemological Problems in Atomic Physics*, pp. 199–241 in Schilpp [**1949**]; reprinted as pp. 32–66 in Bohr [**1958a**] and as pp. 339–381 in Bohr [**1986**], Vol. 7.

[1954] ———, *Unity of Knowledge* (1954), pp. 67–82 in Bohr [**1958a**].

[1955] ———, *Atoms and Human Knowledge*, Daedalus **87** (1958), 164–175; reprinted as pp. 83–93 in Bohr [**1958a**] and as pp. 395–423 in Bohr [**1986**], Vol. 7.

[1956] ———, *Mathematics and Natural Philosophy*, Scientific Monthly **82** (1956), 85–88.

[1957a] ———, *Physical Science and the Problem of Life*, pp. 94–101 in Bohr [**1958a**].

[1957b] ———, *Introduction* (1957), pp. 1–2 in Bohr [**1958a**].

[1958a] ———, *Atomic Physics and Human Knowledge*, originally published in 1958, Science Editions, New York, 1961.

[1958b] ———, *Quantum Physics and Philosophy—Causality and Complementarity*, pp. 308–314 in R. Klibansky, ed., *Philosophy in the Mid-Century*, La nuova Italia editrice, Firenze, 1958 (1958); reprinted as pp. 1–7 in Bohr [**1963**] and as pp. 385–394 Bohr [**1986**], Vol. 7.

[1960a] ———, *The Unity of Human Knowledge* (1960), pp. 8–16 in Bohr [**1963**].

[1960b] ———, *The Connection Between the Sciences*, pp. 17–22 in Bohr [**1963**].

[1960c] _____, *Quantum Physics and Biology*, pp. 1–5 in Symposia of the Society for Experimental Biology # 14, *Modern Analogies in Biology* (1960), Academic Press, New York.

[1961] _____, *The Rutherford Memorial Lecture 1958: Reminiscences of the Founder of Nuclear Science and Some Developments Based on His Work* (1961), pp. 30–73 in Bohr [**1963**].

[1962a] _____, *The Genesis of Quantum Mechanics* (1962), pp. 74–78 in Bohr [**1963**].

[1962b] _____, *The Solvay Meetings and the Development of Quantum Physics* (1962), pp. 79–100 in Bohr [**1963**].

[1962c] _____, *Light and Life Revisited* (1962), pp. 23–29 in Bohr [**1963**].

[1963] _____, *Essays 1958–1962 on Atomic Physics and Human Knowledge*, John Wiley & Sons, New York, 1963.

[1986] _____, *The Collected Works of Niels Bohr*, Vols. 1–10, North Holland Publ. Co., Amsterdam, 1972–1986.

Bohr's Major Writings with other Authors

[1924] N. Bohr, H. A. Kramers and J. C. Slater, *The Quantum Theory of Radiation*, Philosophical Magazine **47** (1924), 785–802; reprinted as pp. 99–118 in Bohr [**1986**], Vol. 6.

[1933] N. Bohr and L. Rosenfeld, *Zur Frage der Messbarkeit der Elektromagnetischen Feldgrossen*, Det. Kgl. Danske Videnskabernes Selskab. Math.-fys. Meddelelser **XII # 8** (1933), 1–65; reprinted with an English translation as pp. 55–166 in Bohr [**1986**], Vol. 7.

[1939] N. Bohr and J. A. Wheeler, *The Mechanism of Nuclear Fission*, Physical Review **56** (1939), 926–950; reprinted as pp. 363–389 in Bohr [**1986**], Vol. 9.

[1950] N. Bohr and L. Rosenfeld, *Field and Charge Measurements in Quantum Electrodynamics*, Physical Review **78** (1950), 794–798; reprinted as pp. 211–216 in Bohr [**1986**], Vol. 7.

The Bohr Archive

[Arch] Bohr Archive on Microfilm, *Set I, Set II, Set III: Bohr's Scientific Correspondence*, access by courtesy of John Heilbron and the University of California, Office for the History of Science and Technology, University of California, Berkeley, California.

Works by Other Authors

On Bohr

[1964] D. Adler, *Childhood and Youth*, pp. 11–37 in Rozental [**1964**].

[1985] J. de Boer, E. Dal and O. Ulfbeck, eds., *The Lesson of Quantum Theory: Niels Bohr Centenary Symposium, October 3–7, 1985*, North-Holland Publ. Co., Amsterdam, The Netherlands, 1986.

[1964] Hans Bohr, *My Father*, pp. 325–339 in Rozental [**1964**].

[1994] C. Chevalley, *Niels Bohr's Words and the Atlantis of Kantianism*, pp. 33–55 in Faye and Folse [**1994**].

[1976] D. Favrholdt, *Niels Bohr and Danish Philosophy*, Danish Yearbook of Philosophy **13** (1976), 206–228.

[1991] _____, *Remarks on the Bohr-Høffding Relationship*, Studies in History and Philosophy of Science **22** (1991), 399–414.

[1992] _____, *Niels Bohr's Philosophical Background*, vol. 63, 1992.

[1994] _____, *Niels Bohr and Realism*, pp. 77–96 in Faye and Folse [**1994**].

[1991]   J. Faye, *Niels Bohr: His Heritage and Legacy: An Anti-Realist View of Quantum Mechanics*, Kluwer Academic Publishers, Dordrecht, 1991.
[1994]   J. Faye and H. J. Folse, *Niels Bohr and Contemporary Philosophy,*, Boston Studies in the Philosophy of Science, Vol. 153, Kluwer Academic Publishers, Dordrecht, 1994.
[1961]   P. K. Feyerabend, *Niels Bohr's Interpretation of the Quantum Theory*, pp. 371–390 in Feigl and Maxwell [**1961**].
[1978]   H. Folse, *Kantian Aspects of Complementarity*, Kantstudien **69** (1978), 58–66.
[1985]   _____, *The Philosophy of Niels Bohr: The Framework of Complementarity*, North-Holland Physics Publishing, Amsterdam, The Netherlands, 1985.
[1994]   _____, *Bohr's Framework of Complementarity and the Realism Debate*, pp. 119–139 in Faye and Folse [**1994**].
[1969]   J. Heilbron and T. Kuhn, *The Genesis of the Bohr Atom*, pp. 211–290 in R. McCormack, ed., Historical Studies in the Physical Sciences, Vol. 1 (1969), Philadelphia University Press, Philadelphia, Pennsylvania.
[1984]   J. Hendry, *The Creation of Quantum Mechanics and the Bohr-Pauli Dialog*, D. Reidel Publ. Co., Dordrecht, 1984.
[1970]   G. Holton, *The Roots of Complementarity*, Daedalus **99** (1970), 1015–1055.
[1987]   J. Honner, *The Description of Nature: Niels Bohr and the Philosophy of Quantum Physics*, Clarendon Press, Oxford, England, 1987.
[1994]   _____, *Description and Deconstruction: Niels Bohr and Modern Philosophy*, pp. 141–153 in Faye and Folse [**1994**].
[1994]   C. A. Hooker, *Bohr and the Crisis of Empirical Intelligibility: An Essay on the Depth of Bohr's Thought and our Philosophical Ignorance*, pp. 155–199 in Faye and Folse [**1994**].
[1994]   D. Kaiser, *Niels Bohr's Conceptual Legacy in Contemporary Particle Physics*, pp. 257–268 in Faye and Folse [**1994**].
[1964]   O. Klein, *Glimpses of Niels Bohr as a Scientist and Thinker*, pp. 74–93 in Rozental [**1964**].
[1992]   H. Kragh, *Bohr's Quantum Philosophy: On the Shoulders of a Giant?*, Danish Yearbook of Philosophy **27** (1992), 109–118.
[1966]   R. Moore, *Niels Bohr, the man, his science & the world they changed*, Knopf, New York, 1966.
[1985]   D. Murdoch, *Niels Bohr's Philosophy of Physics*, Cambridge University Press, Cambridge, England, 1985.
[1964]   A. Pais, *Reminiscences from the Post-war Years*, pp. 215–226 in Rozental [**1964**].
[1991]   _____, *Niels Bohr's Times, in Physics, Philosophy, and Polity*, Clarendon Press, Oxford, England, 1991.
[1963]   A. Petersen, *The Philosophy of Niels Bohr*, Bulletin of the Atomic Scientists **19** # **7** (1963), 8–12.
[1993]   S. Petruccioli, *Atoms, Metaphors and Paradoxes: Niels Bohr and the construction of a new physics*, Cambridge University Press, Cambridge, 1993.
[1963a] L. Rosenfeld, *Niels Bohr's Contribution to Epistemology*, Physics Today **16** # **10** (1963), 47–54.
[1967]   _____, *Niels Bohr in the Thirties: Consolidation and Extension of the Concept of Complementarity*, pp. 114–136 in Rozental [**1964**].
[1964]   S. Rozental, *Niels Bohr*, John Wiley & Sons, New York, 1967; this book first appeared in Danish in 1964.
[1967]   V. F. Weisskopf, *On Niels Bohr*, N. Y. Review of Books, April 20, 1967, pp. 26–30 (1967).

Philosophy

[1956] H. G. Alexander, ed., *The Leibniz-Clarke Correspondence*, Manchester University Press, Barnes & Noble, New York, 1956.
[1956] P. Alexander, *Complementary Descriptions*, Mind **65** (1956), 145–165.
[1958] W. P. Alston, *Ontological Commitments*, Philosophical Studies **9** (1958), 8–17.
[1959] A. J. Arberry, *The Romance of the Rubáiyát: Edward Fitzgerald's First Edition Reprinted with Introduction and Notes*, George Allen & Unwin Ltd, London, 1959.
[Phys] Aristotle, *Physics*, pp. 257–355 in *Aristotle I* published by Great Books of the Western World, Vol. 8 (1952), New York: Encyclopedia Brittanica Press, Inc., 1952..
[1936] A. J. Ayer, *Language, Truth and Logic*, (1936), Victor Gollancz, Ltd., London, 1958; an essay, "The A Priori," is reprinted as pp. 289–301 in Benacerraf and Putnam [**1964**].
[1963] B. Baumrin, ed., *The Philosophy of Science: The Delaware Seminar, Vol. 2, 1962–1963*, Interscience, New York, 1963.
[1961] H. Bedau and P. Oppenheim, *Complementarity in Quantum Mechanics: A Logical Analysis*, Synthese **13** (1961), 201–232.
[1987] J. S. Bell, *Speakable and Unspeakable in Quantum Mechanics*, Cambridge University Press, Cambridge, 1987.
[1964] P. Benacerraf and H. Putnam, *Philosophy of Mathematics*, Prentice-Hall, Inc., Englewood Cliffs, New Jersey, 1964.
[1709] G. Berkeley, *Theory of Vision ... Vindicated and Explained*, printed as pp. 249–276 in Luce and Jessop [**1948**], Vol. I (1948).
[1710] _____, *A Treatise Concerning the Principles of Human Knowledge*, printed as pp. 21–113 in Luce and Jessop [**1948**], Vol. I.
[1713] _____, *Three Dialogues between Hylas and Philonous*, printed as p. 115 in Luce and Jessop [**1948**], Vol. II.
[1721] _____, *De Motu*, printed as pp. 31–52 in Luce and Jessop [**1948**], Vol. V.
[1882] E. du Bois-Reymond, *Über die Grenzen des Naturerkennens*, Verlag von Veit & Co., Leipzig.
[1905] L. Boltzmann, *Populäre Schriften*, J.A. Barth, Leipzig, 1905.
[1953a] M. Born, *The Conceptual Situation in Physics and the Prospects of Its Future Development*, Guthrie Lecture, Proceedings of the Physical Society (London) **A66** (1953), 501–512.
[1953b] _____, *Physical Reality*, Philosophical Quarterly **3** (1953), 139–149.
[1953c] _____, *The Interpretation of Quantum Mechanics*, British Journal for the Philosophy of Science **4** (1953), 95–106.
[1964] _____, *Natural Philosophy of Cause and Chance*, Dover Publ. Inc., New York, 1964.
[1953] L. de Broglie, *La Physique Quantique Restera-t-elle Indeterministe?*, Gauthier-Villars, Paris, 1953.
[1965] S. G. Brush, *Kinetic Theory*, volumes 1–3, Pergamon Press, London.
[1955] M. Bungé, *Strife about Complementarity, I*, British Journal for the Philosophy of Science **6** (1955), 1–12.
[1956] _____, *Strife about Complementarity, II*, British Journal for the Philosophy of Science **6** (1956), 141–154.
[1964] _____, *The Critical Approach to Science and Philosophy (Essays in Honor of Karl Popper)*, The Free Press, New York, 1964.
[1967a] _____, *Delaware Seminar in the Foundations of Physics*, Springer Verlag, New York, 1967.
[1968] _____, *Analogy in Quantum Theory: From Insight to Nonsense*, British Journal for the Philosophy of Science **18** (1968), 265–286.

[1986a] R. E. Butts, *Introduction: Kant's Quest for a Method for Metaphyics*, pp. 1–22 in Butts [**1986c**].
[1986b] _____, *The Methodological Structure of Kant's Metaphysics of Science*, pp. 163–199 in Butts [**1986c**].
[1986c] _____, ed., *Kant's Philosophy of Physical Science*, D. Reidel Publishing Co., Dordrecht, 1986.
[1920] N. R. Campbell, *Foundations of Science (Physics: The Elements)*, Dover Publ. Co., New York, 1920.
[1975] F. Capra, *The Tao of Physics*, Shambala Press, New York, 1975.
[1950] R. Carnap, *Empiricism, Semantics and Ontology*, pp. 233–248 in Benacerraf and Putnam [**1964**].
[1963] _____, *My Views on Ontological Problems of Existence*, pp. 868–873 in Schilpp [**1963**].
[1985] H. G. B. Casimir, *Epistemological Considerations*, pp. 13–20 in de Boer, Dal and Ulfbeck [**1985**].
[1923a] E. Cassirer, *Substance and Function and Einstein's Theory of Relativity*, Dover Publications, Inc., New York, 1953; this is a translation by W. C. Swabey and M. C. Swabey in 1923 of "Substanzbegriff and Funktionsbegriff" (1910) and "Zur Einstein'schen Relativitätstheorie" (1923).
[1923b] _____, *Language and Myth*, Dover Publications, Inc., New York, 1963; translated by S. Langer from "Sprache und Mythos" (1923).
[1923c] _____, *The Philosophy of Symbolic Forms, Vol. I, Language*, Yale Univ. Press, New Haven, Connecticut, 1955; translated by R. Manheim from the German edition of 1923.
[1968] C. Castañada, *The Teachings of Don Yuan: A Yaqui Way to Knowledge*, University of California Press, Berkeley, California, 1968.
[1989] J. Casti, *Paradigms Lost: Tackling the Unanswered Mysteries of Modern Science*, Avon Books, New York, 1989.
[1958] A. Church, *Ontological Commitment*, Journal of Philosophy **55** (1958), 1008–1014.
[1962] R. G. Colodny, ed., *Frontiers of Science and Philosophy*, University of Pittsburgh Press, Pittsburgh, Pennsylvania, 1962.
[1965] _____, *Beyond the Edge of Certainty*, Prentice-Hall, Englewood Cliffs, New Jersey, 1965.
[1953] W. Craig, *On Axiomatizability within a System*, Journal of Symbolic Logic **18** (1953), 30–32.
[1956] _____, *Replacement of Auxiliary Expressions*, Philosophical Review **65** (1956), 38–55.
[1986] J. Cramer, *The Transactional Interpretation of Quantum Mechanics*, Reviews of Modern Physics **58** (1886), 647–687.
[1949] M. Delbrück, *A Physicist Looks at Biology*, Transactions of the Connecticut Academy of Arts and Sciences **38** (1949), 173–190.
[1965] B. D'Espagnat, *Conceptions de la physique contemporaine*, Actualités Scientifique et Industrielles No. 1320, Hermann et Cie, Paris, 1965.
[1995] _____, *Veiled Reality: an analysis of present-day quantum mechanical concepts*, Addison-Wesley Publ. Co., Reading, Mass., 1995.
[1899] P. E. Deussen, *The Philosophy of the Upanishads*, Dover Publications, Inc., New York, 1966; translated in 1906 by A. S. Geden from "Die Philosophie der Upanishads," Vol. 1, pt. 2, of *Allgemeine geschichte der Philsophie* published by F. A. Brockhaus, Leipzig, 1899.
[1963] P. A. M. Dirac, *The Evolution of the Physicist's Picture of Nature*, Scientific American **208** # **5** (1963), 45–53.

[1957]   W. Dray, *Laws and Explanations in History*, Oxford University Press, Oxford, 1957.
[1906]   P. Duhem, *The Aim and Structure of Physical Theory*, (1906), Atheneum, New York, 1962.
[1923]   A. Einstein, *The Principle of Relativity*, Methuen, London, 1923.
[1936]   _____, *Physics and Reality*, Journal of the Franklin Institute **221** (1936), 349–382.
[1949]   _____, *Reply to Criticisms*, pp. 663–668 in Schilpp [**1949**].
[1938]   A. Einstein and L. Infeld, *The Evolution of Physics*, Simon and Schuster, New York, 1938.
[1951]   W. M. Elsasser, *Quantum Mechanics, Amplifying Processes and Living Matter*, Philosophy of Science **18** (1951), 300–320.
[1953]   _____, *Les measures et la realité en mecanique quantique*, pp. 87–108 in George [**1953**].
[1958]   _____, *The Physical Foundations of Biology*, Pergamon Press, New York, 1958.
[1961]   _____, *Quanta and the Concept of Organismic Law*, Journal of Theoretical Biology **1** (1961), 27–58.
[1966]   _____, *Atom and Organism*, Princeton University Press, Princeton, New Jersey, 1966.
[1961]   H. Feigl and G. Maxwell, eds., *Current Issues in the Philosophy of Science*, Holt, Reinhart and Winston, New York, 1961.
[1962]   _____, *Scientific Explanation, Space and Time*, Minnesota Studies in the Philosophy of Science, University of Minnesota Press, Minneapolis, Minnesota, 1962.
[1958]   H. Feigl, M. Scriven and G. Maxwell, eds., *Concepts, Theories and the Mind-Body Problem*, Minnesota Studies in the Philosophy of Science, University of Minnesota Press, Minneapolis, Minnesota, 1958.
[1949]   H. Feigl and W. Sellars, eds., *Readings in Philosophical Analysis*, Appleton-Century-Crofts, Inc., New York, 1949.
[1958a] P. K. Feyerabend, *Complementarity*, Aristotelian Society Supplement **32** (1958), 75–104.
[1958b] _____, *An Attempt at a Realistic Interpretation of Experience*, Proceedings of the Aristotelian Society **58** (1958), 143–170.
[1962]   _____, *Problems of Microphysics*, pp. 189–283 in Colodny [**1962**].
[1964]   _____, *Realism and Instrumentalism: Comments on the Logic of Factual Support*, pp. 280–308 in Bungé [**1967b**].
[1968]   _____, *On a Recent Critique of Complementarity, I*, Philosophy of Science **35** (1968), 309–331.
[1966]   P. K. Feyerabend and G. Maxwell, eds., *Mind, Matter and Method: Essays in Philosophy and Science in Honor of Herbert Feigl*, University of Minnesota Press, Minneapolis, Minnesota, 1966.
[1986]   A. Fine, *The Shaky Game: Einstein, Realism and the Quantum Theory*, University of Chicago Press, Chicago, 1986.
[1638]   Galileo Galilei, *Dialogues Concerning Two New Sciences*, Dover Publications, Inc., New York.
[1963]   P. Gardiner, *Schopenhauer*, Penguin Books, Inc., Baltimore, Md., 1963.
[1994]   M. Gell-Mann, *The quark and the jaguar: adventures in the simple and the complex*, W.H. Freeman, New York, 1994.
[1963]   D. E. Gershenson and D. A. Greenberg, eds., *The Natural Philosopher*, Vol. 1, Blaisdell Publishing Co., New York, 1963.
[1962]   I. J. Good, *The Scientist Speculates*, Heinemann, London, 1962.
[1957]   A. Grünbaum, *Complementarity in Quantum Physics and Its Philosophical Generalization*, Journal of Philosophy **54** (1957), 713–727.

[1958a] N. R. Hanson, *Patterns of Discovery*, Cambridge University Press, Cambridge, 1958.
[1958b] ———, *The Logic of the Correspondence Principle*, Scientia **52** (1958), 1–8.
[1959] ———, *The Copenhagen Interpretation of Quantum Mechanics*, American Journal of Physics **27** (1959), 1–15.
[1962] ———, *The Concept of the Positron*, Cambridge University Press, Cambridge, 1962.
[1936] M. Hartmann, *Die Kausalität in Physik und Biologie*, Sitzungsberichte der Preuessischen Akademie der Wissenshaften, Physikalisch-mathematische Klasse, Berlin (1936), XXXIX–LIII.
[1998] R. A. Healey and G. Hellman, *Minnesota Studies in the Philosophy of Science, volume XVII, Quantum Measurement: Beyond Paradox*, University of Minnesota Press, Minneapolis, 1998.
[1965] P. A. Heelan, *Quantum Mechanics and Objectivity: A Study of the Physical Philosophy of Werner Heisenberg*, Martinus Nijhoff, The Hague, 1965.
[1930] W. Heisenberg, *Physical Principles of Quantum Theory*, University of Chicago, Chicago, 1930.
[1952] ———, *Philosophic Problems of Nuclear Science*, Pantheon, New York, 1952.
[1955] ———, *The Development of the Interpretation of the Quantum Theory*, pp. 12–29 in Pauli [**1955**].
[1958a] ———, *Physics and Philosophy*, Harper & Bros., New York, 1958.
[1958b] ———, *The Physicist's Conception of Nature*, Harcourt, Brace & Co., New York, 1958.
[1960] ———, *Physics and Beyond*, Harper and Row, New York, 1960.
[1873] H. von Helmholtz, *Popular Lectures on Scientific Subjects*, translated by E. Atkinson, Appleton & Co., New York, 1873.
[1878] ———, *Selected Writings of Hermann von Helmholtz*, edited by Russell Kahl, Wesleyan University Press, Middletown, Conn., 1971.
[1942] C. G. Hempel, *The Function of General Laws in History*, Journal of Philosophy **39** (1942), 35–48.
[1958] ———, *The Theoretician's Dilemma*, reprinted as pp. 37–98 in Feigl, Scriven and Maxwell [**1958**].
[1962] ———, *Deductive-Nomological vs. Statistical Explanation*, reprinted as pp. 98–169 in Feigl and Maxwell [**1962**]..
[1948] C. G. Hempel and P. Oppenheim, *Studies in the Logic of Explanation*, Philosophy of Science **15** (1948), 135–175.
[1953] M. B. Hesse, *Models in Physics*, British Journal for the Philosophy of Science **4** (1953), 198–214.
[1966] E. L. Hill, *Classical Mechanics as a Limiting Form of Quantum Mechanics*, pp. 430–448 in Feyerabend and Maxwell [**1966**].
[1920] J. Hjort, *The Unity of Science*, Gyldendal, London, England, 1920.
[1882a] H. Høffding, *Outlines of Psychology*, Macmillan, London, England, 1892; it is a translation of the German version "Psychologie im Umrissen auf Grundlage der Ehrfahrung," 1882.
[1882b] ———, *A History of Modern Philosophy*, Macmillan, London, England, 1900; the Danish original appeared in 1882.
[1902] ———, *The Problems of Philosophy*, Macmillan, London, England, 1905; the Danish original appeared in 1902.
[1904] ———, *Modern Philosophers and Lectures on Bergson*, includes lectures on modern philosophers delivered at the University of Copenhagen in 1902 and Lectures on Bergson delivered in 1913, Macmillan, London, England, 1915; the Danish originals appeared in 1904 and 1914, respectively..

[1910] ———, *La pensée humaine*, Librarie Felix Alcan, Paris, France, 1911; the Danish original appeared in 1910.
[1917] ———, *Totalität als Kategorie*, published in French translation in Høffding [**1924**].
[1918] ———, *Humor als Lebensgefühl (Der Grosse Humor) eine psychologische studie*, published in Danish in 1916, B. G. Teubner, Leipzig, 1918.
[1922] ———, *Relation als Kategorie*, published in French translation in Høffding [**1924**].
[1923a] ———, *Le Concept d'Analogie*, Librarie Philosophie J. Vrin, Paris, France, 1931; the Danish original and a German translation, "Der Begriff der Analogie" appeared in 1923.
[1923b] ———, *Harold Höffding*, printed as pp. 74–97 in Schmidt [**1923**].
[1924] ———, *La relativité philosophique: totalité et relation*, Librarie Félix Alcan, Paris, 1924.
[1925] ———, *Emile Meyerson's erkenntnistheoretische Arbeiten*, Kant Studien 30 (1925), 484–494.
[1930a] ———, *Zur Stellung Erkenntnistheorie in Unsere Zeit*, Kant Studien **35** (1930), 480–495.
[1930b] ———, *Erkenntnistheorie und Lebensauffassung*, O. R. Reisland, Leipzig, Germany, 1930.
[1970] C. A. Hooker, *Concerning Einstein's, Podolsky's and Rosen's Objection to Quantum Theory*, American Journal of Physics **38** (1970), 851–857.
[1972] ———, *The Nature of Quantum Mechanical Reality: Einstein versus Bohr*, pp. 67–302 in R. Colodny, ed., *Paradigms and Paradoxes*, Pittsburgh Series in the Philosophy of Science, Pittsburgh University Press, Pittsburgh, Penn., 1972.
[1994] D. Howard, *What Makes a Classical Concept Classical?*, pp. 201–229 in Faye and Folse [**1994**].
[1748] D. Hume, *An Inquiry Concerning Human Understanding*, The Library of Liberal Arts, Bobbs-Merrill Co., Indianapolis, Indiana, 1955.
[1874] T. H. Huxley, *On the Hypothesis that Animals are Automata, and its History*, reprinted as pp. 199–250 in T. H. Huxley, *Method and Results: Essays*, Appleton & Co., New York 1894.
[1678] C. Huyghens, *Treatise on Light*; this is an English translation printed as pp. 373–386 in G. Swartz and P. W. Bishops, eds., *Moments of Discovery: The Origins of Science*, vol. 1, Basic Books, New York, 1958.
[1907] W. James, *Pragmatism*, New American Library, Inc., 1955.
[1911] ———, *Essays in Radical Empiricism*, containing the reprinted essays "Does 'Consciousness' exist?," (1904), pp. 1–38, "A World of Pure Experience," (1904), pp. 39–91, and "The Thing and Its Relations," (1905), pp. 92–122, Longmans, Green & Co., New York, 1922.
[1957] M. Jammer, *Concepts of Force*, Harper Torchbooks, Harper and Brothers, New York, 1962.
[1966] ———, *The Conceptual Development of Quantum Mechanics*, McGraw-Hill, New York, 1966.
[1974] ———, *The Philosophy of Quantum Mechanics*, John Wiley & Sons, New York, 1974.
[1985] ———, *The EPR Paradox in Historical Development*, pp. 129–149 in P. Lahti and P. Mittelstadt, eds., *Symposium on the Foundations of Modern Physics*, World Scientific Publishing, Singapore, 1985.
[1973] A. Janik and S. Toulmin, *Wittgenstein's Vienna*, Simon and Schuster, New York, 1973.
[1968] J. M. Jauch, *Foundations of Quantum Mechanics*, Addison Wesley & Co., Reading, Massachusetts, 1968.

[1967]   E. T. Jaynes, *Foundations of Probability Theory and Statistical Mechanics*, pp. 77–101 in Bungé [**1967b**].
[1933]   P. Jordan, *Die Physik und das Geheimnis des organischen Lebens*, 6th edition, F. Vieweg & Sohn, Brauschweig, 1948.
[1948]   ———, *Verdrängung und Komplementarität*, Strom Verlag, Hamburg, 1948.
[1965]   F. A. Kaempfer, *Concepts in Quantum Mechanics*, Academic Press, New York, 1965.
[1990]   M. Kafatos and R. Nadeau, *The Conscious Universe: Part and Whole in Modern Physical Theory*, Springer-Verlag, New York, 1990.
[1781]   I. Kant, *Critique of Pure Reason*, translated by N. K. Smith, Macmillan & Co., London, 1963.
[1783]   ———, *Prolegomena to Any Future Metaphysics*, translated by L. W. Beck, Bobbs-Merrill Co., New York, 1950.
[1786]   ———, *Metaphysical Foundations of Natural Science*, translated with an introduction by James Ellington, Bobbs-Merrill, Indianapolis, Indiana, 1970.
[1790]   ———, *Critique of Practical Judgment*, translated by J. H. Bernard, Hafner Publishing Co., New York, 1951.
[Rub1]   Omar Khayyám, *Rubáiyát*, translated in 1859 by Edward Fitzgerald and the first edition is reprinted as pp. 149–183 in Arberry [**1959**].
[Rub2]   ———, *Rubáiyát of Omar-Khayyám*, in Persian, English, German, and French, including a reproduction of the 1868 second edition of the Edward Fitzgerald translation along with translations by Friedrich Rosen and others, Tahrir-Iran Co., Teheran, Iran, 1964.
[1963]   M. J. Klein, *Planck, Entropy and Quanta, 1901–1906*, pp. 83–108 in Gershenson and Greenberg [**1963**].
[1970]   ———, *The First Phase of the Bohr-Einstein Dialogue*, pp. 1–39 in R. McCormmach, ed., Historical Studies in the Physical Sciences **2**, University of Pennsylvania Press, Philadelphia, 1970.
[1970]   J. M. Koller, *Oriental Philosophies*, Charles Scribner's Sons, New York, 1970.
[1957]   S. Körner, *Observation and Interpretation in the Philosophy of Physics*, reprinted in 1962 by Dover Publications, Inc., Dover Publishing Co., New York, 1957.
[1957]   A. Koyré, *From the Closed World to the Infinite Universe*, Harper & Bros. Publishers, New York, 1957.
[1962]   T. Kuhn, *The Structure of Scientific Revolutions*, Chicago University Press, Chicago, Illinois, 1962.
[1964]   ———, *A Function for Thought Experiments*, pp. 307–334 in *Melanges Alexandre Koyré*, Vol. II, "L'Adventure de l'esprit," Histoire de la Pensée, XIII, Herman et Cie, Paris, 1964.
[1978]   ———, *Black-body Theory and the Quantum Discontinuity 1894–1912*, At the Clarendon Press, Oxford, 1978.
[1949]   C. H. Langford, *A Proof That Synthetic A Priori Propositions Exist*, Journal of Philosophy **46** (1949), 20–24.
[1819]   P. S. Laplace, *A Philosophical Essay on Probabilities*, translated by F. W. Truscott and F. L. Emory from the sixth French edition, Dover Publications, Inc., New York, 1951.
[1980]   A. J. Leggett, *Macroscopic Quantum Systems and the Quantum Theory of Measurement*, Progress of Theoretical Physics, Supplement **69** (1980), 80–100.
[1985]   ———, *Quantum Mechanics at the Macroscopic Level*, 35–57 in Boer, Dal and Ulfbeck [**1985**].
[1998]   ———, *Macroscopic Realism. What Is It, and What Do We Know about It from Experiment?*, pp. 1–22 in R. A. Healey and G. Hellman [**1998**].

[1923] C. I. Lewis, *A Pragmatic Conception of the A Priori*, pp. 286–294 in Feigl and Sellars [**1949**].
[1985] J. Lindhard, *"Complementarity" between Energy and Temperature*, 91–112 in Boer, Dal and Ulfbeck [**1985**].
[1939] F. London and E. Bauer, *La Theorie de l'Observation en Mecanique Quantique*, Actualites Scientifique et Industrielles No. 775, Hermann et Cie., Paris, 1939.
[1948] A. A. Luce and T. E. Jessop, *The Works of George Berkeley Bishop of Cloyne*, Thos. Nelson and Sons, Ltd., New York, 1948.
[DRN] Lucretius, *De Rerum Natura*, translated and discussed under the title *Lucretius* by W. H. Mallock, John B. Alden, Publisher, New York, 1889.
[1883] E. Mach, *The Science of Mechanics*, (1883), Open Court Publishing Co., Evanston, Ill., 1960.
[1905] _____, *Erkenntnis und Irrtum: Skizzen zur Psychologie der Forschung*, J. A. Barth, Leipzig, 1905.
[1910] _____, *Die Leitgedanken: Meiner Naturwissenshaftlichen Erkenntnislehre und ihre Aufname durch die Zeitgenossen*, Scientia **7** (1910), 225–240.
[1957] D. M. MacKay, *Complementary Descriptions*, Mind **66** (1957), 390–394.
[1958] _____, *Complementarity*, Aristotelian Society Supplement **32** (1958), 105–122.
[1982] E. MacKinnon, *Scientific Explanation and Atomic Physics*, Univ. of Chicago Press, Chicago, Illinois, 1982.
[1944] H. Margenau, *The Exclusion Principle and its Philosophical Importance*, Philosophy of Science **11** (1944), 187–208.
[1950] _____, *The Nature of Physical Reality*, McGraw-Hill Book Co., New York, 1950.
[1963] _____, *Measurements and Quantum States. I, II*, Philosophy of Science **30** (1963), 1–15, 138–151.
[1962a] G. Maxwell, *Theories, Frameworks and Ontology*, Philosophy of Science **29** (1962), 132–138.
[1962b] _____, *The Ontological Status of Theoretical Entities*, pp. 3–27 in Feigl and Maxwell [**1962**].
[1954] B. Mayo, *The Existence of Theoretical Entities*, Science News **32** (1954), 7–18.
[1956] _____, *More About Theoretical Entities*, Science News **39** (1956), 42–55.
[1967] H. Mehlberg, *The Problem of Physical Reality in Contemporary Science*, pp. 45–65 in Bungé [**1967b**].
[1965] K. M. Meyer-Abich, *Korrespondenz, Individualität und Komplementarität*, Franz Steiner Verlag GHBH, Wiesbaden, 1965.
[1930] E. Meyerson, *Identity and Reality*, first edition 1908, translated by Kate Lowenberg from the third edition in 1930, Dover Publications, Inc., New York, 1962.
[1846] J. S. Mill, *A System of Logic, Ratiocinative and Inductive; Being a connected view of the Principles of Evidence and the Methods of Scientific Investigation*, Harper and Bros., New York, 1846.
[1944] E. Nagel, *Logic Without Ontology*, pp. 302–321 in Benacerraf and Putnam [**1964**].
[1961] _____, *The Structure of Science*, Harcourt, Brace & World, Inc., New York, 1961.
[1994] R. Omnès, *The Interpretation of Quantum Mechanics*, Princeton University Press, Princeton, New Jersey, 1994.
[1986] K. Okruhlik, *Kant on Realism and Methodology*, pp. 307–329 in Butts [**1986c**].
[1946] W. Pauli, *Remarks on the History of the Exclusion Principle*, Science **103** (1946), 213–215.
[1950] _____, *Die Philosophische Bedeutung der Idee der Komplementarität*, pp. 149–158 in Pauli [**1955**].
[1955] _____, ed., *Niels Bohr and the Development of Physics*, Pergamon Press, Inc., New York, 1955.
[1892] K. Pearson, *The Grammar of Science*, Meridian Books, New York, 1957.

PHILOSOPHY

[1989] R. Penrose, *The Emperor's New Mind*, Oxford University Press, Oxford, England, 1989.
[1994] _____, *Shadows of the Mind*, Oxford University Press, Oxford, England, 1994.
[1968] A. Petersen, *Quantum Physics and the Philosophical Tradition*, M.I.T. Press, Cambridge, Mass., 1968.
[1909] M. Planck, *The Unity of the Physical Universe*, pp. 1–26 in M. Planck, *A Survey of Physical Theory*, translated from the German, Dover Publications, Inc., New York, 1960.
[1913] _____, *New Paths of Physical Knowledge*, pp. 45–55 in M. Planck, *A Survey of Physical Theory*, translated from the German, Dover Publications, Inc., New York, 1960.
[1899] H. Poincaré, *La thorie de Maxwell et les oscillations Hertziennes. La tlgraphie sans fil*, L'Institut Scientia, Paris, 1899.
[1905] H. Poincaré, *Science and Hypothesis*, Dover Publications, Inc., New York, 1952.
[1912] _____, *Science and Method*, Dover Publications, Inc., New York, 1952.
[1934] K. R. Popper, *The Logic of Scientific Discovery*, (1934), Science Editions, New York, 1961.
[1962] _____, *Conjectures and Refutations*, Basic Books, New York, 1962.
[1967] _____, *Quantum Mechanics without the Observer*, pp. 7–44 in Bungé [**1967b**].
[1965] H. Putnam, *Craig's Theorem*, Journal of Philosophy **52** (1965), 251–260.
[1953] W. V. O. Quine, *From a Logical Point of View*, Harper Torchbook, New York, 1953.
[1960] _____, *Word and Object*, M.I.T. Press, Cambridge, Mass., 1960.
[1855] W. J. M. Rankine, *Outlines of the Science of Energetics*, New Philosophical Journal **2** (1855), 120–141.
[1944] H. Reichenbach, *Philosophical Foundations of Quantum Mechanics*, University of California Press, Berkeley and Los Angeles, 1965.
[1946] L. Rosenfeld, *Niels Bohr*, first edition 1946, North-Holland Publishing Co., Amsterdam, 1961.
[1961a] _____, *Questions of Irreversibility and Ergodicity*, pp. 1–20 in Caldirola [**1961**].
[1961b] _____, *Foundations of Quantum Theory and Complementarity*, Nature **190** (1961), 384–388.
[1963b] _____, *Strife about Complementarity*, Science Progress **41** (1963), 393–410.
[1986] L. M. Roth, *Buddhist Madyamika Philosophy as Therapy for Realistic Views*, pp. 319–329 in L. M. Roth and A. Inomata, eds., *Fundamental Questions in Quantum Mechanics*, Gordon and Breach Science Publishers, New York, 1986.
[1962] W. Rozeboom, *The Factual Content of Theoretical Concepts*, pp. 273–357 in Feigl and Maxwell [**1962**].
[1945] B. Russell, *A History of Western Philosophy*, Simon and Schuster, New York, 1945.
[1967] R. Schiller, *Relations of Quantum to Classical Physics*, pp. 149–160 in Bungé [**1967b**].
[1949] P. A. Schilpp, *Albert Einstein: Philosopher Scientist*, Tudor Publ. Co., New York, 1949.
[1963] _____, *The Philosophy of Rudolph Carnap*, Vol. XI in the Library of Living Philosopher, Open Court Press, Evanston, Ill., 1963.
[1923] R. Schmidt, ed., *Die Philosophie der Gegenwart im Selbstdarstellungen, Vol. 4*, Felix Meiner, Leipzig, 1923.
[1847] A. Schopenhauer, *The Fourfold Root of the Principle of Sufficient Reason*, originally published in German in 1813, revised 1847, Open Court, LaSalle, Illinois, 1974.

[1859] _____, *The World as Will and Representation*, originally published in German in 1819, revised 1859, The Falcon's Wing Press, Clinton, Mass., 1958.
[1928a] E. Schrödinger, *Conceptual Models in Physics and Their Philosophical Value*, reprinted as pp. 148–165 in E. Schrödinger, "Science and the Human Temperament" New York: W. W. Norton Co., 1935.
[1935a] _____, *Die Gegenwärtige Situation in der Quantenmechanik*, Naturwiss. **23** (1935), 807–812, 823–828, 844–849; reprinted as pp. 484–501 in Schrödinger [**1984**], Vol. 3, and in an English translation as pp. 152–167 in Wheeler and Żurek [**1983**].
[1950] _____, *What is an Elementary Particle?*, Endeavor **9** (1950), 109–116; reprinted as pp. 456–463 in Schrödinger [**1984**], Vol 4.
[1952] _____, *Are There Quantum Jumps? I, II*, British Journal for the Philosophy of Science **3** (1952–53), 109–123, 233–242; reprinted as pp. 478–402 in Schrödinger [**1984**], Vol. 4.
[1962] M. Scriven, *Explanations, Predictions and Laws*, pp. 170–230 in Feigl and Maxwell [**1962**].
[1980] J. Searle, *Minds, brains and programs*, The Behavioral and Brain Sciences **3**, 417–458; it is reprinted D. R. Hoffstadter and D. C. Dennett, *The Mind's I*, Basic Books, Inc., New York , 1981.
[1953] W. Sellars, *Is There a Synthetic A Priori?*, Philosophy of Science **20** (1953), 121–138.
[1963] R. S. Shankland, *Conversations with Albert Einstein*, American Journal of Physics **31** (1963), 47–57.
[1963] A. Shimony, *Role of the Observer in Quantum Theory*, American Journal of Physics **31** (1963), 755–773.
[1998] _____, *Comments on Leggett's "Macroscopic Realism"*, pp. 23–31 in R. A. Healey and G. Hellman [**1998**].
[1956] J. J. C. Smart, *The Reality of Theoretical Entities*, Australasian Journal of Philosophy **34** (1956), 1–12.
[1975] G. S. Stent, *Limits to the Scientific Understanding of Man*, Science **187** (1975), 1052–1057.
[1983] R. Torretti, *Relativity and Geometry*, Dover Publ. Inc., New York, 1996.
[1955] R. Traill, *The Existence of Theoretical Entities*, (Letter), Science News **38** (1955), 117–119.
[1955] J. Turner, *A Note on Maxwell's Interpretation of Some Attempts at Dynamical Explanation*, Annals of Science **11** (1955-56), 238–245.
[1953] A. P. Ushenko, *The Principles of Causality*, Journal of Philosophy **50** (1953), 85–101.
[1989] B. A. Wallace, *Choosing Reality*, Shambhala, Boston, Mass., 1989.
[1958] V. F. Weisskopf, *Review of Heisenberg "Physics and Philosophy"*, Scientific American **199** # 3 (1958), 215–221.
[1952] C. F. von Weizsäcker, *The World View of Physics*, University of Chicago Press, Chicago, Ill., 1952.
[1955] _____, *Komplementarität und Logik*, Naturwissenschaften **42** (1955), 521–529, 545–555.
[1847] W. Whewell, *The Philosophy of the Inductive Sciences, Founded upon their History*, volumes 1 and 2, J. W. Parker, London, 1847.
[1962] E. P. Wigner, *Remarks on the Mind-Body Question*, pp. 284–302 in Good [**1962**].
[1963] _____, *The Problem of Measurement*, American Journal of Physics **31** (1963), 6–16.
[1967] _____, *Symmetries and Reflections: Scientific Essays*, Indiana University Press, Bloomington, Indiana, 1967.

[1956]   A. D. Winspear, *The Roman Poet of Science Lucretius: De Rerum Natura*, S. A. The Harbor Press, New York, 1956.
[1922]   L. Wittgenstein, *Tractatus Logico-Philosophicus*, Routledge, London, 1961.
[1953]   _____, *Philosophical Investigations*, Macmillan Co., New York, 1953.
[1967]   _____, *Lectures and conversations on aesthetics, psychology, and religious belief*, edited by Cyril Barrett from notes taken by R. Smythies, R. Rhees, and J. Taylor, University of California Press, Berkeley, 1967.
[1997]   P. Yarn, *Bringing Schrödinger's Cat to Life*, Scientific American **276**, #6, 124–129.
[1964]   W. Yourgrau, *On the Reality of Elementary Particles*, pp. 360–381 in Bungé [**1964**].
[1991]   W. H. Żurek, *Decoherence and the Transition from Quantum to Classical Physics*, Physics Today **44** (1991), 36-44.

Physics
[1959]   Y. Aharonov and D. Bohm, *Significance of Electromagnetic Potentials in Quantum Theory*, Physical Review **115** (1959), 485–491.
[1961a] _____, *Time in the Quantum Theory and the Uncertainty Relation for Time and Energy*, Physical Review **122** (1961), 1649–1658.
[1961b] _____, *Further Considerations on Electromagnetic Potentials in the Quantum Theory*, Physical Review **123** (1961), 1511–1524.
[1962]   _____, *Remarks on the Possibility of Quantum Electrodynamics without Potentials*, Physical Review **125** (1962), 2192–2193.
[1963]   _____, *Further Discussion of the Role of Electromagnetic Potentials in the Quantum Theory*, Physical Review **130** (1963), 1625–1632.
[1964]   _____, *Answer to Fock Concerning the Time Energy Indeterminacy Relation*, Physical Review **134** (1964), B1417–B1418.
[1961]   J. Albertson, *Von Neumann's Hidden-Parameter Proof*, American Journal of Physics **29** (1961), 478–484.
[1969]   G. R. Allcock, *The Time of Arrival in Quantum Mechanics, I. Formal Considerations, II. The Individual Measurement, III. The Measurement Ensemble*, Annals of Physics (New York) **53** (1969), 253–285, 286–310, 311–348.
[1960]   H. Araki and M. M. Yanase, *Measurement of Quantum Mechanical Operators*, Physical Review **120** (1960), 622–626.
[1965]   A. B. Arons and M. B. Peppard, *Einstein's Proposal of the Photon Concept—A Translation of the* Annalen der Physik *Paper of 1905*, American Journal of Physics **33** (1965), 367–374.
[1965]   E. Arthurs and J. L. Kelly, Jr., *On the Simultaneous Measurement of a Pair of Conjugate Observables*, Bell System Technical Journal **44** (1965), 725–729.
[1994]   D. Atkatz, *Quantum cosmology for pedestrians*, Am. J. Phys. **62** (1994), 619–627.
[1988]   A. Bach, *The Concept of Indistinguishable Particles in Classical and Quantum Physics*, Foundations of Physics **18** (1988), 639–649.
[1970]   L. E. Ballentine, *The Statistical Interpretation of Quantum Mechanics*, Reviews of Modern Physics **42** (1970), 358–381.
[1958]   G. Beck and H. M. Nussenzveig, *Uncertainty Relation and the Diffraction by a Slit*, Nuovo Cimento **9** (1958), 1068–1076.
[1962]   F. J. Belinfante, *Consequences of the Postulate of a Complete Commuting Set of Observables in Quantum Electrodynamics*, Physical Review **128** (1962), 2832–2837.
[1964]   J. S. Bell, *On the Einstein Podolsky Rosen Paradox*, Physica **I** (1964), 195–200.

[1966] _____, *On the Problem of Hidden Variables in Quantum Mechanics*, Reviews of Modern Physics **38** (1966), 447–452.
[1999] Charles H. Bennett, Peter W. Shor, John A. Smolin and Ashiah V. Thaplial, *Entanglement-Assisted Classical Capacity of Noisy Channels*, Physical Review Letters **83** (1999), 3081–3084.
[1936] G. Birkhoff and J. von Neumann, *The Logic of Quantum Mechanics*, Annals of Mathematics **37** (1936), 832–843.
[1959] J. M. Blatt, *An Alternative Approach to the Ergodic Problem*, Progress in Theoretical Physics **22** (1959), 745–756.
[1952] J. M. Blatt and V. Weisskopf, *Theoretical Nuclear Physics*, John Wiley & Sons, New York.
[1968] D. I. Blokhintsev, *Interaction of a Microsystem with a Measuring Instrument*, Soviet Physics Uspekhi **11** (1968), 320–327.
[1960] H. Boersch, H. Hamish, D. Wholleben and K. Grobmann, *Antiparallele Weissche Bereiche als Biprisms für Electroneninterferenzen*, Zeitschrift für Physik **159** (1960), 397–404.
[1951] D. Bohm, *Quantum Theory*, Prentice-Hall, Englewood Cliffs, New Jersey, 1951.
[1952a] _____, *A Suggested Interpretation of the Quantum Theory in Terms of Hidden Variables, I*, Physical Review **85** (1952), 166–179.
[1952b] _____, *A Suggested Interpretation of the Quantum Theory in Terms of Hidden Variables, II*, Physical Review **85** (1952), 180–193.
[1957a] _____, *Causality and Chance in Modern Physics*, D. van Nostrand, New York, 1957.
[1957b] _____, *A Proposed Explanation of Hidden Variables as a Sub-Quantum Mechanical Level*, pp. 33–40 in Körner [**1957**].
[1962a] _____, *On the Relationship Between Methodology in Scientific Research and the Content of Scientific Knowledge*, British Journal of the Philosophy of Science **12** (1962), 103–116.
[1962b] _____, *Classical and Non-Classical Concepts in Quantum Theory*, British Journal of the Philosophy of Science **12** (1962), 265–280.
[1957] D. Bohm and Y. Aharonov, *Discussion of Experimental Proof of the Paradox of Einstein, Rosen and Podolsky*, Physical Review **108** (1957), 1070–1076.
[1960] _____, *Further Discussion of Possible Experimental Proof of the Paradox of Einstein, Rosen and Podolsky*, Nuovo Cimento **17** (1960), 964–976.
[1966] D. Bohm and J. Bub, *A Proposed Solution of the Measurement Problem in Quantum Mechanics by a Hidden Variable Theory*, Reviews of Modern Physics **38** (1966), 453–469.
[1968] _____, *On Hidden Variables—A Reply to Comments by Jauch and Piron and by Gudder*, (Letter), Reviews of Modern Physics **42** (1968), 358–381.
[1872] L. Boltzmann, *Weitere Studien über das Wärmegleichgewicht unter Gasmolekülen*, Sitzungsberichte der Kaiserlichen Akademie der Wissenshaft, Mathematisch-Naturwissenhaftliche Classe **66**, **II** (1872), 275–370; it is printed in an English translation as "Further Studies on the Thermal Equilibrium of Gas Molecules" in S. G. Brush [**1965**], Vol. 2, pp. 88–175.
[1926] M. Born, *Zur Quantenmechanik der Stossvorgänge*, Zeitschrift für Physik **37** (1926), 863–867.
[1927] _____, *Physical Aspects of Quantum Mechanics*, Nature **119** (1927), 354–357.
[1954] _____, *The Statistical Interpretation of Quantum Mechanics*, a translation of Born's Nobel Prize Address, Science **122** (1954), 675–679.
[1925] M. Born and P. Jordan, *Zur Quantenmechanik*, Zeitschrift für Physik **35** (1925), 858–888.

[1925]   M. Born, W. Heisenberg and P. Jordan, *Zur Quantenmechanik II*, Zeitschrift für Physik **35** (1925), 557–615.
[1925]   W. Bothe and H. Geiger, *Über das Wesen des Comptons effeckts: ein experimentaller Beitrag zur Theorie der Strahlung*, Zeitschrift für Physik **33** (1925), 639–663.
[1968]   T. Boyer, *Quantum Electromagnetic Zero-Point Energy and Retarded Dispersion Forces*, Physical Review **174** (1968), 1631–1638.
[1965]   E. Breitenberg, *On the So-Called Paradox of Einstein, Podolsky and Rosen*, Nuovo Cimento **38** (1965), 356–360.
[1923]   L. de Broglie, *Ondes et Quanta*, Comptes rendus hebdomadaires des Seances de l'Academie des Sciences **177** (1923), 507–510.
[1924]   _____, *A tentative theory of light quanta*, Philosophical Magazine **47** (1924), 446–458.
[1925]   _____, *Recherches sur la théorie des quanta*, Annales de Physique **3** (1925), 22–128.
[1926]   _____, *Sur la possibilitie de relier les phenomenes d'interference et de diffraction a la theorie des quanta de lumière*, Comptes rendus hebdomadaires des Seances de l'Academie des Sciences **183** (1926), 447–448.
[1927]   _____, *La Structure atomique de la matiere du rayonnement et la Mecanique ondulatoire*, Comptes rendus hebdomadaires des Seances de l'Academie des Sciences **184** (1927), 273–274.
[1957]   _____, *La Theorie de la Mesure en mecanique ondulatoire*, Les Grandes Problemes des Sciences VII, Gauthier-Villars, Paris, 1957.
[1960]   _____, *Non-Linear Wave Mechanics*, Elsevier, New York, 1960.
[1969]   _____, *Sur l'interpretation des relations incertitude*, Comptes rendus hebdomadaires des Seances de l'Academie des Sciences **268B** (1969), 277–280.
[1968]   J. Bub, *The Daneri-Loinger-Prosperi Quantum Theory of Measurement*, Nuovo Cimento **57B** (1968), 503–520.
[1969]   _____, *What is a Hidden Variable Theory of Quantum Phenomena?*, International Journal of Theoretical Physics **3** (1969), 101–123.
[1963]   J. M. Burgers, *The Measuring Process in Quantum Theory*, Reviews of Modern Physics **35** (1963), 145–150.
[1961]   P. Caldirola, ed., *Ergodic Theories*, Proceedings of the International School of Physics "Enrico Fermi," XIV course, 1960, Academic Press, New York, 1961.
[1921]   W. Campbell, *Atomic Structure*, (Letter), Nature **107** (1921), 170.
[1926]   _____, *Time and Chance*, Philosophical Magazine **1** (1926), 1106–1117.
[1968]   P. Carruthers and M. M. Nieto, *Phase and Angle Variables in Quantum Mechanics*, Reviews of Modern Physics **40** (1968), 411–440.
[1960]   R. G. Chambers, *Shift of an Electron Interference Pattern by Enclosed Magnetic Flux*, Physical Review Letters **5** (1960), 3–5.
[1965]   Z. Chylinski, *Uncertainty Relation Between Time and Energy*, Acta Physica Polonica **23** (1965), 631–638.
[1969]   J. F. Clauser, M. A. Horne, A. Shimony and E. A. Holt, *Proposed Experiment to Test Local Hidden-Variable Theories*, Physical Review Letters **23** (1969), 880–884.
[1978]   J. F. Clauser and A. Shimony, *Bell's theorem: experimental tests and implications*, Reports on Progress in Physics **41**, 1881–1927.
[1962]   W. L. Clinton, *Volume Dependence of the Energy of an Enclosed Quantum Mechanical System*, Physical Review **128** (1962), 2837–2841.
[1925]   A. H. Compton and A. W. Simon, *Directed Quanta of Scattered X-rays*, Physical Review **26** (1925), 289–299.
[1969]   L. N. Cooper and D. van Vechten, *On the Interpretation of Measurement within Quantum Theory*, American Journal of Physics **37** (1969), 1212–1220.

[1953] E. Corinaldesi, *Some Aspects of the Problem of Measurability in Quantum Electrodynamics*, Nuovo Cimento **10** (1953), 83–100.
[1962] A. Danieri, A. Loinger and G. M. Prosperi, *Quantum Theory of Measurement and Ergodicity Conditions*, Nuclear Physics **33** (1962), 297–319.
[1966] _____, *Further Remarks on the Relations Between Statistical Mechanics and Quantum Theory of Measurement*, Nuovo Cimento **44** (1966), 119–128.
[1931a] C. G. Darwin, *Examples of the Uncertainty Principles*, Proceedings of the Royal Society (London) **A130** (1931), 632–639.
[1931b] _____, *The Uncertainty Principle*, Science **73** (1931), 653–660.
[1927] C. J. Davisson and L. H. Germer, *Diffraction of Electrons by a Crystal of Nickel*, Physical Review **30** (1927), 705–740.
[1966] B. D'Espagnat, *Two Remarks on the Theory of Measurement*, Nuovo Cimento Supplemento **4** (1966), 828–838.
[1971a] _____, *Conceptual Foundations of Quantum Mechanics*, W. A. Benjamin, Inc., Menlo Park, California, 1971.
[1971b] _____, ed., *Foundations of Quantum Mechanics, Course IL, 1970 Enrico Fermi Summer School*, Academic Press, New York, 1971.
[1962] B. S. DeWitt, *Quantum Theory without Electromagnetic Potentials*, Physical Review **125** (1962), 2189–2191.
[1968] _____, *The Everett-Wheeler Interpretation of Quantum Mechanics*, pp. 318–332 in DeWitt and Wheeler [**1968**].
[1968] C. S. DeWitt and J. A. Wheeler, *Battelle Recontres: 1967 Lectures in Mathematics and Physics*, W. A. Benjamin, New York, 1968.
[1957] R. H. Dicke, *Gravitation without Equivalence*, Reviews of Modern Physics **29** (1957), 363–376.
[1925] P. A. M. Dirac, *The Fundamental Equations of Quantum Mechanics*, Proceedings of the Royal Society (London) **A109** (1925), 642–653.
[1930] _____, *The Principles of Quantum Mechanics*, 4th edition, Oxford University Press, Oxford, 1930.
[1938] _____, *Classical theory of radiating electrons*, Proc. Roy. Soc. London **A167** (1938), 148–169.
[1968] J. Earman and A. Shimony, *A Note on Measurement*, Nuovo Cimento **54B** (1968), 332–334.
[1921] P. Ehrenfest, *Le Principe de Correspondence*, pp. 248–254 in Institut Internationale de Physique Solvay [**1923**].
[1927] _____, *Bemerkung über die angenaherte Gültigkeit der klassischen Mechanik innerhalb der Quantenmechanik*, Zeitschrift für Physik **45** (1927), 455–457.
[1905] A. Einstein, *Über einen die Erzeugung und Verwandlung des Lichtes betreffenden heuristischen Gesichtspunkt*, Annalen der Physik **17** (1905), 132–148; this is reprinted as pp. 149–169 in Vol. 2 of Einstein [**1987**]. An English translation appears as pp. 86–103 in volume 2 of the English translations of these papers.
[1907] _____, *Die Planckesche Theorie der Strahlung und die Theorie der spezifischen Wärme*, Annalen der Physik **22** (1907), 180–190; this is reprinted as pp. 378–391 in Vol. 2 of Einstein [**1987**]. An English translation appears as pp. 214–224, in volume 2 of the English translations of these papers.
[1911] _____, *Über den Einfluss der Schwerkraft auf die Ausbreitung des Lichtes*, Annalen der Physik **35** (1911), 898–908; this is reprinted in Einstein [**1987**], Vol. 3, pp. 485–497; an English translation titled "On the Influence of Gravitation on the Propagation of Light" appears on pp. 97–108 in Einstein [**1923**] and another in Einstein [**1987**], English Translations, Vol. 3, pp. 379–387.

[1916] _____, *Zur Quantentheorie der Strahlung*, Mitteilungen der Physikalische Gesellschaft (Zürich) **18** (1916), 47–62; this is reprinted as pp. 381–396 in Einstein [**1987**], Vol. 6.

[1923] _____, *The Meaning of Relativity*, Princeton University Press, Princeton, New Jersey, 1955.

[1987] _____, *The Collected Papers of Albert Einstein,*, published between 1987 and 1996 with accompanying volumes of English Translations, Princeton University Press, Princeton, New Jersey, 1987.

[1935] A. Einstein, B. Podolsky and N. Rosen, *Can Quantum Mechanical Description of Reality Be Considered Complete?*, Physical Review **47** (1935), 777–780.

[1931] A. Einstein, R. C. Tolman and B. Podolsky, *Knowledge of the Past and Future in Quantum Mechanics*, Physical Review **37** (1931), 780–781.

[1999] J. Eisert, M. Wilkens and M. Lewenstein, *Quantum Games and Quantum Strategies*, Physical Review Letters **83** (1999), 3077–3080.

[1937] W. M. Elsasser, *On Quantum Measurement and the Role of the Uncertainty Relations in Statistical Mechanics*, Physical Review **52** (1937), 987–999.

[1968] _____, *Theory of Quantum Mechanical Description*, Proceedings of the National Academy of Sciences **59** (1968), 738–744.

[1970] H. Erlichson, *Aharonov-Bohm Effect—Quantum Effects on Charged Particles in Field-Free Regions*, American Journal of Physics **38** (1970), 162–173.

[1957] H. Everett III, *"Relative State" Formulation of Quantum Theory*, Reviews of Modern Physics **29** (1957), 454–462.

[1948] R. P. Feynman, *Space-time approach to non-relativistic quantum mechanics*, Reviews of Modern Physics **20** (1948), 367–387; It is reprinted as pp. 321–341 in J. Schwinger, *Selected Papers on Quantum Electrodynamics,* Dover Publications, Inc., New York 1958.

[1965] R. P. Feynman and A. Hibbs, *Quantum Mechanics and Path Integrals*, McGraw-Hill, New York, 1965.

[1970] A. Fine, *Insolubility of the Quantum Measurement Problem*, Physical Review **2D** (1970), 2783–2787.

[1957] V. A. Fock, *The Interpretation of Quantum Mechanics*, Advances in Physics (U.S.S.R.) **62** (1957), 556–573; also printed in Czechoslovakian Journal of Physics **7** (1957), 643–656..

[1962] _____, *Criticism of an Attempt to Disprove the Uncertainty Relation between Time and Energy*, Soviet Physics J.E.T.P. **15** (1962), 784–786.

[1947] V. A. Fock and N. Krylov, *On the Uncertainty Relation Between Time and Energy*, Journal of Physics (U.S.S.R.) **11** (1947), 112–120.

[1936] R. H. Fowler, *Statistical Mechanics: The Theory of Properties of Matter in Equilibrium*, 2nd edition (1st edition 1929), Cambridge University Press, Cambridge, 1936.

[1957] H. Freistadt, *The Causal Formulation of Quantum Mechanics of Particles (The Theory of DeBroglie, Bohm and Takabayasi)*, Nuovo Cimento Supplemento **5** (1957), 1–70.

[1936a] W. H. Furry, *Note on the Quantum-Mechanical Theory of Measurement*, Physical Review **49** (1936), 393–399.

[1936b] _____, *Remarks on Measurement in Quantum Theory*, Physical Review **49** (1936), 467.

[1960] W. H. Furry and N. F. Ramsey, *Significance of Potentials in Quantum Theory*, Physical Review **118** (1960), 623–626.

[1933] R. Fürth, *Über einige Beziehungen Zwischen klassischen Statistik und Quantenmechanik*, Zeitschrift für Physik **81** (1933), 143–162.

[1902]   W. Gibbs, *Elementary Principles in Statistical Mechanics developed with especial reference to the rational foundation of thermodynamics*, Yale Univ. Press, New Haven, R. I., 1902; it was reprinted in 1981 by Ox Bow Press, Woodbridge, Connecticut.
[1975]   D. L. Goodstein, *States of Matter*, Dover Publications, Inc, New York, 1985.
[1968]   S. P. Gudder, *Hidden Variables in Quantum Mechanics Reconsidered*, (Letter), Reviews of Modern Physics **40** (1968), 229–231.
[1970]   _____, *On Hidden-Variable Theories*, Journal of Mathematical Physics **11** (1970), 431–436.
[1968]   J. B. Hartle, *Quantum Mechanics of Individual Systems*, American Journal of Physics **36** (1968), 704–712.
[1925]   W. Heisenberg, *Über quantentheoretischen Undeutung kinematischer und mechanischer Beziehungen*, Zeitschrift für Physik **33** (1925), 879–893.
[1927]   _____, *Über den Anschaulichen Inhalt der Quanten Theoretischen Kinematik und Mechanik*, Zeitschrift für Physik **43** (1927), 172–198.
[1943]   _____, *Die Beobachtbaren Grössen in der Theorie der Elementarteichen, I, II, III*, Zeitschrift für Physik **120** (1943), 513–538, 673–702; Ibid. **123** (1944), 93–112.
[1847]   H. von Helmholtz, *Über der Erhaltung der Kraft*, W. Engelmann, Leipzig, 1889; an English translation appears in J. Tyndall and W. Francis [**1853**] under the title "The Conservation of Force". A partial English translation appears as pp. 89–100 in Brush [**1965**], Volume 1.
[1894]   H. Hertz, *The principles of mechanics presented in a new form*, translated into English by D. E. Jones and J. T. Walley, Macmillan and Co., New York, 1956.
[1968]   D. H. Holze and W. T. Scott, *The Consequences of Measurement in Quantum Mechanics. II.*, Annals of Physics (New York) **47** (1968), 489–515.
[1992]   D. Home and M. A. B. Whitaker, *Ensemble interpretation of quantum mechanics. A modern perspective*, Physics Reports **210**, 224–317.
[1955]   L. van Hove, *Quantum-Mechanical Perturbations giving rise to a Statistical Transport Equation*, Physica **21** (1955), 517–540.
[1921]   Institut Internationale de Physique Solvay, *Atomes et Electrons*, (1921), Gauthier-Villars et Cie., Paris, 1923.
[1930]   _____, *Le Magnetisme*, (1930), Gauthier-Villars et Cie., Paris, 1932.
[1968]   R. Jackiw, *Minimum Uncertainty Product, Number-Phase Uncertainty Product, and Coherent States*, Journal of Mathematical Physics **9** (1968), 339–346.
[1995]   R. L. Jaffe, *Where Does the Proton Really Get its Spin?*, Physics Today, September (1995), 24–30.
[1964]   R. C. Jaklevic, J. J. Lambe, A. H. Silver and J. E. Mercereau, *Quantum Interference from a Static Vector Potential in a Field-Free Region*, Physical Review Letters **12** (1964), 274–275.
[1964]   J. M Jauch, *The Problem of Measurement in Quantum Mechanics*, Helvetia Physica Acta **37** (1964), 293–316.
[1963]   J. M. Jauch and C. Piron, *Can Hidden Variables be Excluded in Quantum Mechanics*, Helvetia Physica Acta **37** (1963), 827–837.
[1968]   _____, *Hidden Variables Revisited*, (Letter), Reviews of Modern Physics **49** (1968), 228–229.
[1955]   J. M. Jauch and F. Rohrlich, *The Theory of Photons and Electrons*, Addison-Wesley Publ. Co., Cambridge, Mass., 1955.
[1967]   J. M. Jauch, E. P. Wigner and M. M. Yanase, *Some Comments Concerning Measurements in Quantum Mechanics*, Nuovo Cimento **48B** (1967), 114–151.
[1957a] E. T. Jaynes, *Information Theory and Statistical Mechanics. I*, Physical Review **106** (1957), 620–630.

[1957b] ———, *Information Theory and Statistical Mechanics. II*, Physical Review **108** (1957), 171–190.
[1936] P. Jordan, *Anschauliche Quantentheorie*, Verlag von Julius Springer, Berlin, 1936.
[1930] P. Jordan and V. A. Fock, *Neue Unbestimmtheiteigenshaften des Electromagnetischen Feldes*, Zeitschrift für Physik **66** (1930), 206–209.
[1929] E. C. Kemble, *The Pendulum Problem in Wave Mechanics*, Journal of the Franklin Institute **207** (1929), 503–508.
[1935] ———, *The Correlation of Wave Functions with the States of Physical Systems*, Physical Review Letters **47** (1935), 973–974.
[1937] ———, *The Fundamental Principles of Quantum Mechanics*, McGraw-Hill Book Co., New York, 1937.
[1994] C. Kiefer, *Quantum Cosmology and the Emergence of a Classical World*, pp. 104–119 in E. Rudolph and I.-O. Stamatescu, eds., *Philosophy, Mathematics, and Modern Physics*, Springer-Verlag, Berlin, 1994.
[1874] G. Kirchhoff, *Vorlesungen über matematische Physik, Band I, Mechanik*, 4th edition, B. G. Teubner, Leipzig, 1897.
[1967] S. Kochen and E. P. Specker, *The Problem of Hidden Variables in Quantum Mechanics*, Journal of Mathematics and Mechanics **17** (1967), 59–87.
[1962] A. Komar, *Indeterminate Character of the Reduction of the Wave Packet in Quantum Mechanics*, Physical Review **126** (1962), 365–369.
[1965a] M. Kretzschmar, *Must Quantal Wave Functions be Single Valued?*, Zeitschrift für Physik **185** (1965), 73–83.
[1965b] ———, *Aharonov-Bohm Scattering of a Wave Packet of Finite Extension*, Zeitschrift für Physik **185** (1965), 84–96.
[1965c] ———, *On the Aharonov-Bohm Effect for Bound States*, Zeitschrift für Physik **185** (1965), 97–110.
[1996] P. Kwait, H. Weinfurter and A. Zeilinger, *Quantum Seeing in the Dark*, Scientific American **275** # **5** (1996), 72–78.
[1958] L. Landau and E. H. Lifshitz, *Statistical Physics*, Pergamon Press, Ltd., London, 1958.
[1931] L. Landau and R. Peierls, *Erweiterung des Unbestimmtheitsprinzip für die relativische Quantentheorie*, Zeitschrift für Physik **69** (1931), 56–69.
[1955] A. Landé, *Foundations of Quantum Theory*, Yale University Press, New Haven, Conn., 1955.
[1960] ———, *From Dualism to Unity in Quantum Physics*, Cambridge University Press, Cambridge, 1960.
[1965] ———, *Quantum Fact and Fiction I*, American Journal of Physics **33** (1965), 123–127.
[1966] ———, *Quantum Fact and Fiction II*, American Journal of Physics **34** (1966), 1160–1163.
[1969] ———, *Quantum Fact and Fiction III*, American Journal of Physics **37** (1969), 541–548.
[1900] J. Larmor, *Aether and Matter: A Development of the Dynamical Relations of the Aether to Material Systems on the Basis of the Atomic Constitution of Matter including a Discussion of the Influence of the Earth's Motion on Optical Phenomena being an Adam's Prize Essay in the University of Cambridge*, Cambridge University Press, Cambridge, 1900.
[1932] M. von Laue, *Zu den Erorterung über Kausalitat*, Naturwissenschaften **20** (1932), 915–916.
[1934] ———, *Über Heisenbergs Ungenauigkeitsbeziehungen und ihre Erkenntnistheoretische Bedeutung*, Naturwissenschaften **20** (1934), 915–916.

[1955] H. Lehman, K. Symanzik and W. Zimmerman, *Zur Formulierung quantisierter Feldtheorien*, Nuovo Cimento **1** (1955), 205–223.
[1962] F. Lenz, *Zur Phasenschiebung von Electronenwellen im feldfrien Raum durch Potentiale*, (Letter), Naturwissenschaften **49** (1962), 82.
[1929] G. N. Lewis and J. E. Mayer, *The Quantum Laws and the Uncertainty Principle of Heisenberg*, Proceedings of the National Academy of Science **15** (1929), 127–139.
[1968] B. Liebowitz, *Significance of the Bohm-Aharonov Effect*, Nuovo Cimento **38** (1968), 932–950.
[1968] A. Loinger, *Comments on a Recent Paper Concerning the Quantum Theory of Measurement*, Nuclear Physics **A108** (1968), 245–249.
[1938] F. London, *On the Bose-Einstein Condensation*, Physical Review **54** (1938), 947–954.
[1909] H. A. Lorentz, *The theory of electrons, and its applications to the phenomena of light and radiant heat*, second edition (1915; first edition 1909), Dover Publications, Inc., New York, 1952.
[1912] H. A. Lorentz, *Les théories statistique en thermodynamique*, B. G. Teubner, Leipzig, 1916.
[1961] G. Ludwig, *Axiomatic Quantum Statistics of Macroscopic Systems (Ergodic Theory)*, pp. 57–132 in Caldirola [**1961**].
[1963] G. W. Mackey, *Mathematical Foundations of Quantum Mechanics*, W. A. Benjamin, Inc., New York, 1963.
[1968] _____, *Induced Representations of Groups and Quantum Mechanics*, W. A. Benjamin, Inc., New York, 1968.
[1999] L. Mandel, *Quantum effects in photon interference*, Reviews of Modern Physics **71** (1999), S274–S282.
[1962] B. Mandelbrot, *The Role of Sufficiency and of Estimation in Thermodynamics*, Annals of Mathematical Statistics **33** (1962), 1021–1038.
[1945] L. Mandelstam and I. G. Tamm, *The Uncertainty Relation between Energy and Time in Non-Relativistic Quantum Mechanics*, Journal of Physics (U.S.S.R.) **9** (1945), 249–254.
[1962] S. Mandelstam, *Quantum Electrodynamics without Potentials*, Annals of Physics (New York) **19** (1962), 1–24.
[2000] H. C. Manoharan, C. P. Lutz and D. M. Eigler, *Quantum mirages formed by coherent projection of electronic structure*, Nature **403** (2000), 512–515.
[1860] J. C. Maxwell, *Illustrations of the Dynamical Theory of Gases*, pp. 148–171 in Brush [**1965**], Vol. 1.
[1866] _____, *On the Dynamical Theory of Gases*, first published in 1866 and reprinted as pp. 23–87 in Brush [**1965**], Vol. 2.
[1877] _____, *Matter and Motion*, Dover Publications, Inc., New York, 1952.
[2002] P. McEvoy, *The Theory of Interacting Systems, Vol. 2, Classical Theory*, (CIS), MicroAnalytix, San Francisco, 2002.
[—] _____, *The Theory of Interacting Systems, Vol. 3, Equilibrium Theory*, (EIS) to be published, MicroAnalytix, San Francisco.
[—] _____, *The Theory of Interacting Systems, Vol. 4, Quantum Theory*, (QIS) to be published, MicroAnalytix, San Francisco.
[—] _____, *The Theory of Interacting Systems, Vol. 5, Quantum Thermodynamics*, (QTS) to be published, MicroAnalytix, San Francisco.
[1962] E. Merzbacher, *Single Valuedness of Wave Functions*, American Journal of Physics **30** (1962), 237–247.
[1961] A. Messiah, *Quantum Mechanics*, Vols. I and II, North Holland Publishing Co., Amsterdam, 1961.
[1999] D. A. Meyer, *Quantum Strategies*, Physical Review Letters **82** (1999), 1052–1055.

[1935] R. A. Millikan, *Electrons (+ and −), Protons, Photons, Neutrons and Cosmic Rays*, University of Chicago Press, Chicago, Ill., 1935.
[1948] E. A. Milne, *Kinematic Relativity*, Oxford University Press, Oxford, 1948.
[1967] B. Misra, *When can Hidden Variables be Excluded in Quantum Mechanics*, Nuovo Cimento **47** (1967), 841–859.
[1961] H. E. Mitler, *Electromagnetic Potentials in Quantum Mechanics*, Physical Review **124** (1961), 940–944.
[1962] G. Mollenstedt and W. Bayh, *Messung der kontinuierlichen Phasenschiebung von Electronenwellen im kraftfeldfreinen Raum durch das magnetische Vektorpotential einer Luftspunkte*, (Letter), Naturwissenschaften **49** (1962), 81–82.
[1929] N. F. Mott, *The Scattering of Fast Electrons by Atomic Nuclei*, Proceedings of the Royal Society (London) **A129** (1929), 425–442.
[1965] N. F. Mott and H. F. W. Massey, *The Theory of Atomic Collisions*, Oxford University Press, Oxford, 1965.
[1962] R. A. Mould, *Quantum Theory of Measurement*, Annals of Physics **17** (1962), 404–417.
[1998] M. A. Nielsen, E. Knill and R. Laflamme, *Complete quantum teleportation using nuclear magnetic resonance*, Nature **396** (1998), 52–55.
[1927] J. von Neumann, *Wahrscheinlichkeitstheoretisher Aufbau der Quantenmechanik*, Nachrichten der Gesellschaft der Wissenshaften zu Göttingen, Mathematisch-Physikalishe Klasse **1927, Heft 1**, 245–272.
[1932] _____, *The Mathematical Foundations of Quantum Mechanics*, translated by R. T. Beyer, Princeton University Press, Princeton, New Jersey, 1955.
[1687] I. Newton, *Philosophae Naturalis Principia Mathematica*, (1687), translated by A. Mott and revised with notes by F. Cajori as "Sir Isaac Newton's Natural Philosophy and His System of the World,", University of California Press, Berkeley and Los Angeles, 1934.
[1704] _____, *Opticks*, 4th edition 1730, Dover Publications, Inc., New York, 1964.
[1962] P. D. Noerdlinger, *Elimination of the Electromagnetic Potentials*, Nuovo Cimento **23** (1962), 158–167.
[1962] V. I. Ogievestskii and I. V. Polubarinov, *Quantum Electrodynamics in terms of Electromagnetic Field Intensities*, Soviet Physics J.E.T.P. **16** (1962), 969–972.
[1993] R. Omnès, *Consistent interpretations of quantum mechanics*, Reviews of Modern Physics **64** (1993), 339–382.
[2000] J-W. Pan, D. Bouwmeester, M. Daniell, H. Weinfurter and A. Zeilinger, *Experimental test of quantum nonlocality in three-photon Greenberger-Horne-Zeilinger entanglement*, Nature **403** (2000), 515–519.
[1962] D. Pandres, *Derivation of Admissibility Conditions of Wave Functions from General Quantum-Mechanical Principles*, Journal of Mathematical Physics **3** (1962), 305–308.
[1968] J. L. Park, *Nature of Quantum States*, American Journal of Physics **36** (1968), 211–226.
[1991] _____, *Quantum Assembly Semantics: The Fallacious Lingo of Occupation Numbers*, Foundations of Physics **21** (1991), 83–92.
[1986] H. Paul, *Interference between independent photons*, Reviews of Modern Physics **58**, 209–231.
[1932] W. Pauli, *Les theories quantique du magnetisme: l'electron magnetique*, pp. 175–238 in Institut Internationale de Physique Solvay [**1930**].
[1933] _____, *Die Allgemeinen Prinzipien der Wellenmechanik*, pp. 83–272 in H. Geiger and J. Scheel, eds., Handbüch der Physik, Vol. 24, Part I, second edition, J. Springer, Berlin, 1933.

[1936] ———, *Raum, Zeit und Kausalität in der Modernen Physik*, reprinted as pp. 737–748 in Pauli [**1964**].
[1939] ———, *Über ein Kriterium für Ein-oder Zweiwertigkeit der Eigenfunctionen in der Wellenmechanik*, Helvetia Physica Acta **12** (1939), 147–168.
[1964] ———, *Collected Scientific Papers*, 2 volumes, edited by R. Kronig and V. F. Weisskopf, Interscience Publ. Co., New York, 1964.
[1980] A. Peres, *Can We Undo Quantum Measurements?*, Physical Review **D22** (1980), 879–883; it is reprinted as pp. 692–696 in Wheeler and Żurek [**1983**].
[1964a] A. Peres and N. Rosen, *Macroscopic Bodies in Quantum Theory*, Physical Review **135** (1964), B1486–B1488.
[1964b] ———, *Measurement of a Quantum Ensemble by a Classical Apparatus*, Annals of Physics (New York) **29** (1964), 366–377.
[1960] A. Peres and P. Singer, *On Possible Experimental Tests for the Paradox of Einstein, Podolsky and Rosen*, Nuovo Cimento **15** (1960), 907–915.
[1961] M. Peshkin, I. Talmi and L. J. Tassie, *The Quantum Effects of Magnetic Fields Confined to Inaccessible Regions*, Annals of Physics (New York) **12** (1961), 426–435.
[1967] R. L. Pfleegor and L. Mandel, *Interference of Independent Photon Beams*, Physical Review **159** (1967), 1084–1088.
[1965] J. Picht, *Überlegungen zur "Unbestimmtheitsrelation" in der Matrizenmechanik*, Acta Physica Polonica **27** (1965), 25–35.
[1900] M. Planck, *Über eine Verbesserung der Wienschen Spektralgleichung*, Verhandlungen der Deutschen Physikalische Gesellschaft **2** (1900), 202–204.
[1963] R. E. Pugh, *Finite Formulation of Quantum Field Theory*, Annals of Physics (N.Y.) **23** (1963), 335–373.
[1965] B. Rankin, *Quantum Mechanical Time*, Journal of Mathematical Physics **6** (1965), 1057–1071.
[1962] O. Redlich, *Generalized Coordinates and Forces*, Journal of Physical Chemistry **65** (1962), 585–588.
[1968] ———, *Fundamental Thermodynamics Since Carathéodory*, Revs. of Modern Physics **40** (1968), 556–563.
[1953] M. Renninger, *Zum Wellen-Korpuskel-Dualismus*, Zeitschrift für Physik **136** (1953), 251–262.
[1960] ———, *Messung ohne Störung des Messobjects*, Zeitschrift für Physik **158** (1960), 417–421.
[1916] O. W. Richardson, *The Electron Theory of Matter*, second edition, Cambridge University Press, Cambridge, 1916.
[1969] M. C. Robison, *A Thought Experiment Violating Heisenberg's Uncertainty Principle*, Canadian Journal of Physics **47** (1969), 963–967.
[1965] F. Rohrlich, *Classical Charged Particles*, Addison-Wesley Publ. Co., Reading, Mass., 1965.
[1964a] N. Rosen, *Identical Motion in Classical and Quantum Mechanics*, American Journal of Physics **32** (1964), 377–379.
[1964b] ———, *The Relation Between Classical and Quantum Mechanics*, American Journal of Physics **32** (1964), 597–600.
[1965] ———, *Mixed States in Classical Mechanics*, American Journal of Physics **33** (1965), 146–150.
[1968] R. Rosen, *Some Comments on the Physico-Chemical Description of Biological Activity*, Journal of Theoretical Biology **18** (1968), 380–386.
[1953] L. Rosenfeld, *Strife About Complementarity*, Science Progress **41** (1953), 393–410.
[1955] ———, *On Quantum Electrodynamics*, pp. 70–95 in Pauli [**1955**].

[1965] _____, *The Measuring Process in Quantum Mechanics*, Progress in Theoretical Physics Supplement (Japan) **34** (1965), 222–231.

[1968] _____, *Questions of Method in the Consistency Problem of Quantum Mechanics*, Nuclear Physics **A108** (1968), 241–244.

[1928] A. E. Ruark, *A Critical Experiment on the Statistical Interpretation of Quantum Mechanics*, Proceedings of the National Academy of Science **14** (1928), 328–330.

[1972] A. Salam and E. P. Wigner, *Aspects of Quantum Theory*, Cambridge University Press, Cambridge, 1972.

[1988] F. Salleri, ed., *Quantum Mechanics Versus Local Realism: The Einstein-Podolsky-Rosen Paradox*, Plenum Press, New York, 1988.

[1925] E. Schrödinger, *Quantisierung als Eigenwertproblem. I, II*, Annalen der Physik **79** (1925), 361–376, 489–527; reprinted as pp. 82–97, 98–136, in Schrödinger [**1984**], Vol. 3.

[1926a] _____, *Quantisierung als Eigenwertproblem. III, IV*, Annalen der Physik **80** (1926), 437–490; Ibid. **81** (1926), 109–139; reprinted as pp. 166–219, 220–250, in Schrödinger [**1984**], Vol. 3.

[1926b] _____, *Über das Verhältnis der Heisenberg-Born-Jordanschen Quantenmechanik zu der meinen*, Annalen der Physik **79** (1926), 734–756; reprinted as pp. 143–165 in Schrödinger [**1984**], Vol. 3.

[1927] _____, *Energieaustausch nach der Wellenmechanik*, Annalen der Physik **83** (1927), 956–968; reprinted as pp. 267–279 in Schrödinger [**1984**], Vol. 1.

[1928b] _____, *Collected Papers on Wave Mechanics*, Blackie & Son, London, 1928.

[1933] _____, *The Fundamental Idea of Wave Mechanics*, (1933), Nobel Prize Lecture, pp. 305–316 in Nobel Foundation [**1965**]; the German version appears under the title "Der Grundgedanke der Wellenmechanik" as pp. 570–582 in Schrödinger [**1984**], Vol. 3.

[1934] _____, *Über die Unanwendbarkeit der Geometrie im Kleinen*, Naturwissenschaften **22** (1934), 518–520; reprinted as pp. 342–344 in Schrödinger [**1984**], Vol. 4.

[1935b] _____, *Discussion of Probability Relations between Separated Systems*, Cambridge Philosophical Society **31, Part iv** (1935), 555–563; reprinted as pp. 424–431 in Schrödinger [**1984**], Vol. 1.

[1936] _____, *Probability Relations between Separated Systems*, Cambridge Philosophical Society **32** (1936), 446–452; reprinted as pp. 433–439 in Schrödinger [**1984**], Vol. 1.

[1954] _____, *Measurement of Length and Angle in Quantum Mechanics*, (Letter), Nature **173** (1954), 442; reprinted as pp. 723 in Schrödinger [**1984**], Vol. 3.

[1958] _____, *Might Perhaps Energy be a Statistical Concept?*, Nuovo Cimento **9** (1958), 162–170; reprinted as pp. 502–510 in Schrödinger [**1984**], Vol. 1.

[1984] _____, *Gesammelte Abhandlungen*, Vols. 1–4, Verlag der Österreichischen Akademie der Wissenshaften, Friedr. Vieweg & Sohn, Braunschweig, 1984.

[1969] R. J. Sciamanda, *Dirac and Photon Interference*, American Journal of Physics **37** (1969), 1128–1130.

[1987] M. D. Semon and J. R. Taylor, *Expectation Values in the Aharonov-Bohm Effect I, II*, Nuovo Cimento **97B** (1987), 25–40, 389–401.

[1960] R. Serber and C. H. Townes, *Limits on Electromagnetic Amplifications due to Complementarity*, pp. 233–255 in C. H. Townes, ed., "Quantum Electronics," New York: Columbia University Press, 1960 (1960).

[1966] C. Y. She and H. Hefner, *Simultaneous Measurement of Noncommuting Observables*, Physical Review **152** (1966), 1103–1110.

[1959] J. R. Shewell, *On the Formation of Quantum Mechanical Operators*, American Journal of Physics **27** (1959), 16–21.

[1924] J. C. Slater, *Radiation and Atoms*, Nature **133** (1924), 307–308.

[1929] ———, *Physical Meaning of Wave Mechanics*, Journal of the Franklin Institute **207** (1929), 449–455.
[1970] H. Stein and A. Shimony,*Limitations on Measurement*, pp. 56–76 in B. D'Espagnat [**1971b**].
[1950] R. Stogis, ed., *Les Particules Elementaires*, no.8, edited by R. Stogis, Institut Internationale de Physique Solvay, Paris, 1950.
[1877] P. G. Tait, *Sketch of Thermodynamics*, second edition, revised and extended (first edition: 1868), D. Douglas, Edinburgh, 1877.
[1961] L. J. Tassie and M. Peshkin, *Symmetry Theory of the Aharonov-Bohm Effect: Quantum Mechanics of a Multiply Connected Region*, Annals of Physics (New York) **16** (1961), 177–184.
[1951] L. Tisza, *The Thermodynamics of Phase Equilibrium*, Annals of Physics (New York) **13** (1951), 1–92.
[1966] ———, *Generalized Thermodynamics*, M I T Press, Cambridge, Mass., 1966.
[1963] L. Tisza and P. M Quay, *The Statistical Thermodynamics of Phase Equilibrium*, Annals of Physics (New York) **25** (1963), 48–90.
[1913] J. J. Thomson, *On the Structure of the Atom*, Philosophical Magazine **26** (1913), 792–799.
[1962] S. Tomonaga, *Quantum Mechanics*, Vol. 1, North-Holland Publ. Co., Amsterdam, 1962.
[1964] G. T. Trammel, *Aharonov-Bohm Paradox*, Physical Review **134** (1964), B1183–B1184.
[1853] J. Tyndall and W. Francis, *Scientific memoirs, selected from the transactions of foreign academies of science, and from foreign journals: Natural Philosophy*, first published in 1853 by Taylor and Francis, London, Johnson Reprint Corp., New York, 1966.
[1968] W. F. Vinen, *Macroscopic Quantum Effects in Superfluids*, pp. 61–121 in "Reports on Progress in Physics," XXXI, part 1, 1968 (1968).
[1929] J. H. van Vleck, *The Statistical Interpretation of Various Formulations of Quantum Mechanics*, Journal of the Franklin Institute **207** (1929), 475–494.
[1967] B. L. van der Waerden, *Sources of Quantum Mechanics*, Dover Publ. Co., New York, 1967.
[1960] F. G. Werner and D. R. Brill, *Significance of Electromagnetic Potentials in the Quantum Theory in the Interpretation of Electron Interferometer Fringe Observations*, Physical Review Letters **4** (1960), 344-347.
[1957] J. A. Wheeler, *Assessment of Everett's "Relative State" Formulation of Quantum Theory*, Reviews of Modern Physics **29** (1957), 463–465.
[1945] J. A. Wheeler and R. P. Feynman, *Interaction with the absorber as the mechanism of radiation*, Reviews of Modern Physics **17** (1945), 157–181.
[1983] J. A. Wheeler and W. H. Żurek, eds., *Quantum Theory and Measurement*, Princeton University Press, Princeton, New Jersey, 1983.
[1952] G. C. Wick, A. S. Wightman and E. P. Wigner, *Intrinsic Parity of Elementary Particles*, Physical Review **88** (1952), 101–105.
[1952] E. P. Wigner, *Die Messung Quantenmechanischer Operatoren*, Zeitschrift für Physik **133** (1952), 101–108.
[1970] ———, *On Hidden Variables and Quantum Mechanical Probabilities*, American Journal of Physics **38** (1970), 1005–1009.
[1972] ———, *On the Time-Energy Uncertainty Relation*, pp. 237–247 in Salam and Wigner [**1972**].
[1950] C. S. Wu and I. Shaknov, *The Angular Correlation of Scattered Annihilation Radiation*, Physical Review (Letter) **77** (1950), 136.

[1961] M. M. Yanase, *Optimal Measuring Apparatus*, Physical Review **123** (1961), 666–668.
[1964] _____, *Remarks on the Theory of Measurement*, American Journal of Physics **32** (1964), 208–211.
[1981] W. H. Żurek, *Pointer basis of quantum apparatus: Into what mixture does the wave packet collapse?*, Physical Review **D24** (1981), 1516–1525.

Mathematics
[1961] N. I. Akhiezer and I. M. Glazman, *Theory of Linear Operators in Hilbert Space*, I, II, Frederick Ungar Publishing Co., New York, 1961.
[1961] R. P. Feynman, *The Concept of Probability in Quantum Mechanics*, pp. 533–541 in Neyman **[1961]**.
[1957] A. M. Gleason, *Measures on the Closed Subspaces of a Hilbert Space*, Journal of Mathematics and Mechanics **6** (1957), 885–893.
[1961] J. Neyman, ed., *Second Berkeley Symposium on Mathematical Statistics and Probability*, University of California Press, Berkeley and Los Angeles, 1961.
[1972] L. J. Savage, *The Foundations of Statistics*, Dover Publications, Inc., New York, 1972.
[1963] P. Suppes, *The Role of Probability in Quantum Mechanics*; pp. 319–337 in Baumrin **[1963]**.
[1962] V. S. Varadarajan, *Probability in Physics and a Theorem on Simultaneous Observability*, Communications on Pure and Applied Mathematics **15** (1962), 189–271.

Language
[1976] H. Aarsleff, *An Outline of Language-origins Theory since the Renaissance*, pp. 4–17 in S. R. Harnad, H. D. Steklis and J. Lancaster, eds., *Origins and Evolution of Language and Speech* (1976), New York Academy of Sciences, New York.
[1959a] M. Black, *Linguistic Relativity: The Views of Benjamin Lee Whorf*, Philosophical Review **68** (1959), 228–238.
[1959b] _____, *Language and Reality*, Proceedings and Addresses of the American Philosophical Association, Vol. XXXII, October, 1959.
[1943] V. Brøndal, *Essais de Linguistique Generale*, Munksgaard, Copenhagen, 1943.
[1970] J. Bronowski and U. Bellugi, *Language, Name and Concept*, Science **168** (1970), 669–673.
[1959] N. Chomsky, *A Review of B. F. Skinner's Verbal Behavior*, reprinted as pp. 547–578 in Fodor and Katz **[1964]**.
[1966] _____, *Cartesian linguistics: a chapter in the history of rationalist thought*, Harper & Row, New York, 1966.
[1968] _____, *Language and Mind*, Harcourt, Brace & World, New York, 1968.
[1953] L. S. Feuer, *Sociological Aspects of the Relation Between Language and Philosophy*, Philosophy of Science **20** (1953), 85–100.
[1960] J. A. Fishman, *A Systematization of the Whorfian Hypothesis*, Behavioral Science **5** (1960), 323–339.
[1964] J. A. Fodor and J. J. Katz, *The Structure of Language*, Prentice-Hall, Englewood Cliffs, New Jersey, 1964.
[1966] H. G. Furth, *Thinking without Language, Psychological Implications of Deafness*, Free Press, New York, 1966.
[1868] L. Geiger, *Ursprung und Entwicklung der menschlichen Sprache und Vernuft*, J. G. Cotta'schen, Stuttgart, 1868.

[1836] W. von Humboldt, *Linguistic Variability and Intellectual Development*, a translation of *Über die Kawisprache auf der Insul Java, nebst einer Einleitung über die Vershiedenheit des menschlicher Sprachbaues und ihren Einfluss auf die geistige Entwicklung des Menschengeshlects*, Vol. I, Einleitung published posthumously in Berlin, 1836, Univ. of Miami Press, Coral Gables, Florida, 1971.
[1922] O. Jespersen, *Language: Its Nature, Development and Origin*, The Macmillan Co., New York, 1922.
[1971] K. F. Johansen, *J. N. Madvig Sprachtheorestische Abhandlungen*, Munksgaard, Copenhagen, 1971.
[1960] E. Lenneberg, *The Capacity for Language Acquisition*, pp. 570–603 in Fodor and Katz [**1964**].
[1861] F. M. Müller, *Lectures on the Science of Language*, Longman, Green, Longman and Roberts, London, England, 1861.
[1864] _____, *Lectures on the Science of Language, Second Series*, Longman, Green, Longman and Roberts, London, England, 1864.
[1869] _____, *Chips from a German Workshop, Vol. I, Essays on the Science of Religion*, Charles Scribner & Co., New York, 1869.
[1887] _____, *The Science of Thought*, in 2 volumes, Charles Scribner's Sons, New York, 1887.
[1885] L. Noiré, *Logos: Ursprung und Wesen der Begriffe*, Wilhelm Engelmann, Leipzig, 1885.
[1928] E. Sapir, *The Status of Linguistics as a Science*, first published in 1928, and reprinted as pp. 65–77 in E. Sapir "Culture, Language and Personality" Berkeley and Los Angeles: The University of California Press, 1961.
[1976] J. H. Stam, *Inquiries into the Origin of Language: The Fate of a Question*, Harper & Row, New York, 1976.
[1927] V. Thomsen, *Geschichte der Sprachwissenshaft bis zum Ausgang des 19. Jahrhunderts: kurzgefasste Darstellung der Hauptpunkte*, 1927; translated into German from the 1902 Danish edition by Hans Pollak, Max Niemayer Verlag, Halle (Saar).
[1934] L. S. Vygotsky, *Thought and Language*, (1934), M.I.T. Press, Cambridge, Mass., 1962.
[1970] G. Weiler, *Mauthner's Critique of Language*, Cambridge University Press, Cambridge, 1970.
[1867] W. D. Whitney, *Language and the Study of Language*, Charles Scribner's Sons, New York, 1867.
[1892] _____, *Max Müller and the Science of Language*, Appleton and Co., New York, 1892.
[1939] B. L. Whorf, *The Relation of Habitual Thought and Behavior to Language*, pp. 134–159 in Whorf [**1956**].
[1940] _____, *Science and Linguistics*, pp. 207–219 in Whorf [**1956**].
[1941] _____, *Languages and Logic*, pp. 233–245 in Whorf [**1956**].
[1942] _____, *Language, Mind and Reality*, pp. 246–270 in Whorf [**1956**].
[1956] _____, *Selected Writings of Benjamin Lee Whorf*, M.I.T. Press, Cambridge, Mass., 1956.

Biology

[1864] C. Bernard, *An Introduction to the Study of Experimental Medicine*, translated by H. C. Green, MacMillan, New York, 1927.
[1866] _____, *Leçons sur les Propriétés des Tissus Vivant*, Germer Bailliere, Paris, 1866.

[1885] ———, *Leçons sur les phénomènes de vie*, vol. 1, J. B. Bailliere et Fils, Paris, 1885.
[1907] H. Driesch, *Science and the Philosophy of the Organism*, Vols. 1 and 2, the Gifford Lectures of 1907 and 1908, University of Aberdeen, Aberdeen, 1908–1909.
[1969] W. M. Elsasser, *The Mathematical Expression of Generalized Complementarity*, Journal of Theoretical Biology **25** (1969), 276–296.
[1969] D. Fleming, *Émigré Physicists and the Biological Revolution*, pp. 152–189 in D. Fleming and B. Bailyn, eds., *The Intellectual Migration: Europe and America 1930–1960*, Harvard Univ. Press, Cambridge, Mass, 1969.
[1931] J. S. Haldane, *The Philosophical Basis of Biology*, Doubleday, Doran & Co., New York, 1931.
[1930] L. Hogben, *Principles of Animal Biology*, Christophers, London, 1930.
[1964] P. T. Landsberg, *Does Quantum Mechanics Exclude Life?*, Nature **203** (1964), 928–930.
[1965] E. Mendelsohn, *Physical Models and Physiological Concepts: Explanation in Nineteenth-Century Biology*, British Journal of the History of Science **2** (1965), 201–219.
[1928] C. Joh. Petersen, *On Some Biological Principles*, Det Kgl. Danske Videnskabernes Selskab., Biologiske Meddelelser **VII**, 2 (1928), 1–54.
[1968] M. Polyani, *Life's Irreducible Structure*, Science **160** (1968), 1308–1312.
[1930] E. S. Russell, *The Interpretation of Development and Heredity*, At the Clarendon Press, Oxford, 1930.
[1968] G. S. Stent, *That Was the Molecular Biology That Was*, Science **160** (1968), 390–395.
[1929] J. H. Woodger, *Biological Principles: A Critical Study*, Harcourt, Brace & Co., New York, 1929.

History

[1969] M. Born, *Physics in My Generation*, Springer Verlag, New York, 1969.
[1971] J. Bromberg, *The Impact of the Neutron: Bohr and Heisenberg*, Historical Studies in the Physical Sciences **3** (1971), 307–341.
[1996a] C. Carson, *The Peculiar Notion of Exchange Forces—I: Origins in Quantum Mechanics, 1926–1928*, Studies in History and Philosophy of Modern Physics **27** (1996), 23–45.
[1996b] ———, *The Peculiar Notion of Exchange Forces—II: From Nuclear Forces to QED, 1929–1950*, Studies in History and Philosophy of Modern Physics **27** (1996), 99–131.
[1962] E. U. Condon, *60 Years of Quantum Physics*, Physics Teacher **15** # 10 (1962), 37–49.
[1957] P. Cranefield, *The Organic Physics of 1847 and the Biophysics of Today*, J. History of Medicine and Allied Sciences **12** (1957), 407–423.
[1967] K. Damodaran, *Indian Thought: A Critical Survey*, Asia Publishing House, New York, 1967.
[1931] H. Gowen, *A History of Indian Literature from Vedic times to Present Day*, Greenwood Press, New York, 1931.
[1983] John L. Heilbron, *The origins of the exclusion principle*, Historical Studies in the Physical Sciences **13:2** (1983), 261–310.
[1972] J. Mehra, *The Golden Age of Theoretical Physics*, pp. 23–49 in A. Salam and E. P. Wigner [**1972**].
[1987] J. Mehra and H. Rechenberg, *The Historical Development of Quantum Theory*, Volumes 1–5, Springer-Verlag, Berlin, 1987.

SUPPLEMENT 507

[1914] J. T. Merz, *A History of European Thought in the Nineteenth Century*, in four volumes, Blackwood, Edinburgh, 1903–1914.
[1956] J. Needham, *Science and Civilization in China*, Vols. 1–4, Cambridge University Press, Cambridge, England, 1956.
[1920] E. Nordenskiöld, *The History of Biology*, Alfred A. Knopf, New York, 1928.
[1994] S. Schweber, *QED and the Men Who Made It: Dyson, Feynman, Schwinger, and Tomonaga*, Princeton University Press, Princeton, New Jersey, 1994.
[1910] E. T. Whittaker, *A History of Theories of Aether and Electricity*, T. Nelson, London, 1951.
[1967] L. P. Williams, *Michael Faraday and the Physics of 100 Years Ago*, Science **156** (1967), 1335–1342.

Other

[1939] F. Brandt, Hans Høffding and J. Adigard Des Gautries, eds., *Correspondence entre Harald Høffding et Emile Meyerson*, Einar Munksgaard, Copenhagen, Denmark, 1939.
[1960] W. N. Dember, *Psychology of Perception*, Holt, Reinhart and Winston, Inc., New York, 1960.
[1964] ———, *Visual Perception: The Nineteenth Century*, John Wiley & Sons, New York, 1964.
[1962] L. Festinger, *Cognitive Dissonance*, Scientific American **207** #4 (1962), 93–102.
[1953] A. George, *Louis de Broglie: Physicien et Penseur*, Editions Albin Michel, Paris, 1953.
[1992] S. S. Hall, *Mapping the Next Millenium*, Random House, New York, 1992.
[1881] W. James, *Psychology : briefer course*, reprinted in W. James, *Selections. 1992: Writings, 1878-1899 / William James*, Library of America, New York, 1992.
[1890] ———, *The Principles of Psychology*, Harvard Univ. Press, Cambridge, Mass., 1981.
[1913] O. Lodge, *Continuity*, inaugural address to the British Association for the Advancement of Science, Nature **92** (1913), 33–48.
[1840] J. Müller, *Of the Senses*, a selection taken from Johannes Müller, *Elements of Physiology*, which is an English translation of Johannes Müller, *Handbuch der Physiologie des Menschen für Vorlesungen*, Hölscher, Coblenz, 1834–1840; this selection is taken from volume II, pp. 1059–1087, of the English translation and appears as pp. 35–69 in Dember [**1964**].
[1964] Nobel Foundation, *Nobel Lectures in Physics 1942–1962*, Elsevier Publ. Co., New York, 1964.
[1965] Nobel Foundation, *Nobel Lectures in Physics 1922–1941*, Elsevier Publ. Co., New York, 1965.
[1973] E. Rosch, *Natural Categories*, Cognitive Psychology **4** (1973), 328–350.

Supplement

[1956] A. J. Ayer, *The Problem of Knowledge*, Penguin Books, Baltimore, Maryland, 1956.
[1962] M. Brodbeck, *Explanation, Prediction and "Imperfect Knowledge,"*, pp. 231–272 in Feigl and Maxwell [**1962**].
[1930] L. de Broglie, *An Introduction to the Study of Wave Mechanics*, Dutton & Co., New York, 1930.
[1939] ———, *Matter and Light*, Norton Co., New York, 1939.
[1967b] M. Bungé , ed., *Quantum Theory and Reality*, Springer Verlag, Berlin, 1967.

[1967c]   ———, *Physical Axiomatics*, Reviews of Modern Physics **39** (1967), 463–474.
[1942]   P. A. M. Dirac, *The Physical Interpretation of Quantum Mechanics*, Proceedings of the Royal Society (London) **A180** (1942), 1–40.
[1949]   P. Frank, *Modern Science and Its Philosophy*, Harvard University Press, Cambridge, Massachusetts, 1949.
[1810]   J. W. Goethe, *Zur Farbenlehre*, Theory of Colours. Translated from the German, with notes, by Charles Lock Eastlake. Reprinted from the 1840 edition, M.I.T. Press, Cambridge, Massachusetts, 1970.
[1958]   H. S. Green, *Observation in Quantum Mechanics*, Nuovo Cimento **9** (1958), 880–889.
[1965]   R. Hall, *Philosophical Basis of Bohr's Interpretation of Quantum Mechanics*, American Journal of Physics **33** (1965), 624–627.
[1927]   P. Jordan, *Philosophic Foundations of Quantum Mechanics*, Nature **119** (1927), 566–569.
[1969]   W. E. Lamb, jr., *An Operational Interpretation of Non-relativistic Quantum Mechanics*, Physics Today **22** #4 (1969), 23–28.
[1964]   J. Losee, *The Use of Philosophical Arguments in Quantum Physics*, Philosophy of Science **31** (1964), 10–17.
[1962]   H. Putnam, *A Philosopher Looks at Quantum Mechanics*, pp. 75–101 in Colodny [**1965**].
[1966]   A. Shimony, *Basic Axioms of Microphysics*, Physics Today **19** # 9 (1966), 85–90.
[1959]   V. F. Weisskopf, *Quantity and Quality in Quantum Physics*, Daedalus **88** (1959), 592–605.
[1950]   W. H. Werkmeister, *An Experimental Basis of Quantum Physics*, Philosophy of Science **17** (1950), 1–25.
[1949]   H. Weyl, *Philosophy of Mathematics and Natural Science*, Princeton University Press, Princeton, New Jersey, 1949.
[1967]   E. E. Witmer, *Interpretations of Quantum Mechanics and the Future of Physics*, American Journal of Physics **35** (1967), 40–52.

Index

abyss of language 245, 259, 337
acausal changes 388
actor 220, 254, 283
Adigard Des Gautries, Jean 21
Aharonov-Bohm effect 94–96, 428, 429, 436
Aharonov, Yakir 61, 78, 95, 105, 106, 427–429, 434
ahistorical assumptions 454
AI (artificial intelligence) 471, 472
Akhiezer, N. I. 52
Akshapada 202, 203
Albert-Aharonov-D'Amato thought experiment 420
Albertson, J. 69, 116
Allcock, G. R. 61, 62
Alston, William P. 134
Ampére, André-Marie 25
amplification 149, 394
analogy 11, 31, 32, 38, 40, 45, 54, 62, 63, 78, 81, 93, 136, 138, 144, 145, 163, 167, 169, 183, 192, 203, 214, 215, 224, 233, 240, 245, 249, 261, 262, 276, 286, 287, 293, 296, 300, 306, 315, 316, 322–325, 334, 343, 345, 373, 429, 457, 470, 471
Analogy of Experience 233, 240, 247
analytic/synthetic 457
Anaxagoras 214
Anaxamander 214
anthropic principle 218, 457, 458
antirealism 7, 313, 314
antisymmetry 53, 58, 94, 168, 427, 435, 437
apparatus-object 243
apperception 240, 241, 246–249
Araki, Huzihiro 373, 375, 383, 384
Arberry, Arthur J. 220

archetypes 215, 217
Archimedes 257
Aristotle 68, 192, 216–218, 221, 227, 232, 233, 257, 266, 270, 279, 308, 311, 446, 467
Arons, Arnold B. 37
asymptotic states 31, 49, 146, 358
Atkatz, David 410
Avenarius, Richard 284, 308
axioms 69, 116–119, 123, 229, 230, 241, 278, 302, 377, 473
Ayer, Alfred Jules 235
azimuthal angle 170
Bach, Alexander 422, 437
Ballentine, Leslie E. 74, 113, 114
Bauer, Edmond 386, 387, 417, 439
Beck, G. 371
Bedau, Hugo 157, 162
behaviorism 296, 325
Belinfante, Frederik J. 55, 428, 429
Bell, John 57, 92, 106, 107, 116–120, 174, 327, 376, 387, 406, 407, 414, 418
Bellugi, Ursula 336
Bennett, Charles H. 421
Berkeley, George 21, 224–227, 455, 458, 463
Bernard, Claude 268, 269
Bhagavad-Gita 253
Bichat, Xavier 268
BKS (Bohr-Kramers-Slater) 37, 38
Black, Max 335
Blatt, John M. 125, 409
Bohm, David 61, 74, 78, 79, 95, 96, 105, 106, 112, 115, 116, 120, 161, 311, 327, 427–429, 434, 445, 450, 453
Bohr, Christian 474

Bois-Reymond, Emil du 268, 277
Boltzmann, Ludwig 25, 59, 85, 301–303, 342, 345–349, 352, 356, 357, 391, 406, 424, 437–439
Born, Max 16, 44, 46, 54, 75, 80, 95, 96, 115, 139, 172, 185, 193, 311, 312, 415, 418, 448
Boscovich, Roger 273, 449
Bose-Einstein statistics 436
Bose, Satyendra Nath 168
Bothe, Walther 39
Boyd, Richard 107
Boyer, Timothy H. 78
Boyle, Robert 224
Brahe, Tycho 221
Brahman 203, 204, 206
brain 212, 222, 224, 264, 266, 323, 330, 406, 426, 470, 472
Brandt, Frithiof 21
Breitenberg, E. 67
Breit-Wigner formula 126
Broglie, Louis de 37, 41, 45, 62, 79, 95, 115, 160, 453
Brøndal, Viggo 23, 327
Bronowski, Jacob 336
Brownian motion 78, 360
Brücke, Ernst von 268
Bub, Jeffrey 114–116, 171, 311, 403
Buddhism 192, 201, 202, 207–211, 218, 223, 444, 457, 459, 467
Bungé, Mario 135, 154, 164, 360, 475
Butts, Robert 229, 230, 236–238, 246
caloric 272, 454
Campbell, Norman Robert 32
Campbell, W. 32
canonical state 58, 76, 302, 348, 349, 354, 359, 401, 429, 440
Capra, Fritjof 201, 457
Carnap, Rudolph 134
Carnot, Sadi 85
Carruthers, Peter 66
Cartesian dualism 309

Casimir, Hendrik B. G. 168
Cassirer, Ernst 307, 308, 371
Cauchy, Augustin-Louis 52
cells 268, 270, 317, 319, 320, 373, 393
chairness 208
chemistry 250, 256, 266–270, 288, 298–300, 304, 316, 320, 322
Chievitz, I. H. 296
Chinese philosophy 201, 211, 213, 445
Chinese room 471, 473
choice 70, 89, 95, 104, 125, 130, 131, 140, 141, 152, 174, 180, 187, 188, 227, 279, 288, 302, 358, 364, 385, 386, 389, 406, 411, 419, 420, 431, 441, 449, 460
Chomsky, Noam 227, 469
Christiansen, Christian 20
CIS (TIS: Classical Theory) 7, 351, 353, 357, 364, 367, 391, 393, 394, 397, 439
Clarke, Samuel 222, 223, 272
Clauser, J. F. 120, 415
Clausius, Rudolph Julius Emmanuel 344
Clinton, W. L. 433
closure 10, 15, 148, 149, 185, 342, 349, 352, 383, 389, 391–394, 397, 398, 413, 445, 474
coarse-grained distributions 373, 411
coarse-grained entropy 357
cognitive dissonance 326
cognitive powers 314, 326, 335, 445
coherence theory 145, 214, 238, 394, 403, 405, 407–409, 413
coincidence 163, 451
Coleman-Hepp theory 406
Coleridge, Samuel 273
combinatorial methods 344
Como Lecture 43, 63, 64, 70, 73, 121, 157, 178, 179, 185
complementarity 6, 11, 14, 18, 21–23, 34, 35, 39, 64, 70, 71, 76, 77, 93,

Index

97, 98, 104, 134, 148, 157–166, 169–171, 174, 178, 179, 181, 185, 188–190, 194, 200, 242, 246, 248, 249, 276, 282, 287, 288, 295, 301, 302, 310, 315–329, 338, 342, 347, 348, 353, 358, 361, 362, 364, 395, 399, 415, 432, 452, 474, 477
complementary descriptions 71, 112, 113, 131, 148, 149, 158–160, 162, 165, 170, 171, 183, 201, 242, 247, 284, 287, 293, 294, 318–322, 324–328, 347, 352, 362, 418, 476
complexity 162, 268, 298, 301, 318, 319, 321, 322, 364, 396, 404, 406, 426, 470
comprehensibility 112, 138, 144, 163, 204, 222, 250, 274, 275, 439, 452, 453, 477
Compte, August 273, 308
Compton, Arthur H. 39, 364, 371, 477
conceptual framework 4, 8, 18, 25, 26, 70, 71, 97, 109, 110, 112, 132, 134, 135, 138, 139, 143, 144, 161, 163, 164, 173, 177, 178, 180–183, 186, 194, 228, 238, 242, 244, 247, 253, 267, 269, 279, 291, 294, 295, 303, 308, 325, 328, 329, 334, 336, 367, 370, 390, 399, 423, 440, 444–451, 457, 460, 470, 476
Condillac 258
conditionalism 269
Condon, Edward U. 44
Confucianism 201, 211, 212, 253
consciousness 15, 21, 22, 89, 91–93, 134, 150, 165, 185, 204–209, 213, 222, 224, 226, 230, 240–242, 245, 246, 258, 271, 277, 283, 284, 287, 293–298, 309, 315, 331, 337, 365, 386–388, 401, 409, 417, 418, 439, 440, 445, 458, 461, 465, 472
conservatism 453

contextual theories 119, 120, 191, 269, 275
contrafactual definiteness 415
conventionalism 450, 455
Cooper, Leon 98
Copernicus, Nicolaus 221, 229, 271, 308, 467
Corinaldesi, Ernesto 87
corpuscular theories 62, 63, 68, 138, 272, 273
correlations 87, 106, 125, 143, 144, 161, 194, 348, 385, 395, 402, 404, 415, 417, 423
correspondence principle 30, 34–38, 40, 49, 55, 63, 86, 116, 145, 164, 202, 222, 223, 242, 271, 272, 314, 316, 418, 445, 447, 454, 457
cosmogonism 206
Craig, William 135
Cramer, John G. 413–421, 423
Cranefield, Paul F. 268
cut 89, 91, 93, 182, 332, 333, 379, 445, 466
Damodaran, K. 202
Danieri, A. 403
Darwin, Charles Galton 75, 168, 256, 269, 298
Davisson, C. J. 41
Davisson-Germer experiment 37, 41, 195
Davy, Humphry 273
deaf and language 222, 260, 262, 336
De Anima 257
Debye, Peter 4
decoherence 15, 185, 378, 379, 402, 404–413, 424, 439
definiteness 150, 378, 379, 415
Delbrück, Max 23, 317–319, 322
Dember, William N. 263, 330
Democritus 214

Descartes, René 221–225, 227, 230, 256, 258, 265, 266, 272, 277, 329, 443, 463, 471

D'Espagnat, Bernard 92, 98, 112, 174, 312, 387, 401, 402, 409, 415, 439, 456

detached observer 241, 246, 249, 368, 455

determinism 56, 78, 79, 113, 114, 144, 177, 289, 311, 323, 343, 344, 346, 445, 449

Deussen, Paul 203–206

DeWitt, Bryce S. 98, 409, 428, 429

dharmas 208, 209

dialectical method 215, 234

Dicke, Robert H. 450

diffraction gratings 165, 382

Dirac, Paul A. M. 45, 46, 53, 73, 79–81, 84, 96, 131, 133, 167, 168, 173, 349, 418, 426, 430

disciplines 157, 164, 191, 253, 256, 257, 327, 444, 473, 474

dissipation of the wavefunction 404, 424

dissolution of the universe 219

disturbance theory 75, 99

dogmatism 222, 229

double-slit experiment 70, 96, 333, 395, 419, 430

Driesch, Hans 269–271, 286, 297, 304

dualism 4, 37, 184, 185, 206, 207, 250, 273, 284, 286, 471

duality 11, 37, 41–43, 45, 51, 70, 80, 94, 136, 137, 154, 156, 157, 165, 188, 211, 284, 305, 312, 395, 420, 423, 424, 431, 436, 465, 466, 469, 477

Duhem, Pierre 307, 371, 454, 455

Dummett, Michael 107, 313, 314

Earman, John 92

echoes 124, 225, 478

Eddington, Arthur Stanley 154

Ehrenfest, Paul 49, 51, 110

Einstein, Albert 4, 5, 16, 17, 23, 26, 32–35, 37, 39, 41, 42, 45, 46, 67, 68, 70, 73, 79, 92, 93, 99, 100, 106–113, 121, 131–133, 152, 158, 165, 168, 173, 190, 238, 241, 243, 244, 281, 308, 450, 453, 457

Eisert, Jens 421

EIS (TIS: Equilibrium Theory) 7, 346, 347, 353, 357, 393, 397, 401, 403, 439

Ekliptika 18, 327

Elsasser, Walter M. 23, 113, 157, 162, 301, 311, 316, 318, 319, 322

Empedocles 214

empiro-criticism 174

Energetics 274, 276

ensembles 56, 117, 317, 359, 360

entanglement 107, 402, 404, 407, 411, 421, 422

entelechy 266, 269–271

entropy 15, 26, 58, 59, 78, 342, 343, 349, 352, 353, 356–359, 364, 366, 367, 372, 373, 385, 391–394, 397, 398, 406, 412, 413, 433, 438, 439

Epicurean philosophy 218, 220

epiphenomena 297, 466

EPR (Einstein-Podolsky-Rosen) 57, 92, 100–103, 105–114, 120, 123–125, 141, 149, 174, 402, 421, 429, 441, 449, 453, 466

ergodic theory 15, 98, 185, 347, 378, 379, 394–396, 402–404

Erlichson, Herman 96, 427

esse est sentiri 286

esse est percipi 225

essences 258, 443, 454

ethical philosophy 213, 277, 287

Euclid 216, 257, 302

Euler, Leonard 106

Everett, Hugh 409, 410, 424

extraphysical interventions 401

Faraday, Michael 25, 93, 273
Favrholdt, David 16–19, 21, 22, 142, 191, 265, 282, 287–289, 296, 315, 327, 456, 457
Faye, Jan 16–19, 21, 70, 107, 112, 132, 145, 160, 282, 288, 289, 313, 314, 323, 327, 454
Fechner, Gustav Theodor 283
Fermi-Dirac statistics 436
Fermi, Enrico 168
Festinger, Leon 326
Feuer, Lewis Samuel 335
Feyerabend, Paul 124, 135, 157, 164, 192, 193, 250
Feynman, Richard 409, 410, 414, 426, 427, 439
Fick, Ludwig 268
Ficte, Johann Gottlieb 253
Filosofikum 18, 20
Fine, Arthur 402
Fishman, Joshua A. 330, 336
Fitzgerald, Edward 219, 220
Fleming, Donald 317
fluctuation 26, 68, 69, 78, 115, 349, 360–362, 370
Fock, Vladimir A. 61, 80, 81, 111, 173, 174
Folse, Henry 16, 107, 238, 245, 246, 314, 450, 454
forms of perceptions 142
Fowler, Ralph Howard 349
Frassen, Bas van 107
Freedman-Clauser 417, 419
freewill 220
free will 287, 323
freewill 287, 323
Freistadt, H. 112, 116
Furry, Wendel H. 94, 105, 106, 417, 427
Furth, Hans G. 336
Fürth, Reinhold 78

Galileo Galilei 26, 68, 133, 192, 221, 224, 225, 227, 271, 308, 452, 463, 467
Gamow, George 80
Gardiner, Patrick 244, 254
gauge transformations 428, 429
Gauss, Carl Frederick 345
Geiger, Hans 39, 259, 325
Gell-Mann, Murray 402, 409–413, 422, 424
Genauigheitsgrenzen 75
George, André 115
Germer, Lester 41
Gibbs, Willard van Ormand 302, 303, 317, 343, 346–348, 351–354, 357–359, 372, 393, 448
Glazman, I. M. 52
Gleason, Andrew 117, 118
gnat-interests 299
Gödel, Kurt 473
Goethe, Johann Wolfgang 275
Goodstein, David L. 96, 360
Gordon, W. 81
Goudsmidt, Samuel 167
Gowen, Herbert 201
gravity 110, 218, 222, 224, 226, 272, 303, 308, 467
Grünbaum, Adoph 135, 161, 171, 475
Hahn, Otto 408, 409
Haldane, John Scott 265, 266, 269, 286, 298–301, 304
half-silvered mirror 131, 173, 312, 424, 430, 431
Hall, Stephen S. 472
Hamilton-Jacobi equations 40, 45, 49
Hanbury-Brown-Twiss experiment 420
Hanson, Norwood Russell 34, 333, 457
Hartle, James B. 402, 409, 410, 413
Hartmann, Max 319
Harvey, William 266
Hawking, Steven 410
Heelan, Patrick 34, 238

Hefner, H. 77
Hegel, George William Frederick 253, 254, 267
Heidegger, Martin 241
Heilbron, John 28
Heisenberg, Werner 9, 16, 20, 34, 43–46, 49, 59, 60, 62–64, 66–70, 74–77, 80, 81, 88, 99, 115, 130, 131, 153, 157, 160, 168, 169, 174, 180, 192, 193, 238, 250, 302, 307, 311, 348, 360, 362, 396, 415–419, 432, 459, 468
Helmholtz, Hermann von 59, 265, 268, 273–275, 278, 283, 303
Heraclitus 214, 216, 257
Herbert, N. 420
hermeneutic circle 241
Hermogenes 257
Hertz, Heinrich 25, 276, 278, 302, 303
Hesse, Mary B. 39, 59
Hibbs, Albert R. 409
Hilbert, David 44, 116–119, 173, 383
Hilbert space 52–56, 90
Hill, Terrell 34
Hindu philosophy 192, 201, 444
Hjelmslev, Louis 261
Hjort, Johan 59, 298
Hobbes, Thomas 224
Høffding, Harald 14, 16–22, 132–134, 222, 224, 229, 230, 232, 238, 245, 253, 256, 267, 274, 276, 282–289, 297–300, 303–305, 309, 316, 322–324, 381, 457, 463
Hogben, Lancelot Thomas 299
holism 242, 253, 288, 298, 300, 304, 317
Holt, E. A. 120
Holton, Gerald 16, 17, 22, 164, 191
Home, D. 113
Homer 257
Honner, John 8, 13, 16, 19, 20, 177, 238, 241–243, 313, 314, 451, 465

Hooker, Clifford Allen 99, 105, 110, 164, 165, 236–238, 313
Hopi language 332, 333, 335, 336
Horne, M. A. 120
Hove, Leon van 438
Humboldt, Wilhelm von 258, 259, 262
Hume, David 21, 225–227, 229, 248, 256, 279, 463, 467
Husserl, Edmund 263
Huxley, Thomas Henry 222, 266, 269, 297, 298
Huyghens, Christian 68, 136, 221, 222, 272
hypothetico-deductive method 274
idealism 7, 19, 202, 203, 205–209, 212, 213, 227, 250, 254, 294, 314, 451, 452, 458–460, 463, 475
idealizations 49, 67, 88, 150, 151, 172, 239, 390
identity 204, 206, 223, 229, 241, 330, 389, 420, 430, 435, 461, 466
Ignorabimus 278
imagination 226, 240, 365, 377, 447
independence 100, 126, 245, 275, 398, 452, 469
indeterminacy relations 70, 77, 94, 134, 292, 312
indeterminateness 70, 76, 114, 348
indeterminism 114
Indian philosophy 201, 202, 206, 210, 213, 218, 330, 332, 463, 466, 467
indistinguishable outcomes 185, 378, 407, 408
individuality 10, 13, 51, 104, 121, 132, 138, 163, 187, 190, 192, 200, 223, 245, 253, 259, 260, 271, 279, 283, 284, 287, 288, 300, 303–305, 317
Indra's palace 223
inertial frames 26, 353, 449
infinite regress 99, 172, 217, 323, 381, 390
information bandwidth 366, 426

insensible world 215
inseparability 145, 202, 316, 392
inseparable states 260
instrumentalism 7, 131, 313, 452, 454–457
intelligibility 5, 18, 46, 192, 203, 205, 212, 215, 226, 232, 239, 242, 254, 279, 457
interconnectedness 223
intersubjective meaning 290, 456
intrinsic-values theory 378, 379
introspection 265, 271, 283, 288, 323, 386, 443, 444, 465
intuition 6, 8, 46, 57, 59, 71, 94, 96, 172, 193, 216, 217, 224, 232, 233, 237, 239–241, 245–247, 284, 326, 362, 399, 405, 441, 443
invariance 419
invariants 226, 311, 396, 415
irrational 10, 13, 138, 179, 200, 230, 255, 256, 283–285, 300, 303–305
irreversibility 15, 91, 149, 150, 176, 178, 185, 342, 349, 357, 374, 383, 391–398, 417, 419, 477
irreversible registration 99, 148–150, 349, 393, 419
isospin 169, 170
Jackiw, Roman 66
Jacobi, Carl Gustav Jacob 40
Jaffe, Robert L. 435
Jainism 210
Jaklevic, R. C. 428
James-Lange theory 283
James, William 16–19, 21, 22, 283, 286, 294, 309, 323, 324, 440, 450, 459, 461
Jammer, Max 16, 17, 25, 27, 29, 30, 32, 41, 44, 54, 100, 124, 157, 221, 222, 225, 278, 379, 467
Janik, Allan 263, 290
Jauch, Josef M. 77, 98, 117, 387, 437, 439

Jaynes, Edwin T. 162, 359
Jeans, James 25, 31
jen 212
Jespersen, Otto 262
Johansen, Karsten 261
Johnson, Samuel 458
Jordan, Pascual 23, 44, 54, 80, 81, 324
joy/sorrow 324
Kaempfer, F. A. 66
Kafatos, Menas 328
Kaiser, David 125, 126
Kantian Categories 18, 109, 217, 230, 232–234, 236, 237, 239–241, 243, 244, 246, 248–250, 261, 279, 282, 286, 292, 333, 451, 453, 455
Kant, Immanuel 13, 16, 18, 19, 21, 22, 109, 132, 142, 184, 186, 199, 204, 205, 207, 227–241, 243–251, 253, 254, 256, 260, 261, 266–268, 273, 278, 279, 282, 284–286, 297, 298, 365, 426, 449, 463–465, 469, 474
Karika 210
Kelly, J. L. 77
Kelvin, William Thomson Lord 59, 453
Kemble, Edwin C. 113
Kepler, Johannes 221, 271, 274, 308, 467
Khayyám, Omar 219, 220
Kiefer, Claus 410
Kierkegaard, Søren 16–18, 133, 191, 289
Kirchhoff, Gustav Robert 269, 275, 276, 278, 301–303, 308
Klein-Gordon equation 73, 418
Klein, Martin 20, 22, 25, 30, 37, 81, 245, 438
Knill, E. 407, 409
koans 211
Kochen, S. 117, 171
Koller, John M. 202, 207–210

Körner, Steven 116
Koyré, Alexandre 59
Kramers, Hendrik Anton 20, 37–40, 63, 133, 137
Kretzschmar, Martin 95, 427
Kroman, Kristian 282
Krönig, August 344
Krylov, Nikolai Alekseevich 61
Kuhn, Thomas 20, 25, 28, 68, 132, 192, 195, 328, 371, 447
Laflamme, R. 407, 409
Lagrange, Joseph Louis 272
Lambe, J. J. 428
Landau, Lev 61, 73, 80–86, 360
Landé, Alfred 113, 115
Lange, Carl 283, 296
Langford, Cooper Harold 235
language-game 292
Laplace, Pierre Simon, Marquis de 256, 272, 330, 342, 343, 445
Laue, Max von 74
laughter/tears 324
Leggett, Anthony J. 123, 135, 161, 374, 375, 406, 459
Lehman, H. 146
Leibniz-Clarke correspondence 222, 272, 447
Leibniz, Gottfried Wilhelm 134, 221–224, 253, 258, 260, 272, 273, 277, 304, 387, 435, 436
Lenin, Vladimir 174
Lenneberg, Eric 336
Leucippus 214
Lewenstein, Maciej 421
Lewis, Clarence Irving 235
Lewis, G. N. 64
Liebowitz, B. 427
Lifshitz, Evgenii Mikhailovich 360
Lindhard, Jens 362
linearity 371
linguistic framework 134, 135, 242, 260–262, 332, 333, 336, 337, 471
linguistics 256, 260, 262, 327, 332, 453
Liouville, Joseph 355, 396
locality 96, 98, 100, 107, 110, 120, 327, 414, 415, 427, 430, 436, 441, 445, 447, 477
localizability 49, 145, 429
localization 26, 27, 42, 49, 81, 152, 157, 162, 172, 270, 312, 331, 418, 425, 430, 434, 440, 448
Locke, John 21, 224–227, 258, 260, 279, 463
Lodge, Oliver 31
lógos 257, 260
Loinger, A. 98, 403
London, Fritz 161, 386, 387, 417, 439
Lorentz, Hendrik Antoon 25, 26, 31, 168, 302, 303, 360, 426–428
Lorentz, Henrik Antoon 133
Lotze, Hermann 261
Lucretius 218–221
Ludwig, Carl 265, 267, 268
Mach, Ernst 18, 271, 275, 276, 278, 283, 284, 303, 308, 454, 455
MacKay, D. M. 327
Mackey, George W. 69, 77, 434, 439
MacKinnon, Edward 238
macrorealism 375
Madhyamika 209–211, 459
Madvig, Johann Nicolai 260–262, 309
Magendie, Francois 268
Mahavira 210
Mahayana 208, 223
Majorana, Ettore 81
Mallock, William Hurrell 218, 220
Mandelbrot, Benoit 359, 362
Mandel, Leonard 430–432, 477
Mandelstam, Stanley 61, 62, 427–429
Mandelstam-Tamm paper 61
Massey, Harrie Stewart Wilson 168
materialism 26, 97, 98, 134, 174, 202, 214, 219, 220, 256, 273, 279, 308, 314, 315, 376, 401, 424, 441, 445,

447–449, 451, 453, 454, 458–460, 464, 466
Mauthner, Fritz 262, 263
Maxwell, James Clerk 25, 34, 59, 136, 271, 276, 302, 342, 343, 345–347, 351, 362, 363, 406, 436, 448, 449
Maxwell's demon 271
mâyâ 205, 452
Mayer, J. E. 64
measurability 75, 81, 98, 147, 168, 373
mechanism 37, 89, 122, 125, 194, 265–267, 269–271, 286, 296, 297, 308, 321, 327, 349, 394, 403, 406, 407, 411, 412, 421, 449, 467
Mehra, Jagdish 44
Mendelsohn, Everett 267, 268
Mercereau, J. E. 428
Mersenne, Marin 258
Merzbacher, Eugen 95
Merz, John T. 275
metaphors 223, 293, 359
metaphysics 26, 108, 109, 125, 144, 177, 211, 217, 225, 226, 229, 230, 232, 234, 236–239, 242, 243, 253, 275, 286, 308, 315, 328, 335, 336, 376, 389, 401, 406, 424, 441, 444–451, 453, 454, 458, 460, 464, 466
methodology 191, 236, 237, 239
Meyer-Abich, Klaus 16, 30, 32, 36, 99, 132, 138, 148, 153, 157, 159, 164, 238, 248, 293, 415
Meyer, David A. 421
Meyerson, Emile 18, 21, 130, 255, 256, 286, 304, 308
Michelson, Albert Abraham 136
microcanonical state 302, 349, 354
microscopic/macroscopic 377
Millikan, Robert Andrews 165
Mill, John Stuart 134, 256, 259, 274, 276, 457
Milne, Edward A. 450
mind/matter 309

Misra, B. 116
Mitler, Henri E. 427
mixtures 56, 91, 92, 105, 113, 114, 117, 185, 358, 378, 379, 394–396, 401, 402, 410, 411, 413, 421, 437, 459
models 34, 59, 68, 77–79, 112, 125, 126, 169, 189, 194–196, 247, 294, 366–368, 371, 379, 381, 382, 386, 390, 396, 399, 406, 414, 422–424, 448, 454
molecular chaos 424, 437, 438
Møller, Poul 17, 191, 240, 323
monads 223, 224, 387
monism 465
Moore, Ruth 22
Moreley, Edward Williams 136
Mott, Nevill Francis 168
Müller, Johannes 263, 264, 267, 268, 298, 454
Müller, Max 201, 260, 262
multivalued functions 293
Murdoch, David 16, 160, 378, 379, 450, 451
Nadeau, Robert 328
Nagarjuna 209, 210
Nagel, Ernest 313, 456
Nataputta 210
Naturphilosophie 268
Navaho language 335
negative-result experiments 419
Neo-Confucianism 211
neo-platonism 221
Neumann, John von 9, 14, 15, 46, 52, 55–57, 66, 67, 69, 73, 82, 89–93, 98, 99, 101, 107, 115–119, 122, 123, 130, 140, 149, 150, 157, 166, 171–174, 185, 191, 194–196, 295, 296, 315, 327, 338, 351, 357, 358, 368, 370, 372, 373, 377–392, 398, 401, 408–410, 412, 416, 417, 433,

438, 439, 445, 465, 468, 472, 474, 478
Newtonian mechanics 25, 26, 38, 98, 132, 133, 223, 234, 236, 272, 273, 291, 300, 401, 436, 447, 451, 454
Newton, Issac 26, 68, 136, 216, 218, 222, 223, 230, 236, 271, 272, 277, 279, 297, 308, 449, 467
Nicolson, J. W. 32
Nielsen, M. A. 296, 407, 409
Nieto, Michael Martin 66
Noerdlinger, P. D. 428
Noiré, Ludwig 260
nonadditivity of operators 118
noncausal behavior 92, 93, 385
nonclassical behavior 53, 164, 169, 170, 364, 403, 434, 435
non-coherent measures 171
noncommuting operators 69, 101, 103, 118, 438, 439
non-decohering states 411
non-dualism 203
nonequilibrium thermodynamics 352, 433
nonlocality 10, 87, 110, 112, 124, 415–417, 419, 428, 429, 436, 477
nonmaterial soul 223
nonphysical factors 270, 301, 318, 458
nonsense 261
nonseparable states 121
Nordenskiöld, Erik 268, 269
noumena 229, 230, 461
Nussenzveig, H. M. 371
Nyaya 202, 203
objecthood 145, 299, 366
objective-values 378, 379
objectivity 98, 187, 191, 192, 217, 227, 243, 245, 246, 254, 287, 293–295, 307, 309, 443
objectless subject 206
observability 136
Occam, William of 221, 409

Ogievestskii, V. I. 428
Okruhlik, Kathleen 236
Omnès, Roland 402, 456
ontology 36, 40, 68, 69, 98, 99, 134, 135, 145, 194, 217, 257, 314, 327, 401, 413, 417, 439, 440, 447, 452, 456, 459
operationalism 60, 67, 115, 148, 153
Oppenheim, Paul 157, 162
Oracle at Delphi 257
organisms 162, 213, 260, 261, 266, 267, 269–271, 282, 284, 285, 297, 298, 300, 301, 304, 315–319, 321, 322, 365
Ostwald, Wilhelm 276, 308
Pais, Abraham 20, 21
Pandres, D. 95
pantheism 206
paradigmatic experiments 68, 136, 303, 325, 382, 390, 469
parity 169
Park, James L. 57–59, 113, 422
Parmenides 204, 205, 214–216
participatory reality 458, 460, 461, 464, 471
partitions 354, 361
Paul, Harry 135, 431
Pauli, Wolfgang 9, 16, 20, 45, 61, 62, 70, 77, 80, 85, 93, 95, 130, 160, 168, 169, 246, 392, 394, 416, 434, 438
Pearson, Karl 455
Pedersen, Holger 261
Peierls, Rudolph 61, 73, 80–86
Penrose, Roger 135, 402, 471, 472
Peppard, M. B. 37
percepts 283, 288
Peres, Asher 106, 395–397, 404, 460
permutations 80, 427
Persian science 13, 219
perturbation theory 438

Petersen, Åage 16, 20, 135, 148, 157, 180, 282, 291–293, 296–299, 334
Petruccioli, Sandro 16, 28
Pfleegor, R. L. 430–432, 477
phenomena 159
phenomenalistic 135
phenomenologists 265, 443, 445
phenomenology 236, 263
phenomenon 10, 32, 105, 122, 136, 137, 141, 144, 148–150, 158, 159, 173, 223, 239, 298, 304, 325, 391, 392
Piaget, Jean 331
Picht, J. 67
Planck, Max 4, 23, 25, 26, 28–30, 32, 36, 78, 86, 121, 138, 281, 302, 303, 364, 406, 424
Plato 204, 205, 215, 216, 226, 230, 235, 257
pluralism 205, 208, 286, 465
pockets 366
Podolsky, Boris 73, 92, 93, 99, 100, 111, 121, 133, 152, 158, 190, 281, 453
poetry 4, 15, 218–220, 257, 273, 275, 443, 478
Poincaré, Henri 26, 85, 130, 396, 403, 438, 449, 450, 454, 455
Polubarinov, I. V. 428
Polyani, Michael 317
polytheism 213
Popper, Karl 67, 74, 88, 157, 164, 476
positivism 7, 12, 19, 142, 265, 415, 419, 443, 445
positron 73, 79, 126, 414, 427
Posterior Analytics 216, 217
potentia 311, 459
pragmatism 19, 286
preacceleration 426
predestination 220
preestablished harmony 223, 224, 387
prelinguistic thought 260

Principia 218, 230, 271
Prosperi, G. M. 403
Protagoras 216, 364
psyche 269, 299
psychic experiences 183, 203, 269, 284, 287, 297, 323, 324
psychophysical 223, 386
psycho-physical parallelism 323
Putnam, Hilary 107
Pythagorean philosophy 226
QIS (TIS: Quantum Theory) 7, 9, 40, 46, 49, 51, 81, 95, 96, 312, 364, 377, 379, 391, 402, 418, 423, 429, 432, 437–439
QTS (TIS: Quantum Thermodynamics) 7, 9, 26, 32, 376, 377, 391, 393, 432
qualities 112, 214, 219, 224–226, 264, 272, 285, 337, 443, 463
quanton 154
quantum interference 403
quarks 454, 459
Quay, Paul M. 348, 359
Quine, William van Ormond 134, 135, 459
Ramsey, Norman Foster 94, 427
random events 68, 69, 78, 169, 216, 348, 358, 359, 406, 412, 417, 419, 423, 438
randomness 348, 406–408, 424
Rankin, B. 61
Rankine, William John Macquorn 274, 308
Rask, Rasmus 260
rationalism 213, 215, 222, 226, 227, 229, 250, 258, 261, 262, 279, 283, 469
realism 7, 109, 174, 202, 208, 209, 212, 222, 236, 294, 313–315, 401, 415, 449–454, 456, 457, 459, 460, 464
Rechenberg, H. 44

reciprocity 157, 288
recurrence paradox 85, 349, 357, 403, 409, 438
Redlich, Otto 153
Reichenbach, Hans 111, 166
reifications 217, 311, 337, 366, 401, 440, 441, 443, 460, 464
religion 219, 220, 327
Renninger, M. 111, 115, 419
representationalism 209, 314
reversibility paradox 349, 357, 477
Richardson, Owen Willans 38
Riemannian surface 293
RIS (TIS: Relativity Theory) 7
Robison, M. C. 67
Rohrlich, Fritz 426
Roman thought 13, 218
romanticism 250, 253, 256, 268
Rosch, Eleanor 335
Rosenfeld, Leon 12, 16, 17, 20, 22, 61, 70, 85–88, 98, 131, 148, 153, 157, 171, 172, 180, 187, 290, 293, 323, 334, 349, 360–362, 364
Rosen, Nathan 49, 56, 73, 92, 93, 99, 100, 111, 121, 133, 152, 158, 190, 281, 318, 453
Roth, L. M. 457
Rozental, Stefan 16, 20, 22
Ruark, A. E. 113
Rubáiyát 219, 220
Rubin, Edgar 18, 19
Rüdinger, Erik 20
runaway solutions 414, 426
Russell, Bertrand 215, 217, 457
Russell, Edward Stuart 299
Rutherford, Ernest 5, 27, 130
Sāṅkhya 207
Sakur-Tetrode entropy 439
Sanskrit 201, 260, 459
Sapir, Edward 332, 334, 335
Sautrantika 208, 209, 214
Savage, Leonard J. 344

scenarios 328, 366
Schelling, Friedrick Wilhelm Joseph 253
schemata 237, 246
schematized categories 237, 330
Schiller, Friedrich 275
Schiller, R. 168
scholastic philosophy 222, 224, 225, 272, 279, 308, 467
Schopenhauer, Arthur 204, 205, 244, 254
Schrödinger, Erwin 44–46, 48–53, 61, 67, 80, 89–91, 95, 106, 107, 113, 115, 122, 124, 125, 131, 137, 141, 165, 174, 176, 177, 195, 311, 358, 371–373, 376, 379–386, 388, 390–392, 395, 402, 403, 408–410, 417–422, 424, 429, 432, 436, 440, 441, 453, 468, 474
Schrödinger's cat 122, 211, 376, 420, 440
Schwan, Theodore 268
Schweber, Silvan S. 426
Sciamanda, R. J. 430, 431
Scriven, Michael 451
Searle, John 471, 473
self-consciousness 241
self-energy 81, 414
self-reference 243
Sellars, Wilfrid 235
semantics 18, 189, 257, 471
Semon, M. D. 374
sensation 108, 109, 186, 219, 224, 225, 231–233, 237, 244, 256, 259, 263, 264, 266, 274–276, 283, 284, 286, 290, 303, 323, 330–332, 334, 387, 443, 454, 463
sensitivity 317
sensorium 223, 263, 264, 330
sentience 365, 366, 376, 398, 457, 458, 463, 466, 469, 471, 472, 477

Index

separability 98, 100, 107, 112, 117, 327, 380
Shaknov, I. 106, 120
Shankland, 106
Shewell, J. R. 377
Shimony, Abner 92, 98, 119, 120, 161, 317, 374, 386, 387, 415, 439, 440
Shor, Peter W. 421
silver, 428
Silver, A. H. 393, 394
Simon, A. W. 39
singlevaluedness 95
single-valued states 51, 94–96, 177, 293
singularity 95, 115, 293
skepticism 20, 227, 242
Slater, John C. 37–40, 63, 113, 133, 137
smeared operators 79
Smolin, John A. 421
Socrates 215, 216, 257
Solvay Conferences 73, 79, 168
Sommerfeld, Arnold 30, 33, 41
sophistications of reason 235, 472
soul 202, 204, 206, 207, 213, 222–224, 226, 261, 309
spaceless forces 208
special metaphysics 236, 237
Specker, Ernst P. 117, 171
spectator 201, 283
Spencer, Herbert 256
spin-echo experiment 408, 409
spiritual issues 253, 452
spontaneity 217, 273, 401, 402, 421
spontaneous events 32, 37, 403, 448
Stam, James H. 257
Stapp, Henry P. 415
Stark, Johannes 40
stationary states 27–31, 33, 35, 36, 38, 40, 41, 45, 50, 111, 122, 130, 131, 138, 146, 147, 150–152, 157, 182, 193, 434
Stein, H. 374

Stent, Gunther 23, 317, 392, 394
Stern-Gerlach experiment 118, 121, 168, 169, 172, 371, 380, 382
stimuli 256, 264, 270, 271, 303, 304, 336
stochastic 393
Stoicism 220
strangeness 169, 170
Strawson, P. F. 242
Strutt, John William (Lord Rayleigh) 25
Strutt, William (Lord Rayleigh) 25
subjectivity 92, 98, 112, 192, 246, 254, 443
subject/object 4, 5, 8, 11, 13–15, 18, 89, 99, 110, 145, 149, 164, 179–182, 184, 188–190, 192, 199, 201, 209, 211, 213, 242, 244, 245, 247, 249, 253, 254, 279, 283, 294, 300, 303, 305, 307, 309, 329, 332, 338, 342, 350, 352, 362–364, 367, 368, 378–380, 385, 424, 440, 446, 448, 469, 474, 475, 477
sub-quantal level 78
substantialism 108, 312, 387, 401, 422–424, 449, 459, 460
substantialistic 375, 401, 413, 416, 417
substantive 229, 313, 454, 474
supernatural 218, 272, 444
superselection 405, 406, 413, 436
Suppes, Patrick 69, 438
Sutras 202, 205–207, 223, 466
S'vetâs'vatara 207
Symanzik, K. 146
symbolism 153, 154, 290
symbolization 121, 138, 139, 154, 239, 470
symplectic structures 434
synonyms 59, 259
Szilard, Leo 391
Tait, Peter Guthrie 278
Tamm, Igor Evgenevich 61, 62

Taoism 192, 201, 202, 211, 457
Taylor, J. R. 374
teleology 266–269, 271, 298, 300, 304, 316, 319
telepathy 470
teleportation 407, 421, 422
temperature/energy 362
Tetens, Johann Nicolaus 457
Thales 213, 214
Thaplial, Ashiah V. 421
theism 202, 203, 206, 207
theory-laden perception 458
Theravada 208
things-in-themselves 204, 227, 229–231, 282, 284, 330, 443, 464
Thomas, Llewellyn Hilleth 168
Thompson, D'Arcy 299
Thomsen, Vilhelm 19, 261, 262
Thomson, Joseph J. 27, 31, 278
thought-pictures 302
three-valued logic 166, 292
time-energy uncertainty 170
timeless forces 208
time-reversal 414, 418
time-symmetry 418
TIS (Theory of Interacting Systems) 6, 7, 29, 353, 356, 357, 363, 364, 370, 393, 469
Tisza, Lazlo 348, 359
Tomonaga, Sin-itiro 45
Torretti, Roberto 450
totality 34, 35, 109, 204, 232, 253, 258, 260, 261, 269, 271, 285, 286, 298, 299, 441
Toulmin, Stephen 263, 290
Tractatus Logico Philosophicus 290, 291, 332, 454
Trammel, G. T. 427
transactional interpretation 413–415, 418–421
Transcendental Aesthetic 231, 239
Transcendental Analytic 232, 239, 241

transcendental arguments 11, 177, 230, 232, 234, 235, 239–243, 248, 249, 277
transcendental deduction 240
transcendental idea 234, 235
transcendentalism 7, 242, 267, 277, 291, 304, 309, 313, 331, 461
Transcendental Logic 232
Tse, Lao 4, 201, 211, 253, 478
tunneling 152, 366, 434
turner 25
Tzu, Chang 211
Uexküll, Jakob Johann 299, 365
Uhlenbeck, George Eugene 167
Unbekanntheit 70
Unbestimmtheit 70
Unbestimmtheitsprinzip 70
uncertainty relations 43, 46, 61–68, 70, 73–86, 88, 93, 94, 96, 97, 99, 105, 113–115, 121, 134, 139, 146, 149, 151, 163, 168–170, 172, 301, 305, 361, 362, 371, 415, 417, 418, 432, 433, 438, 439, 453
unconditioned statements 209, 235
uncontrollable disturbances 64, 75, 114, 124, 138, 468
undetermined phases 55, 146, 468
unfathomability 258, 259, 308
Ungenauigheit 70
unintelligibility 225, 248
unknowability 70, 206, 304
unmeasurability 168
unobservables 44, 45, 136, 151, 236
unpicturizability 144
unreality 206, 254
unreturnability 397, 398
unsharpness 35
Unsicherheitsrelation 70
unvisualizability 144, 287
Upanishad 203–207, 210
Vaibhashika 208, 209, 214
Vaiseshika 202, 203

Van Vleck, John H. 113
Varadarajan, V. S. 69, 439
Vechten, D. van 98
Vedânta 203, 204, 207
Vedas 203, 207
Vedic philosophy 201, 202, 207, 208, 210
verificationism 7, 75, 77, 226, 318, 419
Verworn, Max 269
virial theorem 29
virtual processes 37, 38, 40, 152
visualizability 46, 57, 59, 144, 241, 245, 314, 323
visualization 40, 56, 71, 123, 195, 226, 414, 476
vitalism 268–271, 274, 286, 296, 298, 299, 301, 304
Volta, Alessandro 264
vortex theories 222
Vygotsky, Lev S. 331
Waerden, Bartel Leendert van der 31–33, 44
walalata 333, 334
Wallace, B. Allan 457–459
walls 320, 321
watchmaker 223
wave-particle duality 11, 45, 51, 70, 80, 94, 136, 137, 154, 156, 157, 160, 165, 167, 188, 312, 395, 423, 424, 431, 436, 469, 477
wavicle 154
Weiler, Gershon 262, 263
Weisskopf, Victor 20, 125, 180, 311
Weizsäcker, Carl-Friederich von 16, 20, 22, 157, 159–161, 166, 180, 193, 233, 238, 250, 265, 290, 311, 333, 334
Wheeler-DeWitt equation 410
Wheeler-Feynman Theory 414, 418, 420, 426
Wheeler, John Archibald 126, 409, 414, 426, 427

Whewell, William 256, 273, 274, 276, 454
Whitaker, M. A. B. 113
Whitehead, Alfred North 298
Whitney, William Dwight 261, 262, 336, 470
wholeness 10, 13, 138, 139, 157, 163, 190, 192, 271, 288, 298–300, 303, 304, 418
Whorf, Benjamin Lee 332–336
Wick, Gian Carlo 436
Wien, Wilhelm 25
Wightman, Arthur 436
Wigner, Eugene P. 61, 92, 98, 168, 372–375, 384, 387, 414, 416, 417, 419, 420, 436, 439
Wilkens, Martin 421
Williams, L. P. 272
Wilner, Partus 285
Winspear, Alban Dewes 218
wisdom 13, 217, 445, 461
Wittgenstein, Ludwig 14, 133, 165, 179, 191, 192, 263, 290–292, 294–296, 309, 323, 325, 327, 331–333, 444, 451, 454, 457, 470
Woodger, Joseph Henry 299, 300
word play 205
worldview 113, 191, 219–221, 272, 277, 299, 336, 451, 456
Wu, Chien-shiung 106, 120
Wundt, Wilhelm 283
Yâjña-valkhya 205, 206
Yanase, Mutsuo M. 98, 374, 375, 383, 384
Yarn, Phillip 405, 406
yes/no questions 372
Yoga 211
Yogacarin 209
Yourgrau, Wolfgang 115
Zen 211
zero-point energy 81, 84
Zimmerman, W. 146

www.ingramcontent.com/pod-product-compliance
Lightning Source LLC
Chambersburg PA
CBHW031539300426
44111CB00006BA/115